TEXAS EVIDENTIARY FOUNDATIONS

Third Edition

David A. Schlueter
Hardy Professor of Trial Advocacy and Director of Advocacy Programs
St. Mary's University

John F. Onion, Jr.
Presiding Judge
Texas Court of Criminal Appeals (Ret.)

Charles W. Barrow
Justice
Texas Supreme Court (Ret.)

Edward J. Imwinkelried
Barrett Professor of Law and Director of Trial Advocacy
University of California at Davis

LexisNexis™

QUESTIONS ABOUT THIS PUBLICATION?

For questions about the **Editorial Content** appearing in these volumes or reprint permission, please call:

Renita Sandosham, Editor .... 1-800-424-0651 Ext. 3204
Dana Vinicoff, J.D. .... 1-800-424-0651 Ext. 3258
Outside the United States and Canada please call .... (415) 908-3200

For assistance with replacement pages, shipments, billing or other customer service matters, please call:

Customer Services Department at .... (800) 833-9844
Outside the United States and Canada, please call .... (518) 487-3000
Fax number .... (518) 487-3584
Customer Service Website .... http://www.lexisnexis.com/custserv/

For information on other Matthew Bender publications, please call:
Your account manager .... (800) 223-1940
Outside the United States and Canada, please call .... (518) 487-3000

Library of Congress Cataloging-in-Publication Data

Texas evidentiary foundations / David A. Schlueter ... [et al.].--3rd ed.
p. cm.
Includes index.
ISBN 0-8205-7453-8 (hardbound)
1. Evidence (Law)--Texas. I. Schlueter, David A.
KFT1740.T49 2004
347.764'06--dc22

2004030546

MATTHEW BENDER

(Pub.66890)

Summary Table of Contents

Table of Contents

Chapter 5: Credibility Evidence

CHAPTER 7: PRIVILEGES AND SIMILAR RULES OF EXCLUSION

PART 1 PRIVILEGES

CHAPTER 10: THE HEARSAY RULE AND ITS EXEMPTIONS

PART 1 THE HEARSAY RULE

Chapter 12: Substitutes for Evidence

Chapter 13: Constitutional Privileges—The Exclusionary Rules

PART 1 THE PRODUCTS OF SEARCHES AND SEIZURES

FOREWORD TO FIRST EDITION

One who presents or defends a lawsuit is telling the story of something that has happened. *Texas Evidentiary Foundations* is a unique new resource that explains how to tell the story in a way that will move it forward with few interruptions, false starts, or distractions. The problem is that the story in court must come from evidence that initially meets certain standards of reliability. When done wrong, the story quickly becomes dull, tedious, and ineffective. Even a good story becomes boring if it is told in an inept and stumbling manner.

As a trial judge, I discovered more than 45 years ago that most lawyers in court are well prepared with the substantive law and the applicable rules of evidence. Too many lawyers, however, obscure the point of their cause by faltering in the technique of talking and walking a piece of evidence into the record. After I had observed this recurring scene and made a list of those subjects which repeatedly caused difficulty, I prepared a series of lectures to explain the stops in laying predicates for the presentation of evidence.

The lectures went through the process of publication in the *Texas Bar Journal*, private printings, and finally became an article entitled "Presenting and Excluding Evidence," published in the *Texas Tech Law Review*. I learned from that experience that lawyers not only need but want this kind of text. Now, for the first time, Texas students, lawyers, and judges have a complete text that covers almost the whole body of evidentiary material, and it is adapted to the Texas Rules of Evidence.

The first two chapters of this book should be required reading for every Texas lawyer. Chapter 1 gives some simple rules for avoiding the careless and distracting practice of asking leading questions. It also explains the simple steps by which one talks and walks a piece of evidence into the official record. It shows how and when the court reporter, the opposing counsel, the judge, and finally, the jury become involved in the preliminary steps of introducing any kind of evidence. Chapter 2 teaches the same lessons about the exclusion of evidence.

Some kind of predicate or foundation is necessary for any piece of evidence. The proofs vary with the many different kinds of evidence. Different proofs must be made prior to the admission into evidence of such items as lay and expert statements, writings, handwritings, business records, official and public documents, diagrams, still or motion pictures, computer records, demonstrations, exhibitions, models, voiceprints, radar readings, and scores of other items. Predicates are also essential when one moves to exclude evidence by motion in limine, certain objections, a motion to strike, a request to take a witness on voir dire, or a motion for limiting instructions. This book has samples for these and many other types of evidence.

The format used in this book for all of the kinds of evidence is a three-step discussion. First, there is a discussion of the relevant doctrine. There is than a checklist of the foundation elements for each kind of evidence. Finally, there is an actual question and answer example of what should be said and done to lay the correct foundation. No other Texas book has come to my attention that includes the second and third steps.

Each of the four authors of *Texas Evidentiary Foundations* has brought scholarship and practical evidence to this book. Professor David Schlueter, Professor of Law at St. Mary's University, is already well known to Texas lawyers as the coauthor of *Texas Rules of Evidence Manual* and for his many helpful articles on evidence that are published regularly in the *Texas Bar Journal*. He has mastered the art of plain talk.

Judge Onion has honorably served the Texas judiciary for 38 years as a trial and appellate judge. He was the Presiding Judge of the Court of Criminal Appeals for 18 years, and even after his retirement he is, by appointment, still writing opinions and sitting as a trial judge. He has seen the growth of the law and has had a firm hand in its development.

Charles Barrow was a successful trial lawyer before he became Judge of the 45th District Court. He then served as a Justice of the Court of Civil Appeals and later as Chief Justice for 11 years. He concluded his long judicial career by service on the Texas Supreme Court, from which he resigned in 1984 to become Dean of the School of Law, Baylor University. His impact upon the law extends beyond, but certainly includes, his knowledge and experience with the Texas Rules of Evidence. Like Judge Onion, he sits from time to time as a trial judge.

Professor Imwinkelried is Professor and Director of Trial Advocacy at the University of California at Davis. He is a nationally recognized expert on evidence and has authored and coauthored such books as *Criminal Courtroom Evidence, Scientific Evidence*, and a book which serves as the genesis to this, entitled *Evidentiary Foundations*. That book applies the foundation rules to the Federal Rules of Evidence. With others, he has written three other books which focus directly upon the evidence rules of California, Florida, and Illinois.

These legal scholars have fashioned a book that is needed, information, easy to read; one that will surely become a standard reference for proving up evidence in Texas courtrooms.

Jack Pope
Chief Justice Texas Supreme Court,
Retired

Preface

Texas Evidentiary Foundations is designed to help all but the most accomplished Texas attorney successfully participate in the real world of Texas trial practice. This text is designed for the recent law graduate, the rookie, and the experienced attorney whose practice has not brought him or her into such frequent contract with the courtroom so as to become a seasoned veteran. Each section of this text reviews a Texas evidentiary doctrine. The text then explains how the litigator can convert that doctrine into a concrete line of questions for use in the courtroom.

This text is based in part on *Evidentiary Foundations* (5th ed. 2002). That text discusses the process of laying foundations under the Federal Rules of Evidence. Many users of that text commented that although the text was useful, it would be more helpful if there were a text tailored to state court practice. That comment obviously has merit even in states such as Texas that have an evidence code patterned after the Federal Rules of Evidence. The evidentiary rules themselves and the specific procedures used in Texas often differ significantly from federal practice. We initially attempted to adapt *Evidentiary Foundations* to state practice in California. My colleagues, Richard Wydick and James Hogan, helped me prepare *California Evidentiary Foundations.* That text proved to be a success; California trial judges began recommending the text to attorneys appearing in their courts, and California appellate courts began citing the text as authority in their opinions. There are now state adaptations in Alabama, Colorado, Florida, Illinois, Minnesota, Missouri, New Jersey, New York, and North Carolina.

Encouraged by that success, we decided to adapt *Evidentiary Foundations* to state practice in other leading jurisdictions. As soon as LexisNexis suggested doing so in Texas, I immediately thought of my old friend, Professor David A. Schlueter. I asked Dave if he would agree to head a team to draft *Texas Evidentiary Foundations*. He was kind enough to do so. Dave took the lead on the first edition and this new edition as well.

Before drafting the first edition of *Texas Evidentiary Foundations*, Dave and I decided that to ensure that the draft reflected the realities of Texas practice, we needed to recruit distinguished state judges who have experience using Texas civil and criminal evidence on a daily basis. We were fortunate enough to persuade Judge John Onion and Justice Charles Barrow to collaborate in drafting *Texas Evidentiary Foundations*.

Although the organization of *Texas Evidentiary Foundations* is similar to that of *Evidentiary Foundations*, the content of this text has been thoroughly tailored to Texas practice. The tailoring required considerable effort, and I must give all the credit for that effort to Professor Schlueter, Judge Onion, and Justice Barrow.

Mastering this text will certainly not make the reader a polished, veteran litigator. I sincerely hope, however, that this text will help Texas attorneys successfully participate in the real world of Texas trial practice.

Edward J. Imwinkelried
Davis, California

ACKNOWLEDGMENTS

We gratefully acknowledge the vital assistance provided by a number of individuals on this project. First, in addition to those who worked on the second edition (Sam Lock, Steve Lovett, Erin McAuliffe, and Heather Tessmer) we recognize the excellent research skills and editorial assistance of Gregory Eyster and Danielle Copes.

Dedication

Dave Schlueter dedicates his work on this book to his wife, Linda.

John Onion dedicates his work on this book to his wife, Nancy.

Charles Barrow dedicates his work on this book to his wife, Sugie.

Ed Imwinkelried dedicates his work on this book to Cindy, Marie, Ken, and Rory; his parents, the late John and Enes Imwinkelried; and his parents-in-law, the late Lyman (Brownie) and Mary Jane Clark.

CHAPTER 1
INTRODUCTION: THE MECHANICS OF INTRODUCING EVIDENCE

§ 1-1 INTRODUCTION

The purpose of this text is to apply Texas evidence law in order to lay sufficient foundations, or predicates, for the introduction of items of evidence as well as to oppose admission of evidence. Most sections of the text use the following format:

First, at the beginning of each section there is a discussion of the applicable *evidentiary doctrine*. The discussion almost always cites the applicable Texas

Rule of Evidence, or, where no rule currently exists, the applicable Texas case law. Because the principal purpose of the text is to present trial technique rather than evidentiary doctrine, this portion is relatively short; and there are few case citations. When citations are used, they are usually in footnotes to make the text more readable.[1]

Second, the text breaks the doctrine down into a list of *foundation elements.* These elements are the historical facts and events which constitute the foundation, or the predicate. Each element is numbered.

Finally, the section contains a *sample foundation* for the evidentiary doctrine. Each question in the body of the sample foundation is numbered, with the number corresponding to the element in the foundation to which the question relates. Thus, the numbered foundation demonstrates how each element in the doctrine converts into concrete questions in the courtroom. In the sample foundations, the following key is used:

— "J" means judge;

— "W" means witness;

— "P" is the proponent of the evidence;

— "O" is the opponent of the evidence;

— "CR" is the court reporter; and

— "D" is the defendant.

The foundations assume that a jury is present. Thus, they tend to reflect a more formal style of introducing evidence. The procedure might be a bit more informal in a bench trial.

§ 1-2 LAYING A FOUNDATION: IN GENERAL

§ 1-2(A) LEGAL RULES

For the purposes of this text, the most important procedural rule is that the proponent of an item of evidence must ordinarily lay the foundation, or the predicate, before formally offering the item into evidence. This process is also sometimes referred to as "proving up" the evidence. For example, the proponent of a letter must present proof of its authenticity before offering the letter into evidence. Proof of the letter's authenticity is part of the letter's "foundation" or "predicate." Substantive evidence law makes proof of authenticity a condition

[1] The reader can find ample authority for the substantive propositions of evidence law in WENDORF, SCHLUETER & BARTON, TEXAS RULES OF EVIDENCE MANUAL (6th ed. 2002) and MCCORMICK, EVIDENCE (5th ed. 1999). The Texas Rules of Evidence are included in this text at Appendix A.

precedent to the letter's admission into evidence. Whenever evidence law makes proof of a fact or event a condition to the admission of an item of evidence (sometimes referred to as a "preliminary" fact), that fact or event is part of the foundation for the evidence's admission.

As in most jurisdictions, Texas trial judges have discretion to deviate from this procedural rule and may vary the order of proof and admit the evidence subject to the subsequent proof of the foundation. Judges may be reluctant, however, to delay the laying of the foundation because proof of the foundation before the evidence's admission is usually the more logical order of presentation. Moreover, if the judge admits the evidence subject to subsequent proof of the foundation and the proponent later fails to present the proof, the judge will be in an awkward position. At the very least, the judge will have to instruct the jurors to disregard the evidence they have already heard. If the judge believes that the instruction will be ineffective and the jurors will be unable to put aside the evidence, the judge may have to grant a mistrial. Thus, whenever possible, the proponent should lay the foundation, or predicate, before formally offering the piece of evidence.

§ 1-2(B) PRACTICAL RULES

There are four rules for drafting a line of questioning: simplicity, brevity, and preparation.

First, Always Use the Simplest, Most Easily Understood Term[2]

The trial attorney must communicate effectively with lay witnesses and jurors. Effective communication with lay persons requires that the trial attorney use lay diction. Jonathan Swift quite properly condemned the attorneys of his day for using "a peculiar Cant and Jargon of their own that no other mortal can understand . . . ." Sadly, many modern trial attorneys are guilty of the same literary sin. There is no need to resort to "prior" and "subsequent" if "before" and "after" will do quite nicely. There is no need to refer to a "motor vehicle" when the word "car" is available. There is no justification for using "altercation" when the attorney could say "fight." Trial attorneys should realize that the examination of witnesses is a test of communicative skill rather than vocabulary.

Second, Always Make Each Question as Short as Possible

One writer has observed that there is an inverse relation between the length of a sentence and its comprehensibility: the longer the sentence, the lower the level of reader or hearer comprehension.[3] Reading psychology studies indicate

[2] *See generally* WYDICK, PLAIN ENGLISH FOR LAWYERS, Chapter 7 (4th ed. 1998).

[3] *See* FLESCH, HOW TO WRITE PLAIN ENGLISH: A BOOK FOR LAWYERS AND CONSUMERS 20–32 (1979).

that the maximum length of a written sentence should be 25 words.[4] If the sentence is any longer, reader comprehension drops off markedly. It is more difficult for a hearer to absorb a spoken sentence than it is for a reader to absorb a written sentence. Consequently, many experienced trial attorneys strive to limit their questions to 10 or 15 words in length. If the spoken question exceeds 15 words, it can be very difficult for the witness and jurors to follow. One way to test this is to practice asking the questions aloud; in many instances it will be readily apparent to the speaker that fewer words would be easier to understand.

The Third Cardinal Rule is Preparation

Both the attorney and the witness must be well prepared for trial. The first step is to research the law, or legal doctrine, governing the necessary foundation or predicate. That will almost always require an examination of the applicable rules of evidence.[5] Without knowing the proper legal basis for introducing the evidence, counsel will often find it difficult to respond to the objection, "We object, your Honor. Counsel has not proved up the document," or "Counsel has not laid a sufficient predicate, your Honor." In preparing for trial, it is often helpful to practice asking the foundation questions aloud until they sound natural.

Practice should also include actually handling any exhibits and visualizing where to stand and what to say. As noted in later discussion of this point *infra* § 1-6(B), exhibits do not talk or walk themselves into evidence. If the attorney falters or pauses too long during direct examination, the examination loses its flow and rhythm. If the witness appears uncertain during questioning, at the very least the jurors will doubt the quality of the witness's memory. Good pretrial preparation should also include reviewing the contemplated testimony with the witness. For example, the attorney should tell the witness what foundation or predicate questions will be asked. All too often a trial attorney learns, after the witness takes the stand, that he or she cannot lay a foundation by that witness. Another common problem occurs when the witness is so awkward in answering the foundation or predicate questions that the credibility of the evidence finally admitted is severely limited in the jurors' minds. It is also appropriate to have the witness review the witness's deposition and other pretrial statements to refresh the witness's recollection.[6]

---

[4] *See* WYDICK, *supra* note 2, at Chapter 7.

[5] The Texas Rules of Evidence are included in this text at Appendix A.

[6] Counsel should be careful, however, on this point. Under Texas Rule 612, if a witness's memory has been refreshed before trial by reviewing a document, the trial court in its discretion may order production of that document, even if it contains otherwise privileged material. *See* Belcour, *Use It and Lose It—Privileged Documents, Preparing Witnesses, and Rule 612 of the Federal Rules of Evidence*, 31 FED. B. NEWS & J. 171, 172 (1984).

Fourth, Counsel Should Always Have a Purpose for Introducing the Evidence.

Trial lawyers must have a clear and beneficial purpose for examining any witness, on either direct or cross-examination. And that purpose must be understandable to the finder of fact. Pretrial preparations should include notations concerning what counsel hopes to accomplish with each witness, and what each witness or exhibit will contribute to developing the counsel's theory of the case. This means more than simply determining the relevance of a particular piece of evidence. In determining the purpose for introducing a particular piece of evidence, counsel might find it helpful to ask, "How can I use this in closing argument?" Indeed, some experienced counsel believe that the best way to focus on the purpose of evidence is to first work out the closing argument. Before trial, counsel should strategically evaluate the case to identify a coherent theory that rests on common sense or substantive justice. And everything counsel does at trial should be calculated to develop that theory. Unless trial lawyers and witnesses understand why the testimony is offered, and how it fits into counsel's overall theory, jurors will likely disregard the testimony or perceive counsel as ineffective.

§ 1-3 LAYING A FOUNDATION ON DIRECT EXAMINATION

The general rules for laying foundations apply to direct examination. The proponent, here the direct examiner, should lay a foundation before offering the evidence, and the examiner should observe the cardinal rules of simplicity and brevity. There are some additional rules, however, with which the direct examiner must be familiar.

§ 1-3(A) LEGAL RULES

§ 1-3(A)(1) Evidence Rules May Not Apply to Foundation Questions

One rule the direct examiner should become familiar with is that the technical evidentiary rules do not apply to some foundational questions. For instance, Texas Rule of Evidence 104(a) provides: "Preliminary questions concerning . . . the admissibility of evidence . . . shall be determined by the court . . . . In making its determination [the court] is not bound by the rules of evidence except those with respect to privileges." For example, suppose that the proponent is offering a witness's former testimony at a prior trial. Part of the foundation for the former testimony exception to the hearsay rule is proof that the witness is unavailable at the present trial. In a jurisdiction where the hearsay rule does not apply to foundational evidence, the proponent could ask an investigator on the witness stand to relate a third party's statement that the former witness had moved to Sweden. The third party's statement would usually be inadmissible hearsay. The third party was outside the courtroom when he or she made the statement, and the proponent is offering the statement for the truth of its assertion. The assumption here, however, is that the hearsay rule is inapplicable to the question of whether a foundation has been laid for admission of the former testimony.

§ 1-3(A)(2) Burden of Proof

In deciding whether a foundational or predicate fact has been established, the trial judge will ordinarily apply a preponderance of the evidence standard. Thus, where the admissibility of evidence is exclusively a question for the judge, for example, whether a witness is competent or a privilege exists, the trial judge applies a preponderance of the evidence standard and makes a final decision. In contrast, where the admissibility of the evidence depends on showing preliminary facts, as noted in Rule 104(b), the judge decides whether the proponent has provided enough evidence to permit the jury to decide by a preponderance of the evidence that the offered exhibit is authentic.[7] A typical example of this would be the issue of the authenticity of a letter purportedly written by one of the parties. The proponent shoulders the burden of convincing the judge, as the initial screener of evidence, that the letter is authentic, using one of the techniques discussed in Chapter 4. The opponent, of course, is free to challenge the foundation or predicate. If the judge decides that the proponent has provided enough proof to go to the jury, the question of whether the letter is authentic will ultimately be decided by the jury.

§ 1-3(A)(3) Use of Leading Questions

The second rule to bear in mind is that leading questions are usually forbidden on direct examination. Leading questions suggest the desired answer to the witness. Because the witness is presumably friendly to the direct examiner, the witness will probably follow the lead. Suppose that the plaintiff's brother was a witness to the accident. The plaintiff alleges that the defendant was speeding. The plaintiff calls her brother as a witness. It would be impermissibly leading for the plaintiff's attorney to ask, "Isn't it true that the defendant was going 80 miles an hour?" There is a serious risk that the witness, the plaintiff's brother, will simply follow the attorney's lead rather than attempting to give the most accurate testimony. It would also normally be impermissible for the proponent to hand an unauthenticated letter to the witness and say, "This is the letter you signed, isn't it?" On direct examination, the law prefers that the attorney use the nonleading question. Thus, in the two examples above it would be better

---

[7] *See* WENDORF, SCHLUETER & BARTON, TEXAS RULES OF EVIDENCE MANUAL I-71 to I-74 (6th ed. 2002).

to ask, "In your opinion, what was the defendant's speed?" And, "Do you recognize plaintiff's exhibit number three for identification?"

In addition to knowing the general prohibition of leading questions on direct examination, the direct examiner must realize that the prohibition is merely a norm rather than an absolute rule. There are numerous exceptions to the norm. One notable exception is that the direct examiner may use leading questions on preliminary matters. Most judges limit the scope of this exception to such matters as the witness's occupation and setting the scene for events. However, some judges construe "preliminary" very broadly and liberally permit leading questions on foundational matters. Another exception is that the direct examiner may use mildly leading questions to refresh the memory of a forgetful witness.

§ 1-3(B) PRACTICAL RULES

Whenever possible, counsel should comply with the technical evidentiary rules. Even if the local practice permits counsel to disregard those rules in laying a foundation, disregard of the rules will often prompt an objection. The opponent may not realize that the technical rules are inapplicable or relaxed in that court. Or the opponent may be searching for any pretext to disrupt the direct examination. The ideal direct examination is flowing and uninterrupted. Without distracting objections, the direct examiner gives the witness an opportunity to tell a story to the jurors. Counsel should minimize the risk that the opponent will interrupt his or her foundation with an objection. Every time the proponent disregards the technical rules in the foundational questions, there is a risk of a distracting objection.

The same practical considerations lead to the conclusion that, whenever possible, counsel should use nonleading questions on direct examination. Again, the key is to reduce the risk that the foundation will be interrupted by a leading question objection. Moreover, if counsel has a good witness, let the witness do the talking. By using leading questions which must be answered "Yes" or "No," counsel restricts the witness's opportunity to speak. And the jurors may suspect that counsel is putting words in the witness's mouth. If the witness projects honesty and intelligence, counsel should use open-ended, nonleading questions. The witness should be, as they say in the theater, "center stage."

Juror psychology studies suggest a further reason to avoid leading the witness. One study found that astute jurors note the difference between leading and nonleading questioning. More important, when the jurors note that the attorney is leading a particular witness, they tend to infer that the attorney is doing so because the attorney lacks faith in the witness. Understandably, after drawing that inference, the jurors discount the witness's "credibility." Tactically, nonleading questions are preferable on direct examination.

To ensure that questions are nonleading, it is better to begin as many as possible with the words, "who," "what," "which," "when," "where," "how," and "why." If a question begins with one of these words, counsel will find that it is very difficult to make the question leading. Indeed, many trial judges use the rule of thumb that questions beginning with these words are not leading.

In this text, we have made a conscious effort to begin every question in the sample foundations for direct examination with one of these words. In the sample foundations, the word is in capital letters. Our hope is that reading questions beginning with these words will help the practitioner develop the skill and habit of phrasing nonleading questions.

We are not advocating the practice of beginning every sentence of direct examination with one of these words, because that practice would make direct examination annoyingly monotonous. As professional writers say, counsel should use elegant variation in phrasing questions. By way of example, counsel should ordinarily use an interrogatory sentence. But when background information is desired, counsel can use imperative sentences. For instance, the witness can be instructed to "Please tell us where you work." Furthermore, to highlight the subdivisions of direct examination, declarative sentences may be appropriate. For example, "Now I want to ask you a few questions about what happened at the hospital." Even when counsel use interrogatory sentences, as we have seen, evidence law sometimes permits use of gently leading questions. Most new trial attorneys, however, pay insufficient attention to the phrasing of their questions on direct examination. This text uniformly uses nonleading phrasing to help the reader develop a habit of consistently phrasing nonleading questions.

§ 1-4 LAYING A FOUNDATION ON CROSS-EXAMINATION

The general rules for laying a foundation also apply here. Most of the general rules apply with even greater force on cross-examination. On cross, judges may be reluctant to permit the examiner to introduce an item of evidence before presenting the foundational proof. On cross-examination, the witness is often hostile to the examiner, and the judge may be more skeptical of the examiner's assurance that the witness will give favorable testimony at a later point in the examination. The norms of simplicity and brevity similarly apply with greater force on cross-examination. The hostile witness will often strain to misinterpret the question; the cross-examiner wants to frame questions that are so clear and so short that they cannot be misinterpreted. In addition to knowing the general rules for laying foundations, however, the cross-examiner must be cognizant of several special rules for cross-examination.

§ 1-4(A) LEGAL RULES

The practitioner may occasionally encounter a trial judge who believes that an attorney may not introduce an exhibit during the cross-examination of an opposing witness. That belief is erroneous.[8] Texas Rule of Evidence 611(b) permits wide open cross-examination on any matter relevant to the case, and Rule 611(a) gives the judge discretionary control over the order of proof. Thus, the permissibility of introducing exhibits during the cross-examination rests within the discretion of the judge.

Because the witness is often hostile to the cross-examiner, the law permits leading questions on cross-examination. While leading questions are permissible on cross, argumentative questions are still objectionable. An argumentative question challenges the witness about an inference from the facts in the case. Assume that the witness testifies on direct examination that the defendant's car was going 80 miles an hour just before the collision. You want to impeach the witness with a prior inconsistent statement. It would be permissible, leading cross-examination to ask, "Isn't it true that you told your neighbor, Mrs. Ashton, at a party last Sunday that the defendant's car was going only 50 miles an hour?" The cross-examiner may legitimately attempt to force the witness to concede the historical fact of the prior inconsistent statement. Now assume that the witness admits the statement. Some trial judges would consider it impermissibly argumentative to ask, "How can you reconcile that statement with your testimony on direct examination?" The cross-examiner is not seeking any additional facts. Instead, the cross-examiner is challenging the witness about an inference from the facts already in evidence. Questions such as "How can you expect the jury to believe that?" or "When were you lying, then or now?" may be similarly considered argumentative and objectionable. There are two schools of thought here. One school believes that the attorney should avoid confronting the impeached witness further and argue the inferences during summation or closing argument. The other school believes that even when the witness has admitted the inconsistency, something should be said at that point, lest the jurors forget what took place. While asking the witness, in a nonconfrontational manner, how he or she can reconcile the inconsistency may risk an objection that the question is argumentative, many counsel are willing to take that risk.

§ 1-4(B) PRACTICAL RULES

Negatively, the cross-examiner should scrupulously avoid argumentative questions. If a hostile witness is intelligent, the witness usually will not easily concede the favorable inference counsel wants to draw. An argumentative question often prompts a heated exchange between the cross-examiner and the

---

[8] J. TANFORD, THE TRIAL PROCESS: LAW, TACTICS AND ETHICS 289–90 (3d ed. 2002).

witness. If that happens, lay jurors may sympathize with the lay witness, and counsel can antagonize the jurors by arguing with the witness. Unless the witness has a particularly abrasive personality, arguments or heated exchanges between the attorney and witness are usually "no-win" situations for the attorney.

If the attorney appears to dominate the exchange, the jurors may infer that the attorney does not want the witness to tell the whole truth. But if the witness appears to dominate, the jurors may conclude that the attorney is diffident, perhaps because the attorney lacks faith in his or her case. Counsel should elicit the historical facts which he or she is morally certain the witness will concede. Closing argument can then be used to draw inferences.

Affirmatively, as a general proposition, the practitioner should consistently use leading questions on cross-examination. Ordinarily, counsel should not give a hostile witness any opening. For example, it can be dangerous to give that witness an opportunity to explain by asking, "Why?" If counsel wants to impeach a witness with a conviction, it is better to ask, "Isn't it true that you have been convicted of perjury?" To prove a prior inconsistent statement, ask, "Isn't it a fact that right after the fight, you told the officer that the hallway was so dark that you couldn't identify your attacker?"

Questions should be prefaced with "Isn't it true . . . ?" "Isn't it correct . . . ?" or "Isn't it a fact . . . ?" to maintain control over the witness. Counsel can also make a declarative statement and add a tag sentence such as "Isn't that true?" at the very end of the question.

We have attempted to begin as many questions as possible in the sample foundations for cross-examination with leading prefatory language. The preface is in capital letters. Our purpose is to help the reader develop the habit of consistently using leading questions on cross-examination. Again, we do not advocate beginning every question with blatantly leading introductory language. Sometimes the practitioner will want to use nonleading questions. For instance, if it appears that an adverse child witness has a memorized story, the cross-examiner might pose an open-ended, nonleading question to the witness to give the child another opportunity to repeat the story verbatim.[9] In other cases, if the topic is safe, counsel can use gently leading questions, beginning with such words as "Is," "Was," and "Did."

The primary failing of neophyte cross-examiners, however, is that they do not lead enough. We have deliberately exaggerated and begun every cross-examination question with blatantly leading language to underscore the importance of maintaining witness control. Albert Krieger, the former president of the

[9] This tactic has been described in many continuing legal education seminars. But it poses some problems. First, the child may not repeat the story verbatim, thus deflating the argument that the story is canned. Second, if the child is a sympathetic witness, the jury may turn on the questioner who appears willing to put the child through seemingly unnecessary questioning.

National Association of Criminal Defense Lawyers, has remarked that under the guise of asking questions, a good cross-examiner actually makes factual assertions and forces the witness to express assent on the record.

Finally, counsel's demeanor and tone should ordinarily be friendly even when using narrowly-phrased, leading questions. In many cases, the key is to get the opposing witness to cooperate. Using combative or offensive language will not do the trick. Quite to the contrary, if counsel's demeanor is aggressive, the witness will put up his or her defenses, and counsel will have a very difficult time eliciting favorable information. Sometimes the practitioner will want to make a show of righteous indignation at an opposing witness caught in an obvious lie. But when using the opposing witness to lay a foundation, the wisest tactic is to be friendly and low-key.

§ 1-5 LAYING MULTIPLE FOUNDATIONS

Any given piece of evidence potentially requires more than one foundation or application of several evidence rules, depending on its use at trial. For example, in laying the foundation for any document, the proponent must show not only that the document is relevant under Texas Rule of Evidence 401, but also that it is authentic under Rule 901 or 902. But counsel should also be prepared to lay a foundation for showing that the document satisfies the hearsay rule[10] and the original document (best evidence) rule.[11] And if the document contains privileged information, counsel should be prepared to satisfy any foundation requirements for showing that no privilege exists.[12] Multiple foundations might be analogized to conditions analysis in contracts cases. The plaintiff must demonstrate that every condition precedent or concurrent has been either fulfilled or excused. Similarly, the proponent of evidence must show that every foundational fact has been established under Rule 104. In this text, we will occasionally point out the need for determining not only what foundation to lay, but that multiple foundations may be required.

§ 1-6 LAYING A FOUNDATION: THE MECHANICS OF HANDLING, MARKING, AND INTRODUCING EXHIBITS

§ 1-6(A) LEGAL RULES

There are few legal rules governing the handling, marking, and formal introduction of exhibits. The Rules of Evidence speak in terms of authenticating

[10] *See* Chapter 10.

[11] *See* Chapter 8.

[12] *See* Chapter 7.

or identifying evidence, but offer no legal guidelines on *how* it must be done. And the various rules of procedure, both civil and criminal, are generally silent on the subject. Despite the absence of clear legal rules, nothing can be more frustrating to the trial process than confusion over the method of marking an exhibit, laying the foundation, and, ultimately, introducing it into evidence.

§ 1-6(B) PRACTICAL RULES: TALKING AND WALKING THE EXHIBIT INTO EVIDENCE

A general set of practical rules for actually handling an exhibit in the courtroom has emerged over the years. While the practice will vary from courtroom to courtroom, a number of well-accepted principles should be followed, unless the court tells counsel otherwise. The following discussion focuses on the "how to" of laying evidentiary foundations for tangible exhibits.

In their insightful article on presenting evidence, Justice Jack Pope and Charles Hampton point out that exhibits do not talk themselves into the record of trial.[13] Counsel must "talk" the exhibits in. What that means is that the proponent should not assume that everyone in the courtroom automatically knows what the exhibit is, or what it represents. Likewise, the process of laying foundations for evidence requires counsel literally to walk the exhibit between the reporter, the opposing counsel, the witness, and the jury.

Although it may seem awkward, it is better to err on the side of formality in presenting the exhibit. Thus, the proponent should indicate, "Please let the record reflect that I am handing plaintiff's exhibit seven for identification to the opposing counsel." In that way, not only will the reporter and other trial participants be alerted to the fact that a piece of tangible evidence is being presented, but the appellate record will also reflect counsel's actions in handling the exhibit. It should be noted, however, that many judges will not say anything in response to the "let the record reflect" language. Nonetheless, the record will indeed reflect that point. Throughout this text, we have included suggested language in the sample foundation questions that counsel may use in "talking" the exhibit into evidence.

§ 1-7 A FOUR-STEP PROCESS FOR HANDLING EXHIBITS: IN GENERAL

There are a number of ways of describing the pattern for handling exhibits at trial. The process we suggest here is perhaps more formal than most trial judges would require, but it seems to work best. Again, it is normally better to err on the side of formality than to have the trial judge remind counsel that it is required.

---

[13] *See* Pope & Hampton, *Presenting and Excluding Evidence*, 9 TEX. T. L. REV. 403, 408 (1978). This is a "must read" article for Texas practitioners.

In some courts, the trial judges expect that counsel will request permission to move around the courtroom, especially in approaching the bench or the witness. That practice obviously varies and counsel should, as a part of pretrial preparation, determine what the trial judge prefers.

§ 1-7(A) STEP ONE: MARKING THE EXHIBIT AND SHOWING IT TO OPPOSING COUNSEL AND THE WITNESS

Assuming that the exhibit has not been marked before trial, counsel should normally request the court reporter to mark it for identification and numbering. In effect, the letters or numbers affixed to the exhibit become a convenient shortcut for referring to the exhibit. Thus, in a case involving dozens of letters, counsel and the court may simply refer to "Defense Exhibit 12." Typically, the processing of "marking" the exhibit consists of attaching some sort of pre-printed label with a space for inserting a number. Each exhibit is numbered sequentially, to permit the participants to locate quickly a particular exhibit. Many courts refer to the exhibit as being one "for identification," until it is actually admitted as an exhibit. At that point the words "for ID" or "for identification" are lined through, to show that the exhibit was admitted into evidence.

While there are some advantages to marking the exhibits before trial, it is almost always better to have the court reporter do so. Reporters have their own system of marking and numbering exhibits and can quickly determine how the exhibit ought to be designated. If counsel has marked the exhibits beforehand and then decides not to introduce a specific exhibit, all of the subsequent numbered exhibits will be off.

In asking that the exhibit be marked, counsel should hand the exhibit to the court reporter and clearly ask that the reporter mark the exhibit. Counsel may say, "We request that this be marked as an exhibit for identification for the plaintiff." Or, counsel may hand the exhibit to the court reporter and, in doing so, state, "Your Honor, we request that this exhibit be marked by the court reporter." In no case should counsel simply stand in front of the reporter and expect him or her to know what counsel wants. Having marked, i.e., numbered, the exhibit, some reporters will announce how the exhibit has been designated. If that is not the case, counsel should examine the exhibit, determine what number or letter has been assigned and thereafter refer to the exhibit by that designation. Counsel should, as a part of pretrial preparation, determine what process is used in that particular court. If there are related exhibits, it may be preferable to have them marked at one time, especially if counsel intends to show them as a group to the witness.

Regardless of the system of marking the exhibit, once it is marked, it takes on the identity of that number or letter. Thereafter, counsel should, at a minimum, refer to it by its number or letter.

Once the exhibit is marked, the proponent should "walk" the exhibit and show it to the opposing counsel. This action is usually reflected with language to the effect, "Please let the record reflect that I am now showing defense exhibit one for ID to [the opposing counsel]." Again, this announcement makes clear on the record what is happening to the exhibit in question. Showing the exhibit to the opposing counsel presents the image of fairness: the proponent is not trying to sneak anything past the opposing counsel.

There are at least two schools of thought on the advisability of showing the exhibit to the opposing counsel at this point. Some counsel will not show the exhibit to opposing counsel until after they have laid the foundation, discussed *infra* § 1-7(B), and just before they formally offer it into evidence. Before that point, they assert, any objections to the exhibit would be premature. A second approach, and the one used in this text, recognizes that although an objection to the exhibit would usually be premature, the opposing counsel is given an opportunity at least to see what evidence the foundation witness is talking about. As noted above, it gives the appearance of being "up front" with the evidence. It also precludes the opposing counsel from interrupting the process of laying the foundation by asking to see the exhibit.

Assuming the opponent offers no objections at the point of examining the exhibit, the proponent should next carry the exhibit and show it to the foundation or sponsoring witness. As before, the proponent should "talk" the exhibit into the record by indicating, "Please let the record reflect that I am now showing [the numbered exhibit] to [the witness]." In showing the exhibit to the witness, the proponent should avoid leading the witness (or testifying) by telling the witness what the exhibit is. Instead, counsel should hand the exhibit to the witness and ask the witness to tell the jury what the exhibit is. It is always acceptable to refer to the exhibit by its number for purposes of the record.

§ 1-7(B) STEP TWO: LAYING THE FOUNDATION OR THE PREDICATE

The terms "foundation" and "predicate" refer to the testimony the proponent must elicit from the witness before offering the exhibit into evidence. The process of asking the foundation or predicate questions is often referred to as "proving up" the evidence or the exhibit. The type of foundation or predicate will depend on the type of evidence. Sample foundation questions are noted throughout this text. During this process, the proponent should continue to be sensitive about "talking" the exhibit into evidence, referring to it by its assigned number or letter and by the witness's characterization of it. This is particularly important, for example, where counsel is asking the witness questions about several exhibits. The better practice is to lay the foundation for exhibits one at a time to avoid confusion.

§ 1-7(C) STEP THREE: FORMALLY OFFERING THE EXHIBIT INTO EVIDENCE

After laying the necessary foundation, counsel should formally offer the exhibit into evidence. For example, counsel should state, "Your Honor, we now offer defense exhibit number one for identification into evidence." The offer should be short and to the point. Using long, involved language may only confuse the participants as to whether the exhibit is being offered. Now is not the time for an editorial comment on the evidence. This offer, or tender, should serve as a clear signal to the opponent to make any appropriate objections, or to risk waiver. It also alerts the trial judge that a ruling will be required. If the trial judge decides to defer ruling on the exhibit, the proponent must be prepared to remind the court later of the deferral and, if necessary, to persist in requesting a ruling. Failure to obtain a ruling may act as a waiver. If the court reporter has marked and accounted for the exhibit, it should be easier to track which exhibits have been admitted or excluded. Before resting his or her case, counsel should carefully determine that the judge has ruled upon all exhibits offered into evidence.

If the judge admits the exhibit into evidence, it should normally be handed back to the court reporter for additional annotation. For example, most court reporters have some method for indicating that the exhibit was admitted or excluded.

§ 1-7(D) STEP FOUR: SHOWING OR READING THE EXHIBIT TO THE JURY

If the trial judge admits the exhibit into evidence, the proponent must ensure that the jury sees or hears the exhibit, either immediately or later in the trial. This process is sometimes referred to as "publishing" the exhibit. Although the term is rarely used, it serves as a useful reminder that the jury is entitled to examine exhibits admitted into evidence. They may even take them into their deliberations. When the exhibit is a piece of physical evidence such as a piece of rope, counsel should ask, "Your Honor, I request permission to hand this exhibit to the jurors for their inspection." When the exhibit is a document, counsel may ask, "I request permission to read [the pertinent portions] to the jury, your Honor." Occasionally, an opposing attorney will object that the document speaks for itself. That objection is bogus.[14] The judge has the discretion to permit the witness or the attorney to quote from a document which has already been admitted into evidence. In the case of any documentary or physical evidence, when the

[14] *See, e.g.*, Moss, *Beyond the Fringe: Apocryphal Rules of Evidence in Texas*, 43 BAYLOR L. REV. 701, 726 (1991).

proponent has completed using the exhibit, it should be handed back to the court reporter or clerk.[15]

§ 1-8 A SAMPLE "WALK-THROUGH"

The following is a short example of how a proponent might walk and talk an exhibit into evidence. Assume that plaintiff's counsel wishes to introduce a letter through the testimony of a Mr. Smith. Following some preliminary questions, the proponent (i.e., plaintiff's counsel) picks up the letter from the counsel table and carries it to where the court reporter is sitting:

P [*Speaking to court reporter*] Would you please mark this as an exhibit for the plaintiff? [*Court reporter marks exhibit and hands it back to proponent.*]

P Thank you. [*Counsel examines document to determine how it has been designated.*] Please let the record reflect that I am now handing what has been marked as plaintiff's exhibit number one for identification to the opposing counsel. [*Opposing counsel inspects exhibit and hands it back to the proponent.*]

P Now, Mr. Smith, I show you what has been marked as plaintiff's exhibit number one for identification. Do you recognize it?

At this point, the proponent lays whatever predicate or foundation is necessary for this particular type of evidence. That is, counsel proves up the evidence. After the foundation or predicate has been laid, the proponent continues as follows:

P Thank you, Mr. Smith. Your Honor, we now offer into evidence plaintiff's exhibit number one for identification.

J Are there any objections?[16]

O No, your Honor.

J Plaintiff's exhibit number one will be received into evidence. [*Proponent hands exhibit to court reporter for further annotation.*]

P Your Honor, we now request permission for Mr. Smith to read a portion of plaintiff's exhibit number one [*the letter*] to the jury.

---

15 During trial, there should be *one* depository for exhibits admitted or exhibits marked for identification but not admitted for one reason or another. Frequently, the exhibits may be used more than once, and the attorneys must know to whom they must look for the availability of the exhibits. The court reporter has long occupied this role in Texas court proceedings although it is now apparently the clerk to whom the exhibits are eventually transferred after trial. Exhibits should not be left with a bailiff. In some courts there are no bailiffs and, even if there are, they frequently change.

16 If there are objections, the proponent should be prepared to answer them.

J Proceed.

CHAPTER 2
PRESERVING ERROR: OBJECTIONS, OFFERS OF PROOF, AND MOTIONS

§ 2-1 INTRODUCTION

Most practitioners realize the importance of learning the procedures that the proponent must use to present evidence. The subsequent chapters outline those procedures. There is a related topic, however, which cannot be overemphasized in any discussion on the admissibility of evidence: the need to preserve error. An in-depth discussion of that topic is beyond the scope of this text. Instead, the discussion here will briefly focus on two sets of procedural rules a trial attorney must master:

1. the procedures the opponent uses to object to the admission of the proponent's evidence; and
2. the procedures the proponent uses if the trial judge sustains the opponent's objection.

The purpose of this chapter is to familiarize the practitioner with these two sets of very important procedural rules. Sections 2-3 through 2-4 describe the procedures that the opponent must invoke to exclude evidence. Section 2-5 illustrates the procedures that the proponent resorts to if the judge sustains an objection by the opponent. Finally, § 2-7 addresses the importance of requesting limiting instructions.

§ 2-2 PRETRIAL MOTION IN LIMINE BY THE OPPONENT

§ 2-2(A) The Doctrine

If the opponent anticipates an evidentiary issue arising at trial, the opponent need not wait until trial to voice the objection. The opponent may raise the objection by a pretrial motion in limine.[1] Although the proponent may make a motion in limine to obtain an advance ruling of the evidence's admissibility, such motions are more frequently used by the opponent to suppress evidence before the trial begins. As a practical matter, such motions are used most frequently to secure a pretrial or early ruling requiring the proponent of the evidence that the opponent hopes to exclude to approach the bench before mentioning or offering such evidence. The motion itself may include this point as the primary prayer, or it may include the request for a preliminary order as an alternate prayer.

The opponent may use the motion for such purposes as preventing any mention of a wrongful death plaintiff's remarriage, a civil defendant's liability insurance, a criminal defendant's prior convictions or extraneous offenses, or the results of a polygraph test.

There are several tactical reasons why the opponent may employ a motion in limine. The most obvious reason is that the objectionable evidence might be highly prejudicial. If the opponent delays objecting until trial, the jurors may, at least, hear some mention of the evidence. It would be preferable to litigate the issue before trial and to preclude the proponent from even mentioning the evidence during trial. If the jurors hear any mention of the evidence, they may conclude that the opponent is hiding the truth from them. Further, the opponent may need an advance ruling to make strategy decisions for trial. For example, a criminal defense attorney must address the issue of whether or not to put his or her client on the stand. In making that decision, the defense attorney must

---

[1] *See* Hazel, *The Motion in Limine: A Texas Proposal,* 21 Hous. L. Rev. 919 (1984).

consider the risk that if the client testifies, the judge may permit the prosecutor to impeach the client with prior convictions. If the judge grants a pretrial motion in limine to exclude the convictions, the defense attorney can confidently place the client on the stand. Without the benefit of the pretrial ruling, the defense attorney must gamble that the judge will exclude the convictions on objection.

Finally, when the attorney is relying on a novel theory to exclude the evidence, making an in limine motion can increase the probability that the judge will exclude the evidence because it gives the judge a chance to think through the theory. If the attorney springs the theory on the judge for the first time at trial, the judge will likely reject the theory and admit the evidence. Submitting the motion before trial demonstrates that the attorney has enough confidence in the theory to allow the judge time to think it through.

How does the opponent make a motion in limine? As a matter of fairness, the opponent should give advance notice. The better practice, if the court does not already require it, is to reduce the motion to writing. The opponent may make the motion either weeks or days before the trial, or on the day of trial before the proceedings begin either in open court or when the attorneys and the judge meet in the judge's chambers.

The trial judge has discretion whether to entertain the motion. In some cases, the judge may prefer to rule on the issue during trial, after the issues become clearer. If the judge entertains the motion, there are several possible rulings:

1. the judge may deny the motion;
2. the judge may enter an absolute order prohibiting the proponent from mentioning the evidence during the trial; or
3. the judge may enter a preliminary order.

On the one hand, a preliminary order prohibits the proponent from mentioning the evidence to the jury without the judge's consent. The order can be worded to apply not only to witnesses' testimony, but also to any reference to the evidence by the attorney during voir dire examination and opening statement. On the other hand, a preliminary order permits the proponent to request a hearing out of the jury's presence during the trial. At that hearing, the proponent may attempt to persuade the judge to admit the evidence. A preliminary order is appropriate when the judge finds that the evidence is prejudicial but does not want to rule finally until he or she knows the final state of the evidence at trial.

Because of the nonbinding nature of the motion in limine in Texas practice, a ruling on the motion does not, in itself, preserve error. In other words, if counsel is successful in obtaining a favorable ruling in limine, an objection to the evidence at trial will still be necessary if the opposing counsel nonetheless attempts to introduce it. And, if the in limine ruling is unfavorable, counsel must renew the objection at trial when the evidence is offered.

There is an additional requirement to preserve error when the motion challenges convictions offered as impeachment evidence under Rule 609. The requirement was first discussed in *Luce v. United States.*[2] In that case, the defense moved in limine to exclude the defendant's conviction on the ground that the prejudicial character of the evidence outweighed its probative value. The defense argued that the prospect of the admission of the conviction would deter the defendant from testifying and would thereby deprive the jury of the defendant's valuable testimony. The trial judge denied the motion, and the defendant elected not to testify. On appeal, the defense challenged the denial of the motion. The United States Supreme Court held that the alleged error would not be reviewed unless the defendant actually testified at trial. Texas case law seems to follow this rule.[3]

§ 2-2(B) Elements of a Motion in Limine

The following are the elements of a motion in limine to exclude evidence:

1. The opponent states his or her intent to move in limine to exclude certain evidence.
2. The opponent has reason to believe that the proponent possesses the evidence and will offer the evidence at trial.
3. The opponent briefly states the ground on which the evidence is inadmissible. The opponent must state the ground with the same specificity with which he or she would make a trial objection. See *infra* § 2-3.
4. The opponent explains why an ordinary trial objection would be inadequate protection for the opponent.
5. The opponent presents the legal argument in favor of the motion.

After the proponent's response, the judge either rules or defers ruling.

§ 2-2(C) Sample Motion in Limine

The fact situation is a criminal prosecution. The defendant is charged with armed robbery. The defendant has a prior, 2000 conviction for armed robbery in Alabama. The judge has already begun the in-chambers conference before trial. The opponent is the defense counsel.

J Are there any other matters either of you think we should take up before trial begins?

---

[2] 469 U.S. 38 (1984).

[3] *See, e.g., Benavides v. State*, 763 S.W.2d 587 (Tex. App.—Corpus Christi 1988, pet. ref.); *Richardson v. State*, 733 S.W.2d 947 (Tex. App.—Austin 1987), *judgment vacated on other grounds*, 761 S.W.2d 19 (Tex. Crim. App. 1988).

O Yes, your Honor. I would like to make a motion in limine to absolutely preclude the prosecutor from mentioning my client's 2000 armed robbery conviction. (1) Pursuant to a Rule 609 request,[4] the prosecutor has informed me that she has a certified copy of the judgment of conviction. I assume that if my client takes the stand, the prosecutor will attempt to use the conviction to impeach my client. (2) I have given the prosecutor a week's advance notice of my intention to make this motion. I have also given her a copy of the memorandum of law, citing the cases I'm relying on as authority.

J [*To the prosecutor*] Did you receive the advance notice?

P Yes.

J And is it your intention to use the conviction?

P Yes, your Honor. It is well-settled in Texas that you can use a felony conviction to impeach a witness, even a criminal defendant. Under Alabama law, this type of armed robbery is a felony. Here is a copy of the latest version of the Alabama penal code which makes our point.

J Defense counsel, have you seen this?

O Yes, your Honor, I have. And I'm aware of the usual rule in Texas. However, our position is that because the 2000 conviction is for the same type of crime my client is now charged with, the conviction is too prejudicial. There's too great a risk that the jurors will misuse this impeachment evidence and treat it as evidence of the defendant's bad character. (3)

J I normally defer ruling on this type of issue until trial.

O I'm aware of that, your Honor. However, I would urge you to dispose of this issue before trial begins. A trial objection won't adequately protect my client. In this case, the charged crime and the crime my client was previously convicted of are absolutely identical. If there's any mention of this conviction at trial, the jurors simply won't be able to follow any curative instruction you give to disregard the evidence if you decide that it is inadmissible. Moreover, I am trying to decide whether to put my client on the stand. Your ruling is going to be a major factor in my decision. (4)

J Do you have any authority to support your motion?

O I've cited the most important cases in my memorandum of law. As pointed out on page two of my memo, Rule 609(a) provides that, as trial judge, you have discretion to balance a conviction's probative value against its prejudicial character. And, under that rule, the conviction should not be

---

[4] *See* TEX. R. EVID. 609(f) (notice provision).

admissible unless the probative value of the evidence outweighs the prejudicial effects. (5)

P Your Honor, all you have to do is give the jurors a limiting instruction. They can be told that they are to consider the conviction solely as impeachment evidence. Further, they can be told that they're not to use the conviction as evidence of the defendant's bad character. That is, they're not to infer that he committed the charged robbery because he committed a previous robbery or because he is a bad person.

O As the cases point out, we can't trust a limiting instruction here. The crimes are identical, and we consequently can't assume that the jurors will follow the limiting instruction. (5) In fact, we should assume that they will improperly consider the conviction.

P My last point, your Honor, is that we have a substantial need for this evidence. There's only one eyewitness, the victim. This trial is going to be a classic swearing contest. The outcome is going to turn on whom the jury believes. We need all the impeaching evidence at our disposal.

J I think that this is an appropriate case for a preliminary rather than an absolute order. I agree that since the crimes are identical, the conviction has tremendous potential for prejudice. Yet, I don't want to absolutely preclude any use of the conviction. If the trial becomes the swearing contest the prosecutor predicts, the prosecution's need for the impeaching evidence may outweigh its prejudicial character. I am going to enter a preliminary order. I don't want any mention of the conviction in the jury's hearing without my prior permission. Ms. Prosecutor, if at any point during the trial you think that the record establishes your need for the evidence, I want you to request a hearing out of the jurors' presence. You can make an offer of proof at the hearing, and then I'll finally rule whether you can use the conviction.

§ 2-3 OBJECTIONS AT TRIAL BY THE OPPONENT

§ 2-3(A) The Doctrine

If the opponent does not move in limine or the judge refuses to entertain the pretrial motion, the opponent must object at trial. When the opponent objects, the opponent in effect asserts that it is improper to admit the proponent's evidence. The American litigation system is patterned after an adversary model: the burden of presenting evidence is on the proponent, and the burden of excluding evidence is on the opponent. In rare cases, an error can be so plain and prejudicial that the judge will exclude the evidence on his or her own motion. Given our adversary model, the opponent must ordinarily assume the responsibility for excluding evidence by objecting.

Any objections made by the opponent must be *courteous, timely*, and *specific*. The following discussion addresses those requirements.[5]

An Objection Must Be Courteous

The opponent owes a duty of courtesy to the trial judge and to the proponent. The opponent should stand to state any objection and preface the objection with "your Honor . . . ." Rambo-like tactics in making objections should be avoided. They can alienate the trial judge and the jury. In a courtroom, it is always better to assume, until instructed otherwise, that all formalities will be followed. That holds true for making objections.

An Objection Must Be Timely

The objection must be neither too early nor too late. The rule is that counsel must object as soon as the grounds for the objection become apparent. That usually means objecting as soon as the evidence is offered. For example, suppose that the objection relates to a foundational issue such as authentication, best evidence, or hearsay. Foundational objections are premature until the questioning attorney attempts to elicit the objectionable testimony. Thus, if the opposing attorney believes that there is an inadequate authentication foundation for a letter, the attorney must reserve the objection until the questioning attorney offers the letter into evidence. Similarly, when the opposing attorney believes that there is an inadequate hearsay foundation for an out-of-court statement, the attorney must reserve the objection until the questioning attorney asks the witness to state the contents of the out-of-court statement. In contrast, if the objection relates to a form problem such as leading or argumentative questioning, the opponent should state the objection immediately after the improper question and before the witness begins the answer. If the opponent delays the objection, the opponent has waived the objection unless he or she can show good reason for the delay.

An Objection Must Be Specific

The opponent must specify both what he is objecting to and why he is objecting. A general objection normally presents nothing for review on appeal. The opponent should identify the word, phrase, or question to which he or she is objecting. In addition, he or she must state the legal ground for the objection. Texas Rule of Evidence 103(a)(1) requires that the opponent state "the specific ground of objection, if the specific ground [is] not apparent from the context." An objection citing the generic evidentiary doctrine may be sufficient to preserve error. For example, the opponent may claim that the proponent is violating the

---

[5] For a more complete discussion of the requirements of preserving error through objections to evidence, *see* WENDORF, SCHLUETER & BARTON, TEXAS RULES OF EVIDENCE MANUAL I-26 to I-58 (6th ed. 2002).

"best evidence" or "hearsay" rules. A better objection, however, would direct the judge's attention to a particular rule of evidence. On the other hand, simply citing one of the Texas Rules of Evidence may not be sufficient. Where the objection is "generic," counsel may have difficulty in determining what response or further questioning may be required. In that case, it may be appropriate to ask the opponent, through the judge, to state why he or she feels, for example, that the evidence is inadmissible hearsay.

In the presence of the jury, the opponent should slightly vary the objection's wording to ensure that the jury does not gain the impression that the opponent is invoking technical rules to suppress or hide the truth. For example, the opponent should state that the proponent is "unfairly" leading the witness or attempting to introduce "unreliable" hearsay. While tailoring the objection's phrasing for the jury, the opponent must not make a "speaking objection." This expression refers to long-winded objections where the opponent makes a speech rather than briefly stating the legal ground for the objection. Trial judges will generally not tolerate speaking objections.

If counsel contemplates making a "running objection" to a series of questions, he or she should first seek permission from the court to do so to ensure that the participants understand what is being objected to, and when.

§ 2-3(B) Elements of an Objection

A proper objection includes the following elements:

1. The opponent addresses the judge.
2. The opponent indicates that he or she is raising an objection.
3. The opponent specifies what he or she is objecting to, e.g., the particular word, phrase, or question.
4. The opponent specifies the legal ground for the objection, that is, the evidentiary doctrine or rule of evidence the proponent is violating.

§ 2-3(C) Sample Objections

Some of the opponent's objections will claim violations of substantive evidentiary doctrines. The following objections are illustrative:

Your Honor, (1) I object (2) to any testimony by this proposed witness (3) on the ground that this person is incompetent under Rule 601 to be a witness. (4) (See *infra* Chapter 3.)

Your Honor, (1) I object (2) to the admission of plaintiff's exhibit number six (3) on the ground that there has been insufficient authentication. (4) (See *infra* Chapter 4.)

Your Honor, (1) I object (2) to the admission of defense exhibit number ten (3) on the ground that it is only a copy and, therefore, not the original writing. (4) (See *infra* Chapter 8.)

Your Honor, (1) I object (2) to counsel's question concerning the defendant's demeanor (3) on the ground that it calls for improper opinion. (4) (See *infra* Chapter 9.)

Your Honor, (1) I object (2) to counsel's question (3) on the ground that it calls for hearsay. (4) (See *infra* Chapter 10.)

Your Honor, (1) I object (2) to counsel's question of the defendant concerning what his wife said to him (3) on the ground that it calls for disclosure of a privileged communication. (4) (See *infra* Chapter 7.)

Many of the objections made during the typical trial relate to matters of form rather than substance. The following are examples of form objections:

Your Honor (1), I object (2) to that question (3) on the ground that it is vague and ambiguous. (4)

Your Honor (1), I object (2) to that question (3) on the ground that it is leading. (4)

Your Honor (1), I object (2) to that question (3) on the ground that it is compound. (4)

Your Honor (1), I object (2) to that question (3) on the ground that it has already been asked and answered. (4)

Your Honor (1), I object (2) to that question (3) on the ground that it is argumentative. (4)

Your Honor (1), I object (2) to that question (3) on the ground that it calls for a narrative answer. (4)

Your Honor (1), I object (2) to that question (3) on the ground that it assumes facts not in evidence. (4)

§ 2-4 MOTIONS TO STRIKE AT TRIAL BY THE OPPONENT

§ 2-4(A) THE DOCTRINE

In most cases, when the opponent desires to exclude the proponent's evidence, the opponent uses the procedural device of an objection. In three situations, however, the opponent must use the procedural device of a motion to strike.

The first situation is the case in which the question is proper, but the witness's answer is improper. Second, the witness answers so rapidly that the opponent did not have a fair opportunity to interpose an objection. Finally, after the witness has given apparently proper testimony, it develops that the testimony was improper. For example, on direct examination, the lay witness purports to testify from personal knowledge. But on cross-examination, the witness makes the surprise concession that he was actually relating what he was told by third parties. In all three instances, the opponent should "move to strike" the earlier answers rather than "object."

Like an objection, a motion to strike must be courteous, timely, and specific. The general requirements for objections apply to motions to strike. If the witness's answer is improper, the opponent should move to strike immediately after the answer and before the next question. If the judge grants the motion, the opponent should then request a curative instruction to disregard. The judge informs the jury that the answer was improper and orders the jurors to disregard the answer, or answers, for any purpose whatsoever in their deliberations.[6]

§ 2-4(B) Elements of a Motion to Strike

The elements of a motion to strike are roughly the same as those of an objection:

1. The opponent addresses the judge.
2. The opponent indicates that he or she is moving to strike.
3. The opponent specifies what he or she is moving to strike.
4. The opponent specifies the legal ground for the motion.
5. If the judge grants the motion, the opponent requests a curative instruction to disregard, followed by a motion for a mistrial.

The opponent should seriously consider moving for a mistrial if the improper remark was highly inflammatory or if it appears that a curative instruction will be ineffective.

§ 2-4(C) Sample Motion to Strike

The fact situation is a burglary prosecution. The defendant has a number of previous burglary arrests. The prosecution witness is the arresting officer. The officer testifies that he observed the burglary in progress. The proponent is the prosecutor.

P Officer Jordan, WHERE were you when the defendant left the building?

W I was standing across the street, maybe 50 feet away.

P WHAT did you observe the defendant do?

---

[6] The fact that the judge grants the motion to strike does not mean that the answer is literally stricken from the reporter's notes or the transcript. Similarly, an attorney's request following an awkward question, "Strike that," will show up in the transcript.

W I saw him place a bag in the truck, look all around, and then enter the truck to start the engine. Knowing the defendant's long arrest record for burglaries, I immediately concluded that he had just completed a burglary.

O Your Honor, (1) I move to strike (2) that last sentence (3) on two grounds. First, the answer is nonresponsive. Second, the answer is clearly improper character evidence. (4)

J Motion granted. Officer, I want to caution you very strongly just to answer the questions asked. Do not volunteer information.

O Your Honor, would you please instruct the jury to disregard the answer? (5)

J Ladies and gentlemen of the jury, the officer just made a reference to the defendant's arrest record. I have stricken that statement from the record, and I instruct you to disregard it. The only testimony you may consider is the officer's testimony about what he personally saw the defendant do.

§ 2-5 REQUEST BY OPPONENT TO TAKE A WITNESS ON VOIR DIRE

§ 2-5(A) THE DOCTRINE

There are two types of preliminary facts which condition the admissibility of evidence. One type of fact conditions only the logical relevance of the evidence. For example, if the item of evidence is a letter, one preliminary fact conditioning its admissibility is its authenticity. The letter is inadmissible unless it is authentic. If the letter is not genuine, it has no logical relevance or probative value in the case. If the fact falls within this category, the judge uses the following procedure.

First, the judge listens to only the proponent's evidence and decides the question of law whether that evidence has sufficient probative value to support a rational jury finding of the fact's existence. Texas Rule of Evidence 104(b) states that "[w]hen the relevancy of evidence depends upon the fulfillment of a condition of fact, the court shall admit it upon, or subject to, the introduction of evidence sufficient to support a finding of the fulfillment of the condition." Is there enough evidence to support a rational finding that the letter is authentic? If so, the judge submits the letter to the jury.[7]

Second, the opponent submits any controverting evidence to the jury, and the jury finally decides whether the letter is genuine. Rule 104(b) applies to such foundational facts as to whether a letter is genuine or whether a lay witness has personal knowledge of the facts she intends to testify about. These facts condition the logical relevance of the evidence. These decisions are entrusted to the jury

---

[7] *See also* § 1-3(A)(1).

because the courts are confident that if the jury decides that the letter is a fake or that the witness lacks firsthand knowledge, common sense will lead the jury to disregard the testimony during deliberations.

The other type of preliminary fact conditions the application of doctrines which exclude logically relevant evidence: the best evidence, hearsay, opinion, and privilege rules. These rules exclude relevant evidence either because the evidence presumably is unreliable, such as hearsay, or to promote social policies, such as the protection of confidential relations. If the fact falls within this category, the judge listens to the evidence on both sides and finally decides whether the fact exists. Texas Rule of Evidence 104(a) provides that when the fact falls within this category, the trial judge makes the final decision. Thus, the judge finally decides whether the original document was destroyed, whether a witness qualifies as an expert, whether a communication was intended to be confidential, whether an out-of-court declarant was excited when he made a hearsay statement, or whether at the time of the statement the declarant was the member of the same criminal conspiracy to which the defendant belonged.[8]

When the fact falls within the second category, the opponent has the right to interrupt the process and show that the evidence is inadmissible. As previously stated, the judge must listen to both sides' evidence before ruling. So how does the opponent interrupt the proponent's direct examination to present the contrary evidence? The opponent interrupts by requesting the judge's permission to take the witness on voir dire examination before the judge rules on the evidence's admissibility. The Rules of Evidence do not specifically address this point, but the practice is long-standing.

In one respect, the voir dire is functionally a restricted cross-examination during the proponent's direct examination. The opponent conducting the voir dire may ordinarily use leading questions. The opponent must remember, however, that the voir dire's limited purpose is to test the competency of the witness or evidence. The voir dire has a limited scope, and the opponent may not conduct a general cross-examination on the case's merits under the guise of voir dire.

§ 2-5(B) Sample Request to Take a Witness on Voir Dire

The fact situation is a homicide prosecution. The prosecution witness is an ambulance attendant. The prosecutor hopes to elicit the ambulance attendant's testimony that he heard the decedent identify the defendant as the assailant. The prosecutor's theory is that the decedent's statement falls within the dying declaration exception to the hearsay rule. See *infra* Chapter 11. The proponent is the prosecutor.

P WHAT is your occupation?

---

[8] *Bourjaily v. United States*, 483 U.S. 171 (1987).

W I am an ambulance attendant employed by the emergency ward of General Hospital.

P WHAT were you doing on the evening of January 19 last year?

W I was on duty when we received a call about a shooting at the Senator Hotel downtown.

P WHAT did you do then?

W We responded to the call.

P WHAT did you find when you arrived at the scene?

W We found Mr. Jones there.

P WHAT was his condition?

W He had a gunshot wound. He'd lost a lot of blood. You could hardly make out what he was talking about.

P WHAT, if anything, did he talk about?

W He talked about the fight in which he received the wound.

P WHO did he say had shot him?

O Your Honor, I object to that question on the ground that it calls for inadmissible hearsay. I request permission to take the witness on voir dire before you rule on my objection.

J Very well.

O ISN'T IT TRUE THAT before he died, Mr. Jones said he was going to get the person who had shot him?

W Yes.

O ISN'T IT ALSO A FACT THAT he wanted to be rushed into surgery as soon as possible so he could get home?

W Right.

O Your Honor, I renew my objection. The witness's testimony shows that the decedent did not believe that imminent death was certain. The declarant had not abandoned all hope of recovery. For that reason, the dying declaration exception is inapplicable.

J Objection sustained.

§ 2-6 OFFER OF PROOF BY THE PROPONENT

§ 2-6(A) THE DOCTRINE

Assume that the judge grants the opponent's pretrial motion in limine or sustains an objection at trial. The trial judge thus precludes the proponent from pursuing the line of inquiry. What should the proponent do at this point? The rule is clear. In order to preserve error, the proponent must make an offer of proof.

There are two senses of the expression "offer of proof." The first is the broad, nontechnical meaning. The proponent "offers" proof whenever he or she presents evidence. Here, the expression is used in the second, technical sense. That is, the proponent formally states what the evidence would have shown and why the proponent wanted to introduce the evidence. Texas Rule of Evidence 103(a)(2) requires that the proponent ensure that "the substance of the evidence was made known to the court by offer . . . ."

Why should the proponent make an offer of proof? There are several reasons. When the proponent makes the offer of proof, the judge may reconsider and change the ruling. Until the offer of proof, the judge may not have realized where the line of questioning was leading. The offer of proof is also important if there is an appeal. If there is no offer of proof, the appellate court will have a difficult time evaluating the propriety and effect of the judge's ruling. With an offer of proof in the record of trial, the appellate court can intelligently decide whether there was error, whether the error was prejudicial, and whether the appropriate disposition of the case is simply to remand or enter judgment for a party.

The proponent should make the offer of proof out of the jury's hearing. If the proponent anticipated the unfavorable ruling, the proponent could prepare a written offer of proof for insertion in the record. Otherwise, the proponent usually makes an oral statement at a sidebar conference. If the expected testimony is complex, the proponent may request to make the offer in question-and-answer form. In that format, the proponent actually elicits the testimony out of the jury's hearing. Note that the judge, either sua sponte or at the request of the opponent, could require under Texas Rule of Evidence 103 that the proponent do so. This would be appropriate, for example, where there is reason to believe that the evidence does not match the proponent's optimistic characterization of the evidence.[9] Rule 103(b) also permits the judge to reflect on the record "the character of the evidence, the form in which it was offered, the objection made, and the ruling thereon."

§ 2-6(B) ELEMENTS OF AN OFFER OF PROOF

An offer of proof contains the following elements:

1. The proponent asks for permission to approach the bench or for a hearing with the jury excused.
2. The proponent states that he or she intends to make an offer of proof.

[9] *See* TEX. R. EVID. 103(b).

3. The proponent states what the witness would have testified to if the judge had permitted the proponent to pursue the line of inquiry, or requests permission to offer evidence in question and answer form.
4. The proponent states the purpose for which he or she wanted to offer the testimony.
5. If the judge sustained the objection on the ground of a competence doctrine such as hearsay, the proponent explains why the evidence is admissible. When counsel moves to sidebar, it is important that the court reporter is in a position to hear the conference. Unless the court reporter records the conference, the appellate court will never learn the tenor of the offer of proof at trial.

§ 2-6(C) SAMPLE OFFER OF PROOF

The fact situation is a civil case involving an automobile accident. The defense counsel attempts to cross-examine a key witness for the plaintiff, Mr. Swart, about his prior relationship with the defendant.

P Mr. Swart, ISN'T IT TRUE that you and the defendant had a business relationship several years ago entailing the sale of goods imported from Mexico?

W Yes.

P And ISN'T IT TRUE that some of these goods were damaged?

O Your Honor, we object. This evidence is obviously irrelevant to this case.

J Objection sustained.

P Your Honor, may we approach the bench? (1)

J Yes.

P Your Honor, I would like to make an offer of proof for the record. (2)

J Very well. Could we have the court reporter over here?

CR Yes, your Honor.

J The defense counsel wants to make an offer of proof. Would you please record this?

P Your Honor, if you permit us to continue with this line of questioning we will show that Mr. Swart and the defendant had a business relationship that required the defendant to inspect goods they were importing from Mexico. After several months, Mr. Swart accused the defendant of not holding up his end of the bargain. Bad blood developed between them and Mr. Swart vowed that he would never forgive the defendant for his actions. (3) Our purpose here is to show that the witness has a bias against the defendant which casts doubt on his testimony against the defendant.

(4) Under Texas Rule of Evidence 613(b) we are permitted to cross-examine witnesses about possible bias or motive. In doing so, we may inquire into specific "circumstances." In this case, their prior dealings are highly relevant on the issue of credibility. (5) Even if the witness denies all of this, he will have had the opportunity to deny or explain the relationship. If he does, we intend to offer extrinsic evidence of the circumstances under Rule 613(b).

J I can see what you're driving at. I tend to agree with you. I'm going to change my ruling and permit you to pursue this line of questioning.

P Mr. Swart, let me repeat the question. Isn't it true that some of these imported goods were damaged?

While it is almost always assumed that the offer of proof will relate to evidence elicited during direct examination, this example shows that the "proponent" may be the cross-examiner. To be able to argue on appeal that the trial judge erroneously blocked otherwise admissible impeachment evidence, the cross-examiner has to make an offer of proof. Making offers of proof on cross-examination can be problematic, however, where counsel is not sure what the questions will show.

§ 2-7 LIMITING INSTRUCTIONS

§ 2-7(A) THE DOCTRINE

Texas Rule of Evidence 105 addresses the use of limiting instructions where a piece of evidence may be admissible for only a limited purpose or against one party, but not another. For example, evidence that a criminal defendant has committed other, uncharged criminal acts, is not admissible to prove that he has a bad character. But that evidence could be admissible for the limited purpose of showing the absence of mistake or accident. Another common example of limited admissibility is the use of a witness's out-of-court statements for the limited purpose of impeaching the witness. Because limited admissibility is commonly encountered during a trial, Rule 105 is a very important rule for preserving error.

Rule 105 requires that upon request, the trial judge is to instruct the jury that it may consider the evidence only for a specified purpose. The rule places the burden for requesting the limiting instruction on the losing party. That is, if the proponent offers evidence which has limited admissibility, the judge's decision to exclude the evidence is not a ground for appellate relief unless the proponent "expressly" offered the evidence for its limited purpose. On the other hand, if the trial judge admits such evidence, the opponent cannot complain on appeal unless he or she requested a limiting instruction. The timing of these limiting instructions is left to the discretion of the trial judge. Counsel should, nonetheless, immediately request the instruction and ask the judge to give it while the matter is still fresh in the jurors' minds.[10]

Tactically, the proponent may find that the trial judge is more inclined to admit questionable evidence where he or she has made the effort to suggest the language for the judge's limiting instruction. Whether language is suggested or not, counsel should determine just what the limiting instruction will be.

§ 2-7(B) ELEMENTS OF A REQUEST FOR A LIMITING INSTRUCTION

The following are the elements for requesting a limiting instruction:

1. The counsel addresses the judge.
2. The counsel requests that the judge give a limiting instruction to the jury or objects to the failure of the charge to the jury to include a limiting instruction.
3. The counsel suggests the nature of the limiting instruction.
4. The court determines the nature of the limiting instruction, if any, to be given.

§ 2-7(C) SAMPLE REQUEST FOR A LIMITING INSTRUCTION

The following fact situation arises from a Texas civil case for personal injuries sustained in a car accident. The witness, Mr. Watson, has testified that at the time of the accident the traffic light was red. The proponent is the cross-examiner who questions Mr. Watson about an inconsistent statement he made at the time of the accident.

P On direct examination, you testified that the light was red at the time of the accident, ISN'T THAT CORRECT?

W Yes.

P ISN'T IT A FACT THAT right after the accident you spoke with Officer Jones?

W Yes, that's right.

P ISN'T IT A FACT THAT you told Officer Jones that the light was green at the time of the accident?

W That's right.

P ISN'T IT TRUE THAT at the time of your statement to Officer Jones your memory was fresher?

---

[10] A party may be entitled to an oral instruction at the time of the request and a written instruction in the court's charge.

W I guess you could say that.

O Your Honor, (1) I request that you give a limiting instruction to the jury (2) that they may not consider this witness's statement to Officer Jones as the truth of the matter. It is obviously hearsay. (3)

J Ladies and gentlemen, you have heard testimony that this witness previously stated that the light was green at the time of the accident. You may not consider that statement as being true. You may only consider that statement, if at all, on the issue of the witness's credibility. (4)

O Thank you, your Honor.

CHAPTER 3
THE COMPETENCY OF WITNESSES

§ 3-1 INTRODUCTION

Some evidentiary doctrines can keep a prospective witness off the stand altogether.[1] These doctrines govern the competency of the person to be a witness and can prevent the person from giving any testimony at all in the case.

To prove that a witness is competent under the common law, the proponent must show that the person possesses the following abilities:

[1] For a discussion of the issue of competency of a witness to testify, *see* WENDORF, SCHLUETER & BARTON, TEXAS RULES OF EVIDENCE MANUAL VI-1 TO VI-14 (6th ed. 2002).

1. to observe—the testimonial quality of perception;
2. to remember—the testimonial quality of memory;
3. to relate—the testimonial quality of narration; and
4. to recognize a duty to tell the truth—the testimonial quality of sincerity.

These abilities ensure that the witness's testimony will have at least some reliability. If the person lacks one or more of these capacities, the person is incompetent to be a witness.

Even if the person was competent in the sense that he or she possesses these four capacities, the law may have rendered the person otherwise incompetent as a witness. For example, before the promulgation of the former Texas Rules of Criminal Evidence, spouses were disqualified from testifying against each other in criminal cases.[2]

Now, under Texas Rule 504(b), the testifying spouse in a criminal case has a testimonial privilege to decide whether to testify or not against the other spouse. No such spousal privilege or disqualification exists in Texas civil trials.

Even if the witness is competent, other evidentiary doctrines may prevent the witness from testifying to certain facts. In this chapter, we are concerned with competency doctrines that have the more drastic effect of keeping the witness off the stand.

Texas Rule of Evidence 601 replaces most of the traditional common-law requirements for competency. The witness must have personal or firsthand knowledge under Rule 602. Rule 603 requires that each witness take an oath or affirmation to testify truthfully. But the proponent need not demonstrate that the prospective witness satisfies the other common-law requirements.[3]

Rule 601 states that "[e]very person is competent to be a witness except as otherwise provided by these rules." In effect, Rule 601 assumes that all persons are competent to testify. The rule, however, does recognize that certain categories of individuals may be disqualified: insane persons and children or other persons who do not appear to have sufficient intellect to testify. Rule 601(b) also contains the long-standing "dead man's rule."

How does the opponent challenge the prospective witness's competency under Rule 601? Normally, the opponent must raise the objection as soon as the person is called to the stand or as soon as it becomes apparent that the witness is not competent to testify. The opponent is permitted to object before the person is

---

[2] *See* TEX. CODE CRIM. PRO. art. 38.11 (Vernon) (repealed).

[3] An argument could be made that a judge could bar a witness from the stand. The argument is that the trial judge has the power to do so under Rule 403 when it is clear as a matter of law that the prospective witness lacks one of the testimonial abilities required at common law. Chapter 5 discusses Rule 403.

even sworn as a witness. The opponent both objects and requests a voir dire of the person concerning his or her qualifications to be a witness. Whether the voir dire examination is under oath is left to the discretion of the judge.

There is generally no set pattern as to who should conduct the examination of the witness, except in those cases where the witness is a child. In that case, Rule 601(a)(2) indicates that the trial judge should examine the child witness.

Competency doctrines do not simply condition the testimony's logical relevance. Rather, they fall within the category of doctrines designed to ensure the reliability of concededly relevant evidence. For that reason, the trial judge decides the question of the witness's competency under Rule 104(a). In doing so, the trial judge may permit the opponent to present extrinsic evidence, such as a psychiatrist's testimony. If, at the end of the presentation of the evidence, the judge decides that the person is incompetent, the judge sustains the objection and directs the person to leave the witness stand. If the judge finds that the person is competent, the judge overrules the objection, and the person then takes the normal oath in the case and testifies.

§ 3-2 THE VOIR DIRE OF A CHILD TO DETERMINE COMPETENCY

§ 3-2(A) THE DOCTRINE

In some jurisdictions, there may be a presumption that a child of a certain age is competent to testify. Such a presumption is usually rebuttable. Rule 601(a) indicates that "every person is competent to be a witness except as otherwise provided in these rules." Even if the child is presumed competent because of his or her age, the proponent may attempt to show that in fact, the child possesses the four requisite abilities. Assuming the opponent has raised the issue by objecting to a child's competency, there is a question of fact whether the child has the requisite capacities under Rule 601(a)(2). The trial judge decides the question of competency under Rule 104(a).

§ 3-2(B) ELEMENTS OF THE FOUNDATION

When the opponent challenges the competency of the proponent's child witness, the judge must determine if the witness possesses sufficient intellect to relate transactions with respect to which they are interrogated. Although Rule 601 does not list the four common-law factors for competency, they should, nonetheless, be helpful in assessing whether a child witness is competent under that rule:

1. The child has the capacity to observe.
2. The child has the capacity to remember.

3. The child has the capacity to relate.
4. The child recognizes a duty to tell the truth.

§ 3-2(C) SAMPLE FOUNDATION

The fact situation is a personal injury action arising from a traffic accident. The plaintiff, the proponent, calls a child who saw the accident as a witness.

P As our next witness, we call Jimmy Gillespie.

O Your Honor, we object to any testimony by this child on the ground that the child is incompetent to be a witness under Rule 601. We request that you conduct a voir dire examination of the child concerning his competency.

J Request granted. [*Some judges may indicate that the oath should be given at this point.*]

J WHAT is your name and address?

W My name is Jimmy Gillespie. I live here in Lubbock.

J And you live with your parents?

W Yes, sir.

J Jimmy, HOW well do you see? (1)

W I can see real well.

J HOW well do you hear? (1)

W Just great.

J HOW old are you, Jimmy? (2)

W I am five years old. I had my birthday last month.

J WHAT day is your birthday? (2)

W I think it's September 28th, just after my mommy's birthday.

J WHERE do you live? (2)

W Here in Lubbock, on Elm Street.

J HOW do you know that you live on Elm Street?

W My mommy made me remember that in case I got lost.

J HOW long have you lived there? (2)

W I can't remember.

J Well, have you ever lived anywhere else?

W No.

J Jimmy, HOW many brothers and sisters do you have? (2)

W I have one sister.

J WHAT is her name? (2)

W Amy.

J HOW old is Amy? (2)

W She's older than me. She's almost eight.

J WHAT school do you go to? (2)

W Horace Mann Elementary School.

J WHERE is that school located? (2)

W I think it's on Fourth Street.

J WHAT grade are you in? (2)

W I'm in the first grade.

J WHO is your teacher? (2)

W Her name is Mrs. Lopez. She's real nice.

J WHAT do you learn in school? (3)

W We learn how to make numbers and words. And we started reading.

J WHAT do you learn to read? (3)

W We learn about words and sentences and stuff.

J WHAT grades do you get in school? (3)

W I do real well. I got a big red check mark yesterday.

J WHAT does that mean? (3)

W It means I did good on my paper.

J Jimmy, do you know WHAT a car is? (3)

W My dad has one. You drive around in them. They take you places.

J WHAT does "fast" mean? (3)

W Well, when you drive, you should go slow. You can get hurt if you don't go slow, if you go too fast.

J Jimmy, do you know WHAT an intersection is? (3)

W No, sir.

J Do you know WHAT a stop sign is? (3)

W Oh, yes, sir. That is a big red sign by the road telling cars to stop first.

J WHERE do you see stop signs? (3)

W I think where streets come together. That's where kids can cross the street.

J WHAT is the truth? (4)

W The truth is what really happens, not a story you come up with.

J WHAT is a lie? (4)

W That's when you don't tell the truth.

J WHAT happens when you don't tell the truth? (4)

W Your parents can get real mad at you, and God can get unhappy with you.

J HOW do you know that? (4)

W I learned that at Sunday School.

J WHERE do you go to Sunday School? (4)

W At our church.

J WHICH church is that? (4)

W I think . . . it sounds like Holy Comforter.

J WHAT do you learn at Sunday School? (4)

W We learn that you have to be good. You gotta obey your parents and tell the truth and stuff like that.

J Do you know WHAT an oath is? (4)

W I promise to tell the truth to the judge.

J Have you ever been in a court before? (4)

W No, sir.

J WHAT happens if you don't tell the truth in this court? (4)

W I guess I could get punished.

J I have no further questions. Does either side have any suggested questions?

P No, your Honor.

O I have no questions. I renew my objection on the ground that this child is too young to be a witness. He obviously is not sure about several key points in his life, and we believe that in a case of this magnitude, he does not have sufficient intellect to understand what this case is all about.

P Your Honor, I think the child's answers demonstrate the capacities to observe, remember, and relate, and his recognition of a duty to tell the truth. He was obviously a little nervous. Rule 601 does not require that the witness understand fully all of the legal consequences of this case. All that is required is that he has sufficient intellect to relate what he saw and experienced.

J I agree. The objection will be overruled. Clerk, please administer the oath to Jimmy.

§ 3-3 THE QUESTIONING OF A LAY WITNESS BY THE PROPONENT TO DEMONSTRATE PERSONAL KNOWLEDGE

§ 3-3(A) THE DOCTRINE

All courts agree that a lay witness must have personal or firsthand knowledge of facts or events to testify about them at trial. Although the Texas Rules of Evidence generally abolish the traditional competency requirements, Rule 602 still insists upon personal knowledge. Before questioning a lay witness about an event, the proponent should show that the witness has personal knowledge of the event. Under Rule 104(b), the jury ultimately decides whether the witness had personal knowledge.

§ 3-3(B) ELEMENTS OF THE FOUNDATION

To establish that a witness has personal knowledge, the proponent should show that:

1. The witness was in a physical position to perceive the event. The witness normally observes the event by the sense of sight, but the witness may use any sense to perceive the event.
2. The witness actually perceived the event.

§ 3-3(C) SAMPLE FOUNDATION

The following sample foundation is a continuation of the previous hypothetical in § 3-2(C), in which Jimmy Gillespie has been called to the stand.

Assume the judge rules that the child is a competent witness. The child takes the oath and begins testifying. Now the plaintiff wants to elicit the testimony about the accident. The accident occurred at the intersection of Fourth and Main Streets.

P Jimmy, do you remember seeing a car accident in front of your school one day? (1)

W Yes, sir.

P WHERE did it happen? (1)

W In front of our school.

P WHERE is your school located? (1)

W It's on Fourth Street.

P WHERE on Fourth Street? (1)

W Next to the McDonald's. There's lots of cars in the street.

P WHAT happened that day? (2)

W There was this big crash.

P WHERE were you at the time of the crash? (1)

W I was standing on the corner.

P WHAT were you doing there?

W Waiting to go across the street.

P WHAT crashed? (2)

W Two cars.

J Do you know WHAT color they were? (2)

W Yes, one was bright red. And one was yellow, I think.

P WHO was driving the cars? (2)

W The man over there and that lady.

P Please let the record reflect that the witness has pointed to the plaintiff and defendant.

J It will so reflect.

P HOW do you know they were driving the cars? (2)

W I ran up right after the big noise, and I saw them get out of their cars.

P HOW well could you see the cars? (2)

W I got a good look. They were real close to me when they crashed. I was real scared!

P HOW well could you see the drivers? (2)

W Gee. I got right up close to them. I ran up right after the big noise, and I saw them get out of their cars.

P HOW much time passed between the crash and the time when you ran up to see the drivers? (2)

W Not very long.

P Jimmy, now I want to ask some questions about how the crash happened.

§ 3-4 THE OPPONENT'S PRESENTATION OF PSYCHIATRIC TESTIMONY ATTACKING A PROSPECTIVE WITNESS'S COMPETENCY

§ 3-4(A) The Doctrine

Trial judges rarely sustain objections to an adult witness's competency. But Rule 601 recognizes that an adult could be questioned in the same way as a child witness if there were some indication that the adult witness did not have a sufficient intellect to testify. Rule 601(a)(1) also indicates that "insane persons" may be incompetent witnesses. A witness may be incompetent either because he or she was insane at the time of the event or at the time of trial. In those instances, the opponent may challenge the witness's competency by offering evidence of recent adjudications of insanity, such as civil commitments. These adjudications are relevant to prove incompetency. But, as a practical matter, the opponent may have to present expert, psychiatric testimony attacking the witness's competency. The psychiatrist could testify, for example, that the person is suffering from a full fledged psychosis and that the psychosis grossly interferes with one of the testimonial qualities such as perception or memory. Again, Rule 601 does not require that the witness fully comprehend the legal significance of the case.

§ 3-4(B) Elements of the Foundation

The opponent should demonstrate that:

1. The witness is a qualified psychiatrist.
2. The psychiatrist has examined the prospective witness.
3. The prospective witness has certain symptoms.
4. The symptoms lead to the conclusion that the prospective witness is suffering from a psychosis.
5. The psychosis grossly interferes with one or more of the prospective witness's testimonial qualities, such as perception or memory.

§ 3-4(C) Sample Foundation

The fact situation is a rape prosecution. The prosecution calls Ms. Janet Lincoln as a witness. Ms. Lincoln has told the police that she witnessed the rape. Her window overlooks the park, and she saw the defendant attack the alleged victim. The defense counsel objects to any testimony by Ms. Lincoln. Counsel contends that she is incompetent to be a witness. The defense counsel has already taken Ms. Lincoln on voir dire and questioned her outside the presence of the jury.

J Do you have anything further you'd like to present on the issue of Ms. Lincoln's competency?

O Yes, your Honor. At this point, I would like to call Dr. Kenneth Rogers.

J Proceed.

CR Please raise your right hand. Do you swear or affirm that the evidence you will give in the case now in hearing will be the truth, the whole truth, and nothing but the truth?

W I do.

O WHAT is your name?

W Kenneth Rogers.

O WHERE do you live?

W I reside at 1774 Club Drive.

O WHAT is your occupation? (1)

W I am a physician.

O WHERE are you licensed to practice medicine? (1)

W Here in Texas and in New York.

O WHEN did you obtain your license here in Texas? (1)

W Approximately 10 years ago.

O WHAT medical school did you attend? (1)

W Baylor Medical School. I received my M.D. in 1990.

O WHERE did you intern? (1)

W I interned at South Texas Medical Center in San Antonio.

O HOW long did you intern there? (1)

W Approximately one year.

O WHAT field of medicine, if any, is your specialty? (1)

W Psychiatry.

O WHAT is the subject matter of that specialty? (1)

W A psychiatrist studies the diseases and disorders of the mind.

O WHAT special training have you had in psychiatry? (1)

W I spent three years as a resident in psychiatry.

O WHERE did you take this residence? (1)

W At Bellevue, in New York City.

O WHAT other special training have you had in psychiatry? (1)

W I'm a diplomate with the American Board of Psychiatry. I passed the oral and written examinations for the diploma. I've taught psychiatry at two medical schools and I've written 13 articles for psychiatric journals.

O WHO is Janet Lincoln? (2)

W She's a woman I've had occasion to interview several times.

O WHY did you interview her? (2)

W One of the local judges, Judge Lopardo, asked me to do so. It was a court appointment.

O HOW many times did you interview her? (2)

W Three times.

O WHEN was the first interview? (2)

W Approximately three months ago.

O HOW long did this interview last? (2)

W Roughly two and a half hours.

O WHAT was her appearance at the time of the interview? (3)

W It was rather unkempt. She was rather dirty.

O WHAT was her general attitude? (3)

W At first, she seemed rather detached and distant. She became excited and angry whenever I tried to question her about sexual subjects.

O WHAT, if anything, did she say during the interview? (3)

W At first, she just told me to keep my distance.

O WHAT did she say then? (3)

W She said that all men were sex fiends and could not be trusted. She said that for as long as she could remember, at least once a day a man had attempted to assault her.

O HOW would you characterize her statements? (3)

W They were delusional. A delusion is a belief that a rational person would not entertain under the same circumstances. The person persists in the belief although all the evidence is to the contrary.

O WHY did she have this belief? (3)

W She said that voices told her to distrust all men.

O WHO were the voices? (3)

W She didn't know.

O HOW would you characterize those statements? (3)

W They are hallucinations. She has auditory experiences when, in fact, there is no voice or sound.

O WHAT did you do after you interviewed Ms. Lincoln? (3)

W I tried to gather her history.

O WHAT is a history? (3)

W The background of an illness. You trace it through the years and its various stages.

O HOW did you gather Ms. Lincoln's history? (3)

W I spoke with her brother, Vance Lincoln.

O WHO is he? (3)

W He's a certified public accountant in town.

O WHAT was her background or history? (3)

W Evidently she had made numerous rape complaints to the police. In each case, the police or medical investigation had shown the complaint was groundless. She had spent almost a year in a hospital in Pennsylvania for mental illness.

O WHAT did you do then? (3)

W I conducted further interviews with Ms. Lincoln.

O WHAT happened during those interviews? (3)

W She repeated her beliefs. She told me about some incidents in her life, sometimes giving me conflicting stories about the same incident. On several occasions, she accused me of making advances toward her. She again became quite restless.

O WHAT, if anything, did you do to lead her to believe that you were making an advance toward her? (3)

W Nothing, as far as I could tell. My mere physical presence seemed to trigger that belief.

O WHAT, if any, diagnosis have you reached of Ms. Lincoln's psychiatric condition? (4)

W I would diagnose her condition as a schizophrenic reaction of the paranoid type.

O WHAT does that mean? (4)

W A schizophrenic person has a sort of split personality. She lives in two worlds: one, the world of fantasy; the other, the world of reality. She has lost contact with reality to a severe extent. Her disorder manifests itself in paranoid beliefs that men are persecuting and constantly attacking her.

O WHAT leads you to this diagnosis? (4)

W The irrational content of her statements, for one thing. I also consider her appearance and attitude. Finally, I attach particular importance to her delusions and hallucinations. Her history confirms the diagnosis.

O Doctor Rogers, in this case, Ms. Lincoln wants to testify about a sexual assault she allegedly observed. WHAT effect, if any, would her psychosis have on her ability to accurately observe an encounter between a man and a woman? (5)

W The psychosis grossly interferes with that capacity. She's going to see things that didn't really happen, just as she hears voices when they're not there. Every male-female encounter tends to become an assault in her mind.

O WHAT effect, if any, would her psychosis have on her ability to accurately remember a male-female encounter she had observed? (5)

W It's going to severely distort the memory process. A psychosis of this magnitude is going to affect her abilities to perceive and remember. Her purported recollections will be untrustworthy. In the process of remembering, she'll add assaultive aspects to the encounter.

O Thank you, Doctor. Your witness.

After the prosecutor's cross-examination of the expert witness, the judge would rule on Ms. Lincoln's competency as a witness.

§ 3-5 THE DEAD MAN'S RULE

§ 3-5(A) THE DOCTRINE

§ 3-5(A)(1) In General

Suppose that two parties enter into a contract. One dies, and the other files suit for breach of contract against the decedent's estate. The decedent can no longer testify to rebut any false claims. Is it fair to permit the survivor to testify against the estate?

Roughly half the states have enacted some form of dead person's or survivor's evidence statutes. These statutes represent a judgment that it is unfair to permit the survivors to testify in these circumstances. Even though the witness is otherwise competent, fairness dictates the exclusion of the witness's testimony.

The rule in Texas is known as the Dead Man's Rule and is now found in Texas Rule of Evidence 601(b).[4] The current rule is a greatly relaxed version of its statutory predecessor. While under the Texas statute, survivors were prohibited from testifying as to any transaction with the decedent, the rule now only bars uncorroborated oral statements. The title "Dead Man's Rule" may be misleading. The testimonial disqualification in Rule 601(b) also extends to statements made by "wards." It is important to note that no such rule exists for criminal cases. Nor is there any codified federal version of the rule.[5]

---

[4] Before the Rules of Evidence were adopted, the rule appeared in TEX. REV. CIV. STAT. ANN. art. 3716 (repealed in 1983), and was known as the "Dead Man's Statute." For a complete discussion of the rule as it now appears, *see* WENDORF, SCHLUETER & BARTON, TEXAS RULES OF EVIDENCE MANUAL VI-8 to VI-14 (6th ed. 2002).

[5] Federal Rule of Evidence 601 does recognize, however, that a state's competency rules might apply in federal proceedings.

Although a detailed discussion of this rule is beyond the scope of this text, it is important to highlight briefly the key provisions in Rule 601(b).

§ 3-5(A)(2) Types of Actions in Which the Dead Man's Rule Applies

Rule 601(b) is specifically limited to those cases where an action has been brought by, or against, an executor, administrator, or guardian, and a judgment can be rendered for, or against, them in that capacity. Any actions brought in their own right would not fall within the rule. For example, a wrongful death action would not normally fall within Rule 601(b). In that instance, the cause of action stems from an independent statutory right and not from an inherited right.

§ 3-5(A)(3) Witnesses Covered by the Dead Man's Rule

Rule 601(b) indicates that the rule applies only to the testimony of a party to the action. For purposes of the rule, that would probably also include not only named parties, but also those having an actual and direct interest in those matters which pertain to the testator, intestate, or ward. If the witness is not a party and has no interest in the case, he or she is competent to testify.

§ 3-5(A)(4) Evidence Covered by the Dead Man's Rule

Rule 601(b) covers only uncorroborated oral statements made by the testator, intestate, or ward. Thus, if the statements in question were written, the rule does not apply. If the statements were oral, the proponent can introduce other evidence, including the testimony of another witness, which corroborates the oral statements. Evidence is corroborative if it tends to strengthen and confirm the witness's testimony. The trial judge should determine whether the oral statements are corroborated. Note that Rule 601(b) does not keep the witness off the stand altogether. The witness is still permitted to testify about any transactions with the testator, intestate, or ward.

§ 3-5(A)(5) Waiver of the Dead Man's Rule

The rule may be waived by calling the opposing party to the stand to testify about oral, uncorroborated statements. As with other rules of evidence, the Dead Man's Rule may also be waived by failing to object.

§ 3-5(A)(6) Instructions Concerning the Dead Man's Rule

Finally, Rule 601(b) provides that the court may instruct the jury about the operation of the rule. This would normally be appropriate when the court has sustained an objection under the Dead Man's Rule and the jury would be left to speculate why a party was not permitted to testify about certain statements.

§ 3-5(B) ELEMENTS OF THE FOUNDATION

To invoke the Dead Man's Rule under Rule 601(b), the opponent of the evidence must show that:

1. The Rule applies to this cause of action—an action by or against an executor, administrator, or guardian.
2. The witness is a party or an interested person.
3. The witness is testifying about an uncorroborated oral statement made by a testator, intestate, or ward.

The first element presents a question of law. The judge construes the rule and compares its coverage to the pleadings on file in the case. The opponent may have to voir dire the witness, however, to develop factual support for the second and third elements of the foundation.

§ 3-5(C) SAMPLE FOUNDATION

The first hypothetical is a contract action against the decedent's estate. The decedent is John Grant. The plaintiff is Miles Dalton. Grant and Dalton had entered into a contract. Dalton alleges that Grant, the decedent, breached the contract. Dalton takes the stand to testify that Grant had told him that he intended to renege on the contract because he was tired of dealing with Dalton. The plaintiff is the proponent of the witness. The opponent is the defendant, the administrator of the Grant estate.

P HOW did you learn that Mr. Grant intended to breach the contract?

W We had a conversation about that on May 1st, about one month before he died.

P Specifically, WHAT did he say to you?

O Your Honor, I object to the last question on the ground that under the Dead Man's Rule, this witness is incompetent to testify about the decedent's oral statements.

P Your Honor, may I be heard?

J Yes.

P It's true that the Rule applies to contract actions against the decedent's estate (1) and that the rule prohibits testimony by a party (2) about oral statements of a decedent. (3) But the rule only applies to uncorroborated oral statements of the decedent. We intend to offer corroborating evidence in the form of a written memorandum that the decedent, Mr. Grant, prepared the same day he made the oral statements to Mr. Dalton. We intend to authenticate this letter through the testimony of Mr. Grant's secretary, who prepared the memo. If you desire, we can cite recent Texas cases on this point.

J Well, I am not sure that will be necessary at this point. I am going to permit the questioning to continue about the decedent's oral statements on the condition that you are able to authenticate the memo.[6]

P Mr. Dalton, let me repeat the question. WHAT did the decedent say to you?

The second hypothetical is a wrongful death action brought by the decedent's heirs. They allege that the defendant, Steven Pollet, negligently caused the death of the decedent, Kathryn Manning, in a traffic accident. The defense attorney calls the defendant as a witness. The defense attorney is the proponent. The defendant has already testified about what happened earlier in the day. The defendant has just testified that he reached a narrow curve in the road. The collision occurred as he rounded the curve.

P WHAT happened when you rounded the curve?

W I saw Ms. Manning's car coming.

P HOW did you maneuver your car after you saw this other car coming?

O Your Honor, I object to that question on the ground that under the Dead Man's Rule, the witness is incompetent to testify about that topic. Ms. Manning is deceased and can no longer give her version of what took place.

P Your Honor, may I be heard?

J Yes.

P Under Rule of Evidence 601(b), the Dead Man's Rule is not applicable here. First, the plaintiffs are not in this suit as executors, administrators, or guardians. They are here in their individual capacity. Second, the rule now only prohibits evidence of uncorroborated oral statements of a decedent. We do not intend to introduce such evidence. Further, Rule 601(b) now specifically recognizes that a party may testify about "transactions" with a decedent.

J The objection is overruled.

---

[6] Some judges may be very reluctant to make this sort of ruling. Instead, they will wait to see if the proponent can authenticate the memo before admitting the statements.

CHAPTER 4
AUTHENTICATION, IDENTIFICATION, AND VERIFICATION OF EVIDENCE

§ 4-1 INTRODUCTION

This chapter deals with the authentication of evidence. The term *authentication* is a generic term used to describe the process of proving that the evidence is the real thing. Here, we use the term authentication in relation to writings. The terms *identification* and *verification* are used to describe the process of authenticating other evidence, such as physical evidence and photographs.

The law generally requires that the proponent of evidence prove the evidence's authenticity as a condition to its admission. To authenticate an item of evidence, the proponent must present proof that the article is what the proponent claims. In Texas courtrooms, that process is sometimes referred to as "proving up" the evidence. Texas Rule 901(a) states: "[t]he requirement of authentication or identification as a condition precedent to admissibility is satisfied by evidence sufficient to support a finding that the matter in question is what its proponent claims." Thus, if the proponent claims that the decedent signed a letter, the proponent must prove that the document is a genuine letter signed by the decedent. If the proponent offers a photograph of an intersection, the proponent must show that the photograph accurately depicts the intersection. Or, if the prosecutor alleges that a pistol is the defendant's pistol, the prosecutor must present evidence tracing the pistol to the defendant's possession.

In addition to stating the requirement for authentication, Texas Rule 901(a) outlines the procedure for determining the evidence's authenticity. Rule 901(a) prescribes the same procedure as Rule 104(b). The test is whether the proponent has presented sufficient evidence to support a rational jury finding that the letter is genuine or the photograph is accurate. The trial judge looks to only the proponent's evidence and asks that question of law. Of course, the opponent may have controverting evidence. For example, although the proponent has a lay witness prepared to identify a friend's handwriting on a letter, the opponent may have an expert questioned document examiner ready to testify that the letter is a forgery. In this circumstance, the trial judge would admit the letter, and the opponent would present his or her controverting evidence to the jury. The trial judge would instruct the jurors that they must finally decide whether the letter is genuine.

The mechanics of presenting physical or documentary evidence are discussed in more detail in Chapter 1. As noted in that chapter, one of the keys to laying the predicate, or foundation, for a piece of evidence successfully is *practice*. Practice means literally handling the exhibits and working out the actual predicate or foundation questions to be asked. It also means talking to the predicate witness beforehand to ensure that the witness can fully answer the necessary predicate questions.

§ 4-2 AUTHENTICATION OF PRIVATE WRITINGS

§ 4-2(A) In General

There are several well-settled techniques for authenticating private writings. These techniques are alternate methods of establishing the writing's authenticity.

It is important to note here that the practitioner should develop the habit of automatically thinking of *authentication, best evidence*, and *hearsay* whenever a document is used in the courtroom. Whenever a document is used, the proponent will have to authenticate it. If the document's terms are in issue, the proponent will have to comply with the best evidence rule. Finally, if the proponent wants to use the document's contents as substantive evidence, the proponent will probably have to show that the document falls within a hearsay exception. In short, the proponent offering a document will often have to lay three separate foundations: authenticity, best evidence, and hearsay. The proponent should thus consult Chapters 8, 10, and 11 as well as this chapter.

§ 4-2(B) Authentication of Private Writings—Testimony of Witness Who Observed the Document's Execution

§ 4-2(B)(1) The Doctrine

The proponent can use direct evidence to authenticate a document. If a witness observed the writing's execution and recognizes the document executed, the witness's testimony is sufficient authentication. Texas Rule 901(b)(1) permits authentication by a witness with knowledge. In other words, the witness presents testimony that a "matter is what it is claimed to be."

§ 4-2(B)(2) Elements of the Foundation

The following are the elements of the foundation for using a witness who observed the execution of the private writing:

1. Where the witness observed the document's execution.
2. When the witness observed the execution.
3. Who was present.
4. What happened, i.e., the writing's execution.
5. The witness recognizes the exhibit as the document previously executed.

6. How the witness recognizes the document.

§ 4-2(B)(3) Sample Foundation

Assume that one issue in a commercial case is whether the defendant signed a certain check. The defendant's acquaintance, Mr. Bucher, observed the defendant sign the check. The plaintiff is the proponent.

P WHERE were you on the afternoon of February 4, 2005? (1), (2)

W I was at the defendant's house in Texarkana.

P WHO was there? (3)

W It was just me, the defendant, and his wife, Ruth.

P WHAT, if anything, happened while you were there? (4)

W The defendant was writing out some checks to pay his monthly bills.

P [*To court reporter*] We request that this be marked as an exhibit.

CR This will be plaintiff's exhibit seven for identification.

P Please let the record reflect that I am showing plaintiff's exhibit number seven for identification to the opposing counsel. [*Shows to counsel.*]

P I request permission to approach the witness.

J Permission granted.

P Mr. Bucher, I now hand you plaintiff's exhibit number seven for identification.

P Do you recognize it?

W Yes, I do.

P Would you please tell the jury WHAT it is? (5)

W It's one of the checks the defendant signed that afternoon.

P HOW do you recognize it? (6)

W Well, the defendant handed it to me and asked me to take a look at it. I recognize the signature and other writing on it.

P HOW long did you have to examine it? (6)

W About a minute or so.

P HOW carefully did you examine it? (6)

W Closely enough to recognize it now.

P WHAT characteristics of the exhibit are you relying on as the basis for your identification? (6)

W I remember the amount of the check, the payee, the defendant's rather peculiar signature, and the color of the check.

P Your Honor, I now offer plaintiff's exhibit number seven for identification into evidence.

J It will be received.

P I request permission to hand the exhibit to the jurors for their inspection.

J Permission granted.

§ 4-2(C) AUTHENTICATION OF PRIVATE WRITINGS—WITNESS FAMILIAR WITH HANDWRITING

§ 4-2(C)(1) The Doctrine

Even if the proponent cannot locate a person who observed the writing's execution, the proponent may be able to find someone familiar with the author's handwriting style. In that case, the witness expresses an opinion on whether the handwriting belongs to a particular person.[1] The primary problem of proof for the proponent is establishing that the witness is sufficiently familiar with the author's handwriting style to recognize that style. Ideally, the witness will have observed the author sign his or her name on several previous occasions.

It is sufficient if the witness has seen the author's signature under reliable circumstances. For example, a corporate executive's secretary may have seen documents bearing the signature of another executive of the same corporation on hundreds of prior occasions. Even if the witness has never seen that second corporate executive sign a document, the witness is sufficiently familiar with the executive's handwriting style. Texas Rule of Evidence 901(b)(2) recognizes this authentication technique. The Rule permits "[n]onexpert opinion as to the genuineness of handwriting, based upon familiarity not acquired for purposes of the litigation."

§ 4-2(C)(2) Elements of the Foundation

The foundation is very simple. The elements are:

1. The witness recognizes the author's handwriting on the document.
2. The witness is familiar with the author's handwriting style.
3. The witness has a sufficient basis for familiarity.

§ 4-2(C)(3) Sample Foundation

The following fact situation is a variation of the original hypothetical, used above. Assume that the witness, Mr. Bucher, did not observe the check's execution, but is familiar with the author's handwriting style:

[1] *See* TEX. R. EVID. 701, which addresses lay opinion testimony. Opinion testimony is discussed in Chapter 9.

P [*To court reporter*] We request that this be marked as an exhibit for the plaintiff. [*Court reporter marks exhibit and hands it back to counsel, who determines what the number is on the exhibit.*]

P Please let the record reflect that I am showing plaintiff's exhibit number seven for identification to the opposing counsel. [*Counsel shows exhibit to opposing counsel.*]

P I request permission to approach the witness.

J Request granted.

P Mr. Bucher, I now hand you plaintiff's exhibit number seven for identification. Would you please examine it? WHAT is it?

W It seems to be a check.

P Do you know WHO signed the check? (1)

W I'd say that the defendant signed it.

P WHY do you say that? (2)

W I recognize the defendant's handwriting style on the check.

P HOW well do you know the defendant's handwriting style? (3)

W Very well.

P HOW did you become familiar with his handwriting style? (3)

W We've been friends for years.

P HOW many years? (3)

W About 10.

P And, during that time, HOW often have you seen the defendant sign his name? (3)

W Tens, maybe hundreds.

P Your Honor, I now offer plaintiff's exhibit number seven for identification into evidence.

J Plaintiff's exhibit number seven will be received.

P I request permission to hand plaintiff's exhibit number seven to the jurors for their inspection.

J Permission granted.

§ 4-2(D) AUTHENTICATION OF PRIVATE WRITINGS—THE REPLY LETTER DOCTRINE

§ 4-2(D)(1) The Doctrine

The courts assume that the mails are reliable.[2] Given that assumption, the courts have developed the so-called reply letter doctrine. Suppose that the witness sent a letter to a certain person. In the due course of mail, the witness receives a letter. The letter purports to be signed by the person to whom the witness sent the first letter, and the second letter refers to, or at least purports to respond to, the first letter. The courts generally hold that this fact pattern creates a sufficient circumstantial inference that the second letter is authentic.

§ 4-2(D)(2) Elements of the Foundation

The predicate for the reply letter doctrine contains several elements:

1. The witness prepared the first letter.
2. The witness placed the letter in an envelope and properly stamped the envelope.
3. The witness addressed the letter to the author.
4. The witness mailed the letter to the author.
5. The witness subsequently received a letter.
6. The letter arrived in the due course of mail.
7. The second letter referred to the first letter or was responsive to it.
8. The second letter bore the name of the author.
9. The witness recognizes the exhibit as the second letter.
10. The witness specifies the basis on which he or she recognizes the exhibit.

§ 4-2(D)(3) Sample Foundation

The fact situation is a contract case. The plaintiff wants to prove that the defendant sent a letter containing an express warranty of the goods' condition. The plaintiff had not had previous dealings with the defendant, and, therefore, cannot recognize the defendant's handwriting style. The witness is the plaintiff. The plaintiff has just testified that he had a telephone conversation with the defendant. The plaintiff's attorney is the proponent.

P WHAT did you do after this telephone conversation? (1)

---

[2] *See, e.g.*, *Cliff v. Huggins*, 724 S.W.2d 778 (Tex. 1987) (presumption that properly addressed and mailed letter was received by addressee).

W I decided to send the defendant a letter requesting some specific assurances and warranties about the goods.

P HOW did you do that? (1)

W I typed it up and then signed it.

P WHAT did you do with it after you signed it? (2), (3), (4)

W I stuck it in an envelope. I stamped the envelope, addressed it, and stuck it in the mail.

P WHERE did you get the defendant's address? (3)

W Out of the telephone book.

P WHEN did you mail the letter? (4)

W I think it was that afternoon. Yes, it was Monday afternoon.

P WHAT happened then? (5)

W I got a reply letter.

P WHEN did the letter arrive? (6)

W The following Monday.

P HOW often have you exchanged letters with people in Dallas? (6)

W I've done it hundreds of times in the course of business.

P HOW long does it usually take to get a reply from Dallas? (6)

W About a week.

P HOW much time passed between the time you mailed your letter and the time when you received this second letter? (6)

W About a week. It was right on time.

P WHY did you refer to the letter as a reply letter? (7)

W Well, it referred to my letter. It said it was going to answer my questions.

P WHOSE name appeared on this second letter? (8)

W The defendant's.

P [*To court reporter*] Would you please mark this as an exhibit for the plaintiff? [*The court reporter marks exhibit and hands it back to the proponent.*]

P Thank you. Please let the record reflect that I am showing plaintiff's exhibit number eight for identification to the opposing counsel. [*Proponent shows exhibit to counsel.*]

P I request permission to approach the witness.

J Permission granted.

P I now hand you plaintiff's exhibit number eight for identification. Do you recognize it?

W Yes.

P WHAT is it? (9)

W It's the letter I just referred to.

P HOW can you recognize it? (10)

W I remember the contents, and the signature on the bottom is rather unique.

P Your Honor, I now offer plaintiff's exhibit eight for identification into evidence.

J It will be received.

P I request permission to have the witness read the last paragraph and signature block from that exhibit, your Honor.

J Permission granted.

P [*To the witness*] Would you please read this passage to the jurors?

O We object, your Honor. The letter can speak for itself.

J Your objection is overruled. Counsel, the letter has been admitted and the jury is entitled to hear and see what the letter says. You may proceed.

W It reads: "I guarantee that it's a first-rate product. Nobody makes a better shingle. They'll last at least 15 years. Sincerely yours, John Bettencourt."

P Your Honor, I now request permission to hand plaintiff's exhibit eight to the jurors for their inspection.

J Permission granted.

§ 4-2(E) AUTHENTICATION OF PRIVATE WRITINGS—COMPARISON BY EXPERT

§ 4-2(E)(1) The Doctrine

In § 4-2(C), *supra*, the discussion addressed the issue of how a proponent could authenticate a writing by using nonexpert lay opinion testimony about the author's handwriting style. The proponent may also use expert testimony rather than lay testimony. Texas Rule of Evidence 901(b)(3) allows a "[c]omparison by . . . expert witness with specimens which have been found by the court to be genuine." Before presenting the expert questioned document examiner, the proponent must authenticate the other specimens or exemplars. The proponent may use any authentication technique other than expert comparison to establish the exemplars' genuineness. Determination of the authenticity of the exemplars is governed by Rule 104(a).[3] The judge admits the exemplars so long as there is sufficient evidence to support a permissive inference of their genuineness. The expert will compare the questioned document with these exemplars.

The proponent then calls the expert to the stand. After qualifying as an expert, the witness compares the exemplars with the questioned document. On the basis of this comparison, the expert may testify whether, in his or her opinion, the same person who wrote the exemplars authored the questioned document. In most cases, the expert has viewed the documents before trial. Pretrial comparison makes the in-court testimony more reliable and credible.

§ 4-2(E)(2) Elements of the Foundation

The elements of the foundation for authenticating a writing by having an expert make a comparison are as follows:

1. The proponent authenticates the exemplars.
2. The proponent shows that the witness qualifies as an expert questioned document examiner.
3. The witness compares the exemplars and the questioned document.
4. After the comparison, the witness concludes that the same person who wrote the exemplars authored the questioned document.
5. The witness specifies the basis for his or her opinion, namely, the similarities between the exemplars and the questioned document.

§ 4-2(E)(3) Sample Foundation

Assume that the proponent has already authenticated the exemplars. Someone who saw the defendant sign two letters authenticated the letters. The letters are marked plaintiff's exhibits three and four. The plaintiff will mark the disputed check as plaintiff's exhibit number five for identification. The plaintiff is the proponent. The next witness is the questioned document examiner. The witness has already identified himself as John Glenn and stated his address.

P WHAT is your occupation? (2)

W I am a technician with Richard Whaley and Associates.

P WHAT line of business is that firm in? (2)

W It is a private forensic laboratory. We do all sorts of scientific work for legal cases.

P HOW long have you worked there? (2)

---

[3] *See* WENDORF, SCHLUETER & BARTON, TEXAS RULES OF EVIDENCE MANUAL IX-22 to IX-23 (6th ed. 2002).

W For about 12 years.

P WHAT are your duties there? (2)

W I do mainly questioned document examination.

P WHAT does a questioned document examiner do? (2)

W Among other things, we attempt to determine who signed writings.

P WHAT is your formal education? (2)

W I have a bachelor of science degree from Pennsylvania State University.

P WHAT other training, if any, have you had? (2)

W I attended several two-week courses on questioned document examination at Northwestern University. I've also attended many seminars on the subject sponsored by the Law Enforcement Assistance Administration.

P HOW long have you been a questioned document examiner? (2)

W The whole time I've had my present position, roughly 7 years.

P WHAT part of your working time do you devote to questioned document examination? (2)

W All of it. It's my specialty.

P HOW often have you testified as an expert questioned document examiner? (2)

W At least 100 times.

P WHERE have you testified? (2)

W Mainly in the courts in Texas.

P WHEN was the last time you testified as a questioned document examiner? (2)

W Last month.

P WHERE was that? (2)

W In another courtroom here in Tyler.

P Your Honor, permission to approach the witness?

J Granted.

P Mr. Glenn, I now hand you plaintiff's exhibits number three, four, and five for identification. WHAT are they?

W They're handwriting specimens.

P HOW many times have you seen these documents? (3)

W Once before.

P WHEN was that? (3)

W An investigator brought them to my office.

P WHAT happened when the investigator came to your office? (3)

W Well, I examined them. I studied them under an optical microscope to determine whether they had a common authorship.

P HOW long did you study them? (3)

W I spent the better part of the afternoon, maybe three hours, working on the comparison.

P HOW did you make the comparison? (3)

W I studied the documents. I had some blown up into enlarged photographs and studied the enlargements as well.

P HOW can you recognize these documents as the ones you previously examined? (3)

W I noted the peculiarities of the handwriting style. They were uniform throughout each document. They're quite distinctive.

P Do you have an opinion on the question whether the author of exhibits three and four also wrote plaintiff's exhibit five for identification?

W Yes.

P WHAT is that opinion? (4)

W I'm convinced that it was the same author.

P WHAT is the basis for your opinion? (5)

W In all, I detected five unique writing characteristics common to all three documents. There was a common misspelling, a spacing peculiarity, the tail on each "y," the pronounced loop on each "o," and the unique way in which they are written. These characteristics all point to common authorship.[4]

P Your Honor, I now offer plaintiff's exhibit number five for identification into evidence.

J It will be received.

P I now request permission to hand exhibits three, four, and five to the jurors for their inspection.

J Permission granted.

---

[4] Practitioners will sometimes have these types of exhibits blown up to poster-sized displays so that the jury can follow along with the witness's explanation. This can be an extremely effective use of the exhibits.

§ 4-2(F) AUTHENTICATION OF PRIVATE WRITINGS—ANCIENT DOCUMENTS OR DATA COMPILATIONS

§ 4-2(F)(1) The Doctrine

Texas Rule of Evidence 901(b)(8) provides that certain documents and data compilations may be authenticated by showing, inter alia, that they are at least 20 years old at the time they are offered into evidence. The underlying theory of this method of authentication is that it is often difficult, if not impossible, to authenticate older documents by direct evidence: those witnesses who might have been able to lay the foundation by one of the other methods of authentication are no longer available. Thus, it may be necessary to rely upon circumstantial guarantees of genuineness.[5] Although the age of the document is one factor to be considered, Rule 901 requires more.

If the proponent lays a satisfactory foundation under Rule 901, the authentication requirements are met. There may be a best evidence issue if the proponent is offering a copy of an ancient document or data compilation. If the proponent is offering a statement in the document or compilation for the truth of the matter asserted, there may be a hearsay issue. There is a specific hearsay exception in Rule 803(16) for statements in ancient documents that may be relied upon if the document has been in existence 20 years or more and its authenticity is established. Thus, laying a foundation that meets the requirements of Rule 901 will normally suffice to lay the foundation for the hearsay exception as well.

§ 4-2(F)(2) Elements of the Foundation

The elements of the foundation for authenticating an ancient document or compilation are as follows:

1. The document is in such a condition that it does not create a suspicion regarding its authenticity.
2. The document was found in a place where, if authentic, it would likely be found.
3. The document has been in existence 20 years or more at the time the proponent offers it at trial.

§ 4-2(F)(3) Sample Foundation

In the following sample foundation the proponent wishes to introduce a one-page personal typewritten letter written in 1974 concerning the disposition of property at issue in the case. The foundation witness, Ms. Woodnut, is a relative

[5] *See* 2 McCORMICK ON EVIDENCE § 223 (5th ed. 1999).

of the recipient of the letter and is not able to authenticate the signature of the sender.

P [*To court reporter*] We request that this exhibit be marked as an exhibit for the plaintiff. [*Court reporter marks exhibit and hands it back to counsel who determines what the number is on the exhibit.*]

P Please let the record reflect that I am showing what has been marked as plaintiff's exhibit number eight for identification to defendant's counsel. [*Counsel examines exhibit and hands it back to proponent.*]

P I request permission to approach the witness.

J Request granted.

P Ms. Woodnut, I now hand you plaintiff's exhibit number eight for identification. Would you please examine it. WHAT is it?

W This is a letter I found in my cousin Emily's attic some time ago.

P Do you know WHO signed the letter?

W Well, there is a signature on the letter, but I do not personally know that person.

P WHO is the letter addressed to? (2)

W It is addressed to my uncle Charles Woodnut, who died last year.

P HOW can you tell that? (2)

W Well, that is my uncle's full name and that is the address where he was living in 1974, when this letter was apparently written.

P Would you please tell us HOW you happened to find this letter. (2)

W Several months ago, his daughter, my cousin Emily and I were asked by my uncle's personal attorney to look through his things for any correspondence relating to rental property he used to own on Century Avenue. After my uncle died last year, we cleaned out his house and moved a lot of boxes containing letters and correspondence to my cousin's house. We found a storage box in her attic that was marked as containing papers for 1974 and 1975. Inside we found this letter in a file marked "Century Avenue." So we gave the letter to my uncle's attorney.

P WHY did you look in your cousin's attic? (2)

W Well, she remembered that we had put my uncle's boxes in her attic and she told me that that was the first place we should look.

O Objection, your Honor, that is hearsay and we ask that you strike that last answer.

P Your Honor, it is not being offered to prove the truth of the matter asserted. It is being offered to show information acted upon by this witness, that is, why she happened to search the attic.

J Objection overruled.

P WHAT was the condition of the box where you found the letter? (1), (2)

W The outside of the box was very dusty, and as I recall, it was taped shut. We had to find a knife to open the box.

P WHAT was the general condition of the other contents in the storage box? (1), (2)

W There were various file folders and large manila envelopes, all organized by subject matter and date. The file names appeared to involve other pieces of property. All of the contents had a very fine layer of dust on them.

P Ms. Woodnut, WHAT is the date on the letter? (3)

W July 15, 1974.

P And Ms. Woodnut, would you please describe for us the general condition of this letter. (1)

W The paper is yellowed and it seems a bit brittle around the edges.

P Your Honor, we offer plaintiff's exhibit eight for identification into evidence.

O We object, your Honor. There has been no showing that this letter is authentic. The witness cannot even identify the signature on the letter. In addition, we object on hearsay grounds.

P Your Honor, we believe we have sufficiently authenticated this letter under Rule 901(b)(8). There is nothing on the face of the letter, nor in its condition, to cause any question about its authenticity. (1) The date on the letter indicates that it was written in July of 1974, which is more than 20 years ago. (3) And the witness found the letter where such a letter or other similar correspondence would be found. (2) Concerning the hearsay aspects, the statements in the letter, which we do intend to introduce, fall within a specific hearsay exception in Rule 803(16).

J Objection is overruled. Plaintiff's exhibit number eight for identification is received into evidence.

P Ms. Woodnut, would you please read aloud the second paragraph of the letter.

§ 4-3 AUTHENTICATION OF BUSINESS WRITINGS

§ 4-3(A) In General

The preceding sections focused on the various methods available for authenticating private writings. The following sections discuss the methods for authenticating business writings such as ledgers, hospital records, and time sheets. The first method discussed, the more traditional method, is for the proponent to call a predicate or foundation witness to the stand who can authenticate the business writing. The second method recognizes the value of being able to "self-authenticate" business records under Texas Rule of Evidence 902. Finally, the issue of authenticating computerized business records is addressed.

§ 4-3(B) AUTHENTICATION OF BUSINESS WRITINGS—PREDICATE WITNESS

§ 4-3(B)(1) The Doctrine

Authenticating an ordinary business record through the testimony of a predicate, or sponsoring, witness is a simple matter. It is sufficient if the witness is familiar with the business's filing system, took the record from the right file, and recognizes the exhibit as the record removed from the files. The basis for this form of authentication can rest on Rule of Evidence 901(b)(1), which recognizes that evidence may be authenticated by "testimony of a witness with knowledge." The personal knowledge requirement focuses on the creation or filing of the document. It is not necessary that the witness is personally familiar with the contents of the writing. Again, it is important to note that authenticating the business record does not necessarily overcome whatever hearsay and best evidence objections might exist.

§ 4-3(B)(2) Elements of the Foundation

The foundation for authenticating a business record by using a foundation witness is brief; the elements are as follows:

1. The witness has personal knowledge of the business's filing or records system.
2. The witness removed a record from a certain file.
3. It was the right file.
4. The witness recognizes the exhibit as the record he or she removed from the files.
5. The witness specifies the basis on which he or she recognizes the exhibit.

§ 4-3(B)(3) Sample Foundation

In a contract action, counsel for the plaintiff, Collegiate Clothing Manufacturers, wants to authenticate a bill prepared in December 2004. The proponent calls Ms. Peters as its witness.

P WHAT is your occupation? (1)

W I am a chief bookkeeper for Collegiate Clothing Manufacturers.

P WHERE do you work? (1)

W I work at the main office of the company.

P HOW long have you worked there? (1)

W About seven years.

P WHAT are your duties? (1)

W As chief bookkeeper, I ensure that we have proper records of all the money and goods flowing into and out of the company. I supervise the records' preparation, maintenance, and eventual destruction.

P HOW well do you know the company's filing system? (1)

W I know it backwards and forwards. In fact, I helped design the system.

P Ms. Peters, WHERE were you this morning? (3)

W I was picking up the records I thought we would need for the trial today.

P WHERE did you go to get the files? (3)

W I went to the file cabinet for our 2004 records. I was particularly interested in the records for December of that year.

P WHAT did you find in the file? (3)

W I located all the bills and invoices we needed.

P [*To court reporter*] Would you please mark this as an exhibit for the plaintiff? [*Reporter marks exhibit and hands it back to counsel.*]

P Thank you. Please let the record reflect that I am now showing plaintiff's exhibit number three for identification to the opposing counsel. [*Opposing counsel examines exhibit and hands it back to the proponent.*]

P I request permission to approach the witness.

J Permission granted.

P Ms. Peters, I now hand you plaintiff's exhibit number three for identification. WHAT is it? (4)

W It's one of the bills I removed from the file for December 2004.

P HOW can you recognize it? (5)

W I recognize the handwriting of the clerk, John Winters. I've known him for years. In addition, I can generally recall the contents of each of the bills I took out of the file cabinet.

P Your Honor, I now offer plaintiff's exhibit number three for identification into evidence.

J It will be received.

P I now request permission to hand plaintiff's exhibit number three to the jurors for their inspection.

J Permission granted.

§ 4-3(C) AUTHENTICATION OF BUSINESS WRITINGS—USING AN AFFIDAVIT

§ 4-3(C)(1) The Doctrine

While the proponent can almost always count on finding a predicate witness to lay the foundation for a business writing, as demonstrated *supra* at § 4-3(B), Texas Rule of Evidence 902(10) provides a convenient short cut to the authentication process. That rule, however, only applies to documents which would otherwise satisfy the business records exception to the hearsay rule.[6] Assuming the document falls into that category, the rule permits the proponent to obtain an affidavit from the person who would otherwise lay the foundation for the document by testifying at trial. The Rule sets out the requirements for using an affidavit and even provides a sample form for the practitioner's convenience. Both originals and copies may be authenticated by this method. If, for some reason, the trial court concludes that the affidavit is not sufficient, or that Rule 902(10) has not been followed, the proponent can always fall back on the traditional method of calling the predicate witness to the stand.

§ 4-3(C)(2) Elements of the Foundation

The elements of the foundation are specified in Rule 902(10):

1. The business document must be a business record within the definition of Texas Rule of Evidence 803(6).
2. The business record, either the original or an exact copy, must be accompanied by an affidavit, completed by the custodian or another person with knowledge about the record, which specifies that the document was kept in accordance with Rule 803(6).
3. The proponent must show that the affidavit and document were filed with the clerk of the court at least 14 days prior to trial.
4. The proponent must give prompt notice to the opponent of the filing and provide the name and employer, if any, of the person executing the affidavit.

---

[6] *See* TEX. R. EVID. 803(6) (Business Records Exception).

§ 4-3(C)(3) Sample Foundation

The fact situation is the same as the one used *supra* at § 4-3(B)(3) for authenticating a business record by using a predicate witness. Now assume that instead of calling the witness, Ms. Peters, the plaintiff obtained a Rule 902(10) affidavit from her.

P [*To court reporter*] Could we have this exhibit marked, please? [Court reporter marks exhibit as plaintiff's exhibit and hands it back to the proponent.]

P Thank you. Please let the record reflect that I am now showing the exhibit to the opposing counsel.

J The record will so reflect. [*Opposing counsel examines exhibit and hands it back to the proponent.*]

P I now offer into evidence plaintiff's exhibit number three for identification into evidence.

O Your Honor, I object. There has been no predicate witness for this exhibit.

P Your Honor, we are offering this exhibit under Texas Rule of Evidence 902(10). That rule provides for self-authentication by affidavit of the person who could otherwise serve as the predicate witness. (2) As Ms. Powers' affidavit indicates, she is the bookkeeper for the plaintiff and is familiar with its record keeping. (2) Further, the affidavit follows the suggested form provided in Rule 902, and it was filed with the clerk's office over two months ago. (3) We also gave timely notice to the opposing counsel as required by the rule. (4)

J May I see the exhibit, please?

P Yes, your Honor.

J This affidavit seems to be in order. Counsel, I am going to overrule your objection. Plaintiff's exhibit three for identification is received into evidence.

P Your Honor, may I show the exhibit to the jury?

J Yes.

§ 4-3(D) AUTHENTICATION OF BUSINESS WRITINGS—COMPUTER RECORDS AND DATA

§ 4-3(D)(1) The Doctrine

Computer-generated evidence is a species of scientific evidence. The process of generating data by computer is beyond the knowledge of most laypersons. As § 4-11, *infra*, explains, the presentation of scientific evidence usually requires proof of: (1) the validity of the underlying theory; and (2) the reliability of the instrument. Computers are so widely accepted and used, however, that the proponent of computer evidence may not need to prove those two elements of the foundation for computerized business records. Even assuming the court requires that predicate, the trial judge can judicially notice the validity of the theory underlying computers and the general reliability of computers.

In the past, there was some Texas case law that required the proponent of a computerized business record to establish the underlying reliability of the computer system and the competency of its operators.[7] There is more recent Texas authority for the proposition, however, that computerized business records may be authenticated simply by showing that the records otherwise meet the traditional requirements for authenticating business records.[8] With the proliferation of "user friendly" business records software, the need for showing the reliability of the system and the competency of the operator seems less important. Virtually anyone can operate this software, although he or she may not fully understand how it works. It is important to note that while the Rules of Evidence are silent on electronically stored business records, Rule 901(b)(9) recognizes that the proponent may authenticate evidence by showing how a particular process or system works and that it produces accurate results.

While the predicate for authenticating computerized business records may be relaxed, an argument could be made that where the computerized data is not a traditional business entry, a more exacting predicate should be shown. With the advent of computerized graphics, for example, the proponent should always be prepared to establish how the system works and that it produces an accurate result.[9]

It is important to remember that the computer readout may not be comprehensible to a layperson. The readout may use symbols and terminology that only an expert can understand. If this is the case, after introducing the record, the proponent must ask the expert to explain the record to the trier of fact.

---

[7] *See, e.g., Railroad Com'n of Tex. v. Southern Pac. Co.*, 468 S.W.2d 125 (Tex.Civ.App.—Austin 1971), *writ refused n.r.e.*, 471 S.W.2d 39 (Tex. 1971).

Some courts now require a more extensive foundation. *See, e.g.*, Peritz, *Computer Data and Reliability: A Call for Authentication of Business Records Under the Federal Rules of Evidence*, 80 Nw. U. L. Rev. 956 (1986). These courts require the proponent to authenticate a computer record by proving the reliability of the particular computer used, the dependability of the business's input procedures for the computer, the use of proper procedures to obtain the document offered in court, and the witness's recognition of that document as the readout from the computer.

[8] *See, e.g., Longoria v. Greyhound Lines, Inc.*, 699 S.W.2d 298 (Tex. App.—San Antonio 1985, no writ) (court noted that reliability of system and competency of operator go to weight of evidence, but not to its admissibility).

[9] *See*, e.g., *Burleson v. State*, 802 S.W.2d 429 (Tex. App.—Fort Worth 1991, pet. ref.) (good discussion of computerized records; proponent authenticated computerized accounting system).

§ 4-3(D)(2) Elements of the Foundation

Note that in listing the elements of the predicate for a computerized record, we have included predicate facts which show how the system works, that it is reliable, and that the operator is competent to use it. We have chosen the more conservative path because, in some cases, the trial court may be inclined to view the computerized data as something other than a typical business record. In that instance, the proponent should be prepared to lay a more detailed foundation. The elements of the foundation are as follows:

1. The business uses a computer.
2. The computer is reliable.
3. The business has developed a procedure for inserting data into the computer.
4. The procedure has built-in safeguards to ensure accuracy and to identify errors.
5. The business keeps the computer in a good state of repair.
6. The witness had the computer readout of certain data.
7. The witness used the proper procedures to obtain the readout.
8. The computer was in working order at the time the witness obtained the readout.
9. The witness recognizes the exhibit as the readout.
10. The witness explains how he or she recognizes the readout.
11. If the readout contains strange symbols or terms, the witness explains the symbols or terms for the trier of fact.

§ 4-3(D)(3) Sample Foundation

Suppose that Acme Corporation brings an antitrust suit against Bechtor, Inc. To prove its damages, Acme wants to show that its gross sales declined from 2002 to 2004. Acme wants to use a computer printout to show its gross sales in those two years. As its witness, Acme calls Mr. Schons. Counsel for Acme is the proponent.

P Mr. Schons, WHAT is your occupation?

W I am one of the accountants from Acme Corporation.

P HOW long have you worked for Acme Corporation?

W Roughly 10 years.

P HOW long have you worked for Acme Corporation as an accountant?

W Again, roughly 10 years.

P WHAT are your duties with Acme Corporation?

W My specialty is the maintenance of our computer records.

P HOW does Acme maintain its business records? (1)

W We maintain the overwhelming majority of our data in our computer.

P WHICH computer do you use? (1)

W We use an IBM System 38.

P HOW long have you used that computer? (2)

W For the last 3 years.

P HOW widely used is that model computer? (2)

W There are hundreds in use throughout the country. When it was first marketed, it was the top of the line. There's a somewhat more sophisticated model available now, but the 38 is still regarded as one of the most dependable models on the market.

P WHAT procedure does Acme have for using the computer to maintain its records? (3)

W When an order comes in from a customer, we ship it straight to the sales department. They check it to ensure that the order has the correct spelling of the product name.

P WHAT does the sales department do with the order then? (3)

W They send it to the computer center. The center personnel enter the data into the computer memory. The computer is used to make certain that the merchandise is available and that the purchaser's credit is good. If the order passes those tests, the computer then makes entries on the customer's account and stores data for statistical and management reports.

P HOW do you know that this is the procedure? (3)

W I helped design the procedure. As I said, computer record maintenance is my specialty.

P WHAT safeguards, if any, do you use to ensure that your records are accurate? (4)

W There are double checks at several points. For example, one computer center employee enters the data and another randomly checks the data on the order slip. Perhaps the most important safeguard is the customers' review of the bills we print out and then send them. If anything's wrong, they let us know right away.

P HOW many complaints, if any, have you received about the printouts?

W I would say less than two or three a year. And those complaints are usually the result of errors in the original sales data which was provided to the computer operators.

P HOW is the computer maintained? (5)

W It's checked nightly for any obvious problems. Whenever an operator encounters a mechanical problem, they call maintenance immediately. In addition, IBM personnel visit the center every two weeks and check the system thoroughly.

P WHERE were you yesterday afternoon? (6)

W I was at my office.

P WHAT were you doing there? (6)

W I was trying to get the data I thought we'd need today in court.

P WHAT data was that? (6)

W I knew we'd need the total sales figures for 2002 to 2004.

P HOW did you obtain the data? (6)

W I had the computer print it out.

P HOW did you obtain the printout? (7)

W I went to the terminal, set it in the printout mode, and then requested the sales figures.

P HOW many times did you request the data from the computer? (7)

W Twice.

P WHY did you do it twice? (7)

W I wanted to make certain I had the right figures.

P WHAT was the result of your double check? (7)

W The computer read out the same data both times.

P WHAT condition was the computer in at the time? (8)

W It seemed to be fine. There were certainly no obvious problems. It had been checked the night before, and we'd used it several times already that day without any difficulty.

P Your Honor, we request that this be marked as an exhibit for the plaintiff. [*Proponent hands exhibit to court reporter, who marks it and hands it back to the proponent. Proponent examines it to determine what the exhibit number is.*]

P Please let the record reflect that I am showing exhibit number 10 to the opposing attorney. [*Proponent hands exhibit to counsel for inspection.*]

J It will so reflect.

P I request permission to approach the witness.

J Permission granted.

P Mr. Schons, I now hand you plaintiff's exhibit number 10 for identification. Do you recognize it? (9)

W Yes, I do.

P WHAT is it? (9)

W It's the second printout I just referred to.

P HOW can you recognize it? (10)

W I put my initials and the date in that corner. I can easily recognize them.

P Your Honor, I now offer plaintiff's exhibit number 10 for identification into evidence.

J It will be received.

P Now, Mr. Schons, directing your attention to this notation on the exhibit, WHAT does it say there? (11)

W It reads "MER S."

P WHAT does that mean? (11)

W It means sales of merchandise.

P HOW do you know that? (11)

W I helped select the symbols and terminology the computer would use in printouts.

P WHAT are these figures? (11)

W They're the dollar amounts of sales for the years indicated, for example, $3,675,334 in 2004.

P Your Honor, may exhibit number 10 be handed to the jurors for their inspection?

J Yes.

§ 4-4 AUTHENTICATION OF OFFICIAL AND PUBLIC WRITINGS

§ 4-4(A) THE DOCTRINE

The government often possesses information relevant to the outcome of civil and criminal actions. Thus, it often becomes necessary for one of the parties to introduce an official record. It would obviously be inconvenient to require public officials to appear in court to authenticate official records; their appearance would not only divert them from their official duties but also create the risk of the records' loss.

To remedy this problem, Texas Rule of Evidence 902 provides for self-authentication of certain public and official documents or records. Specifically,

Rule 902(4) provides that a properly attested copy of an official record is self-authenticating. The proponent obtains a copy of the official record from the official custodian, and the custodian attaches an attesting certificate. The certificate reads along these lines:

> I, Robert Dondero, certify that I am the County Clerk of Medina County, Texas, and that the attached document is a true and accurate copy of an original, official record in my custody.

The certificate is signed and often bears the seal of the official's office. The courts have developed the doctrine that the purported signature or seal of an official is presumed to be authentic.

§ 4-4(B) ELEMENTS OF THE FOUNDATION

The mechanics of introducing a properly attested copy of an official or public record are as follows:

1. The document purports to be a copy of an official record.
2. A certificate is attached to the copy.
3. The certificate states that the signatory is a public custodian of official records.
4. The certificate states that the document is a true and accurate copy of an original, official record.
5. The certificate bears a presumptively authentic signature and/or seal.

§ 4-4(C) SAMPLE FOUNDATION

The fact situation is a probate contest. At one point in the trial, the contestant must prove that a Jean Simmons was born in Houston, Texas, in 1956. The contestant is the proponent. The contestant is attempting to introduce a copy of a birth certificate in the custody of the Harris County Clerk. The hearing is a bench trial without a jury.

P Your Honor, I request that this be marked contestant's exhibit number four for identification. [*Proponent hands exhibit to court reporter for marking.*]

J It will be so marked.

P Please let the record reflect that I am showing the exhibit to the opposing counsel. [*Proponent hands exhibit to opposing counsel for inspection.*]

P I now offer contestant's exhibit number four for identification into evidence.

O I object on the ground that there has been insufficient authentication. No sponsoring witness has come forward to verify the authenticity of this document.

J [*To the contestant*] What is your response to the objection?

P Your Honor, live testimony is unnecessary. The law generally presumes that public officials have properly performed their duty and that their purported signatures and seals are genuine. This document bears both a purported official signature and seal. (5) The signature and seal authenticate the certificate itself. The certificate states that the attached document is a true and accurate copy of an official record in Mr. Dondero's custody. (1) (2) (3) (4) Thus, the certificate serves to authenticate the attached copy.

J Objection overruled.

P Your Honor, at this point I would like to invite the court's attention to the body of exhibit number four.

J Yes.

P I would like to point out that it states that a Jean Simmons was born in Houston, Texas, on September 19, 1956.

J I have noted that.

This hypothetical example is so short because the proponent needed only an attesting certificate to make the document self-authenticating. In an attesting certificate, the signatory writes that he or she is the custodian or deputy custodian of a set of official records and that the attached document is an original official record or a copy of an original official record in his or her custody. If the court can presume the authenticity of the signature or seal on the attesting certificate, that presumption authenticates the certificate. In turn, the attesting certificate authenticates the attached document.

Suppose, however, that the document originates in a foreign country. The presumption of authenticity may not attach to a foreign official's signature; consequently, a foreign official's attesting certificate will probably not suffice to authenticate the attached document. In that event, Rule 902 provides that the proponent will need a chain of certificates, usually culminating in an authenticating certificate executed by an American official. In an authenticating certificate, one official writes that he or she is familiar with the position and handwriting of another official and that the signature attached to another certificate in the chain is the signature of that other official. The chain used to authenticate a foreign record might include an attesting certificate by a local foreign official, an authenticating certificate by a national foreign official, and, finally, an authenticating certificate by an American consular officer.

§ 4-5 AUTHENTICATION OF ORAL STATEMENTS

§ 4-5(A) In General

Like written statements, oral statements must be authenticated. In the case of a written statement, authentication consists in identifying the author. In the case of an oral statement, authentication consists in identifying the speaker. To do so, the proponent may use several techniques. The following sections discuss those techniques.

§ 4-5(B) Authentication of Oral Statements—Witness Familiar with Speaker's Voice

§ 4-5(B)(1) The Doctrine

The proponent may use lay opinion testimony to authenticate an oral statement just as the proponent may use lay opinion testimony to authenticate a writing. In the case of a writing, the witness must testify that he or she is familiar with the author's handwriting style. Here, the witness must testify that he or she is familiar with the person's voice. Texas Rule of Evidence 901(b)(5) recognizes this method of voice identification.

§ 4-5(B)(2) Elements of the Foundation

The foundation, or predicate, for using lay opinion testimony to authenticate oral statements contains these elements:

1. At a specific time and place, the witness heard a voice.
2. The witness recognized the voice as that of a certain person.
3. The witness is familiar with that person's voice.
4. The witness explains the basis for his or her familiarity with that person's voice.
5. The person made a statement during the conversation.

§ 4-5(B)(3) Sample Foundation

The fact situation is a tort action for slander. The plaintiff, Mr. Brown, sues the defendant, Ms. Nolan. The plaintiff alleges that Ms. Nolan slandered the plaintiff during a telephone conversation with Mr. Parish. The plaintiff calls Mr. Parish to the stand.

P Mr. Parish, WHERE were you on the evening of April 6 of this year? (1)

W I was at home.

P WHAT, if anything, happened while you were home? (1)

W I received a phone call.

P WHO was the caller? (2)

W It was the defendant, Ms. Nolan.

P HOW do you know that it was Ms. Nolan? (3)

W I recognized her voice, and she said it was Ms. Nolan.

P HOW did you become familiar with her voice? (4)

W We've known each other for years.

P HOW many years? (4)

W Easily 15.

P HOW often have you spoken with her? (4)

W I can't answer that. We've spoken hundreds of times, I guess. We're neighbors. I see her at least a couple of times a week.

P WHAT condition was your telephone in when you received this call?

W It was in good working condition. There was no static or anything.

P HOW much noise was there in the background?

W None that I could tell. I didn't have the stereo on or anything like that, and I couldn't hear any noise at the other end other than Ms. Nolan talking.

P WHAT did Ms. Nolan say during this telephone conversation? (5)

W She said that she had a hot item of news for me.

P WHAT was that? (5)

W She said that the plaintiff, Mr. Brown, had paid $6,000 to bribe one of the city councilmen to get favorable zoning on some commercial property he owns.

§ 4-5(C) AUTHENTICATION OF ORAL STATEMENTS—TELEPHONE DIRECTORY DOCTRINE

§ 4-5(C)(1) The Doctrine

The telephone directory doctrine parallels the reply letter doctrine, discussed *supra* at § 4-2(D). Under the reply letter doctrine, the courts trust the reliability of the Postal Service. Under this doctrine, the courts place their faith in the accuracy of telephone directories. Texas Rule of Evidence 901(b)(6) describes the doctrine; the proponent may authenticate a telephone conversation by "evidence that a call was made to the number assigned at the time by the telephone company to a particular person or business, if . . . in the case of a person, circumstances, including self-identification, show the person answering to be the one called." This fact pattern creates a circumstantial inference that the person answering the telephone was the person the telephone number is assigned to.

§ 4-5(C)(2) Elements of the Foundation

The predicate for this method of authenticating an oral statement includes these elements:

1. The telephone directory assigns a certain number to the person.
2. The witness called that number.
3. The witness asked for the person to whom the number is assigned.
4. The person answering identified himself or herself as the person to whom the number is assigned.
5. Any other circumstances indicating that the person answering was the person to whom the number was assigned.

§ 4-5(C)(3) Sample Foundation

The following fact situation is a tort action arising from an automobile accident. The expert testimony indicates that the failure of the defendant's brakes caused the crash. One issue is whether the defendant knew his brakes were defective. The plaintiff wants to elicit Mr. Martinez's testimony that he worked on the defendant's car, found the brakes defective, and notified the defendant by telephone. The telephone conversation was Mr. Martinez's only contact with the defendant, Mr. Jackson. The plaintiff is the proponent.

W After examining the brakes, I concluded that they were in a dangerous condition.

P WHAT did you do then?

W I decided to notify the owner, this fellow Jackson.

P HOW did you notify him?

W I wanted to phone him and let him know.

P HOW did you do that? (1)

W First, I checked the telephone directory to get his number.

P WHAT did you do then? (2)

W I dialed the number.

P WHERE was the directory when you were dialing? (2)

W It was right in front of me. I was looking at it as I dialed.

P WHAT happened next? (3)

W It rang, and a man answered.

P WHAT did you say? (3)

W I asked to speak to Mr. Jackson, the owner of the silver Corvette.

P HOW did the person answering the phone identify himself? (4)

W He just said he was Jackson, the person I wanted to talk to.

P WHAT, if anything, did he say about the Corvette? (5)

W He told me that he realized that it had some problems.

P WHAT problems? (5)

W He mentioned a problem with the exhaust and the windshield wipers.

P HOW accurate were those statements? (5)

W The guy was right. I'd looked at the car, and I'd seen those problems, among others. The guy I was talking with was obviously familiar with the car.

P WHAT did you say then?

W I told him about the brakes.

P Specifically, WHAT did you tell him?

W I said that they were defective and dangerous. I told him that they could fail anytime and that he should have them repaired immediately.

§ 4-5(D) Authentication of Oral Statements— Voiceprints or Sound Spectrography Expert

§ 4-5(D)(1) The Doctrine

The sound spectrography expert is to the identification of speakers what the questioned document examiner is to the identification of writers. The voiceprint witness is the supposed expert. There are two theoretical premises underlying sound spectrography. The first premise is that interspeaker variability exceeds intraspeaker variability. This theory presumes that even though a person's voice pattern changes from time to time, the voice pattern differences among speakers are greater than the variations in a single speaker's voice pattern. The second premise is intraspeaker invariant speech: each voice has certain unique characteristics that it will invariably display under spectrographic analysis. Most speech scientists accept the first premise, but there is still a good deal of controversy in scientific circles over the second premise. Many critics of sound spectrography argue that there has been insufficient experimental verification of the theory of invariant speech. A report of a committee of the National Academy of Sciences found insufficient verification.

The spectrograph instrument includes: (1) a magnetic recording device; (2) a variable electronic filter; (3) a paper-carrying drum coupled to the magnetic recording device; and (4) an electronic stylus that marks the paper as the drum rotates.

The spectrograph operates in the following fashion. The operator starts with a tape of commonly used English cue words such as "the," "and," "me," "on," "is," "it," "I," "a," and "you." The cue words are static-state words. The words preceding and following them have little effect on their pronunciation and, hence, on the spectrograms they produce. The operator prepares the tape by having the suspect read the words into the tape or excerpting the words from a tape of the known suspect's speech. The operator plays the tape repeatedly on the magnetic recording device. The device is attached to the electronic filter. Each time the operator replays the tape, the filter lets another frequency pass through. The frequencies pass through to an electronic stylus. As the frequencies pass through, the stylus marks the paper-carrying drum. The stylus thus produces a spectrogram, a graphic depiction of the voice pattern.

The usual spectrogram is a bar spectrogram. The vertical axis is frequency, the horizontal axis is time, and the darkness is the voice's amplitude.

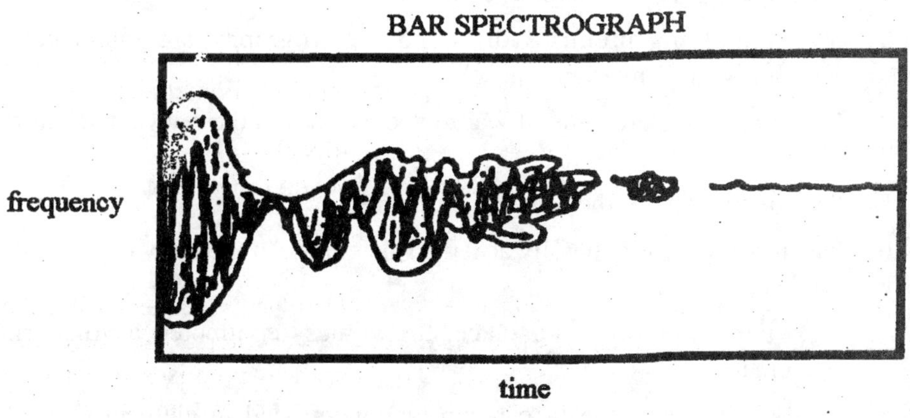

The operator then takes the unknown voice, for example, the tape of a bomb threat or an obscene telephone call. The operator excerpts the same words from the tape of that voice and prepares another spectrogram in the same fashion. The operator then compares the two spectrograms and forms an opinion whether the same voice produced the two spectrograms. Experts vary on the number of points of similarity required for a match. Some will accept as few as 16, while others insist upon as many as 33.

Given the division in the scientific community over sound spectrography, it is understandable that the courts are also split. Some courts reject the evidence.

In *People v. Kelly*,[10] the California Supreme Court excluded the evidence. Courts in the District of Columbia, Louisiana, Maryland, Michigan, New Jersey, and Pennsylvania have followed *Kelly*. Other courts continue to accept the evidence. For example, the Federal Court of Appeals for the Second Circuit, the Maine Supreme Judicial Court, and the Rhode Island Supreme Court have sustained the admission of sound spectrography evidence.

Whether Texas will accept this evidence is unclear at this point.[11] One fact is clear: if the proponent plans to offer sound spectrography evidence, the proponent must lay a complete foundation. Because sound spectrography is a scientific technique, the proponent must lay the foundation outlined *infra* at § 4-11(B).

§ 4-5(D)(2) Elements of the Foundation

The elements of a foundation for sound spectrography evidence include:

1. The tape recordings used to produce the spectrograms are authentic. See *infra* § 4-6.
2. The witness has the qualifications to explain sound spectrography's underlying premises and to conduct the test.
3. The underlying premises of sound spectrography are interspeaker variability and invariant speech.
4. Those premises are generally accepted as valid in the relevant scientific circles.
5. The instrument is the sound spectrograph.
6. The instrument is generally accepted as reliable in the relevant scientific circles.
7. At a particular time and place, the witness conducted a voiceprint examination.
8. The witness used the tape recordings mentioned in element #1.
9. The witness excerpted the cue words from both tapes.
10. The witness used a spectrograph to analyze the tapes of the cue words.
11. The spectrograph was in good working condition at the time.

---

[10] 17 Cal.3d 24, 549 P.2d 1240, 130 Cal.Rptr. 144 (1976).

[11] *See, e.g.*, *Lewis v. State*, 815 S.W.2d 560 (Tex. Crim. App. 1991) (en banc) (court noted but did not decide issue of whether voiceprint evidence was admissible); *Pope v. State*, 756 S.W.2d 401 (Tex. App.—Dallas 1988, pet. ref.) (noting that issue of admissibility of voiceprint was case of first impression, court declined to address it). *See* 1 PAUL C. GIANNELLI & E. IMWINKELRIED, SCIENTIFIC EVIDENCE § 10–6 (3d ed. 1999).

12. The witness used the proper procedures.
13. The analysis produced two spectrograms.
14. The witness identifies the spectrograms.
15. There are several points of similarity between the two spectrograms.
16. In the witness's opinion, the same voice produced the two spectrograms.

§ 4-5(D)(3) Sample Foundation

The following is a sample foundation. The fact situation is a bomb threat prosecution. A police officer recorded the threat and authenticated the tape recording as State's exhibit number one. Another officer obtained a voice exemplar recording from the defendant. The officer has authenticated that tape recording as State's exhibit number two. Thus, the two officers have laid the first element of the foundation. The prosecution now calls Mr. James Cottrell, a sound spectrography expert. The prosecution is the proponent. Mr. Cottrell has already identified himself and stated his address.

P WHAT is your occupation? (2)

W I am a member of the staff of the Fort Worth Police Department Laboratory.

P HOW long have you worked there? (2)

W For the past six years, ever since I graduated from college.

P WHERE did you attend college? (2)

W I attended Texas A & M University.

P WHAT was your undergraduate major? (2)

W I was a science major, specializing in speech science and acoustics.

P WHAT are your present duties? (2)

W I do all the sound spectrography or voiceprint analysis for the Fort Worth Police Department.

P WHAT is sound spectrography? (3)

W It's a scientific technique for identifying a speaker.

P WHAT is the basis of this technique? (3)

W It has two premises. One is interspeaker variability.

P WHAT does that mean? (3)

W It means simply that the difference between my voice and yours is greater than the fluctuations in my voice. Depending on whether I'm alert or sleepy, my voice pattern changes. But the differences between our two voices are still greater than the changes in my voice pattern from time to time. That's one of the two major premises of sound spectrography.

P WHAT is the other premise? (3)

W Invariant speech.

P WHAT does that mean? (3)

W Each person's voice has some unique characteristics, and you'll always be able to detect those characteristics with the instrument we use, the spectrograph.

P WHAT experiments have been conducted to verify these theories? (3)

W There has been extensive experimentation at Stanford, Michigan State, and a number of industrial laboratories.

P WHAT has been the outcome of these experiments? (3)

W They show that if you have a trained examiner, the examiner will ordinarily be able to determine whether the same voice produced two spectrograms, the charts of the voice patterns.

P HOW high has the error rate been? (3)

W It depends on the type of error you're talking about. If you're talking about false identifications, erroneously identifying a suspect as the person who produced the unknown spectrogram, it's pretty low. If you give the examiner the right to say that a particular test is too close to call, the error rate is likely to be only one or two percent.

P HOW widely are these theories accepted? (4)

W There's still some controversy. However, I think that the people who are knowledgeable, who have read the available data, accept both premises.

P HOW do you apply these theories to a particular case? (5)

W As I said, you use a spectrograph. In our laboratory, we use a Series 700 Sound Spectrograph manufactured by Voiceprint Laboratories in New Jersey.

P WHAT is a sound spectrograph? (5)

W It has four basic components. First, there's a magnetic recording device. Then there's an electronic filter. Third, the machine has a stylus. Finally, it has a paper-carrying drum.

P HOW does the spectrograph operate? (5)

W You put a tape on the recording device. You play it again and again. Every time you play it, the filter lets a different frequency of the voice through. The frequencies activate the stylus, and the stylus marks the paper. The end result is a sort of chart that we call a spectrogram. In effect, it's a visual display of a voice pattern. You compare two charts. If there are enough points of similarity, you conclude that the same voice produced the two spectrograms and, hence, the two tape recordings.

P WHAT experiments have been conducted to verify the spectrograph's reliability? (6)

W Basically, the same ones I mentioned before. The researchers have tested both the theory and the instrument. The test results I mentioned before tend to validate the instrument as well.

P HOW widely is the spectrograph accepted? (6)

W I'd say that its reliability is accepted to the same extent as the underlying theories—generally accepted by the really knowledgeable people in the field.

P Mr. Cottrell, WHERE were you on the morning of July 17 of this year? (7)

W I was at my office at the lab.

P WHAT happened while you were there? (7)

W A police officer dropped by some tape recordings for spectrographic analysis.

P I now hand you State's exhibits numbers one and two. WHAT are they? (8)

W They're the tape recordings I was given.

P HOW can you recognize them? (8)

W I remember the notations on the containers, and I marked my initials on the label and on the reels themselves.

P WHAT did you do with the tapes? (8)

W I proceeded to conduct the analysis.

P HOW did you do that? (8)

W First, I had to excerpt common words from both tapes. That took a little while.

P Then WHAT did you do? (10)

W One at a time, I put the new tapes of the excerpts on the spectrograph.

P WHAT condition was your spectrograph in at the time? (11)

W It was in good working condition.

P HOW do you know that? (11)

W I ran through the manufacturer's maintenance checklist before I used the spectrograph. The instrument checked out fine.

P HOW are you supposed to operate the machine? (12)

W You let it warm up a bit, mount the tape you're analyzing, activate the machine, and then let it run until the spectrogram is complete.

P WHAT procedure did you use on this occasion? (12)

W I followed the proper procedure exactly. I did just what I outlined for you.

P WHAT was the result of the test? (13)

W At the end, I had two spectrograms, two visual displays of voice patterns.

P [*To court reporter*] Would you please mark these as State's exhibits? [*Court reporter determines numbers to be assigned, marks them, and hands them back to the prosecutor.*] Thank you.

P Please let the record reflect that I am showing these exhibits to the opposing attorney. [*Counsel shows exhibits to opponent.*]

J It will so reflect.

P Mr. Cottrell, I now hand you State's exhibit number three for identification. Would you please tell us WHAT it is? (14)

W It's the spectrogram of that tape, State's exhibit number one.

P HOW can you recognize the spectrogram? (14)

W As you can see, on the other side, I marked my initials, the date, and the number of the tape it corresponded to.

P I now hand you State's exhibit number four for identification. WHAT is it? (14)

W It's the spectrogram produced by analyzing the other tape, State's exhibit number two.

P HOW can you recognize it? (14)

W I made the same sort of notations on the back here.

P Your Honor, I now offer State's exhibits three and four for identification into evidence.

J They will be received.

P Mr. Cottrell, WHAT did you do with the spectrograms? (15)

W I compared them.

P WHAT was the result of your comparison? (15)

W I found a large number of points of similarity between the two spectrograms.

P HOW many points of similarity? (15)

W Thirty-two in all.

P Do you have an opinion on the question as to whether the same voice produced the two spectrograms? (16)

W Yes.

P WHAT is that opinion? (16)

W In my judgment, it was the same voice.

P WHAT is the basis of that opinion? (15)

W Not just the number of points of similarity, but the fact that some of them were really unique. I'm confident that the same person who phoned in this bomb threat made this other voice exemplar.

P Your Honor, I request permission to hand State's exhibits three and four to the jurors for their inspection.

J Permission granted.

§ 4-6 AUTHENTICATION OF RECORDINGS: AUDIO AND VIDEO

§ 4-6(A) THE DOCTRINE

Like computers, tape recorders present scientific evidence issues. The same is true for video recorders. But the validity of the underlying theory and the reliability of recorders in general are so well accepted that the judge may judicially notice those elements of the foundation. Texas courts, however, have traditionally taken a more strict attitude towards audio and videotape recordings. The courts realize that tapes can be tampered with. For that reason, the courts have generally insisted on a more complete foundation.

The seven-pronged predicate for audiotape and videotape recordings is essentially the same and finds its genesis in *Cummings v. Jess Edwards, Inc.*,[12] which, in turn, relied upon a widely used annotation at 58 A.L.R.2d 1024. The Court of Criminal Appeals subsequently adopted that predicate for audio recordings in *Edwards v. State.*[13] And the Supreme Court adopted it in *Seymour v. Gillespie.*[14] Subsequent decisions have applied the predicate to videotapes with sound.[15] The predicate for videotapes without sound is the same as the predicate for photographs and silent motion pictures.[16] In summary, the *Cummings-*

---

12 445 S.W.2d 767 (Tex.Civ.App.—Corpus Christi 1969, writ refused n.r.e.). *See also Seymour v. Gillespie*, 608 S.W.2d 897 (Tex. 1980) (tape recordings must be shown to be fair representation of the conversation or event).

13 551 S.W.2d 731 (Tex. Crim. App. 1977).

14 608 S.W.2d 897, 898 (Tex. 1980).

15 *Roy v. State*, 608 S.W.2d 645 (Tex. Crim. App. 1980).

16 *Huffman v. State*, 746 S.W.2d 212 (Tex. Crim. App. 1988).

Edwards predicate requires the proponent to show the operator's qualifications, the equipment's working condition, the custody of the tape, the identification of the speakers on the tape, and the evidence that the tape is accurate.

In applying the predicate, several Texas courts have recognized that some of the foundation facts may be inferred from the tapes. For example, courts have inferred that the recorder was working,[17] that the operator was competent,[18] and that the speakers were speaking voluntarily.[19]

If the opponent seriously contests a tape's accuracy, he or she can use an expert to detect the tampering. Ultimately, the test for admissibility of video and audio recordings is whether they are authentic. As § 4-1, *infra*, emphasizes, the test for authentication is lax. The question is whether the proponent has presented sufficient evidence to support a rational finding of fact that the recording is authentic. Given that test, if a witness testifies that he or she heard a conversation and that the tape accurately reproduced the conversation, there is a permissive inference of the tape's genuineness.

Finally, it is important to note that, assuming the recording can be authenticated, there may still be hearsay and best evidence issues to be resolved.

It is important to note that the Texas Court of Criminal Appeals abandoned the formal seven-pronged *Edwards* predicate for audio and video recordings. In *Stapleton v. State*,[20] the court held that *Edwards* is "no longer needed as an authoritative guide for the admissibility of electronic recordings because it has been superseded by the Rules of Evidence."[21] The court also noted that the Rules of Evidence had nonetheless "incorporated substantially the seven-pronged test of *Edwards*."[22] Applying the Rules of Evidence, the Court ultimately concluded that an audiotape recording of a phone call to the police station was not admissible under the facts of the case.

The question of whether *Edwards* still applied to videotapes in criminal cases was addressed in *Kephart v. State*.[23] Citing its decision in *Stapleton, supra*, and other cases addressing the authentication of videotapes, the Court of Criminal Appeals concluded that a proponent is simply required to establish that the videotape is what it is claimed to be, e.g., a witness who could verify that the videotape was what the State claimed it to be—evidence of drug use. In this

[17] *Hinote v. Local 4–23*, 777 S.W.2d 134 (Tex. App.—Houston [14th Dist.] 1989, writ denied).

[18] *Id.*

[19] *Tims v. State*, 779 S.W.2d 517 (Tex. App.—Beaumont 1989, no pet.)

[20] 868 S.W.2d 781 (Tex. Crim. App. 1993).

[21] 868 S.W.2d at 786.

[22] *Id.* The court cited Rules 803(6), 901(a), 901(b)(4) (distinctive characteristics), (b)(5) (voice identification), (b)(6) (telephone conversations), and (b)(9) (process or system).

[23] 875 S.W.2d 319 (Tex. Crim. App. 1994) (per curiam).

case, however, the prosecution failed to present a sufficient predicate. Prosecution witnesses could only establish that the tape in question had been seized from a video camera found in the defendant's motel room. There was no testimony concerning where or when the tape was made or that it accurately portrayed the event. More recently, the Court in *Angleton v. State*[24] overruled *Kephart*. The Court held that the proponent could use a number of illustrations in Rule 901 to authenticate a recording, even if the predicate witness does not have personal knowledge about the preparation of the tape. The court said that the question is whether the voices on the tape are identified and that the tape is accurate and not altered. The court specifically noted that using the *Edwards* test will only confuse counsel and the courts.

Although these cases provide greater flexibility for authenticating audio and video recordings in criminal cases, cautious counsel should still find the *Edwards* seven-pronged predicate useful as a sort of checklist. What is clear from these recent cases is that in criminal cases, the following predicate is not mandatory.

§ 4-6(B) ELEMENTS OF THE FOUNDATION

The traditional *Cummings-Edwards* predicate includes the following elements:

1. The recording device was actually capable of recording.
2. The operator of the equipment was competent.
3. The recording is authentic and correct.
4. No changes, additions, or deletions have been made.
5. A showing of the manner of preservation of the recording.
6. The speakers and participants are identified.
7. The statements on the tape were voluntarily made.

§ 4-6(C) SAMPLE FOUNDATIONS

The first fact situation is a contract action and demonstrates a slightly longer and more detailed foundation. The contracting parties were rather suspicious of each other, and they had a private investigator make an audiotape of a key negotiating session.

P WHAT is your occupation? (2)

W I'm a private investigator.

P WHO is your employer? (2)

W I work for the Stead Detective Agency downtown.

---

[24] 971 S.W.2d 65 (Tex. Crim. App. 1998).

P HOW long have you worked there? (2)

W For about 10 years now.

P WHAT are your duties for your employer? (2)

W My real specialty is electronic surveillance and tape recording.

P HOW long have you worked in that field? (2)

W About 15 years.

P WHEN did you begin working in that field? (2)

W When I was in the military service.

P WHICH military service were you in? (2)

W I was in the Army.

P WHAT did you do while you were in the service? (2)

W I specialized in radar.

P WHAT training did you receive in that specialty? (2)

W I took a four-month course and was even able to get a first-class license from the Federal Communications Commission.

P WHAT additional training have you had in the field? (2)

W Since leaving the service, I've taken several college level courses in electronics. I've also attended a number of seminars on tape recording and electronic surveillance techniques.

P WHERE were you on the morning of January 17, 2005? (2)

W I went to the offices of Atco Corporation.

P WHY did you do that? (6)

W The president of the corporation, Mr. Semegen, had asked me to come and record a negotiating session between him and a Mr. Heiser, the head of another corporation.

P WHAT did you do while you were at the offices of Atco Corporation? (6)

W I did what I'd been asked to do. I recorded their conversation.

P WHAT equipment did you use to record the conversation? (1)

W I used a Uher recorder, microphones, and a seven-inch reel of Ampex audio tape.

P WHAT do "Uher" and "Ampex" mean? (1)

W They're trade names. They are two of the most dependable manufacturers in the field.

P HOW often had you used that equipment in the past? (2)

W Hundreds of times. I really trust their equipment. It's very reliable.

P WHAT condition was the equipment in that morning? (1)

W It was in good condition.

P HOW do you know that? (1)

W Well, I checked out the recorder and microphones. I test recorded some conversation and replayed it. It was a good quality reproduction. I took the tape out of the original wrapper. It was fresh and had never been used before.

P HOW did you use the equipment? (1), (2)

W I followed my standard procedure. First, I plugged the recorder into a wall outlet. Then I attached the mikes. After I'd test recorded some sound on one track—that is, half of the width of the tape, I turned the reel over, threaded the tape again, and set up to record on the second track.

P WHAT did you do then?

W Before I started recording the conversation, I asked the parties, Mr. Semegen and Mr. Heiser, to speak into the microphones. I got the right voice level, and then I was all set to record.

P WHAT happened then? (5)

W They spoke continuously for about half an hour. I then read my name, the date, and the address into the tape. After doing that, I turned off the recorder.

P HOW well did the recorder work during the conversation? (3)

W Very well.

P HOW do you know that? (3)

W In the first place, I didn't experience any technical or mechanical difficulties during the recording session. Second, right after the session, I rewound the tape onto the feeder reel and replayed it.

P WHAT happened when you replayed the tape? (3)

W I could hear the recording of the conversation.

P WHAT was the quality of the recording? (3)

W Excellent. As far as I could tell, the recorder picked up everything, and the recording was loud and clear.

P WHAT, if any, changes, additions, or deletions have been made to the tape? (4)

W None whatsoever.

P WHAT did you do with the tape after you replayed it? (5)

W I put it in an envelope and wrote my name, the parties' names, the date, and address on it.

P WHAT did you do with the envelope? (5)

W I took it back to my office.

P WHERE did you put it in your office? (5)

W In my evidence locker.

P HOW many people have access to the locker? (5)

W Only me. I have a combination lock on it, and I'm the only one who knows the combination.

P WHAT happened to the tape after you placed it in your evidence locker? (5)

W With one exception until today, it's been in the locker the whole time.

P WHAT was that exception? (5)

W You and I took it out several months ago and listened to it.

P WHO was present during that playing of the tape? (5)

W You and I were the only two people present.

P WHERE were you while the tape was out of the evidence locker? (5)

W I was present the whole time. I took it out, played it for you, and then immediately put it back.

P WHERE has the tape been since then? (5)

W In the locker the whole time.

P Did the speakers on the audiotape speak voluntarily? (7)

W Yes, by all means.

P [*To court reporter*] I request that this tape be marked as a plaintiff's exhibit for identification. [*Court reporter marks exhibit and hands it back to proponent.*]

P Please let the record reflect that I am showing plaintiff's exhibit number 10 for identification to the opposing counsel. [*Proponent shows exhibit to opposing counsel for examination.*]

P I request permission to approach the witness.

J Permission granted.

P I now hand you plaintiff's exhibit number 10 for identification. WHAT is it?

W It's the tape I've been talking about.

P HOW can you recognize it?

W I recognize my handwriting. I made those markings on the label on the reel.

P WHAT condition is the tape recording in? (3)

W It's in excellent condition.

P HOW do you know that? (3)

W When I removed it from the locker this morning, I replayed it.

P WHAT was the quality of the recording? (3)

W It hasn't changed at all. It was and is an excellent reproduction of the conversation.

P Your Honor, I now offer plaintiff's exhibit number 10 for identification into evidence.

J It will be received.

P I request permission to have the bailiff play the exhibit for the jury.

J Permission granted.

The second foundation is a simpler and shorter foundation, but uses the same predicate elements. This example focuses on a videotape recording of a "sting" operation during which the defendant sold stolen goods to police undercover agents posing as pawnshop owners. The proponent is the prosecutor. The witness is Officer Jones, who operated the video camera from behind a two-way mirror in an adjoining room. The officer has just finished describing how the sting operation worked.

P Officer Jones, HOW did you record the sting operation?

W We set up a video camera on a tripod in the back room and pointed it through a two-way mirror. The people bringing the stolen goods into the store thought they were dealing with members of organized crime interested in buying stolen goods. They had no idea they were being filmed.

P Please describe WHAT type of camera equipment you used. (1)

W We used a Sony Digicam, hi-8 mm, with a zoom lens and 2 Lux power. That means that it is capable of picking up pictures in very low lighting conditions. And we used a remote microphone to pick up all of the voices in the room. This type of equipment is available in any neighborhood electronics store.

P WHAT was the condition of the equipment? (1)

W It worked excellently. I ran several trial tapes and sound checks before the defendant came in. The quality was very impressive.

P WHAT, if any, training have you had in operating this equipment? (2)

W No formal training as such. Several of us worked with one of our electronics people to become familiar with the equipment and we have used this operation at least fifteen times without any problems. The system is extremely simple to operate.

P [*To court reporter*] Would you please mark this as an exhibit for the State? [*Court reporter marks exhibit as State's exhibit number 3 for identification and hands it back to the proponent.*]

P Thank you.

P Please let the record reflect that I am showing State's exhibit number 3 to opposing counsel. [*Shows to counsel.*]

P Your Honor, I request permission to approach the witness.

J Granted.

P Officer Jones, I now show you what has been marked as State's exhibit number 3 for identification. Would you tell us, please, WHAT this is?

W This is the tape we ran on the defendant.

P HOW do you know that?

W My initials are on the tape, here.

P WHAT, if any, changes have been made to the tape? (4)

W Absolutely none.

P WHERE has the tape been since the recording? (5)

W In our police files under lock and key. We did remove it only once and that was to show it to you and the defense counsel last month.

P WHO is on the tape? (6)

W Officers Schmedlapp and Wartsville, the two undercover officers posing as the buyers, and the defendant.

P WHAT, if any, inducements were offered to get the defendant to participate in this transaction? (7)

W The only thing we did was to get the word on the street that we were offering cold cash for hot merchandise. Everything on this tape is voluntarily done and said by the defendant and the officers.

P Officer Jones, is this tape a correct and accurate recording of what took place when the defendant came into the store? (3)

W Absolutely.

P HOW can you be so sure? (3)

W Well, for one thing, this equipment has a date and time feature on it, which means that once you turn it on, it runs continuously until the switch is turned off. By watching the tape you can see that the date and time indicator is on continuously from when the defendant walked in the store until we arrested him ten minutes later. There is no break in the action.

P Thank you. Your Honor, we now move for the admission of State's exhibit number 3 for identification into evidence.

J Any objections from the defense?

O We have none, your Honor.

J Very well. State's exhibit number 3 for identification will be admitted into evidence.

P At this time, your Honor, we would like to use the television monitors to show the videotape to the jury.

J That will be fine. Would the bailiff get the lights, please?

It is important to remember that even if the tape is authenticated, there may still be hearsay and best evidence issues.

§ 4-7 AUTHENTICATION OF FACSIMILE TRANSMISSIONS

§ 4-7(A) The Doctrine

The use of facsimile machines as a means of transmitting documents is becoming more and more prevalent. Indeed, they are an important, and sometimes an indispensable element, of efficient business operations. The facsimile ("fax") machine, which uses regular telephone connections, works in a particular manner. First, the sender determines the fax number of the person to whom the document is to be transmitted. Second, the sender prepares a cover sheet to precede the document to be sent. The cover sheet includes identifying information which indicates the name of the sender, the sender's fax number, the sender's telephone number, and the name and fax number of the person receiving the faxed document. The cover sheet also notes how many pages are being transmitted. Third, the cover sheet and document are inserted into the feeder mechanism for the fax machine. Fourth, the fax number of the receiving party is entered into the fax machine using the keys arranged in the same fashion as those on a regular telephone. Fifth, when the telephone connection is made, the sender's fax machine signals that the document is ready to be transmitted and the sender presses the appropriate key on the fax machine to begin transmission. Any errors in transmission are normally noted on the sender's fax machine. The person receiving the document can determine who sent the transmission by reading the cover sheet or reading the data which sometimes automatically registers on the transmitted document itself.

Fax machines are normally very reliable and require no real expertise in operation. If for some reason the fax transmission is in error, the receiver immediately notifies the sender to try again.

Despite their simplicity of operation, there appears to be no set method of authenticating facsimile transmissions. While an argument could be made that a facsimile transmission could be authenticated under the methods used for reply letters,[25] computer records,[26] or telephone conversations,[27] the faxed document could also be authenticated by relying upon Rule 901(b)(4) and identifying the document's distinctive characteristics and evaluating the surrounding circumstances.[28]

The transmission can also be authenticated under Rule of Evidence 901(b)(9), which permits the proponent to show how a particular process or system works and that it produces accurate results. That is the method discussed in the following sections.

§ 4-7(B) ELEMENTS OF THE FOUNDATION

The elements for showing that the facsimile machine is a process or system which produces accurate results are as follows:

1. The individual or organization uses a facsimile machine.
2. The facsimile machine is standard equipment that can both send and receive documents by telephone.
3. The facsimile machine accurately transmits by telephone to other facsimile machines copies of original documents inserted into that facsimile machine to be so transmitted, and accurately receives such documents as well.
4. A procedure exists for detecting mechanical and human error.
5. The facsimile machine accurately and automatically records the time and date of transmittal.
6. A "fax" cover sheet, sent with the "faxed" document, shows the phone number of the originating facsimile machine and the name of the person or organization to whom the document is directed, as well as the facsimile number of that person or organization.

---

25 *See supra* § 4-2(D).

26 *See supra* § 4-3(D).

27 *See infra* § 4-5(C). One Texas case has held that a fax transmission is a telephone conversation for purposes of TEX. R. EVID. 901(b)(6). *Tyson v. State*, 873 S.W.2d 53 (Tex. App.—Tyler 1993, pet. refused).

28 *See, e.g., Tyson v. State*, 873 S.W.2d 53 (Tex. App.—Tyler 1993, pet. refused) (trial court impliedly found a faxed document authentic under Rule 901(b)(4)).

§ 4-7(C) SAMPLE FOUNDATION

The fact situation involves an order placed by Sunlight Manufacturing with one of its suppliers, Bearings, Inc., for 3,000 ball bearings. As part of its case, Bearings wishes to show that Ms. Baker, a Bearings employee, received a "faxed" letter from Sunlight containing an order for 3,000 ball bearings. Sunlight has alleged that it never placed the order. Assume that the original document is not available to the proponent. Bearings' lawyer is the proponent, and Ms. Baker is the witness. Assume that Ms. Baker has already identified herself.

P Ms. Baker, WHERE do you work?

W At Bearings, Inc.

P WHAT is your position there?

W I am the executive secretary and assistant to the president of the company, George Wilson.

P As of September 11, 2004, the date in question here, DID Bearings own a facsimile machine? (1)

W Yes.

P As of that date, HOW long had Bearings had that facsimile machine?

W At least three or four years prior to that date.

P WHAT brand is the machine?

W It's a Murata 3000.

P WHAT, if any, experience have you had with that machine? (2)

W I have used it dozens, perhaps hundreds, of times, both sending and receiving.

P Ms. Baker, please describe HOW you fax a document to someone. (2), (3), (5), (6)

W I fill out a cover sheet indicating the person to whom the document is directed and that person's fax number and phone number. The cover sheet also contains other information, such as the total number of pages being transmitted, the date and time of the transmission, and any additional routing information. I also include a statement that in case of poor transmission the party receiving the document should call me at the number written on the cover sheet so that I can fax the document again. I then feed the cover sheet and the document to be transmitted into the facsimile machine and it transmits them to the number I dialed. The machine automatically records the time and date of transmittal on the documents being faxed.

P WHAT is the procedure when you receive faxed documents? (2)

W The same as I described, only in reverse. The fax machine rings several times to let us know that a document is being received. When the fax comes out of the machine, we get the cover sheet that the person faxing the document has filled out followed by a copy of the document.

P HOW can you be sure that what you have sent or received is an accurate transmission of the original document? (3), (4)

W Well, during the course of my handling the paperwork regarding Sunlight's contracts, I often see documents that I have faxed to some third party that are being returned to me by mail with some additional writing on them. I can readily tell by looking at the documents that they were accurate transmissions.

P WHAT, if any, errors are likely to occur during transmissions? (4)

W Well, sometimes the pages run together or the paper feeder jams and the lettering is hard to read. In that case we do not rely on the faxed document. If the faxed document is not clear to read, we call the transmitter of the document and ask them to send it again until we do get a clean copy.

P HOW often do you experience such problems? (4)

W Very rarely.

P Directing your attention to September 11, 2004, did you receive a document by fax transmission?

W Yes.

P [*To court reporter*] Would you please mark this as plaintiff's exhibit next in order? [*Reporter marks exhibit and hands it back to counsel.*]

P Thank you. Please let the record reflect that I am now showing what has been marked as plaintiff's exhibit number four for identification to the counsel for the defense. [*Opposing counsel examines exhibit and hands it back to the proponent.*]

P Request permission to approach the witness.

J Granted.

P Ms. Baker, I now hand you plaintiff's exhibit number four for identification. Have you ever seen this exhibit before?

W Yes, I have.

P WHAT is this exhibit? (2)

W This is the four-page document and the cover sheet that I received on our facsimile machine on September 11, 2004. It indicated it was being sent from Sunlight's facsimile machine. Our machine had been called and this document was transmitted to it.

P Is this document in the same or substantially the same condition today as it was when you received it on September 11, 2004? (3)

W Yes, it is.

P WHAT information, if any, is there on the document concerning the date and time and telephone number? (5)

W There is a date and time entry located here at the top of the page, along with the phone number of the transmitter.

P HOW accurate is that information? (3), (5)

W It is very accurate.

P Regarding the telephone number shown printed on the document, WHOSE fax number is that? (5)

W It is the fax number of our company.

P Your Honor, I offer into evidence plaintiff's exhibit number four for identification.

J Any objections, counsel?

O No, your Honor.

J Then plaintiff's exhibit number four for identification is admitted into evidence as plaintiff's exhibit number four.

§ 4-8 AUTHENTICATION OF E-MAIL TRANSMISSIONS

§ 4-8(A) THE DOCTRINE

Section 4-7, *supra*, discusses the fax technology. A fax is a graphic image that is digitized and sent over regular telephone lines by modem. Like fax, electronic mail (e-mail) poses special evidentiary issues.[29] To appreciate the authentication problem posed by e-mail, we must first understand e-mail technology. E-mail is more versatile than fax; it can be sent over a variety of network links, ranging from dial-up to fiber optic lines. E-mail is ordinarily text, but other things can be transmitted, including graphic images.

The mechanics of a simple e-mail system are straightforward. To send e-mail, the user first opens her e-mail application. The user next sees the e-mail screen, which has two parts: a heading and the body.

The visible part of a typical heading includes at least three lines. One is a line for the sender's e-mail address. That line has usually been automatically completed already, but it is generally a simple matter for the sender to change

[29] Note, *When the Postman Beeps Twice: The Admissibility of Electronic Mail Under the Business Records Exception to the Federal Rules of Evidence*, 64 FORDHAM. L. REV. 2285 (1996).

the entry in that line. There is a second line for the recipient's address. An Internet e-mail address consists of a local part and a host part: username@hostname. The local part is the mailbox, log-in name, or user identification of the intended recipient. The host name indicates the network serving the user. For example, Professor Imwinkelried's address is "ejimwinkelried@ucdavis.edu" (his host is U.C. Davis in the larger educational domain). The Internet provides online directory service databases of varying reliability—"white pages"—for locating e-mail addresses. The third line is provided for a brief summary or title of the message.

After completing the heading, the sender composes the body of the message. Once the sender completes the message, she ordinarily types "send" or clicks on a "send" button. Alternatively, the user might press a "queue" button and then later send queued messages before signing off. The program routes the message through the computer networks connecting the source (the sender) and destination (the intended recipient). Service providers (servers) intervene between the sender and recipient to transmit the message. After traveling through various servers and networks, the message reaches the recipient's in-box. When that person logs on and checks for mail, he will be told that he has new mail. At that point, the recipient may open the message and read it. Most e-mail programs have a reply feature. To use this feature, the recipient types "reply" or clicks a "reply" button. Depending on the program, the recipient then types the reply immediately before or after the message received. The program then automatically sends the reply to the original sender. The original sender receives e-mail consisting of both her message and the recipient's reply.

One fundamental difference between e-mail systems and fax is that it is usually easier to change the e-mail address of the sender. When the sender is completing the heading, it is a simple matter to enter a fictitious name or someone else's name. Section 4-7, *supra*, noted that some fax machines automatically imprint the sending number on the pages printed out at the recipient's end. Although a sophisticated fax user might be able to either disable that function or change the number, doing so requires a level of expertise above and beyond the elementary knowledge needed to send a fax message. Thus, in laying a foundation to show that a fax was sent by a particular person, the proponent can rely in part on the sender's fax address automatically printed on the received form. It is less justifiable to rely on the sender's address appearing in the heading of an e-mail message. With many of the most popular, less sophisticated systems, many e-mail users possess the knowledge needed to change the e-mail sender's address. In short, it is less justifiable to accept an e-mail message at face value than to presume the authenticity of a fax. Accordingly, there is an even greater need to lay additional foundation establishing the authenticity of the message.

§ 4-8(B) ELEMENTS OF THE FOUNDATION

Although e-mail is a relatively new technology, the pertinent evidentiary principles are old and well settled. In many instances, the proponent can authenticate an e-mail message by adapting a traditional doctrine.

Reply Letter Doctrine

Section 4-2(D) discusses the reply letter doctrine. This doctrine can also be applied by analogy to e-mail. The proponent makes a foundational showing that she obtained the address from an online directory or other reliable source, sent an e-mail message to that address, and in due course received a message responsive in terms to her earlier message. In the context of e-mail (and fax), "due course" will ordinarily be a shorter period of time than in the case of conventional mail. When the doctrine is applied to letters, it might take several days for the response to reach the original sender. When the doctrine is applied to e-mail, only a few minutes or hours might be required.

Content

The proponent can authenticate a writing by showing that only the purported author was likely to know the information found in the message. That technique also extends to e-mail. There are at least three fact situations in which that technique would come into play. First, the substantive content of the message might be information with which only the purported sender was familiar. Second, if the recipient used the reply feature to respond, the new message may include the sender's original message. If the sender dispatched that message to only one person, its inclusion in the new message indicates that the new message came from the original recipient. Finally, an encrypted message might be openable only by the encryption pass phrase or PIN of a particular person. Standing alone, that fact can identify the sender and/or recipient. Encryption is discussed in greater detail in the immediately ensuing paragraphs.

Cryptography

The proponent can sometimes lay a foundation to authenticate an e-mail message by presenting testimony about the cryptography used in transmitting the message. While it is true that cryptography is employed in only a small percentage of e-mail communication, that percentage is growing. Moreover, many important electronic transactions—the kinds of transactions likely to generate litigation—utilize cryptography.

In most cryptography, the communicating parties use a key which encrypts or scrambles the message. There are two basic types of key cryptography: the single-key system and the public/private two-key system. In single-key cryptography, the communicating parties use the same key; the sender utilizes the key to encrypt the message, and the recipient employs the same key to decipher or decrypt it. One difficulty with single-key cryptography is that before using the key, the parties must have a secure communication channel to exchange the key. It can be difficult to obtain access to such a channel. Sending the private key under secure channels can be expensive and slow.

A public/private two-key system provides an additional level of security at the price of some computational complexity. One key is the public key, and the other is the private or secret key. The keys are complementary; each unlocks the code which the other key makes. A person can use commercially available software such as PGP (Pretty Good Privacy) to create the two keys.[30] The person who is the key owner will publish one key and keep the other private. The person can use the private key to send messages which could be sent only by her;[31] because those messages can be decrypted only by using the sender's public key, the fact that the recipient successfully opened the message by employing that public key identifies the key owner as the sender.

However, there is a problem: How can the recipient determine that the purported sender is indeed the owner of that public key?

> The problem facing [the recipient] in this scenario . . . is that there is no more reason to trust an e-mail message purporting to be from Bob that says here is my public key than there is to trust any other e-mail message purporting to be from Bob.[32]

To overcome that problem, a new industry has emerged—the business of certification authorities (CAs).[33] These companies are in the business of verifying that a particular person owns a certain public key. Thus, after receiving a request from the person owning the public key, the company would conduct an inquiry to verify the identity of the key owner. Having done so, the company can provide third parties with assurance of the person's key ownership by issuing identifying certificates to that effect.[34] In effect, the CA certifies the connection between the owner and the public key.

> The CA might publish the resulting certificate on a World Wide Web site available to anyone with Internet access, or give the certificate to [the owner],

---

[30] Technically, PGP is a "hybrid" system: the program uses public/private key encryption to encrypt a session key—a one-time, disposable key—which is then used by IDEA, a strong single key algorithm, to encrypt the actual message. PGP employs this two-step process because public/private key encryption can be very slow when utilized on long messages.

[31] A. Michael Froomkin, *Regulation of Computing and Information Technology*, 15 J. LAW. & COMMERCE 395, 419 n.74 (1996); A. Michael Froomkin, *The Essential Role of Trusted Third Parties in Electronic Commerce*, 75 ORE. L. REV. 49, 52 (1996).

[32] Froomkin, *The Essential Role of Trusted Third Parties*, at 52.

[33] *Id.* at 49.

[34] *Id.* at 60.

or contract with [the owner] to honor e-mailed requests for the certificate from all comers.[35]

Given this technology, the proponent could authenticate an e-mail message by laying the following foundation:

1. In Utah there is a state statute regulating CAs;[36] however, CAs are unregulated in most states. The proponent can call a representative of a certain CA as a witness, introduce the relevant part of a transcript of the representative's deposition, or proffer a stipulation as to the existence and operation of the CA.
2. The CA received a request to verify that a particular person owned a specified public key. The request itself is nonhearsay under Federal Rule 801(a). The request is not a declarative statement asserting any facts. The CA's record reflecting receipt of the request qualifies as a business entry under Rule 803(6).
3. The CA conducted an inquiry to verify that the person in question owned that public key. The CA might conduct varying levels of inquiry. For instance, VeriSign offers four classes of certificates corresponding with differing levels of inquiry.[37] If the CA has retained the records reflecting the inquiry, the records themselves are admissible under Rule 803(6). If the CA no longer has those records, under Rule 406 the proponent can elicit the representative's testimony about the CA's routine practices for conducting inquiries.
4. As a result of the inquiry, the CA issued an identifying certificate verifying that the person in question owns the specified public key. There are various types of certificates,[38] but for our purpose an identifying certificate is of greatest interest. An identifying certificate establishes the connection or link between a specified public key and a particular person. In essence, the certificate vouches that the person is the key owner. Like the records reflecting the CA's receipt of the request (element #2) and its inquiry (element #3), the certificate itself will qualify as a business entry under Rule 803(6). The CA is not only in the business of conducting the inquiries; another essential part of its business is issuing the certificates and thereby giving third parties assurance of the key owner's identity. (Note that the proponent could dispense with the preceding foundational elements if the opponent were

---

35 *Id.*

36 UTAH CODE ANN. § 46-3-309 (1996).

37 Froomkin, *The Essential Role of Trusted Third Parties*, at 58–59.

38 *Id.* at 59–65 (identifying certificates, authorizing certificates, transactional certificates, and digital time-stamping devices).

willing to stipulate that the person in question was the owner of the specified public key.)

5. The recipient of the message to be authenticated had previously learned of the person's identity as the owner of the specified public key. The recipient might have obtained the information from any of many sources, including a telephone call or a page on the World Wide Web. In many cases, in an earlier e-mail message, the recipient received the plain text of the sender's public key.[39] The recipient's testimony about his discovery of the key owner's identity is not subject to a hearsay objection. The testimony is proffered only for the nonhearsay purpose of explaining the recipient's subsequent conduct under Rule 801(c), namely, later using that public key to decrypt the message in question. On request by the opponent, the trial judge would give the jury a Rule 105 limiting instruction about the nonhearsay status of the recipient's testimony. Of course, the proponent must present independent, admissible evidence of the person's identity as the key owner. However, the prior four foundational elements furnish that evidence.
6. The recipient received the message in question.
7. When the recipient received the message, the recipient used the person's public key to decrypt or decipher it.
8. When the recipient used the specified public key, the key successfully unscrambled the message.
9. The message identified the key owner as the sender. Standing alone, foundational elements 1–8 support this inference. However, when the message itself identifies the originator, the proponent should elicit this foundational testimony to strengthen the inference.

The proponent would use the above foundation to authenticate an encrypted e-mail message. A variation of this foundation can be used to present testimony about a digital signature to authenticate an unencrypted message.[40] Although the body of the message itself is unencrypted, the sender can use her private key to encrypt the digital signature.[41] If the recipient can successfully use the person's public key to decrypt the signature, the circumstances uniquely identify the sender and relate the sender to the message.[42]

Suppose that following receipt of the message, the purported sender takes action consistent with the content of the message. In a business context, the action

[39] *Id.* at 52.

[40] *Id.* at 54.

[41] *Id.*

[42] *Id.*

might be the delivery of merchandise mentioned in the message. That conduct could also provide circumstantial authentication of the source of the message.

Chain of Custody

The chain of custody technique can be used to authenticate a document.[43] Even if a person did not read the letter within an envelope, the person's testimony about the physical handling of the envelope can help establish a chain of custody for the enclosed letter. Suppose, for instance, that B testifies that she received an envelope from A and that she later handed it to C. In turn, C testifies that he received the envelope from B and later delivered it to D. D testifies that he accepted the envelope from C, opened it, and found a letter purportedly signed by A. Even though neither B nor C saw the contents of the envelope, their testimony suffices to establish that the letter D received was in fact authored by A.

Analogously, the proponent of an e-mail message may authenticate the message by showing its electronic handling. The proponent can use the business records of all the systems which transmitted the message to trace the message back to the source computer. As long as those records show that each system handled a message originating from the purported sender's computer, it is immaterial that no one at the intermediate systems actually opened and read the message. At the recipient's end, using proper commands, the computer can print out the information indicating the handling of the message between its dispatch and receipt. For example, the computer might print out the following:

From aamerson@oxy.edu; Fri June 7 16:51:49 1998
Received: from guilder.ucdavis.edu by peseta.ucdavis.edu (8.76/UCD3.5.6)
id QAA24323; Fri, 7 Jun 1998 16:31:30-0700 (PDT)
Received: from bobcat.cc.oxy.edu by guilder:ucdavis.edu (8.7.5/UCD3.5.4)
id QAA24807; Fri, 7 June 1998 16:31:26-0700 (PDT)
Received (from aamerson@localhost)
by bobcat.cc.oxy.edu (8.61.11/8.6.11) id QAAA21403
for sdlangford@ucdavis.edu; Fri, 7 June 16:31:22-0700
From Andy Amerson<aamerson@oxy.edu.

This string traces a message from Andy Amerson (aamerson@oxy.edu) to Steve Langford (sdlangford@ucdavis.edu). The message initially went from Amerson's computer to bobcat, the e-mail server for Amerson's organization, Occidental College. In turn, the bobcat server routed the message to guilder, the e-mail hub for Langford's organization, the University of California at Davis. Next, guilder routed the message to the peseta network on the Davis campus. Peseta is the e-mail server for that campus. Finally, peseta routed the message to the recipient's e-mail account. Each server in this chain is maintained by a

---

[43] *United States v. Thomas*, 54 F.3d 73 (2d Cir. 1995).

regularly conducted activity such as a department of a college or business. That department generates records documenting the receipt and transmittal of the message in question.

When the server receives the message, it assigns the message an identification number and notes the time and date of its processing of the message. Those records should qualify as business entries admissible under Rule 803(6) when testified to by the appropriate custodians or other qualified witnesses. Unless the server's administrator has "flushed" or disposed of the records, the records should still be available to help lay the foundation for an e-mail passage which was handled by the server.

Thus, if every other authentication technique fails, the proponent can lay the foundation for an e-mail message by:

1. Asking the recipient to print out the entire routing of the message;
2. Introducing the routing records for each server which handled the message to verify that the message was processed as the recipient's printout indicates; and
3. Establishing that the alleged author had primary or exclusive access to the computer which, according to the records, originated the message.

§ 4-8(C) SAMPLE FOUNDATIONS

§ 4-8(C)(1) Regular E-mail Transmission

The following example involves a contract lawsuit. The case involves an order placed by the University of Texas Purchasing Office with one of its suppliers, Intel Company, for computer parts. As part of its case, the University of Texas wishes to show that Mr. Langford, its employee, received an e-mail message. The message purportedly came from Intel and contained an offer to sell the computer components in question. The university's lawyer is the proponent.

Langford has already testified. During his testimony, he testified that: On September 12, 2004, he received an e-mail message on his personal computer at work; the university hub is "guilder.unut.edu"; the university server is "peseta.unut.edu" the message purported to come from Mr. Mishkin, a representative of Intel; the message was an offer to sell the computer parts. At the attorney's request (to establish element #1 of the foundation, *supra*) Langford printed out all the routing information for the message and he recognizes an exhibit as the printout. The printout includes seven entries. Three entries represent Langford's address, which is "sdlangford@utdallas.edu" and the identifications for the university's hub and server. A fourth line of the printout indicates that the message in question was routed by "orgmail.intel.com." That line lists

OAA23641 as the identification number for the message and indicates that the message was routed on September 12, 2004 at 2:02 P.M. That line represents Organization Mail, the external server intermediate between the plaintiff's e-mail system and the defendant's. The other three lines correspond to the Internet address and identification identified in the stipulation, *infra*. The printout was admitted as plaintiff's exhibit number eight.

In addition, the plaintiff introduces a stipulation of fact between the parties to establish element #3 of the foundation. The stipulation is to the effect that: On September 12, 2004, Jerome Mishkin was one of the defendant's employees. He is now deceased. As of September 2004, he had been assigned the Internet address "jeromemishkin@ccm.jf.intel.com;" the identification for Intel's server is "ccm.jf.intel.com;" and the identification for Intel's hub is "relay.jf.intel.com." (That address and those identifications correspond with three lines on the heading which Langford printed out.)

The next witness is Ms. Carlton, the employee in charge of records for the Organization Mail company. Organization Mail is an e-mail server for users in the commercial, governmental, and educational domains.

P WHAT is your name? (2)

W My name is Elise Carlton.

P WHO do you work for? (2)

W I work for Organization Mail.

P WHAT is the nature of your company's business? (2)

W We are an Internet service provider. We're sometimes called an external server. We get e-mail messages from one company or agency and transmit them to another. We take the message from the sender's mail system and transmit it to the intended recipient's system.

P WHAT is your job title there? (2)

W I'm chief of records for serving operations.

P WHAT are your responsibilities as chief? (2)

W I oversee the generation and maintenance of our records of all the messages we receive and send to destinations.

P WHAT kinds of messages do you handle? (2)

W All kinds—government, commercial, and educational.

P When your company handles an e-mail message, HOW, if at all, will your firm's handling be reflected at the message's final destination? (2)

W Well, when they print out the heading at the final destination, the word "orgmail" will be included in an entry indicating that we were a server.

P When you receive a message for transmission, WHERE, if at all, would the word "orgmail" appear on the message? (2)

W It automatically becomes part of the larger heading. It shows that we handled the message.

P Specifically, WHAT would the heading say about the message? (2)

W It gives it an identification number and notes the date and time of handling the message.

P Your Honor, I request that this be marked as plaintiff's exhibit number nine for identification. (2)

J It will be so marked.

P Please let the record reflect that I am showing the exhibit to the defense attorney. [*Proponent shows exhibit to opposing counsel.*]

J The record will so reflect.

P Permission to approach the witness?

J Granted.

P Ms. Carlton, I now hand you what has been marked as plaintiff's exhibit number nine for identification. WHAT is it? (2)

W It is one of our logs of e-mail messages.

P WHAT is a "log?"

W It's a printout of the information relevant to the handling of a message. At the end of every 12-hour period, someone in my office prints out the log listing all the messages received or sent on our server system. (2)

P WHAT does this log show? (2)

W It documents the handling of messages on a particular date.

P WHICH date? (2)

W September 12, 2004.

P WHAT types of messages does this log list? (2)

W As I said, it lists all the outgoing and incoming messages routed by our server "orgmail" on that date.

P WHY does your company prepare these logs? (2)

W For quality control and business reasons. To begin with, the logs help us determine whether our equipment is working properly, that is, whether we're sending messages to the right destinations. Moreover, we obviously have to monitor the volume of traffic for each customer for billing purposes. That's how we determine how much to charge each customer. These logs are absolutely essential in our business.

P HOW do you prepare these logs? (2)

W As I mentioned, at the end of each day, we print out our e-mail records and store them.

P WHO prepares them? (2)

W One of our employees, one of the people I supervise.

P HOW often do you prepare this type of record? (2)

W We do it every day, twice a day. Again, we do it at the end of every 12-hour period.

P HOW do you recognize this record? (2)

W I recognize the contents. You told me that you were interested in the e-mail log for a particular day. I personally went to the file to pull the log. I went to the file cabinet in my office where we store the logs for September 2004. I can vouch that this is the log I took out of the file for that date.

P Your Honor, I now place plaintiff's exhibit number nine for identification into evidence as plaintiff's number nine. (2)

J Any objection?

O None, your Honor.

J Very well. The exhibit will be received as plaintiff's number nine.

P Ms. Carlton, I'd like to take a look at the third entry on the second page of the log.

W Yes.

P According to that entry, WHAT message did your server handle on September 12, 2004? (2)

W According to the entry, we routed a message from the computer used by one of Intel's employees, a person named Jerome Mishkin. The entry is "jeromemishkin@ccm.jf.intel.com."

P According to your log, WHO was the intended recipient of that message? (2)

W The log says that the recipient's e-mail address was "sdlangford@utdallas.edu."

It is true that neither Carlton nor any other Organization Mail employee read the content of the e-mail message handled by her company. However, cumulatively, the stipulation and Langford's and Carlton's testimony support a permissive inference that the message Langford received on September 12, 2004 originated from Mishkin, Intel's employee. Based on the stipulation and the testimony, the plaintiff can now successfully introduce the e-mail message. The information in a heading can be forged, but the possibility of forgery affects the weight of the evidence rather than its admissibility.

§ 4-8(C)(2) E-MAIL TRANSMISSION WITH KEY CRYPTOGRAPHY

The foundation in § 4-8(C)(1) illustrated one method of authenticating an e-mail message. That foundation necessitated testimony by an employee from an Internet service provider. There are other methods of establishing the authenticity of an e-mail message. The following foundation is an example of another method. Like the previous foundation, this foundation is based in part on key cryptography. However, this foundation also relies on a certifying authority's (CA's) certificate with a DS (digital signature). The foundational elements relate to the CA, the Sender of a message, and the Recipient of the message. The assumption is that the CA, Sender, and Recipient use compatible public-key cryptographic software.

THE CERTIFYING AUTHORITY (CA)

1. There is a CA which is in the business of certifying, inter alia, the identity of the holders of public keys.
2. The CA itself has a public key and a private key.
3. The CA makes its public key accessible. For example, a bank might include some sort of key "fingerprint" in its bank statements. Alternatively, a CA can publish its own public key at its World Wide Web site available to anyone with Internet access.
4. A person (Sender) requests a certificate from the CA.
5. The CA requests certain proof of identity from Sender.
6. Sender furnished the requested proof.
7. CA:
   a. generates a certificate attesting that Sender has a certain public key;
   b. digitally signs the certificate. A hash function is used to produce the DS. The hash function utilizes the text of the certificate as an input and produces a hash number, for instance, a 500-digit number which is probabilistically unique. A hash function is a one-way function. In other words, knowing the text, the function allows you to determine the hash number, but knowing the number does not allow you to reproduce the text; and
   c. Uses its private key to encrypt the DS.

THE END RESULT of this step is both a certificate with unencrypted text and an encrypted hash number.

8. CA can make the certificate accessible by the following means, inter alia:
   a. publishing the certificate on its World Wide Web site;
   b. giving the certificate to Sender who requested the certificate; or
   c. contracting with Sender to honor E-mailed requests for the certificate from all comers.

SENDER

9. Sender later generates a message to Recipient. Just as CA digitally signed the certificate, Sender digitally signs the message. Thus, Sender uses a hash function to produce its DS. The hash function utilizes the text of the message as an input and produces a hash number. Sender uses its private key to encrypt the DS. THE END RESULT of this step is both a message with unencrypted text and an associated DS.
10. Sender sends Recipient both the message with unencrypted text and the DS. (If Sender has CA's certificate, Sender sends the certificate as well. Alternatively, Sender might inform Recipient that CA has posted the certificate at its Web site or will honor Recipient's request for the certificate.)

RECIPIENT

11. One way or another Recipient obtains CA's digitally signed certificate.
12. Recipient checks CA's certificate revocation list (CRL). In its CRL, CA lists any certificates that have been compromised. If the certificate in question is not on the list, Recipient has reason to believe that the certificate was in effect at the time Sender sent the message.
13. Recipient knows or learns CA's public key. (By way of example, Recipient might have previously contacted CA, Recipient might find CA's public key on an Internet directory, or Recipient can go to CA's Web site.)
14. *CA's Certificate.* Recipient uses CA's public key to decrypt the DS appended to CA's certificate. The decryption reveals the hash number for the certificate. Recipient then independently hashes the text of the certificate, yielding a hash number. If the two numbers match, the certificate is presumed valid when created. (If anyone had altered the text of the certificate, in all probability the two numbers would not match.)
15. *Sender's Message.* Again, CA's certificate states that Sender owns a certain public key. Recipient next uses that public key to decrypt the

DS appended to Sender's message. The decryption reveals the hash number for the message. Recipient then independently hashes the text of the message, yielding a hash number. If the two numbers match, the message is presumed authentic. (If anyone had altered the text of the message, in all probability the two numbers would not match.)

The proponent of the e-mail message would initially call an expert to educate the judge and jury about certificates and digital signatures:

Q WHAT is your name? Please state your full name and spell your last name for the record.

A Gina Martinez. My surname is spelled M-A-R-T-I-N-E-Z.

Q Ms. Martinez, WHAT is your current address?

A 4502 Shenandoah Place here in El Dorado.

Q WHERE do you work?

A I'm on the faculty of El Dorado State University.

Q WHAT do you teach?

A Computer science. I'm the assistant chair of that department.

Q WHAT, if any, specialties do you have?

A My specialty has been electronic commerce.

Q WHAT does that specialty involve?

A I study the way in which computers are used to conduct commerce, including the way messages are authenticated.

Q WHAT do you mean by "the way messages are authenticated?"

A Suppose that you are a seller. You receive a message that purports to come from a potential buyer. Before you rely on that message and ship goods, you want to be sure that the message really came from that person. You could be shipping the goods to an imposter, and you might not get your money. In short, you have to "authenticate" the message—in other words, you have to establish that that person was really the individual who sent the message. If that person can't prove his or her identity to your satisfaction, you're not going to supply them with goods or services.

Q HOW can you do that?

A There are several ways, but the one I've studied most intensely is the use of digital signatures.

Q HOW is a digital signature used to authenticate an electronic message?

A It's a complicated process involving several parties.

Q WHICH parties?

A There are basically three—you have a certifying authority, a sender, and a recipient.

Q Your Honor, I request that this be marked plaintiff's exhibit number one for identification.

J It will be so marked.

Q Your Honor, I request that the record reflect that I am showing the exhibit to the opposing counsel.

J The record will so reflect.

Q Permission to approach the witness?

J Granted.

Q Ms. Martinez, I now hand you what has been marked as plaintiff's exhibit number one for identification. WHAT is it?

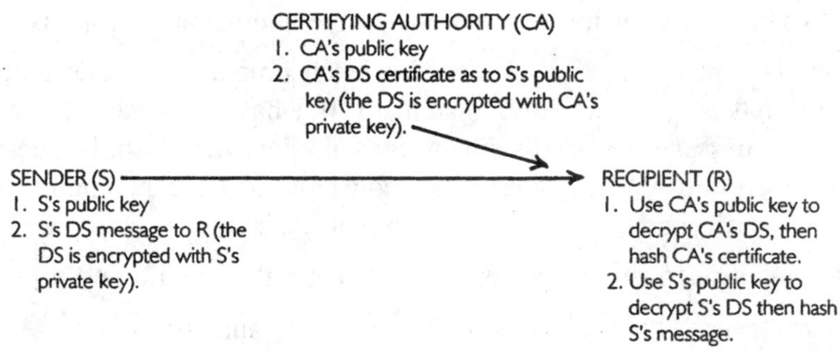

A It's a simple chart depicting the relationship among a certifying authority, the sender of a message, and the recipient of a message. Using the chart will help me explain the process.

Q All right. I notice that this chart three times uses the expression, "public key," and twice uses the expression, "private key." What do those expressions mean?

A The basic problem is this. You're in business in the market place; and when you send messages to other businesses such as orders for supplies, you want them to believe that you're really the sender. Again, if they can't trust those messages when you send them, you can't do business with them. You have to be able to provide these other businesses with proof that you are who you say you are in your messages—you are in fact ABC Software at 123 Adams Street in San Francisco. If you can't prove that to them, they're not going to respond to your messages and give you the goods and services you need. Pardon my pun, but the key to understanding how you prove your identity to other businesses is key cryptography.

Q I think we can excuse the pun, but please explain what you mean by "key cryptography."

A "Cryptography" is a term which used to be associated only with military codes. One military unit would use code or cryptography to send a message to another military unit. The first platoon on the west side of the hill uses the code to send a message to the second platoon on the east side. Today cryptography is used extensively by civilians, especially businesses. In most cases key cryptography involves the use of a public and a private key. One key is public; you make it available to everyone. The other key is private or secret. The relationship between the two keys has special properties or characteristics. Special software programs create the keys. The two keys are created by a single process and have a complementary property.

Q What do you mean by the expression, "a complementary property?"

A The complementary characteristic is that each unlocks the code that the other key makes. The two keys match up. If I have a private key and I send you a message encoded with my private key, there's only one way you can open and read my message—you have to have my public key. That's the sense in which they complement each other.

Q You just mentioned this businessperson "creating" a public and a private key. How does someone get these keys?

A There are commercially available software programs specially designed to create these keys. You buy the program, and the program will create for you a public key and a complementary private key. The programs use algorithms to create the keys.

Q Professor, I vaguely recall the term "algorithm" from high school. However, could you refresh my memory as to what that term means?

A Sure. Simply stated, it's a type of mathematical concept or formula. The software uses this formula to generate a long number—which is in all probability unique—and it programs that number into both the public and the private key. When someone attempts to use the public key to open a message coded with the private key, the private key recognizes the number, opens, and allows you to read it. But if you don't have the right public key, there's no way to open the message without destroying it.

Q But couldn't someone just get a person's public key, figure out what the number is, and then open messages coded with the private key?

A No.

Q Why not?

A As I said, there's a very special relationship between the public and private keys. This works only one way. There's no way to just extract the number from the public key. You can use the public key to open messages coded with the private key; but even if you know someone's public key, you can't determine what number the public and private key share. Again, that sort of key cryptography is the key to understanding this process.

Q Now let's take the parties one by one. Let's start in the middle of the chart by talking about a certifying authority. To begin with, WHY is that person in the middle of the chart? (1)

A The chart shows them between the sender and the recipient. They allow the sender and the recipient to communicate with confidence. In a sense, the CA intervenes between the two and serves as an intermediary, enabling the recipient to trust the messages the sender sends the recipient. Again, in the market the basic problem facing a businessperson is to get the recipient to trust his or her messages. If the recipient can't trust the messages, they won't do business with the sender. The CA or certifying authority enables the recipient to trust the sender's message.

Q WHAT does the term "certifying authority" mean? (1)

A A certifying authority is a company which is in the business of certifying or attesting to the identity of holders or owners of public keys.

Q Again, WHAT do you mean by a public key? (2)

A This is the core concept, so it probably bears repeating. During a war, each combatant uses cryptography or codes to "encrypt" or scramble important messages. Today businesses also use cryptography to protect their messages. The public key is part of a technique—the public key/private key technique—used in modern cryptography. The public and private keys are complementary; each unlocks the codes that the other key makes. The key owner makes one key publicly available and keeps the other key secret. The first key is the public one, and the second is the private key. The owner can use the private key to send messages which could be sent only by that person. Messages coded with that person's private key can be decoded only by using that person's public key. Therefore, the fact that the recipient can successfully open the message by employing that public key helps identify the key owner as the sender. Certifying authorities establish that a particular person owns a certain public key and issue certificates to that effect.

Q HOW can someone trust the certificate and know that the certificate actually came from the certifying authority?

A You can trust it because of the way the certifying authorities generates and issues the certificate.

Q Specifically, HOW does the certifying authority do that?

A Well, the certifying authority or CA itself has a public and private key.

Q Again, WHY do you call it a public key? (2)

A It's accessible to the public.

Q HOW does the CA make it accessible to the public? (3)

A There are a number of ways it can be done. For example, a bank might include the key in the bank statements it sends out. Alternatively, a CA can publish the public key at its World Wide Web site available to anyone with Internet access.

Q HOW does the process of certification begin? (4)

A The CA receives a request from someone who wants to send messages. We'll call them Sender. Sender requests that CA issue a certificate to the effect that Sender owns or holds a certain public key. [*The request is admissible nonhearsay, as information acted upon, under Texas Rule of Evidence 801(d).*]

Q WHAT does CA do after receiving the request? (5)

A The CA requests certain proof of identity from Sender? [*Like the sender's request, the CA's request is nonhearsay under Rule 801(a).*]

Q WHAT happens next? (6)

A If Sender supplies the requested proof of identity, CA generates a certificate that Sender owns that key. [*Because the CA is in the business of issuing such certificates, the certificate qualifies as a business entry under Texas Rule of Evidence 803(6). The CA does not accept the sender's representation as to sender's identity at face value. Rather, CA demands independent proof of identity. The inquiry arguably satisfies the requirement for personal knowledge under Rule 803(6).*]

Q WHAT does CA do next? (7)

A CA digitally signs the certificate. As the chart shows, at the end of this part of the process CA generates and issues a digitally signed certificate.

Q WHAT do you mean by the expression, "digitally signs the certificate?" (7)

A CA uses a hash function to produce the digital signature.

Q WHAT does "a hash function" do? (7)

A It takes the text of the certificate as an input and uses it to produce a hash number.

Q WHAT do you mean by "hash number?" (7)

A For instance, it might convert the wording of the certificate into a 500-digit number that is probabilistically unique.

Q WHAT do you mean by "probabilistically" unique? (7)

A The number could include 500 digits. It's possible—in the same sense that virtually anything is possible—that just by chance someone could come up with the same number. But when you're talking about a 500-digit number, the odds against that are absolutely astronomical. For all practical purposes, the number is unique to that message. If you have software using that hash function, you can convert the text of the certificate into that number; but if the text were changed in even the slightest—one letter in one word or even a comma—you'd come up with a different hash number. That's the way you generate the digital signature for the certificate.

Q WHAT does the CA do with this digital signature? (7)

A It uses its own private key to encrypt the digital signature.

Q WHAT does the CA do with the certificate and the digital signature? (8)

A It can do one of several things. It could publish the certificate on its World Wide Web site. Or it could contract with Sender to honor any requests from third parties for the certificate. Or it might give the certificate to Sender.

Q We've been talking about the role of the first person, the certifying authority. Now let's shift and talk in more detail about the second person shown on the left hand side of the chart, Sender.

A Sure. This is the businessperson who needs to convince the recipient that the sender really is ABC Software on Adams Street in San Francisco. Sender needs to prove his or her identity to potential suppliers and customers.

Q WHAT does the Sender do after the CA generates the certificate with the digital signature? (9)

A As I said at the outset, Sender will want to engage in some business transaction. So just as CA generated a certificate, Sender generates a message—perhaps an offer to buy some goods.

Q WHAT does Sender do with the message? (10)

A Before sending it, Sender will digitally sign the message just as CA digitally signed the certificate. As the chart indicates, while CA generates and issues a digitally signed certificate, Sender is going to generate and send out a digitally signed message.

Q HOW does Sender digitally sign the message? (10)

A In roughly the same way as CA digitally signs the certificate. Again, Sender uses a hash to produce a hash function. The hash function uses the text of Sender's message as an input and yields a hash number.

Q WHAT does Sender do next? (10)

A There's another parallel to what the certifying authority does. As I said, the CA uses its private key to encrypt the digital signature on the certificate. For his or her part, Sender uses its private key to encrypt the digital signature on the message.

Q WHAT does Sender do next? (10)

A Well, we call this person Sender because they send both the message and the digital signature to the third party, Recipient.

Q WHAT else, if anything, would Sender provide to Recipient? (10)

A Sender might send Recipient the certificate from CA. Or, as I testified previously, Recipient could find the certificate on CA's World Wide Web site. Alternatively, CA might furnish the certificate in response to a specific request by Recipient.

Q Finally, let's consider the role of the third part shown on the right hand side of the chart, Recipient in this transaction. WHO is this person?

A In the business world, this is the person sender has to convince of sender's identity. For example, Recipient could be the supplier of goods or services Sender needs to keep his or her business going. If Recipient doesn't trust the messages Sender sends, Sender can't do business.

Q WHAT does Recipient do after getting CA's certificate? (11), (12)

A To begin with, as the chart shows, if he or she has any sense, the Recipient will check CA's CRL.

Q WHAT is a "CRL?" (12)

A That's CA's certificate revocation list. In a CRL, a CA lists any certificates that have been compromised. [*Since the CRL is prepared in the regular course of CA's business, the entries on the CRL also qualify as business entries under Texas Rule 803(6).*]

Q WHAT do you mean by "compromised?" (12)

A If CA learns that some third party has learned Sender's private key, the public key is compromised. Some impostor could then use the private key. If CA learns that the private key has been compromised, the CA should immediately announce that you can no longer rely on the certificate. The certificate stated that Sender owned that public key—and implied that Sender was the only one who knew the corresponding private key. If that's no longer true, CA will include the certificate on the CRL.

Q WHAT happens if Recipient checks the list and the certificate in question is not on the list? (12)

A Recipient should then conclude that the certificate is still good. If the certificate is good, Recipient has reason to conclude that Sender is still the owner and holder of that public key.

Q If Recipient reaches that conclusion, WHAT does Recipient do next? (13)

A Recipient will use CA's public key to decrypt the digital signature on the certificate.

Q WHAT happens when Recipient does that? (14)

A The decryption reveals the hash number for the certificate.

Q WHAT does Recipient do after it learns the hash number for the certificate? (14)

A Using compatible software, Recipient independently hashes the text of the certificate.

Q WHAT happens when Recipient does that? (14)

A Recipient gets another hash number. If the two hash numbers match, Recipient will conclude that the certificate is valid. No one has tampered with the text of the certificate. Again, if you changed the text in any way, in all probability you'd get two different numbers.

Q WHAT does Recipient do if Recipient concludes that the certificate is valid? (15)

A Remember that the certificate states that Sender owns a certain public key. Recipient will next use that public key to decrypt the digital signature appended to the message.

Q WHAT happens when Recipient does that? (15)

A The decryption reveals the hash number for the message.

Q WHAT does Recipient do next? (15)

A Just as Recipient independently hashed the text of the certificate, Recipient does the same thing to the wording of the message.

Q WHAT happens when Recipient does that? (15)

A You get another hash number. If the two numbers match, Recipient can now conclude that no one has tampered with the text of the message. If no one has tampered with the text of the message and CA's certificate establishes that Sender holds that public key, Recipient will conclude that he or she has an authentic message from Sender. If that message is a purchase order for a certain number of goods, now Recipient can rely on the order and get ready to ship to Sender.

After the expert has taught the judge and jury about the technology, the proponent calls a second witness to explain how the technology was used in the instant case.

Q WHAT is your name? Please state your full name and spell your last name for the record.

A Jane Stevick. My last name is spelled S-T-E-V-I-C-K.

Q WHAT is your current address?

A 440 West Point Court in Morena.

Q WHERE do you work?

A I work for the plaintiff, Furnish Company.

Q WHAT do you do for Furnish Company?

A I'm in charge of monitoring all the messages we receive and send through the Internet. We conduct a large percentage of our business that way.

Q WHERE were you on the morning of January 13, 2005?

A I was at work.

Q WHAT were you doing?

A I was in my office monitoring our Internet communications.

Q WHAT, if anything, happened at roughly 10:00 a.m. that morning?

A We received a communication.

Q WHAT was in the communication? (10)

A It consisted of two things—first an unencrypted message with an associated digital signature and second a certificate with a digital signature.

Q Your Honor, I request that these be marked as plaintiff's exhibits number two and three for identification.

J They will be so marked.

Q Your Honor, please let the record reflect that I am showing the exhibits to the opposing counsel.

J The record will so reflect.

Q Your Honor, may I have permission to approach the witness?

J Yes.

Q Ms. Stevick, I now hand out what have been marked as plaintiff's exhibits numbers two and three for identification. WHAT are they? (10)

A Two is the printout of the certificate, and three is the printout of the accompanying message.

Q HOW do you recognize them? (10)

A They have distinctive contents. I've never seen any other message or certificate with the same appearance. [*This testimony suffices to satisfy Rule of Evidence 901(b)(4).*]

Q WHOM did the message, exhibit three for identification, purport to come from? (10)

A Martinez Construction.

Q WHOM did the certificate, exhibit two for identification, purport to come from? (10)

A Cyberspace Certification.

Q Now, Ms. Stevick, let me first ask you some questions about exhibit two for identification, the certificate purportedly from Cyberspace. WHAT did you do after you received this certificate? (11)

A I contacted Cyberspace.

Q HOW did you do that? (11)

A I went to their Website.

Q HOW did you know the address of their Website? (11)

A We've dealt with them on numerous prior occasions. Many of our customers use Cyberspace as the certifying authority. I have their address in my personal directory of Website addresses.

Q WHY did you go to Cyberspace's Website? (12)

A I wanted to check their certificate revocation list.

Q WHY did you want to check the list? (12)

A I wanted to see if their certificate for Martinez Construction was listed as having been compromised.

Q WHAT did you learn when you checked the list? (12)

A That certificate was not on the list. So I figured that the certificate in question was still good and in effect.

Q After learning that, WHAT did you do? (13)

A I used Cyberspace Certification's public key to decrypt the digital signature appended to the certificate.

Q HOW did you learn their public key? (13)

A As I said, we've dealt with them on numerous prior occasions. I also have that in my office records.

Q WHAT happened when you used their public key to decrypt the signature? (14)

A It yielded a hash number.

Q WHAT did you do next? (14)

A I independently hashed the text of the certificate.

Q WHAT happened when you did that? (14)

A Again, I got a hash number.

Q HOW did the two numbers compare? (14)

A They were identical.

Q So at that point, WHAT did you conclude? (14)

A That exhibit two for identification was the real McCoy, a genuine certificate from Cyberspace Certification.

Q Your Honor, I request that plaintiff's exhibit two for identification be accepted into evidence as plaintiff's exhibit number two.

J It will be received.

Q WHAT, if anything, did exhibit two, the certificate, state? (15)

A It identified Martinez Construction as the holder of a certain public key.

Q I've asked you some questions about what you did with exhibit two, the certificate which purported to come from Cyberspace Certification. Now I'd like to shift topics and ask you some questions about what you did with exhibit three for identification, the message that purported to come from Martinez Corporation. After you read Cyberspace's certificate, WHAT did you do? (15)

A I used that public key—the public key for Martinez Construction—to decrypt the digital signature associated with the message.

Q WHICH message? (15)

A The one that said that it came from Martinez Construction.

Q WHAT happened when you used that public key to do that? (15)

A I got a hash number.

Q WHAT did you do next? (15)

A I independently hashed the text of the message that purported to come from Martinez Construction.

Q WHAT happened when you did that? (15)

A I got another hash number.

Q HOW did the two numbers compare? (15)

A They were identical.

Q At that point, WHAT did you conclude? (15)

A That the message had in fact come from Martinez Construction.

Q Your Honor, I now request that plaintiff's exhibit number three for identification be accepted into evidence as plaintiff's exhibit three.

J It will be received.

Q Ms. Stevick, I'd now like you to read plaintiff's exhibit number three to the jury.

§ 4-9 AUTHENTICATION OF CALLER IDENTIFICATION

§ 4-9(A) THE DOCTRINE

Like fax and e-mail, caller identification (caller ID) technology has made its advent. Caller ID units or boxes are now widely available commercially. A prospective user can purchase a unit from a variety of vendors that merchandise telephones and telephone accessories. After purchasing the unit, the user installs the unit and informs her telephone company that she desires caller ID service. The telephone company then activates the service for the user. The caller ID information is transmitted as a burst of a modem signal to the unit. Once service has been activated, whenever someone places a call to the user, the user's caller ID unit will automatically display the caller's telephone number.[44] More sophisticated caller ID units have the capability of time stamping and storing the number for later retrieval and printout.

Suppose that at trial, the proponent wants to prove that a certain call to the proponent's home or business originated from a certain number. In a contract action, the proponent might be the plaintiff contending that the telephone call (the alleged offer) came from the defendant's corporate headquarters.[45] To help prove up that contention, the plaintiff could rely on caller ID technology.

Caller ID is already in such widespread use that many judges would be willing to judicially notice this proposition under Rule 201(b). The reliability of the technology is both a matter of common knowledge under Rule 201(b)(1) and a "verifiable certainty" under Rule 201(b)(2). The problem facing the proponent is that to date, there are no published opinions upholding an authentication based on caller ID. Given the dearth of precedent, a cautious trial judge might insist that the proponent present live expert testimony to establish this element of the foundation. In that event, the proponent could call a telephone company representative. The representative would qualify as an expert under Texas Rule 702, and

---

[44] Some callers, though, have "blocking." They can block the transmission of their phone number either in all cases or for a particular call. If the caller has the latter type of blocking, she must dial a special code at the time of the call in order to prevent the transmission of her phone number.

[45] Some callers have PBX, private branch exchanges. If so, the number transmitted to the user might be the main number for the corporation rather than the number of the specific phone from which the call was actually originated.

the hypothesis of the reliability of the technology would undoubtedly qualify as "scientific knowledge."

§ 4-9(B) ELEMENTS OF THE FOUNDATION

To lay a proper foundation, the proponent is required to show the following:

1. In general, caller ID technology is reliable.
2. Prior to the telephone call in question, the user acquired and installed a caller ID unit or box.
3. The caller ID unit in question is a reliable one.[46]
4. On the occasion in question, the caller ID unit displayed a particular telephone number.[47]
5. That displayed telephone number belongs to a particular person or business.[48]

---

[46] Even if the judge is willing to judicially notice the first element of the foundation, she will probably hesitate at noticing this proposition. To be on the safe side, just as for element #1, the proponent could call an expert witness. In this case, the ideal expert would be a representative of the manufacturer. A salesperson at a telephone store would also probably qualify as an expert if he had substantial experience with the make and model in question. The judge might not demand the appearance of an expert to testify directly to the reliability of a caller ID unit installed at the plaintiff's office. Instead, the judge might well be content with circumstantial proof. For example, one of the plaintiff's agents could testify that she has used the unit in question for several months or years; when she receives a telephone call, the unit regularly displays a telephone number; and on numerous occasions, the circumstances have indicated that the number displayed was in fact the number from which the call originated.

A myriad of circumstances might suffice. The circumstance might be that when the agent answered, she recognized the voice as that of the person whose number was displayed. Or the caller might have disclosed information known only to employees of the business whose number was displayed. Or at a later point in time, the agent called the number previously displayed by the caller ID unit, and in that subsequent conversation, the respondent referred to the earlier telephone call.

[47] If the user recalls the number displayed, she can testify to that number on the basis of personal knowledge under Rule 602. If the unit has logging and printout capability, the proponent can offer the printout into evidence so long as the foundational witness satisfies Rule 901 by identifying the exhibit as the printout from the user's caller ID unit. If, as is often done in the business world, the user has connected the caller ID unit to a computer which stores a history of the telephone numbers, the proponent can offer the computer printout.

[48] The witness could testify from personal experience that that number belongs to that individual or business. Failing that, the proponent could introduce a telephone directory. Telephone directories fall within the hearsay exception codified in Rule 803(17), and the inscription on the directory would make it self-authenticating under Rule 902(7). In many cases, the two parties can reach a stipulation that the phone number has been assigned to a particular person or business.

§ 4-9(C) SAMPLE FOUNDATION

The fact situation is a civil contract action. The plaintiff, Arnett Corporation, alleges that the defendant, Balantine Corporation, breached a contract with the plaintiff. The plaintiff contends that on June 15, 2005, the defendant telephoned the plaintiff and placed an order for custom merchandise to be manufactured by the plaintiff. Before trial, the parties stipulated that the main telephone number for the defendant's purchasing department is (512) 555-0727. At a pretrial hearing, the judge accepted the stipulation. In addition, at the same hearing, the judge granted the plaintiff's request for judicial notice of the general reliability of caller identification technology. The next witness is Ms. Amann. Just before calling her, the plaintiff's attorney states:

P Your Honor, as you will recall, at our pretrial conference, you granted our request for judicial notice. I would ask that at this point, you instruct the jury on the judicially noticed proposition. (1)

J Very well. Ladies and gentlemen, I am going to give you an instruction now. The instruction is that you are to assume that in general, caller identification units for telephones are reliable. You are to assume that when a unit is working properly, it correctly displays the number of the incoming telephone call. You must assume the truth of that fact even though you will not hear any live testimony about it. All right, let's proceed.

P Thank you, your Honor. As our next witness, we call Ms. Holly Amann.

J Ms. Amann, please approach the witness stand. [*Ms. Amann is sworn and identifies herself. The plaintiff's direct examination continues.*]

P Ms. Amann, WHERE do you work? (2)

W I work for Arnett Corporation in Plano.

P HOW long have you worked there? (2)

W I've been employed there for 15 years.

P WHAT is your current position with Arnett Corporation? (2)

W I'm the head of the order department.

P HOW long have you held that position? (2)

W I've been in orders for 10 years, and I've headed the department for the past 3 years.

P WHAT is the job of the order department? (2)

W We take all the incoming orders for merchandise. We make sure that the order is sent on to records, bookkeeping, and the plant.

P HOW do you receive these orders? (2)

W Lots of ways.

P Such as WHICH ways? (2)

W We get them by personal contact, e-mail, fax, telephone—basically, if the means of communication exists, we use it to get orders.

P WHAT percent of your orders come over the telephone? (2)

W The vast majority. Most people still use the good old telephone rather than the fancier stuff like e-mail.

P WHAT type of telephone equipment do you use in your department? (2)

W We have a phone hooked to a caller identification unit.

P HOW long have you had a caller ID unit in your department? (2)

W We've used one for over 3 years now.

P WHAT type of unit do you have? (2)

W It's a standard caller ID box manufactured by AT&T.

P WHAT does the unit do? (2)

W Since we're a business, we use one of the more advanced models.

P WHAT do you mean by "advanced?" (2)

W A basic caller ID unit—like the one I have at home—just displays the incoming call number. However, as a business, we need to keep a record of our calls. So we have a caller unit with a history capability.

P WHAT do you mean by "history capability?" (2)

W It does more than just display the incoming caller number. It logs or records the number in memory and time stamps it—indicating the date and time the call came in. At a later point, you can retrieve the number and time stamp from memory; you can either display it again or print it out.

P HOW reliable is your caller ID unit? (3)

W It's very trustworthy.

P HOW do you know that? (3)

W On many occasions, the information I've gotten from the unit has checked out.

P HOW has it checked out? (3)

W Someone will tell me something over the phone, and it will turn out to be true.

P WHAT would be an example? (3)

W Well, I'll get a call, and someone will tell me to expect an order from their business. Then in a couple of days I'll get that order, and I'll recognize the telephone number on the order. Or they'll say that a check is on the way, and a check will show up from that very company.

P HOW often, if ever, has the caller ID unit malfunctioned? (3)

W As I recall, there was one day in 2005 when it went down. It's not that it malfunctioned in the sense of giving you the wrong number. It shorted and didn't work at all. We immediately called the repairman and got the unit fixed. Since then we've had no problems at all.

P Ms. Amann, WHERE were you on June 15 of 2005? (4)

W I was at work at the office.

P WHAT, if any, telephone calls did you receive that day? (4)

W I got one from a person who said he was a buyer for Balantine.

P Before that telephone call, HOW much contact, if any, had you had with that person? (4)

W I have to say honestly that I didn't recognize his voice.

P WHO did the caller say he worked for? (4)

W He said he was calling on behalf of Balantine to place an order.

P At the time of the call, WHAT telephone number was the caller ID unit displaying? (4)

W It was displaying Balantine's number.

P WHAT is that number? (5)

W It's (512) 555-0727.

P HOW do you know that? (5)

W I've dealt with them on dozens of occasions before.

P HOW do you know that the caller ID unit displayed that number? (4)

W As I said, I didn't recognize this person's voice. However, I always make it a practice to check the caller ID display whenever I don't recognize the voice. You have to make sure who you're dealing with. If it hadn't displayed that number, I'd remember that. That would have been a red flag for me.

P WHERE were you before coming to court this afternoon? (4)

W I was at the office.

P WHY were you there? (4)

W You asked me to stop by and print out the history log from the caller ID unit for June 15, 2005.

P WHAT did you do? (4)

W I did as you asked. I went to the unit, called up the log for that date, and printed it out.

P Your Honor, I request that this be marked plaintiff's exhibit number three for identification. [*Proponent hands exhibit to court reporter, who marks exhibit and hands it back to proponent.*]

P Thank you. Please let the record reflect that I am showing the exhibit to the opposing counsel. [*Opposing counsel examines exhibit and hands it back to proponent.*]

J The record will so reflect.

P Permission to approach the witness?

J Granted.

P Ms. Amann, I now hand you what has just been marked as plaintiff's exhibit number three for identification. Do you recognize it?

W Yes I do.

P WHAT is it? (4)

W It's the printout of the history log from the caller ID unit in my department.

P HOW can you recognize it? (4)

W To begin with, I read it as soon as it printed out. I recognize the contents. In addition, just to be on the safe side, I wrote my initials and today's date on the page. They're right here. I recognize them as well.

P Your Honor, I now offer plaintiff's exhibit number three for identification into evidence as plaintiff's three.

J Any objection?

O No, your Honor.

J Very well, it will be received.

P Ms. Amann, I'd like you to read to the jury the third entry on this page. (4)

W Certainly. It reads: "June 15 0930 hours (512) 555-0727."

P WHAT does that entry mean? (4)

W It means that at 0930 hours—that is, 9:30 in the morning—we received a telephone call from that number.

P Thank you, Ms. Amann. Your Honor, as you know, at the pretrial hearing you accepted a stipulation between the parties. I would request that at this point, you inform the jury of the stipulation.

J [*Judge gives standard instruction on stipulations.*]

§ 4-10 INFORMATION POSTED AT BUSINESS WEB SITE

§ 4-10(A) The Doctrine

E-commerce has become one of the most important types of business activity. In order to participate in E-commerce, many businesses have established web sites that customers can visit. The information posted at these sites can become relevant as evidence in litigation. In some cases, the proponent may want to use assertions posted at a web site as substantive evidence and will hence need to lay a foundation for a hearsay exception. In other cases, though, the proponent can put the assertion to a nonhearsay use. For example, in a suit for breach of warranty, the plaintiff-customer might want to prove that in purchasing the defendant manufacturer's goods, the customer relied on an assurance posted on the defendant's web site. In that situation, the assurance would be admissible as nonhearsay, since it would be a verbal act; the assurance is the warranty. Or in a trade libel case, a plaintiff competitor might allege that an assertion posted on the defendant's web site defamed the plaintiff's product. Here again the assertion would be admissible as a nonhearsay verbal act; in this hypothetical trade libel action, the last thing the plaintiff wants to prove is the truth of the assertion defaming its product. Truth is a defense, and the plaintiff would be proving itself out of court.

Whatever the hearsay status of the proposed testimony about the information posted at the web site, in most cases the proponent must authenticate the information as posted on the business' site and emanating from the business. On the one hand, some courts are quite skeptical about proffers of testimony about web site data:

> While some look to the Internet as an innovative vehicle for communication, the Court continues to warily . . . view it largely as one catalyst for rumor, innuendo, and misinformation . . . . Anyone can put anything on the Internet. No web-site is monitored for accuracy and nothing contained therein is under oath or even subject to independent verification absent underlying documentation. Moreover, the Court holds no illusions that hackers can adulterate the content of any web-site from any location at any time.

St. Clair v. Johnny's Oyster & Shrimp, Inc., 76 F.Supp.2d 773, 774–75 (S.D.Tex. 1999).

On the other hand, in the final analysis, like other questions discussed in this problem, this authentication issue is governed by the lax standard set out in Texas Rules of Evidence 104(b) and 901(a).

§ 4-10(B) ELEMENTS OF THE FOUNDATION

To authenticate testimony allegedly describing information posted at a web site, the proponent should lay the following foundation:

1. The Internet exists and is an effective medium for electronic communication. This proposition is so well known that it qualifies for judicial notice under Texas Rule of Evidence 201(b).
2. On the Internet, a person or entity can establish a web site that other persons can visit. This proposition is also so well established that it is judicially noticeable.
3. A certain person or entity operates a web site with a particular universal resource locator (URL) address, usually prefaced with "www." If the site purports to be operated by a government entity, the documents posted there are arguably self-authenticating under Rule of Evidence 902(5).[49] Likewise, if a site includes a company's "inscription" or "label," the self-authentication provision of Rule 902(6) might come into play. If the court demands extrinsic proof of the identity of the operator of the site and the alleged operator is the opposing litigant, an out-of-court admission would be sufficient authentication. Moreover, circumstantial evidence will suffice. If only that person or entity is likely to possess the information posted at the site, that fact can establish the identity of the site's operator. Or if persons have visited that site, ordered merchandise from a particular company, and later received merchandise from that company, that course of conduct identifies the operator of the site.
4. At a certain time, a person visited the web site.
5. When the person visited the web site, he or she found certain information posted there. There are several methods of proving that the information was posted there. First, the proponent could call the "web master" responsible for maintaining the site. If he or she recalled the posting of the information, he or she could testify to that from personal knowledge under Rule 602. Alternatively, if the web master maintained records of postings, the records would qualify as business records under Rule 803(6). (The records would have to be those of the web master rather than the Internet service provider.) The person who visited the site could also testify from firsthand knowledge if he or she remembered the contents of the posting the person found at the site. Better

[49] *L.P. v. Banco de la Nacion*, 194 F.R.D. 116, 121 (S.D.N.Y. 2000) (prime rates published on a Federal Reserve Board web site); *Sannes v. Jeff Wyler Chevrolet, Inc.*, 107 Misc.2d 6, 736 N.E.2d 112 (1999) (FTC press releases printed from the FTC's world wide web page).

still, if the person printed out the information, he or she could authenticate the printout as an accurate copy of the data he or she read at the site at that time.

6. The information in question is attributable to the business. In large part, the attribution depends on the part of the web site where the information was posted. Some web sites feature chat rooms, which third parties can visit and in which they can post messages. Without a manifestation of adoption by the business, a chat room posting cannot be imputed to the business. However, if the information appears in a part of the site purportedly maintained by the business itself, the information can be attributed to the business.[50]

§ 4-10(C) SAMPLE FOUNDATION

The following fact situation is a breach of warranty action. The Ajax Corporation alleges that: It purchased tires from the Fassel Corporation; in so doing, it relied on a representation about the quality of the tires posted on the Fassel Corporation's web site; and the tires the defendant delivered did not live up to the representation. The witness is Ms. Stewart, the head of Ajax Corporation's Purchasing Department. Assume that elements (1) and (2) have been judicially noticed by the trial judge.

P WHAT is your name?

W Donarae Stewart.

P WHERE do you live?

W Right here in Texarkana.

P WHERE do you work?

W I've worked for Ajax Corporation for the past 15 years. We retail car supplies.

P WHAT are your job duties?

W I'm the head of our purchasing department. I'm responsible for ordering all the supplies from manufacturers and wholesalers.

P WHAT contact, if any, have you had with Fassel Corporation?

W They're one of our regular suppliers.

P WHAT do they supply you with?

W Primarily tires.

---

[50] GREGORY P. JOSEPH, MODERN VISUAL EVIDENCE 15-4-6 (rev. 2001) (if the information appears in a part of the site where the postings are ordinarily made by the owner of the site, there should be a presumption that information appearing there was posted by the owner).

P When you want to contact Fassel Corporation, HOW do you reach them?

W In the old days, I used to phone them. However, for the past three years they've maintained a web site; and I ordinarily deal with them by visiting their site.

P WHAT is the address of their web site? (3)

W The address is "www.fasseltires.com."

P HOW do you know that? (3)

W As I testified a few moments ago, I've been dealing with them through their web site for the past three years. On numerous occasions I've ordered goods from them over the site and later received both their merchandise and their bills.

P HOW do you know it was their merchandise? (3)

W All the tires arrived in boxes with Fassel labels, and the tires themselves bore the company inscription. [*Under Texas Rule of Evidence 902(7), "[i]nscriptions, signs, tags, or labels purporting to have been affixed in the course of business and indicating ownership, control, or origin" are self-authenticating.*]

P All right. WHAT contact, if any, did you have with Fassel Corporation on September 19, 2005? (4)

W My boss, Ms. Clark, told me to place an order for 500 tires for large pickup trucks, and I decided to order the tires from Fassel. Consequently, I visited the Fassel web site.

P HOW did you do that? (4)

W As usual, I just logged on to my computer, went to the Internet, and typed in the address of the Fassel site.

P WHAT happened after you did that? (4)

W Everything worked fine, and in a matter of moments I was at the site.

P WHAT did you do after you reached the site? (5)

W I went to their product list, particularly their tires suitable for large pickups.

P HOW many parts of the web site are there? (6)

W There are a number of parts. There's even a chat room where customers can exchange views or submit questions to company representatives. Then there are all the sections maintained by the Fassel Corporation itself, including the listing and description of products.

P WHICH part of the web site did you go to? (6)

W Well, I wasn't in a chatty mood. So I went straight to the listing and description of pickup truck tires.

P HOW can you as a customer post anything there? (6)

W Simply stated, you can't. You can post messages in the chat room, but in the part I visited all you can do is read the information the company has posted and print out what's posted.

P When you went to the part of the web site, WHAT, if anything, did you find? (5)

W I found a description of several types of pickup truck tires, including one that I was particularly interest in.

P WHY were you particularly interested in that description? (5)

W The description indicated that that particular model of tire was especially suitable for use by large pickups that went off road. We have a lot of customers who have that type of vehicle.

P WHAT did you do when you came up upon that description? (5)

W to begin with, I read it very carefully to make certain that the specifications would meet our needs.

P WHAT else, if anything, did you do? (5)

W I was confident that the boss, Ms. Clark, would be very interested in that model tire. However, since it was a little more expensive than the other models, I wanted her to make the final decision whether to order that model. Consequently, I printed out the description from the web site.

P Your Honor, I request that this be marked as Plaintiff's Exhibit #3 for identification.(5)

J It will be so marked.

P [*Proponent hands exhibit to court reporter, who marks the exhibit and hands it back to counsel*]. Thank you. Your Honor, please let the record reflect that I am showing what has been marked as Plaintiff's Exhibit #3 for ID to opposing counsel. (5)

J It will so reflect. [*Opposing counsel examines exhibit and hands it back to the Proponent*].

P Permission to approach the witness? (5)

J Granted.

P Ms. Stewart, I now hand you what has been marked as Plaintiff's Exhibit #3 for identification. Do you recognize this exhibit? (5)

W Yes, I do.

P WHAT is it? (5)

W It's the printout of the description of that tire.

P HOW can you recognize the exhibit? (5)

W First, I remember the contents. They're pretty distinctive. The unique qualities of the tire are what caught my attention. In addition, immediately after printing it out and before showing it to Ms. Clark, I placed my initials and the date in the upper, right hand corner. They're still there. That's why I can recognize the printout so easily.

P Your Honor, I now offer Plaintiff's Exhibit #3 for identification into evidence as Plaintiff's #3.

J Any objection?

O No, your Honor.

J In that event, the exhibit will be received.

P Ms. Stewart, I'm handing you Exhibit #3. With her Honor's permission, I'd like you to read the second full paragraph of the printout to the ladies and gentlemen of the jury. (5)

W Certainly.

§ 4-11 DEMONSTRATIVE EVIDENCE

§ 4-11(A) In General

The types of articles discussed up to this point in this chapter are tangible evidence, sometimes referred to as "original" or "real" evidence. The articles have a historical connection with the transaction giving rise to the case. For example, the document is a will the decedent signed before death, or the item is the very pistol the defendant used during the assault.

Sometimes the proponent may use an item even if the item has no connection with the case. Suppose, for example, that the police never found the pistol used in the assault. The trial judge might permit an eyewitness to the assault to use another, similar pistol to illustrate his or her testimony. The courts often refer to this latter type of evidence as "demonstrative." The article helps the witness to demonstrate or illustrate oral testimony. The only limits on the use of demonstrative evidence are the trial judge's discretion and the trial attorney's imagination.

The following sections discuss the methods of authenticating such demonstrative evidence. Later sections discuss the process of identifying real physical evidence.

§ 4-11(B) DEMONSTRATIVE EVIDENCE—VERIFICATION OF A DIAGRAM

§ 4-11(B)(1) The Doctrine

The verification of a diagram, drawing, or illustration is very similar to the verification of a photograph. The sponsoring or predicate witness must testify that the diagram is generally a "true," "accurate," "good," or "fair" depiction of the scene or object shown. Normally, diagrams and illustrations need not be to scale. An exception could arise where the exact dimensions or distances were crucial. In any event, if the diagram is not to scale and the relative distances are important, the opposing counsel should request a limiting instruction.

§ 4-11(B)(2) Elements of the Foundation

The elements of the foundation for using a chart or diagram are:

1. The diagram depicts a certain area or object.
2. The witness is familiar with that area or object.
3. The witness explains the basis for his or her familiarity with the area or object.
4. In the witness's opinion, the diagram is an accurate depiction of that area or object.

§ 4-11(B)(3) Sample Foundation

The fact situation is an assault prosecution. The indictment alleges that the defendant attacked the victim, Mr. Williams, in a bathroom in the Senator Hotel in Amarillo. The prosecutor wants to use a chart to illustrate the victim's testimony. The witness is the victim. The prosecutor is the proponent. The victim has just testified that he was attacked.

P WHERE did this attack occur?

W As I said, it occurred in the bathroom on the second floor of the hotel.

P Your Honor, we request that this be marked as State's exhibit number three for identification. [*Court reporter marks exhibit.*]

P Please let the record reflect that I am showing the exhibit to the defense attorney. [*Counsel shows chart to opposing counsel for inspection.*]

J The record will so reflect.

P I request permission to approach the witness.

J Permission granted.

P Mr. Williams, I hand you State's exhibit number three for identification. WHAT is it? (1)

W It's a chart of the bathroom I was just referring to.

P HOW do you recognize it? (2)

W I know that hotel very well.

P HOW did you become familiar with the hotel? (3)

W I've lived in it for two years. It's a boarding hotel.

P HOW many times have you been in that bathroom? (3)

W Lots of times. I couldn't give you a specific figure.

P HOW accurate is the diagram? (4)

W Well, it's not to scale. That's for sure.

P Otherwise, HOW accurate is the diagram? (4)

W It's correct. It shows everything in roughly the right place.

P Your Honor, I now offer State's exhibit number three for identification into evidence.

O Your Honor, may a limiting instruction be given that the diagram is not to scale?

J Yes. The exhibit will be received. [*To the jurors*] Ladies and gentlemen of the jury, the prosecutor is now going to show you a diagram of the bathroom in the Senator Hotel. The witness has testified that the diagram is basically accurate, but the witness also stated that the diagram is not to scale. In deciding what weight to attach to the diagram, you should consider the fact that the diagram is not to scale.

P Your Honor, I now request permission to hand State's exhibit number three to the jurors for their inspection.

J Permission granted.

To effectively use a chart, the proponent will sometimes have to ask the witness to mark on the chart. The marking will help the jury visualize the testimony. Moreover, the marking will help the appellate court understand the record of trial. Unless the diagram is clearly marked, in conjunction with counsel's narrative description of the marking, the record of trial may be positively confusing to the appellate court. The court will not know where "here" or "there" was on the map. The proponent should give the witness specific instructions as to how to mark the chart.

To illustrate these techniques, we will use the original hypothetical:

P Mr. Williams, would you please go and stand by the chart (State's exhibit number three).[51] Thank you. Now, using the chart, WHERE were you when the defendant first walked into the bathroom?

---

[51] The chart should be large enough for the jury to see. Having the witness simply mark on a standard sheet of paper while seated in the witness chair is rarely effective.

W I was standing over here by the front door. [*Witness points.*]

P Please take this pen, place a circle where you were standing, and write the letter W in the circle. [*The witness complies.*] Thank you. Please let the record reflect that the witness has so marked the chart. Mr. Williams, would you please draw a circle with a D in it where the defendant was standing when you first saw him?

W Right here. [*Witness marks chart as requested.*]

P Thank you. Now, Mr. Williams, WHAT direction was the defendant Mr. Dugan walking in when he first entered the room?

W He was going that way. [*Witness points.*]

P Please use the pen again, and draw an arrow showing that direction. Start the arrow in the circle you just drew with the D in it. [*The witness complies.*] Please let the record reflect that the witness complied with my direction.

J The record will so reflect.

The reader should bear in mind two important caveats. First, some trial judges prefer that the chart be completely marked before it is formally offered into evidence. These judges will not permit any further marking after the exhibit has been received into evidence. If the practitioner contemplates using a chart during a trial, he or she should inquire about the judge's preference during the chambers conference before the trial begins. The second caveat is that if counsel ultimately wants the judge to send the chart to the jury during deliberation, he or she may want to add a legend at the bottom of the chart. Of course, the jurors may remember that "W" represents Williams and "D" the defendant Dugan. To ensure that the jury correctly interprets the markings on the chart, however, the witness can be instructed to indicate on the bottom of the chart the significance of each mark. For example, the prosecutor might add, "Mr. Williams, would you please indicate on the bottom of the chart that the letter 'D' represents or equals the defendant?"

After counsel has finished using the chart, there is the very practical problem of how the exhibit should be handled and preserved for the appellate record. If counsel has used a chalkboard for the chart, there is also the question of preserving the chart from one day to the next without it being erased. If the chart is bulky, it is usually a good idea to request permission to have a photograph taken of the chart and included in the record of trial. That may mean that counsel will have to make some arrangements beforehand to have a camera available. Or, if the chart is on large paper, it can be folded and included in the record of trial.

§ 4-11(C) DEMONSTRATIVE EVIDENCE—MODELS

§ 4-11(C)(1) The Doctrine

The use of models is becoming increasingly common in courtrooms. The proponent may use a skeletal model or a model of a house or machine. Models present more logistical problems for trial courts than simple diagrams. For that reason, some judges are more reluctant to permit the use of models. Indeed, to be on the safe side, the proponent might be prepared to show affirmatively that the witness needs the model to explain his or her testimony adequately.

§ 4-11(C)(2) Elements of the Foundation

The foundation for the use of a model should include the following elements:

1. The witness needs the visual aid to explain his or her testimony.
2. The aid depicts a certain scene or object.
3. The witness is familiar with the scene or object.
4. The witness explains the basis for his or her familiarity with the scene or object.
5. In the witness's opinion, the aid is a true, accurate, good, or fair model of the scene or object.

§ 4-11(C)(3) Sample Foundation

The fact situation is a tort action for injuries. The plaintiff, Ms. Graham, suffered extensive bone damage. The witness is Dr. Miller, a bone specialist. In general terms, Dr. Miller has already described the extensive nature of the bone damage.

P Now, Doctor, in detail, WHAT are the injuries to Ms. Graham's bones? (1)

W That question is really difficult to answer orally.

P WHY? (1)

W Well, in the first place, a large number of bones have been damaged. Second, it's sometimes difficult for me to explain the precise location of the bone. Finally, some of the damage is really to the way bones work and fit together. It's hard to put all that into words.

P HOW could you explain the detailed injuries more effectively? (1)

W It would be much better if I were permitted to use a skeletal model.

P [*To court reporter*] Would you please mark this as an exhibit for the plaintiff? [*Reporter marks exhibit and hands it back to proponent, who examines it to determine how it has been marked.*] Please let the record reflect that I am now showing plaintiff's exhibit number seven for identification to opposing counsel.

J The record will so reflect.

P Doctor, I now show you plaintiff's exhibit number seven for identification. WHAT is it? (2)

W It's the sort of skeletal model I just mentioned.

P HOW do you know that? (3), (4)

W I'm not only a medical doctor; I'm a bone specialist. I've studied and used models such as this one for years. In fact, I've consulted with some of the art companies that manufacture these models.

P HOW accurate is this skeletal model? (5)

W It's quite good. It depicts the bone structure of a female of the approximate height and build of the plaintiff, Ms. Graham.

P HOW helpful would this be to illustrate your testimony about the specific bone injuries? (1)

W Very. I can point to the location of the bones, show you what they look like, and demonstrate how they're supposed to fit together with adjacent bones.

It may be possible to use models such as the one in the hypothetical without even marking them for identification. But that practice makes it difficult for the appellate court to understand the record of trial. It would be better at least to mark the model as an exhibit for identification. If the exhibit is merely marked for identification and is never formally admitted into evidence, however, it cannot be sent to the jury for use during deliberation. If counsel wished to offer it formally into evidence, the sample foundation would continue:

P Your Honor, I now offer plaintiff's exhibit number seven for identification into evidence.

J It will be received.

P I now request permission to use the model to illustrate Dr. Miller's testimony.

J Permission granted.

One final point is that the proponent does not always have to leave the model in the court's possession after trial. The trial judge has discretion to permit the proponent to substitute a photograph or written description later for insertion in the record of trial. If the proponent wishes to do so, after the judge receives the exhibit into evidence, the proponent should state, "I request permission to substitute a photograph of this model later into the record of trial and to secure a ruling on the same."

§ 4-12 COMPUTER ANIMATIONS AND SIMULATIONS

§ 4-12(A) THE DOCTRINE

Rather than offering motion pictures or videotapes of historical events, attorneys frequently offer computer animations of the events.[52] A computer animation is the display of a sequence of computer-generated images. The use of computer-generated animation (CGA) is becoming widespread. In a 1992 study, the American Bar Association reported that attorneys at 13 percent of medium sized litigation firms had already used computer animation. Even more significantly, attorneys at 45 percent of the firms indicated that they intended to use computer animation in the near future. Some law firms now have entire departments devoted to the preparation of trial exhibits, including computer animations.

There are several reasons for the growing use of computer animations. First, when there is no movie or video of the event being litigated, a computer animation is a superior method of communicating the information to the trier of fact. A computer animation in effect condenses the information into a single evidentiary package. In part due to television, the typical American is a primarily visual learner, and for that reason many jurors find the animation more understandable than charts or oral testimony. Furthermore, computer animation technology is becoming more affordable.[53] In the early days of computer technology, the price of a quality animated exhibit might have been as much as $500,000. However, there are now numerous, commercial CAD/CAM (computer-assisted design and manufacturing) programs such as Applecrash, Mannequin, and 3D Studio. Some programs even allow the computer operator to scan or digitize external images from artwork or photographs into the computer's memory. Today, the total cost of the hardware and software necessary to generate computer animations can be less than $10,000, and that figure is likely to decrease in the future.

In part, computer animations are so popular because the medium is so flexible. The animation can adopt almost any conceivable vantage point or angle. For instance, the animation can depict the perspective of the person behind the wheel of a car or portray an aerial overview of two cars approaching each other. The animation can pan or zoom in. The animation can even display an impossible

[52] Henke, *Admissibility of Computer-Generated Animated Reconstructions and Simulations*, 35 TRIAL LAW. GUIDE 434 (1991).

[53] Keriger, *Sophisticated Computer Graphics Come of Age—And Evidence Will Never Be the Same*, 78 A.B.A.J. 92 (Dec. 1992).

perspective, that is, the inner working of a piece of machinery. The split screen capability permits the simultaneous display of several perspectives; one perspective can be that of the airline pilot, and the other of a ground observer watching the airplane descend for landing. The technology is also flexible in a temporal sense; the animation can be real time, time lapse (accelerated), slow motion (decelerated), or freeze frame. Finally, the animation can be combined with other media. The trial exhibit can begin with a photograph of the actual object involved in the case and then fade or dissolve into a photorealistic animation. Given this flexibility, animations have already been employed in court to depict a wide range of events, including plane crashes, highway accidents, murders, gas well explosions, product failures, the movement of contaminating particles in the soil, and the progress of diseases.

§ 4-12(B) ELEMENTS OF THE FOUNDATION

The foundation depends upon the purposes for which the proponent proffers the animation. The animation can be offered either as illustrative demonstrative evidence or as a substantive computer simulation.

Illustrative Evidence

Suppose that a lay or expert witness is prepared to describe an event and that the witness did not initially obtain his or her information about the event by viewing any computer animation. A lay witness might simply have seen the accident. For his or her part, a scientist might have derived an opinion about the event by merely sitting down, reading the police report describing the accident, and applying the laws of physics to the data in the report. Assume further, though, that after hearing the witness's description of the event before trial, the attorney has a computer animation prepared to depict that description. In that event, the attorney could offer the animation as purely demonstrative evidence to illustrate the witness's description. When that is the proponent's theory of admissibility, the foundation is minimal.[54] It suffices if the witness testifies that he or she has viewed the animation and that the animation fairly and accurately depicts the witness's version of the event.[55] In the words of one court:

> The evidence sought to be introduced here is more akin to a chart or diagram than a scientific device. Whether a diagram is hand drawn or mechanically drawn by means of a computer is of no importance. What is important is

---

[54] Comment, *Admission of Computer Generated Visual Evidence: Should There Be Clear Standards?*, 6 SOFTWARE L.J. 325, 333–34 (1993).

[55] Dilworth, *Computer Animations Reach Criminal Court*, 28 TRIAL 26 (Sept. 1992).

[that] the presentation . . . fairly and accurately reflect the oral testimony offered and that it be an aid to the jury's understanding of the issue.[56]

As a practical matter, it may be safer to call the animator as well as the lay or expert witness to overcome any objections under Rule 403; but if the proponent offers the animation strictly as illustrative evidence, the lay or expert witness can give sufficient sponsoring testimony to authenticate the animation. That testimony should satisfy Rule of Evidence 104(b) when the proponent is content to introduce the animation as demonstrative evidence to illustrate testimony by a lay or expert witness.

There are, of course, procedural downsides to proffering the animation purely as an illustrative, demonstrative exhibit. Under Rule 105, on the opponent's request, the trial judge will have to give the jury a limiting instruction as to the evidentiary status of the animation. Moreover, purely illustrative exhibits cannot accompany the jury into the deliberation room.[57] However, offering the animation for such a limited purpose obviates the necessity for testimony validating the scientific assumptions programmed into the software that generates the animation.

Substantive Evidence

In other cases, the proponent will want to offer the animation as substantive evidence. In these cases, it is often said that the proponent is proffering a computer "simulation." Computer simulation software includes scientific equations and principles, such as the law of Newtonian physics, that predict the behavior of, for example, automobiles; accepts input of the data, such as skidmark length required to apply the scientific principles and equations; and converts the mathematical predictions into images on the computer's screen. When the proponent offers an animation as an accurate computer simulation, the inference of accuracy does not arise from the simulation's correspondence with a description of the same event by any lay or expert witness. Rather, the bases of the inference are the validity of the pertinent scientific principles and the trustworthiness of the input data. Consequently, the foundation for a simulation differs from that for a merely demonstrative, illustrative exhibit. The simulation foundation must include a showing of the principle's validity and the data's trustworthiness. If the proponent can lay the necessary foundation, there will be no need for a limiting instruction under Rule 105. The judge might decide to read the jury a cautionary instruction against giving the simulation undue weight,[58] but it would

[56] *People v. McHugh*, 476 N.Y.S.2d 721, 722–23 (1984).

[57] TEX. R. CIV. P. 281. *Cf. Speier v. Webster College*, 616 S.W.2d 617 (Tex. 1981) (not error to admit chart showing summary of testimony). *See also* Brain & Broderick, *The Derivative Relevance of Demonstrative Evidence: Charting Its Proper Evidentiary Status*, 25 U.C. DAVIS L. REV. 957, 965–66 (1992).

[58] *Datskow v. Teledyne Continental Motors*, 826 F.Supp. 677, 685 (W.D.N.Y. 1993).

be inappropriate to deny the simulation the status of substantive evidence. As substantive evidence, the simulation could be taken into the jury room and viewed during deliberation.[58]

Unfortunately, the published cases offer little specific guidance as to the foundational requirements for computer simulations.[59] However, in principle, the following foundation should suffice:

1. There are certain valid scientific equations and principles such as the Newtonian laws of motion. These equations and principles will have to pass muster under the tests for validating scientific evidence. See § 9-3, *supra*. If the principle or equation in question is widely accepted, it may be judicially noticeable, and live testimony on this foundational element would therefore be unnecessary.
2. Computer technology is capable of producing simulations or models based on scientific equations and principles. This proposition may be judicially noticeable under Rule 201.[60]
3. The equations and principles mentioned in foundational element #1 have been programmed into a particular computer program.
4. To generate a mathematical representation, the equations and principles require certain input.[61]
5. The software in question is capable of converting its mathematical predictions of behavior into accurate images.[62]

---

58 Henke, *Admissibility of Computer-Generated Reconstructions and Simulations*, at 437.

59 Comment, *Admission of Computer Generated Visual Evidence: Should There Be Clear Standards?*, 6 SOFTWARE L.J. 325, 327 (1993).

60 *Id.* at 339.

61 The program may require numerical data about measurements of dimensions of objects, human beings, and the environment in which the objects and human beings are moving or acting. For example, to produce a virtual reality (VR) simulation of a room, "everything in the room is measured, and each object's position relative to all other objects—including the VR user—is calculated." Dilworth, *Virtual Reality: Coming Soon to a Courtroom Near You?*, 29 TRIAL 13, 14 (July 1993).

62 Some programs produce a picture—an individual computer graphic—every thirtieth of a second. When the software is in widespread, commercial use, the judge may treat its widespread acceptance as circumstantial evidence of its accuracy. If a defective program were used widely, presumably the defect would have caused problems for its users; and the program would have been corrected or withdrawn. When the software has not yet come into widespread use, the proponent should present expert testimony vouching for the program's accuracy. For instance, one of the computer experts who helped develop an accident reconstruction program could testify that she had verified the program's accuracy by comparing its output with data from test crashes of automobiles.

6. Someone input all the data needed to use the principles or equations programmed into the software.[63]
7. The data input was trustworthy.[64]
8. The computer operator checked to ensure that the data was properly entered. The operator could simply call the data up on the screen and doublecheck the accuracy of the input data against the police reports that were the source of the data.
9. After inputting the data, the operator asked the computer to perform the function of generating a simulation or model of the relevant behavior.
10. The computer recorded the images of the simulation on videotape or laser disc.[65] However, many practitioners prefer laser disc:

   > [T]he far better quality is . . . laser disc format[] . . . . You get much better definition . . . than videotape, plus you have much more flexibility because you can use bar codes to jump to any sequence in the animation.
   >
   > King, *Animation Seizes Jury, Judge's Attention*, MERRILL'S ILLINOIS LEGAL TIMES 1, 10 (May 1993).

11. The witness on the stand recognizes the videotape or laser disc as the output produced when the operator asked the computer to perform the function of generating a simulation of the relevant behavior.

In some cases, a single witness is qualified to lay the entire foundation. However, in a given case, multiple witnesses may be necessary: one to validate the pertinent scientific principles and equations, another to verify the part of the program that generates the mathematical representation of behavior, still another to vouch for the part of the program converting the mathematical prediction into visual images, a further witness to describe the collection of the input data, and a final witness to testify to the inputting of the data and the production of the videotape or laser disc.

§ 4-12(C) SAMPLE FOUNDATION

The fact situation is a civil tort action. The plaintiffs allege that a truck driver for the defendant negligently lost control of his truck and allowed it to drift into

---

[63] *Schaeffer v. General Motors Corp.*, 360 N.E.2d 1062 (Mass. 1977) (the data must be complete).

[64] *Id.* This foundational element reflects "the GIGO principle: garbage in, garbage out." Comment, *Admission of Computer Generated Visual Evidence: Should There Be Clear Standards?*, 6 SOFTWARE L.J. 325, 346 n.144 (1993).

[65] Videotape is more popular. Krieger, *Photorealistic Computer Graphics: New Horizon for Evidence*, 29 TRIAL 46, 48 (Feb. 1993).

a bike lane, where the truck struck and killed the plaintiffs' daughter. The proponent is the defense. The defense calls Professor Ernest Kelly as its next witness.

P Please state your full name and spell your last name for the record.

W My name is Ernest Kelly. My last name is spelled K-E-L-L-Y.

P WHERE do you live?

W I live and work in College Station, Texas.

P WHAT is your place of work?

W I teach in the Engineering Department of Texas A & M University.

P WHAT is your educational background?

W I obtained my bachelor of science degree in engineering from Iowa State University in 1990.

P In general terms, WHAT is engineering?

W Engineers are specialists in using the laws of physics to create machines for human use.

P WHAT did you do after you obtained your bachelor's degree?

W We moved to College Station so that I could begin my graduate studies at A & M. I wanted to get my master's degree and then a doctorate. I got the master's in 1992 and the doctorate in 1994.

P WHAT subjects did you study in the course of obtaining those degrees?

W I pretty much specialized in vehicle dynamics and computer graphics related to vehicle dynamics.

P WHAT do you mean by the expression "vehicle dynamics?"

W That's the study of how vehicles like cars behave as they move and travel down a highway.

P WHAT do you mean by "computer graphics?"

W That's the use of computer programs to create sequences of images that depict the movement of automobiles such as trucks on a road or highway.

P WHAT professional licenses, if any, do you hold in this state?

W I'm registered as an engineer.

P HOW many professional papers, if any, have you had published?

W Approximately 20.

P WHAT topics did those papers relate to?

W They all deal with vehicle dynamics, and the vast majority of them relate more specifically to computer animation of vehicle dynamics.

P WHAT professional engineering organizations, if any, do you belong to?

W For years I've been a member of the Society of Automotive Engineers and the American Society of Mechanical Engineers. I've served as the president of the state chapter of the SAE, the Society of Automotive Engineers.

P WHAT practical experience, if any, do you have in vehicle dynamics?

W I've consulted with major manufacturers such as General Motors and Chrysler on a number of design projects. My contribution was determining how a design change would affect the dynamics of the vehicles in question.

P HOW many times, if ever, have you qualified as an expert witness in a court of law?

W On over 40 occasions.

P WHAT topics did you testify about as an expert witness?

W On each occasion, the testimony related to some aspects of vehicle dynamics.

P HOW many times, if ever, did you testify about computer animation of vehicle dynamics?

W The majority of the time.

P WHAT do these computer animations do? (1)

W The ones that I prepare do more than simply illustrate a version of an accident. The ones I develop are intended to use the laws of physics to accurately recreate and portray accidents.

P WHAT laws of physics are you referring to? (1)

W To begin with, you have Newton's laws of motion. Those are fundamental tenets of modern physics. In addition, there are other rules of auto dynamics physics that have been empirically derived.

P WHAT do you mean by "empirically derived?" (1)

W People have conducted experiments to establish that these other propositions are true. You run tests with autos, trucks, and bicycles to prove that the proposition is valid.

P HOW well accepted are these propositions? (1)

W They're universally accepted by engineers in my specialty.

P HOW thoroughly have these propositions been established by the experiments you referred to? (1)

W There are some that are still in the debatable stage, but the ones I use in my computer programs have been proven beyond any doubt.

P HOW can a computer apply these propositions? (2)

W You simply program the principle or equation into the software. The software contains the instructions for the computer, and you include the various principles and equations as part of the instructions. Using these principles and equations, the computer can create a mathematical representation of a vehicle such as a truck. The simulation program utilizes an "icon" of the vehicle and the computer simulates the motion of the icon.

P WHAT experience, if any, do you have programming these principles and equations into computer software? (2)

W In large part, that's what I did during my master's and doctoral work at A & M. I know programming language, and I've developed dozens of programs based on the principles of auto dynamics.

P WHAT is "Autodynam?" (3)

W That's the name of a program I've developed for computer simulations of auto dynamics.

P WHAT laws and equations is that program based on? (3)

W It's one of my most conservative programs.

P WHAT do you mean by "conservative?" (3)

W As I said a little while ago, some propositions about vehicle dynamics are still debatable; the research into the validity of those propositions is still incomplete and inconclusive. None of those propositions is included in Autodynam. It's a conservative program in the sense that it rests on the original laws of motion, propositions deduced directly from those laws, and further propositions that have clearly been established by ample research.

P HOW accurately does the Autodynam program state those propositions? (3)

W Not just accurately, but perfectly.

P HOW do you know that? (3)

W To begin with, I have access to a number of databases on actual and test auto crashes. I've checked the results of the program against the databases, and on each occasion the result of using the program has checked out and been confirmed. More importantly, I periodically print out the program itself and review the portion of the program setting out the propositions. I can read programming language, and as a scientist, I also know the propositions. I can personally vouch that the program is 100 percent accurate in that regard. If you input the right information about an accident, you're going to get an accurate reconstruction of the event.

P WHAT do you mean by "input?" (4)

W The laws and equations are general propositions about vehicle dynamics. If you're going to make some findings about a specific accident, you need some of the data about that accident—where the vehicles came to rest, the extent of the damage to the vehicles, the length and direction of skidmarks, the drag factor of the road surface, that sort of thing.

P Suppose that you wanted to use Autodynam to create a computer animation of an accident involving a truck and a bicycle and you wanted to use Autodynam to determine how fast the truck was going. WHAT input would you have to give the computer to determine that? (4)

W I'd need to tell the computer the final resting place of the truck, bicycle, and rider, the extent and nature of any personal injuries suffered by the bicyclist, the extent and location of the damage to the truck and bicycle, the road drag factor, the point where the rider's body first struck the ground, the relative angle of the bicycle and truck at impact, and the length and direction of any skidmarks. Given that information, the computer can create a valid, mathematical representation of the dynamics of the two vehicles.

P All right. You have this mathematical representation in the computer. HOW does the computer convert that into an image on the screen? (5)

W The program also does that. The program creates a sequence of images on the screen. It creates a new picture every thirtieth of a second. Autodynam is a sophisticated program, and its images are photorealistic—they look awfully close to the real thing.

P HOW accurate are these images? (5)

W They're quite accurate.

P HOW do you know that? (5)

W I previously mentioned test crashes. We have a lot of test crashes on videotape. I've often used Autodynam to generate a computer animation and then compared it to a videotape of the same accident. The computer simulation produces amazingly accurate images of the crash.

P Professor, WHERE were you on January 19, 2005? (6)

W I was in my office at Texas A & M.

P WHAT happened that day? (6)

W That's the day I received the Federal Express package with photocopies of all the police reports and depositions in this case.

P WHAT do you mean by "this case?" (6)

W This lawsuit. You had phoned me the week before, and during our telephone conversation I had agreed to use Autodynam to generate a computer simulation of the truck-bicycle collision involved in this lawsuit.

P WHAT reports and depositions did you receive on January 19? (6)

W The stack included the official police report on the accident, the truck driver's deposition, and the deposition of two eyewitnesses to the accident.

P WHAT did you do with the reports? (6)

W I carefully reviewed every page of every document and then extracted the information Autodynam needs.

P HOW much of the necessary information did you find in the reports? (6)

W They contained all the information the program requires.

P In particular, WHICH reports did you take the information from? (7)

W I gathered all the information from the police report and the eyewitness accounts.

P WHY didn't you take any information from the truck driver's deposition? (7)

W You instructed me not to.

P WHAT reason did I give you? (7)

W You said that you didn't want the simulation to represent simply your client's driver's version of the accident; you said that there might be questions about his bias. So you expressly instructed me to use the police report and the depositions given by the two eyewitnesses, who had no connection with either party.

P WHAT did you do with the information after you extracted it from the report and depositions? (8)

W I inputted it.

P HOW did you do that? (8)

W I used the computer keyboard.

P HOW accurately did you input the data? (8)

W It was all correct.

P HOW do you know that? (8)

W You put the data into a particular file on the computer. I called that file back on the screen and double checked each entry against the original police report and depositions. Every entry was right.

P WHAT did you do after you double checked the data input to the computer? (9)

W I entered a command, directing Autodynam to apply the programmed propositions of physics to that data to first determine where the truck and bicycle collided and then to produce a computer animation showing the point of collision.

P WHAT happened then? (9)

W The computer generated the animation I had requested.

P HOW, if at all, was the animation recorded? (10)

W I'm pretty traditional. Some researchers put it on laser disc, but I still like videotape. So I recorded it on a videotape.

P [*Speaking to the court reporter*] Would you please mark this as a defense exhibit for identification? [*Court reporter marks exhibit and hands it back to the proponent.*]

P Thank you. [*Counsel examines exhibit to determine how it has been marked.*] Please let the record reflect that I am handing what has been marked as defense exhibit C for identification to opposing counsel. [*Opposing counsel examines exhibit and hands it back to proponent.*]

P Professor, I now hand you what has been marked defense exhibit C for identification. WHAT is it? (11)

W It's the videotape I just mentioned.

P HOW do you know that? (11)

W A couple of ways.

P Namely?

W To begin with, I recognize the markings on the label affixed to the tape. That's my handwriting. In my own handwriting, I noted the case name and the date on which I prepared the videotape. In addition, we viewed this tape in its entirety in the judge's chambers about three hours ago, and I recognize the tape as the one Autodynam produced after I input the data about this accident.

P Your Honor, I now offer defense exhibit C for identification into evidence as defense exhibit C.

J Any objections?

O No, your Honor.

J Defense exhibit C for Identification is admitted as defense exhibit C.

P Your Honor, I would now like to have this witness run the videotape, that is defense exhibit C, on the monitors in the courtroom.

J You may proceed.

§ 4-13 IDENTIFICATION OF REAL OR ORIGINAL EVIDENCE

§ 4-13(A) IN GENERAL

Section 4-10, *supra*, discusses demonstrative physical evidence. Demonstrative evidence has two characteristics. On the one hand, it illustrates or demonstrates the witness's testimony. On the other hand, the object itself has no historical connection with the facts of the case. It is not the actual pistol or knife used in the crime.

In contrast, real or original physical evidence has a connection with the case. For example, the prosecutor may contend that it is the very pistol or knife used. If the prosecutor makes this claim, the prosecutor must authenticate the evidence by proving the claim. The prosecutor must demonstrate the object's connection with the case. The process of demonstrating this historical connection is usually termed the identification of the physical evidence. There are two recognized methods of identifying physical evidence: establishing that the physical evidence is readily identifiable or establishing a chain of custody.

§ 4-13(B) READILY IDENTIFIABLE PHYSICAL EVIDENCE

§ 4-13(B)(1) The Doctrine

The first method of identifying real or original physical evidence is ready identifiability. If the article has a unique, one-of-a-kind characteristic, that characteristic makes the article readily identifiable. The foundation, or predicate, is complete so long as the witness testifies that he or she previously observed the characteristic and presently recalls the characteristic. An identification resting on that characteristic is sufficient. The foundation is sufficient to establish the exhibit's identity as the object the witness previously observed. Texas Rule of Evidence 901(b)(4) expressly permits identification of an object by its distinctive characteristics.[66]

§ 4-13(B)(2) Elements of the Foundation

The predicate for establishing that an item of physical evidence is readily identifiable is very simple:

1. The object has a unique characteristic.
2. The witness observed the characteristic on a previous occasion.
3. The witness identifies the exhibit as the object.

---

[66] *See* WENDORF, SCHLUETER & BARTON, TEXAS RULES OF EVIDENCE MANUAL IX-23 (6th ed. 2002).

4. The witness rests the identification on his or her present recognition of the characteristic.

5. As best as he or she can tell, the exhibit is in the same condition as it was when he or she initially received the object.

§ 4-13(B)(3) Sample Foundation

The fact situation for the readily identifiable foundation is a civil tort case. The complaint alleges that the defendant assaulted the plaintiff with a knife. The witness is a police officer who investigated the complaint. The proponent is the plaintiff. The officer has just testified that she reported to the scene and began inspecting the scene.

P WHAT did you do during this inspection?

W I was looking for any evidence.

P WHAT, if anything, did you find?

W I found a knife answering the description the plaintiff, Ms. Brown, gave me.

P WHERE did you find it?

W Right at the corner of the building where the alleged assault occurred.

P WHAT did you do with the knife? (1)

W I followed standard operating procedure.

P WHAT is that procedure? (1)

W I marked it for identification.

P HOW did you do that? (1)

W In the case of a relatively inexpensive item such as this one, I tagged it and scratched my initials and the date onto the wooden handle.

P WHEN did you do this? (2)

W As soon as I found it.

P HOW much time passed between your discovery of this knife and your marking it? (2)

W No more than a couple of minutes.

P Your Honor, I request that this be marked as a plaintiff's exhibit for identification. [*Court reporter marks exhibit.*] Thank you.

P Please let the record reflect that I am showing plaintiff's exhibit number two for identification to the opposing counsel. [*Proponent shows exhibit to opposing counsel.*]

J The record will so reflect.

P I request permission to approach the witness.

J Permission granted.

P I now hand you plaintiff's exhibit number two for identification. WHAT is it? (3)

W It's the knife I found.

P HOW can you recognize it? (4)

W As I testified, I marked my initials and the date on the handle. They're right there.

P WHAT condition is the exhibit in? (5)

W It's in good condition.

P HOW has it changed, if at all, since you found it at the scene? (5)

W It doesn't appear to have changed at all. It seems to be in the same condition.

P WHERE has it been since you found it?

W It has been in our property room, in a drawer.

P Your Honor, I now offer plaintiff's exhibit number two for identification into evidence.

J It will be received.

P I request permission to hand the exhibit to the jurors for their inspection.

J Permission granted.

In the foregoing fact situation, the predicate witness had personally marked the exhibit and thus gave it the unique characteristic which permitted in-court identification. The same method can be used, however, where no identifying marks have been placed on the evidence, but its coloring, weight, texture, and other characteristics permit the witness to state that the object is what counsel purports it to be. Because the relevancy of the knife did not depend on any fungible characteristics which might have been altered, no chain of custody was required. If, however, the proponent had wished to prove that blood found on the knife belonged to the victim, a chain of custody would normally have to be shown from the time the knife was seized until it reached the laboratory for testing. That issue is discussed in § 4-12(C).

§ 4-13(C) CHAIN OF CUSTODY

§ 4-13(C)(1) The Doctrine

Suppose that one of the elements of the foundation for ready identifiability is missing. That is, either the object lacks a unique characteristic, the witness did not observe the characteristic on the previous occasion, or the witness cannot presently recall the characteristic. Or, suppose that the proponent is interested in the object's condition rather than in its simple identity. The proponent might want a laboratory technician to testify about a chemical analysis of the object. In these circumstances, the proponent must establish a "chain of custody." Chain of custody is the second method of identifying physical evidence.

Who are the links in the chain? The links are people who actually handle the object. Other persons who merely have access to the object are not considered links. Thus, even if two other laboratory technicians know the combination to the safe where the witness kept the object, the other technicians are not deemed links. The only link would be the technician who physically handled the object. The proponent would have to account for that technician's handling of the object.

How does the proponent account for handling? The proponent must show the link's initial receipt of the object, ultimate disposition of the object (retention, destruction, or transfer), and safekeeping of the object between receipt and disposition. The witness can keep the object in a locked safe, a secure evidence container, or any other place where substitution and tampering are unlikely.

Ideally, the proponent should call each link to the stand in the sequence in which they handled the object. The proponent would mark the object for identification and hand it to the first link for identification. The proponent would also hand it to every intermediate link for identification. The proponent does not formally tender the exhibit into evidence, however, until the last link's testimony.

At that point, the foundation is complete. Normally, breaks in the chain will only affect the weight of the evidence, not its admissibility.

§ 4-13(C)(2) Elements of the Foundation

The predicate for chain of custody must be laid during the testimony of each link in the chain:

1. The witness initially received the object at a certain time and place.
2. The witness safeguarded the object; the witness testifies to circumstances making it unlikely that substitution or tampering occurred.
3. The witness ultimately disposed of the object (retention, destruction, or transfer to another person).
4. As best as he or she can tell, the exhibit is the object he or she previously handled.
5. As best he or she can tell, the exhibit is in the same condition as it was when he or she initially received the object.

§ 4-13(C)(3) Sample Foundation

The fact situation is a criminal assault prosecution. The State alleges that the defendant, Mr. Morris, used his feet to kick and beat the victim, Mr. Navin. The prosecutor wants to show that the blood grouping of stains on the defendant's shoes matches the victim's blood grouping. As a predicate for that scientific analysis, the State must establish a chain of custody for the shoes. The State must demonstrate that the shoes were in the same condition at the time of analysis as they were when they were seized from the defendant. The seizing police officer, Officer Stevens, has already testified. He testified that he seized the shoes from Mr. Morris, kept them safe, and then delivered them to the laboratory technician, Ms. Quinn. Ms. Quinn is the next witness. The prosecutor is the proponent. The shoes have already been marked as State's exhibit number four for identification and have been shown to the opposing counsel for examination.

P WHAT is your occupation?

W I am a laboratory technician with the local police department.

P HOW long have you worked for the police department?

W About six years.

P WHAT are your duties?

W I specialize in blood and stain analysis.

P HOW long have you done that sort of work?

W About six years—ever since I graduated.

P WHAT school did you graduate from?

W Texas Tech University.

P WHAT was your major area of study?

W Chemistry, especially organic chemistry.

P Ms. Quinn, WHERE were you on the afternoon of February 12, 2005? (1)

W I was on duty at work at the laboratory.

P WHAT, if anything, happened that afternoon? (1)

W Officer Stevens delivered some shoes to me for analysis.

P WHO is Officer Stevens? (1)

W He is an officer on the police force. I believe he just testified in here.

P WHAT did you do with the shoes when he delivered them to you? (2)

W I followed standard practice. The very first thing I did was initial the evidence slip that's attached.

P WHAT is an evidence slip? (2)

W It's a chain of custody receipt. You sign off on it when you receive the attached object.

P WHAT did you do with the shoes after you initialed the evidence slip? (2)

W I immediately conducted an analysis of some stains on the soles of the shoes.

P HOW much time passed between his delivery of the shoes and your analysis? (2)

W Only about five minutes. I wasn't very busy when he walked in.

P WHAT did you do after you conducted the analysis? (2)

W I put the shoes in my evidence locker.

P WHERE is this locker? (2)

W It's in my work area in the lab.

P HOW secure is this locker? (2)

W Well, I have a combination lock on it.

P WHO knows the combination? (2)

W Just me and the head of the Fluids section of the lab, Mr. Guinn.

P WHAT happened to the shoes after you put them in the locker? (3)

W They've just been sitting there until today.

P HOW often have you opened the locker between the time you placed the shoes there and today? (2)

W Probably hundreds of times.

P WHAT procedure do you use to open the locker? (2)

W I use the combination to open it, remove what I want, and immediately close and lock it.

P HOW have the shoes changed since you placed them in the locker? (2)

W They're certainly a little dustier than before, but otherwise they haven't changed.

P Your Honor, I request permission to approach the witness.

J Permission granted.

P I now hand you State's exhibit number four for identification. WHAT is it? (4)

W They seem to be the shoes I analyzed.

P HOW can you recognize them? (4)

W I notice my handwriting on the attached slip, and I recognize their general appearance, including the scrapes and the stains on the soles.

P HOW did the shoes get out of the evidence locker? (4)

W I removed them just before coming here to testify.

P WHO has had possession of them since you removed them from the locker? (4)

W I had possession until I got here.

P WHAT did you do then? (4)

W I placed them on your counsel table so you could use them.

P WHAT condition are the shoes in? (5)

W They seem to be in the same condition as when Officer Stevens delivered them to me.

P WHAT condition are the stains in? (5)

W They're a bit changed because I had to scrape some off to analyze the stains. Otherwise they're in the same condition.

P Your Honor, I now offer State's exhibit number four for identification into evidence.

J They will be received.

P Your Honor, I request permission to hand the exhibit to the jurors for their inspection.

J Request granted. [*The jurors inspect the shoes.*]

P Now, Ms. Quinn, I'd like to ask you a few questions about your analysis of the shoes.

§ 4-13(D) SIMILAR PHYSICAL EVIDENCE—PROPS

§ 4-13(D)(1) The Doctrine

If, for some reason, the proponent is not able to introduce the actual piece of physical evidence, the courts may permit use of a replica for illustrative purposes. The court in *Miskis v. State*[67] recognized that an object which is not the actual piece of physical evidence may be admitted into evidence if the proponent can confirm that: (1) the original is not available; (2) if the original were available, it would be admissible; (3) the offered exhibit is relevant, and its probative value outweighs its prejudicial effect; and (4) the jury is instructed that the item is being admitted only for illustrative purposes. In effect, the exhibit

[67] 756 S.W.2d 350 (Tex. App.—Houston [14th Dist.] 1988, pet. ref.)

becomes a prop, or a pedagogical device for counsel. If admitted, the exhibit can be taken by the jury into the deliberation room.

§ 4-13(D)(2) Elements of the Foundation

The foundation for similar physical evidence is as follows:

1. The original piece of physical evidence is not available.
2. If available, the original would be admissible.
3. The replica piece of evidence is relevant.
4. Its probative value outweighs any inflammatory effect.[68]
5. The jury is instructed that the evidence is not actually connected with the case, but is being admitted for illustrative purposes only.

§ 4-13(D)(3) Sample Foundation

The following fact situation is a criminal case in which the victim, Mr. Wells, has testified that he was assaulted by the defendant, who was swinging a hammer at him. The hammer actually used in the assault cannot be found. The victim has identified the defendant in court and the questioning continues with identification of a hammer similar in appearance to the one used in the assault. The proponent is the prosecutor.

P [*To the court reporter*] Would you please mark this as a State's exhibit? [*Court reporter marks exhibit for identification and hands it back to prosecutor.*] Thank you.

P Please let the record reflect that I am handing what has been marked as State's exhibit number five for identification to the defense counsel for his examination. [*Prosecutor hands exhibit to counsel.*]

J The record will so reflect.

P Now, Mr. Wells, I show you State's exhibit number five for identification. Do you recognize this?

W Yes.

P Would you please tell the court WHAT it is?

W It's a hammer that is almost exactly like the one that the defendant swung at me.

P WHAT leads you to that conclusion?

---

[68] This element, although noted by the court in *Miskis* is at odds with Texas Rule of Evidence 403, which assumes that relevant evidence is admissible. The burden usually rests on the opponent to show that otherwise relevant evidence is inadmissible because its prejudicial dangers substantially outweigh its probative value.

W The hammer he used on me was mine. I had it for several years and used it all the time. It was a Stanley claw hammer, just like this one, with a rubber handle. It's pretty standard.

P WHERE is the actual hammer the defendant swung at you? (1)

W It's lost. After the police came, we never could find my hammer. We looked everywhere.

P Your Honor, we offer into evidence State's exhibit number five for identification.

O Your Honor, we object. This witness has admitted that this is not the hammer that was allegedly used. We have no idea where this hammer came from. Because it is not the real hammer, it should not be admitted.

P Your Honor, this hammer is admissible as a replica of the one that was used in the assault. We have shown that the original is not available. (1) Second, this evidence is relevant because it tends to show what sort of implement was used in the assault. (3) Clearly, if this were the real hammer, it would be admissible; the witness identified the real hammer as a Stanley claw hammer with which he was familiar. And clearly, the probative value of this exhibit outweighs any possible prejudice.

J State's exhibit number five for identification is admitted into evidence.

O Your Honor, may we have a limiting instruction under Rule 105 which indicates that this exhibit is being admitted only for illustrative purposes.

J Yes. I will include that instruction in my charge to the jury.

P Your Honor, may I hand State's exhibit number five to the jury for their examination?

J Yes, you may.

If the trial judge had ruled that the exhibit was not admissible, the prosecutor should still be able to use the replica hammer as a prop for purposes of demonstration.

§ 4-14 VERIFICATION OF PHOTOGRAPHS AND MOTION PICTURES

§ 4-14(A) IN GENERAL

The process of authenticating photographs and motion pictures is the same,[69] and is generally referred to as *verification*. That is, the proponent must verify, usually through the testimony of a witness, that the photograph or motion picture

[69] *See, e.g., Associated Employers Ins. Co. v. Burris*, 321 S.W.2d 112 (Tex.Civ.App.—Amarillo 1959, writ ref.).

accurately and fairly depicts the scene in question. Over the years, two common methods of verifying photographs have developed: the pictorial testimony method and the silent witness method.

§ 4-14(B) THE PICTORIAL TESTIMONY METHOD

§ 4-14(B)(1) The Doctrine

The pictorial testimony method of verifying photographs and motion pictures simply requires a witness to testify that the photograph fairly and accurately depicts the scene. This method assumes that the witness is personally familiar with the scene depicted and can testify to that fact. Under this theory of admissibility, the picture is illustrating what the witness could have testified to. The proponent need not produce the person who actually took the picture. Any person familiar with the scene or object depicted may verify the photograph. Likewise, the proponent should not have to present detailed evidence about the type of camera used. If there is no witness who can verify the photograph in this method, it may be necessary to verify the photograph by showing that properly working equipment recorded the scene. That method is often referred to as the silent witness method.

§ 4-14(B)(2) Elements of the Foundation

The foundational elements for a still photograph or a motion picture, using the pictorial testimony method, are as follows:

1. The witness is familiar with the object or scene.
2. The witness explains the basis for his or her familiarity with the object or scene.
3. The witness recognizes the object or scene in the photograph or motion picture.
4. The photograph or movie is a fair, "accurate," "true," or "correct" depiction of the object or scene at the relevant time.

§ 4-14(B)(3) Sample Foundation

The fact situation is a civil tort action arising from a collision. The collision occurred at the intersection of A and Third Streets. The plaintiff calls a witness to verify a photograph of the intersection. The witness has already identified himself as Mr. Donald Adams. The accident occurred in 2005.

P WHERE do you work? (1), (2)

W Downtown. I'm a teller at the First National Bank on Third Street.

P WHERE is the bank located on Third Street? (1), (2)

W The address is 401 Third Street. The bank is between A and B Streets.

P HOW long have you worked there? (1), (2)

W A good seven years.

P Your Honor, I request that this be marked as a plaintiff's exhibit for identification. [*Court reporter marks exhibit.*] Please let the record reflect that I am showing plaintiff's exhibit number three for identification to the opposing counsel.

J The record will so reflect.

P Your Honor, I request permission to approach the witness.

J Permission granted.

P I now hand you plaintiff's exhibit number three for identification. WHAT is it? (1), (3)

W It's a photograph of the intersection of A and Third Streets.

P HOW can you recognize it? (2)

W As I said, I've worked in that area for years.

P HOW often have you passed that intersection? (2)

W I couldn't give you a figure. I've been there hundreds of times.

P WHAT perspective or viewpoint does this photograph show? (3)

W Let's see. Third Street runs north-south. A Street runs east-west.

P WHICH corner are you on? (3)

W You're on the southwest corner.

P In WHICH direction are you facing? (3)

W You're facing north; you're looking up Third Street.

P HOW accurate is this photograph? (4)

W Very. It's a correct and true depiction as far as I can tell.

P HOW accurately does it show the intersection as it was in 2005? (4)

W Well. It's a good photograph for that purpose. I worked downtown then, and I think it shows how the intersection looked then.

P HOW has the intersection changed since 2005? (4)

W Some of the signs have changed; businesses come and go. However, the intersection itself really hasn't changed. As best I can recall, it's the same size, the street markings are the same, and traffic flows the same way.

P Your Honor, I now offer plaintiff's exhibit number three for identification into evidence.

J It will be received.

P I request permission to hand the exhibit to the jurors for their inspection.

J Permission granted.

The following fact situation is a civil tort action. The plaintiff's theory is that the defendant, Polecat Motors, defectively designed the 2005 Sport Sprint. The plaintiff wants to introduce films depicting impact experiments with a 2005 Sport Sprint. The plaintiff calls an eyewitness who observed the tests and later reviewed the films of the tests. The witness has already identified himself as Mr. Blair McIntosh.

P Mr. McIntosh, WHERE were you on the morning of August 17th of this year? (2)

W I was at Abbott Laboratories on Industrial Street, here in Galveston.

P WHY did you go there? (2)

W You asked me to go there to watch some experiments.

P WHAT experiments? (2)

W It was an impact experiment with a 2005 Polecat Sport Sprint.

P WHAT did you do when you arrived at Abbott Laboratories? (2)

W I was introduced to the engineer in charge of the tests along with the man who was photographing the tests, a Mr. Wilson, I believe.

P WHAT did you see at the laboratories? (1)

W I saw three different tests being run over a period of two hours.

P Your Honor, I request that this be marked as plaintiff's exhibit number P-2 for identification.

J It will be so marked. [*Court reporter marks exhibit.*]

P Please let the record reflect that I am showing the exhibit to counsel for the defendant.

J So reflected.

P May I approach the witness, your Honor?

J Yes.

P Mr. McIntosh, I now show you what has been marked as plaintiff's exhibit number P-2 for identification. Do you recognize it?

W Yes, this is a film of the experiments I just described.

P WHAT does this film represent? (3)

W It shows the three tests that were run on the Sprint.

P Would you please tell us HOW you know that? (3)

W Well, this is the same film that I personally reviewed last week and it has my initials on the side of the reel, here. The contents of the film match what I saw in the laboratory.

P HOW accurate is the film? (4)

W It is extremely accurate.

P Is this film a true and accurate representation of what you saw at the tests run at Abbott Laboratories on August 17th? (4)

W Definitely.

P Your Honor, I move for the admission of plaintiff's exhibit number P-2 for identification into evidence.

O Your Honor, we object. Counsel has not shown a sufficient predicate.

P Your Honor, all that is required to lay a predicate for a silent motion picture in Texas is to have a witness verify that the movie accurately and correctly depicts the event. The witness has clearly stated that he personally saw the tests and that this film is an accurate portrayal of the tests. It is well settled that we do not need to produce the person who took the movie.

J The exhibit will be admitted.

P Your Honor, we would now request permission to show the movie to the jury and ask the witness to describe the tests shown on the movie.

§ 4-14(C) THE SILENT WITNESS METHOD

§ 4-14(C)(1) The Doctrine

The silent witness method of verifying photographs is becoming increasingly popular with automated photography systems. Under this theory, the picture speaks for itself, even where no human was present to see what took place. This method would be available, for example, where the proponent is attempting to show who made a withdrawal from an automatic teller machine. This method requires the proponent to show what process or system was used to record the event and that the resulting photograph was reliable.[70] This usually means that the proponent will call a witness competent to testify about the system used.[71] While the focus under the pictorial testimony method is on the witness on the stand, under the silent witness method, the focus is on the reliability of the camera system.

[70] *See* TEX. R. EVID. 901(b)(9).

[71] *See United States v. Taylor*, 530 F.2d 639 (5th Cir. 1976).

§ 4-14(C)(2) Elements of the Foundation

The foundation for using the silent witness method is as follows:

1. The manner of loading the film into the camera.
2. How the camera system works and is activated.
3. How the film was removed.
4. How the film was handled afterwards.
5. Whether the development process produced reliable results.

Note that this foundation could also be used to verify x-rays, discussed *infra* at § 4-15.

§ 4-14(C)(3) Sample Foundation

The next example relates to a surveillance video taken of the defendant breaking into an automatic teller machine late at night when no one else was present. The proponent is the prosecutor and the witness is the bank security guard, Mr. Jay Morkes, who has already described his position and relationship to the bank.

P Mr. Morkes, WHAT, if any, photographic system does the bank have for recording what takes place at the teller machine? (2)

W The system consists of a small video camera located behind protective Plexiglas.

P HOW does it work? (2)

W The camera is set to record continuously whenever anyone comes within three feet of the machine. It continues to run until the person leaves. It uses regular VHS film, but it does not pick up any sounds.[72]

P WHO manufactures the camera? (2)

W It's a Sony 2000-7 system.

P HOW is the camera loaded? (1)

W In the same way as any other video camera. It is really a very simple operation. We load a cassette at least once a day. A separate monitoring system indicates when the camera is running low on film.

P WHO removes the film? (3)

W Either I or the other two security personnel who are responsible for the system.

---

[72] Because Texas courts seem to make a distinction between videos with sound and those without, if the proponent wanted to show that the participants on the video said something, the predicate for videotapes, discussed *supra* at § 4-6, would probably apply.

P [*To court reporter*] Would you please mark this as a State's exhibit? [*Reporter marks exhibit and hands it back to proponent.*] Thank you.

P Please let the record reflect that I am showing what has been marked as State's exhibit number seven for identification to the defense counsel. [*Proponent hands exhibit to defense counsel, who examines it.*]

J The record will so reflect.

P May I approach the witness?

J Yes, you may.

P Mr. Morkes, do you recognize WHAT State's exhibit number seven for identification is?

W Yes. This is the video of a person attempting to pry into the automatic teller machine at our bank.

P HOW do you know that?

W Well, I have watched it several times over the last several months.

P HOW accurate is this tape? (5)

W Well, of course, I was not there, but the quality of the tape is certainly very good. You can clearly see the person's face and the date and time stamp on the screen. You can even see small fragments of the machine go flying when the person took a hammer to it.

P WHO processed this video? (4)

W I did. I marked my initials on the outside of the cassette to indicate that on that particular date, it was my responsibility to load and unload the camera.

P WHERE has this video been since you removed it?

W It has been in our bank records section. I took it from there this morning before coming to court. Oh, I should add that I believe that the police made a copy of it for their records several months ago.

P Your Honor, we now offer State's exhibit number seven for identification into evidence.

§ 4-14(D) ENHANCED PHOTOGRAPHS

§ 4-14(D)(1) The Doctrine

The proponent may not be content to proffer the original photograph developed from the film. There are several possibilities. First, the proponent might offer a simple enlargement of the photograph. Enlargement is a multiplication process; an enlargement merely increases the size of the photograph. The foundation for an enlarged photograph can be relatively short, since the trial judge may judicially notice the validity of the technique for enlarging a photograph.

Second,[73] the proponent may attempt to introduce an enhanced photograph. Image enhancement is a subtractive process, which improves image contrast by removing "interfering colors and background patterns."[74] Testimony based on image enhancement technology is admissible provided that a sufficient foundation is laid that validates the underlying scientific process.[75]

Image enhancement technology was developed during the late 1960s and early 1970s for the NASA space program.[76] The Jet Propulsion Laboratory of the California Institute of Technology was instrumental in pioneering image enhancement.[77] Due to the weight and power limitations of spacecraft, it was impractical for NASA to use state-of-the-art camera systems on unmanned craft.[78] The cameras used produced somewhat degraded photographs. Image enhancement reverses the degradation. Initially, researchers study the degradation properties of the use of a particular type of photographic equipment to capture a certain type of image: When this type of camera is used to photograph distant objects, what type of degradation can be anticipated? Then, the researchers design computer software to reverse the degradation and thereby improve the sharpness and image contrast of the photograph[79] by eliminating background patterns and colors.[80]

Before the image on a normal analog photograph could be enhanced, the photographic image would have to be digitized.[81] "Digital images are composed of millions of tiny dots, referred to as 'pixels.' "[82] Digital photography "can capture approximately 16 million different colors and . . . differentiate between 256 shades of gray."[83] Then, based on degradation models developed in

---

[73] There is a third possibility, namely, image restoration. *State v. Hayden*, 950 P.2d 1024, 1028 (Wash.App. 1998). That process is additive. The process adds details "based upon preconceived ideas about what the end result should look like . . . ." *Id.* The use of image restoration computer software presents a significant problem in the validation of the scientific process. To add details, the software predicts the missing details. The proponent must point to a body of solid empirical research validating the "preconceived idea about what the end result should look like . . . ." *Id.*

[74] *Id.*

[75] *See Wagner v. State*, 707 So.2d 827 (Fla.App. 1988).

[76] *State v. Hayden*, 950 P.2d 1024, 1026 (Wash.App. 1998).

[77] GREGORY P. JOSEPH, MODERN VISUAL EVIDENCE 8–22 (1999).

[78] *Id.*

[79] *State v. Hayden*, 950 P.2d 1024, 1028 (Wash.App. 1998).

[80] *Id.* at 1025.

[81] *Dolan v. State*, 743 So.2d 544, 545 (Fla.Dist.Ct.App. 1999).

[82] *Id.*

[83] *State v. Hayden*, 950 P.2d 1024, 1028 (Wash.App. 1998).

research,[84] computer software manipulates the pixels to filter out[85] graininess and improve brightness and contrast.[86]

Although image enhancement technology was developed for the space program to isolate distant galaxies,[87] the technology now has a wide variety of applications. The technology has been "applied in numerous areas, including medicine, physics, meteorology, resource exploration, factory automation and robotics control."[88] For instance, forensic scientists utilize the technology to enhance photographs of finger and palm prints.[89] When the proponent has made a proper showing of the reliability of the technology, the courts have been receptive to enhanced photographs.[90] Indeed, in several cases, trial judges have ordered that photographs be enhanced prior to trial.[91]

§ 4-14(D)(2) Elements of the Foundation

Assume that a prior witness has laid the foundation for the introduction of a normal analog[92] photograph. To justify the introduction of an enhanced version of that photograph, the proponent should lay the following foundation:

1. The witness is an expert in photography.
2. The witness describes image enhancement technology. The technology is a process including two steps: the creation of a digital photograph consisting of pixels and the computer manipulation of the pixels.
3. In general, both steps of image enhancement technology are valid. The proponent must demonstrate that the underlying hypothesis has sufficient assurances of reliability in the sense that experts have verified the hypothesis by sound scientific methodology.
4. There has been adequate research into the specific application of image enhancement technology involved in the case.
5. The research resulted in the development of computer software for this application of image enhancement technology.

---

[84] GREGORY P. JOSEPH, MODERN VISUAL EVIDENCE 8–22 (1999).

[85] *State v. Hayden*, 950 P.2d 1024, 1026 (Wash.App. 1998).

[86] *Nooner v. State*, 907 S.W.2d 677, 686 (Ark. 1995).

[87] *State v. Hayden*, 950 P.2d 1024, 1026 (Wash.App. 1998).

[88] GREGORY P. JOSEPH, MODERN VISUAL EVIDENCE 8–22 (1999).

[89] *State v. Hayden*, 950 P.2d 1024, 1025 (Wash.App. 1998).

[90] *Id.*; *Dolan v. State*, 743 So.2d 544 (Fla.Dist.Ct.App. 1999); *Wagner v. State*, 707 So.2d 827 (Fla.Dist.Ct.App. 1998); *Nooner v. State*, 907 So.2d 677 (Ark. 1995); *English v. State*, 422 S.E.2d 924 (Ga.App. 1992). *But see State v. Swinton*, 847 A.2d 921 (Conn. 2004).

[91] GREGORY P. JOSEPH, MODERN VISUAL EVIDENCE 8-24.2, at n.22 (1999), *citing Pyka v. Village of Orland Park*, No. 92-C-7888, 1995 U.S. Dist. LEXIS 17050 (N.D. Ill., Nov. 14, 1995) and *State v. Newman*, 1994 Minn.App. LEXIS 1246 (Minn.App., Dec. 13, 1994).

[92] *State v. Hayden*, 950 P.2d 1024, 1028 (Wash.App. 1998).

6. At a given time and place, the witness received the analog photograph previously introduced.
7. The witness followed proper procedure in digitizing the analog photograph.
8. The witness also followed proper procedure in using the computer software to enhance the analog photograph.
9. The witness recognizes the exhibit proffered at trial as the photograph which he or she produced when he or she used the software to enhance the analog photograph.

§ 4-14(D)(3) Sample Foundation

The fact situation is a criminal prosecution for burglary. The prosecution alleges that on February 22, 2005, the defendant broke into a residence in Austin. Earlier in the trial, a crime laboratory technician, Officer O'Grady, testifies that she: visited the burglary scene, detected a fingerprint on a sheet in the master bedroom, and took an analog photograph of the fingerprint. She adds that she later took the film back to the crime laboratory, developed the film, produced a photograph of the print, and delivered that print to Mr. Julio Mendez on February 23, 2005. Before the technician leaves the stand, the prosecution lays the foundation for and introduces State's Exhibit No. 3, the analog photograph of the fingerprint found at the burglary scene. The prosecution calls Mr. Mendez as its next witness.

P WHAT is your educational background? (1)

W I obtained a B.A. in Fine Arts from Texas A & M University in 1990.

P WHAT area, if any, did you specialize in while you were working on your degree? (1)

W Photography. I had always loved that as a kid, and I thought that I might be able to turn my love for photography into a profession.

P WHAT did you do after you obtained your B.A.? (1)

W I took some additional college photography courses at the University of Texas.

P WHY did you do that? (1)

W Well, my parents lived near campus, and it was convenient to continue my course of studies there. More importantly, though, Texas had some advanced courses on new photographic technologies. I hadn't taken those courses while I was a student at A & M. I just couldn't fit them into my schedule while I was working on my degree at A & M. However, I decided that I really needed to master those technologies before I opened my own photographic business.

P WHAT did you do after you completed those courses? (1)

W I opened up a full-service photographic business here in town.

P WHAT do you mean by a "full-service photographic business?" (2)

W I mean that I offer virtually every type of photography—not just the conventional analog photography which most people are familiar with but also digital photography and techniques such as image enhancement. If you need virtually any type of photographic service, I can provide it.

P You just mentioned "image enhancement." WHAT do you mean by that term? (2)

W It's a technology that was developed for the NASA space program. It was pioneered by the Jet Propulsion Laboratory at the California Institute of Technology. Unmanned spacecraft have severe power and weight limitations. For that reason, NASA couldn't put heavy, state-of-the-art film and photographic equipment on the craft. The practical limitations dictated that they use less than state-of-the-art equipment.

P WHY was their use of that type of equipment important? (2)

W In practical terms, what it meant is that they later needed to enhance the photographs produced by the equipment installed on the craft.

P HOW do you "enhance" a normal photograph? (2)

W It requires a couple of first steps. The first step is digitizing the images on the normal or analog photograph. You convert each image into lots of dots called pixels. Sophisticated equipment can tell the difference between the pixels comprising thousands of different colors. In fact, the equipment can differentiate among over 250 shades of gray.

P WHAT is the second step? WHAT do you do after you have digitized a normal photograph? (2)

W After you've digitized the photograph, you're ready for the second step. Simply stated, you use computer software to reverse the degradation of the photograph. Especially when you use less than state-of-the-art cameras, you're not going to get ideal contrast and brightness—the term of art is "degradation." However, you can direct the computer to manipulate the pixels for certain shades of gray in a particular part of the normal photograph. Doing so eliminates some of the graininess and improves the contrast. You filter out the background colors that make it difficult to make out the details in the photograph.

P HOW do you know that the computer software does that? (2)

W You need scientific research. You have to engage in research and develop a degradation model. The research tells you what type of degradation to expect if you use a certain type of camera on a particular type of subject. If you can predict the type of expected degradation, you can program a computer to eliminate some of that degradation and thereby improve the photograph. In a nutshell, that's how you produce an enhanced photograph.

P WHAT, if any, details does enhancement add to the photograph? (2)

W None. It subtracts graininess caused, for example, by the presence of certain shades of gray in the photograph. But it doesn't add any details. If you put the normal photo side by side with the enhanced photo, you'll be able to find every detail shown in the enhanced photo in the normal photo. It's just easier to see those details because enhancement improves the brightness in the other areas and therefore the contrast between those areas and the details you're interested in.

P HOW valid is the first step in this process, digital photography? (3)

W There's no question about the validity of the technology. It's universally accepted by experts in the field, and it's in worldwide use.

P HOW valid is the second step of the process, using computer software to enhance photographs? (3)

W The second step is also very reliable if the photographer applying the process has adequate training and knows what he or she is doing.

P HOW do you get that training? (3)

W You can get it on the job, or you could get it the way I did by taking advanced courses at a college such as at A & M or Texas. One of my courses was in digital photography, and another dealt with advanced techniques such as image enhancement. I took courses in both steps of the technology. Again, I went to Texas because I wanted to learn those advanced techniques.

P HOW widely accepted is the first step in the process, the technology of digital photography? (3)

W As I said, there's no question that it's accepted. Its use was formerly confined to professional photographers. Now the leading companies are making digital cameras that are commercially available to even amateur photographers. You can go down to your local camera store today and buy a digital camera off the shelf.

P HOW widely accepted among photographers is the second step, the use of computer software for image enhancement? (3)

W It's not only accepted among photographers. It's accepted in lots of professional fields. NASA has used it for years. It's also been applied in medicine, physics, meteorology, resource exploration, factory automation, and robotics control.

P WHAT application, if any, does image enhancement have in fingerprint analysis? (4)

W You can use it to enhance poor quality normal photographs of fingerprints.

P HOW do you know that? (4)

W Because photography is both my love and my line of work, I try to stay on top of developments in the field. In the last ten years forensic experts—scientists interested in legal cases—have adapted photographic enhancement techniques to many of their tasks, including fingerprint analysis.

P HOW do you know that? (4)

W Several ways. First, I read the literature. The photographic and forensic journals contain tons of articles about photo enhancement in various forensic fields. Second, I've attended specialized short courses offered by both the photographic equipment companies and police agencies such as the Federal Bureau of Investigation. In fact, I've served as an instructor at some of those courses. Finally, in several civil and criminal cases, I've had occasion to use the technique myself.

P HOW valid is the use of enhancement technology to improve photographs of fingerprints? (4)

W I consider it to be a very reliable adaptation of the technology.

P WHY do you say that? (4)

W As I said before, the technology depends on developing a degradation model. There's been a lot of research—a lot of time and effort—invested in determining the type of degradation you can expect when you take a normal photograph of a fingerprint on various types of surfaces such as linen sheets.

P HOW widely accepted is this adaptation of photographic enhancement technology? (4)

W If you do sophisticated photographic work, as I do, you know the technique, and you accept the technique.

P In your work, HOW do you use the technique? (5)

W I employ computer software specifically developed for this adaptation of photographic enhancement.

P WHO developed the software? (5)

W It was perfected and then marketed by Phototek, one of the leading companies in the field.

P HOW widely used is that software? (5)

W It's commercially available, and it's employed at laboratories throughout the United States and overseas as well.

P Mr. Mendez, I've asked you some questions about photographic enhancement technology. Now I'd like to shift topics. Do you remember WHERE you were on the afternoon of February 23, 2005? (6)

W Yes.

P WHERE were you? (6)

W At my office downtown here.

P WHAT, if anything, happened that afternoon? (6)

W Probably the only thing worth mentioning was that I had a visit from Officer O'Grady.

P WHAT was the purpose of her visit? (6)

W She gave me a normal analog photograph of a fingerprint taken at a burglary scene and asked that I enhance it.

P [*To court reporter*] Would you please mark this as State's Exhibit for Identification next in order? [*Reporter marks the exhibit and hands it back to the proponent who examines it to determine the number assigned to the exhibit.*] Thank you. Please let the record reflect that I am showing State's Exhibit No. 3 for Identification to the defense counsel. [*Proponent hands exhibit to defense counsel who examines it and then hands it back to the proponent.*]

J The record will so reflect.

P May I approach the witness, Your Honor?

J Yes.

P Mr. Mendez, I now hand you what has been marked as State's Exhibit No. 3 for Identification. Do you recognize it? (6)

W Yes.

P WHAT is it? (6)

W It's the photograph which Officer O'Grady gave me.

P HOW do you recognize it? (6)

W To begin with, I recognize the contents. I've never seen a photograph quite like that before. In addition, I placed my initials and the date on the reverse side. That's my handwriting right there on the other side of the exhibit.

P WHAT did you do with this photograph after Officer O'Grady gave it to you? (7)

W I had agreed to enhance it for my regular fee. As I said before, the first step in enhancement is to convert it into a digital image. You digitize the normal photo into all those dots or pixels.

P HOW did you do that? (7)

W I used my specialized digital photography equipment.

P HOW well was that equipment working that day? (7)

W As far as I could tell, it was fine. I always check specialized equipment like that before I use it. I don't have occasion to use that sort of sophisticated instrument every day. I therefore inspected it, and it checked out just fine. I didn't encounter any problems preparing the digital photograph.

P WHAT did you do after you prepared the digital photograph of the fingerprint? (8)

W As I said before, the second step is using computer software to do the enhancement. It manipulates the pixels to eliminate certain dark shading and thereby improves brightness and contrast.

P WHAT condition was that computer equipment in that day? (8)

W It also seemed fine. I ran a diagnostic when I booted up, and the diagnostic indicated that everything was in working order. In addition, everything went smoothly during the process. For example, I didn't get any error messages on the screen.

P WHAT was the result of your use of the software? (9)

W It produced an enhanced photograph.

P [*To court reporter*] Would you please mark this as State's Exhibit next in order? [*Reporter marks exhibit and hands it to proponent who determines what number the court reporter used.*] Thank you. Please let the record reflect that I am showing what has been marked as State's Exhibit No. 4 for Identification to the defense counsel. [*Proponent hands exhibit to defense counsel who examines it and returns it to proponent.*]

J The record will so reflect.

P Permission to approach the witness?

J Permission granted.

P Mr. Mendez, I now hand you State's Exhibit No. 4 for identification. Do you recognize this exhibit?

W Yes, I do.

P Would you please tell us WHAT it is. (9)

W It's the enhanced photo.

P HOW can you recognize it? (9)

W As in the case of the other exhibit, Number 3, I recognize its contents and appearance. Moreover, as in the case of the analog photo, I placed my initials and the date on the back. That's also my handwriting right there. [*Witness points to notation.*]

P Mr. Mendez, HOW well does the enhanced photograph compare with the normal photograph? (9)

W You can see for yourself. There are areas of brightness on the enhanced photo and therefore more contrast with the details of the fingerprint. However, if you compare the two photos carefully, you'll see that every detail reflected in the enhanced photo is also shown in the normal photo, the one which Officer O'Grady gave me.

P Thank you. Your Honor, we offer into evidence State's Exhibits 3 and 4.

J Any objections, defense counsel?

O None, Your Honor.

J Then State's Exhibits 3 and 4 will be admitted into evidence.

P Your Honor, may we hand them to the jury?

J Yes, you may.

§ 4-15 VERIFICATION OF X-RAYS

§ 4-15(A) THE DOCTRINE

X-rays are also a form of photographs. In many cases, the counsel stipulate to the authenticity of x-rays in the case. Occasionally, however, the proponent will have to authenticate the x-ray. The authentication of an x-ray is a rather peculiar process. No one can testify that he or she saw what the x-ray depicts and verify the x-ray on that theory. Thus, it is very much like the silent witness theory used to verify other photographic evidence, where no person actually saw the event or scene.

Because of that peculiarity, the proponent must resort to some other authentication technique. Some judges treat x-rays as business records of the hospital. In those instances, the x-rays could be self-authenticated under Texas Rule of Evidence 902(10).[93] They accept authentication by the testimony of the hospital's x-ray librarian that he or she removed the x-ray from the right file.

Other judges view x-ray evidence as presenting both scientific and physical evidence problems. In that case, the proponent must show the operator's qualifications, the working order of the x-ray, and a chain of custody for the

[93] *See supra* at § 4-3(C) for a discussion on how the proponent can use an affidavit to authenticate business records.

x-ray cassette. In many hospitals, however, the x-ray technician uses an identification assembly during the x-ray. The assembly is composed of lead letters and numbers and casts a shadow of the letters and numbers on the cassette. In effect, the letters and numbers make the cassette a readily identifiable article.

§ 4-15(B) ELEMENTS OF THE FOUNDATION

If the hospital follows the customary practice of using an identification assembly, the complete foundation for the x-ray would include the following elements:

1. The operator was a qualified x-ray technician.
2. The operator filmed a certain part of a person's body at a certain time and place.
3. The operator used certain equipment.
4. The equipment was in good working condition.
5. The operator used the correct procedures.
6. The operator used an identification assembly on the cassette.
7. The operator accounts for the cassette's custody between filming and trial; the chain of custody includes proof of the proper development of the cassette.
8. The witness recognizes the exhibit as the cassette.

§ 4-15(C) SAMPLE FOUNDATION

The fact situation is a civil action and demonstrates the more stringent form of verification of an x-ray. The plaintiff contends that as a result of the tort, she suffered severe personal injuries, including bone fractures. The plaintiff wishes to introduce an x-ray to depict some of the fractures. The plaintiff calls Mr. Paul Nesbitt. Mr. Nesbitt has already identified himself.

P WHAT is your occupation? (1)

W I am an x-ray technician at Sharp Hospital downtown.

P HOW long have you worked as an x-ray technician? (1)

W For seven years.

P WHAT is your formal education? (1)

W I have a degree from the University of Houston.

P WHAT was your major field of study? (1)

W Science.

P WHAT other training have you had as an x-ray technician? (1)

W I attended a three-month course at U.C.L.A. Medical School, and I've also attended numerous seminars on the subject.

P WHERE were you on the afternoon of July 7, 2005? (2)

W As I recall, I was on duty at the x-ray lab.

P WHAT, if anything, happened that afternoon? (2)

W Doctor Bertrand asked me to take the plaintiff's x-ray, and the plaintiff stopped by for the x-ray.

P WHO is the plaintiff? (2)

W The woman at the table to the right over there.

P WHAT is she wearing? (2)

W The green dress and yellow scarf.

P Your Honor, please let the record reflect that the witness has identified the plaintiff, Ms. Wohlmuth. (2)

J It will so reflect.

P WHAT did you do when Ms. Wohlmuth arrived at the lab? (3)

W I showed her how to position herself on the table to enable me to get a good x-ray of her right leg.

P WHAT happened then? (3)

W Then I set up the equipment.

P WHAT equipment? (3)

W The x-ray machine and the cassette with identification assembly.

P WHAT is the x-ray machine? (3)

W It's the camera that you use to take an x-ray.

P WHAT is the cassette? (3)

W It's the film. The x-rays make the impression on the cassette.

P WHAT is the identification assembly? (6)

W It consists of lead numbers and letters. The lead casts shadows on the cassette; you sort of outline the letters and numbers.

P WHAT are these letters and numbers? (6)

W The practice varies from hospital to hospital. Some hospitals use the numbers for the patient's file number. Each patient has a different file number. We usually spell out the patient's name if it's short and then list the date of the x-ray in numbers.

P WHAT condition was the equipment in? (4)

W It was in fine condition.

P HOW do you know that? (4)

W I had checked it myself the day before. I always check it Monday morning. I took this x-ray on a Tuesday.

P HOW did you learn to check the equipment? (4)

W That was one of the subjects we studied at U.C.L.A.

P HOW did you take the plaintiff's x-ray? (5)

W After I set up the equipment, I told the plaintiff to position her leg. Then I stepped behind the lead and leaded glass. I viewed the plaintiff during the x-ray. I adjusted the amperage and voltage settings, and then I turned the machine on to make the exposure.

P WHAT did you do then? (5)

W I reentered the room and removed the cassette.

P WHAT did you do with the cassette? (7)

W I put it in a corner in the room and developed it that afternoon.

P WHAT happened to the cassette between the filming and development? (7)

W As far as I know, nothing. It was just there in the room.

P WHO handled the cassette between the filming and development? (7)

W As far as I can tell, I was the only one.

P HOW did you develop the x-ray? (7)

W I went into the darkroom, removed the film from the cassette, and then put it through the developing process.

P HOW did you learn to develop x-rays? (7)

W That was another subject we studied in detail at U.C.L.A.

P WHAT did you do with the film after you developed it? (7)

W I brought it down to our x-ray records library on the second floor.

P WHAT happened then? (7)

W I gave it to the clerk and asked her to file it under the plaintiff's name.

P Your Honor, I request that this be marked as plaintiff's exhibit number four for identification.

J It will be so marked. [*Reporter marks exhibit.*]

P Please let the record reflect that I am showing the exhibit to the opposing counsel.

J It will so reflect.

P I request permission to approach the witness.

J Permission granted.

P Mr. Nesbitt, I now hand you plaintiff's exhibit number four for identification. WHAT is it? (8)

W It's the x-ray I took of the plaintiff's leg.

P HOW can you recognize it? (8)

W I recognize this type of film, and I see the plaintiff's name and the date just as I set them up in the identification assembly. I also recognize the general appearance of the bones depicted.

P HOW did the film get to court today? (7)

W I went to the file for that month and looked for the x-ray with the plaintiff's name and the date.

P HOW many were there? (7)

W Only the one I took.

P HOW many times have you used that filing system in the past? (7)

W Hundreds.

P WHO taught you how to use the system? (7)

W The x-ray records librarian herself, Dr. Riley.

P Your Honor, I now offer plaintiff's exhibit number four for identification into evidence.

J It will be received.

The proponent will use the x-ray later during a doctor's testimony. The doctor will testify about the extent of injury and use the x-ray to illustrate the injuries.

§ 4-16 IN-COURT EXHIBITIONS

§ 4-16(A) THE DOCTRINE

The proponent will sometimes want to display something other than a normal, inanimate, physical exhibit to the jurors. For example, in a personal injury case, the plaintiff's attorney may want the plaintiff to display the injured part of the body to the jurors. Such an exhibition can be helpful to the jury in determining the damages in the case. The probative danger is that the exhibition will inflame the jurors. After viewing a badly mangled limb, the jurors may not be able to dispassionately weigh the evidence on liability or damages.

Under Texas Rule of Evidence 403, the trial judge has wide discretion in deciding whether to permit an exhibition. The judge ordinarily considers three factors: (1) whether the object to be exhibited is relevant to the case; (2) whether the jurors need to see the object to understand the oral testimony about the object; and (3) the risk that viewing the object will inflame the jurors' emotions.

§ 4-16(B) ELEMENTS OF THE FOUNDATION

In requesting permission to conduct an in-court exhibition the proponent should be prepared to show the following:

1. The object to be exhibited is relevant to the case.
2. The object will assist the jury in understanding the facts in the case.
3. The object will not unduly inflame the jury.

§ 4-16(C) SAMPLE FOUNDATION

The fact situation is a products liability action. The plaintiff, Mr. Jansen, brought the action against Kenway, Inc., which manufactures electrical saws. The plaintiff alleges that the defendant defectively designed the saw and that the design defect caused the blade to come loose and slice the plaintiff's arms. The plaintiff takes the witness stand. When he does so, the plaintiff is wearing a jacket. The plaintiff has testified about his injuries in general terms. The proponent, the plaintiff's attorney, now wants to exhibit the injuries to the jurors.

P WHAT were your injuries?

W The blade sliced both of my arms very badly.

P Mr. Jansen, would you please take off your jacket and show your arms to the jurors?

O Your Honor, may we approach the bench?

J Certainly.

O Your Honor, I strenuously object to this exhibition.

P Your Honor, the plaintiff's arms were injured in this accident, and it's certainly logically relevant to show the jurors what the arms look like now. (1)

O I admit that the exhibition would be relevant, but I object on the ground that the sight of the plaintiff's badly cut arms will arouse the jurors' emotions and prejudice my client.

P The jurors simply won't understand the extent of the plaintiff's injuries unless they actually see the arms. (2) Additionally, the mere fact that the jury may be bothered by the injured arms is not the test. Under Rule 403, the opponent must show that the prejudicial dangers of the evidence substantially outweigh the probative value. In this instance, we believe the probative value is very high. (3)

J The objection is overruled. You may proceed with the exhibition.

§ 4-17 IN-COURT DEMONSTRATIONS

§ 4-17(A) The Doctrine

A demonstration is a step beyond an exhibition. In an exhibition, the proponent merely displays something for the jurors' view. In a demonstration, the proponent demonstrates some physical or mechanical process in action. The proponent may want to demonstrate how poorly the plaintiff can move his limbs or how a particular machine operates. Once again, under Rule 403, the trial judge has wide discretion in deciding whether to permit the demonstration. In exercising his or her discretion, the judge looks to the factors relevant to exhibitions, plus an additional factor. The fourth factor is the risk that the party demonstrating a physical process may be feigning or may present a misleading version of the process. A plaintiff can easily feign the extent of his or her disability, and it will be very difficult to expose the feigning plaintiff during cross-examination. If the demonstration is an exhibition of what has occurred at another place and time, the proponent must also be prepared to show that the in-court demonstration is substantially similar to the event or process it is intended to depict.

§ 4-17(B) Elements of the Foundation

If counsel wishes to conduct an in-court demonstration, he or she should be prepared to show the following:

1. The demonstration is relevant to the case.
2. The demonstration will assist the jury in understanding the facts in the case.
3. The demonstration will not unduly inflame the jury.
4. The demonstration is a substantially correct depiction of the process or event.

§ 4-17(C) Sample Foundation

The following is a continuation of the preceding hypothetical. Suppose that the plaintiff claims that as a result of the saw accident, he can no longer straighten his arms.

P Mr. Jansen, let me repeat my request. Please show your arms to the jurors. [*The witness does so.*] HOW has the accident affected your arms?

W I have a good deal of pain, and I can't straighten them all the way anymore.

P Please show us how far you can straighten your arms.

O Your Honor, may we approach the bench again?

J Yes.

O I hate to object again, your Honor, but I feel compelled to register my objection to this demonstration.

P Your Honor, this demonstration is indisputably logically relevant. (1) To show the plaintiff's disability, we have to show the extent to which he's lost the use of his arms.

O Your Honor, how can I cross-examine a demonstration? There's too great a risk that the plaintiff will be able to feign the extent of his disability. The demonstration also poses problems of inflaming the jury.

P We need this demonstration to help the jury understand our medical testimony about the extent of disability, and the defendant can cross-examine the experts about whether the plaintiff is faking. (2), (4) Regarding the possible prejudicial effect of the demonstration, this is the sort of condition the plaintiff must now live with. Yes, it is not a pretty sight, but that is not the test for whether the demonstration should be conducted. (3)

J The objection will be overruled. The demonstration may proceed.

§ 4-18 EVIDENCE OF AN OUT-OF-COURT EXPERIMENT

§ 4-18(A) THE DOCTRINE

Suppose that in a particular case, the central issue is whether a traffic accident occurred in a certain manner, and that the plaintiff and defendant advance conflicting theories as to how the accident occurred. To corroborate her theory, the plaintiff might offer testimony about an out-of-court experiment.[94] The plaintiff would hire an expert to design and conduct an experiment duplicating the conditions which existed at the time of the accident in question. If the result of the experiment indicated that the accident occurred in the manner claimed by the plaintiff, it might be important corroboration for the plaintiff's theory of the case. At trial, the plaintiff could present an expert witness or witnesses to provide an oral description of the experiment. In addition, the plaintiff could offer a photograph[95] or videotape[96] depicting part or all of the experiment.

[94] C. Phillip Colver, *The Persuasive Impact of Simulation Experimentation*, 17 TRIAL 64 (Nov. 1981).

[95] *Reed v. Tiffin Motor Homes, Inc.*, 697 F2d 1192 (4th Cir. 1982).

[96] *Miles v. Ford Motor Co.*, 922 S.W.2d 572 (Tex. App.—Texarkana 1996), *rev'd in part on other grounds*, 967 S.W.2d 377 (Tex. 1998).

In an accident reconstruction case, the proponent might be attempting to introduce the expert's testimony about an experiment involving braking distance. The witness would testify that the following factors, inter alia, determine braking distance: the type of road surface, the amount of moisture on the surface, the condition of the tire tread, and the amount of pressure which the driver applies to the brake. The witness might explicitly or implicitly rely on a scientific hypothesis about the factors which determine the outcome of the experiment. When the expert relies on a purportedly scientific hypothesis, the expert must be prepared to testify to the empirical validation as discussed at Chapter 9, *infra*.

In laying the foundation for an out-of-court test or experiment, the proponent must generally be prepared to show that the conditions which existed at the time of the event and the conditions recreated during the experiment were the same. The two sets of conditions, however, need not be perfectly identical.[97] The judge has discretion in assessing the degree of similarity between the two sets of conditions,[98] if the differences are minor or subject to explanation.[99] The Texas courts recognize that an affirmative acknowledgment by the proponent to the jury that there are dissimilarities will alleviate any unfairness in the experiment.[100]

In most of the published opinions, the appellate courts assert that when the experiment is offered to establish how the particular incident occurred, the trial judge must find substantial similarity.[101] On the other hand, some courts tend to accept a lesser degree of similarity when the experiment is for the limited purpose of demonstrating the operation of a scientific law.[102] If the proponent offered the experimental evidence for that purpose, the opponent would be entitled to a limiting instruction under Rule 105. In the instruction, the judge would inform the jury that although the experiment illustrates the operation of a scientific law relevant to the accident, the experiment is not intended to duplicate the accident.

The proponent must also be prepared to show the basis for the expert's information about the conditions existing at the time of the accident. Under Rule 703, the expert may gain his information about the accident from three sources. First, the expert can rely on personal knowledge. For instance, the expert might

---

97 *Garza v. Cole*, 753 S.W.2d 245, 247 (Tex. App.—Houston [14th Dist.] 1987, writ refused).

98 *City of Dallas v. Cox*, 793 S.W.2d 701, 734 (Tex. App.—Dallas 1990, no writ).

99 *Id.*

100 *Miles v. Ford Motor Co.*, 922 S.W.2d 572, 595 (Tex. App.—Texarkana 1996), *rev'd in part on other grounds*, 967 S.W.2d 377 (Tex. 1998). *Lopez v. Foremost Paving, Inc.*, 796 S.W.2d 473, 480 (Tex. App.—San Antonio 1990, writ dism'd).

101 *Kainer v. Walker*, 377 S.W.2d 613 (Tex. 1964); *Rodriguez v. Hyundai Motor Co.*, 944 S.W.2d 757 (Tex. App.—Corpus Christi 1997).

102 *Robinson v. Audi NSU Auto Union, A.G.*, 739 F.2d 1481 (10th Cir. 1984); *Brandt v. French*, 638 F.2d 209 (10th Cir. 1981); *Carr v. Suzuki Motor Co.*, 280 Ark. 1, 655 S.W.2d 364 (1983).

personally visit the accident scene or go to the mechanic's shop to inspect the vehicles involved in the accident. Second, the expert could rely on facts that would be posited to him at trial in the form of a hypothetical question. When the proponent opts to rely on this source, she will, of course, have to introduce admissible evidence of all the facts stated in the hypothesis posed to the expert. Ordinarily, the trial judge will require that the proponent present the admissible evidence before calling the expert. In many cases, if not most, in wording the hypothesis the proponent specifies the facts which she wants the expert to assume. In other cases, the judge exempts the expert from being placed under "the Rule,"[103] and the proponent then invites the expert to assume the truth of particular testimony the expert has heard in court. Third, the expert may rely on hearsay sources of information. The expert certainly can do so when the hearsay would be independently admissible under Rules 803 and 804. Moreover, by the terms of Rule 703, the expert may even rely on hearsay information that would not be independently admissible so long as that type of information is reasonably relied on by experts in that particular field. Thus, an accident reconstruction expert might testify that he read the police report containing the officer's description of the accident scene.

Once the foundation is laid, the proponent could present the experiment's outcome to the trier in several different ways. The simplest way is to elicit a description of the outcome from a witness with personal knowledge. In addition, under Rule 901, the same witness could lay the foundation to authenticate a photograph or videotape of the experiment. The proponent usually prefers incorporating the latter method of presentation. A photograph or videotape helps the trier visualize the expert's testimony, and in turn usually enhances the trier's immediate understanding of the testimony.

§ 4-18(B) ELEMENTS OF THE FOUNDATION

To lay a proper predicate for evidence of an out-of-court experiment, the proponent must lay the following foundation:

1. The witness possesses the expertise to design and conduct the experiment.[104]
2. The proponent asked the witness to design and conduct an experiment.[105]

---

[103] *See* TEX. R. EVID. 614.

[104] The witness must qualify as an expert under Texas Rule of Evidence 702. In the accident reconstruction context, the witness might have prior experience as a traffic police officer and a background in engineering, notably physics. *Adams v. Smith,* 479 S.W.2d 390 (Tex. App.—Amarillo 1972).

[105] The request itself is not an assertive statement under Rule 801(a). Hence, the witness may testify to the request without violating the hearsay rule. Further, the witness may testify that he agreed to comply with the request without violating the hearsay rule. The promise to comply is a verbal act which is nonhearsay under Rule 801(c).

3. The witness studied the accident which the proponent asked the witness to duplicate.[106]
4. After studying the accident, the witness identified the variables which would have to be duplicated to replicate the accident. In laying this element of the foundation, the witness testifies as an expert.
5. In designing the experiment, the witness ensured that the experimental conditions were "substantially similar" to those at the time of the accident.[107]
6. The witness later conducted the experiment or supervised the experiment.[108]
7. The experiment yielded a particular result.

§ 4-18(C) SAMPLE FOUNDATION

The fact situation is a civil tort action. The plaintiff alleges that the defendant was driving inattentively and negligently rear-ended the plaintiffs car. In particular, the complaint alleges that but for his negligence, the defendant could have stopped his car in time to avoid striking the rear of the plaintiffs car. The proponent (the plaintiff) calls Professor Ernest Kams as her witness. Professor Kams will lay the foundation for an experiment about braking distance.

P Please state your full name and spell your last name for the record.

W My name is Ernest Kams. My last name is spelled K-A-M-S.

P WHERE do you live?

W I live in Houston, Texas.

P WHERE do you work? (1)

W I teach in the Engineering Department of Rice University.

P WHAT is your educational background? (1)

W I obtained my bachelor of science degree in mechanical engineering from Texas A & M University in 1990.

P In general terms, WHAT is engineering? (1)

W Engineers are specialists in using the laws of physics to create machines for human use.

---

[106] At this point, Rule 703 comes into play. *See* the discussion *supra.*

[107] *See* the discussion *supra* regarding the Texas courts' view on the degree of similarity required.

[108] Any instructions the witness issued or received for conducting the experiment would be nonhearsay under Rule 801(a), since they constitute imperative sentences. Furthermore, even if the witness did not personally conduct every facet of the experiment, under Rule 703 he could rely on hearsay reports from the other participants in the experiment.

P WHAT did you do after you obtained your bachelor's degree? (1)

W We moved to Ann Arbor, Michigan so I could begin my Graduate studies at the University of Michigan. I got my master's in 1992 and my doctorate in 1994.

P WHAT subjects did you study in the course of obtaining those degrees? (1)

W I pretty much specialized in vehicle dynamics.

P WHAT do you mean by the expression, "vehicle dynamics?" (1)

W That's the study of how vehicles, like cars, behave as they move and travel down a road.

P WHAT licenses do you hold in Texas? (1)

W I'm a licensed professional engineer.

P HOW many professional papers, if any, have you had published? (1)

W Approximately 20.

P WHAT topics did those papers relate to? (1)

W They all deal with aspects of vehicle dynamics. The vast majority of them relate to braking.

P WHAT professional engineering organizations, if any, do you belong to? (1)

W For years I've been a member of the Society of Automotive Engineers and the American Society of Mechanical Engineers. I've served as the president of the state chapter of the SAE, the Society of Automotive Engineers.

P WHAT practical experience, if any, do you have in vehicle dynamics? (1)

W I've consulted with major manufacturers such as General Motors and Chrysler on a number of brake system design projects.

P HOW many times, if ever, have you qualified as an expert witness in a court of law? (1)

W On over 50 occasions.

P WHAT topics did you testify about as an expert witness? (1)

W On every occasion I've testified about braking vehicles, including both passenger cars and trucks.

P Professor, WHERE were you on January 19, 2005? (2)

W I was at my office at Rice University in Houston.

P WHAT happened that day? (2)

W That was the day your associate phoned me about this case.

P WHO phoned you? (2)

W Your associate, Ms. Clark.

P WHAT, if anything, did she ask you to do? (2)

W She requested that I study the material about a braking problem in this case with a view to possibly testifying at this trial.

P Specifically, WHAT type of analysis did she ask you to perform? (2)

W Ms. Clark explained that it had been raining the day of the accident and that the defense might contend that the real cause of the accident was the design of the road. She said that the road curves just before the stop sign where the plaintiff's car had stopped. She said that she expected the defense to contend that on a rainy day, given that curve, even an attentive driver wouldn't be able to stop in time to avoid hitting a car sitting at the stop sign.

P WHAT, if anything, did you say to Ms. Clark? (2)

W I agreed to review the problem, conduct the analysis, and testify at trial if necessary.

P WHERE were you earlier today? (3) [*This assumes that the expert was not excluded from the courtroom.*]

W Right here in court.

P WHICH witnesses, if any, did you hear testify? (3)

W I heard the testimony by the witness to the accident, the mechanic, and the police officer.

P HOW well do you remember their testimony about the physical layout of this stretch of road, the type of vehicle, and the condition of both the tire tread and the brake lining? (3)

W I recall it well. I was paying special attention to that testimony.

P WHAT exhibits, if any, did you hear read? (3)

W I heard the weather report read into evidence.

P HOW well do you remember the contents of the report? (3)

W Again, I remember it quite well. I was trying to be especially attentive.

P Professor Kams, WHEN did you first hear this information about the stretch of road and the vehicle? (3)

W Actually, I got a lot of the information a few days after I spoke with Ms. Clark.

P HOW did you obtain the information? (3)

W A few days later Ms. Clark sent me a Federal Express package containing material about the case.

P Specifically, WHAT material did that package contain? (3)

W Let's see. As I recall, it included the police reports, a mechanic's reports on the post-accident inspection of both vehicles, a U.S. Weather Service report about the rain the day of the accident, and the depositions of both the plaintiff and the defendant.

P When you analyze braking problems, WHAT type of material do you ordinarily review? (3)

W Exactly the sort of material which Ms. Clark had sent me. I specifically asked her to send that material.

P HOW many experts in your field make it a practice to consider that type of material? (3)

W Virtually everyone. It would be irresponsible not to gather that type of material.

P WHAT other information, if any, did you gather? (3)

W In March, I drove to Conroe and inspected the stretch of road before I prepared my final design for the experiment.

P WHY did you do that? (3)

W I wanted to measure the coefficient of friction of that stretch of road.

P WHAT is a "coefficient of friction?" (3)

W It's sometimes loosely called the drag factor. In general terms, the type of road surface determines how much horizontal force you need to move an object across the road surface.

P HOW did you determine the coefficient of friction? (3)

W There's an instrument known as a drag sled or box that measures the coefficient. I brought mine with me from Houston, and I used the sled to personally measure the coefficient on the road surface where the accident occurred.

P Professor, for the balance of your testimony, I want you to take into consideration: (1) the coefficient of friction you personally measured; (2) the truth of the prior testimony about the section of road, the model of car, and the condition of the car's tire tread and brake lining; and (3) the truth of the weather report. (3)

W Very well.

P WHAT, if anything, did you do after studying all this written material and measuring the coefficient of friction? (5)

W At that point, I designed an experiment to duplicate the defendant's attempt to brake just before impact.

P HOW did you do that? (5)

W Whenever you design an experiment like this, you're trying to duplicate the conditions that were present at the time of the event. You identify the key conditions and try your best to replicate them.

P WHAT are the key conditions? (4)

W In a braking experiment like this, excluding the human factor, they're the following: the type of road and its coefficient of friction, the wet or dry condition of the surface, the condition of the tire tread, the condition of the brake lining, and the type of vehicle. The literature indicates that those are the most important variables.

P You said "excluding the human factor." WHY do you exclude that factor? (4)

W That's what you're trying to determine by this experiment. You're trying to figure out whether an attentive human could have braked in time. You duplicate the physical conditions in order to draw a conclusion about the other condition, namely, the attentiveness of the human being behind the wheel.

P After you identified these key conditions, WHAT did you do? (5)

W I went about trying to duplicate them.

P In particular, HOW did you do that? (5)

W Well, to begin with, we ran our experiment over the very same stretch of road. Then we got hold of another car of the same year, make, and model as the defendant's. We had the tire tread and brake lining modified by a mechanic to ensure that they were essentially identical to the tread and lining on the defendant's car at the time of this accident. Next, after reading the Weather Service report, we waited to conduct the experiment until there had been the same amount of rain on a given day as there had been the day of the accident. As I said, the wet or dry condition of the road surface will affect braking. I hired six test drivers from local auto manufacturing companies to take turns actually driving the car during the experiment.

P WHEN did you conduct the experiment? (6)

W We had our act together and the weather condition was almost ideal on June 1st. That's when we conducted the experiment.

P HOW did you conduct the experiment? (6)

W We initially coordinated with the Department of Public Safety to briefly block off that section of highway. They were very cooperative. I gave a detailed set of instructions to the test drivers. For example, I instructed the drivers to follow a particular route to the stop sign. It was the same route the defendant took that day. I also instructed them to drive at the same speed that the defendant claimed in his deposition. We had an unoccupied car parked at the stop sign in the same position in which the plaintiff had stopped. We didn't tell the test drivers that a car would be stopped there. We didn't want them to anticipate that and give them an unfair advantage in braking—a forewarning that the defendant did not have on the day of the accident.

P WHAT happened next? (6)

W We actually ran the experiment. Each driver drove the designated route and turned the curve at the speed indicated by the defendant.

P HOW do you know that they had the right speed? (6)

W Each time we ran the test, there was a researcher in the passenger seat. That person's sole responsibility was ensuring that the test driver hit the curve at the right speed. They did every time.

P Professor, at the time of the accident the defendant was the only occupant of his car. You've just said that during the test, there were both a driver and a researcher in the car, HOW might the presence of the second person have affected the outcome of your experiment? (6)

W It really wouldn't.

P WHY not? (6)

W To begin with, the researcher's weight wouldn't have affected the braking distance. Moreover, we instructed the researchers to remain both silent and stationary during the test. Their only function was to passively note the speed of the test car when the driver reached the curve.

P WHAT was the result of your experiment? (7)

W On each occasion, the driver stopped well before hitting the rear of the parked car.

P WHAT do you mean by "well before?" (7)

W The closest any test vehicle came to striking the car was 30 feet away. In the six tests, the average distance was 46 feet.

P WHAT do you mean by "the average distance"—from where to where? (7)

W From the rear of the vehicle parked at the stop sign to the front of the test vehicle.

P WHO measured the distance? (7)

W I did so myself.

P HOW did you measure the distance? (7)

W I used a type of tape measure officially approved by the Society of Automotive Engineers. It's the most accurate one available on the market.

At this point the proponent might lay the foundation for a videotape or photograph of the experiment.

CHAPTER 5
CREDIBILITY EVIDENCE

PART 1
INTRODUCTION TO CREDIBILITY EVIDENCE

§ 5-1 INTRODUCTION

The last chapter focuses on the probative value of evidence. To be admissible, evidence must have probative value in two senses. First, on its face, the evidence must be material. That is, the evidence must have some logical connection with the material facts of consequence in the case. In the words of Texas Rule of Evidence 401, the evidence must have some tendency to make the existence of any fact that is of consequence to the determination of the action more probable or less probable than it would be without the evidence. Secondly, as we have seen, the evidence must have underlying probative value. The common law will not accept evidence at face value and stubbornly insists that the proponent authenticate his or her evidence. As noted in the last chapter, Rules 104(b), 901, and 902 set out the authentication rules.

Even if the evidence is logically relevant in both senses, the trial judge may exclude the evidence on the ground that the evidence is legally irrelevant. The expression *legal irrelevance* is a rubric for excluding evidence on the theory that the probative dangers attending the evidence outweigh the evidence's probative value. Texas Rule of Evidence 403 states the doctrine: "[a]lthough relevant, evidence may be excluded if its probative value is substantially outweighed by the danger of unfair prejudice, confusion of the issues, or misleading the jury, or by considerations of undue delay, or needless presentation of cumulative evidence."

Underlying Rule 403 is a model of optimal jury behavior. Ideally, we want the jury to use admitted items of evidence as proof of only the factual propositions the judge admits them to prove, to ascribe the proper probative weight to each item of evidence, and to concentrate on the historical issues in dispute in the case. Rule 403 empowers the judge to exclude technically relevant evidence which realistically poses a danger to this model. This model not only explains the general discretionary power conferred on the judge under Rule 403. The model also helps explicate many of the more specific doctrines set out in Articles IV and VI of the Texas Rules of Evidence.

To begin with, if the judge admits an item of evidence to prove legitimately one factual proposition, courts do not want the jury to misuse the item as proof of another factual proposition in the case. This probative danger helps to explain the doctrine stated in Texas Rule 411 which generally excludes evidence of a defendant's liability insurance. Evidence of liability insurance creates a grave danger of jury misuse of the testimony. Once the jury learns of the existence of the insurance, they may be tempted to find the defendant liable even though the evidence of fault is weak. Evidence which realistically tempts the jury to decide the case on an improper basis is prejudicial within the meaning of that term in Rule 403.

Moreover, there may be a risk that the jury will overestimate the probative value of the evidence. Psychological studies indicate that, on the one hand, laypersons tend to attach a great deal of weight to evidence of specific instances of a litigant's bad behavior. For instance, after learning of a defendant's criminal record, the jurors may form a simplistic notion of the defendant's character and reason that "if he did it once, he probably did it again." On the other hand, the studies indicate that a person's general character is a poor predictor of the person's conduct in a specific situation. In short, lay jurors could easily overvalue evidence of a party's bad character. That risk, in part, accounts for the restrictions on character evidence in Rules 404 and 405.

Finally, the jurors should concentrate on the historical facts and events in dispute under the pleadings. It is true that the jurors must also resolve incidental disputes over the witnesses' credibility. To the extent that the jurors become bogged down in resolving credibility contests, however, they may lose sight of their primary task—the resolution of the historical merits of the case. This risk accounts for many of the limitations on credibility evidence in Article VI.

As previously stated, these probative dangers help explain the specific rules in Articles IV and VI and also factor into the general balancing test stated in Rule 403. Even when an item of evidence passes muster under the specific rules in Articles IV and VI, in most instances, the judge has discretion to exclude the item if the judge concludes that the probative dangers substantially outweigh the probative value of the item. Note two features of Rule 403. First, the rule is cast in the passive voice, suggesting that the opponent of the admission of the evidence has the burden of persuading the judge that the probative dangers outstrip the probative value. Second, the rule includes the adverb "substantially." The opponent must not only convince the judge that the dangers outweigh the probative value; the opponent must also convince the judge that the dangers do so by a wide margin. Rule 403 thus reflects a marked bias in favor of the admission of logically relevant evidence.

§ 5-2 IMPEACHMENT OF WITNESS BY EITHER SIDE

In discussing foundations for impeaching a witness, it is important to note briefly that under Texas Rule of Evidence 607, either side may impeach a witness, without regard to who called the witness to the stand. In other words, the common-law voucher rule in Texas no longer exists.[1] That is, counsel is not

---

[1] *See generally* WENDORF, SCHLUETER & BARTON, TEXAS RULES OF EVIDENCE MANUAL, VI-34 (6th ed. 2002).

considered to vouch for the credibility of a witness by calling that witness to the stand. Counsel may not, however, call a witness to the stand for the express purpose of impeaching the witness with prior inconsistent statements that counsel wants the jury to hear.[2]

§ 5-3 THE STAGES OF CREDIBILITY ANALYSIS

There are three stages in credibility evidence: *bolstering, impeachment*, and *rehabilitation*. Typically, they arise as follows. If the trial judge rules that the prospective witness is competent,[3] the judge or the clerk administers the oath to the witness. The witness's proponent immediately begins direct examination. As soon as the witness answers one question on direct examination, his or her credibility becomes a relevant issue in the case.

The proponent naturally wants to build up the witness's believability or credibility in the jury's eyes. Conversely, the opponent wants to tear down that credibility. The opponent's attacks on the witness's credibility are termed *impeachment*. If the proponent attempts to build up the witness's credibility before any attempted impeachment, the proponent is said to be *bolstering* the witness's credibility. For example, the proponent might attempt to increase the witness's credibility during the direct examination before the opponent has had any opportunity to cross-examine the witness. If the proponent attempts to repair the witness's credibility after attempted impeachment, the proponent is said to be *rehabilitating* the witness's credibility. If the opponent attempted to impeach during cross-examination, the proponent could attempt to rehabilitate the witness during redirect.

Most of the evidence law dealing with credibility focuses on impeachment. For that reason, most of the sections in this chapter deal with the various impeachment techniques. Some of the impeachment techniques may be used only during cross-examination of the witness to be impeached—intrinsic impeachment. The opponent may use the technique then, but the opponent must accept the witness's answer in the sense that the opponent may not present other evidence to contradict the witness's answer. Section 5-7, *infra*, deals with such a technique, proof that the witness has committed bad acts which have not resulted in a conviction.

Other impeachment techniques necessarily entail extrinsic evidence and cannot be used during cross-examination. Sections 5-8 and 5-9, *infra*, are illustrative. Section 5–8 deals with proof that witness #1 has a character trait of untruthfulness. Use of this technique requires that the opponent present witness #2, a character witness, to testify to the bad character of witness #1. Section 5-9

[2] *Zule v. State*, 802 S.W.2d 28 (Tex. App.—Corpus Christi 1990).

[3] *See* Chapter 3.

discusses specific contradictions. In this technique, the opposing attorney calls witness #2 to contradict facts asserted in witness #1's testimony.

The remaining impeachment techniques permit both cross-examination and extrinsic evidence. Sections 5-10 through 5-13 analyze these techniques:

- prior inconsistent statements,
- convictions,
- bias, and
- attacks on the witness—mental capacity.

In reviewing the credibility doctrines in this chapter, the reader should remember that the doctrines are largely explicable in terms of the model of jury behavior underlying Rule 403. All of the evidence in question is logically relevant to the witness's credibility, but the doctrines discussed in this chapter restrict the admissibility of credibility evidence in the hope that the jury will focus primarily on the historical merits of the case.

PART 2
BOLSTERING WITNESSES BEFORE IMPEACHMENT

§ 5-4 GENERAL RULE—BOLSTERING PROHIBITED

The general rule regarding bolstering is clear: it is prohibited. The reason for the rule rests on the assumption that bolstering a witness before the witness has been attacked may be a waste of valuable time. If the opposing counsel has no intention of impeaching a witness, there is usually no need to make the witness look good in the eyes of the jury. Of course, if the opposing counsel actually attacks the credibility of a witness, then counsel is permitted to rehabilitate that witness. Thus, the distinction between impermissible bolstering and permissible rehabilitation is a question of timing. Impermissible bolstering is premature rehabilitation.

Texas law has recognized two exceptions to the general rule against bolstering. They are discussed in the next sections.

§ 5-5 EXCEPTIONS TO RULE PROHIBITING BOLSTERING

§ 5-5(A) PRIOR IDENTIFICATION

§ 5-5(A)(1) The Doctrine

The general common-law rule is that the proponent may not bolster the witness's credibility before any attempted impeachment. The jurors' principal focus should be on the historical issues in the case rather than on the witness's credibility. To ensure that the jurors maintain that focus, the common law excludes evidence of the witness's believability until the opponent has attacked the witness.

There are special exceptions to the rule. One exception is the prior identification doctrine. In Texas, as in many jurisdictions, if the witness has already made an in-court identification of a person such as the criminal defendant, the witness's proponent may prove that the witness made a pretrial identification of the same person. The prior identification is not admitted as substantive evidence that the prior identification was correct. Instead, the proof is admitted for the limited purpose of increasing the witness's credibility. The fact that the witness identified the same person on a prior occasion tends to strengthen the inference of the witness's credibility. At least the witness is consistent. When the judge admits prior identification evidence on this theory, the opponent is entitled to a limiting instruction under Texas Rule 105. Upon the opponent's request, the judge must instruct the jury that the proof is not admitted as substantive evidence, but only on a bolstering theory.

But the Texas Rules of Evidence, like their federal counterpart, take a step beyond this view and permit the proponent to use the prior identification as substantive evidence that the person identified was the perpetrator or actor. Texas Rule of Evidence 801(e)(1)(C) exempts prior identification evidence from the definition of hearsay. The effect of the exemption is to enable the proponent to use the evidence as substantive proof. On this theory, the opponent has no right to a limiting instruction. Some courts have construed Federal Rule of Evidence 801(d)(1)(C)[4] as applying even when the witness cannot make an in-court identification. The Supreme Court has held that a prior identification may be admitted as substantive evidence even when, at trial, the witness cannot explain the basis for the pretrial identification.[5]

It is important to note, however, that this exception to the general rule against bolstering is not available, at least in criminal cases, where another witness testifies that he or she saw another person make the pretrial identification. Under what has been labeled as the *Lyons* rule,[6] any attempts to use Witness B to show that Witness A made a pretrial identification before Witness A is impeached amount to impermissible bolstering.[7]

---

[4] This is the counterpart to Texas Rule 801(e)(1)(C).

[5] *See United States v. Owens*, 484 U.S. 554 (1988).

[6] *See Lyons v. State*, 388 S.W.2d 950 (Tex. Crim. App. 1965).

[7] *See generally* WENDORF, SCHLUETER & BARTON, TEXAS RULES OF EVIDENCE MANUAL VIII-31 (6th ed. 2002).

§ 5-5(A)(2) Elements of the Foundation

To introduce evidence of a prior identification, the proponent must show that:

1. The witness has already made an in-court identification of the person.
2. The witness had a pretrial opportunity to observe the person.
3. The witness had an adequate opportunity to observe the person.
4. The pretrial encounter was conducted in a fair manner.
5. At the pretrial encounter, the witness identified the same person.

§ 5-5(A)(3) Sample Foundation

The fact situation is a tort action arising from a hit-and-run accident. The plaintiff calls a witness, Jane Morris. The witness is prepared to testify that the defendant was the driver of the hit-and-run car. She is also ready to testify that she identified the defendant at a lineup at the local police station shortly after the accident. The witness has already described the accident which occurred at noontime. The proponent is the plaintiff.

P WHAT did the car do after it struck the plaintiff?

W It sped away from the scene.

P WHO was driving that car? (1)

W The defendant.

P WHERE is he sitting? (1)

W At the end of the table over there to the right.

P HOW is he dressed? (1)

W He's wearing a blue suit, white shirt, and striped tie.

P Your Honor, may the record reflect that the witness has identified the defendant, John Ursin? (1)

J It will so reflect.

P Ms. Morris, HOW many times have you seen the defendant? (2)

W Three times.

P WHAT were those occasions? (2)

W Well, I saw him at the scene of the accident, today in court, and one other time.

P WHAT was that other time? (2)

W It was at a lineup at the police station on Laredo Street.

P WHEN did this lineup occur? (2)

W It was about 5:00 P.M. on the afternoon of the accident.

P WHERE did the police hold this lineup? (2)

W It was on a stage in the big room off the entrance.

P HOW was the lighting in the room? (3)

W It was fine.

P HOW close were you to the stage? (3)

W I was only 10 feet away.

P HOW were you facing? (3)

W I was facing straight ahead and looking at all the men in the lineup.

P HOW long did the police permit you to observe the lineup? (3)

W They gave me as much time as I wanted. I didn't need long.

P HOW many men were in the lineup? (4)

W There were six.

P HOW were they dressed? (4)

W They all were wearing dark clothes.

P HOW tall were they? (4)

W They were roughly the same height, five-ten to six feet.

P WHAT, if anything, did the police say about the men in the lineup? (4)

W They didn't say anything. They just ushered me into the room and asked me if I recognized anyone.

P WHAT did the men in the lineup do while they were on the stage? (4)

W Nothing. They just stood there.

P WHAT happened after the lineup? (5)

W The police asked me if I recognized the driver of the car in the lineup.

P WHAT did you say? (5)

W I told them that I did.

P WHOM did you identify at that lineup? (5)

W The defendant, the same person I just pointed out in court.

O Your Honor, at this time, I would request a limiting instruction under Rule 105.

P Your Honor, may we be heard?

J Yes.

P Under Texas Rule of Evidence 801(e)(1)(C), we are permitted to introduce this witness's pretrial identification as nonhearsay, substantive evidence.

Thus, opposing counsel is not entitled to a limiting instruction. Indeed, because it is admissible as substantive evidence, the jury may also consider it on the issue of the weight to attach to the witnesses' credibility.

J The request for a limiting instruction is denied.

§ 5-5(B) Sexual Assault Victim's Complaint

§ 5-5(B)(1) The Doctrine

Another exception to the rule against bolstering is the fresh complaint doctrine, sometimes also referred to as "outcry evidence." Although there is no specific Texas Rule of Evidence covering this exception, Texas case law has recognized it in cases involving rape, or what is now more commonly referred to as sexual assault.[8]

The underlying assumption is that the victim of this type of offense is likely to make an immediate report or complaint about the offense. The fact of a fresh complaint or outcry by the victim tends to strengthen the inference of the truthfulness of the complainant. Moreover, especially in sex offense cases, there is often a need for credibility evidence. There are rarely eyewitnesses, and the trial usually becomes a swearing contest between the victim and the alleged assailant.

Under this theory, the Texas courts usually restrict the evidence to proof that the victim made a complaint about a sexual assault and identified a certain person as the perpetrator. The other details of the offense are normally inadmissible. As in the case of prior identification evidence, the opponent is entitled to a limiting instruction. The judge is admitting the proof as credibility evidence rather than as substantive proof that a certain person committed the offense. On the other hand, the fresh complaint may also qualify as an excited utterance. As Chapter 11 notes, excited utterances fall within an exception to the hearsay rule. If the outcry, or fresh complaint, statement qualifies as an excited utterance, all the details about the offense are admissible and, more importantly, the details are admissible as substantive evidence. If they are admissible, the jury may also consider the victim's statements in assessing credibility.

§ 5-5(B)(2) Elements of the Foundation

To introduce evidence that a victim made a complaint, the proponent must show that:

1. The victim made a complaint.
2. The victim made the complaint shortly after the offense.

---

[8] *See generally* Ray, Texas Law of Evidence § 775 (West Tex. Prac. Vol. 1, 3d ed. 1980).

3. The victim made the complaint to the authorities or to the first person he or she encountered after the offense.
4. The report stated that the complainant was the victim of an offense.
5. The report identified the perpetrator of the offense.

§ 5-5(B)(3) Sample Foundation

The fact situation is a criminal prosecution for kidnapping and rape. The victim, Ms. McDonald, is on the stand on direct examination. She has already testified that the defendant abducted her, drove her to a remote cabin, raped her, and then left her tied in the cabin. The proponent is the prosecutor.

P WHAT did you do after the defendant left?

W I struggled to get free from the ropes. Fortunately, the knot was so loose that I got free.

P WHAT did you do next?

W I got out of the cabin and started running down the dirt road. I wanted to escape and get back to safety.

P WHAT, if anything, happened while you were running down the road?

W I ran into a fellow driving a Jeep.

P WHO was this person? (3)

W He told me that his name was Jeff Seltzer.

P Between the time you escaped from the cabin and the time you met Mr. Seltzer, HOW many people had you met? (3)

W None. He was the very first person I met after escaping.

P HOW much time elapsed between the rape and the time you met Mr. Seltzer? (2)

W About an hour.

P HOW much time elapsed between your escape from the cabin and the time you met Mr. Seltzer? (2)

W Only about five minutes. I hadn't run very far before I met him.

P WHAT, if anything, happened after you met Mr. Seltzer? (1)

W I told him everything that had happened. Then he gave me a ride back to town and took me to the hospital.

P Precisely WHAT did you tell him? (4)

W I said I had just been raped at a cabin just up the road.

P WHO did you say had raped you? (5)

W I said it was the defendant, Henry Miles.

O Your Honor, at this time I request a limiting instruction under Rule 105.

J Ladies and gentlemen of the jury, you have just heard Ms. McDonald testify that she made a complaint to Mr. Seltzer shortly after the alleged offense. In this complaint, she said she had been raped and that the defendant was the rapist. You may not consider her testimony as proof that, in fact, a rape occurred or that the defendant was the rapist. I'm admitting the testimony only for whatever light, if any, it sheds on Ms. McDonald's credibility. You must decide whether the fact that she made this complaint affects her credibility.[9]

PART 3
IMPEACHMENT OF WITNESSES

§ 5-6 IMPEACHMENT TECHNIQUES—IN GENERAL

The next sections discuss the foundations or predicates which must be established to impeach a witness through one or more impeachment techniques. In each of these techniques, it is important to remember that even assuming counsel has complied with the evidence rules or law governing the particular technique, the trial court has the discretion to exclude the evidence under Texas Rule of Evidence 403, discussed *supra* at § 5-1. For example, the court may limit the number of character witnesses counsel intends to call to impeach another witness. Or, the court may determine that otherwise admissible impeachment evidence is too prejudicial because it will unnecessarily and improperly stir the emotions of the jury. The impeachment techniques discussed in the following sections are as follows:

- specific acts of a witness
- character evidence
- contradiction of testimony
- prior inconsistent statements
- prior conviction
- proof of bias
- attacks on element of witness's competency

[9] Note that in this case the proponent is not attempting to introduce the victim's statement as an exception to the hearsay rule. Thus, the jury is not entitled to consider her statement for its substantive truth.

§ 5-7 SPECIFIC ACTS THAT HAVE NOT RESULTED IN A CONVICTION

§ 5-7(A) THE DOCTRINE

§ 5-7(A)(1) The Federal Rule

Many jurisdictions permit the opponent to impeach the witness with proof that the witness has committed untruthful acts, i.e., acts which are probative of truthfulness. Under Federal Rule of Evidence 608(b), the opponent may do so even if the acts have not resulted in the witness's conviction. That Rule states the prevailing view:

> Specific instances of conduct—Specific instances of the conduct of a witness, for the purpose of attacking . . . the witness' character for truthfulness, other than conviction of crime as provided in Rule 609, may not be proved by extrinsic evidence. They may, however, in the discretion of the court, if probative of . . . untruthfulness, be inquired into on cross-examination of the witness . . . concerning the witness' character for . . . untruthfulness . . . .

Under the Federal Rule, the theory of logical relevance is simple: if the witness has been willing to commit untruthful and deceitful acts in the past, the witness may be willing to lie on the witness stand. Of course, the doctrine is limited to acts which reflect adversely on the witness's truthfulness.

The opponent, under the Federal Rule, is ordinarily restricted to cross-examination. On cross-examination, the opponent may inquire whether the witness committed the act. However, the opponent must accept, or take, the answer in the sense that the opponent cannot use extrinsic evidence to contradict the answer. Thus, if witness #1, the witness to be impeached, denies committing the deceitful act, the opponent cannot call witness #2 to testify that he or she was an eyewitness to witness #1's act. This restriction is a remnant of the broader, common-law collateral fact rule. The collateral fact rule announces that the impeaching attorney is limited to intrinsic impeachment when the impeaching fact relates only to the witness's credibility. An untruthful act may reflect adversely on the witness's credibility; however, the argument runs that when the act has no relevance to the merits of the case, it would be an undue expenditure of time to allow the impeaching attorney to present extrinsic evidence. By banning the use of extrinsic evidence, the first sentence of Federal Rule 608(b) codifies this application of the collateral fact rule.

§ 5-7(A)(2) The Texas Rule

The Texas rule governing impeachment through evidence of prior specific acts is contrary to the Federal rule, *supra* at § 5-7(A)(1). Texas Rule of Evidence

608(b) specifically prohibits counsel from attacking (or supporting) a witness's credibility by inquiring into that witness's specific instances of conduct. Nor may counsel prove such acts by extrinsic evidence.

Despite the limitations in Texas Rule 608(b), counsel may, nonetheless, find support in other rules for using specific instances of conduct to impeach a witness. First, Texas case law recognizes the ability of counsel to introduce evidence of specific instances of conduct to rebut a witness's blanket denial of wrongdoing.[10] This evidence is considered admissible to rebut the false impression left by the witness's testimony and is usually raised by statements such as "I have never done anything like that." Second, under Texas Rule of Evidence 613, counsel may inquire into circumstances or statements showing a witness's bias. That would include specific acts or instances of conduct which demonstrate a particular bias. The topic of impeaching a witness through bias evidence is discussed *infra* at § 5-12. Third, a witness's specific instances of conduct might be otherwise admissible under Rule 404(b) to show motive, plan, intent, etc. Admissibility of evidence under Rule 404(b) is discussed in Chapter 6. Finally, inquiry into specific instances of conduct can be used to test a character witness's testimony. But the specific instances of conduct in that situation are not those of the character witness. Instead, the questioner asks the character witness if he or she has heard about, or knows about, the target or principal witness's specific instances of conduct in an attempt to challenge the basis of the character witness's opinion or reputation testimony. This point is discussed in more detail *infra* at § 5-8(D).

§ 5-7(B) ELEMENTS OF THE FOUNDATION

Assuming that under the Texas Rules, counsel is able to introduce evidence of a person's specific acts for impeachment, the following elements must generally be shown:

1. When the witness committed the act.
2. Where the witness committed the act.

§ 5-7(C) SAMPLE FOUNDATION

The following scenario demonstrates use of a witness's prior specific instances of conduct to rebut the false impression left by the witness's direct examination. The fact situation is a criminal case in which the defendant, Emile Swart, has testified on direct examination that he has never been in trouble with the law before. The prosecutor is the opponent and is cross-examining the defendant.

O Now, Mr. Swart, you testified that you have never been in trouble before with the law, ISN'T THAT CORRECT?

[10] *See, e.g., Trans-State Pavers, Inc. v. Haynes*, 808 S.W.2d 727 (Tex. App.—Beaumont 1991, writ den.); *Cevallos v. State*, 755 S.W.2d 901 (Tex. App.—San Antonio 1988, pet. ref.).

W Yes.

O ISN'T IT CORRECT THAT on May 2, 2004, you were arrested by the Oklahoma City police? (1)

W Yes.

P And ISN'T IT A FACT THAT you were eventually indicted by Oklahoma authorities for illegal transfer of cocaine to your roommate? (2)

W Yes. But the charges were later dismissed.

P Well, even so, ISN'T IT TRUE that, in fact, you have been in trouble with the law before?

W If you say so.

§ 5-8 PROOF OF THE CHARACTER TRAIT OF UNTRUTHFULNESS

§ 5-8(A) In General

To impeach the witness, the opponent may prove that the witness has a character trait of untruthfulness. The opponent uses the proof of the character trait as circumstantial proof of conduct. The opponent reasons that if the witness has that character trait, the character trait increases the probability that the witness is lying, or acting in conformity with the character trait.

Unlike the last impeachment technique, the technique of using character evidence is not limited to the cross-examination of the witness to be impeached. Quite to the contrary, the opponent usually resorts to extrinsic evidence. To impeach witness #1, the opponent calls witness #2 who testifies that witness #1 has a character trait of untruthfulness. The courts usually term witness #2 a *character witness*. Witness #1 can be labeled as either the *principal witness* or the *target witness*. In Texas, under Rule 405(a), the character witness may present either *opinion* or *reputation* evidence about the target witness. In the former case, the character witness describes witness #1's reputation for untruthfulness in the community. In the latter case, the character witness expresses his or her personal opinion of witness #1's truthfulness.

§ 5-8(B) Reputation Testimony

§ 5-8(B)(1) The Doctrine

As noted in § 5-8(A), *supra*, a character witness may impeach another witness by offering testimony that the target witness does not have a good reputation for telling the truth. Under Texas Rule of Evidence 405, the character witness must have some basis for knowing the target witness's reputation. Although the character witness need not know the target witness personally, he or she must have been in a position to hear what others have said about the target witness.

§ 5-8(B)(2) Elements of the Foundation

The foundation for introducing reputation evidence about a witness's character trait for truthfulness includes these elements:

1. Witness #2 is a member of the same community (residential or social) as witness #1. Modernly, any large social group can qualify as a community. For instance, a church congregation or the student body of a school can constitute a community. In a Texas criminal case, the character witness must have been familiar with witness #1's reputation before the date of the charged offense.[11]
2. Witness #1 has a reputation for untruthfulness in the community.
3. Witness #2 knows witness #1's reputation for untruthfulness.

Some courts may permit witness #2 to add that, in light of witness #1's poor reputation for truthfulness, witness #2 would not believe witness #1's testimony.

§ 5-8(B)(3) Sample Foundation

The following is a reputation foundation. The witness to be impeached is Mr. Harding:

P WHO is Mr. Harding?

W He's a fellow office worker at Lobbs Electric.

P WHEN is the last time you saw him?

W Here in the courtroom. He testified for the other side a couple of hours ago.

P WHERE does he live? (1)

W Here in El Paso.

P HOW long have you known Mr. Harding? (2)

W For over 10 years.

P Does Mr. Harding have a reputation for truthfulness or untruthfulness at Lobbs Electric? (2)

W Oh, yes.

P WHAT is that reputation? (2)

W It's bad. He's known as an untruthful person.

---

[11] *See* TEX. R. EVID. 405(a).

P Given Mr. Harding's reputation, would you believe him under oath? (3)

W No.

§ 5-8(C) OPINION TESTIMONY

§ 5-8(C)(1) The Doctrine

As noted *supra* at § 5-8(A), a character witness may impeach another witness (a target witness) through opinion testimony. The character witness testifies that he or she is personally familiar with the target witness and has a low opinion of that witness's character for truthfulness.

§ 5-8(C)(2) Elements of the Foundation

The foundation for presenting a character witness's opinion testimony about another witness includes the following elements:

1. Witness #2 is personally acquainted with witness #1.
2. Witness #2 knows witness #1 well enough to have formed an opinion of witness #1's truthfulness.
3. Witness #2 has an opinion of witness #1's untruthfulness.
4. Witness #2 has the opinion that witness #1 is an untruthful person.

Some courts may permit witness #2 to opine whether, given that opinion, he or she would believe witness #1 under oath.

§ 5-8(C)(3) Sample Foundation

The following fact situation demonstrates use of a character witness's opinion testimony about a Mr. Harding:

P WHO is Mr. Harding? (1)

W He's an acquaintance of mine.

P WHEN is the last time you saw him?

W Here in the courtroom. He testified for the other side a few hours ago.

P HOW did you come to know him? (2)

W We've worked in the same company for a long time. I've had a lot of contact with him.

P HOW many years have you known him? (2)

W I'd say easily nine years.

P In WHAT contexts have you known him? (2)

W As I said, we've worked for the same company, Lobbs Electric, for a long time. I see him at least several times a day around the plant.

P HOW often do you talk with him? (2)

W Usually several times a week. We're always bumping into each other on various projects.

P Do you have an opinion of his truthfulness? (3)

W Yes, I do.

P WHAT is that opinion? (4)

W In my opinion, he's an untruthful person.

P Given that opinion, would you believe Mr. Harding under oath? (4)

W No.

Note that the courts will normally not permit counsel to inquire into what specific instances of conduct or acts have led the character witness to have a poor opinion of the target witness's character for truthfulness. That limitation is another example of the collateral fact rule, discussed *supra* at § 5-7(A)(1). That is, permitting counsel to spread out a witness's prior acts would further detract from the historical facts before the jury. But, as the following discussion points out, the cross-examiner may ask the character witness "have you heard" and "did you know" questions.

Even if Harding were a party to the litigation, this evidence would be admissible only for the limited purpose of aiding the jury in assessing his credibility. Thus, even if Harding were a civil defendant in a tort action (not involving moral turpitude, see Rule 404(a)(1)(B)), on request the trial judge would give the jurors a limiting instruction that they could not treat this testimony as proof that Harding is a bad person and therefore more likely to have committed the alleged tort. For the same reason, during closing argument it would be objectionable for the proponent to indicate to the jury that Harding's reputation for untruthfulness was evidence that he committed the tortious conduct alleged by the plaintiff.

§ 5-8(D) Impeachment of Character Witnesses

When a character witness takes the stand to impeach another witness, he or she also becomes vulnerable to impeachment. Thus, a character witness could be impeached by showing that the witness has made prior inconsistent statements or has a prior felony conviction. A very common way of impeaching the character witness is to show that despite their adverse testimony, they really do not know the reputation of witness #1, nor do they know witness #1 well enough personally to form an opinion about that witness's character for truthfulness. Texas Rule of Evidence 405(a) specifically recognizes this form of impeachment of character witnesses. The classical way of doing this is to ask the character (reputation) witness, i.e., witness #2, whether he or she has heard about acts of witness #1 that are probative of truthfulness.

Having asked the question, counsel is usually stuck with the answer. That is, counsel may not introduce extrinsic evidence of the specific instance of conduct in an attempt to impeach the character witness.

Likewise, in the case of a character witness who has expressed an opinion about witness #1, the cross-examiner is permitted to ask the witness whether he or she knows that witness #1 has done something which exhibits truthfulness, e.g., made a truthful statement at great personal risk. In either case, the cross-examiner must (1) have a good faith basis for asking the question, and (2) be prepared to show that the incident in question is relevant to the character witness's testimony, i.e., it relates to the character trait of truthfulness.

The Texas courts generally do not permit cross-overs on cross-examination. Thus, the cross-examiner may not attempt to convert a reputation witness into an opinion witness by the form of the cross-examination questions.[12]

§ 5-9 IMPEACHMENT BY CONTRADICTION

Although there is no specific Texas Rule of Evidence addressing the point, a traditional impeachment technique is to show that a witness's testimony is contradicted by another witness's testimony. For example, witness #1 testifies to *A*, and the opposing attorney calls witness #2 to testify to non-*A*. The impeaching effect of witness #2's testimony is indirect and inferential: if witness #2 is correct, witness #1 must be mistaken or lying.

Suppose, for example, that plaintiff's witness #1 testifies that the traffic light facing the defendant's car was red. The defense calls witness #2, who testifies that the light facing the defendant's car was green. Because witness #2's testimony is logically relevant to the historical merits, it is admissible both to prove that the light was green and to impeach witness #1 by contradiction.

The problem arises when witness #2's testimony is logically relevant only to witness #1's credibility. Suppose a traffic accident occurred in a rural area near Bryan, Texas. During his direct examination, witness #1 testified that he was walking near the intersection where the collision occurred. Witness #1 adds that in the adjacent field, there were about 20 head of cattle grazing. During the defense case-in-chief, the defense calls the rancher who owns the field. The rancher is prepared to testify that there were only 10 head of cattle grazing at the time. The rancher's testimony would specifically contradict witness #1's testimony. The rancher's testimony is logically relevant to impeach witness #1; if the rancher is correct, witness #1 erred in perception or memory. The rancher's testimony has no logical relevance to the historical merits, however, because the

---

[12] *See* WENDORF, SCHLUETER & BARTON, TEXAS RULES OF EVIDENCE MANUAL IV-106 TO IV-108 (6th ed. 2002).

number of cattle in the field has no impact on the facts relating to the traffic accident. The common-law collateral fact rule would have mandated the exclusion of the farmer's testimony.

An argument can be made, however, that such evidence would be governed by Rule 403. The judge weighs the importance of the witness and the strength of the inference that the witness is wrong about the historical merits if the witness is wrong about the detail in question. When the witness is the star witness for one side and the inference is strong, the judge can admit the extrinsic evidence. As an earlier edition of the McCormick hornbook explained:

> Suppose a witness has told a story of a transaction crucial to the controversy. To prove him wrong in some trivial detail of time, place or circumstance is collateral. But to prove untrue some fact recited by the witness that if he were really there and saw what he claims to have seen, he could not have been mistaken about, is a convincing kind of impeachment that the courts must make place for . . . . To disprove such a fact is to pull out the linchpin of the story. [W]e must recognize this . . . type of allowable contradiction . . . of any part of the witness's account of the background of a material transaction, which as a matter of human experience he would not have been mistaken about if his story were true.[13]

Suppose, for example, that in the hypothetical, witness #1 testified that there is a large, red barn at the intersection. The rancher will testify that the fields near the intersection are vacant and that the nearest red barn is two miles away at another intersection. If witness #1 is mistaken about the barn, he may be testifying about another collision at another intersection. Under Rule 403, the trial judge would probably be justified in admitting the rancher's testimony to contradict witness #1.

If the extrinsic evidence in question passes muster under Rule 403, the proponent must simply ensure that he or she lays all of the other foundations normally required for that type of evidence. In the case of the rancher's testimony, the only required foundation would be firsthand knowledge of the vicinity. Assume, for instance, that all the intersections in question are located within Meridian Township. The proponent might establish the rancher's personal familiarity:

P WHERE do you live?

W I live just outside Bryan.

P HOW long have you lived there?

W All my life. I was raised right here.

---

[13] C. McCORMICK, EVIDENCE § 47, at 111–12 (3d ed. 1984).

P HOW many years have you lived here?

W Fifty-two years, give or take a couple of months.

P HOW familiar are you with the roads in this area?

W Real familiar. At one time or another, I've probably driven every one of them a time or two.

P HOW well do you know the intersection of FM 1111 and 9999?

W Real well. I live only about three miles from there. In fact, it's on the route I take to town almost every weekday.

P HOW well do you know the intersection formed by FM 1111 and 8888?

W Just about as well. That's right on the way we take to church on Sundays.

At this point, the proponent would elicit the rancher's testimony. A common technique for highlighting the contradiction is to preface the questions to the rancher with references to the contradictory testimony by the earlier witness:

P Earlier today, a plaintiff's witness, Mr. Greenfield, testified that there's a large red barn at the intersection of FM 1111 and FM 9999. WHAT buildings, if any, are there at that intersection?

Some judges permit such references. The proponent certainly has no right, however, to make such cross-references. The cross-references are declarative statements about witness #1's testimony, and the only right the proponent has during the examination of witness #2 is to put questions to witness #2.

During closing argument, the proponent would tell the jury that the farmer's testimony establishes that Greenfield was mistaken about the existence of a large red barn at the intersection of FM 1111 and FM 8888. The proponent would argue that Greenfield's mistake calls into question the reliability of his testimony on the merits about the accident. The proponent would explain that if Greenfield was mistaken about the barn, he might have been at another intersection and witnessed an accident other than the one involving the plaintiff and defendant.

§ 5-10 IMPEACHMENT BY PRIOR INCONSISTENT STATEMENT

§ 5-10(A) IN GENERAL

The issue of impeachment by showing a witness's specific instances of conduct is discussed in § 5-7. As previously stated, that technique, if it can be used at all, is ordinarily limited to intrinsic impeachment, that is, the cross-examination of the witness to be impeached. At the opposite extreme are the impeachment techniques discussed *supra* at §§ 5-8 and 5-9: proof of witness #1's character trait of untruthfulness, and witness #2's testimony specifically contradicting witness #1's testimony. Those techniques require extrinsic evidence. This section begins a discussion of a series of impeachment techniques which can be developed by either cross-examination or extrinsic evidence. The first such technique is proof that the witness made a prior statement inconsistent with his or her trial testimony.

Consider the following hypothetical. Mr. Miller's car collided with Ms. Dolan's van at the intersection of University and Felton Streets. Mr. Miller's car is red and Ms. Dolan's van is blue. Mr. Williams happened to be standing at a corner of the intersection when the collision occurred. Later that day, he had a conversation with his neighbor, Mr. Jensen. During the conversation, he told Mr. Jensen that he witnessed the collision and that the collision occurred because the red car (Mr. Miller's car) ran a red light. Mr. Miller files a personal injury action against Ms. Dolan. At the trial, Mr. Miller calls Mr. Williams as a witness. On direct examination, Mr. Williams testifies that he witnessed the collision and that Ms. Dolan's van caused the accident by running a red light. On cross-examination, may the defense attorney call Mr. Jensen as a defense witness to testify to Mr. Williams's earlier statement? As noted in the last section, counsel may call witness #2 specifically to contradict witness #1's testimony. May counsel similarly prove that witness #1 has contradicted himself or herself by making an inconsistent statement?

§ 5-10(B) Cross-Examination Eliciting a Witness's Concession of an Inconsistent Statement

§ 5-10(B)(1) The Doctrine: An Overview

As soon as Mr. Williams testifies at the trial, his credibility becomes one of the relevant facts in issue in the case. Common sense suggests that the jury is entitled to know that Mr. Williams made an earlier, inconsistent statement. The fact that he has made inconsistent statements about the same fact calls into question his memory and sincerity. In everyday life, if a person tells us differing stories about the same event, we pause before deciding to believe either story. For that reason, the Texas Rules permit the defense attorney to cross-examine Mr. Williams about his statement to Mr. Jensen. Texas Rule 613(a) makes it clear that the cross-examination of Williams about the earlier statement is a proper method of impeachment.

The goal is to obtain a concession from the witness that he or she made the prior inconsistent statement. That failing, counsel may be able to introduce extrinsic evidence of the prior inconsistent statement. That point is discussed *infra* at § 5-10(F).

The jurors can infer from Williams' inconsistency that he is either uncertain or lying. Thus, the fact of the inconsistent statement is relevant to credibility even if the facts mentioned in the statement are false. The proponent may mention the statements during closing argument, but the proponent must make it clear that he or she is asking the jury to consider the statements for the purpose of evaluating the witness's consistency and credibility. It would be objectionable for the proponent to suggest to the jury that it could treat the statements as proof of the facts asserted in the statements.

§ 5-10(B)(2) Hearsay Issues; Limiting Instructions

As discussed in Chapter 10, whenever counsel introduces evidence of an out-of-court statement, there are potential hearsay issues. If Ms. Dolan's attorney forced Mr. Williams to concede the earlier statement to Mr. Jensen, Mr. Miller's attorney may be entitled to a Rule 105 limiting instruction if the statement does not otherwise satisfy the hearsay rule, either as an exemption or as an exception. In the instruction, the judge would tell the jurors that they could not use Mr. Williams's earlier statement to Mr. Jensen as evidence that, in fact, Mr. Miller ran a red light. The judge would instruct the jurors that they could consider the evidence only for the limited purpose of deciding whether they want to believe the testimony that it was green. So limited, the evidence would not be subject to a hearsay objection. Quite apart from its truth or falsity, the statement to Jensen is logically relevant. Mr. Williams's credibility is an issue, and the fact that he said one thing at one time and another thing at another time about the same subject lowers his credibility. On that reasoning, the prior inconsistent statement is not hearsay because the proponent is not asking the jury to believe the truth of the prior statement.

Under Texas Rule of Evidence 801, however, the impeaching attorney need not be content to offer the prior inconsistent statement for the limited purpose of attacking Williams's credibility. As noted in Chapter 10, Texas Rule 801(e)(1)(A) provides that if a statement qualifies as a prior inconsistent statement of an in-court witness, in some circumstances the statement is admissible as substantive evidence. Under Rule 801, Williams's out-of-court statement could be used as substantive evidence that the light was red if he had made the prior statement under oath in a formal proceeding. That is, counsel could argue to the jury that they should believe Williams's out-of-court statement as being true. The person is available for questioning, and the cross-examiner can ask the witness about both the witness's direct testimony and the witness's earlier statements. Furthermore, the drafters of Federal Rule 801 (which served as the model for the Texas version) doubted that many jurors could follow a judge's limiting instruction admitting a prior inconsistent statement merely as credibility evidence.

§ 5-10(C) PRIOR ORAL INCONSISTENT STATEMENT

§ 5-10(C)(1) Elements of the Foundation

Texas Rule of Evidence 613(a) requires that before introducing extrinsic evidence of a prior inconsistent statement, the witness is to be given notice of the particulars of the alleged statement and an opportunity to explain the statement. Counsel seeking to cross-examine a witness about a prior inconsistent statement should lay the following foundation:

1. Counsel should get the witness committed to the testimony he or she gave on direct examination.[14]
2. The witness made an earlier oral statement at a certain place.
3. The witness made the statement at a certain time.
4. The statement was made to a certain person.
5. The statement was of a certain tenor.[15]

§ 5-10(C)(2) Sample Foundation

The following fact situation involves impeachment with an oral inconsistent statement. The opponent is the defense counsel who is cross-examining Mr. Williams.

O Mr. Williams, if I correctly understood your testimony on direct examination, my client's car was the car that ran a red light. IS THAT CORRECT? (1)

---

[14] Unless the opponent does so, the witness may later attempt to explain away the inconsistency by testifying that he or she innocently misspoke. The opponent might attempt to commit the witness by asking directly, "ISN'T IT TRUE THAT on direct examination you testified that . . .?" Some experienced trial attorneys counsel against such direct questions because they alert the proponent, often the witness, that the opponent is going to use a prior inconsistent statement. Moreover, on various theories, trial judges may consider the question objectionable. In the interest of completeness, the question is included in the sample foundations, but be aware that this tactic can be dangerous.

[15] Some might add a sixth element: the prior statement is more likely to be reliable than the present testimony. In the sample foundations that follow, the counsel attempts to force the witness to concede that the witness's memory was fresher at the time of the inconsistent statement than at the time of the trial. Many experienced counsel prefer not to attempt to force that concession. These counsel elicit the facts about the statement's timing and then argue the relative reliability of the statements during closing argument. These attorneys forego attempting to force the concession in part because they realize that some judges regard such questions as objectionably argumentative. There is also a real problem with the witness giving a plausible reason why the prior statement was not reliable, i.e., it was blurted out without any thinking and that the witness immediately realized that it was a mistake. If this element is added as part of the foundation, counsel should be aware that, as with element #1, this tactic can be dangerous.

W Yes.

O ISN'T IT A FACT THAT on the afternoon of the accident, you had a conversation with a Mr. Walter Jensen at your house? (2), (3), (4)

W Yes.

O ISN'T IT CORRECT THAT during that conversation, you discussed the collision between my client's car and the plaintiff's car? (5)

W Right.

O ISN'T IT ALSO TRUE THAT during the conversation, you told Mr. Jensen that it was the defendant's car that had run a red light? (5)

W Yes.

O ISN'T IT A FACT that, in point of time, that conversation was closer to the accident than your testimony today? (6)

W Yes.

O ISN'T IT CORRECT that your memory was fresher then? (6)

W Yes.

P Your Honor, may I please have a limiting instruction under Rule 105 that the jurors may use this evidence only in evaluating Mr. Williams's credibility? Mr. Williams wasn't under oath at the time of the statement, and Texas Rule 801(e)(1)(A) is therefore inapplicable.

J The court will grant the request for a limiting instruction. Ladies and gentlemen of the jury, you've heard Mr. Williams tell you that before trial, Mr. Williams told a Mr. Jensen that the defendant's car ran the red light. That testimony is not being admitted to prove that in fact the defendant's car ran the red light. The testimony is being admitted solely for the purpose of helping you, if it does, to evaluate Mr. Williams's credibility. If you decide that his prior statement is inconsistent with his testimony in court today, you may consider that inconsistency in deciding whether to believe Mr. Williams and how much weight, if any, to give to his testimony.

Note that in this scenario the witness unequivocally admitted making the inconsistent statement. Once he did so, the impeachment was complete and counsel was not permitted to introduce extrinsic evidence of the statement. That is, he may not now call another person who heard the statement to repeat what the witness said.

§ 5-10(D) PRIOR WRITTEN INCONSISTENT STATEMENT

§ 5-10(D)(1) Elements of the Foundation

If counsel is going to impeach a witness with a prior written inconsistent statement, the following elements should be established:

1. Counsel should commit the witness to the testimony he or she gave on direct examination.[16]
2. The witness wrote an earlier statement. (For a written prior inconsistent statement, the place where the witness wrote the document may not be essential.)
3. The witness wrote the statement at a certain time.
4. The statement was written in a specified document.
5. The statement was of a certain tenor.[17]

If the prior inconsistent statement is written, there is an additional element: if the opponent proposes to hand the writing to the witness, the opponent should first show the writing to the other counsel. Under Texas Rule 613(a), the opponent need not show the writing to the witness.

§ 5-10(D)(2) Sample Foundation

In the following hypothetical, Mr. Williams made an inconsistent statement in a letter that he mailed to Mr. Jensen.

O Mr. Williams, if I correctly understood your testimony on direct examination, my client's car was the car that ran a red light. IS THAT CORRECT? (1)

W Yes.

O Your Honor, we ask that the court reporter mark this as a defense exhibit for identification. [*Counsel hands exhibit to court reporter, who marks*

---

[16] Unless the opponent does so, the witness may later attempt to explain away the inconsistency by testifying that he or she innocently misspoke. The opponent might attempt to commit the witness by asking directly, "ISN'T IT TRUE THAT on direct examination you testified that . . .?" Some experienced trial attorneys counsel against such direct questions because they alert the proponent, often the witness, that the opponent is going to use a prior inconsistent statement. Moreover, on various theories, trial judges may consider the question objectionable. In the interests of completeness, the question is included in the sample foundations, but be aware that this tactic can be dangerous.

[17] Some might add a sixth element: the prior statement is more likely to be reliable than the present testimony. In the sample foundations which follow, the counsel attempts to force the witness to concede that the witness's memory was fresher at the time of the inconsistent statement, than the memory is at trial. Many experienced counsel prefer not to attempt to force that concession. These counsel elicit the facts about the statement's timing and then argue the relative reliability of the statements during closing argument. These attorneys forego attempting to force the concession in part because they realize that some judges regard such questions as objectionably argumentative. There is also a real problem with the witness giving a plausible reason why the prior statement was not reliable, i.e., it was blurted out without any thinking and that the witness immediately realized that it was a mistake. If this element is added as part of the foundation counsel should be aware that, as with element #1, this tactic can be dangerous.

it and hands it back.] Please let the record reflect that I am showing what the court reporter has marked as defense exhibit F for identification to the opposing counsel.

J The record will so reflect.

O Mr. Williams, I now hand you defense exhibit F for identification. WHAT is it?

W It's a letter.

O ISN'T IT TRUE THAT the letter is in your handwriting?

W Yes.

O ISN'T IT A FACT THAT you wrote that letter?

W Yes.

O ISN'T IT CORRECT THAT on the day of the collision between my client's car and the plaintiff's car, you wrote that letter at your house? (2), (3)

W Right.

O ISN'T IT A FACT THAT you then sent the letter to your friend, Mr. William Jensen? (4)

W Yes.

O Let me direct your attention to the third paragraph on page one of the exhibit. Please read that paragraph silently to yourself. ISN'T IT TRUE THAT in that paragraph, you wrote that it was the red car, the plaintiff's car, that ran a red light? (5)

W Yes.

O Your Honor, I now offer paragraph three of the exhibit into evidence.

P Your Honor, counsel is not permitted to introduce extrinsic evidence of the statement under Texas Rule 613(a) because the witness admitted making the statement.

J The exhibit will not be received.

P Your Honor, we also request that you instruct the jury that they may not consider the statement as substantive evidence.

J I will give that instruction in my charge to the jury at the close of the case.

O Mr. Williams, ISN'T IT CORRECT THAT, in point of time, the date of the letter was closer to the accident than your testimony today? (6)

W Yes.

O ISN'T IT ALSO A FACT THAT your memory was fresher then?

W Yes.

As in the case of the oral inconsistent statement, on request the judge would give the jury a limiting instruction about the evidentiary status of the statement. In closing argument, the proponent could invite the jury to consider the written inconsistent statement in evaluating Williams's credibility. It would be objectionable, however, for the proponent to suggest to the jurors that Williams' written statement was itself evidence that the red car ran a red light.

§ 5-10(E) INCONSISTENT STATEMENT IN DEPOSITION

§ 5-10(E)(1) Elements of the Foundation

If the witness made the prior statement at a deposition hearing, the opponent should elicit the following facts, in addition to the foregoing elements which generally draw the witness's attention to the circumstances of the deposition testimony:

1. Confirm that the witness made the statement on direct examination.
2. Inform the witness of the time and place of deposition.
3. Confirm that the witness's attorney was present at the deposition.
4. Confirm that a court reporter was also there.
5. The reporter administered an oath to the witness.
6. At the beginning of the deposition, the opposing attorney told the witness that if any question was unclear, the witness should request clarification.
7. The opposing attorney asked whether the witness was experiencing any mental or physical problem that would interfere with testifying at the deposition; the witness assured the attorney that there was none.
8. The reporter later prepared a transcript of the questions and answers at the deposition.
9. The reporter gave the witness a copy of the transcript to review, and the witness signed the transcript without making any changes.

§ 5-10(E)(2) Sample Foundation

In this example, counsel cross-examines Mr. Williams about a prior statement made during a deposition.

O Mr. Williams, if I correctly understood your testimony on direct examination, my client s car was the car that ran a red light. IS THAT CORRECT? (1)

W Yes.

O ISN'T IT TRUE THAT you appeared at a deposition hearing in April of this year at our law offices? (2)

W Yes.

O ISN'T IT TRUE THAT there were several people at that deposition, including myself, opposing counsel, and a court reporter? (3), (4)

W Yes.

O ISN'T IT CORRECT THAT you were placed under oath? (5)

W Right.

O ISN'T IT A FACT THAT you were told that if any questions were unclear to you, you should ask for clarification? (6)

W Yes.

O ISN'T IT ALSO TRUE that you had no problem answering the questions put to you? (7)

W That is also correct.

O And ISN'T IT A FACT that several weeks later you were presented with a copy of your deposition testimony for your review and any corrections? (8), (9)

W Yes.

O IT IS TRUE, IS IT NOT, that you had no corrections and that you signed the transcript without making any changes? (9)

W That's correct.

O Your Honor, we ask that the court reporter mark this as a defense exhibit for identification, next in order. [*Counsel hands exhibit to court reporter, who marks it and then hands it back to counsel.*] Please let the record reflect that I am showing what has been marked by the court reporter as defense exhibit D for identification to the opposing counsel. Mr. Williams, I now hand you defense exhibit D for identification. WHAT is it?

W It appears to be part of my deposition testimony.

O I direct your attention to the last page. That is your signature, IS IT NOT?

W It is.

O Let me direct your attention to the third paragraph on page one of the exhibit. Please read that paragraph silently to yourself. ISN'T IT TRUE THAT in that paragraph you testified, under oath, that it was the red car, the plaintiff's car, that ran a red light? (5)

W Yes.

O Your Honor, I would now like permission to read to the jury the pertinent deposition statements made by this witness.[18]

P Your Honor, counsel is not permitted to introduce extrinsic evidence of the statement under Texas Rule 613(a) because the witness admitted making the statement.

J The objection will be sustained.

P Your Honor, we also request that you instruct the jury that they may not consider the statement as substantive evidence.

O May we be heard, your Honor?

J Yes.

O Your Honor, this witness's prior deposition testimony is admissible for the substantive truth of the matter asserted. Under Rule 801(e)(1)(A), the prior inconsistent statement qualifies as nonhearsay. The statement was given under oath, subject to the penalty of perjury at a deposition.

J I will not give the limiting instruction.

O Mr. Williams, ISN'T IT CORRECT THAT, in point of time, the date of the deposition was closer to the accident than your testimony today?

W Yes.

O ISN'T IT ALSO A FACT THAT your memory was fresher then?

W Yes.

§ 5-10(F) EXTRINSIC EVIDENCE OF PRIOR INCONSISTENT STATEMENT

§ 5-10(F)(1) The Doctrine

In the variations of the hypothetical in the last subsection, the witness obligingly admitted that he made the prior inconsistent statement. When the witness makes that concession, the impeachment is complete. If the witness denies the statement or equivocates, however, the opponent has a choice. If the statement is in writing and the opponent has not yet shown the writing to the witness, the opponent can immediately confront the witness with the writing and attempt to refresh the witness's memory. Section 11-5(B)(3), *infra*, contains a sample foundation for present recollection refreshed. Alternatively, the opponent may attempt to introduce extrinsic evidence of the inconsistent statement after

[18] Note that the jury is not entitled to take with them into the deliberation room the depositions of witnesses. TEX. R. CIV. P. 281; *Harvey v. Culpepper*, 801 S.W.2d 596, 601 (Tex. App.—Corpus Christi 1990, no writ) (the trial court should not have allowed the jury to retire with the depositions); *Mid-South Bottling Co. v. Cigainero*, 799 S.W.2d 385, 387 (Tex. App.—Texarkana 1990, writ denied) (unquestionably, the trial court erred in furnishing the jury a written portion of the deposition testimony of the witness). Deposition testimony is to be read to the jury. TEX. R. CIV. P. 287.

the witness leaves the stand. Extrinsic evidence refers to any other evidence of the inconsistent statement that Ms. Dolan's attorney might offer after Mr. Williams leaves the witness stand. For example, if the defense attorney called Mr. Jensen to testify to Mr. Williams's oral inconsistent statement, Mr. Jensen's testimony would be extrinsic evidence. Or suppose that the defense attorney called another of Mr. Williams's acquaintances, Ms. Bigelow, to identify Mr. Williams's handwriting on a written inconsistent statement. Again, the writing would be extrinsic impeachment of Mr. Williams.

There are two restrictions on the admissibility of extrinsic evidence of a prior inconsistent statement. First, extrinsic evidence of the prior inconsistent statement is only admissible if the opponent laid a foundation while cross-examining the witness to be impeached. The theory is that fairness dictates giving the witness an opportunity to explain or deny the impeaching evidence. This is different from the Federal Rules, which relax that requirement.[19]

There is another possible hurdle. The common-law collateral fact rule decreed that if the statement related to a purely collateral fact, with no relevance to the historical merits, extrinsic evidence was automatically inadmissible. As previously stated, the Texas Rules do not explicitly codify the collateral fact rule. Only Rule 403 remains. If the trial judge believes that the issue is important enough to an assessment of the witness's credibility, the judge may permit the introduction of extrinsic evidence of the prior statement.

§ 5-10(F)(2) Elements of the Foundation

In order to introduce extrinsic evidence of a prior inconsistent statement, counsel must first satisfy the following elements:

1. Draw the witness's attention to elements listed above for the witness's prior statement (i.e., the time, place, persons present, tenor).
2. Give the witness an opportunity to deny or explain the statement.
3. Authenticate the statement.

---

[19] In federal court, if the opponent is attacking an in-court witness's credibility, the Federal Rules recognize alternatives to a traditional foundation on cross-examination. Federal Rule 613(b) requires only that the witness be afforded an opportunity to explain or deny the statement. The opponent attacking the witness's credibility can afford the witness that opportunity by having the witness excused subject to recall. If the judge excuses the witness subject to recall, the witness's proponent can later recall the witness to deny the statement or to explain away the apparent inconsistency. Even when there is no foundation on cross and the witness has been permanently excused, the judge retains discretion to admit extrinsic evidence, "in the interests of justice," under Rule 613(b). Despite the exercise of due diligence, the party seeking to introduce the statement may not have learned of its existence until after the witness has left the witness stand.

§ 5-10(F)(3) Sample Foundations

The following three foundations illustrate the presentation of extrinsic evidence of a prior inconsistent statement. For purposes of each foundation, assume that the defense attorney has satisfied Rule 613(a). That is, assume that counsel has already drawn the witness's attention to the time, place, persons present, and tenor of the statement. Also, assume that counsel further offered the witness an opportunity to explain or deny the statement and that the witness either denied making the statement or equivocated on making it. Initially, suppose that the defense calls Mr. Jensen to testify to Mr. Williams's oral prior inconsistent statement.

O WHERE were you on the afternoon of January 15, 2005? (3)

W At Mr. Williams's house.

O WHO was there? (3)

W Just Mr. Williams and myself.

O WHAT happened while you were there? (3)

W We just talked.

O WHAT did you talk about? (3)

W A lot of things, including the accident he evidently witnessed that morning.

O WHAT did Mr. Williams say about the accident? (3)

W He said that the guy in the red car had clearly caused the accident by running a red light.

In the next variation of the hypothetical, Mr. Jensen will authenticate a letter containing the inconsistent statement that Mr. Williams sent to Mr. Jensen.

O [*To court reporter*] Would you please mark this as a defense exhibit for identification? [*Reporter marks exhibit and hands it back to counsel.*] Thank you. Please let the record reflect that I am showing what has been marked as defense exhibit F for identification to the opposing counsel. [*Counsel shows exhibit to opposing counsel for inspection.*] Mr. Jensen, I now hand you defense exhibit F for identification. WHAT is it? (3)

W It's a letter I received.

O WHEN did you receive it? (3)

W It was in January of this year. It arrived in the mail at my apartment. (2)

O WHOSE handwriting is the letter in? (3)

W Mr. Williams's handwriting.

O HOW do you know that? (3)

W We've worked together for years in different offices of the same company.

O HOW many times have you seen Mr. Williams's handwriting? (3)

W Hundreds of times. We exchange business memos. Sometimes we'll be at each other's office, and I'll be present when he signs documents.

O HOW familiar are you with his handwriting style?

W Very.

O Your Honor, I now offer defense exhibit F for identification into evidence.

J Any objections?

P No, your Honor.

J Defense exhibit F for identification will be received into evidence.

O Mr. Jensen, permit me to direct your attention to the second sentence in paragraph three of the exhibit. WHAT does that sentence say?

W It reads, "The guy in the red car ran right through a red light."

O Your Honor, I now request permission to submit defense exhibit F to the jurors for their inspection.

J Permission granted.

In the final version of the hypothetical, the written statement is in the form of a deposition transcript. The notary public's certificate at the end of the transcript makes the transcript self-authenticating under Rule 902. After the witness to be impeached leaves the stand, the opponent may request the judge's permission to read the inconsistent passage to the jurors. When the opponent makes the request, the opponent should specify the page and lines to be read. If the transcript has already been filed with the court, there is no need to mark the transcript even for identification. In some cases, however, the transcript has not been filed with the court. In that event, the opponent should have the transcript marked for identification:

O Your Honor, we request that this be marked defense exhibit F for identification. [*Counsel hands exhibit to court reporter, who marks exhibit and hands back to counsel.*] Thank you. Please let the record reflect that I am showing defense exhibit F for identification to the opposing counsel. I now offer page 8, lines 17 through 23 of defense exhibit F for identification into evidence and request permission to read those lines to the jurors.

J The passage will be admitted, and you may read the passage to the jury.

§ 5-11 PROOF THAT THE WITNESS HAS BEEN CONVICTED

§ 5-11(A) THE DOCTRINE

If the witness has suffered a conviction, the conviction tends to impeach the witness's credibility. Proof of the conviction creates a general inference that the witness is sometimes willing to disobey social norms. The conviction thus strengthens the inference that the witness is violating another norm and lying during his or her testimony. Of course, the conviction has much more probative value if the underlying offense is a crime such as perjury or embezzlement involving an element of deceit or fraud. All jurisdictions recognize this method of impeachment, but they differ on the types of convictions usable to impeach. Texas Rule of Evidence 609 provides in part:

> For the purpose of attacking the credibility of a witness, evidence that he has been convicted of a crime shall be admitted if elicited from him or established by public record but only if the crime was a felony or involved moral turpitude, regardless of the punishment, and the court determines that the probative value of admitting this evidence outweighs its prejudicial effect to a party.

As in the case of prior inconsistent statement impeachment, this technique permits the opponent to both cross-examine the witness to be impeached and use extrinsic evidence. In Texas, the opponent may choose between cross-examination and extrinsic evidence. There is no requirement that the opponent lay a foundation on cross-examination as a condition to introducing extrinsic evidence. If the opponent does cross-examine the witness, however, and the witness admits all the facts about the conviction, a court should normally prohibit the introduction of extrinsic evidence. The rationale is simply that it would be cumulative and a waste of time to introduce the extrinsic evidence after the witness has conceded all the facts.

When the opponent resorts to extrinsic evidence, the evidence usually takes the form of an attested copy of the judgment of conviction. The properly attested copy is self-authenticating. The opponent does not need a live, sponsoring witness to authenticate the copy. In rare cases, the opponent will present live testimony, such as the testimony of someone who was present in the courtroom when the witness was convicted.

The courts differ on the number of details the opponent may prove about the conviction. Some courts limit the opponent's proof to evidence that in a certain jurisdiction in a certain year, the witness suffered a felony conviction. Most courts, however, permit the opponent to identify the crime of which the witness was convicted. Some courts also allow the opponent to prove the sentence the witness suffered. But the consensus seems to be that the opponent may not inquire about other details, especially any aggravating facts about the particular manner in which the witness committed the crime.[20]

---

[20] *See generally* WENDORF, SCHLUETER & BARTON, TEXAS RULES OF EVIDENCE MANUAL, VI-49 (6th ed. 2002).

§ 5-11(B) ELEMENTS OF THE FOUNDATION

In order to impeach a witness by showing that the witness has been convicted, the opponent must establish the following foundation:

1. The witness is the person who suffered the prior conviction.
2. The conviction is for one of the crimes Texas holds to be impeaching, i.e., a felony or a crime involving moral turpitude.[21]
3. The conviction was entered in a certain jurisdiction.
4. The conviction was entered in a certain year.
5. The conviction is final.

If the opponent is using a copy of the judgment of conviction, there are two other elements of the foundation:

6. On balance, the probative value of the conviction outweighs its prejudicial effect to a party.[22]
7. The copy of the judgment of conviction is authentic.

§ 5-11(C) SAMPLE FOUNDATIONS

The first sample foundation illustrates cross-examination about a conviction. The case is a civil case and the opponent is the defense attorney attempting to impeach the witness who has testified for the plaintiff.

P ISN'T IT TRUE THAT you are the same Steven Giles who once was convicted of a felony? (1), (2)

W Yes.

P ISN'T IT A FACT THAT the felony was a robbery? (2)

W Yes.

P ISN'T IT CORRECT THAT you were convicted of that crime in 1988 in a New York Supreme Court in Cause No. 12345? (3), (4)

W Yes.

P ISN'T IT ALSO A FACT THAT you were sentenced to 15 years in state prison for that robbery?

W Yes.

---

[21] For a list of crimes involving moral turpitude, see WENDORF, SCHLUETER & BARTON, TEXAS RULES OF EVIDENCE MANUAL VI-52, n. 10 (6th ed. 2002).

[22] The balancing test noted in Rule 609(a) inferentially places the burden on the proponent to show that the value of the conviction outweighs its costs. In contrast, the Rule 403 balancing test places the burden on the party seeking to exclude otherwise admissible evidence to show that the costs substantially outweigh the benefits of the evidence.

P And ISN'T IT ALSO CORRECT that the conviction is final? (5)

W Yes.

The next foundation illustrates the use of an attested copy of a judgment of conviction to impeach. Assume that the witness, Mr. Giles, has already left the stand.

O Your Honor, we request the court reporter to mark this exhibit as a defense exhibit. [*Counsel hands exhibit to court reporter, who marks it and hands exhibit back to counsel.*] Thank you. Please let the record reflect that I am showing the exhibit to the opposing counsel. I now offer defense exhibit D for identification into evidence.

P Your Honor, I object on the ground that there's insufficient authentication of this document.

O Your Honor, the exhibit includes a properly executed attesting certificate. The certificate makes the exhibit self-authenticating under Rule 902. (7)

P Your Honor, we would also object that whatever possible probative value this conviction might have is outweighed by its prejudicial effect.

O Your Honor, may we be heard?

J Yes.

O Your Honor, the fact that the witness has a prior felony conviction is extremely probative of the fact that the witness is inclined to disregard social norms. (6) The jury should be entitled to take that into consideration in deciding whether the oath he took earlier today actually means anything to him. The witness is not on trial in this case, and there is little danger that admission of the conviction will prejudice the plaintiff. (6)

J May I see the exhibit, please? [*Judge examines exhibit.*] The objection will be overruled. Defense exhibit D for identification will be received into evidence.

O Your Honor, may I read these two sentences to the jury?

J Permission granted. Ladies and gentlemen of the jury, I have just accepted into evidence defense exhibit D. This exhibit is a properly authenticated copy of a judgment of a conviction of a crime. You will please bear in mind that the last prosecution witness was Mr. Steven Judson Giles, Jr. You may proceed.

O Ladies and gentlemen, the exhibit reads, On this day, July 13, 2005, the Supreme Court of the State of New York, Hudson County, the Honorable Paul Wilson presiding, duly found the defendant, Steven Judson Giles, Jr., guilty of the crime of robbery. (1), (2), (3), (4), (5). For this crime, the defendant is hereby sentenced to 15 years' confinement in the prisons of the State of New York.

Even if the witness were a party, the evidence of the conviction would be admissible solely on a credibility theory. Therefore, even if Giles were a criminal defendant, on request the judge would give the jury a limiting instruction that it could not use the evidence as a basis for concluding that Giles was a bad person and therefore more likely to have committed the charged offense. The judge would explain to the jurors that they could consider the evidence only for the purpose of deciding whether to believe Giles' testimony and how much weight to give to his testimony. During closing argument, the opponent could treat the conviction as credibility evidence; but it would be objectionable if he or she suggested to the jurors that the conviction showed that Giles was the sort of person likely to commit the type of crime he was charged with.

§ 5-12 PROOF THAT THE WITNESS IS BIASED

§ 5-12(A) THE DOCTRINE

Unlike the Federal Rules, Texas Rule of Evidence 613(b) specifically addresses the issue of impeaching a witness through evidence of bias. Bias may affect the witness consciously or subconsciously, and the courts typically grant the opponent great latitude in proving bias. In fact, the courts often allow the opponent to use bias impeachment as a method of circumventing other evidentiary rules. For example, there is a general rule that in a civil action, the plaintiff may not prove that the defendant has settled any other claims arising from the same accident. The justification for the rule is that the admission of such evidence would discourage desirable, out-of-court settlements. Suppose, though, that the defendant calls a witness who has settled his or her claim with the defendant. The fact of the settlement is logically relevant and admissible to show the witness's bias in the defendant's favor. Another illustration is the rule that the plaintiff ordinarily may not prove that the defendant has liability insurance. The admission of such evidence would tempt the jury to decide the case on an improper basis; they might find in the plaintiff's favor because in reality, the insurance company will pay the judgment. Assume, however, that the defendant calls one of the insurance company's investigators as a witness. The plaintiff should be able to prove the defendant's liability insurance. The fact that the witness works for the defendant's liability carrier is logically relevant to show the witness's bias in favor of the defendant.

This impeachment technique is similar to conviction impeachment in another respect: the opponent may both cross-examine the witness to be impeached and use extrinsic evidence. On cross-examination, the courts grant the opponent a very wide scope of inquiry. Texas follows the traditional view, which requires that the opponent lay a foundation on cross-examination as a predicate for extrinsic evidence. The underlying theory is that as a matter of fairness, the opponent should give the witness an opportunity to explain or deny the impeaching facts. If the witness fully admits all the facts, the judge may exercise discretion to limit or exclude extrinsic evidence. When the witness denies any of the relevant impeaching facts or equivocates, however, the opponent may introduce extrinsic evidence.

§ 5-12(B) PROOF OF BIAS THROUGH STATEMENT

§ 5-12(B)(1) Elements of the Foundation

The foundational requirements for bias evidence are almost identical to those for showing a prior inconsistent statement:

1. The witness made an earlier statement at a certain place.
2. The witness made a statement at a certain time.
3. The statement was made to a certain person.
4. The statement was of a certain tenor.

§ 5-12(B)(2) Sample Foundation

The following fact sample is a criminal case in which the defense counsel wishes to show that a prosecution witness made a statement evidencing bias against the defendant. The defense counsel is the opponent and the prosecution witness is Mr. Juarez.

O ISN'T IT TRUE, Mr. Juarez, that several months ago you had a conversation concerning this case with a Ms. Smith at her apartment? (1), (2), (3)

W I did.

O And ISN'T IT ALSO CORRECT that Mr. Williams was also present? (3)

W Yes.

O IT IS TRUE, ISN'T IT, Mr. Juarez, that you told Ms. Smith and Mr. Williams that you had a score to settle with the defendant in this case? (4)

W Well, maybe not in those exact words.

O WHAT words did you use? (4)

W I said that I was mad at the defendant and that I was going to make life very hard for him. I didn't say anything about settling any scores.

§ 5-12(C) PROOF OF BIAS THROUGH CIRCUMSTANCE, EVENT, OR CONDITION

§ 5-12(C)(1) Elements of the Foundation

The foundation for showing bias through circumstance, event, or condition include the following elements:

1. Where the event or condition occurred.
2. When the event or condition occurred.
3. Who was present.
4. What occurred.

Many counsel attempt to lay an additional element: they seek the witness's concession that the fact or event will tend to bias the witness. Others avoid such attempts. The witness will often not make that concession. And in the attempt to force the concession, the counsel might become argumentative. Those who prefer to seek the concession believe that waiting until closing argument may be too late. By then, the jury may have forgotten about the bias issue.

§ 5-12(C)(2) Sample Foundation

The fact situation is a civil suit between Mr. Martinez and Mr. Saltzman, and demonstrates use of an event to show the witness's bias. Mr. Martinez calls Mr. Fargo as a witness. After the direct examination, Mr. Saltzman's attorney begins cross-examination. Mr. Saltzman's attorney is the opponent. Note that this particular sample also includes reference to a statement made by the witness that also reflects some bias.

O ISN'T IT TRUE THAT on July 4, 2005, you attended a party at Jane Fleming's house? (1), (2)

W Yes.

O ISN'T IT A FACT THAT Ms. Fleming and Mr. Saltzman, the defendant in this case, were at the party? (3)

W Yes.

O ISN'T IT CORRECT THAT during the party, you and Mr. Saltzman got into an argument? (4)

W Yes, sort of.

P And ISN'T IT TRUE THAT you punched Mr. Saltzman? (4)

W Yes.

O ISN'T IT ALSO TRUE THAT before you left the party, you told Ms. Fleming that you had a strong, personal dislike for Mr. Saltzman? (4)

W Yes.

Assume that the witness had denied the impeaching facts. Under Texas Rule 613(b), the opponent could present extrinsic evidence, such as Ms. Fleming's testimony:

O WHERE were you on the evening of July 4, 2005? (1), (2)

W At my house. I was throwing a party for some friends.

O WHO attended the party? (3)

W There were a lot of people. Mr. Fargo, the last witness, was there. The defendant, Mr. Saltzman, was also there.

O WHAT, if anything, unusual happened during the evening? (4)

W I couldn't believe it, but Mr. Fargo actually punched Mr. Saltzman. They were just standing talking pretty loudly, and all of a sudden Mr. Fargo slugged him.

O WHAT happened then? (4)

W I asked Mr. Fargo to get out.

O WHAT, if anything, did Mr. Fargo say? (4)

W He said he'd be glad to. He said that he had a strong, personal dislike for Mr. Saltzman and that he, Mr. Fargo, wouldn't stay under the same roof as Mr. Saltzman. Mr. Fargo said that if he'd known Mr. Saltzman was going to be at the party, he never would have accepted my invitation.

On request, the judge would have to give the jury a limiting instruction explaining that it could consider the bias evidence only for the purpose of evaluating Fargo's credibility. Likewise, in closing argument the opponent could treat the testimony solely as credibility evidence. Even if the witness were a party to the litigation, the opponent could not invite the jury to treat the evidence as proof of the party's bad character and therefore evidence that it is more likely that the party committed the criminal or tortious conduct alleged in the pleadings.

§ 5-13 PROOF THAT A WITNESS IS DEFICIENT IN AN ELEMENT OF COMPETENCY

§ 5-13(A) THE DOCTRINE

Section 3-1 listed the elements of competency. At common law, to be a competent witness, a person must possess the testimonial qualities of perception, memory, narration, and sincerity. If the opponent can negate one or more of those elements, the person is incompetent; the person cannot testify at all during the trial. Even if the opponent's evidence does not completely negate one of the elements, however, the evidence may be logically relevant on an impeachment theory. For example, a color-blind person is a competent witness. But the color blindness is a deficiency which can tend to reduce the value of the witness's testimony.

The courts liberally admit evidence of deficiencies in elements of competency. The courts have admitted evidence that the witness was intoxicated when he or she observed the event they testified about, that the witness has a psychiatric disorder affecting his or her testimonial qualities, and that the witness is mentally retarded.

As a general proposition, the opponent may use either cross-examination or extrinsic evidence. For example, on cross-examination, the opponent may attempt to force a witness to concede that he or she was intoxicated at the time of the event.

§ 5-13(B) Elements of the Foundation

This impeachment technique often requires proof of a particular historical event, such as an occasion when the witness was drunk. The normal foundation will include:

1. Where the event occurred.
2. When the event occurred.
3. Who was present.
4. What happened.
5. What happened may have affected the accuracy of his testimony.

In addition, if expert testimony is being used, Chapter 9 illustrates the foundations for lay and expert testimony. When such testimony is necessary, the opponents will also have to establish:

6. The qualifications of the expert, if expert testimony is necessary.
7. The basis for the opinion.
8. The opinion itself.

§ 5-13(C) Sample Foundations

The first sample is cross-examination to attack a deficiency in the witness's competency. The fact situation is a tort case arising from a traffic collision. The plaintiff, Ms. Schmitt, sues the defendant, Mr. Jackson. The plaintiff calls a witness, Mr. Oser. On direct examination, Mr. Oser testifies that he observed the accident from 150 feet away. He testifies that the defendant swerved into the plaintiff. The defendant is the opponent.

O ISN'T IT TRUE THAT on direct examination, you testified that on January 4th, you observed a collision between the plaintiff's and defendant's cars just outside the Sports Arena? (1), (2), (3)

W Yes.

O Mr. Oser, ISN'T IT CORRECT THAT you are nearsighted? (4)

W Yes.

O ISN'T IT A FACT THAT as a nearsighted person, you have difficulty seeing anything at a distance? (4)

W Yes.

O ISN'T IT CORRECT THAT your doctor has prescribed glasses for you to correct your nearsightedness? (4)

W Yes.

O ISN'T IT ALSO TRUE that when you supposedly saw the collision, you weren't wearing your glasses? (4)

W Yes.

O Finally, ISN'T IT A FACT THAT you were at least 150 feet away from the collision when you supposedly saw it? (5)

W Yes.

The next scenario is an example of extrinsic testimony impeaching a prior witness. Mr. Oser has left the witness stand. The defendant calls Mr. Thelan. The defendant is still designated the opponent. The defendant is conducting the direct examination of Mr. Thelan.

O WHERE were you on the evening of January 4 of this year? (1), (2)

W I was downtown with Mr. Oser.

O WHO is Mr. Oser? (3)

W He's Ed Oser, the last witness in this case.

O WHAT were you and Mr. Oser doing? (4)

W We had a bite and some drinks at a bar. Then we were going home to our respective wives.

O WHEN did you and Mr. Oser start drinking? (7)

W At about 5:30 in the early evening.

O HOW many drinks did Mr. Oser have? (7)

W He was really putting them away. I'd say he had five before we left.

O WHAT was he drinking? (7)

W He was having screwdrivers, orange juice, and vodka.

O WHEN did you leave the bar? (7)

W At about seven o'clock. Maybe a little later.

O WHAT was Mr. Oser's appearance when you left?

W His face was a little red.

O HOW was he acting? (7)

W Pretty silly. He was stumbling and acting giddy.

O HOW did his breath smell? (7)

W He had a strong odor of alcohol on his breath.

O WHAT was his speech like? (7)

W It was slurred. He was having trouble pronouncing words.

O WHAT, if anything, happened after you left the bar?

W Just down the street a collision occurred.

O WHAT collision? (5)

W The collision Ed testified about, the one between the plaintiff and the defendant.

O WHEN did you see this collision? (5)

W Maybe five minutes after we left the bar.

O In your opinion, WHAT was Mr. Oser's condition when the collision occurred? (5), (8)

W I hate to say it, but I think he was drunk.

The preceding foundation illustrates lay opinion testimony attacking the witness's credibility. The opponent may also use expert opinion testimony. For example, § 3-4(C), *supra*, contains a sample foundation for a psychiatrist's testimony. In this example, the opponent used the testimony to attack the prospective witness's competency. The opponent could use the very same foundation to show a deficiency in the witness's competency.

The above evidence is admitted solely on a credibility theory. Thus, even if the witness being impeached were a party, on request the trial judge would give the jury a limiting instruction under Rule 105 that it could consider the evidence only for the purpose of evaluating the credibility of the witness's testimony. Given the instruction, in closing argument the opponent could urge the jury to discount the witness's testimony for the reason that the witness was intoxicated at the time the witness supposedly observed the accident. However, even if the witness were a party, in closing argument it would be objectionable for the opponent to suggest to the jury that the evidence of drinking shows that the witness is a bad person and therefore more likely to have committed the criminal or tortious misconduct alleged in the pleadings.

PART 4
REHABILITATION OF WITNESS AFTER IMPEACHMENT

§ 5-14 PRIOR CONSISTENT STATEMENT

§ 5-14(A) THE DOCTRINE

After the opponent attempts to impeach the witness's credibility, the witness's proponent may attempt to repair the damage. These attempts are called *rehabilitation*. One of the most common rehabilitation techniques is proof of a prior consistent statement. Texas Rule of Evidence 613(c) and Rule 801(e)(1)(B) address the use of prior consistent statements. The proponent shows that the witness testified to the fact at the time of trial and that the witness made a pretrial statement to the same effect. Just as inconsistency has an impeaching effect, consistency has a rehabilitating effect.

The courts do not want trials to be bogged down, however, with proof of all of the witness's pretrial statements. For that reason, Texas evidence case law imposes timing requirements on prior consistent statements. For example, assume that the opponent impeached the witness with a prior inconsistent statement. Texas courts take the position that the proponent may rehabilitate with a prior consistent statement only if the consistent statement preceded the allegedly inconsistent statement. Or, assume that the opponent charged that the witness recently fabricated his or her testimony. Again, Texas law permits the proponent to rehabilitate by prior consistent statement only if the witness made the statement before he or she had any motive to lie. As with prior inconsistent statements, if the prior consistent statement is otherwise admissible and it was given under oath at a prior proceeding, the statement may be admitted as substantive evidence.

§ 5-14(B) ELEMENTS OF THE FOUNDATION

The statement itself is an event. For that reason, the foundation includes the normal foundational elements for proof of any statement:

1. Where the statement was made.
2. When the statement was made.
3. Who was present.
4. The tenor of the statement.
5. The statement preceded (a) the prior inconsistent statement or (b) any motive on the part of the witness to fabricate.

§ 5-14(C) SAMPLE FOUNDATION

The fact situation is a tort action arising from a collision on December 14. The plaintiff, Mr. Gillis, alleges that the defendant, Ms. Bollack, negligently caused the accident by crossing over into his lane. On direct examination, Mr. Gillis testifies to that effect. On cross-examination, the defense attorney charges that Mr. Gillis fabricated his story. Specifically, the defense attorney asked this question, "ISN'T IT TRUE THAT you never thought of that story until you consulted your attorney, Mr. Clark?" The plaintiff now begins redirect examination. The plaintiff is the proponent.

P Mr. Gillis, WHAT happened after the accident?

W The police arrived, and I went down to the nearest station with them.

P WHERE is the station located? (1)

W I think it's at the intersection of Elm and Main.

P WHEN did you arrive there? (2)

W About two hours after the accident. It might have been three in the afternoon.

P WHO was there? (3)

W A lot of police officers, myself, and Ms. Bollack.

P WHO were the officers? (3)

W There was one named Jorgenson, and then there was Desk Sergeant Allen.

P WHAT, if anything, did Desk Sergeant Allen do?

W He questioned me about the accident.

P Again, on WHAT day did you have this conversation with Desk Sergeant Allen? (2)

W December 14th.

P WHEN was the first time you ever consulted me about this case? (5)

W I guess it was three weeks after my conversation with Desk Sergeant Allen.

P So WHICH came first—your conversation with Desk Sergeant Allen or your conversation with me? (5) [*Many trial attorneys omit this question. They feel that the timing is obvious and that the question will offend judges or jurors by insulting their intelligence.*]

W As I just said, my conversation with Allen.

P WHAT, if anything, did you tell Allen? (4)

W I told him about the accident. I said that the other driver caused it by coming into my lane. I was minding my own business, and then this car is coming across the lane right at me.

Now assume that in the same fact situation, the defendant attempted a different impeachment technique. On cross-examination, the defendant asked this question, "ISN'T IT TRUE THAT on Christmas Day that year, you told your brother that the accident occurred because your brakes failed?" This question amounts to attempted impeachment by prior inconsistent statement. The foundation would be exactly the same until the last three questions. Now the foundation on redirect would read:

P WHEN did you have the conversation with your brother the defense attorney mentioned? (5)

W I'm pre'ty sure it was on Christmas Day, December 25th.

P So WHICH came first, your conversation with Desk Sergeant Allen or your conversation with your brother? (5)

W My conversation with Allen—it was about a week and a half before I saw my brother over the holidays.

P WHAT, if anything, did you tell Allen? (4)

W I told him about the accident. I said that the other driver caused it by coming into my lane. I was minding my own business, and then this car is coming across the lane right at me.

§ 5-15 PROOF OF THE CHARACTER TRAIT OF TRUTHFULNESS

§ 5-15(A) THE DOCTRINE

Many of the impeachment techniques available to the opponent are express or implied attacks on the witness's character. If the opponent calls a character witness to testify to witness #1's character trait of untruthfulness, the testimony is an express attack. If the opponent proves convictions, there is an implied attack on the witness's character. Even bias impeachment sometimes involves an attack on the witness's credibility. For instance, the proof of bias may be evidence of a corrupt financial motive. In all these cases, the judge will permit the proponent to rehabilitate by proving a character trait of truthfulness. The sequence would be the following. The proponent, perhaps the plaintiff, calls witness #1 to testify about the historical merits of the case. The opponent then calls witness #2, a character witness. Witness #2 testifies that witness #1 has a reputation for untruthfulness. To rehabilitate witness #1, the proponent calls witness #3, another character witness. Witness #3 contradicts witness #2. Witness #3 testifies that witness #1 has a good reputation for truthfulness.

In general, the rules governing the opponent's character evidence also apply to the proponent's character evidence. Those rules are outlined *supra* at § 5-8. There is only one other rule the proponent should bear in mind: the trial judge is likely to limit the proponent's character evidence to the same type, time, and community as the opponent's evidence. If the opponent used reputation evidence, the judge may not permit the proponent to use opinion evidence. The judge may limit the proponent's character evidence to roughly the same time period and community as the opponent's evidence. If the opponent presented character evidence about the witness's reputation in Houston within the past five years, the judge might exclude the proponent's character evidence relating to the witness's reputation in Dallas ten years before. The courts do not want trials to bog down in collateral disputes over witnesses' credibility. The proponent should respond in kind to the opponent's attacks on the witness's credibility.

§ 5-15(B) Elements of the Foundation

The foundational elements are the same as in § 5-8(B)(2) (reputation testimony) and § 5-8(C)(2) (opinion testimony), *supra.*

§ 5-15(C) Sample Foundation

With one exception, the foundations are the same as in § 5-8(B)(3) (reputation testimony) and § 5-8(C)(3) (opinion testimony), *supra.* The exception is that the final answers will be favorable to witness #1 rather than unfavorable. Thus, the reputation foundation would end in this fashion:

P WHAT is that reputation? (4)

W It's good. He's known as a truthful person.

P Given Mr. Harding's reputation, would you believe him under oath? (5)

W Yes.

The opinion foundation would conclude in this fashion:

P WHAT is that opinion? (4)

W In my opinion, he's a truthful person.

P Given that opinion, would you believe Mr. Harding under oath? (5)

W Yes.

Like impeaching evidence of a witness's character trait of untruthfulness, rehabilitating evidence of a witness's character trait of truthfulness is admissible solely on a credibility theory. Thus, even if the witness were the civil or criminal defendant in the case, on request the trial judge would instruct the jury that the jurors could not treat the evidence as proof that the defendant did not commit the criminal or tortious (moral turpitude) act alleged in the pleadings. The judge would direct the jury to consider the evidence only for the purpose of evaluating Harding's credibility. In closing argument, the proponent could put the evidence only to that limited use. It would be objectionable for the proponent to suggest to the jury that it should treat the evidence as substantive proof on the merits of the case.

CHAPTER 6

CHARACTER, HABIT, AND OTHER ACTS EVIDENCE

§ 6-1 INTRODUCTION—RELATIONSHIP OF CHARACTER EVIDENCE AND RULE 403

This chapter addresses the topic of introducing several types of evidence which may demonstrate the propensity of a person to act in a particular way. As the discussion will point out, this type of evidence can present dangers that the jury will improperly jump to the conclusion, for example, that if the defendant has done this sort of act before, she must certainly have done it this time. Before addressing the particular foundations for these types of evidence, it is important to note briefly the potential interplay between these doctrines and Texas Rule of Evidence 403.

The last chapter pointed out that the dangers listed in Rule 403 can lead to the exclusion of evidence that is logically relevant to the witness's credibility. The "legal relevance" doctrine codified in Rule 403 is not limited to credibility evidence. The doctrine can also apply to evidence that is logically relevant to the historical merits.

The premier danger noted in Rule 403 is "prejudice." In this context, "prejudice" refers to the evidence's tendency to tempt the jury to decide the case on an improper, usually emotional, basis. For instance, in a homicide prosecution, gruesome photographs of the victim could be excluded if, after viewing them, the jurors could no longer dispassionately evaluate the evidence of guilt or innocence. Most of the types of evidence analyzed in this chapter present the danger of prejudice. Several sections discuss evidence of other misdeeds by a criminal defendant. Such evidence creates a risk that the jurors will convict, not because they are convinced beyond a reasonable doubt of the defendant's commission of the charged crime, but rather because they conclude that the defendant is a bad person who should be behind bars.

Simply stated, Rule 403 embodies the doctrine that the trial judge may exclude logically relevant evidence if, in his or her judgment, the evidence's dangers substantially outweigh its probative value. The judge's application of the doctrine involves several steps. At the outset, the trial judge must determine the probative value of the evidence. How clear is the evidence? How strong is the logical link between the evidence and the fact it is offered to prove? How positive is the witness? These are just some of the questions the judge asks in evaluating probative value. Then the judge identifies the countervailing dangers and, finally, balances the probative value against the dangers.[1] For some types of evidence, such as inflammatory photographs, the doctrine remains highly discretionary. Trial judges resolve the questions case-by-case. For other types of evidence, including most of those examined in this chapter, relatively rigid rules have evolved.

It is important to recognize that even if the proponent can surmount the exclusionary rules codified in specific rules of evidence, such as the rules governing character evidence, the opponent can still invoke Rule 403.

§ 6-2 CHARACTER EVIDENCE—INTRODUCTION

§ 6-2(A) IN GENERAL

Texas Rule of Evidence 404(a) states the general rule that character evidence to show a person's propensity to act in a particular manner is inadmissible. But that rule also recognizes several exceptions. For example, Rule 404(a)(3) permits counsel to introduce character evidence of a witness, a topic discussed in Chapter 5.[2] Under that theory of admissibility, the opponent of the witness uses the witness's character trait of untruthfulness as circumstantial proof of the witness's conduct in an attempt to impeach the witness. The opponent reasons that because the witness has a character trait of untruthfulness, the witness's present testimony is probably untruthful.

Rule 404(a) also states other exceptions to the general rule of exclusion. Under Rule 404(a), counsel may introduce character evidence where a party has been accused of acts involving moral turpitude. And where a party has been accused of assaultive conduct, counsel may introduce character evidence about the alleged victim. Rule 404(a) permits the defendant to offer pertinent character evidence. This rule also includes a provision for introducing character evidence of a victim.

This chapter focuses on the admissibility of character evidence on the historical merits of the case. Much of what was said about character on a credibility theory in Chapter 5 applies here as well. Here, however, the character evidence is being used as evidence of conduct. For example, a criminal defendant may introduce

---

[1] *See generally* WENDORF, SCHLUETER & BARTON, TEXAS RULES OF EVIDENCE MANUAL IV-29 to IV-30 (6th ed. 2002); Schlueter, *Rule 403—The Great Balancing Act*, TEX. B.J. 698 (July 1990).

[2] *See supra* § 5-8.

testimony that he or she is a moral, law-abiding person. The defendant reasons that if he is that type of person, he would probably not commit the crime for which he has been charged. In a prosecution for a violent crime, the defendant may introduce evidence that the alleged victim is an aggressive person. The defendant is inviting the jury to infer that the alleged victim was, in reality, the aggressor on the occasion in question.

§ 6-2(B) METHODS OF PROOF

The rules governing character evidence on the merits resemble the rules for character evidence of untruthfulness in another respect: the methods of proof. In Chapter 5, we noted that the opponent presenting evidence of the witness's character trait of untruthfulness is ordinarily restricted to reputation and opinion evidence. The same restriction generally applies to character evidence on the historical merits. Thus, under Texas Rule of Evidence 405(a), the criminal defendant is usually limited to reputation or opinion evidence of moral, law-abiding character. The major difference in methods of proof is that when character is an essential element of a claim or defense, Rule 405(b) indicates that character may be proved through specific instances of conduct.

§ 6-2(C) DIFFERENCES BETWEEN CREDIBILITY AND CONDUCT THEORIES

There is often confusion in distinguishing between character evidence that is admissible on the issue of credibility and character evidence that is introduced to show an individual's propensity. There are, however, some key differences. The following points highlight those differences.

§ 6-2(C)(1) Whose Character Is Relevant?

On a credibility theory, the character of any witness in any type of case is relevant. Once the person takes the witness stand and gives any testimony in the case, his or her credibility becomes one of the material facts of consequence. On a character theory on the merits, the rules are quite different. The following statements are over-simplifications, but it is generally true that:

1. in Texas civil cases the parties only use character evidence as circumstantial proof of conduct on the merits, regarding the conduct of a victim or regarding a party charged with conduct involving moral turpitude; and
2. in Texas criminal cases, we may use character evidence as circumstantial proof of the conduct of only the defendant and the alleged victim.

§ 6-2(C)(2) What Part of the Person's Character Is Relevant?

On a credibility theory, the focus is squarely on the witness's character trait of truthfulness. That is the only part of the witness's character that is relevant. In contrast, on a character theory on the merits, we are interested in different parts of the person's character. If the person is the criminal defendant, we may be interested in the defendant's general moral, law-abiding character. On the other hand, we may focus on a specific character trait relevant to the nature of the offense, such as peacefulness in an assault prosecution or honesty in a theft prosecution.

§ 6-2(C)(3) When Does the Person's Character Become Relevant?

On a credibility theory, the witness's character trait of truthfulness becomes relevant as soon as the witness gives any testimony in the case. In Texas, the defendant's character on the merits does become relevant until the defendant affirmatively presents character evidence. It is not enough that the defendant has taken the witness stand. The defendant has the choice whether to place his or her character in issue on the merits. The prosecution ordinarily may present evidence of the defendant's immoral, law-breaking character only as rebuttal to defense character evidence.[3] When a person's character itself is on trial, such as in a child custody hearing or in a defamation case, character is obviously in issue as part of the case-in-chief.

§ 6-3 CHARACTER AS DIRECT EVIDENCE—CHARACTER AS ESSENTIAL ELEMENT OF CLAIM OR DEFENSE

§ 6-3(A) THE DOCTRINE

It is important to draw a distinction between those cases where the party's character is not the focus of the case and counsel is using character evidence to prove circumstantially that the party must have acted in a particular way, and those cases where the person's character is an essential element of a claim or a defense. In the former case, Rule 404 places limits on when character evidence may be used. In the latter case, there are no applicable character evidence rules save for Rule 405(b), which states that counsel may prove character either through reputation, character, or specific act evidence. The types of cases which involve this type of direct evidence of character are few. In the civil arena, they arise typically in defamation cases and in child custody cases. In both instances, the party's character will become the focus of the trial. In criminal cases, the list is even shorter, and for all practical purposes, is limited to insanity cases. Character evidence is also generally relevant on sentencing.

---

[3] *See also* TEX. R. EVID. 404(c) (evidence of defendant's character admissible on sentencing).

§ 6-3(B) ELEMENTS OF THE FOUNDATION

To prove character through direct evidence, the proponent should be prepared to lay the following foundation:

1. The person has a particular character trait.
2. The witness has (a) an opinion about the person's character trait, or (b) is familiar with the person's reputation concerning that particular character trait, or (c) can testify as to specific acts which are relevant to the character trait. (In a criminal case, a character witness testifying about an accused must have been familiar with the accused's reputation or the facts supporting the witness's opinion before the date of the offense)[4]
3. The witness (a) states an opinion about the character trait, or (b) relates the reputation of the person, or (c) testifies about the person's specific instances of conduct which are relevant to the character trait in issue.

§ 6-3(C) SAMPLE FOUNDATION

The following fact situation involves a defamation case in which the plaintiff, Mr. Jim Scotts, has alleged that the defendant newspaper published an account in which the plaintiff was labeled as a "liar and a cheat." The defendant has called a witness to the stand to testify about specific instances of conduct which are relevant to the question of whether the plaintiff is indeed a liar and a cheat. The defense counsel is the proponent.

P Mr. Williams, WHO is Mr. Jim Scotts? (2)

W He is a fellow worker in the Ajax Company.

P HOW long have you known him? (2)

W At least five years.

P HAVE you ever known him to tell a lie? (1)

W Yes.

P WHAT were the circumstances? (2), (3)

W Well, about two years ago, he gave me a copy of a resume that he had already sent to another company, hoping to get a better job. I read it and pointed out to him that he did not have a master's degree, like the resume said.

P WHAT, if anything, did he say about that? (1)

---

[4] *See* TEX. R. EVID. 405(a). *See generally* WENDORF, SCHLUETER & BARTON, TEXAS RULES OF EVIDENCE MANUAL IV-102 et seq. (6th ed. 2002).

W He said that what the company did not know would not hurt them. He added that he really needed the new job.

§ 6-4 CIRCUMSTANTIAL CHARACTER EVIDENCE OF DEFENDANT OR PERSON ACCUSED OF CONDUCT INVOLVING MORAL TURPITUDE

§ 6-4(A) THE DOCTRINE

Texas Rule of Evidence 404 makes provisions for introducing character as circumstantial evidence of a party. In civil cases, Rule 404(a)(1)(B) permits a party accused of acts involving moral turpitude to introduce evidence of a pertinent character trait. If such evidence is admitted, the accusing party can offer rebuttal character evidence. In criminal cases, Rule 404(a)(1)(A) permits the defendant to open the door to character evidence of a pertinent character trait. In both instances, the proponent hopes to convince the fact finder that the party is not the kind of person who would commit the alleged acts. Under Rule 405(a), the proponents would be limited to using either reputation or opinion evidence.

§ 6-4(B) ELEMENTS OF THE FOUNDATION

The foundation for character evidence of a party on the historical merits is strikingly similar to the foundation for character evidence on credibility. In order to present character evidence about a party, counsel should show that:

1. The defendant or party has a relevant specific character trait (e.g., honesty).[5]
2. The witness knows about the character trait, either personally or by reputation. [In a criminal case, a character witness testifying about an accused must have been familiar with the accused's reputation or the facts supporting the witness's opinion before the date of the offense.][6]
3. The witness states his or her opinion about the party's character trait, or states what the party's reputation is regarding that character trait.

§ 6-4(C) SAMPLE FOUNDATIONS

The first fact situation is a criminal case involving an assault prosecution. The government has charged Mr. Lowe with a violent assault. During its case-in-chief, the defense calls Mr. Nieman as a character witness who will testify about the

[5] Some older Texas cases refer to the character trait of "honesty and fair dealing." *See, e.g.*, *Grant v. Pendley*, 39 S.W.2d 596 (Tex. Com'n App. 1931, holding approved).

[6] *See* TEX. R. EVID. 405(a).

defendant's reputation. Mr. Nieman has already identified himself. The defense is the proponent.

P WHO is Mr. Lowe?

W He's a neighbor of mine.

P WHEN was the last time you saw him?

W He's in the courtroom right now.

P WHERE is he sitting?

W He's sitting there at the table with you.

P HOW is he dressed?

W He's wearing a brown suit and yellow tie.

P Your Honor, may the record reflect that the witness has identified my client, Mr. Lowe?

J The record will so reflect.

P Mr. Nieman, WHERE does Mr. Lowe live? (2)

W Here in Corpus Christi.

P WHERE do you live? (2)

W I also reside in Corpus Christi.

P HOW close do you live to Mr. Lowe? (2)

W No more than half a mile away.

P HOW long has Mr. Lowe lived in Corpus Christi? (2)

W I'd say easily 7 years.

P HOW long have you lived here? (2)

W For the past 10 years.

P Does Mr. Lowe have a reputation for violence or peacefulness in Corpus Christi? (1) [*Or, Does Mr. Lowe have a reputation as a law-breaking or law-abiding person?*]

W Yes.

P Do you know that reputation? (2)

W Yes.

P WHEN did you learn of his reputation? (2)

W Several years ago. Long before this case came up.

P WHAT is that reputation? (3)

W He's known as a peaceful person. [*Or, He's known as a moral, law-abiding person.*][7]

When this testimony is admitted,[8] during the jury charge, or on both occasions on request the trial judge would give the jury a limiting instruction along these lines:

> Evidence has been received for the purpose of showing the good character of the defendant for those traits involved in the commission of a crime of the kind charged here. Good character for the traits involved in the commission of the crime charged may be sufficient by itself to raise a reasonable doubt as to the defendant's guilt. It may be reasoned that a person of good character as to such traits would not be likely to commit the crime with which the defendant is charged.

During closing argument, the defense attorney could state:

> Ladies and gentlemen, during the trial you heard the testimony of Mr. Nieman. As you'll recall, Mr. Nieman is one of Mr. Lowe's neighbors. They've been neighbors for the better part of a decade; as Mr. Nieman told you, they've both lived in Corpus Christi for over seven years. Mr. Nieman took the stand and told you that Mr. Lowe has an excellent reputation for peacefulness. In Mr. Nieman's words, Mr. Lowe "is known as a peaceful person."
>
> Her Honor read to you the legal instructions that you have to follow during your deliberations. She told you that in deciding Mr. Lowe's innocence or guilt, you may consider this evidence of Mr. Lowe's good character.
>
> Ladies and gentlemen, that instruction makes a lot of sense. Every day in the real world you make decisions about people based on their character. If they have a bad reputation, you think twice; but if they have a good reputation, you trust them because it would be "out of character" for them to violate the law. The uncontradicted evidence—in this case Mr. Nieman's testimony—shows you that Mr. Lowe has an unblemished reputation as a peaceful person. The prosecution has charged Mr. Lowe with an assault, a violent crime. Mr. Lowe simply isn't the kind of man who would commit that type of offense; he's a man with an excellent reputation as a peaceful

---

[7] Note that the sample questions recognize that more than one character trait may be relevant. In this assault case, the defendant's character trait for peacefulness might be more appropriate, although the question about moral, law-abidingness would certainly be permissible.

[8] The Texas Court of Criminal Appeals has held that in Texas criminal cases, the limiting instruction *must* be given, if one is requested, at the time the evidence is admitted. *Rankin v. State*, 974 S.W.2d 707 (Tex. Crim. App. 1996). The court also stated, however, that Article 36.14 of the Texas Code of Criminal Procedure seems to require that the limiting instructions also be given in the jury charge at the conclusion of the trial.

person. Again, remember Her Honor's words that good character "may be sufficient by itself to raise a reasonable doubt . . ."

Assume the same hypothetical assault prosecution. In this example, however, the proponent has called the witness to offer opinion testimony on a character trait.

P WHO is Mr. Lowe? (2)

W He's a neighbor of mine.

P WHEN is the last time you saw him? (2)

W He's in the courtroom right now.

P WHERE is he sitting? (2)

W He's sitting right there at the table with you.

P HOW is he dressed? (2)

W He's wearing a brown suit and yellow tie.

P Please let the record reflect that the witness has identified my client, Mr. Lowe.

J The record will so reflect.

P Mr. Nieman, WHERE does Mr. Lowe live? (2)

W Here in Corpus Christi.

P HOW long has he lived here? (2)

W I'd say easily 7 years.

P WHERE do you live? (2)

W I also reside in Corpus Christi.

P HOW close do you live to Mr. Lowe? (2)

W No more than half a mile away.

P HOW long have you lived in Corpus Christi? (2)

W Over 10 years.

P HOW long have you known Mr. Lowe? (2)

W I guess 7 years—ever since he moved here.

P HOW did you come to know Mr. Lowe? (2)

W We have several mutual acquaintances, and we both are members of some local clubs, including the Optimists.

P HOW often do you see Mr. Lowe? (2)

W At least once or twice each week.

P HOW well do you know him? (2)

W I consider him a good, close friend.

P Do you have an opinion whether he is a violent or peaceful person? [*Or, "Do you have an opinion whether he is a law-breaking or law-abiding person?"*] (1), (2)

W Yes.

P WHAT is your opinion? (1), (3)

W In my opinion, he is a peaceful person. [*Or, In my opinion, he is a moral, law-abiding person.*]

Whether the evidence takes the form of lay or expert opinion, on request the judge would give the jury a limiting instruction similar to the one for reputation character evidence. In closing argument, the defense counsel could then state:

> Mr. Nieman isn't just a passing acquaintance of Mr. Lowe. Mr. Nieman knows him well. The undisputed evidence is that Mr. Nieman has lived a few blocks from Mr. Lowe for over seven years. They have mutual friends, and they belong to some of the same organizations. In Mr. Nieman's words, they see each other "at least once or twice each week." Mr. Nieman knows Mr. Lowe—he knows the type of man Mr. Lowe is. That's why you ought to believe Mr. Nieman when he tells you that Mr. Lowe simply isn't the kind of person who would commit this crime.

The following fact situation centers on a civil lawsuit in which the plaintiff has alleged that the defendant, Ms. Wilson, engaged in fraudulent business practices involving real estate transactions. Assume that the alleged actions by the defendant are considered acts involving moral turpitude. The defense counsel has called an opinion character witness to the stand to testify on behalf of the defendant.

P WHO is Ms. Wilson? (2)

W She is a dear friend of mine.

P HOW long have you known her? (2)

P For over 20 years.

W WHAT, if any, business transactions have you both been involved in? (2)

P We used to routinely work on real estate deals together. I would say that we worked on over 100 different transactions.

W Do you have an opinion on whether Ms. Wilson is an honest and law-abiding person? (1)

P Yes, I do.

W WHAT is it? (3)

P She is very honest and law-abiding.

At least a significant minority of other jurisdictions permit the proponent to use expert opinion testimony as well as lay opinion. Suppose, for example, that a psychiatrist diagnoses the defendant as a passive personality with an aversion to violence. That expert opinion would certainly be relevant evidence to reduce the probability that the defendant initiated a violent, unprovoked attack. If the proponent wanted to present such testimony, the proponent would have to comply with the foundational requirements for an expert opinion described in Chapter 9.

§ 6-5 CIRCUMSTANTIAL CHARACTER EVIDENCE CONCERNING VICTIMS

§ 6-5(A) THE DOCTRINE

Under Rule 404, provision is made for introducing character evidence relating to victims. In Rule 404(a)(2), a party accused of assaultive conduct may introduce character evidence to show that the victim had a character for violence in an attempt to show self-defense. And, under Rule 404(a)(2), the defendant in a criminal case may open the door by introducing character evidence of a pertinent character trait of the victim. In a homicide case, the court may permit evidence of the peaceable character of the victim. Rule 404 notes a special exception for sexual assault victims which is discussed *infra* at § 6-6. The logical relevance of character evidence of victims is that if the alleged victim has a violent personality, for example, that personality increases the probability that the alleged victim threw the first punch and was the aggressor. The Texas Rules limit the defendant to the use of reputation and opinion testimony as methods of proving the victim's violent character. As noted *infra* at § 6-6, a different rule applies where sexual assault victims are involved.

§ 6-5(B) ELEMENTS OF THE FOUNDATION

The elements of the foundation for proving the character of a victim are as follows:

1. The victim has a violent (or peaceable) character.
2. The witness knows about the character trait of violence or peaceableness either personally or by reputation.
3. The witness states his or her opinion about the victim's character trait or states what the victim's reputation is regarding that character trait.

§ 6-5(C) SAMPLE FOUNDATION

Assume that the government charges Mr. Lowe with assaulting Mr. Gamely on December 1, 2004. During the defense case-in-chief, the defense calls Mr.

Nieman as a witness. Mr. Nieman has already identified himself. The defense is the proponent.

P WHO is Mr. Gamely? (2)

W He is my former college roommate.

P HOW long have you known him? (2)

W For the last 14 years.

P HOW well do you know him? (2)

W Very well. We used to see each other at least once a week at Rotary Club meetings. We also worked for a little while at the same company.

P WHAT, if any, opinion do you have about Mr. Gamely's violent or peaceful character? (1), (3)

W He is very violent and prone to starting fights.

Notice that at the end of this line of questioning, the proponent does not attempt to elicit the witness's opinion that given Gamely's violent character, it is more probable that Gamely started the fight. It would be improper opinion for the witness to draw that inference. Moreover, it is unnecessary for the witness to draw that inference at this point. In the subsequent instructions the judge will tell the jury that it may decide whether to draw the inference, and in summation the proponent may expressly argue in favor of the inference.

Thus, when the testimony is admitted, during the jury charge, or on both occasions the judge might tell the jury the following about the evidence:

> In this case, the defendant claims that Mr. Gamely was the aggressor. Evidence has been received for the purpose of showing that Mr. Gamely has a violent character. You may consider that evidence in deciding whether the defendant or Mr. Gamely was the real aggressor.

During final argument, the defense counsel could state:

> Ladies and gentlemen, as I told you in opening statement, this case boils down to a simple question: Who attacked whom? Did Mr. Lowe start the fight, or was Mr. Gamely, the so-called victim, the real aggressor? When you discuss that question in the deliberation room, I ask you to remember the testimony of Mr. Nieman. Mr. Nieman testified about another incident involving Mr. Gamely. It was a relatively recent incident; it happened on December 1st of this year. It started out as a pleasant evening, a party at Tarantino's. Most of us are familiar with that restaurant—it's a great place for a party, good food, nice surroundings, and a peaceful atmosphere with a wonderful view of the Bay. But something shattered the peace that evening. A fight broke out. Remember how it broke out. For no good reason, someone

just started screaming. Then that same person got violent. With no provocation, he threw one punch, then another, and another—and before it was over, he had thrown five or six punches. Who was that person? Mr. Nieman told you that it was none other than Mr. Gamely. Ladies and gentlemen, that incident tells you something about Mr. Gamely. It shows that he has a violent streak. A few minutes ago, her Honor gave you the legal instructions that you have to follow during deliberations. In particular, she told you that you may consider Mr. Nieman's testimony "in deciding whether the defendant or Mr. Gamely was the real aggressor." I want you to do exactly what her Honor tells you. If you do that, if you consider the evidence of Mr. Gamely's violent temper, you'll reach the only reasonable conclusion in this case, namely, that Mr. Lowe was the real victim and that the so-called victim, Mr. Gamely, actually started the fight.

§ 6-6 CHARACTER EVIDENCE REGARDING SEXUAL ASSAULT VICTIMS

§ 6-6(A) THE DOCTRINE

Under Texas Rule of Evidence 412, sometimes referred to as the "rape shield rule," character evidence about the victim of a sexual assault offense is severely limited.[9] Reputation and opinion evidence about the victim's past sexual behavior is absolutely inadmissible. But evidence of prior specific instances of the victim's sexual behavior may be admissible under one of several specific provisions in Rule 412(b). One of those exceptions permits the proponent, usually the defense counsel, to introduce evidence of the victim's prior sexual behavior with the accused on the issue of whether the alleged sexual act was consensual. The line of reasoning is that if the alleged victim consented to intercourse on prior occasions, her prior consent increases the probability that she consented to intercourse with the defendant.

§ 6-6(B) ELEMENTS OF THE FOUNDATION

The proponent of specific acts evidence under Texas Rule 412 would have to establish the following elements:

1. The act is relevant for one of the specified purposes in Rule 412(b).[10]

---

[9] Note that character evidence about a sexual assault victim would not necessarily be blocked in a Texas civil trial under the character evidence rules. That evidence might be excluded, however, under Texas Rule of Evidence 403.

[10] Rule 412 permits introduction of a sexual assault victim's prior specific sexual behavior to: (1) rebut or explain medical evidence offered by the state; (2) prove consent; (3) prove motive or bias; (4) impeach the witness under Rule 609 (impeachment by conviction); or (5) when admission of evidence of such acts is constitutionally required.

2. Where the act occurred.
3. When the act occurred.
4. Who was present.
5. The probative value of this evidence outweighs the danger of unfair prejudice.

§ 6-6(C) SAMPLE FOUNDATION

Assume that the government charges Mr. Lowe with raping Ms. Younger on February 1, 2005. During the defense case-in-chief, the defense calls the defendant, Mr. Lowe, as a witness to testify about prior sexual acts involving the defendant and the victim. The defense is the proponent.

P WHERE were you on the evening of January 2, 2005? (2), (3)

W I was at Gino's bar in downtown Texarkana.

P WHAT were you doing there?

W I was hanging out and looking for some women to pick up.

P WHAT do you mean by "pick up?"

W I was trying to find someone to have some fun with that night.

P WHAT happened after you arrived at the bar?

W I bumped into a woman.

P WHO was the woman? (4)

W Ms. Nancy Younger.

P WHEN did you last see her? (3)

W Today.

P WHERE was she? (3)

W She was testifying for the prosecution a couple of hours ago in this courtroom.

P WHAT happened after you met Ms. Younger? (4)

W We spent a couple of hours at the bar and had some drinks.

P WHAT happened next? (1)

W We went to my apartment.

P WHAT happened then? (1)

W We had a couple more drinks there, and she spent the night.

P WHAT, if anything, happened that night? (1)

W We had sex.

P WHAT do you mean by "we had sex?" (1)

W We had intercourse.

P WHAT was your legal relation to Ms. Younger at that time? (1)

W We didn't have any legal relation. We weren't married, or engaged, or anything like that.

P HOW long had you known her before she had intercourse with you? (1)

W A couple of hours.

P WHAT force did you use to get her to consent to intercourse? (1)

W None.

P WHAT threats did you make against her? (1)

W None. She did it of her own free will.

P WHAT happened the next morning? (1)

W She just left. I didn't see her again until the next week at Gino's Bar.

P WHAT were you doing there? [*Here the proponent repeats the line of questioning to establish that on two other occasions, the defendant met the victim under the same circumstances and that consensual sexual intercourse occurred.*]

P Now, Mr. Lowe, I direct your attention to February 1, 2005, the date you allegedly raped Ms. Younger. WHERE were you at about 10:00 P.M.?

W I was at Gino's Bar, again. [*The proponent now conducts a line of questioning to show that the defendant believed that, based upon the prior sexual conduct with the victim, she was again consenting to the conduct which ultimately resulted in sexual assault charges against the defendant.*]

Notice that at the end of this line of questioning, the proponent does not ask the witness to opine whether Ms. Younger has a propensity for extra-marital sexual intercourse or whether her propensity increases the probability that she consented to intercourse with the defendant. It would be improper opinion for the witness to attempt to draw those inferences. Moreover, it is unnecessary for the proponent to invite the witness to draw the inferences; in the subsequent instructions the judge will tell the jury that it is to decide whether to draw the inferences, and in summation the proponent may expressly argue in favor of those inferences.

When the testimony is admitted, during the jury charge, or on both occasions, the judge might tell the jury the following about the evidence:

> One of the questions in this case is whether Ms. Younger consented to sexual intercourse with Mr. Lowe. You may have heard evidence that on three other occasions, the alleged victim consented to intercourse with Mr. Lowe. You

> may consider that evidence, if at all, in deciding whether Ms. Younger gave her consent to intercourse with Mr. Lowe and for no other purpose.

During closing argument, the defense counsel could state:

> Ladies and gentlemen, as I told you in opening statement, Mr. Lowe admits having had sex with Ms. Younger. It's not a crime to have sex with someone. It's a crime only if you force them to have sex with you. And, again as I said during opening, the only real question in this case is whether Ms. Younger agreed to have sex with Mr. Lowe. In a few minutes her Honor will give you the legal instructions that you must follow during your deliberations in this case. One of those instructions relates to the testimony given by my client, Mr. Lowe, earlier today. As you'll recall, Mr. Lowe told you that on three prior occasions in November he met Ms. Younger at a bar and that later that night they had consensual sex. In her instructions, her Honor told you that you may consider his testimony in deciding whether Ms. Younger consented to having sex with Mr. Lowe on the date in question. Let's talk about Mr. Lowe's testimony. Consider all the striking similarities between Ms. Younger's contacts with Mr. Lowe on those prior occasions. The incidents are incredibly similar. She met him at Gino's bar. They had a few drinks. They then went to his apartment where they spent the night together, having sex. That sexual contact, ladies and gentlemen was completely consensual. No force. No threats. No coercion. Mr. Lowe testified in no uncertain terms that Ms. Younger consented to sex that night. Mr. Lowe took the stand, looked you in the eye, and told you that she also consented on the night in question—December 1st. There are so many parallels between the three prior occasions of sexual intercourse. The evidence shows that she consented in November, and the only reasonable conclusion is that a few weeks later in strikingly similar circumstances she consented again.

§ 6-7 CROSS-EXAMINATION OF A CHARACTER WITNESS

After the proponent conducts the direct examination of a character witness, the opponent has a right to cross-examine the witness. This issue was also discussed briefly in Chapter 5 concerning cross-examination of character witnesses who have testified about another witness's character for truthfulness.

Suppose that on direct examination, the witness testified that the defendant in a criminal case had a reputation for peacefulness. Further assume that the prosecutor knows that the defendant was arrested for a violent assault only two months before the alleged assault. The traditional view is that during the cross-examination, the prosecutor may ask, "Have you heard that the defendant was arrested for assault in October 1999?" If the witness denies hearing about the incident, the denial impeaches the witness. The denial indicates that the witness really is not familiar with the defendant's reputation. If the witness admits hearing about the incident, the admission also impeaches the witness. The admission indicates that the witness has a rather strange standard for evaluating good reputation. The prosecutor may inquire about reports that the defendant committed, or was arrested for, indicted for, or convicted of a crime. Of course, the crime must be logically relevant to the character trait the witness testified to on direct examination. Thus, if on direct examination the witness testifies to the defendant's character trait of peacefulness, the prosecutor may not inquire about an arrest for mere drunkenness.

If on direct examination the witness expresses his or her opinion, the wording of the question on cross-examination is slightly different. The prosecutor no longer uses the "Have you heard?" formula. Rather, the prosecutor may ask, "Do you know that the defendant was arrested for assault in October 1999?" If the witness denies knowing about the arrest, the denial indicates that the witness may not know the defendant well. If the witness admits knowing about the arrest, the admission indicates that the witness has a strange personal standard for evaluating good character. Again, the crime inquired about must be logically relevant to the character trait the witness testified to on direct examination.

Texas Rule of Evidence 405, which governs how character evidence may be introduced, is modeled after Federal Rule 405. The Advisory Committee's Note to the Federal Rule states that the Committee intended to abolish the old, formal distinctions in the phrasing of the questions on cross-examination. The Note asserts that the Committee intended to "eliminate them [the distinctions] as a factor in formulating questions." Thus, under the Federal Rules, it would be permissible to use normal, cross-examination phrasing: "HAVEN'T YOU HEARD THAT the defendant was arrested for assault in October 2004?" Arguably, that same form should be permissible under the Texas Rules.

Of course, the prosecutor in the preceding example must have a good faith basis in fact for inquiring about the incident. The prosecutor cannot smear the defendant's character by inventing derogatory reports about the defendant. Thus, the prosecutor must have a basis in fact for believing that the defendant committed, was arrested for, was indicted for, or was convicted of the crime. The basis in fact need not be admissible evidence. For example, the prosecutor could use an eyewitness's written statement or a police report as the basis in fact. The statement and report would normally be inadmissible hearsay, but they are sufficient to give the prosecutor a good faith belief that the incident occurred. When the defense attorney challenges the prosecutor to show the basis in fact for the belief that the incident occurred, the prosecutor usually makes a statement for the record outside the jurors' hearing. It might be appropriate for the prosecutor to insert any documentary material into the record. The material is not admitted as a formal exhibit to be submitted to the jury. It is usually marked for identification and submitted for purposes of the record only.

Assume that during cross-examination of a character witness, the prosecutor inquired about an arrest of the defendant for assault. The prosecutor might have used the classic language, "Have you heard that the defendant was arrested for assault in October 1999?" As the opponent, the defense counsel objects:

O Your Honor, may we approach the bench?

J Yes.

O [*Outside the hearing of the jury*] Your Honor, I want to object to the last question on the ground that the prosecutor is merely fishing for extraneous offenses allegedly committed by the defendant.

P Your Honor, we do have information that the defendant was indeed arrested for assault in 1999.

O What is the basis of your information?

P We have an arrest report from the Denton Police Department.

O Then we request to see a copy before questioning resumes.

P Your Honor, I would like to mark this document as prosecution exhibit number one for identification.

O What is that document?

P [*Hands to opponent*] It is an arrest report from the Denton Police Department. The report names the defendant, George Larson, as the arrestee and states that he was arrested for assault on a Mr. Dave Langdale.

O This report is inadmissible hearsay, your Honor.

J Let me see the document. [*Judge inspects document.*]

P That would normally be true, but the material creating the basis in fact for believing the incident occurred need not qualify as admissible evidence.

J Do you have any other objections to this document?

O No.

J The objection to the question will be overruled. Prosecution exhibit number one will be admitted for purposes of the record only. It will not be shown to the jury.

P Mr. Stacey, let me repeat the question. Have you heard that the defendant was arrested for assault in October 1999?

W No.

Notice that at the end of this line of questioning; the proponent does not take a further step and ask: "Well, how then can you say that you know the defendant's reputation well?" It would be objectionably argumentative for the proponent to pose that question. Moreover, it is unnecessary for the proponent to put that question to the witness; in the subsequent instructions the judge will tell the jury that it can decide whether to draw the inference, and during summation the proponent may argue in favor of that inference.

When the cross-examiner asks a character witness about an incident, the judge may tell the jury the following—at the time the question is asked, during the jury charge, or on both occasions:

> When on cross-examination, a witness is asked if he has heard reports of certain conduct of a defendant inconsistent with the traits of good character to which the witness has testified, these questions and the witness's answers to them may be considered, if at all, only for the purpose of determining the weight to be given to the witness's testimony about the defendant's good reputation. These questions and answers are not evidence that the reports are true, and you must not assume from them that the defendant in fact committed the act inconsistent with those traits of character.

During closing argument, the prosecutor could state:

> Ladies and gentlemen, as you'll recall, the defense called a Mr. Stacey in an attempt to convince you that Mr. Larson is a peaceful person, not the type of man who would commit the violent battery that Mr. Larson is on trial for. The judge read you the legal instructions that you must follow during your deliberations in this case. One of those instructions deals with Mr. Stacey's character testimony. He told you that you don't have to accept Mr. Stacey's testimony; it's up to you to decide how much weight, if any, to give it. He also told you that in making that decision, you can consider the way Mr. Stacey answered my questions on cross-examination.
>
> Do you remember my cross-examination? On cross-examination, I asked Mr. Stacey whether he'd heard a report that the defendant had been arrested for an assault a mere two years ago. [Mr. Stacey said that he'd never heard any such report. Think about that answer. Mr. Stacey expects you to believe that he knows the defendant's reputation for peacefulness well, but he's never heard a report about an assault only two years ago. An assault is a violent crime. Yet Mr. Stacey claims he never heard of the report. That answer tells you that Stacey really doesn't know the defendant's reputation well. If he knew the defendant's reputation well, he certainly would have heard about that report. And that's why you should reject his testimony.]
>
> OR (assuming that the witness admitted hearing about the assault).
>
> [Stacey admitted that he had heard that report. Think about that answer. On the one hand, he testifies that the defendant had a good reputation for

peacefulness, and he expects you to believe that he's a good judge of character. On the other hand, he admits that he's heard that the defendant was arrested for an assault battery a mere two years ago. Ladies and gentlemen, Mr. Stacey must have a pretty strange standard for deciding whether someone has a good reputation for peacefulness. When someone is reported to have committed a battery, most reasonable people would say that that person had a terrible reputation for peacefulness. But not Mr. Stacey. Either he has a crazy standard for judging character, or he's simply a biased witness. After all, he conceded on cross-examination that he and the defendant have been good friends for almost ten years. In either case, you just can't trust Stacey's testimony].

§ 6-8 HABIT EVIDENCE

§ 6-8(A) THE DOCTRINE

The proponent may use habit evidence as well as character evidence as circumstantial proof of conduct. Texas Rule of Evidence 406 states the habit evidence doctrine:

> Evidence of the habit of a person or of the routine practice of an organization, whether corroborated or not and regardless of the presence of eyewitnesses, is relevant to prove that the conduct of the person or organization on a particular occasion was in conformity with the habit or routine practice.

Although both character and habit evidence serve as circumstantial proof of conduct, there are major differences between the two theories of admissibility.

The first difference is that although character evidence is usually admissible only after the criminal defendant opens the issue, under the modern view, either party in a civil or criminal case may introduce habit evidence. It is true that some jurisdictions admit habit evidence only if there are no eyewitnesses to the conduct in question or only if there is corroboration of the conduct. Rule 406 embodies the emerging view, however, that habit evidence is always admissible to prove the conduct of a person or a business organization.

The second difference is that while character evidence permits the proponent to prove general character or character traits, habit evidence requires proof of a very specific, frequently repeated behavioral pattern. For instance, the proponent may prove the precise manner in which a decedent routinely executed right-hand turns or the specific mailing procedure a business customarily uses.

Finally, the habit and character evidence theories may differ in the method of proof. The proponent of character evidence ordinarily presents reputation or opinion evidence. In contrast, the proponent of habit evidence usually uses opinion evidence or evidence of specific acts, although there is some authority in Texas case law for using reputation evidence. To be qualified to express an opinion on the existence of a habit, the witness must have been familiar with the person or business for a substantial time and observed numerous instances of the person's or business's conduct. Opinion habit evidence is typically presented by a single witness who is familiar with a large number of instances of the conduct of the person or business in question. Habit may also be proved by the testimony of several witnesses. Each witness testifies to the instances of conduct of which he or she knows. If the behavioral pattern is specific enough and the instances numerous enough, the judge allows the jury to infer the existence of the habit.

§ 6-8(B) ELEMENTS OF THE FOUNDATION

The foundation for habit evidence includes these elements:

1. The person or business has a particular habit or routine practice.
2. The witness has observed the person or business act in conformity with the habit on numerous occasions or is familiar with the reputation of the person or business for a habit or routine practice.

§ 6-8(C) SAMPLE FOUNDATION

The fact situation is a tort action. The plaintiff sues the decedent's estate on the theory that the decedent negligently caused the traffic accident. The decedent is Mr. Myles. The collision occurred as the decedent was making a right-hand turn at a stop sign. The estate's personal representative contends that the decedent drove carefully. To support that contention, the representative desires to offer evidence of the decedent's driving habits. To do so, the representative calls Ms. Vincent, an acquaintance of the decedent. The decedent's personal representative is the proponent. Ms. Vincent has already identified herself.

P WHO was Joshua Myles? (1)

W He was a friend of mine. He died in an accident about a year and a half ago.

P HOW long did you know him? (2)

W For about seven years.

P HOW did you come to know him? (2)

W We worked at the same bank. In fact, we were in the same car pool.

P HOW many people were in this car pool? (2)

W Three of us, Joshua, a teller named Kathy Jacobs, and I.

P HOW often did you see the decedent drive a car? (2)

W Hundreds of times. I couldn't give you a precise number.

P WHEN did you see him drive a car? (2)

W He did a lot of the driving in our car pool; he took me to work.

P HOW many times a week did the decedent drive you to work? (2)

W Usually twice.

P HOW many weeks during the year did he drive you to work? (2)

W About 50 per year. You have to exclude our vacation times.

P HOW many years were you in this car pool? (2)

W Roughly five years.

P HOW many years was the decedent in this car pool? (2)

W The same—five years.

P WHAT did the decedent do when he came to a stop sign? (1)

W He came to a complete stop.

P HOW regularly did he do that? (1)

W Always.

P HOW often did you see him do that? (2)

W Hundreds of times.

P HOW did the decedent make right-hand turns after coming to a stop? (1)

W He'd look both ways and start up only after he could see that it was safe.

P HOW fast did he go immediately after starting up? (1)

W Usually quite slowly and cautiously.

P HOW often did you see him make a right-hand turn in that manner? (1)

W All sorts of times.

At the end of this line of questioning, the proponent does not attempt to elicit the witness's opinion that given Myles' driving habit, it is more probable that he drove in the manner alleged in the pleadings. That testimony would amount to an improper opinion. It is unnecessary for the proponent to invite the witness to draw the inference; during the subsequent instructions the judge will instruct the jury that it can decide whether to do draw that inference, and during summation the proponent may expressly argue in favor of the inference.

If the judge admits this testimony then the judge might tell the jury the following—either when the evidence is admitted, during the jury charge, or on both occasions:

> Evidence may have been presented of the decedent's driving habits. You may use that evidence, if any, to infer that a person acts consistently with

> their personal habits. Therefore, you may consider evidence of the decedent's driving habits, if at all, in deciding how the decedent made his right-hand turn on the occasion when his car collided with the plaintiffs' car.

During closing argument, the defense attorney could state:

> Ladies and gentlemen, as I told you in opening statement, this case boils down to the question of whether Mr. Myles used due care in making his right-hand turn at 1st and Martin Streets just before the collision with the plaintiff's car. When you discuss that question in the deliberation room, I want you to consider the testimony of Ms. Vincent. She was the witness who testified about Mr. Myles' driving habits.
>
> The judge gave you the legal instructions that you must follow during your deliberations in this case. One of those instructions concerned Ms. Vincent's testimony about Mr. Myles' driving habits. In the instructions, his Honor told you that you can consider Ms. Vincent's testimony in deciding how Mr. Myles made his right-hand turn that day. How much importance should you attach to her testimony? Think back to the undisputed testimony she gave you. She knew Mr. Myles well for about seven years. They were in the same carpool to work together. They were together in the car—let's do the simple arithmetic [*counsel writes numbers on board*]: five years, 50 times, over 250 times. And on each and every occasion, Mr. Myles always came to a complete stop at the stop sign. And on every occasion, he looked both ways before entering the intersection and started up only after it was clearly safe. In her words, he "would look both ways and start up only after he could see that it was safe." Not just sometimes, not just most of the time, but "all sorts of times"—that was the exact word she used. Common sense tells you that you ought to give Ms. Vincent's testimony a lot of weight. If Mr. Myles followed that practice so religiously so many times, it's ridiculous to think that he'd abandon it for no reason at all on the day of the accident.

§ 6-9 EXTRANEOUS OFFENSES OR UNCHARGED MISCONDUCT IN CRIMINAL CASES

§ 6-9(A) THE DOCTRINE

The prosecution in a criminal case may not prove other crimes by the defendant simply to prove that the defendant is a law-breaking, immoral person, even in rebuttal to defense character evidence. The prosecution may, however, introduce such evidence for other purposes. Texas Evidence Rule 404(b) states:

Evidence of other crimes, wrongs, or acts is not admissible to prove the character of a person in order to show that he acted in conformity therewith.

It may, however, be admissible for other purposes, such as proof of motive, opportunity, intent, preparation, plan, knowledge, identity, or absence of mistake or accident . . .[11]

Thus, if the evidence is logically relevant to a fact in issue other than character, and its probative value is not substantially outweighed by its prejudicial effect, the prosecution may introduce the proof of the uncharged act. The Texas courts tend to follow the inclusionary approach to the uncharged misconduct doctrine; the prosecution may offer the evidence on any noncharacter theory of logical relevance.

A prosecutor offering extraneous offense or uncharged misconduct evidence faces two primary problems. First, the prosecutor must demonstrate that the evidence is logically relevant to a material fact in issue other than character. For example, if the defendant is charged with a specific intent crime, the defendant's commission of similar, deliberate acts may be logically relevant to prove the specific intent. In that instance, the prosecutor is relying on what is often referred to as the "doctrine of chances." That is, the prosecutor is not relying on the defendant's personal, subjective bad character; instead, the prosecutor is attempting to show that it is objectively unlikely that an innocent person would become repeatedly enmeshed in suspicious circumstances. Another example is where the prosecutor uses prior acts to show that the modus operandi used in the case at bar bears a striking resemblance to the modus operandi used by the defendant in other prior acts. Although many criminals may share the same character or character trait, the hypothesis is that one and only one criminal uses the same peculiar modus operandi.

Second, the prosecutor must be prepared to convince the judge that the evidence passes the Rule 403 balancing test. That is, the prejudicial character of the evidence does not substantially outweigh the probative value of the evidence.[12] To be sure, such evidence is highly prejudicial. There is a grave danger that the jurors will misuse it as evidence of the defendant's bad, law-breaking disposition. If the element of the crime the prosecution wants to offer the uncharged misconduct evidence to prove is disputed, however, the judge will probably admit the evidence. Thus, if the prosecution wants to offer the evidence to prove identity and the defendant denied committing the crime, the judge would probably rule in the prosecution's favor.

---

[11] *See generally* WENDORF, SCHLUETER & BARTON, TEXAS RULES OF EVIDENCE MANUAL IV-35 (6th ed. 2002).

[12] There is authority for the proposition that if the defendant does not make a Rule 403 objection, the trial court may not need to conduct the balancing test. *See Montgomery v. State*, 810 S.W.2d 372 (Tex. Crim. App. 1990) (en banc) (opinion on rehearing).

§ 6-9(B) ELEMENTS OF THE FOUNDATION

The foundation for introducing extraneous offense evidence includes these elements:

1. Where the other act occurred.
2. When the act occurred.
3. What the nature of the act was.
4. The defendant committed the other act. Rule 104(b) governs this foundational fact. The judge accepts the prosecution's foundational evidence at face value and asks only whether the evidence is sufficient to permit the jury to find beyond a reasonable doubt that the defendant committed the act.
5. The surrounding circumstances making the uncharged act relevant to the charged crime. The prosecutor must convince the trial judge that the act is logically relevant to a material fact other than the defendant's criminal disposition or propensity.

Even after the prosecutor lays a proper foundation, the defense counsel will have a right to a limiting instruction. Under Rule 105, the judge must inform the jury that they may not use the evidence as general character, i.e., propensity, evidence. Rather, the jury must use the evidence only in deciding the existence of the fact the judge admitted the evidence to prove, e.g., motive, intent, or identity.

§ 6-9(C) SAMPLE FOUNDATION

Suppose that the State has charged the defendant, Mr. Standish, with armed robbery. During the prosecution case-in-chief, a single eyewitness identified the defendant as the robber. She testified that the defendant was wearing a dark green T-shirt, work gloves, and a bright red hat. A police officer also testified on behalf of the prosecution. He testified that he searched the crime scene and found a.32 caliber pistol with the serial number 789444. During the defense case-in-chief, the defendant testified and denied committing the robbery. During the prosecution rebuttal, the prosecution calls Mr. Usher. Mr. Usher has already identified himself. The prosecution is the proponent.

P WHAT is your occupation?

W I own a gun store.

P WHERE were you on March 15th of this year? (1), (2)

W I was at work at my store.

P WHAT, if anything, happened that day? (3)

W I was the victim of a theft that day.

P WHAT was stolen? (5)

W A pistol.

P WHAT pistol? (5)

W It was a .32 caliber pistol, serial number 789444.

P HOW do you know that? (5)

W I handle all my inventory personally, and I refreshed my memory by reviewing my records before trial.

P HOW was the pistol stolen? (4)

W A guy came in in broad daylight, pretended he was looking to buy, and then grabbed the pistol and ran out the door.

P HOW well did you see the thief? (4)

W Very well.

P HOW dose were you to the thief? (4)

W When he was at the counter, he was only about five feet away.

P HOW much time did you have to observe the thief? (4)

W He was in the store for at least a couple of minutes.

P Please describe WHAT he was wearing.

W He was wearing a bright red hat, some sort of heavy-duty gloves, and I believe he was wearing a dark greenish-blue shirt.

P WHO was the thief? (4)

W I'm not sure of his name, but I see him in the courtroom right now.

P WHERE is he sitting? (4)

W At that table over there.

P HOW is he dressed? (4)

W He's wearing a blue suit and green tie.

P Please let the record reflect that the witness has identified the defendant.

O Your Honor, may we approach the bench?

J Yes.

O Your Honor, we object to this witness's identification of the defendant as the person who allegedly stole a pistol. This is clearly inadmissible evidence of an extraneous offense. If the jury is permitted to consider this evidence they will naturally and improperly assume that the defendant has a propensity to commit offenses. Further, Texas case law requires that if the prosecutor is using the evidence to show identity, there must be some distinctively common characteristics between the charged and uncharged offense.

P Your Honor, we believe that there is clearly a distinct signature in these two offenses. The clothing, for example, is almost an exact match. Further, this evidence is clearly relevant to link the defendant with the gun found at the scene of the crime. The fact that the defendant has denied committing the charged offense makes this evidence very important to our case.

O Your Honor, at this point, I would make a Rule 403 objection. The prejudicial effect of this evidence substantially outweighs the probative value, if any.

P Your Honor, as we just pointed out, the defendant's identity is clearly in issue in this case and the evidence we are offering is crucial. Any possible prejudice can be addressed in a limiting instruction.

O We disagree, your Honor. This evidence is extremely prejudicial and will naturally lead the jury to an improper conclusion about the defendant's propensity to commit crimes.

J Your objection is overruled. I will permit inquiry into this other alleged offense.

O Your Honor, we request a limiting instruction under Rule 105.

J Ladies and gentlemen of the jury, you have just heard testimony that the defendant may have stolen a pistol, serial number 789444. You may not infer from that evidence that the defendant is generally a bad person and, for that reason, more likely to have committed the alleged robbery in this case. You may only use Mr. Usher's testimony, if at all, if you first find beyond a reasonable doubt that the defendant stole the pistol. If you so find, then you may only consider that evidence in deciding the issue of identity of the robber in this case.

At the end of this line of questioning, the proponent does not attempt to elicit the witness's testimony that it is therefore more likely that the defendant committed the charged offense. That testimony would amount to improper opinion. It is unnecessary for the proponent to invite the witness to draw that inference—during the subsequent instructions the judge will instruct the jury that it can decide whether to draw the inference, and during summation the proponent may expressly argue in favor of the inference.

During closing argument, the prosecutor could state:

> Ladies and gentlemen, the key issue in this case is identity. This case boils down to the question of whether the defendant is the person who committed the armed robbery at the liquor store. In deciding that question, I want you to especially recall the testimony of three witnesses. One witness was Officer

Salcido. He testified that he arrived at the crime scene a few minutes after the robber made his getaway. Right there on the floor of the liquor store he found State's Exhibit #2—the .32 caliber pistol, serial number 789444, which I'm holding right now. You will be able to take this exhibit with you into the deliberation room, so you can examine the serial number yourself.

We also presented the testimony of Mr. Usher. Now think back to his testimony. He took the stand and told you that he owns a gun store downtown. He testified that in March of this year, the defendant—whom he positively identified in court today—came to his store. He testified that the defendant grabbed a pistol and ran out of the store. Mr. Usher immediately checked his records. And guess what? There was only one missing gun, a.32 caliber pistol, serial number 789444. This is State's Exhibit #3, Mr. Usher's inventory sheet. It lists all weapons in Mr. Usher's inventory that day. You're also going to have this exhibit in the deliberation room. Check it against exhibit #2—the pistol. You'll see that the numbers match perfectly. There's only one pistol out there that perfectly fits that description. It's this one. This is the pistol the defendant stole from Mr. Usher, and it's the same one he used in this robbery. Put the testimony of Officer Salcido and Mr. Usher together, and what do you get? You get the only reasonable conclusion, namely, that the defendant is the man who robbed the liquor store in this case.

Earlier today, the judge gave you legal instructions you have to follow during your deliberations. One of those instructions relates to Mr. Usher's testimony. In her Honor's words, you can consider that testimony only on the question of whether it tends to show the identity of the person who committed the crime of which the defendant is presently accused. I want you to do exactly what the judge said you could do. Think about Mr. Usher's testimony when you deliberate on the question of the identity of the robber. If you do that, I'm confident you'll find that the defendant was the robber and that the defendant is guilty as charged.

§ 6-10 PRIOR ACTS OF DEFENDANT IN ASSAULT CASES—TEXAS CODE OF CRIMINAL PROCEDURE ART. 38.37

§ 6-10(A) THE DOCTRINE

As noted at § 6-9, the prosecution in a criminal case is normally limited to noncharacter use of a defendant's prior extraneous offenses or uncharged misconduct. The typical vehicle for introducing a defendant's extraneous offenses is through Rule 404(b). However, under that Rule, the prosecution may introduce those acts only for noncharacter purposes, such as showing lack of accident or the defendant's intent. If the evidence is admitted under Rule 404(b) the defendant is entitled to an instruction that directs the jury to consider the defendant's acts only for the noncharacter (on nonpropensity) purpose for which it was admitted.

Under article 38.37 of the Code of Criminal Procedure, however, the prosecution may be able to introduce the defendant's prior acts to prove that he or she had the propensity to commit the charged act in the case. That article, which applies to various assaultive and sexual offenses against a child under 17 years of age, provides in pertinent part:

> Notwithstanding Rules 404 and 405, Texas Rules of Criminal Evidence, evidence of other crimes, wrongs, or acts committed by the defendant against the child who is the victim of the alleged offense shall be admitted for its bearing on relevant matters, including:
>
> (1) the state of mind of the defendant and the child; and
>
> (2) the previous and subsequent relationship between the defendant and the child.
>
> * * *

Further, the provision includes a notice provision similar to that of Rule 404(b) and indicates that it does not limit the admissibility of similar evidence under any other applicable law. Due to the wording in article 38.37, specifically the "shall be admitted," the court's discretion in the admission of evidence may be limited. This wording signals that the Legislature believes this type of evidence is relevant and admissible. Although the statute does not indicate whether a Rule 403 balancing test is applicable, recent case law suggests that it does apply.[13] Additionally, the extraneous acts or offenses are admissible in the state's case-in-chief; and this admission does not depend on whether the defense has impeached the victim. The statute is silent on what burden the prosecutor bears in proving the extraneous act or offense. If the evidence is admitted under Rule 404(b), the prosecutor must establish the act beyond a reasonable doubt.[14]

§ 6-10(B) Elements of the Foundation

The foundational elements for proving the defendant's prior acts under article 38.37 are as follows:

1. What the nature of the act was.
2. Where the other act occurred.

---

[13] *See Walker v. State*, 4 S.W.3d 98 (Tex. App.—Waco 1999, pet. ref.) applying Rule 403 balancing test to CCP 38.37 evidence and finding it admissible.

[14] *See Harrell v. State*, 884 S.W.2d 154 (Tex. Crim. App. 1994).

3. When the act occurred.
4. The victim, at the time of the charged offense, was under the age of 17.
5. The defendant committed the other act.

§ 6-10(C) SAMPLE FOUNDATION

In the following sample foundation, the defendant is charged with sexual assault of the victim, a child under the age of 17. The victim is on the stand and has just testified about the charged sexual assault. The defendant is the victim's stepfather. The proponent is the prosecutor.

P Have you ever have been assaulted by the defendant on any other occasion?

O Your Honor, we object to this question. Alleged unadjudicated offenses are not admissible. This is clearly inadmissible evidence of an extraneous offense under Texas Rule of Evidence 404(b). This evidence is highly prejudicial and the jury will assume that the defendant has a propensity to commit such offenses.

P Your Honor, under article 38.37 of the Texas Code of Criminal Procedure, this evidence is permissible in our case-in-chief. This article specifically allows the introduction of prior extraneous offenses and acts in sexual assault cases involving children under the age of 17. In this case, previous evidence has established the victim was under the age of 17 at the time of the charged offense. (4)

J The objection is overruled. I will allow the inquiry into the prior acts of the defendant.

P Again, have you been assaulted previously by the defendant?

W Yes.

P Can you tell us WHERE these other acts occurred? (1)

W In the same place, my bedroom.

P WHEN did these assaults take place? (2)

W It started when I was about 15 years old and continued about once a month until he was arrested. I guess it has been about three years.

P WHAT exactly happened? (3)

W Pretty much the same thing that always happened. He would come in my room after my mom was asleep and get in bed with me. He would then have sex with me.

P To make sure we are clear, could you please identify the person that you are talking about?

W (points to the defendant) He's sitting over there at that table.

P Please let the record reflect that the witness has pointed to the defendant.

O Your Honor, we would request a limiting instruction under Rule 105.

P Your Honor, under article 38.37, we believe that the evidence is admissible to prove that the defendant has a propensity to commit sexual assaults and therefore it is more likely that he committed the charged offense. The article explicitly notes that this evidence is admissible "Notwithstanding Rule 404 and 405 . . . ."

J I will not give the limiting instruction.

Notice that at the end of this line of questioning, the proponent does not attempt to elicit the witness's testimony that the defendant has a propensity to engage in sexual misconduct or that given that propensity, it is more probable that the defendant committed the charged offense. It would be improper opinion for the witness to draw those inferences. Moreover, it is unnecessary for the proponent to invite the witness to draw those inferences; in the subsequent instructions the judge will tell the jury that it is to decide whether to draw the inferences, and during summation the proponent may expressly argue in favor of the inferences.

If this testimony is admitted, the judge may instruct the jury as follows:

> You may have heard evidence that the defendant engaged in a sexual offense on other occasions with the victim, other than that charged in this case. If you find that the defendant committed those prior sexual offenses beyond a reasonable doubt, you may, but are not required, to infer that the defendant had a disposition to commit the same type of sexual offense. If you find that the defendant had this disposition, you may treat it as some evidence that the defendant was likely to commit and did commit the crime he is charged with.

During closing argument, the prosecutor might state:

> Ladies and gentlemen, during the trial you heard the testimony of Ms. Leslie, the victim in this case. You heard her describe a sexual assault—an assault made on her by her stepfather—the defendant—in December of last year. His Honor read to you the legal instructions that you have to follow during your deliberations in the case. He told you that in deciding the defendant's guilt or innocence of the sexual attack on Ms. Chang, you may consider Ms. Leslie's testimony. In particular, his Honor told you the following: "If you find that the defendant committed a prior sexual offense, you may, but are not required, to infer that the defendant committed a prior sexual offense, you may, but are not required, to infer that the defendant had a disposition to commit the same type of criminal offense." If you find that the defendant

had this disposition, you may treat it as some evidence that he was likely to commit and did commit the crime against Ms. Chang.

Ladies and gentlemen, with that instruction in mind, let's consider Ms. Leslie's testimony. Take a look at this chart. Think of all the striking similarities between the attack in this case and the attacks that the defendant committed on his stepdaughter—starting when she was about 15 years old—and continued, as she said, on a monthly basis. On each of those occasions, he would come into her room after her mother was asleep, get in bed with her, and have sex with her. Ask yourselves, ladies and gentlemen: In the words of his Honor's instruction, did the defendant have "a disposition to commit the same type of sexual offense"? You bet he did. A leopard doesn't change its spots. The defendant did exactly the same thing on a monthly basis for almost two years. Ms. Leslie's testimony clearly shows you the type of man the defendant is. He is exactly the kind of person who would commit the assault on Ms. Chang.

§ 6-11 UNCHARGED MISCONDUCT EVIDENCE IN CIVIL ACTIONS

§ 6-11(A) THE DOCTRINE

Rule 404(b) refers not only to evidence of other "crime[s], but also to evidence of other wrong[s] . . . or other act[s]." While most cases involving Rule 404(b) evidence arise in criminal cases, the rule applies to civil actions as well as prosecutions. In a criminal prosecution, the State may not use evidence of a defendant's other crimes as circumstantial proof of conduct. That is, the prosecution may not argue that the defendant has a bad character and that his bad character increases the probability that he committed the charged crime. Similarly, in a tort action, the plaintiff may not use evidence of a defendant's other torts as circumstantial proof of conduct; the plaintiff may not argue that the defendant is a careless driver and that his character trait of careless driving increases the likelihood that he ran the red light. To this extent, the criminal and civil cases are parallel.

As with the application of Rule 404(b) in criminal cases, which tends to follow an inclusionary approach, in civil cases the proponent should not be bound by the exact list of grounds for admission listed in Rule 404(b). Hence, like a criminal prosecutor, the proponent of uncharged misconduct in a civil case should be permitted to introduce the evidence on any noncharacter theory. The proponent should be able to rely on any theory of logical relevance other than the general inference that the person's other negligent or wrongful acts increase the likelihood of fault on the pleaded occasion.[15]

[15] For a discussion of applying Federal Rule 404(b) in civil cases, *see* Annotation, 64 ALR Fed. 648 (1983).

§ 6-11(B) ELEMENTS OF THE FOUNDATION

The list of foundational elements is the same as the list for uncharged misconduct evidence in criminal cases:

1. Where the other act occurred.
2. When the act occurred.
3. What the nature of the act was.
4. The defendant committed the other act.
5. The surrounding circumstances make the extraneous act relevant to the pleaded act. The proponent must convince the trial judge that the act is logically relevant to a material fact other than the defendant's disposition or propensity.

§ 6-11(C) SAMPLE FOUNDATION

The fact situation is a wrongful discharge action. The plaintiff, Morrison, contends that the defendant, Ziegler, fired him because he is black. The petition alleges that the defendant employed the plaintiff as a shop supervisor and that the defendant fired the plaintiff on May 12, 2005. The plaintiff calls Mr. Foote. Mr. Foote has already identified himself.

P WHERE do you work?

W At the moment I'm unemployed.

P WHAT was your last job? (4), (5)

W I worked for the defendant, Ron Ziegler.

P WHERE is he now? (4)

W In the courtroom. He's sitting at the table to my right. He's got on a brown suit.

P Your Honor, please let the record reflect that the witness has identified the defendant.

J It will so reflect.

P WHAT type of work did you do for the defendant? (5)

W I was a shop supervisor from 1995 to 2005. I worked on the assembly line from 1991 to 1995.

P WHY did you stop working for him? (3)

W He fired me.

P WHEN did he do that? (2)

W It was in late April 2005.

P WHERE did it happen? (1)

W One day over the public address system he just called me into his office. I reported there as soon as I heard the call.

P WHAT happened after you reported to his office? (3)

W He said he was firing me.

P WHAT did you do then? (5)

W I demanded an explanation. I'd put in a lot of good years at that company, and I wanted to know why he was letting me go.

P WHAT, if anything, did the defendant say when you demanded an explanation? (5)

W He said he was letting me go because I was black. He said he didn't like me; and since there were no witnesses to our conversation, he didn't mind telling me the real reason he was giving me my walking papers.

O Your Honor, may we approach the bench?

J Certainly.

O Your Honor, I move to strike this entire line of questioning on the ground that it's irrelevant and that it amounts to bad character evidence.

P May I be heard?

J Yes.

P Your Honor, I'm not going to offer this evidence to support a general inference that the defendant is a bad person. I know that it would violate Rule 404(b). Rather, I'm offering this evidence on a non-character theory of logical relevance. The defendant fired Mr. Foote a few days before he fired the plaintiff. Like the plaintiff, Mr. Foote is an African-American. Given the surrounding circumstances, including the defendant's statements to Mr. Foote, the firing of Mr. Foote shows that the defendant had a racial prejudice that motivated him to fire African-American employees. In this case, we have to show that the defendant fired the plaintiff because he was black, and this April incident tends to show the defendant's later intent.

J Motion to strike denied.

O Your Honor, if you're going to overrule my motion, will you at least give the jury a limiting instruction?

J I'll tell them that they can't use it as proof that your client is a bad person. I'll indicate that they may consider the evidence, if at all, only in deciding why your client discharged the plaintiff.

§ 6-12 SIMILAR HAPPENINGS EVIDENCE

§ 6-12(A) THE DOCTRINE

In § 6-9(A), *supra*, we saw that Rule 404(b) applies in a civil case when a party offers evidence of a person's misdeeds that are not mentioned in the pleadings. The first sentence of Rule 404(b) bars the party from using the misdeeds as circumstantial proof of the person's conduct, but the second sentence permits the party to use noncharacter theories of logical relevance to introduce evidence of the misdeeds. Whether the case is a criminal prosecution or a civil action, under Rule 404(b) the focus is on the conduct of some person.

In other cases, the focus is on the qualities or properties of a physical object. Was a sidewalk cracked at the time the plaintiff slipped and fell? Was a steering wheel's design dangerously defective? To prove the quality of the object, the plaintiff may attempt to introduce evidence of other accidents involving the same or similar objects.[16] For example, the plaintiff may offer evidence that the day before her mishap, another passerby slipped and fell at the same location on the sidewalk.

On the one hand, Rule 404(b) does not apply directly when a plaintiff offers evidence of such a similar happening. Rule 404(b) comes into play when the party offers evidence of another incident to prove a person's conduct. The focus is now on the property of an object rather than on any conduct by a person. On the other hand, like evidence of a person's misdeeds used as circumstantial proof of the person's conduct, evidence of the other slip-and-fall poses probative dangers. The presentation of the testimony about the other accident may confuse the trier of fact, consume an undue amount of time, and sidetrack the trial. For that reason, although the evidence of the other slip and fall is relevant to prove the existence of the crack in the sidewalk, the judge might exclude the evidence under Rule 403.

While the Texas courts admit evidence of similar happenings, they have almost always imposed the requirement that there be some special connection between the act alleged and other similar acts or events. That connection may be supplied by showing substantial similarity in the events.

§ 6-12(B) ELEMENTS OF THE FOUNDATION

The foundation for similar happenings is similar to the foundation for evidence of an uncharged crime in a prosecution or tort offered under Rule 404(b):

1. Where the other event occurred.

[16] *See* Worm, *Similar Facts Evidence: Balancing Probative Value Against the Probable Dangers of Admission*, 9 U.C. DAVIS L. REV. 395 (1976).

2. When the event occurred.
3. What the nature of the event was.
4. The person's responsibility for, or connection with, the event.
5. The surrounding circumstances making the unpleaded happening relevant to show the property or quality of the object mentioned in the pleading.

§ 6-12(C) SAMPLE FOUNDATION[17]

The fact situation is a products liability case arising from a traffic accident. The plaintiff, Ms. Ramachotti, alleges that she purchased a Polecat Centuria and that the car's steering mechanism had a design defect. Specifically, the plaintiff contends that the mechanism had a tendency to freeze in lengthy, uphill turns.

The plaintiff has already testified. During her testimony, the plaintiff testified that she was driving north on a freeway and entered an off-ramp leading to the eastbound lane of a street near the freeway. She described the off-ramp as turning to the right, sloping slightly uphill, and being approximately 2,000 feet in length. The plaintiff stated that the steering wheel froze when her car was halfway through the off-ramp. The plaintiff used a chart to illustrate her testimony.

The plaintiff's attorney calls Mr. Dorsey to testify about an uncharged accident involving Mr. Dorsey's Polecat Centuria with a stick shift. The purpose of Mr. Dorsey's testimony is to show the existence of a defect in the Centuria's steering mechanism.

Assume that the witness has already identified himself. As in the criminal case, the next part of the direct examination establishes the witness's personal knowledge of the uncharged accident.

P WHERE were you on the morning of September 19th? (1), (2)

W I drove from my home in Seguin to downtown San Antonio.

P WHO was driving the car?

W I was.

The next part of the direct examination is devoted to showing the similarity of circumstances between the uncharged accident and the accident alleged in the pleading. The plaintiff wants to demonstrate that the physical layout of the site of the uncharged accident is comparable to that of the pleaded accident.

P WHAT route did you take? (1)

W I drove Interstate 10 most of the way.

---

[17] Adapted from 2 E. IMWINKELRIED, UNCHARGED MISCONDUCT EVIDENCE § 9.30 (rev. ed. 1999). Reprinted with permission.

P In WHAT direction were you driving? (1)

W I was traveling west.

P WHEN did you get off Interstate 10? (1)

W I tried to get off at the exit for Interstate 37 headed north.

P HOW can you remember that exit?

W I use it all the time when I go into San Antonio.

P [*To court reporter*] Would you please mark this as an exhibit for the plaintiff? [*Court reporter hands exhibit back to counsel.*]

P Thank you. Please let the record reflect that I am showing what has been marked as plaintiff's exhibit number four for identification to the opposing counsel.

J The record will so reflect.

P Your Honor, I request permission to approach the witness.

J Permission granted.

P Mr. Dorsey, I now hand you what has been marked plaintiff's exhibit number four for identification. WHAT is it? (1)

W It's a map showing Interstate 10 and the exit for going north on Interstate 37.

P HOW can you recognize it? (1)

W As I said, I've used that off-ramp lots of times.

P WHEN you enter this off-ramp, in WHAT direction are you traveling?

W At first, you're still going west and then it turns to the north.

P Please use this blue marker and write "east" at the entrance of the off-ramp.

W Yes.

P Please let the record reflect that the witness has complied with my request.

J The record will so reflect.

P In WHAT direction were you turning on the off-ramp? (1)

W I was turning to the right.

P HOW long is the off-ramp? (5)

W It's pretty long. It's a gradual thing. It's maybe 1,000 feet.

P HOW does the off-ramp slope? (5)

W It slopes up. You're going up maybe 10 feet in all.

P Please draw an arrow from the mouth of the off-ramp to the exit and write "up" next to the arrow.

W O.K.

P HOW steep is the slope? (5)

W I'm no engineer, but it's pretty gradual.

P In general, HOW accurate is this exhibit? (1)

W I don't know if it's to scale, but on the whole it seems correct.

The plaintiff now begins a process-of-elimination reasoning. To single out the defect in the vehicle's steering as the cause of the accident, the plaintiff questions the witness to negate other possible causes of the accident, such as lack of maintenance, speeding, intoxication, poor visibility, and the witness's inattention.

P Now, Mr. Dorsey, I'd like to ask you a few questions about the car you were driving toward this off-ramp. WHERE did you purchase this car? (4)

W From a Polecat dealer in San Antonio.

P Was the car new or used? (4)

W New. I was the first owner.

P HOW long had you owned the car before the accident on September 19th? (4)

W I'd had it for only two months before this occurred.

P HOW often, if at all, had you had the car serviced before the accident? (4)

W I took it in twice. The first time I took it in about two weeks after buying it, and then I took it in about a week before the accident for the 2,500 mile maintenance under the warranty.

P WHERE did you take the car for service? (4)

W I took it back to the same Polecat dealer that I initially bought it from.

P Mr. Dorsey, to the best of your knowledge, WHAT was the condition of your car on the day of the accident?

W As far as I knew, it was in good working order.

P All right, now let's get back to the exhibit. Could you show us approximately WHERE your car was on the map when you were 1,000 feet from the entrance to the off-ramp? (1)

W I'd say right here.

P Please place a large dot and "D-1" at that point

W Here it is.

P Please let the record reflect that the witness has so marked the exhibit.

J The record will so reflect.

P At that point, HOW fast were you going? (5)

W I was doing about 55, but this is the point where I began to slow down.

P WHAT is the posted speed limit along this portion of the interstate? (5)

W Fifty-five miles per hour.

P Now please indicate with a dot and "D-2" WHERE you would be when you were 100 feet from the entrance to the off-ramp. (1)

W Right here.

P Please let the record reflect that the witness has marked the exhibit as requested.

J The record will so reflect.

P HOW fast were you going then? (5)

W I had slowed to 45.

P WHAT is the posted speed limit at the entrance to the off-ramp? (5)

W I'm pretty sure it's 45.

P WHAT was the condition of the pavement? (5)

W It was dry.

P WHEN was the last rain? (5)

W It hadn't rained in weeks.

P HOW well could you see when you reached the mouth of the off-ramp? (5)

W Perfectly.

P WHAT were the lighting conditions at that time? (5)

W It was mid-morning, and it was a beautiful, clear day.

P WHAT, if anything, obstructed your view of the off-ramp? (5)

W Nothing. The only shrubbery in the area is grass. There are no big trees or anything.

P HOW closely were you paying attention to your driving? (5)

W I was watching it closely.

P WHY? (5)

W I wanted to have good control of my car before I got on a busy highway like Interstate 37.

P HOW good was your vision that morning? (5)

W Fine. I have 20-20 vision, and I've never worn glasses.

P WHAT was your physical condition? (5)

W Excellent.

P HOW many drinks, if any, had you had that morning? (5)

W None. None at all.

At this point, the plaintiff elicits the description of the accident itself. The plaintiff wants to make the uncharged accident sound as similar as possible to the pleaded accident.

P WHAT happened after you entered the off-ramp? (3)

W At first, everything was going smoothly.

P WHAT happened next? (3)

W About halfway into the turn, the steering wheel just plain froze.

P WHAT do you mean by "froze?" (5)

W I couldn't move it at all.

P Please indicate by placing "D-3" WHERE you were when the steering wheel first froze. (1)

W Right there.

P Please let the record reflect that the witness has so marked the exhibit.

J The record will so reflect.

P HOW fast were you going then? (5)

W Probably only 40 or 45.

P WHAT did you do then? (5)

W I hit the brakes and tried to move the wheel.

P HOW quickly did you hit the brakes? (5)

W As soon as I realized I was in trouble—immediately.

P HOW did the wheel respond? (5)

W Not at all.

P WHAT happened after you hit the brakes? (5)

W I slowed a bit, but it was just too late.

P WHERE did the car go? (5)

W It plowed through the railing, flew off the off-ramp, and finally stopped over here.

P Please mark the resting point of your car with "D-4."

W Right here.

P Please let the record reflect that the witness has marked the exhibit as requested.

J The record will so reflect.

[*At this point, the plaintiff elicits the witness's testimony that his automobile contained the same design feature as the plaintiff's.*]

P Now the car that you were driving that morning, the car that eventually came to rest at D-4, WHAT was the make of that car? (4), (5)

W It was a Polecat.

P WHAT was the model of Polecat? (5)

W It was the Centuria.

P WHAT was the year of that model? (5)

W 2004.

P Was the car automatic or stick shift? (5)

W Stick shift.

P WHAT, if any, accessories did you have on the car? (5)

W Other than air-conditioning and radio, there were none. It was a basic 2004 Polecat Centuria right off the showroom floor.

P Thank you, Mr. Dorsey. Your Honor, at this point we offer into evidence plaintiff's exhibit number four for identification.

J Any objections?

O No.

J Plaintiff's exhibit number four will be admitted.

CHAPTER 7
PRIVILEGES AND SIMILAR RULES OF EXCLUSION

PART 1
PRIVILEGES

§ 7-1 INTRODUCTION

The last two chapters examined rules based on the concern that the jury will misuse the item of evidence, overestimate the probative value of the evidence, or lose sight of the historical merits of the case. These concerns reflect policies governing the way in which we want jurors to behave. Ideally, we want the jury to use items of evidence properly, to ascribe the proper weight to each item, and to concentrate on the historical merits of the case. When a court excludes evidence under Rule 403 or any of the more specific rules in Articles IV or VI, it is excluding logically relevant evidence for a policy reason—a policy related to the way in which trials should be conducted.

This chapter is devoted to other types of evidentiary doctrines which result in the exclusion of logically relevant evidence for policy reasons. These doctrines bar the evidence in order to promote an extrinsic social policy, that is, a policy related to conduct outside the courtroom. Privileges epitomize this type of rule and are the focus of Part 1 of this chapter. Similarly, the Rules of Evidence may exclude evidence of subsequent remedial measures, pretrial settlement negotiations, and evidence of liability insurance. Those rules, like the rules governing privileges, tend to promote certain extrinsic social policies and are discussed in Part 2 of this chapter.

§ 7-2 PRIVILEGES—IN GENERAL

Privileges reflect a delicate balance between competing interests: the desire to admit helpful evidence at trial and the public's interest in protecting certain relationships or information. Article V of the Texas Rules of Evidence now contains specific privilege rules. One of the most common privileges, the attorney-client privilege in Rule 503, reflects the balance. Suppose that a party makes damaging admissions in a letter to his or her attorney. The party had firsthand, personal knowledge of the facts admitted. The admissions are not only logically relevant, they are highly reliable, because the party had personal knowledge of the facts. The letter will almost always be excluded, however, on the ground that it is a privileged communication. The drafters of the privilege rules want to give clients the assurance that they can disclose all the facts to their attorneys without fear that the facts will be divulged to strangers. With fuller disclosure from their clients, attorneys can render more effective service. The rule thus reflects the belief that the policy is important enough to warrant excluding even relevant, reliable evidence.

Although the most common form of privilege involves confidential communications between individuals, Texas law also recognizes a variety of other privileges. One type of privilege discussed here which does not involve confidential communications is the informant privilege. That privilege, which is discussed *infra* at § 7-7, protects the identity of an informant. One class of privileges which are not discussed here, but which are encountered frequently at the discovery stage of the trial, are the investigative privileges reflected in Rule 192 of the Texas Rules of Civil Procedure: attorney work product, disclosure of information regarding experts and party communications.[1] These privileges are normally not considered "evidentiary" privileges. Indeed, they are listed as "exemptions" to the general rule in Rule 192 requiring full disclosure.

---

[1] For a full discussion of these privileges, *see* ALBRIGHT, HERRING & PEMBERTON, TEXAS PRACTICE: HANDBOOK ON TEXAS DISCOVERY PRACTICE (West Pub 2000).

§ 7-3 PRIVILEGES FOR CONFIDENTIAL COMMUNICATIONS

§ 7-3(A) IN GENERAL

Unlike the Federal Rules of Evidence, which contain no codified privilege rules, Article V of the Texas Rules of Evidence contain a number of rules governing privileges. In federal court, counsel and the judge must refer to federal case law to determine if a particular privilege exists. Counsel and the judge in a Texas court, on the other hand, usually have the benefit of a particular rule of evidence which spells out what the privilege is, who the holder is, and whether any exceptions exist.[2]

The law of privileges can be summarized in this fashion: in certain types of proceedings, the holder has certain privileges with respect to privileged information unless (1) the holder has waived the privilege, or (2) there is an applicable exception to the privilege's scope. This summational sentence raises six issues. Given the potential scope of any discussion on the various privileges for confidential communications privileges, the discussion in this chapter will focus on those six issues as they apply to all of the privileges.

§ 7-3(B) TYPES OF PROCEEDINGS IN WHICH PRIVILEGES APPLY

The first issue is in what types of proceedings privileges apply. The general rule is that privileges apply in any proceeding in which testimony can be compelled. A few privileges have a peculiar, limited scope. For instance, in Texas, the physician-patient privilege does not apply in criminal prosecutions.[3] With such rare exceptions, however, privileges apply in all legal proceedings.

§ 7-3(C) WHO HOLDS THE PRIVILEGE?

The second question is who is the holder of the privilege. The original holder is the intended beneficiary of the privilege. Thus, the client is the holder of the attorney-client privilege, the patient the holder of the physician-patient privilege, and the penitent the holder of the penitent-clergyman privilege. In Texas, the spouse who made confidential marital communications holds the privilege under Rule 504. If the original holder of the privilege becomes mentally incompetent, that person's guardian or conservator becomes the successor holder of the privilege. In some privileges, if the original holder dies, the personal representative, such as the executor or heir, becomes a successor holder of the privilege. Finally, the holder's agent may sometimes assert the privilege on the holder's behalf. The client may authorize the attorney to claim the attorney-client privilege

---

[2] *See* WENDORF, SCHLUETER & BARTON, TEXAS RULES OF EVIDENCE MANUAL V-1 et seq. (6th ed. 2002) (discussion of privilege rules).

[3] *See* TEX. R. EVID. 509 at Appendix A.

for the client at a particular hearing. Under several privilege rules, the agent has implied-in-law authority to do so.[4]

§ 7-3(D) NATURE OF THE PRIVILEGE

The third question is what is the nature of the privilege. The privilege can encompass three rights. The first right is the personal right to testify and to refuse to disclose the privileged information.[5] A judge may neither hold the holder in contempt nor impose discovery sanctions on the holder if he or she is properly invoking a privilege. The second right is the right to prevent third parties from making disclosure. The recipient of the communication, the attorney, physician, or clergyman, is clearly bound. The troublesome question is whether eavesdroppers and interceptors are bound. The traditional view has been that they are not bound and may testify to the privileged communications. The privilege rules in the Texas Rules of Evidence, however, have attached more weight to the interest in privacy, and the trend is to silence eavesdroppers and interceptors. The third and final right is the right to preclude the opposing counsel and the judge from commenting on the invocation of the privilege. This right is recognized in Texas Rule of Evidence 513.

There is one right, however, which the common law and statutory privilege do not encompass; the majority view is that a privilege does not include a right to exclude evidence derived from a violation of the privilege. In this respect, common law and statutory privileges differ from constitutional privileges, such as the Fourth Amendment exclusionary rule. Assume, for example, that the police conduct an illegal, warrantless search of the defendant's apartment and discover a diary showing the location of evidence relating to the crime. The police immediately go to the location and dig up the evidence. The police deliver the evidence to the prosecutor. The defendant can move to suppress not only the diary but also the derivative evidence. The derivative evidence is also suppressible as the fruit of the poisonous tree. In contrast, suppose that one spouse reveals a confidential communication from the other spouse to the police. The police then use that revelation as an investigative lead and uncover other evidence that incriminates the other spouse. In this setting, the derivative evidence is admissible. The defendant spouse could preclude the other spouse from repeating the revelation on the witness stand, but the defendant cannot suppress the evidence the police derived from the violation of the defendant's confidence.

---

[4] *See, e.g.*, TEX. R. EVID. 504 (authority of spouse to claim privilege on behalf of other spouse is presumed).

[5] *See* TEX. R. EVID. 501.

§ 7-3(E) WHAT IS "PRIVILEGED INFORMATION?"

The fourth question is the most difficult: what is privileged information? Simply stated, with regard to communications privileges, the privileged information is a confidential communication between properly related parties and incident to the relation. This question presents several additional points.

§ 7-3(E)(1) Definition of "Communication"

What is a communication? Oral and written statements fall within the definition of communication. In the case of some privileges, however, the rules use extraordinarily broad definitions of communication. In the case of the physician-patient privilege, the privilege extends to any information the physician gains by examining the patient. The physician could not testify about the patient's physical condition even though the observation of the patient's physical condition is not a communication in the orthodox sense of the term.[6]

§ 7-3(E)(2) Definition of "Confidential"

When is a communication confidential? Confidentiality entails two elements: (1) physical privacy, and (2) an intent on the holder's part to maintain secrecy. If third parties are present to the holder's knowledge, the courts usually hold that the communication is not confidential. For practical business reasons, the courts have allowed clerks and secretaries to be present without destroying confidentiality in an attorney-client conversation. The courts realize that attorneys and physicians use assistants to conduct their professional work, and Texas Rule 503 specifically indicates that confidentiality is maintained if disclosure is required for the rendition of legal services.

Even if there was physical privacy at the time of the communication, the communication is unprivileged if the holder intended subsequent disclosure outside the circle of confidence. Suppose that the client gave the attorney information for the specific purpose of including the information in a press release about the case. The normal inference would be that the client never intended confidentiality.

§ 7-3(E)(3) What Are "Protected Relations?"

Next, what are the protected relations? The answer varies. As noted *supra* at § 7-3(A), there are specific Texas Rules of Evidence recognizing privileges for the following relations, among others: attorney-client, physician-patient, psychotherapist-patient, penitent-clergyman, and spouses. The drafters of the Rules believed that these are useful social relationships and that the nature of the

[6] *See* TEX. R. EVID. 509(c)(2) (protects medical records created or maintained by doctor).

relationship requires an element of confidentiality. This belief is the policy judgment underlying the very existence of the privileges.

In applying the relationship requirement, the courts have found two fact situations troublesome. One situation is the case in which a corporate employee communicates with corporate counsel. When is the communication deemed a communication between the corporate client and the corporate counsel? Some jurisdictions limit the corporate attorney-client privilege to communications between corporate counsel and the members of the corporate "control group," the narrow circle of directors, officers, and high-ranking employees needing direct access to corporate counsel. In *Upjohn Co. v. United States*,[7] however, the Supreme Court made it clear that it favors a broader test. Under the *Upjohn* test, a communication between any employee and the corporate counsel constitutes a corporate attorney-client communication if the employee is divulging information which he or she gained in the course of performing employment duties. Although the Texas Supreme Court initially held that Texas Rule of Evidence 503 had adopted the control group test, in the 1998 amendments to the Texas Rules of Evidence, the Court rejected the control group test and adopted what could be termed a "subject matter test." That is, a communication by (or to) an employee for an entity, such as a corporation, will be considered privileged if the employee was acting in the scope of his or her employment at the time of the communication.

The second situation is the case in which the client communicates with an expert hired by the attorney. Suppose, for example, that the defense attorney sends the defendant to a psychiatrist for an evaluation. The client possesses private information, namely, his or her mental condition. The attorney needs an evaluation of the information to prepare for trial. Neither the client nor the attorney, however, possesses the expertise to perform the evaluation. In this situation, the Texas rule is that the privilege does not attach unless the attorney employs the expert. The privilege protects not only the client's revelations to the expert, but also the expert's report to the attorney.

§ 7-3(E)(4) What is "Incident to the Relationship?"

When does a communication occur incident to the relationship? It is not enough that the communication occur between an attorney and his or her client. The client must be consulting the attorney in his or her professional capacity. The incidence requirement necessitates that the court examine the purpose of the communication. Why did the client consult the attorney? If the client was seeking legal information or advice, the communication satisfies the incidence requirement.

[7] 449 U.S. 383 (1981).

§ 7-3(F) Waiver of the Privilege

The fifth issue is waiver. If a holder invokes the right type of privilege in the right type of proceeding to suppress privileged information, there is a prima facie case for privilege. Opposing counsel can defeat the privilege, however, by showing that the holder has waived the privilege. The waiver can occur inside or outside court.[8] On direct examination by his or her attorney, the holder may have referred to the privileged communication. The in-court reference waives the privilege. The court may also find a waiver if the holder voluntarily discloses the privileged information to a third parry outside the courtroom. Not every out-of-court disclosure effects a waiver because the disclosure itself might be a privileged communication; for example, a husband might tell his wife what he previously told his attorney.

Texas has also recognized that by placing privileged information in issue in the case, the holder may have waived the privilege. The courts have indicated that the privilege may not be used both as a sword and a shield.

§ 7-3(G) Exception to Privilege

The sixth and final question is whether there is any special exception to the privilege's scope. The opponent can defeat a privilege by showing either waiver or a special exception. It may not serve the purpose of the privilege to apply it in a particular situation, or there may be a countervailing interest that overrides the privilege. In § 7-6, *infra*, we shall illustrate several special exceptions to the privileges' scope.

§ 7-4 INVOKING A PRIVILEGE

§ 7-4(A) Elements of the Foundation

The claimant has the burden of proving the existence of the elements of the prima facie case for privilege. The prima facie case for privilege includes these elements:

1. The privilege applies to this type of proceeding. The judge makes this determination by examining the pleadings in the case.
2. The claimant of the privilege is asserting the right type of privilege. The judge makes this determination by insisting that the claimant specify the right he or she is claiming, that is, the right to refuse to disclose personally, the right to prevent a third party from disclosing, or the right to comment on the invocation of the privilege.

---

[8] *See* TEX. R. EVID. 511.

3. The claimant is a proper holder.
4. The information the claimant seeks to suppress is privileged information:
    a. It was a communication.
    b. It was confidential.
    c. It occurred between properly related parties.
    d. It was incident to the relation.

Rule 104(a) governs the judge's determination of these preliminary facts.

§ 7-4(B) SAMPLE FOUNDATION

The fact situation is a tort action arising from a collision. The plaintiff, Ms. Cox, alleges that the defendant, Mr. Harty, caused the accident by speeding. Mr. Harty takes the stand during the defense case-in-chief. On direct examination, he testifies that he was going only 20 miles an hour, 5 miles under the speed limit. On cross-examination, the following occurs. The plaintiff's attorney is the proponent:

P Mr. Harty, ISN'T IT A FACT THAT you testified on direct examination that you were going only 20 miles an hour before the collision?

W Yes.

P ISN'T IT TRUE, Mr. Harty, THAT when you spoke with Mr. Riley, you told him that you were going 35 miles an hour?

O Your Honor, I object to that question on the ground that it calls for information protected by the attorney-client privilege. (2) I request permission to take the witness on voir dire examination.

J Permission granted.

O Mr. Harty, WHO is this Mr. Riley? (4c)

W He's a long-time friend of mine.

O WHAT is his occupation? (4c)

W He's an attorney.

O HOW do you know he is an attorney? (4c)

W His office door says "Attorney," he has degrees on his wall, and he's represented my family in court before.

O WHERE and WHEN did you talk to Mr. Riley about this case? (4d)

W I think the first time was January 12th or 13th of 2005, just after the accident occurred.

O WHAT happened during that meeting? (4a)

W I told him about the accident.

O Precisely, HOW did you give him information about the accident? (4a)

W I told him about it. I didn't put it in writing or anything like that.

O HOW many people were present when you had this meeting with Mr. Riley? (4b)

W Just the two of us.

O HOW many doors are there to his office? (4b)

W Just one.

O WHAT position was the door in while you talked with him? (4b)

W It was closed.

O After you told him about the accident, to WHOM did you authorize him to give the information? (4b)

W No one.

O WHAT did you want him to do with the information? (4b)

W Keep it secret, of course. He was my attorney.

O WHY did you talk to him that day? (4d)

W I thought I might need legal help. Even at the accident scene, the plaintiff said something about suing.

O In WHAT capacity did you consult Mr. Riley? (4d), (2)

W I was talking to him as an attorney, not just a family friend.

O Your Honor, I have no further questions on voir dire. I renew my objection and assert my client's privilege to refuse to disclose his communications with his attorney. (1), (2), (3)

J Objection sustained.

§ 7-5 DEFEATING A PRIVILEGE BY PROVING WAIVER

§ 7-5(A) IN-COURT WAIVER

§ 7-5(A)(1) The Doctrine

If the party opposing the privilege claim is going to argue an in-court waiver, that party must be prepared to point to the witness's testimony that effected the waiver. Under Texas Rule of Evidence 511, the party relying on the waiver must show that the holder of the privilege voluntarily disclosed, or consented to the disclosure of, any significant portion of the privileged matter.

§ 7-5(A)(2) Elements of the Foundation

To argue an in-court waiver, the proponent should show the following:

1. When the in-court disclosure was made.
2. The disclosure was voluntary.

§ 7-5(A)(3) Sample Foundation

The following is a continuation of the immediately preceding tort hypothetical. The plaintiff is the proponent and the defendant is the opponent.

P Mr. Harty, ISN'T IT A FACT THAT when you first spoke with your family attorney, Mr. Riley, you told him that you were going 35 miles an hour?

O Your Honor, I object to that question on the ground that it calls for information protected by the attorney-client privilege.

P Your Honor, may we approach the bench?

J Yes.

P Your Honor, I concede that this communication would ordinarily be privileged. However, I contend that the defendant has already waived the privilege. I would request that the court reporter read back the last question and answer on direct examination. (1)

J Very well.

CR It'll take me just a second to find the passage. Yes, here it is. My notes show that the last question was, "What was your speed just before the collision?" The last answer was, "I was going at a safe rate of speed. That's what I told my attorney when I first discussed the accident with him, and it's the same story I'm telling today. That's the truth."

P This shows that on direct examination, the defendant expressly referred to his previous conversation with his attorney about the collision. That reference waives the privilege. (2)

J I agree. The objection is overruled.

P Mr. Harty, let me repeat the question. ISN'T IT TRUE THAT you told your attorney that you were going 35 miles an hour?

W Yes.

§ 7-5(B) OUT-OF COURT WAIVER

§ 7-5(B)(1) The Doctrine

If the proponent is relying upon an out-of-court waiver, he or she must be prepared to show under Rule 511 that the privilege was waived voluntarily by the holder of the privilege, or by his or her predecessor.

§ 7-5(B)(2) Elements of the Foundation

If the party opposing the privilege relies on the theory of out-of-court waiver, the party must lay the following foundation:

1. Where the out-of-court statement was made.
2. When the statement was made.
3. To whom the statement was made.
4. The holder knew that the addressee was outside the circle of confidence.
5. The holder disclosed information to the addressee.
6. The disclosure was voluntary.

§ 7-5(B)(3) Sample Foundation

The previous hypothetical continues. Now the proponent will attempt to show that the holder waived the privilege by an out-of-court disclosure.

P Mr. Harty, ISN'T IT A FACT THAT when you first spoke with your family attorney, Mr. Riley, you told him that you were going 35 miles an hour?

O Your Honor, I object to that question on the ground that it calls for privileged information protected by the attorney-client privilege.

P Your Honor, I request permission to take the witness on voir dire examination before you rule on the objection.

J Granted.

P Mr. Harty, ISN'T IT TRUE THAT on January 19th of this year, you had dinner with your cousin, Mike Hughes? (1), (2), (3)

W Yes.

P ISN'T IT CORRECT THAT during this dinner, you discussed the accident with your cousin? (3)

W Yes.

P ISN'T IT A FACT THAT at the time, you knew your cousin wasn't working for your attorney in this case? (4)

W Right.

P ISN'T IT TRUE THAT you told your cousin what you told your attorney about the accident? (5)

W Yes.

P And no one forced you to tell that to your cousin, DID THEY? (6)

W No.

P And no one made any threats to make you tell your cousin. ISN'T THAT TRUE? (6)

W Yes.

P Your Honor, I have no further questions on voir dire.

J The objection will be overruled.

P Mr. Harty, let me repeat the question. ISN'T IT CORRECT THAT you told your attorney that you were going 35 miles an hour?

W Yes.

§ 7-6 DEFEATING A PRIVILEGE BY PROVING A SPECIAL EXCEPTION

As previously stated, there are numerous special exceptions to the various privileges. Some privileges are virtually riddled with exceptions.[9] The party opposing the claim of privilege usually relies on voir dire examination to show the factual predicate for the exception. The following sections illustrate some of the more important exceptions.

§ 7-6(A) COMMUNICATIONS USED TO FACILITATE A CRIME OR FRAUD

§ 7-6(A)(1) The Doctrine

The courts will not permit holders to abuse and pervert the privileges. For that reason, the courts usually reject a privilege claim if the party opposing the claim shows that at the time of the communication, the holder sought the information or advice to facilitate the commission of a future crime or fraud. The most common example of the "crime or fraud" exception rests in the attorney-client privilege in Texas Rule of Evidence 503.

§ 7-6(A)(2) Elements of the Foundation

The foundation for the crime or fraud exception usually requires proof that:

---

[9] *See, e.g.*, TEX, R. EVID. 509 (exceptions for doctor-patient privilege) at Appendix A.

1. At the time of the communication, the holder knew that the contemplated course of conduct was illegal or fraudulent.
2. The purpose of the communication was to obtain information or advice to facilitate the commission of a future crime or fraud. Because of the difficulty of proving the holder's state of mind, many courts recognize the exception so long as there is a prima facie case or permissive inference of the existence of the improper intent in the holder's mind.

§ 7-6(A)(3) Sample Foundation

The following fact situation is a prosecution for willful tax evasion. Suppose that state law requires that the purchaser of goods pay a 4 percent sales tax unless the goods are intended for interstate shipment. If the goods are intended for interstate shipment, the purchaser obtains a tax exemption form from the seller and submits the completed form to the Franchise Tax Board. The prosecution alleges that in August 2005, the defendant, Mr. Lloyd Marx, purchased goods for intrastate shipment and willfully evaded the tax. The goods were 230 air conditioners. The defendant took the stand during his case-in-chief. On direct examination, the defendant admits that he purchased the air conditioners and neither paid the tax nor filed the exemption form. He also testifies, however, that he did not understand the procedures for filing the form and claiming the exemption. The following occurs on cross-examination. The proponent is the prosecutor. The prosecutor is attempting to prove willfulness.

P Mr. Marx, ISN'T IT TRUE THAT in June 2005, you spoke with Mr. Felton of the local office of the Franchise Tax Board? (1)

W Yes.

P ISN'T IT A FACT THAT during this conversation, you asked him whether you had to pay a sales tax on purchases for intrastate shipments? (1)

W Right.

P AND DIDN'T HE tell you that you had to do so? (1)

W Yes.

P ISN'T IT CORRECT THAT on July 1, 2005, you entered into a contract for the sale of air conditioners to Johnson Construction Company? (2)

W Yes.

P ISN'T IT TRUE THAT Johnson has its office in this city and state? (2)

W Yes.

P ISN'T IT A FACT THAT you promised to deliver the air conditioners in September to their office in this state? (2)

W Yes.

P ISN'T IT CORRECT THAT the number of air conditioners you promised to sell them was 230? (2)

W Yes.

P AND ISN'T THAT the exact number of air conditioners you bought on August 1, 2005? (2)

W Yes.

Later, during the prosecution rebuttal, the prosecutor calls Ms. Celia Waylan as a witness. The prosecutor is still the proponent. Ms. Waylan has already identified herself and stated that she is an attorney.

P Ms. Waylan, WHERE were you on the morning of July 20, 2005?

W I was in my office.

P WHERE is your office?

W Downtown on High Street.

P WHAT happened that morning?

W I had a visit from a client.

P WHO was that client?

W It was the defendant, Mr. Marx.

P WHERE is Mr. Marx now?

W In this courtroom.

P Specifically, WHERE in the courtroom?

W He's sitting right there.

P HOW is he dressed?

W In grey slacks and a blue shirt.

P Your Honor, please let the record reflect that the witness has identified the defendant.

J It will so reflect.

P WHAT happened when the defendant came to your office that morning?

W He asked for some advice.

P WHAT advice?

O Your Honor, I object to that question on the ground that it calls for information protected by the attorney-client privilege under Texas Rule of Evidence 503.

P Your Honor, may we approach the bench?

J Yes.

P Your Honor, I concede that Ms. Waylan is an attorney and that the defendant consulted her as such. However, I offer to prove that the witness will testify that the defendant asked how he could evade paying a tax or filing a form on a shipment. She will further testify that she advised him that there was no way to avoid paying or filing. This conversation occurred in July, well before the purchase of the air conditioners in August. She will finally testify that he said that she obviously misunderstood his question and that he wanted her advice as to the best way to evade the law without getting caught. Since the defendant had already talked with Mr. Felton and had already entered into an intrastate shipment contract, the inference is that the defendant sought Ms. Waylan's advice to facilitate a future crime. Under Texas Rule of Evidence 503(d)(1), there is therefore no privilege.

J I think there's a sufficient showing to invoke the exception. I will overrule the objection.

P Ms. Waylan, WHAT advice did the defendant ask for? (1), (2)

W He asked how he could get around paying a tax or filing a form.

P WHAT did you tell him?

W I said that he couldn't. He had to do one or the other. If the goods were destined for intrastate sale, he had to pay the tax. If the goods were destined for interstate shipment, he had to file a form with the state. It was one or the other.

P WHAT did the defendant say then? (2)

W He told me that I'd obviously misunderstood his question. He said that he'd already entered into a contract for an intrastate shipment and that he wanted my advice as to how to evade the law without getting caught.

§ 7-6(B) The Patient-Litigant Exception

§ 7-6(B)(1) The Doctrine

One of the most important, and common, exceptions to the physician-patient privilege in civil cases is the patient-litigant exception. Under Texas Rule of Evidence 509(d)(4), if the patient sues and tenders the issue of his or her condition, the patient loses the privilege for communications relevant to that condition. The theory is that it would be unfair to permit the patient-litigant to suppress such highly relevant information. In effect, by suing, the patient makes a limited waiver of the privilege. To decide whether this exception applies in a particular case, the judge must examine the complaint and determine whether the complaint tenders an issue of physical condition to which the communication is logically relevant.

§ 7-6(B)(2) Elements of the Foundation

To prove the patient-litigant exception for the physician-patient privilege in a civil case, the proponent must show, under Texas Rule 509(d)(4), that:

1. The patient made a communication to a physician.
2. The communication related to an issue of the patient's physical, mental, or emotional condition.
3. The patient's physical, mental, or emotional condition is being relied upon by a party as a part of its claim or defense.

§ 7-6(B)(3) Sample Foundation

The fact situation is a tort action in which the plaintiff claims extensive personal injuries. In particular, the complaint asks for $90,000 in damages for pain and suffering. The defendant calls Dr. Metal as a witness. Dr. Metal identifies himself and states that he formerly treated the plaintiff. He testifies that he examined the plaintiff two days after the accident. The defendant is the proponent.

P Dr. Metal, during this examination, WHAT, if anything, did the plaintiff say about his pain? (1), (2)

O Your Honor, I object to that question on the ground that it calls for privileged information protected by the physician-patient privilege.

P Your Honor, may we approach the bench?

J Yes.

P Your Honor, I offer to prove that the witness will testify that the plaintiff said his pain was not intense. On page nine of his petition, the plaintiff prays for $90,000 in damages for pain and suffering. As a litigant, the plaintiff tendered the issue of the extent of his pain. (3) The statement he made to his physician is logically relevant to his condition and pain. Under Rule 509, any statements to the physician are not privileged.

J The objection is overruled.

P Dr. Metal, let me repeat the question. WHAT, if anything, did the plaintiff say about his pain?

W He said it wasn't very intense. He felt it occasionally, but it bothered him only off and on.

§ 7-7 PRIVILEGE FOR AN INFORMER'S IDENTITY

§ 7-7(A) THE DOCTRINE

This section deals with the privilege for an informer's identity. In many cases, an informer would not report a law violation unless the government assured him or her confidentiality. The informant sometimes fears reprisals from the person being reported, and in other cases the informer does not want to expose his or her own involvement to public scrutiny. To encourage informants to report violations of the law, Texas Rule of Evidence 508 creates a privilege for the informer's identity. The privilege does not protect the informer's report. Given its narrow purpose, the privilege protects only the identity of a person who confidentially reports a law violation to law enforcement authorities.

Rule 508 indicates that the privilege belongs not to the informer, but to the "United States or a state or subdivision thereof . . . ." That is, a public entity holds the privilege.

The informer privilege can be defeated if a party shows a compelling need for the informant's testimony. If the informer merely supplied an investigative lead and pointed a finger of suspicion at the defendant but did not observe the crime or event, the informer is only a "tipster" and the court will not order the disclosure of the informer's identity unless there is a real question about his or her reliability.

A different rule applies, however, where the informer has something important to say about merits of the case. In a criminal case, the court will find a compelling need when the defendant demonstrates that the informer has personal knowledge of the facts determining the defendant's guilt or innocence. And in a civil case, the court may order disclosure where the public entity is a party and the informer could provide "testimony necessary to a fair determination of a material issue on the merits in a civil case . . . ." When the informer personally observed the facts relevant to the case, the informer is a "percipient witness" and the court will usually order disclosure. In *Roviaro v. United States*,[10] the Supreme Court stated that the defendant has a due process right to discover the identity of a percipient witness. Counsel does not have to make a preliminary showing that the percipient witness testimony will be favorable. He or she need show only that the witness has personal knowledge of facts material to the theory of the case.

§ 7-7(B) ELEMENTS OF THE FOUNDATION

The foundation for establishing the existence of the informer privilege includes these elements:

---

[10] 353 U.S. 53 (1957).

1. The privilege applies in this type of proceeding. Most of the cases recognizing the privilege are criminal prosecutions. The privilege is recognized, however, in both civil and criminal cases.
2. The party claiming the privilege is a proper holder. The government is the formal holder, but the government's agents, including prosecutors, may invoke the privilege on the government's behalf.
3. The holder is asserting the right type of privilege. The government can refuse to disclose the informer's identity. Further, the government can prevent another person from disclosing the informer's identity.

However, the government cannot silence the informer himself. If the informer is brave or foolhardy enough to admit his or her identity, the government loses the privilege.

4. The information is privileged.
   a. A person made a confidential report.
   b. The subject of the report was a violation of law.
   c. The person made the report to a law enforcement agency such as the police, a prosecutor's office, an administrative agency charged with enforcing the law, or a legislative committee investigating law enforcement.

The foundation for the percipient witness exception in a criminal case, where the exception will most often arise, is quite simple. Defense counsel shows that the informer was in a physical position—the proper time and place—to observe the facts determining guilt or innocence. Rule 508 provides for an in camera hearing, without any counsel being present, during which the informer testifies in chambers after the defendant makes the preliminary showing. If, in the judge's mind, the informer's testimony is favorable to the defense, the judge then orders disclosure of the informer's identity to the defense. If the judge concludes that the informer's testimony would not be helpful to the defense, the judge denies the discovery motion. The record of the testimony in chambers is sealed and filed with the regular record of trial. If there is an appeal, the appellate court opens the sealed transcript to review the trial judge's determination.

§ 7-7(C) SAMPLE FOUNDATION

The following fact situation is a drug prosecution. The prosecution alleges that the defendant, Ms. Jane Moreland, wrongfully sold heroin to a Mr. Vincent Styles. The prosecution calls Officer Bernard Lopardo as a witness. Officer Lopardo testifies that he was hiding in the house where the alleged sale occurred and observed the sale. The defense attorney is the proponent and is cross-examining Lopardo. The prosecutor is the opponent.

P Officer Lopardo, ISN'T IT TRUE THAT someone else was with you when you observed the alleged heroin sale?

W Yes.

P WHO was that other person?

O Your Honor, I object to that question on the ground that it calls for privileged information. May we approach the bench?

J Yes.

O Your Honor, on behalf of the government, I claim the privilege for the identity of an informer under Evidence Rule 508. (1), (2), (3) I request permission to take the witness on voir dire examination.

J Permission granted.

O WHEN did you first meet the person who was with you in the house?

W About two months before.

O WHAT happened when you met this person? (4b)

W He told me that he thought a drug sale was going to occur in the neighborhood within the next few months.

O WHERE did he make this report? (4c)

W At the local police station.

O WHOM did he report it to? (4c)

W To me.

P HOW were you dressed at the time? (4c)

W I was wearing my regular police uniform.

P WHO else was present when he made this report? (4a)

W No one else. Just the two of us.

O WHERE did this conversation occur? (4a)

W In a room in the station.

O HOW many doors did the room have? (4a)

W Only one.

O WHAT position was the door in when you met this person? (4a)

W It was closed.

O WHAT, if any, assurances did you give the informant when he made this report to you? (4a)

W I told him that I wouldn't disclose his identity to anyone.

O To WHOM have you revealed his identity? (4a)

W No one. I've worked with him directly. I haven't even revealed his identity to the desk sergeant. I'm the informer's only contact.

O Your Honor, I have no further questions on voir dire. I renew my claim of the privilege for an informer's identity.

Now the defense counsel will attempt to lay the foundation for the percipient witness exception.

P Your Honor, may I also voir dire the witness?

J Very well.

P Officer Lopardo, ISN'T IT TRUE THAT this person accompanied you to the house where the alleged sale occurred?

W Yes.

P ISN'T IT A FACT THAT the informer was standing next to you when you observed the alleged sale?

W Yes.

P ISN'T IT CORRECT THAT, most of the time, the informer was facing in the same direction as you?

W Yes.

P Your Honor, I have no further questions on voir dire examination. Although the privilege for the informer's identity applies in this case, the percipient witness viewed the very transaction that the defendant's guilt or innocence depends on. Under Rule 508, we submit that the informer in this case, in the words of the rule, "may be able to give testimony necessary to a fair determination of the issues of guilt, innocence. . . ."

J I am going to order the prosecutor to make arrangements for the informer to meet with me tomorrow morning. At that time, I shall question the informer in camera and determine whether his testimony would be helpful to the defense. I suggest that someone from the prosecutor's office contact my office and make arrangements for that hearing, so that the identity of the informer will not be compromised. Court will be recessed.[11]

[11] Although Rule 508 makes provision for an in camera hearing, there are obvious problems with conducting such a hearing without the opposing party learning who the informer is. In most cases, the judge will receive affidavits and make his or her ruling based on those documents.

PART 2
OTHER EXCLUSIONARY RULES

§ 7-8 EVIDENTIARY EXCLUSIONARY RULES—IN GENERAL

The following sections analyze several evidentiary doctrines similar to the privileges: subsequent repairs, compromise statements, and evidence of liability insurance. These are doctrines that exclude logically relevant evidence to promote extrinsic social policies. The subsequent repair doctrine bans evidence of subsequent precautionary measures by tort defendants. The primary rationale for the doctrine is that admitting the evidence would discourage desirable safety improvements.

The second doctrine, excluding statements made during civil settlement and criminal plea negotiations, has a similar justification. The doctrine's underlying theory is that the admission of such statements would discourage negotiated settlements and pleas. The adherents of the doctrine argue that settlements and pleas serve the critical function of easing the trial courts' burden.

The third doctrine, excluding evidence of liability insurance, rests on the fear that if the jury hears that a party is insured, it will be more likely to conclude that the party is able to assume the costs of the event. Because, like privileges, these doctrines exclude logically relevant evidence to promote extrinsic policies, some commentators refer to these doctrines as quasi-privileges.

§ 7-9 SUBSEQUENT REMEDIAL MEASURES

§ 7-9(A) THE DOCTRINE

Texas Evidence Rule 407 states the exclusionary rule for subsequent remedial measures: "[w]hen, after an injury or harm allegedly caused by an event, measures are taken that, if taken previously, would have made the injury or harm less likely to occur, evidence of the subsequent measures is not admissible to prove negligence, culpable conduct, a defect in a product's design, or a need for a warning or instruction." It is important to note that although this doctrine most often arises in the context of subsequent repairs, the rule is actually broader than that and could include, for example, an employer firing the employee whose actions led to the lawsuit.

The courts have stated two justifications for the subsequent remedial measures doctrine. One is that the evidence is logically irrelevant. The defendant's subsequent conduct has no bearing on the question of whether the defendant was guilty of antecedent negligence. This justification is flawed. The subsequent remedial measure has some slight probative value on the question of negligence.

At the very least, the evidence suggests that the defendant could have taken steps to eliminate or reduce the danger. Increasingly, however, the courts are relying on a second justification for the doctrine—admitting the evidence would create a disincentive for repairs, and the public interest in safety will not tolerate such a disincentive.

This doctrine bans the evidence only when the evidence is offered for a particular, forbidden purpose. In the words of Texas Rule 407, the evidence is inadmissible when the proponent offers the evidence "to prove negligence or culpable conduct in connection with the event." The exclusionary rule bans the evidence when the only theory of logical relevance the proponent articulates is the general inference that the defendant was negligent or culpable. If the proponent can articulate a different theory of logical relevance, the rule is inapplicable. Texas Rule 407 declares: "[t]his rule does not require the exclusion of evidence of subsequent measures when offered for another purpose, such as proving ownership, control, or feasibility of precautionary measures, if controverted, or impeachment." When the proponent identifies a theory of logical relevance other than a general inference of negligence or fault, the opponent is entitled to a limiting instruction under Rule 105. The trial judge informs the jury of the permissible and impermissible uses of the evidence.

Originally, the Texas drafters specifically exempted products liability causes of action from the scope of Rule 407. But in 2003, they amended the Texas rule to follow the federal rule counterpart. So products liability cases are now covered by the rule.[12]

§ 7-9(B) ELEMENTS OF THE FOUNDATIONS

§ 7-9(B)(1) Invoking the Rule of Exclusion

The party attempting to exclude evidence of a subsequent remedial measure should lay the following foundation:

1. The defendant took a certain action.
2. The defendant took the action as a remedial measure.
3. The defendant took the action after the injury or harm that gave rise to the suit.

The party can assert this doctrine pretrial by a motion in limine. If the issue arises at trial, the party can conduct voir dire examination to lay the foundation.

---

12 *See* WENDORF, SCHLUETER & BARTON, TEXAS RULES OF EVIDENCE MANUAL, 2004 SUPPLEMENT, 52.

§ 7-9(B)(2) Avoiding the Rule of Exclusion

If the party seeking to introduce the evidence is going to invoke an alternate theory of logical relevance, the party must make a proper offer of proof. The offer of proof should include these elements:

1. What the witness will testify to if the judge permits the proponent to pursue the line of inquiry.
2. The evidence is logically relevant to some issue other than the general question of negligence or fault.
3. The issue the evidence relates to is disputed in the case. The proponent of the evidence should point to specific testimony by the opposing witnesses or the pleadings in the case which shows that the issue is controverted.

As previously stated, if the proponent of the evidence successfully invokes an alternate theory of logical relevance, the opponent has the right to insist that the judge give the jurors a limiting instruction under Rule 105.

§ 7-9(C) SAMPLE FOUNDATIONS

The first fact situation illustrates the general rule of exclusion under Rule 407. The fact situation is a tort action arising from a slip and fall on the entrance to a department store. The plaintiff, Mr. Jarvis, alleges that the defendant, Merrill Department Store, had a dangerous and unsafe slope on its entrance. During the defense case-in-chief, the defense calls Ms. Fenton as a witness. Ms. Fenton identifies herself and states that she was the store manager the day of the accident. She describes the day, including her conversation with the plaintiff after the slip and fall. On cross-examination, the following occurs. The proponent is counsel for the plaintiff. The opponent is the defense counsel.

P Ms. Fenton, ISN'T IT TRUE THAT one week after the plaintiff was injured in the accident, you hired a contractor to reduce the slope on the entrance?

O Your Honor, I object to that question on the ground that it calls for evidence of a subsequent repair under Rule of Evidence 407.

J Objection sustained.

O Your Honor, will you please give the jury a curative instruction?

J Yes. Ladies and gentlemen of the jury, the plaintiff's attorney just referred to a change made in the entrance to the defendant's store. I am instructing you to disregard that reference and the question asked. You may not even speculate whether there were any subsequent changes. The only issue before you is whether the defendant was negligent at the time the alleged accident occurred.

If the defendant thought that the reference would taint the rest of the case, the defendant would next move for a mistrial.

O Your Honor, I now move for a mistrial.

If there is any doubt about the soundness of the objection, the opponent should request permission to take the witness on voir dire to lay a complete foundation for the objection.

P Ms. Fenton, ISN'T IT TRUE THAT one week after the plaintiff's accident, you hired a contractor to reduce the slope on the entrance?

O Your Honor, I object to that question. May we approach the bench?

J Yes.

O Your Honor, I object to that question on the ground that it calls for evidence of a subsequent repair. I request that you excuse the jurors and permit me to voir dire the witness before you rule on my objection.

J Very well. Ladies and gentlemen of the jury, I am going to excuse you from the courtroom for a few moments. The bailiff will escort you to the jury room. [*The jurors leave.*]

O Ms. Fenton, WHAT did you hire this contractor to do? (1)

W I hired a Mr. Darby to reduce the angle of the slope on the entrance.

O WHY did you do that? (2)

W We did it as a safety measure. We wanted to ensure that there wouldn't be a recurrence of the accident. We're concerned about the safety of our customers.

O WHEN did you hire Mr. Darby? (3)

W In late February of 2005.

O WHEN did the plaintiff's accident occur? (3)

W In early February. I think it was February 2.

O Your Honor, I have no further voir dire questions of this witness. I renew my objection.

J The objection will be sustained.

The second fact situation is a suit against a railroad company. The plaintiff, Hughes Corporation, sues West Central Railroad. The plaintiff alleges that the defendant's train derailed near the plaintiff's plant and caused extensive property damage. The defendant's answer alleges that the cause of the derailment was the defective condition of the track and that under the railroad's contract with the adjacent landowner, the landowner was responsible for maintaining the track. The plaintiff calls Mr. Karl as a witness. Mr. Karl identifies himself and states that he is one of the plaintiff's employees. He is prepared to testify that on

December 3, 2004, the day after the accident, one of the defendant's work crews repaired the track. The proponent is the plaintiff's counsel and the opponent is the defendant's counsel.

P Mr. Karl, WHERE were you on December 3, 2004?

W I was at work at our main plant in Del Rio.

P WHAT happened that day?

W I was working outside, trying to repair some of the damage caused by the derailment the day before.

P WHAT, if anything, did you see while you were outside?

W I saw some of the defendant's employees arrive.

P HOW do you know that they were the defendant's employees?

W They all had coveralls on, and the coveralls had the defendant's name on them. They drove to the site in a truck with the defendant's name on the side.

P WHAT were the defendant's employees doing?

O Your Honor, I object to that question. May we approach the bench?

J Yes.

O Your Honor, I suspect that the plaintiff is attempting to elicit inadmissible evidence of subsequent repairs to the track.

J [*To the plaintiff's attorney*] Is that your intention?

P Your Honor, I do intend to try to prove a subsequent repair. However, this evidence is clearly admissible under Rule 407. This witness will testify that he saw the defendant's employees repair the track. (1) The evidence is logically relevant to prove that the defendant had control of the track and thus a duty to keep the track in a state of good repair. (2) The defendant's answer specifically denied that it had control of the track or a duty to repair. (3) The defendant's general manager testified to that effect yesterday afternoon. (3) The evidence should be admitted for the limited purpose of proving the defendant's control of the track.

J The objection is overruled.

P Mr. Karl, let me repeat the question. WHAT were the defendant's employees doing?

W They were repairing the track.

O Your Honor, I request a limiting instruction.

J Granted. Ladies and gentlemen of the jury, you have just heard evidence that the day after the accident, the defendant's employees were repairing the track. You are not to use that evidence as proof that the defendant was careless at the time of the accident. You may use the evidence only in deciding whether the defendant had control of the track and a duty to repair it.

Given the judge's instruction, during summation the plaintiff could discuss the testimony when he or she was arguing the question of whether the defendant had control of the defective track which caused the damage to the plaintiff's property. However, it would be objectionable if the plaintiff suggested to the jury that the defendant was somehow admitting fault in the accident by sending its work crew to the site.

The third fact situation is a products liability suit. The plaintiff, Mr. James Barry, sues the defendant, Enright Corporation, on a strict liability theory. The plaintiff alleges that in January 2005, the defendant sold the plaintiff a defectively designed microwave oven and that in February 2005, the oven exploded, injuring the plaintiff. During the defense case-in-chief, the defendant calls Dr. Verna Gunther. Dr. Gunther identifies herself and states that she is the defendant's chief safety engineer. On direct examination she testifies that, in her opinion, the oven was properly designed. She adds that the oven was the safest oven on the market and represented the state of the art. It was as safely designed as the state of the art permitted. The following occurs on cross-examination. The plaintiff is the proponent and the defendant-company is the opponent.

P Dr. Gunther, ISN'T IT TRUE THAT in March 2005, you redesigned the oven?

O Your Honor, may we approach the bench?

J Yes.

O Your Honor, I object to that question on the ground that it calls for evidence of a subsequent remedial measure.

J [*To the plaintiff*] Is that what you're attempting to prove?

P Yes, your Honor. Yes your Honor. Although amended Rule 407 now covers products liability cases, we are offering the evidence to show that it was feasible to make the design changes. Our questions of the witness will go directly to that point.

J The objection will be overruled.

P Dr. Gunther, ISN'T IT A FACT THAT in March 2005, you redesigned the oven?

W Yes.

P AND ISN'T IT CORRECT THAT the part of the oven you redesigned was the heating coil?

W Yes.

P AND DIDN'T the redesign make an accidental explosion less likely?

W Yes.

P And it's a fact, is it not, that it was relatively easy to make the design change?

W I suppose.

P In fact, it took your department only two days to make the design change?

W Yes.

§ 7-10 COMPROMISE STATEMENTS

§ 7-10(A) Statements During Civil Settlement Negotiations

§ 7-10(A)(1) The Doctrine

The courts have long favored the out-of-court settlement of legal claims. That attitude has become even more pronounced in recent years. The trial courts are so badly backlogged that it is imperative that parties be encouraged to make out-of-court settlements. The attitude expresses itself in Texas Rule of Evidence 408, excluding statements made during civil settlement negotiations.[13] The Rule rests on the rationale that if negotiators know that their statements are privileged, their discussions will be more candid and, hopefully, more successful. Texas Rule of Evidence 408 states the general rule of exclusion:

> Evidence of (1) furnishing or offering or promising to furnish, or (2) compromising or attempting to compromise a claim which was disputed as to either validity or amount, is not admissible to prove liability for or invalidity of the claim or its amount. Evidence of conduct or statements made in compromise negotiations is likewise not admissible.

Like the subsequent remedial measure doctrine, this doctrine is not an absolute exclusionary rule. The proponent may offer the evidence on other theories of logical relevance. Rule 408 states in pertinent part: "[t]his rule . . . does not require exclusion when the evidence is offered for another purpose, such as proving bias or prejudice or interest of a witness or a party, negating a contention of undue delay, or proving an effort to obstruct a criminal investigation or prosecution."

This list is not exclusive, however. Counsel should be able to introduce evidence of settlement negotiations on the issue of agency, ownership, or control,

---

[13] Although Rule 408, on its face, applies to both civil and criminal cases, the focus here is on settlement negotiations in civil cases because that is where the Rule finds its greatest utility. Compromise agreements in criminal cases are more likely to fall within Rule 410, discussed *infra*.

if those issues are disputed. In the past, a common exception to the general rule of exclusion was the introduction of what is commonly referred to as a "Mary Carter Agreement."[14] This form of settlement agreement usually involved an agreement between the plaintiff and one of the codefendants where the settling codefendant remained as a party in the case and also retained some financial interest in the case, such that the codefendant had an interest in promoting the plaintiff's case. However, in *Elbaor v. Smith,*[15] the Texas Supreme Court held that Mary Carter agreements are void as against public policy. Thus, the opportunity to use such an agreement under an exception in Rule 408 is slim. But an agreement falling short of a Mary Carter agreement may still fall within the exception in Rule 408 and may be used to show a witness's or party's bias or interest.[16]

§ 7-10(A)(2) Elements of the Foundation—Exclusion of Evidence

The party attempting to exclude the evidence under Rule 408 should lay this foundation:

1. At the time of the statement, there was a dispute over the existence or extent of liability.
2. The party made the statement for the purpose of settling the dispute.
3. The subject matter of the statement is proper. This would include accompanying statements and conduct made in the compromise negotiations.

§ 7-10(A)(3) Elements of the Foundation—Admission of Evidence

The party attempting to introduce the evidence involving compromise negotiations must be ready to make an offer of proof. In the offer of proof, the party should state:

1. What the witness will testify to if the judge permits the party to pursue the line of questioning.
2. The evidence is logically relevant to some issue other than the general question of the claim's validity.

§ 7-10(A)(4) Sample Foundations

The first fact situation is a tort action for personal injuries. The plaintiff, Mr. Emilio Juarez, sues the defendant, Ms. Rachel Damer. The plaintiff alleges that

---

[14] *See Booth v. Mary Carter Paint Co.*, 202 So.2d 8 (Fla. Dist. Ct. App. 1967).

[15] 845 S.W.2d 240 (Tex. 1992).

[16] *See* WENDORF, SCHLUETER & BARTON, TEXAS RULES OF EVIDENCE MANUAL IV-132 (6th ed. 2002).

the defendant caused a collision and that in the collision the plaintiff suffered injuries in the amount of $100,000. The plaintiff takes the witness stand to testify in his own behalf. On cross-examination, the following occurs. The proponent is the defendant and the opponent is the plaintiff.

P Mr. Juarez, ISN'T IT TRUE THAT in your complaint in this case, you claim that you've suffered $100,000 in damages?

W Yes.

P ISN'T IT A FACT THAT on February 17th, you were at my office?

W Right.

P ISN'T IT CORRECT THAT while you were there, you offered to settle your whole claim for only $15,000? (1), (3)

O Your Honor, I object to that question. May we approach the bench?

J Yes.

O Your Honor, I object to that question on the ground that it calls for an inadmissible compromise statement under Texas Rule of Evidence 408. I request permission to voir dire the witness before you rule on my objection. I also request that you excuse the jurors.

J Yes. Ladies and gentlemen of the jury, I am going to ask you to leave the courtroom for a few minutes. The bailiff will accompany you to the deliberation room. [*Jurors leave the courtroom.*]

O Mr. Juarez, WHY did you go to the opposing attorney's office on February 17th? (2)

W I went there to discuss my claim against his client.

O WHAT was your claim? (1)

W I took the position that Ms. Damer was at fault in the accident and caused my injuries.

O WHAT was your belief about the validity of this claim? (1)

W I thought I was in the right. I thought the claim was valid. As I remember the accident, I had the green light.

O WHAT did the defendant say about your claim? (1)

W She denied that she was at fault.

P WHAT was the purpose of the meeting on February 17th? (2)

W We wanted to see if we could settle without going to trial.

O WHY did you want to settle if you thought that your claim was valid? (2)

W You told me that juries are unpredictable and that sometimes it's better to be conservative and accept less money than you ask for in your complaint. I still thought that I had a good claim, but that's why I was willing to talk about settling.

O Your Honor, I have no further voir dire questions. The witness's testimony shows that there was a dispute over his claim's validity and that he made his offer in a bona fide effort to compromise. The question I'm objecting to calls for the settlement offer itself (2), (3). The question is objectionable.

J The objection is sustained.

As in the case of subsequent repair evidence, the opponent should consider moving for a mistrial.

The second fact situation is a contract action. The plaintiff, Mr. John Peterson, sues the defendant, Aramco Construction Company. In its answer, the defendant alleges that the plaintiff did not reasonably mitigate damages. The answer alleges that after the defendant's breach, the plaintiff delayed three months before looking for another contractor. The plaintiff takes the witness stand in his own behalf. The plaintiff has already testified to the contract's formation and the defendant's breach. The plaintiff is the proponent and the opponent is the defendant.

P WHAT happened after the defendant's work crew walked off the site?

W The next day I contacted Mr. Garner, the defendant's president.

P WHAT happened when you contacted him?

W He and I discussed how we might settle my claim against his company.

O Your Honor, I move to strike the last answer. May we approach the bench?

J Yes.

O Your Honor, the answer refers to inadmissible compromise negotiations.

P Your Honor, may I be heard?

J Yes.

P I offer to prove that the witness will testify that the parties began settlement negotiations that day and that the negotiations continued for over two months. (1) The testimony is logically relevant to explain the plaintiff's delay in hiring another contractor. (2) In his answer, the defendant alleged that the plaintiff did not properly mitigate damages. (2) The evidence is admissible for the limited purpose of rebutting the defendant's allegation. (2)

J The motion to strike is denied.

P Mr. Peterson, permit me to repeat the question. WHAT happened when you contacted Mr. Garner?

W We discussed settling my claim against his company.

P HOW long did these discussions last?

W On and off for over two months. I kept trying to get them back on the project. I wanted a warehouse, not a lawsuit.

O Your Honor, I request a limiting instruction.

J Granted. Ladies and gentlemen of the jury, you've just heard testimony about settlement negotiations between the plaintiff and defendant. You are not to use the evidence of the defendant's willingness to negotiate as an admission of liability. You are to use this evidence only for the limited purpose of deciding whether the plaintiff acted with reasonable speed in finding a new contractor to finish the project. The defendant claims that the plaintiff did not. The plaintiff offers these pending settlement negotiations as an explanation for his delay in hiring a new contractor.

The third sample foundation focuses on use of a settlement agreement between the plaintiff and a codefendant. The fact situation arises out of products liability suit. The plaintiff, Mr. Brian Dettmann, has alleged that one of the defendants, Fixit, Inc., sold him defective tools which resulted in damages totaling $50,000. He has also alleged that Tools, Inc., was negligent in manufacturing the tools. One of the former defendants, Tools, Inc., reached a settlement agreement with Mr. Dettmann to the effect that in return for testifying on behalf of the plaintiff, Tools, Inc, will be liable for only $2,500. After settling, Tools, Inc. was dropped from the case. The owner of Tools, Inc., Mr. Jim Olson, has just presented testimony favorable to the plaintiff and is now being cross-examined by the counsel for defendant Fixit, Inc. The opponent is plaintiff's counsel.

P ISN'T IT TRUE, Mr. Olson, that you have reached a settlement agreement with the plaintiff in this case?

O Your Honor, we object. May we approach the bench?

J Yes.

O Your Honor, it is clear that counsel is attempting to violate Rule 408 by introducing evidence of settlement agreements.

P We are attempting to introduce evidence of the agreement, your Honor. We have learned that the plaintiff and the defendant, Tools, Inc., have reached an agreement which amounts to a Mary Carter Agreement. Rule 408 recognizes that one of the legitimate uses of compromise agreements is to show the bias or interest of a party or a witness. Here, we are entitled to show the jury that Mr. Olson is now actually aligned with the plaintiff. (1), (2)

J [*To plaintiff's counsel*] Is that correct, counsel?

O Yes, it is, your Honor.

J I will permit defense counsel to inquire into the general nature of the agreement and the dollar amounts, if any, which are involved. But I will not permit you to introduce any of the agreement itself. I will also instruct the jury on the limited use which they may make of this agreement. In effect, I will instruct them that they may only use evidence of the agreement to assess the credibility of Mr. Olson. You may continue.

P Mr. Olson, let me repeat my question. ISN'T IT TRUE THAT your company has reached an agreement with the plaintiff in this case? (2)

W Yes.

P And, IS IT NOT TRUE THAT as a result of that agreement, you stand to benefit by presenting testimony favorable to the plaintiff? (2)

W I guess you could say that.

§ 7-10(B) STATEMENTS DURING PLEA BARGAINING NEGOTIATIONS

§ 7-10(B)(1) The Doctrine

The last section examined the doctrine excluding statements made during civil settlement negotiations. The reason for that doctrine is that the courts want to encourage out-of-court settlements and save court time. For a similar reason, Texas Evidence Rule 410 recognizes a parallel doctrine excluding statements made during criminal plea bargaining negotiations. Rule 410 places the Texas courts among the ranks of the jurisdictions following the doctrine. The Rule generally excludes: (1) a plea of guilty which was later withdrawn; (2) a plea of nolo contendere;[17] (3) any statement made in the course of any proceedings under Rule 11 of the Federal Rules of Criminal Procedure or comparable state procedure regarding either of the foregoing pleas; or (4) any statement made in the course of plea discussions with an attorney for the prosecuting authority which do not result in a plea of guilty or which result in a plea of guilty later withdrawn.

There is only one exception in Rule 410. A statement made in the course of plea discussions "is admissible in any proceeding wherein another statement made in the course of the same plea or plea discussions has been introduced and the statement ought in fairness be considered contemporaneously with it."

§ 7-10(B)(2) Elements of the Foundation

Counsel attempting to invoke this doctrine must lay this foundation:

1. At a certain time and place, the defendant met with the authorities, that is, the prosecutor or the police acting with the prosecutor's consent.
2. The defendant subjectively believed that the purpose of the meeting was plea bargaining.

---

[17] In criminal cases Rule 410 blocks admission of a plea of nolo contendere which is later withdrawn.

3. The defendant's belief was reasonable. The authorities' statements and conduct reasonably led the defendant to that belief.
4. The defendant made the statement during the plea bargaining session.
5. The subject matter of the statement was proper. Both offers to plead guilty and accompanying statements of fact are protected.

§ 7-10(B)(3) Sample Foundation

The fact situation is a medical aid fraud prosecution. The State alleges that the defendant, Mr. George Aston, is a pharmacist who knowingly filled fraudulent prescriptions for doctors receiving medical aid payments from the state. The State's primary interest is convicting the doctors with whom the defendant conspired. Prior to trial, the defendant makes a motion in limine to suppress certain statements he made to the prosecutor during a meeting at the prosecutor's office. Assume that there are no *Miranda* warnings or voluntariness issues. Rather, the defense counsel rests the motion squarely on the doctrine excluding statements made during plea bargaining negotiations. The defense counsel calls the defendant as a witness in support of the motion. The defendant has already identified himself. The defendant is the proponent.

P Mr. Aston, WHERE were you on the afternoon of April 3rd of this year? (1)

W I went to the D.A.'s office in downtown Texarkana.

P WHO else was there? (1)

W You were there, and the other person present was an Assistant D.A.

P WHO was that? (1)

W I think her name was Hester Martin.

P WHAT was the purpose of this meeting? (2)

W Plea bargaining. I hoped to get some concessions, maybe even immunity.

P WHY did you think that was the purpose of the meeting? (2)

W You told me that before we got there.

P WHAT, if anything, did Ms. Martin say about the purpose of the meeting? (3)

W When we got there, she said that she wanted to be honest with me. She said that I was just a small fish and that they were really interested in nailing all the doctors I had filled false prescriptions for. She said that if I came clean, they might give me a break. She even mentioned some sort of immunity.

P WHAT did you say then? (4), (5)

W With your permission, I told her about my involvement with the doctors. I said that I'd be willing to repeat those statements in court for full immunity.

P HOW did Ms. Martin respond to your offer?

W She said that she'd have to talk it over with her boss, Mr. Chunn, before giving us a final answer.

P WHAT was the final answer?

W Ms. Martin phoned me at work about three days later. She said that her boss would O.K. some sentence concessions but wouldn't buy immunity.

P WHAT, if anything, did you say then?

W I told her that it was too bad because you and I had agreed that I'd talk only if I got immunity.

P WHAT happened to your plea bargaining with the District Attorney's office?

W That conversation ended the negotiations.

P Your Honor, I have no further questions of the defendant. I renew my motion to preclude any reference to my client's statements during the plea bargaining session at the District Attorney's office. Under Rule of Evidence 410(4), those statements are clearly inadmissible.

J Your motion is granted.

§ 7-11 LIABILITY INSURANCE

§ 7-11(A) THE DOCTRINE

A tort plaintiff ordinarily may not prove that the defendant has liability insurance. There is a weak argument that the defendant's liability coverage, or lack thereof, is logically relevant to show the defendant's negligence. Knowing that he or she has liability insurance, the defendant might be less careful. There is a prominent probative danger, however, that the evidence will tempt the jury to decide the case on an improper basis. The jurors may find for the plaintiff, not because they are convinced of the defendant's fault, but rather because they feel the insurance company can better afford to absorb the economic loss. Texas Rule of Evidence 411 states the norm:

> Evidence that a person was or was not insured against liability is not admissible upon the issue whether the person acted negligently or otherwise wrongfully. This rule does not require the exclusion of evidence of insurance against liability when offered for another purpose, such as proof of agency, ownership, or control, or bias or prejudice of a witness.

On the one hand, the evidence of the defendant's liability insurance may not be used to support a generalized inference of the defendant's negligence. On the other hand, as Rule 411 makes clear, the plaintiff may use the evidence for other purposes. For example, it may be used to prove agency, ownership, or control, if those issues are in dispute. As with the exceptions for admitting evidence of subsequent remedial measures, *supra* at § 7-9, the burden is on the counsel seeking admission of liability insurance to show the court that the evidence is being offered to show something other than fault.

§ 7-11(B) Elements of the Foundation

§ 7-11(B)(1) Invoking the Rule of Exclusion

The party attempting to exclude evidence of liability insurance should lay the following foundation:

1. The party has, or does not have, liability insurance.
2. Evidence of liability insurance is not relevant to the case apart from the issue of the party's fault.

The party can assert this doctrine in a motion in limine. If the issue arises at trial, the party can conduct voir dire examination to lay the foundation.

§ 7-11(B)(2) Avoiding the Rule of Exclusion

If the party seeking to introduce evidence of liability insurance is invoking an alternative theory of logical relevance, the party should be prepared to show:

1. What the witness will testify to (or what the evidence will show) if the judge permits the proponent to pursue the line of inquiry.
2. The evidence of liability insurance is logically relevant to some issue other than the general question of negligence or fault.
3. Unless the issue is one of credibility of a witness, the issue the evidence relates to is in dispute. The proponent should point to the specific testimony by the opposing witnesses, or the pleadings, which shows that the issue is controverted.

§ 7-11(C) Sample Foundations

The following foundations illustrate both the rule and two of the more important exceptions to the rule.

The first fact situation is a tort case. The plaintiff, Ms. Greenwich, sues the defendant, Mr. Fenton. The plaintiff alleges that the defendant's negligent driving caused the collision in which she was injured. The defendant takes the stand and denies driving carelessly. The plaintiff then begins cross-examination. The plaintiff is the opponent.

O Mr. Fenton, ISN'T IT TRUE THAT you carry liability insurance?

P Your Honor, I object to that question on the ground that it calls for evidence of liability insurance.

J Objection sustained.

P Your Honor, I request a curative instruction.

J Yes. Ladies and gentlemen of the jury, you have just heard a reference to possible liability insurance in this case. You are to disregard that reference and the question. You may not speculate whether the defendant has insurance, and you may not consider the possible existence of insurance in your deliberations. You are to decide whether the defendant is liable solely on the basis of the evidence admitted in this case.

P Now, your Honor, I move for a mistrial.[18]

J The motion will be denied.

The hypothetical continues. Assume that the defendant called Mr. Graham as a witness. Mr. Graham inspected the accident scene and measured the plaintiff's skid marks. The skid marks supported the defendant's theory that the plaintiff caused the accident by speeding. The plaintiff now takes Mr. Graham on cross-examination.

P Mr. Graham, ISN'T IT TRUE THAT you work for Allied Insurance Company?

W Yes.

P AND ISN'T IT ALSO A FACT THAT your company insures the defendant, Mr. Fenton?

O Your Honor, I object to that question on the ground that it calls for evidence of liability insurance.

P Your Honor, may we approach the bench?

J Yes.

P Your Honor, we are not offering the evidence to support a general inference of negligence on Mr. Fenton's part. Rather, we would offer the evidence to impeach Mr. Graham. (1), (2) Under Rule 411, the evidence is logically relevant to show Mr. Graham's bias in the defendant's favor. (2)

---

[18] Although earlier Texas cases took a very strong view against any improper mention of insurance in a trial, the modern trend has been to give an instruction to disregard, at a minimum. A mistrial may be granted if it appears, inter alia, that the counsel deliberately interjected the subject and a curative instruction to disregard will be ineffective.

J The objection is overruled.

P Mr. Graham, let me repeat the question. ISN'T IT CORRECT THAT your company insures the defendant?

W Yes.

O Your Honor, I request a limiting instruction under Rule 105.

J Very well. Ladies and gentlemen of the jury, you have just heard evidence that the defendant has liability insurance. You may not consider that evidence in deciding whether the defendant was at fault in the accident. You also should not consider whether the insurance company is in a better economic position to absorb any loss than the plaintiff. I am admitting the evidence for one limited purpose, to shed light on Mr. Graham's credibility. You may consider the fact that Mr. Graham works for Mr. Fenton's insurance company in deciding how much weight to attach to Mr. Graham's testimony.

The hypothetical continues. Now assume that Jennings Trucking Company is the codefendant. The codefendant denies that Fenton is its employee. The codefendant calls Mr. Munster as a witness. Mr. Munster testifies that he is the codefendant's general manager. On direct examination, he testifies that although Fenton once worked for Jennings Trucking Company, he was not an employee at the time of the accident. Suppose that the plaintiff gave Jennings notice to produce its insurance policy and thereby satisfied the best evidence rule. The plaintiff now takes Mr. Munster on cross-examination.

P Mr. Munster, ISN'T IT TRUE THAT your company carries liability insurance?

O Your Honor, I object to that question on the ground that it calls for evidence of liability insurance.

P Your Honor, may we approach the bench?

J Yes.

P I offer to prove that if the witness is permitted to answer, the witness will testify that the codefendant's insurance policy listed Mr. Fenton as an employee at the time of the accident. (1), (2), (3) The codefendant denies that Mr. Fenton was its employee at that time, and I am offering the evidence for the limited purpose of showing Mr. Fenton's agency. (3)

J The objection will be overruled.

P Mr. Munster, let me repeat the question. ISN'T IT TRUE THAT your company carries liability insurance?

W Yes.

P ISN'T IT CORRECT THAT you are the custodian of the insurance policy?

W Yes.

P AND ISN'T IT A FACT THAT appendix II to the policy lists the employees covered by the policy?

W That's correct.

P ISN'T IT TRUE THAT at the time of the accident, appendix II to your policy listed Mr. Fenton as one of your employees?

W That's right.

O Your Honor, I would like a limiting instruction.

J Yes. Ladies and gentlemen of the jury, you have just heard a reference to the codefendant's liability insurance. You are not to consider that evidence in deciding whether either defendant acted negligently. You are also not to speculate as to whether the insurance company could absorb the loss resulting from the accident. You are to consider the evidence only for the purpose of deciding whether, at the time of the accident, Mr. Fenton was an employee of Jennings Trucking Company.

CHAPTER 8
THE ORIGINAL WRITING "BEST EVIDENCE" RULE

§ 8-1 INTRODUCTION

The last three chapters analyzed evidence rules which exclude logically relevant evidence for policy reasons—either policies relating to jury behavior or extrinsic social policies. The next three chapters also discuss rules which have the effect of barring the admission of logically relevant evidence. The doctrines discussed in these chapters, however, exclude relevant evidence for a very different reason, namely, doubts about the reliability of certain types of evidence.

The common law prefers that evidence take the form of a witness walking into court, subjecting himself or herself to cross-examination, and either reciting observed facts or quoting a document produced in the courtroom. In the view of the common law courts, that type of testimony is the most trustworthy. Whenever the proponent of evidence attempts to deviate from the norm, the proponent is likely to encounter an exclusionary rule. If the proponent offers testimony about an out-of-court statement rather than calling the declarant as a witness at trial, the proponent may have to surmount the hurdle of the hearsay rule. When the proponent attempts to elicit opinions from the witness rather than statements of observed fact, the proponent may encounter the opinion prohibition. Finally, if the proponent invites the witness to paraphrase a document rather than producing the document in court, the proponent may face a best evidence objection.

The proponent may be able to introduce hearsay, opinion, or paraphrase. But in order to do so, the proponent must establish an exceptional reason for deviating from the preference upon proper and timely objection.

The original writing rule, more often referred to as the best evidence rule, is illustrative. The best evidence rule excludes secondary evidence of a writing's contents. The rule expresses a preference for the more reliable evidence, the writing itself. Texas Rules of Evidence 1001–08 set out the rule.

Briefly, the rule states that when a writing's terms are in issue, the proponent must either (1) produce an original or duplicate, or (2) both excuse the nonproduction of the originals and present an admissible type of secondary evidence. The rule presents five questions:

- What is a "writing" for purposes of the rule?
- When are a writing's terms "in issue?"
- What is an "original" or a "duplicate?"
- What are the admissible types of secondary evidence?
- What are adequate excuses for nonproduction?

§ 8-2 DEFEATING AN ORIGINAL WRITING "BEST EVIDENCE" OBJECTION

The proponent can usually defeat a best evidence objection. The proponent can do so because the five issues convert into several different bases for overriding the objection. The judge can overrule the objection on the grounds that the article involved is not a document; the document's terms are not "in issue"; the document's terms are only collaterally "in issue"; the evidence offered is an "original"; the evidence offered is a "duplicate"; there is an adequate excuse for the nonproduction of the originals; and the proponent is offering an admissible type of secondary evidence.

The following sections illustrate the various bases for defeating best evidence objections.

§ 8-2(A) THE OBJECT INVOLVED IS NOT A "WRITING"

§ 8-2(A)(1) The Doctrine

Reference to the doctrine under consideration as "the best evidence rule" is a misnomer. There is no general requirement that the proponent produce or account for the best, or most persuasive, evidence. The Rule's scope is limited to writings and other similar memorializations, such as videotapes and photographs. The rationale is that detail is often more important in the analysis of writings. Thus, a more accurate title for the doctrine would be the "original writing rule." This is the term used in the Texas Rules of Evidence.

Texas Rule of Evidence 1002 contains a broad definition of the Rule's scope. Rule 1002 applies the Rule to writings, recordings, and photographs. Rule 1001(1) defines writings and records as "letters, words, or numbers, or their equivalent, set down by handwriting, typewriting, printing, photostating, photographing, magnetic impulse, mechanical or electronic recording, or other form of data compilation." Rule 1001(2) defines photographs as "still photographs, X-ray films, video tapes and motion pictures."

§ 8-2(A)(2) Sample Foundation

The following fact situation is a products liability action. The plaintiff, Mr. Konert, brings a tort action against Goodyear Tire Company. He alleges that the defendant negligently manufactured his tire and that the negligent manufacture caused the tire to blow out and thereby cause an accident. The defendant has generally denied liability. The plaintiff calls Mr. Langdale, the police officer who investigated the accident. The witness has already identified himself and generally described the investigation at the accident scene. The officer has stated that he carefully examined the condition of the plaintiff's car. The plaintiff is the proponent.

P WHAT parts of the car did you inspect?

W Any part that might have contributed to the accident—the steering wheel, the engine, and the tires.

P WHAT condition were the tires in?

W Three were O.K.

P WHAT was the condition of the fourth tire?

W It had blown out. There was no air in it, and there was a large hole in it.

P HOW large was the hole?

W I'd say that it was easily two inches in diameter.

P WHERE was the hole located?

W On the tread part of the tire.

P WHAT was written on the tire?

W There were size specifications and a trade name.

P WHAT was the trade name on the tire?

O Your Honor, I object to that question on the ground that it calls for secondary evidence.

P Your Honor, may I be heard?

J Yes.

P In Texas, the best evidence rule does not apply to inscribed chattels such as tires.[1]

---

[1] *See* Hippard, *Article X: Contents of Writings, Recordings, and Photographs*, 20 HOUS. L. REV. 595 (1983).

J Objection overruled.

P Let me repeat the question. WHAT was the trade name on the tire?

W It was "Goodyear."

§ 8-2(B) THE WRITING'S TERMS ARE NOT "IN ISSUE"

§ 8-2(B)(1) The Doctrine

In the words of Texas Evidence Rule 1002, the rule applies only when the proponent attempts "to prove the content of a writing . . . ." There are three situations in which a document's terms are "in issue" for purposes of triggering the original writing rule.

The first situation is the case in which the material facts of consequence automatically place the document's terms in issue. For example, in a forgery prosecution, the terms of the allegedly forged document are automatically in issue. The same analysis applies in a contract action if the complaint alleges that the agreement was a written contract.

We must distinguish this situation from the situation in which a fact exists independently of the writing but the writing is convenient evidence of the fact. Thus, a witness who observed payment of a debt may testify to that fact without producing the receipt; the receipt is merely convenient evidence of payment. Similarly, a witness who attended a wedding ceremony may testify to the marriage without producing the marriage license. Again, the license is convenient evidence, but the wedding is a historical event that occurred independently of the writing.

The second situation is a case in which the witness expressly or impliedly refers to the writing in his or her testimony. Suppose that the proponent attempting to prove the marriage cannot find an eyewitness to the ceremony. The proponent instead calls a deputy county clerk to testify to the contents of the marriage license on file. The clerk will expressly or impliedly rely upon the document's contents. The express or implied reference to the document's contents triggers the original writing rule.

§ 8-2(B)(2) Sample Foundation

The hypothetical fact situation is a probate contest. The contestants are challenging the will and claiming by intestate succession. To prove their right to take by intestate succession, they have to show that on March 1, 1990, Joan Merchant married Thomas Kleven. The contestants call Ms. Trudy Guinn, an eyewitness to the marriage. The contestants are the proponents.

P Ms. Guinn, WHERE were you on March 1, 1990?

W I was in Chicago, Illinois.

P WHAT were you doing there?

W I was attending a wedding.

P WHOSE wedding?

O Your Honor, I object to that question on the ground that it calls for secondary evidence. The marriage license is the best evidence.

P Your Honor, may I be heard?

J Yes.

P The event of the wedding occurred independently of the license or certificate. A witness could observe the wedding ceremony without ever seeing the license. This eyewitness is prepared to testify without relying on the license. Thus, the license's terms are not in issue.

J Objection overruled.

P Ms. Guinn, let me repeat the question. WHOSE wedding?

W The marriage of Joan Merchant and Thomas Kleven.

P HOW can you remember a wedding that occurred almost 14 years ago?

W It sticks in my mind because I was Joan's maid of honor. I knew Joan and Tom well, and Joan asked me to stand up with her.

§ 8-2(C) THE WRITING'S TERMS ARE ONLY COLLATERALLY "IN ISSUE"

§ 8-2(C)(1) The Doctrine

Even if the writing's terms are technically in issue, the judge may dispense with compliance with the original writing rule. Sometimes the writing's terms relate to a minor issue in the case, and the judge concludes that it is not worth the time and inconvenience to require the proponent to comply with the rule. Suppose, for instance, that the opponent wants to impeach the witness with a written prior inconsistent statement. If the opponent is going to use the document solely to impeach the witness, the judge is likely to hold that the document is only collaterally relevant. The opponent could dispense with compliance with the original writing rule and use a photocopy of the written prior inconsistent statement.

Texas Rule of Evidence 1004(4) recognizes this limitation on the scope of the original writing rule. This subsection states that the proponent need not comply with the rule if "[t]he writing, recording, or photograph is not closely related to a controlling issue." The judge considers the importance of the issue which relates to the document. If the judge concludes in his or her discretion that the issue is a minor question in the case, the proponent need not comply with the original writing rule.

§ 8-2(C)(2) Sample Foundation

The following fact situation is a tort action arising from a hit-and-run accident. The plaintiff, Ms. Lopez, alleges that the defendant, Mr. Smith, negligently struck her in a crosswalk. The defendant denies that he was the driver. The plaintiff calls Mr. Meese, an eyewitness to the accident. Mr. Meese has just testified that he saw the accident and observed the car's license number. The plaintiff is the proponent.

P WHAT was that license number?

W I'm sorry, but I can't remember off-hand.

P WHAT, if anything, might help you remember?

W Well, I made a note of the license number right after the accident. If I could see that note, I could probably remember.

P [*To court reporter*] Would you please mark this as an exhibit? [*Court reporter designates exhibit and hands it back to the proponent.*]

P Thank you. Please let the record reflect that I am showing what the Reporter has marked as plaintiff's exhibit number four for identification to the opposing counsel.

O Your Honor, I am going to object to the use of this document to refresh the witness's recollection. It's obvious that this is only a photocopy and not the best evidence.

P Your Honor, may I be heard?

J Yes.

P I intend to use the exhibit solely to refresh the witness's recollection. I am not going to use the exhibit as substantive evidence of its contents. The exhibit is being used only collaterally.

J Objection overruled.

P I request permission to approach the witness.

J Granted.

P Mr. Meese, I now hand you plaintiff's exhibit number four for identification. WHAT is it?

W It's a copy of the note I just mentioned.

P HOW can you recognize it?

W I recognize my handwriting style.

P WHO prepared the note?

W I did.

P WHEN did you prepare it?

W Right after the accident.

P HOW soon after the accident?

W It was a matter of minutes at most.

P Please read the exhibit to yourself silently. [*The witness does so.*]

P Please hand the exhibit back to me. Please let the record reflect that I am holding the exhibit away from the witness and out of the witness's sight.

P Mr. Meese, you've had an opportunity to read the exhibit to refresh your memory. Now, without relying on the exhibit, HOW well can you remember the license number?

W Now it's clear in my mind.

P WHAT was the license number?

W It was a Texas license, FIA 986.

§ 8-2(D) THE EVIDENCE OFFERED IS AN "ORIGINAL"

§ 8-2(D)(1) The Doctrine

If the object involved is a writing and its terms are in issue, the proponent must comply with the original writing rule. The simplest method of complying is by offering an original or duplicate. The "original" is usually the first document prepared, the first writing signed, the first tape recording prepared, or the negative of the photograph.

Bear in mind, however, that the common law test for originality is legal rather than chronological. Suppose that the case is a bomb threat prosecution. The government alleges that the defendant sent a bomb threat through the mail. The defendant first prepared the threat by typing it. The defendant realized, however, that it would be more difficult for a questioned document examiner to identify the paper or typewriter if he mailed a copy rather than the original. Consequently, the defendant made a photocopy of the typed threat and mailed the copy to the bank. For purposes of the original document rule, the photocopy is the original. Although it is a copy in a chronological sense, because it is the very writing the defendant mailed to the bank, the copy is the legal original.

As the preceding paragraph indicates, very often there is only an original writing in the singular. But that is not always the case. The Texas Rules broaden the definition of "original." Rule 1001(3) states: "[a]n 'original' of a writing or recording is the writing or recording itself or any counterpart intended to have the same effect by a person executing or issuing it."

Assume, for example, that the purchaser of a car signs a single copy of the contract of purchase and leaves the writing with the seller. The next day the seller decides that the buyer should have her own copy of the writing. For that reason, the seller makes a photocopy and mails it to the buyer. Because the photocopy is an exact copy made by reliable, mechanical means and it is intended to have essentially the same effect as the copy earlier signed in ink, both writings would be "originals" in Texas practice.

§ 8-2(D)(2) Elements of the Foundation

The foundation for showing that the offered exhibit is the original includes these elements:

1. The witness recognizes the document.
2. The witness specifies how he or she recognizes the document.
3. The witness adds that the document is the original.

§ 8-2(D)(3) Sample Foundation

The fact situation is a contract action. The plaintiff, Mr. Levine, alleges that the defendant, Mr. Gomez, breached a written employment contract by discharging Mr. Levine without cause. The plaintiff's attorney calls the plaintiff to the stand. The plaintiff has already identified himself and described the parties' oral agreement. The plaintiff is the proponent.

P WHAT did you do after you reached an oral agreement?

W Mr. Gomez's secretary reduced the agreement to writing.

P WHEN did she do that?

W The very afternoon we reached the agreement Mr. Gomez had standard forms with blanks, so it didn't take the secretary long to get the contract ready for signature.

P [*To court reporter*] Would you please mark this as an exhibit for the plaintiff? [*Court reporter marks exhibit as "Plaintiff's Exh. No. 1 for ID" and hands it back to proponent.*]

P Thank you. Please let the record reflect that I am showing plaintiff's exhibit number one for identification to the opposing counsel. [*Hands exhibit to counsel, who inspects it.*]

P I request permission to approach the witness.

J Granted.

P Mr. Levine, I now hand you plaintiff's exhibit number one for identification. WHAT is it? (1)

W It's the contract I was just describing.

P HOW can you recognize it? (2)

W I can tell by its general appearance and especially by the signatures on page five. I certainly know my own handwriting.

P HOW many copies of this were made? (3)

W Three. We signed one in ink, and two were photocopies.

P WHICH one is this exhibit, the one in ink or one of the photocopies? (3)

W This is the one in ink.

P WHEN did you sign this one? (3)

W We signed it first.

P HOW did you sign the photocopies? (3)

W Right afterwards.

P Your Honor, I now offer plaintiff's exhibit number one for identification into evidence.

O Your Honor, I object to the introduction of the exhibit on the ground that the plaintiff has not accounted for the other documents.

P Your Honor, may I be heard?

J Yes.

P The testimony shows that this exhibit is the original, the very first writing the parties signed. Thus, we've complied with the original writing rule under Texas Rule of Evidence 1002.

J Objection overruled. The exhibit will be received.

P I request permission to hand plaintiff's exhibit number one to the jurors for their inspection.

J Permission granted.

§ 8-2(E) The Evidence Offered Is a "Duplicate"

§ 8-2(E)(1) The Doctrine

The proponent can comply with the original writing rule by offering a duplicate rather than an original. At Texas common law, a duplicate original was as admissible as the original; the proponent could offer a duplicate original without proving any excuse for the nonproduction of the original. The common law developed a fairly narrow definition of duplicate. The common law insisted that the duplicate be prepared for the same purpose at the same time as the original and executed with roughly the same formalities. Carbon copies signed by the same stroke of the pen as the original were acceptable duplicate originals at common law.

The common law balked, however, at accepting subsequently prepared documents as duplicates. The common law refused to accept subsequently prepared documents even if they were prepared by reliable, mechanical means of reproduction. The trend, however, is to include such documents within the definition of duplicate. Texas Rule of Evidence 1001(4) follows that trend. That subsection defines duplicate as "a counterpart produced by the same impression as the original, or from the same matrix, or by means of photography, including enlargements and miniatures, by mechanical or electronic re-recording, or by chemical reproduction, or by other equivalent techniques which accurately reproduce the original." So long as the writing is prepared by reliable, mechanical means, it qualifies as a duplicate even if it was prepared much later or for a different reason. Finally, Rule 1003 indicates that a duplicate is as admissible as an original unless a question is raised about the authenticity of the original or if, under the circumstances, it would be unfair to admit the duplicate in place of the original.

§ 8-2(E)(2) Elements of the Foundation

To offer a "duplicate," the proponent must lay the following foundation:

1. The witness recognizes the writing.
2. The witness specifies the basis on which he or she recognizes the writing.
3. The writing is a copy of the original.
4. The witness states the time when the copy was made.
5. The copy was made by reliable, mechanical means of reproduction.

§ 8-2(E)(3) Sample Foundation

The following is a continuation of the hypothetical involving the employment contract *supra* at § 8-2(D)(3). The plaintiff has already stated that the parties reached an oral agreement and had the agreement reduced to writing. The plaintiff is still the proponent.

P HOW many documents did you prepare?

W Three—the ink original, and two photocopies.

P [*To court reporter*] We request that this be marked as plaintiff's exhibit number one for identification. [*Court reporter marks exhibit and hands it back to proponent.*]

P Thank you. Please let the record reflect that I am showing what has been marked as plaintiff's exhibit number one for identification to opposing counsel.

P [*To the witness*] I now show you plaintiff's exhibit number one for identification. WHICH one is this? (3)

W It's one of the photocopies.

P HOW can you tell? (1), (2), (3), (5)

W You can tell by its appearance and the feel of the paper. For example, in the bottom left hand corner you can see the type of marks left by a photocopy machine.

P Your Honor, I now offer plaintiff's exhibit number one for identification into evidence.

O I object to the introduction of this exhibit on the ground that it is not the best evidence.

P Your Honor, may I be heard?

J Yes.

P The testimony shows that this exhibit is a duplicate. It is true that it was prepared subsequently. (4) But, under Texas Rules of Evidence 1001(3) and 1003, a duplicate is as admissible as an original so long as it was made by a mechanical means of reproduction. (5)

J The objection will be overruled, and plaintiff's exhibit number one will be received into evidence.

On the one hand, the Texas Rules expand the definition of "duplicate." On the other hand, in Texas practice, a duplicate is not necessarily automatically admissible as an original. Texas Rule 1003 reads: "[a] duplicate is admissible to the same extent as an original unless (1) a genuine question is raised as to the authenticity of the original or (2) in the circumstances it would be unfair to admit the duplicate in lieu of the original."

The opposing attorney might invoke 1003(1) by presenting evidence that the original document was a forgery. The purported author might deny ever signing such a writing. That evidence sharpens the need to examine the original. Similarly, the opposing attorney could resort to 1003(2) if the copy was incomplete and omitted a potentially important part of the original. In either event, the proponent would have to establish excuses for the nonproduction of all originals before introducing a duplicate.

§ 8-3 ADMISSIBLE TYPES OF SECONDARY EVIDENCE

If the object involved is a writing and the writing's terms are in issue, there are two methods of satisfying the original writing rule. Sections 8-2(D) and 8-2(E), *supra*, dealt with the first method: proving that the evidence offered qualifies as an original or duplicate. The second method involves two steps: (1) proving an adequate excuse for the nonproduction; and (2) offering an admissible type of secondary evidence.

There are two admissible types of secondary evidence. The first is an authenticated copy. The witness testifies that the document is an accurate copy of the original. The second is oral recollection testimony. The proponent does not have even a written copy of the original, but the witness can recall the substance of the contents of the original.

§ 8-3(A) AN AUTHENTICATED COPY

§ 8-3(A)(1) The Doctrine

One permissible type of secondary evidence is an authenticated copy. The witness need not have personally prepared the copy. However, the witness must remember the tenor or contents of the original, read the copy, and, finally, testify that the exhibit is a true and accurate copy of the original.

§ 8-3(A)(2) Elements of the Foundation

The elements of the foundation for secondary evidence in the form of an authenticated copy are:

1. On a previous occasion, the witness read the original.
2. The witness still remembers the original.
3. As best he or she can tell, the exhibit is a true and accurate copy of the original.

§ 8-3(A)(3) Sample Foundation

The fact situation is a civil tort action. The plaintiff, Mr. Smythe, alleges that the defendant, Mr. Wiggins, is guilty of libel. The complaint alleges that the defendant committed the libel in a letter to Mr. Jackson. The plaintiff calls Mr. Jackson as a witness. Mr. Jackson first testifies that he received the letter in the defendant's handwriting. The plaintiff then establishes an excuse for the nonproduction of the original letter, such as the loss of the letter. The next section describes the foundation for that excuse. Now the proponent, the plaintiff, will attempt to authenticate a photocopy of the letter.

P WHAT did you do when you first received the letter? (1)

W I read it.

P HOW carefully did you read it? (1), (2)

W Very carefully.

P WHY did you read it carefully? (1), (2)

W It shocked me. I had to read it several times before I could believe what I saw.

P HOW many times did you read it? (1), (2)

W At least three.

P WHY did you read it three times? (1), (2)

W Again, it was hard to believe what I read in that letter.

P HOW well do you remember the contents of the letter? (2)

W Very well. I can't quote it word for word, but I have a distinct recollection of it.

P HOW can you remember it so well? (2)

W Well, it was fairly short, and I read it both carefully and several times.

P [*To court reporter*] Would you please mark this as an exhibit for the plaintiff? [*Court reporter marks exhibit and hands it back to proponent.*]

P Thank you. Please let the record reflect that I am showing what has been marked as plaintiff's exhibit number two for identification to the opposing counsel. [*Hands exhibit to opposing counsel.*]

P I request permission to approach the witness.

J Permission granted.

P Mr. Jackson, I now hand you plaintiff's exhibit number two for identification. WHAT is it? (3)

W It's a photocopy of the letter I just described.

P HOW can you recognize it? (3)

W I recognize the handwriting, the general contents, and some phrases that stick in my mind.

P HOW accurate is this copy? (3)

W As far as I can tell, it's verbatim.

P Your Honor, I now offer plaintiff's exhibit number two for identification into evidence.

O I object to the introduction of this exhibit on the ground that it is does not satisfy the original writing rule. It is only a secondary copy.

P Your Honor, may I be heard?

J Yes.

P It's true that this is secondary evidence. However, we've established the loss of the original, which is an adequate excuse for nonproduction. In addition, the witness has authenticated the copy.

J The objection will be overruled, and plaintiff's exhibit number two for identification will be received into evidence.

P Mr. Jackson, would you please read the last paragraph of the letter to the jurors?

W The paragraph reads, "I heard this juicy rumor about our mutual friend, James Smythe. He evidently slipped $2,000 to Councilman Wild to get a favorable ruling on a zoning application. Old Smythe is a lot slicker, and a lot less honest, than I thought."

P WHOSE handwriting is that letter in?

W The defendant's, Marvin Wiggins.

P I request permission to hand plaintiff's exhibit number two to the jurors for their inspection.

J Granted.

§ 8-3(B) ORAL RECOLLECTION TESTIMONY

§ 8-3(B)(1) The Doctrine

Even if the proponent does not have a copy, the witness can testify to his or her recollection of the original's contents. Again, the proponent must establish an excuse for nonproduction.

§ 8-3(B)(2) Elements of the Foundation

The foundation for using a document to refresh the witness's recollection is quite simple:

1. On a previous occasion, the witness read the original.
2. The witness still remembers the substance of the original's contents.
3. The witness states the substance of the original's contents.

§ 8-3(B)(3) Sample Foundation

The preceding hypothetical can be used to illustrate this type of secondary evidence. Again, assume that the proponent has already established an excuse for nonproduction of the original letter.

P WHAT did you do when you first received the letter? (1)

W I read it.

P HOW carefully did you read it? (1), (2)

W Very carefully.

P WHY did you read it carefully? (1), (2)

W It shocked me. I had to read it several times before I could believe what I saw there.

P HOW many times did you read it? (1), (2)

W At least three times.

P WHY did you read it three times? (1), (2)

W Again, it was so hard to believe what I read there.

P HOW was the letter prepared? Was it printed, written, or typed? (2)

W It was handwritten.

P HOW well do you remember the contents of the letter? (2)

W Very well. I can't quote it word for word, but I have a distinct recollection.

P HOW can you remember it so well? (2)

W It was relatively short and I read it very carefully several times.

P WHAT, if anything, did the letter say about Mr. Smythe? (3)

O Your Honor, I object to that question on the ground that it calls for secondary evidence.

P Your Honor, may I be heard?

J Yes.

P It's true that the witness recollection is secondary evidence. However, we've established the loss of the original, which is an adequate excuse for the nonproduction of the original. In addition, the witness has testified to recalling the substance of the letter.

J Objection overruled.

P Mr. Jackson, let me repeat the question. WHAT, if anything, did the letter say about Mr. Smythe? (3)

W It said that he had bribed Councilman Wild in connection with a zoning application.

P WHOSE handwriting was the letter in?

W The defendant's, Marvin Wiggins.

§ 8-4 EXCUSES FOR NONPRODUCTION

If the proponent's evidence does not qualify as an original or duplicate, the proponent must both authenticate the evidence and establish an excuse for nonproduction of each of the originals.

§ 8-4(A) THE PROPONENT LOST THE ORIGINAL

§ 8-4(A)(1) The Doctrine

An adequate excuse for nonproduction of an original is to establish under Texas Rule of Evidence 1004(1) that "[a]ll originals are lost . . . ." Sometimes the witness can testify directly to the original's loss. For example, perhaps the witness saw the original fall into a sewer. In most cases, however, the proponent will have to rely on circumstantial proof of loss: although the witness conducted a diligent search for the original, the witness could not locate it. The trial judge makes a discretionary determination whether the proponent exercised sufficient diligence to locate the original.

§ 8-4(A)(2) Elements of the Foundation

The foundational elements for showing that the original has been lost include the following:

1. The witness discovered that the original was lost.
2. The witness then searched for the original.
3. The search was reasonably diligent.
4. Despite the search, the witness could not locate the original.

§ 8-4(A)(3) Sample Foundation

The fact situation is a continuation of the previous hypothetical in § 8-3(B)(3). The plaintiff will use Mr. Jackson's testimony to establish the excuse for nonproduction. Mr. Jackson has already testified about receiving a handwritten letter from the defendant.

P WHAT did you do with the letter after you received it? (1)

W I put it in my dresser in our bedroom.

P WHERE is the letter now? (1)

W I don't know.

P WHEN did you discover that the letter was missing? (1)

W I looked for it three weeks ago when you told me we would be going to trial.

P HOW did you discover that the letter was missing? (1)

W I went to the dresser, looked through it, and couldn't find the letter.

P WHAT did you do then? (2)

W I searched for the letter.

P HOW did you conduct this search? (3)

W I went through each drawer in the dresser very carefully.

P HOW carefully? (3)

W I went through it item by item and still couldn't find the letter.

P WHERE else did you search? (3)

W I looked all around the room.

P WHERE else did you look? (3)

W I checked my desk to see if I might have put it there.

P WHAT else did you do? (3)

W I asked my wife if she had seen it.

P WHAT did she say? (3)

W She said she hadn't seen it. [*Note that her response is being offered for a nonhearsay purpose; the purpose is to prove the effect on the hearer's state of mind. Given the wife's response, it was reasonable for the witness not to search further.*]

P WHAT did you do then? (3)

W I stopped searching.

P WHY did you stop the search? (3)

W I just couldn't think of anywhere else to look.

P WHAT was the outcome of your search? (4)

W I couldn't find it. I just don't know where it went.

Authentication of the Secondary Evidence

At this point, the proponent authenticates the secondary evidence. Assume that the proponent authenticates the witness's recollection of the letter's contents.

P WHAT, if anything, did the letter say about Mr. Smythe?

O Your Honor, I object to that question on the ground that it calls for secondary evidence.

P Your Honor, may I be heard?

J Yes.

P It's true that the witness's recollection is secondary evidence. However, we've established the loss of the original which is an adequate excuse for nonproduction. In addition, the witness says he can remember the substance of the letter.

J The objection will be overruled.

P Mr. Jackson, let me repeat the question. WHAT, if anything, did the letter say about Mr. Smythe?

W It said that he had bribed Councilman Wild in connection with a zoning application.

P WHOSE handwriting was the letter in?

W The defendant's.

§ 8-4(B) THE PROPONENT INNOCENTLY DESTROYED THE ORIGINAL

§ 8-4(B)(1) The Doctrine

The early, common law view was that if the proponent intentionally destroyed the original, the proponent could not introduce secondary evidence of the original's contents. Modern courts realize, however, that an intentional destruction might have occurred in good faith. For example, businesses routinely destroy their original records after a number of years. They retain only computer or microfilm copies because they do not want warehouses jammed with voluminous, outdated records. The current test is whether the proponent destroyed the original in bad faith. If the proponent destroyed the original intentionally but in good faith, the secondary evidence is admissible. Texas Evidence Rule 1004(1) adopts this doctrine. The subsection provides that secondary evidence is admissible if "all originals . . . have been destroyed, unless the proponent . . . destroyed them in bad faith."

§ 8-4(B)(2) Elements of the Foundation

The foundation for showing that the proponent innocently destroyed the original includes these elements:

1. The witness had the original.
2. The witness destroyed the original.
3. The destruction was accidental, or the witness's intentional destruction of the original was in good faith.

§ 8-4(B)(3) Sample Foundation

The fact situation is an antitrust action. Belmar Corporation sues Dutton Corporation for various violations of the federal antitrust statutes. Belmar alleges that over a 10-year period, it lost $5,000,000 in sales because of Dutton's anticompetitive practices. To show its damages, the plaintiff calls its chief records custodian, Ms. Gerst. Ms. Gerst has already identified herself and testified to her familiarity with Belmar's records policies. The proponent is the plaintiff.

P WHAT, if any, procedures does Belmar use to record its sales? (1)

W We first prepare sales memoranda.

P WHAT is a sales memorandum? (1)

W It is a permanent record of all the data concerning the sale—customer, product, date, amount, and the like.

P WHO prepares the memorandum? (1)

W One of the people in bookkeeping.

P WHAT do they do with the memorandum? (1)

W They place it in their files.

P WHAT happens to the memoranda after they are inserted in the files? (2)

W They're kept there for two years.

P WHAT happens after two years pass? (2)

W They're transferred to a records holding area in our warehouse.

P WHAT happens to the memoranda after they are stored in the warehouse? (2)

W They're kept there for another two years.

P WHAT happens after that two-year period passes? (2)

W We make microfilm copies of the records and destroy the originals.

P WHY do you do that? (3)

W We just don't have enough room to keep the originals. We don't want warehouses stuffed with nothing but records. We need the warehouse space for equipment and merchandise.

P Ms. Gerst, WHAT were your company's sales in 1999?

W I don't know off-hand.

P WHERE could you find that data?

W Either in the sales memoranda or the microfilm entries.

P WHERE are the sales memoranda for that year? (2)

W They're gone.

P HOW do you know that? (2)

W I searched for them in the warehouse and couldn't find them.

P WHAT happened to them? (3)

W In all probability, they were destroyed after sitting in the warehouse for the two-year period. As I said, that is our customary practice.

P WHEN would they have been destroyed? (3)

W By my estimates, probably in 2001.

P WHEN did you first learn of this lawsuit? (3)

W About a year ago.

P WHAT year was that? (3)

W 2004.

P WHAT did you know about this suit in 2004 when you destroyed the sales memoranda? (3)

W Nothing. I had no notice of the suit at all.

Authentication of the Secondary Evidence

At this point, the proponent authenticates the secondary evidence, the microfilm entries. The proponent marks the microfilm entries as plaintiff's exhibit number three for identification. The witness then describes the reliable equipment and procedures the corporation uses to produce its microfilm copies. Finally, the witness states that she took the copies from the right file cabinet.

P Your Honor, I now offer plaintiff's exhibit number three for identification into evidence.

O Your Honor, I object to the introduction of that exhibit on the ground that the microfilm copies are not the best evidence. The plaintiff intentionally destroyed the originals.

P May I be heard?

J Yes.

P It's true that the microfilm entries are secondary evidence and that the plaintiff intentionally destroyed the original sales memoranda. However, the witness's testimony shows that the destruction was in good faith; the plaintiff did not destroy the originals for the fraudulent purpose of making them unavailable to the defendant.

J The objection will be overruled, and plaintiff's exhibit number three for identification will be received into evidence.

§ 8-4(C) THE ORIGINAL IS IN OFFICIAL CUSTODY

§ 8-4(C)(1) The Doctrine

If the original is in official custody, the original's nonproduction is excused. Texas Rule of Evidence 1005 states:

> The contents of an official record, or of a document authorized to be recorded or filed and actually recorded or filed, including data compilations in any form, if otherwise admissible, may be proved by copy, certified as

correct in accordance with Rule 902 or testified to be correct by a witness who has compared it with the original . . . .

There are several reasons for this doctrine. First, the removal of the original from official custody might inconvenience other persons who wanted to use the original. Second, the removal would create the risk of the loss of the original.

There is one peculiar aspect of this excuse. This excuse does not automatically authorize the admission of any secondary evidence. Rather, Rule 1005 states a preference for attested or compared copies. The Rule ordinarily requires a copy "certified as correct in accordance with Rule 902 or testified to be correct by a witness who has compared it with the original." The Rule states that the proponent may introduce "other evidence of the contents" only if "a copy which complies with the foregoing cannot be obtained by the exercise of reasonable diligence . . . ."

§ 8-4(C)(2) Elements of the Foundation

The foundation for showing that the original is in official custody includes the following elements:

1. The original is in official custody.
2. The copy is properly authenticated.

§ 8-4(C)(3) Sample Foundation

The fact situation is a probate contest. The contestants claim by intestate succession. To establish their claim, they must prove the marriage between Joan Merchant and Thomas Kleven. The contestants want to offer the marriage license to prove the marriage. We shall work the hypothetical first with live testimony and then with an attesting certificate. In the first variation of the hypothetical, the witness is Mr. John Stern, the deputy county clerk. Mr. Stern has already identified himself and has described his duties as deputy county clerk.

P [*To court reporter*] Would you please mark this as an exhibit for the contestants? [*Court reporter marks exhibit and hands it back to proponent.*]

P Thank you. Please let the record reflect that I am showing contestants' exhibit B for identification to the opposing counsel. I request permission to approach the witness.

J Permission granted.

P Mr. Stern, I now hand you contestants' exhibit B for identification. WHAT is it?

W It's a copy of a marriage license.

P HOW can you tell that it is a copy? (1)

W It's obviously a photocopy rather than an original.

P WHERE are the originals of marriage licenses kept in this county? (1)

W In our office.

P WHERE is the original of this license kept? (1)

W In our office.

P HOW do you know that? (1)

W I saw it there only a few days ago when I ran off this copy at your request.

P WHAT did you do when I requested that you copy the original marriage license in this case? (2)

W I made this copy.

P HOW did you make it? (2)

W I did it by mechanical means, with our photocopy machine.

P WHAT condition was the machine in?

W Fine, as far as I could tell. I didn't experience any mechanical difficulties when I used it.

P WHAT did you do with the copy after you made it?

W I compared it with the original to make sure I had a good copy.

P HOW did it compare with the original?

W It was a clear, verbatim copy.

P Your Honor, I now offer contestants' exhibit B for identification into evidence.

O Your Honor, I object to the introduction of this exhibit on the ground that the copy is not the best evidence.

P May I be heard?

J Yes.

P We've shown that the original is in official custody and, under Rule 1005, that is an adequate excuse for nonproduction. We've also authenticated the copy.

J The objection will be overruled, and contestants' exhibit B for identification will be received into evidence.

In the second variation of the hypothetical, the proponent does not use live testimony. Rather, the proponent merely offers a properly attested copy of the original marriage license under Rule 902.

P [*To the court reporter*] Would you please mark this as an exhibit for the contestants? [*Court reporter marks exhibit and hands it back to proponent.*]

P I now offer contestants' exhibit B for identification into evidence.

O Your Honor, I object to the introduction of this exhibit on the ground that it is not the original. On its face, it shows that it is a photocopy rather than an original.

P Your Honor, may I be heard?

J Yes.

P It's true that this is a purported copy of the original. However, there is an attached attesting certificate. The certificate is self-authenticating because it is in proper form, and the certificate states that the original is in official custody of the county clerk.

J I will overrule the objection. Contestants' exhibit B for identification will be received into evidence.

P I request permission to hand contestants' exhibit B to the jurors for their inspection.

J Permission granted.

§ 8-4(D) THE ORIGINAL IS NOT OBTAINABLE BY JUDICIAL PROCESS OR IS OUTSIDE THE STATE OF TEXAS

§ 8-4(D)(1) The Doctrine

Texas Rule of Evidence 1004(2) reads that there is an excuse for nonproduction if "[n]o original can be obtained by any available judicial process or procedure." The proponent usually relies on this excuse when the original is in the possession of a third party beyond the reach of the court's compulsory process. Texas Rule of Evidence 1004(3) excuses nonproduction of the originals where none are located within Texas. In the first instance, the proponent will have to make some showing of a reasonable attempt to use judicial process to obtain an original which is in the State. Usually this means that counsel has attempted to use a subpoena duces tecum or shows that doing so would be futile. If the originals are outside the State, counsel may not even have to show that he or she has attempted to obtain them.[2]

[2] *See* WENDORF, SCHLUETER & BARTON, TEXAS RULES OF EVIDENCE MANUAL X-22 (6th ed. 2002).

§ 8-4(D)(2) Elements of the Foundation

The foundation for showing under Rule 1004(2) that the original is not obtainable by judicial process includes these elements:

1. A third party has the original.
2. The third party resides in a certain place.
3. The proponent unsuccessfully attempted to use a subpoena duces tecum, or the circumstances indicate that it would be futile for the proponent to do so.

The foundation for showing under Rule 1004(3) that the original is in the possession of someone outside the State of Texas is as follows:

1. A third party has the original.
2. That party resides outside the State of Texas.

§ 8-4(D)(3) Sample Foundation

The fact situation is a civil libel action. The plaintiff, Mr. Smythe, alleges that the defendant, Mr. Wiggins, is guilty of libel. The complaint alleges that the defendant committed the libel in a letter to a Mr. Jackson. The witness is the plaintiff, Mr. Smythe. Mr. Smythe has already identified himself. The plaintiff is the proponent. The place of the trial is Lubbock, Texas.

P WHERE were you on the afternoon of January 15, 2005? (2)

W I was visiting Bill Jackson in Dallas.

P WHAT did you do while you visited Mr. Jackson?

W We were just talking about some mutual acquaintances.

P WHICH acquaintances?

W Several, including the defendant, Mr. Wiggins.

P WHAT, if anything, did Mr. Jackson say about Mr. Wiggins? (1)

W He said that Mr. Wiggins had just sent him a handwritten letter about me.

P WHAT did Mr. Jackson do after he told you about the letter? (1)

W He showed it to me.

P WHOSE handwriting was the letter in?

W Clearly the defendant's.

P HOW do you know that?

W I've known the defendant for years, and I've seen him sign his name on innumerable occasions.

P WHAT did you do after Mr. Jackson showed you the letter? (3)

W I asked him if I could have it. I told him it made me real angry and I wanted to use the letter to sue the defendant.

P HOW did Mr. Jackson respond to your request for the letter? (3)

W He refused to let me have it. [*Mr. Jackson's statement is being used for a nonhearsay purpose. The statement is an operative fact; it is the refusal which satisfies the third element of the foundation.*]

P WHY did he refuse to let you have it? (3)

W He said he didn't want to become involved.

P WHAT other efforts did you make to persuade Mr. Jackson to give you the letter? (3)

W I phoned him several times since returning to Lubbock. Each time I asked him to send it to me.

P WHAT was his answer? (3)

W He still insists that he won't send it to me and he said that even if I got a court order he would refuse to give it up.

Authentication of the Secondary Evidence

At this point, the proponent authenticates the witness's oral recollection.

P WHAT, if anything, did the letter say about you?

O Your Honor, I object to that question on the ground that the witness's testimony is not the best evidence.

P Your Honor, may I be heard?

J Yes.

P The testimony shows that a third party, Mr. Jackson, has the original. Although technically it might be possible to eventually gain the original through judicial process, that option would not seem reasonable at this point, given Mr. Jackson's adamant refusal to cooperate. Thus, under Rule 1004(2), the original is not obtainable.

J I will overrule the objection.

P Mr. Smythe, let me repeat the question. WHAT, if anything, did the letter say about you?

W It said that I had bribed Councilman Wild in connection with a zoning application.

P WHOSE handwriting was the letter in?

W The defendant's.

§ 8-4(E) THE PARTY-OPPONENT HAS POSSESSION OF THE ORIGINAL AND FAILS TO PRODUCE IT AFTER NOTICE

§ 8-4(E)(1) The Doctrine

Texas Evidence Rule 1004(4) recognizes an excuse for nonproduction if:

> [a]t a time when an original was under the control of the party against whom offered, that party was put on notice, by the pleadings or otherwise, that the contents would be a subject of proof at the hearing, and that party does not produce the original at the hearing . . . .

Sometimes the proponent has direct evidence of the party-opponent's possession of the original. More often, the proponent must rely on circumstantial evidence, tracing the original to the party-opponent.

The other problem facing the proponent is proving that the party-opponent had fair notice the original would be needed at trial. The proponent can sometimes argue that the terms of the pleadings gave the party-opponent implied notice; the implication would be very strong in a contract action based on breach of a written contract. To be safe, however, the proponent should give the party-opponent express notice that the original will be needed at trial.

§ 8-4(E)(2) Elements of the Foundation

The foundation for showing the party-opponent has the original and failed to produce it includes these elements:

1. The party-opponent has the original.
2. The party-opponent knew that the original would be needed at trial.
3. The party-opponent nevertheless failed to produce the original at trial.

§ 8-4(E)(3) Sample Foundation

The fact situation is a civil contract action. The plaintiff, Mr. Renfield, alleges that the defendant, Mr. Payntor, warranted that the car the defendant sold plaintiff would get at least 25 miles per gallon on the open highway. The complaint alleges that the defendant breached the warranty because, on the open highway, the car gets only 15 miles to a gallon. The plaintiff takes the stand. The proponent is the plaintiff. The plaintiff wants to testify that before agreeing to buy the car, he wrote the defendant and made it clear that he did not want the car unless it got at least 25 miles per gallon. The plaintiff has identified himself and described his preliminary oral negotiations with the defendant.

P WHAT did you do after your oral agreement?

W I thought about the deal and then decided to write the defendant and outline the parts of the deal I was really insistent on.

P WHEN did you write this letter? (1)

W I wrote it on February 14, 2005.

P WHAT did you do with the letter? (1)

W I mailed it to the defendant.

P HOW did you mail it to him? (1)

W I stuck it in an envelope and addressed it to the defendant.

P WHERE did you get the defendant's address? (1)

W From the telephone book.

P WHAT did you do with the letter after you addressed it? (1)

W I stamped it and deposited it in a mailbox.

P WHAT response, if any, did you receive from the defendant? (1)

W I didn't get any written response.

P WHEN, if ever, did you see the letter again? (1)

W Well, when we sat down to sign the final contract, the defendant pulled it out and showed it to me.

P WHEN was the last time you saw the letter? (1)

W The day I signed the contract for the car.

P WHO had the letter? (1)

W The defendant.

P WHERE were you on the morning of November 17 of this year? (2)

W I was here at the courthouse.

P WHY were you here? (2)

W We were having a conference in this case.

P WHO attended the conference? (2)

W You and I were there. The defendant and his attorney were also there.

P WHAT happened during the conference? (2)

W We discussed some aspects of the case.

P WHAT, if anything, did you tell the defendant during the conference about the letter? (2)

W I told him that you and I wanted him to bring the letter to trial.

P WHAT was the defendant's response? (3)

W He said to forget about the letter. [*This statement is being offered for a nonhearsay purpose. The answer is the party-opponent's refusal, the last foundational element.*]

P WHAT, if anything, did you tell the defendant today about the letter? (3)

W I again asked the defendant for the letter.

P WHAT was his response? (3)

W He said he didn't have it.

P WHAT did you tell the defendant in your letter to him?

O Your Honor, I object to that question on the ground that it calls for secondary evidence. The letter is the best evidence.

P Your Honor, may I be heard?

J Yes.

P The testimony shows that the defendant was the last known custodian of the letter. The testimony also indicates that the defendant knew we wanted the original letter at trial today. That amounts to an excuse for the letter's nonproduction under Rule 1004(4).

J The objection will be overruled.

P Mr. Renfield, let me repeat the question. WHAT did you tell the defendant in your letter to him?

P I said that unless the car got at least 25 miles per gallon on highway driving, I didn't want the car at all.

§ 8-4(F) VOLUMINOUS OR BULKY RECORDS

§ 8-4(F)(1) The Doctrine

Texas Rule of Evidence 1006 declares:

> The contents of voluminous writings, recordings, or photographs which cannot conveniently be examined in court may be presented in the form of a chart, summary, or calculation. The originals, or duplicates, shall be made available for examination or copying, or both, to the other parties at a reasonable time and place. The court may order that they be produced in court.

Texas Rule 1006 generally codifies the common law and recognizes the practical problems of requiring the proponent to present all of the original supporting documents in court.

§ 8-4(F)(2) Elements of the Foundation

The foundational elements for introducing summaries under Texas Rule 1006 are as follows:

1. The original entries would be admissible in evidence.

2. The original entries are so voluminous or bulky that it would be inconvenient for the trier of fact to examine them.
3. The witness was qualified to review the records.
4. The witness reviewed the records.
5. The witness's testimony is a summary of the records.

If the proponent offers a written summary, it is not merely demonstrative evidence. In Texas practice, the summary is substantive evidence. Hence, the summary can be formally admitted and sent to the jury during deliberation.

§ 8-4(F)(3) Sample Foundation

The fact situation is a civil action to rescind a corporate merger. The Gemini Corporation was to merge into Rohr Corporation. Gemini sues to rescind the merger agreement; the complaint alleges that the contract is voidable because of Rohr's fraud. Specifically, the complaint alleges that the defendant overstated the amount of its yearly sales. The defendant denies that its representations were false. The defendant is attempting to prove the amount of its annual sales. To prove its annual sales, the defendant would probably call two witnesses. The first witness would be the defendant's bookkeeper or records custodian. The first witness would describe the original records and show that they fall within the business entry exception to the hearsay rule. This testimony would lay the first element of the foundation. The witness would conclude his or her testimony by stating that he gave the second witness access to the relevant records.

The second witness is Mr. Beer. Mr. Beer has already identified himself. The defendant is the proponent.

P WHAT is your occupation? (3)

W I am a certified public accountant.

P WHERE do you work? (3)

W I am self-employed. I own my own C.P.A. firm downtown.

P HOW long have you been a C.P.A.? (3)

W Roughly 10 years.

P WHAT is your formal education? (3)

W I have a bachelor's, a master's, and a doctorate.

P WHAT was your field of study? (3)

W Accounting.

P WHAT school awarded you your degrees? (3)

W Cornell.

P WHERE were you on April 15th of this year? (4)

W I went to the offices of Rohr Corporation.

P WHY did you go there? (4)

W You asked me to review the corporation's sales records from 2000 to the present.

P WHAT did you do when you arrived at the corporation's offices? (4)

W First I met Mr. Gaynor, the head bookkeeper.

P WHAT did he do?

W He led me to the office where all the records are kept.

P WHAT did you do when you arrived at the office? (4)

W I immediately started reviewing the records to compute the annual sales for each year since 2000.

P HOW did you do that? (4)

W I used generally accepted accounting techniques and a calculator to double check my computations.

P HOW many pages of records did you review? (2)

W I couldn't give you a precise number. The number would run into the thousands.

P HOW long did it take you to compute the yearly totals? (2)

W Five workdays.

P HOW long is your workday? (2)

W A solid eight hours a day.

P Mr. Beer, WHAT was the total amount of Rohr Corporation's sales in 2001? (5)

O Your Honor, I object to that question on the ground that it calls for secondary evidence. The best evidence would be the records themselves.

P Your Honor, may I be heard?

J Yes.

P Mr. Gaynor's testimony established that the original records would be admissible. Mr. Beer's testimony shows that the original records are too voluminous to be used in the courtroom. Moreover, last week we offered to let the plaintiff's accountants review the records.

J [*To the opposing attorney*] Is that true?

O Yes, your Honor.

J I think there's an adequate excuse for nonproduction. The objection will be overruled.

P Mr. Beer, let me repeat the question. WHAT was the total amount of Rohr Corporation's sales in 2001? (5)

W It was $5,312,400.

CHAPTER 9
OPINION EVIDENCE

§ 9-1 INTRODUCTION

Like the original writing (best evidence) rule, the general prohibition against opinion evidence is based on doubts about the reliability of a certain type of evidence. The common law reflected doubts about the trustworthiness of opinions. For that reason, the common law preferred that witnesses restrict their testimony to statements of observed fact.[1] The witness stated the primary, sensory data, and the jurors then drew the inferences or conclusions from the underlying data.

The prohibition against opinion testimony is a general norm rather than an absolute, categorical rule. There are two situations in which the law permits opinion testimony. In the first situation, a lay witness may express an opinion on a subject if the lay witness cannot verbalize all the underlying data and communicate the data to the jury. For example, a witness cannot articulate all the sensory impressions which led the witness to the conclusion that a car was going 45 miles per hour rather than 60. The lay witness's inability to verbalize the underlying data necessitates permitting the lay witness to voice an opinion. Texas Evidence Rule 701 allows this type of lay opinion testimony.

In the second situation, the lay trier of fact lacks the knowledge or skill to draw the proper inferences from the underlying data. If the subject matter is technical or scientific, the lay jurors may lack the expertise necessary to evaluate the hard data. Lacking the expert knowledge and skill, they cannot draw reliable inferences or opinions from the facts. In this situation as well, the law sanctions opinion testimony: expert opinion testimony. Texas Evidence Rule 702 authorizes such testimony.

§ 9-2 LAY OPINIONS

§ 9-2(A) In General

As previously stated, Rule 701 governs the admissibility of lay opinion testimony. The Rule reads:

---

[1] *See* Wendorf, Schlueter & Barton, Texas Rules of Evidence Manual VII-1 (6th ed. 2002).

> If the witness is not testifying as an expert, his testimony in the form of opinions or inferences is limited to those opinions or inferences which are (a) rationally based on the perception of the witness and (b) helpful to a dear understanding of his testimony or the determination of a fact in issue.

In practice, the courts have construed the Rule as authorizing two types of lay opinion testimony: (1) collective fact or shorthand rendition opinions; and (2) skilled lay observer opinions.

§ 9-2(B) LAY OPINIONS—COLLECTIVE FACT OPINIONS

§ 9-2(B)(1) The Doctrine

Commentators have coined various titles for this doctrine. They sometimes call it the collective fact doctrine, and on other occasions they refer to it as the shorthand rendition doctrine. The elements of the doctrine are: the witness's opinion is based on perceived facts; the opinion is a type of inference that lay persons commonly and reliably draw; and—the key to the doctrine—that the lay witness cannot verbalize all the underlying sensory data supporting the opinion. This doctrine permits opinions on such subjects as height, distance, speed, color, and identity.[2] The trial judge passes on the second and third elements of the doctrine as questions of law. The judge asks himself or herself whether lay persons commonly draw this type of inference and whether it would be practical for the lay witness to articulate all the underlying factual data.

§ 9-2(B)(2) Elements of the Foundation

The foundation for the collective fact or shorthand rendition doctrine includes proof that:

1. The witness was in a position to observe.
2. The witness in fact observed.
3. The witness observed enough data to form a reliable opinion.
4. The witness states the opinion.
5. The opinion will help the jury understand the witness's testimony or decide a factual issue.[3]

---

[2] *Id.* at VII-6 to VII-7 (citing cases).

[3] Although it will usually be apparent from the lay opinion testimony whether the opinion is helpful, as required by Rule 701, the proponent should be prepared to articulate to the trial judge why the lay opinion is helpful to the jury.

§ 9-2(B)(3) Sample Foundation

The fact situation is a tort action arising from a collision. The plaintiff, Ms. Cook, alleges that the defendant, Mr. Armato, caused the accident by speeding. The accident occurred at the intersection of Pine Drive and Magnolia Street. The plaintiff calls Mr. Carona as a witness. Mr. Carona has already identified himself. The plaintiff is the proponent.

P WHERE were you on the morning of November 17, 2005, at approximately 10 o'clock in the morning? (1)

W I was standing at the intersection of Pine Drive and Magnolia Street in Dickinson.

P HOW were you facing? (1)

W I was ready to enter the crosswalk, so I was facing the intersection itself.

P WHAT, if anything, did you see while you were standing there? (2)

W I saw a red car on Pine Drive approaching the intersection.

P WHAT else did you see? (2)

W There was a blue car approaching the intersection on Magnolia Street.

P HOW far was the red car from the intersection when you first saw it? (3)

W A couple of hundred feet away.

P HOW long did you have to observe the red car before it reached the intersection? (3)

W Several seconds. I had a pretty good chance to eyeball it.

P Do you have an opinion of the red car's speed? (4)

W Yes.

P In your opinion, WHAT was the speed of the red car? (4)

W I'd say 40 miles an hour. It was moving at a pretty good clip.

P WHAT happened when the red car reached the intersection?

W It hit the blue car.

P WHO was the driver of the red car?

W The fellow sitting at the table over there.

P WHAT is he wearing?

W He's wearing a blue suit and a striped tie.

P Please let the record reflect that the witness has identified the defendant, Mr. Armato.

P HOW can you recognize him?

W After the two cars hit, he got out of the car, and I walked over to see what had happened.

P HOW long did you stay at the accident scene?

W About an hour. I talked to the parties and then to the police.

P HOW close were you standing to the defendant?

W At one time, I was talking to him. He was no more than a foot or two away from me.

P WHAT were the lighting conditions?

W It was broad daylight.

P HOW well could you see him?

W Very well.

P WHO was the driver of the blue car?

W That lady over there.

P HOW is she dressed?

W She's wearing a green dress and white shoes.

P Please let the record reflect that the witness has correctly identified the plaintiff, Ms. Cook.

P HOW can you recognize her?

W She was also at the accident scene. I had a chance to look at and talk with her.

§ 9-2(C) LAY OPINION—SKILLED LAY OBSERVER

§ 9-2(C)(1) The Doctrine

The Judge may assume that the witness has enough common, human experience to be able to estimate distance, time, or height. The judge's assumption explains why the foundation for collective fact opinions is so minimal. However, there is a second type of lay opinion testimony under Rule 701 that usually requires a more extensive foundation. The commentators sometimes use the expression "skilled lay observer testimony"[4] to describe this second type of lay opinion. This category includes lay opinions about a person's voice, handwriting style, or sanity. A lay witness cannot express an opinion identifying someone's voice unless the witness has had repeated opportunities to hear that voice. Similarly, a lay witness cannot identify a person's handwriting style unless the witness had numerous occasions to observe that person's writing. Finally, a lay

[4] CARLSON, IMWINKELRIED, KIONKA & STRACHAN, EVIDENCE 598 (5th ed. 2001).

witness cannot express an opinion about a person's sanity unless the witness is intimately familiar with the person. In each of these situations, if the witness has had repeated, prior opportunities for observation, the witness qualifies as a skilled lay observer.

§ 9-2(C)(2) Elements of the Foundation

The foundation for skilled lay observer testimony on voice or handwriting style includes these elements:

1. The witness is familiar with the person or his or her voice or handwriting style.
2. The witness explains how he or she became familiar.
3. The witness states his or her opinion.

§ 9-2(C)(3) Sample Foundation

The following fact situation involves use of skilled lay opinion evidence to authenticate a check. The witness, Mr. Butcher, did not observe the check's execution, but he is familiar with the author's handwriting style. The plaintiff is the proponent.

P [*To court reporter*] Would you please mark this as an exhibit for the plaintiff? [*Court reporter marks exhibit and hands it back to proponent, who examines it to see how it has been marked.*]

P Thank you. Please let the record reflect that I am showing what has been marked as plaintiff's exhibit number seven for identification to the opposing counsel. [*Opposing counsel examines exhibit.*]

P I request permission to approach the witness.

J Permission granted.

P Mr. Butcher, I now hand you plaintiff's exhibit number seven for identification. WHAT is it?

W It is a check.

P Do you have an opinion as to who signed the check? (3)

W Yes.

P In your opinion, WHO signed the check? (3)

W I'd say that the defendant signed it.

P WHY do you say that? (1)

W I recognize his handwriting style on the check.

P HOW well do you know the defendant's handwriting style? (1)

W Very well.

P HOW did you become familiar with his handwriting style? (2)

W We've been friends for years.

P HOW many years? (2)

W About 13.

P HOW often have you seen the defendant sign his name? (2)

W Tens, maybe hundreds, of times.

P Your Honor, I now offer plaintiff's exhibit number seven for identification into evidence.

O Your Honor, we object. Counsel has failed to lay a sufficient foundation.

P Your Honor, this witness is clearly qualified to offer opinion testimony on how he knows who signed the exhibit.

O Simply because the witness and the defendant have been friends for a long time does not a predicate make.

J [*To proponent*] Counsel?

P Your Honor, may we ask several more questions?

J Yes.

P Mr. Butcher, in those instances in which you say you had an opportunity to observe the defendant's signature, HOW closely were you able to see what he wrote? (2)

W I had excellent opportunities and I watched him somewhat closely. Of course, I did not put my nose down on the paper to watch him sign things.

P In examining plaintiff's exhibit number seven for identification, WHAT characteristics or qualities in the signature lead you to believe that it was the defendant's? [*Proponent hands exhibit to witness.*] (2)

W Well. [*Witness examines exhibit more closely.*] Okay, for instance, look at the way he crossed his "t's." He always starts high and goes low, to the right, with a little tail that curves up. I remember seeing that before in letters he had sent me. Also, this signature looks like the signatures that have appeared on letters he has sent me on numerous occasions.

P Your Honor, we again offer plaintiff's exhibit seven for identification into evidence.

O Your Honor, we repeat our objection. Counsel has failed to prove up his exhibit.

J Objection overruled. Plaintiff's exhibit seven for identification will be admitted into evidence.

P I request permission to hand the plaintiff's exhibit number seven to the jurors for their inspection.

J Permission granted.

§ 9-3 EXPERT OPINION TESTIMONY

§ 9-3(A) IN GENERAL

The Texas Rules of Evidence admit expert opinion testimony in addition to lay opinion testimony. The Rule in point is 702: "[i]f scientific, technical, or other specialized knowledge will assist the trier of fact to understand the evidence or to determine a fact in issue, a witness qualified as an expert by knowledge, skill, experience, training, or education, may testify thereto in the form of an opinion or otherwise."

In reality, the proponent may use an expert witness in four different ways. First, the proponent may use an expert purely as a fact witness. Suppose that the defendant is being prosecuted for rape. The complaining witness testifies that during the rape, she scratched the rapist's face and drew blood. It just so happened that the defendant visited his doctor the day after the alleged rape. The defendant could call his doctor and elicit the doctor's testimony that there were no scratches on the defendant's face. The witness certainly did not have to be an expert to observe the defendant's face, but it is equally clear that the witness is not incompetent to testify to facts solely because he or she is an expert.

Secondly, the proponent may use the expert as a teaching witness to explain the scientific or technical principles the jurors need to evaluate the facts in the case. The expert witness explains the principles without applying them to the specific facts of the case. The jurors themselves apply the principles to the facts. This use of expert testimony is quite common. As previously noted in Chapter 4, there is a sharp controversy over the reliability of sound spectrography (voiceprint) evidence. A prosecutor offering sound spectrography evidence must do more than simply have the evidence admitted. More important, the prosecutor must persuade the jurors to believe the evidence. The prosecutor might call several speech scientists to testify solely about the validity of the underlying theories of interspeaker variability and invariant speech. The witnesses might not even refer to the voiceprint examination in that particular prosecution. The expert witness's sole function would be to educate the jurors on the general theories and convince the jurors that the theories are valid.

Third, the proponent may have the expert serve as an evaluator by offering an opinion on the facts in the case. This is probably the most common use of expert testimony. When the proponent uses an expert in this manner, the expert usually employs a general theory or principle to evaluate the facts of the case.

After stating his or her qualifications, the expert's testimony follows a syllogistic structure. The expert describes a general explanatory theory (the major premise), states the case-specific facts to be evaluated (the minor premise), and derives an opinion (the conclusion) by applying the major premise to the minor premise. Experienced litigators often conclude the expert's examination by having the expert explain the opinion.

Finally, the expert may offer lay opinion testimony on facts or matters for which he may not necessarily qualify as an expert or on matters which do not call for expert testimony or evaluation. For example a medical doctor who has treated the victim for her wounds may offer expert testimony on the nature and extent of those wounds—relying on his expertise—and in the process offer lay opinion testimony about the approximate weight and size of a bullet removed from one of those wounds. While not an expert on firearms and ammunition, he should be permitted to offer lay testimony, if the testimony otherwise satisfied Rule 701.

The expert's testimony therefore covers five topics: the witness's qualification as an expert, the general theory, the facts of the case, the opinion, and the explanation of the opinion. Each topic requires a foundation. The following sections analyze the five topics and their respective foundations.

§ 9-3(B) THE EXPERT'S QUALIFICATIONS TO FORM THE OPINION

§ 9-3(B)(1) The Doctrine

The law permits expert opinion testimony because it is believed that the expert can draw inferences beyond the capability of lay jurors. The expert can do so because the expert has knowledge or skill the jurors lack. The expert can acquire the knowledge or skill by education, experience, or a combination of education and experience. The expert's background usually includes theoretical education and practical experience.

The process of spelling out the expert's qualifications may amount to a subtle form of bolstering, to the extent that the qualifications improve the expert's credibility.[5] But the proponent is not required to accept an opponent's offer to stipulate to the qualifications. Indeed, a common response to such offers to stipulate is for the counsel to state that the jury has a right to hear the qualifications so that it can better assess the expert's opinion.

If, for some reason, the trial judge does not permit the witness to testify as an expert, the witness may still be in a position to provide lay opinion testimony under Rule 701.

---

[5] For a discussion of bolstering, *see* Chapter 5.

§ 9-3(B)(2) Elements of the Foundation

In laying the foundation for establishing that a witness is an expert within Rule 702, the proponent has some flexibility. The following is a nonexhaustive list of elements which the proponent might rely upon:

1. The witness has acquired degrees from educational institutions.
2. The witness has had other specialized training in this field of expertise.
3. The witness is licensed to practice in the field.
4. The witness has practiced in the field for a substantial period of time.
5. The witness has taught in the field.
6. The witness has published in the field.
7. The witness belongs to professional organizations in the field.
8. The witness has previously testified as an expert on this subject.

The trial judge decides whether a particular witness is an expert under Rule 702. Unlike federal practice, where counsel normally proffer a witness as an expert after laying the foundation, such proffers are normally not made in Texas courts.

§ 9-3(B)(3) Sample Foundations

The fact situation is a civil personal injury action. The plaintiff, Mr. Nowick, alleges that the defendant, Mr. Johnson, negligently caused the collision in which Mr. Nowick was injured. The complaint alleges that the plaintiff has suffered severe brain injury as a result of the accident. The plaintiff calls Dr. Worth. The plaintiff is the proponent. Dr. Worth has already identified himself.

P WHAT is your formal education? (1)

W I have a bachelor's degree and a medical degree.

P WHICH undergraduate school did you attend? (1)

W Arizona State University.

P WHAT degree did you obtain there? (1)

W I earned a bachelor of science degree.

P WHAT was your major field of study? (1)

W Biology.

P WHICH medical school did you attend? (1)

W The Johns Hopkins University Medical School in Baltimore.

P WHAT degree did you obtain there? (1)

W My M.D.

P WHAT did you do after you graduated from medical school? (2)

W I interned at the University of Southern California Medical Center.

P HOW long was your internship? (2)

W A year.

O Your Honor, we are willing to stipulate to this witness's credentials.

P Your Honor, we appreciate counsel's offer to stipulate to Dr. Worth's qualifications. But we believe it is important that the jury fully appreciate the level of expertise which Dr. Worth has in this area.

J Please continue with your questioning.

P WHAT did you do after your internship? (2)

W I became a resident at Gross Hospital in Lexington, Kentucky.

P WHAT is a residency? (2)

W You specialize in a certain field and get practical experience.

P WHAT was your specialty? (2)

W Neurology, brain problems.

P HOW long was your residency? (2)

W Three years.

P WHEN did your residency end? (2)

W In 1979.

P WHAT did you do when your residency ended? (3)

W I moved to Denver and began practicing.

P WHAT did you have to do to practice in Denver? (3)

W I had to become licensed in Colorado.

P WHEN did you obtain your license in Texas? (3)

W In 1980.

P WHAT did you do after you obtained your license? (4)

W I began my practice, specializing in neurology.

P HOW long have you practiced in Texas? (4)

W Nine years now.

P HOW many clients with neurological problems have you treated? (4)

W I can't name a number. By this time, I've probably treated thousands.

P HOW much of your time do you devote to the practice of medicine? (5)

W About 80 percent of my working time.

P WHAT else do you spend your time on? (5)

W For one thing, I teach at the University of Texas Medical School.

P HOW long have you taught there? (5)

W For four years now.

P WHAT courses do you teach? (5)

W I teach three upper division courses in the field of neurology.

P WHAT else do you spend your professional time on? (6)

W I try to publish with some frequency.

P WHAT journals have published your articles? (6)

W Some of the leading medical and neurological journals, including the A.M.A. Journal.

P What is the "A.M.A.?"

W I'm sorry, it's the American Medical Association.

P HOW many articles have you published? (6)

W Nine.

P WHAT topics did you discuss in these articles? (6)

W All the articles relate to neurology.

P WHAT professional organizations do you belong to? (7)

W Several, including the American College of Neurological Specialists and the American Board of Neurology.

P HOW do you become a member of the American College? (7)

W You have to have specialized in the neurological field for at least five years.

P HOW do you become a member of the Board? (7)

W There are strict requirements. You not only have to have practiced for several years; you also have to pass oral and written examinations.

P HOW often have you testified in court? (8)

W I'd say at least 100 cases in both state and federal courts.

P HOW many times were you permitted to give expert opinion testimony? (8)

W Every time.

P WHAT subjects did you testify on? (8)

W Most of the time I testified on neurology.

Note that the opponent in the preceding hypothetical did not request permission to take the expert witness on voir dire to test his qualifications. The following hypothetical involves a variation on that fact situation. The plaintiff, the proponent, has begun questioning Dr. Worth. The opponent is the defense counsel.

P WHAT is your formal education? (1)

W I have a bachelor's degree from Arizona State University and a medical degree from John Hopkins University.

P WHAT did you do after you graduated from medical school? (2)

W I served for a year in internship in Los Angeles.

P Doctor, WHAT training do you have in the area of brain injuries?

W I took several courses on the subject in medical school and I have kept current on the subject through additional studies and continuing education courses.

P Now, turning to the facts in this case . . .

O Your Honor, we would like to take the witness on voir dire.

J Proceed.

O Doctor Worth, ISN'T IT TRUE THAT your current practice has nothing to do with neurology or brain injuries?

W Well, yes and no. I am not specializing currently in neurology, but I do intend to do so in the near future.

O And Doctor, IT IS A FACT, IS IT NOT, that the area of neurology is constantly developing and changing?

W Yes, that is true.

O And it is TRUE, IS IT NOT, that you took your medical school courses on the changing subject of neurology over 10 years ago?

W Yes.

O Regarding the continuing education courses you have taken, IT IS TRUE, IS IT NOT, that these programs are cruise-type courses where you combine a vacation and some classroom time?

W Some are, yes.

O And ISN'T IT ALSO TRUE that you make a large portion of your annual income testifying in cases such as this?

W Well, I do charge for my time, yes.

O And your typical fee is around $10,000 per case, IS IT NOT?

P Your Honor, how much this witness is being paid, or has been paid, is not at all relevant to whether he is qualified to give an opinion in this case.

O Your Honor, I have no further voir dire questions. But it should be apparent that Dr. Worth should not be permitted to offer expert opinion on this case.

P Your Honor, may we question Dr. Worth further?

J Go ahead.

P Doctor, would you please tell us about your schooling in the area of neurology.

W Yes. I took three advanced courses on the subject while in medical school. In two of the courses I made the highest grade and in the other course I made one of the top grades. In one of the courses I made the top grade in, I wrote a paper and proposal on the diagnosis and treatment of traumatic brain injuries. It was later published in the American Medical Association Journal.

P And please describe in more detail WHAT continuing education courses you have participated in.

W I have attended two neurological training courses for the last two years. Both were week-long courses sponsored by the University of Texas Medical School. In a third course, held six months ago, I conducted one of the sessions myself. The topic of my paper was on the issue of diagnosing and treating brain injuries resulting from auto accidents.

P Your Honor, we believe that Dr. Worth should be permitted to offer his opinions in this case. It is clear that he is qualified under Rule 702.

J You may proceed with your questions.

§ 9-3(C) The General Theory or Principle on Which the Expert Relies

§ 9-3(C)(1) The Doctrine

§ 9-3(C)(1)(i) In General

After describing his or her credentials, the expert often states the major premise, or the general scientific theory or principle that the expert proposes to rely on. If the witness is a psychiatrist, for example, the witness may testify that there is a recognized symptomatology for a particular mental disease or disorder. To be a permissible premise for expert testimony, the theory or principle must, at a minimum, in the words of Rule 702, "assist the trier of fact." If the subject is a matter of common knowledge, there is no need for expert testimony.

§ 9-3(C)(1)(ii) Scientific Evidence

If the underlying premise is scientific in nature, the proponent must be prepared to clear one more hurdle. Until recently most courts applied what has become commonly referred to as the *Frye*[6] test: the proponent of scientific testimony must show that the principle in question is generally accepted within the relevant scientific field. Although most of the cases applying Frye are criminal, *Frye* has also been applied to scientific testimony in civil cases.[7] The trend, however, has been to replace the *Frye* general acceptance test with a reliability test

The *Frye* test was rejected by the United States Supreme Court in *Daubert v. Merrell Dow Pharmaceuticals, Inc.*[8] In *Daubert*, the Court held that *Frye's* general acceptance test has been replaced by the Federal Rules of Evidence. The more rigid *Frye* test, said the Court, is at odds with the liberal thrust of the Federal Rules which generally lower the traditional barriers to "opinion" testimony. The Court, however, noted that the Federal Rules, especially Rule 702, themselves place limits on the admissibility of scientific evidence by assigning the trial judge the task of determining whether the expert's testimony is grounded on a reliable foundation and will be helpful. The trial judge's task under Rule 104(a) is to decide whether the expert will be testifying to "(1) scientific knowledge that (2) will assist the trier of fact to understand or determine a fact in issue."[9] The Court stated that "scientific knowledge" is not a static body of propositions. Rather, according to the Court, a scientific proposition is one derived by a particular methodology—the process of formulating hypotheses and then conducting experimentation to validate or disprove the hypotheses. Under Rule 104(a), the trial judge must make "a preliminary assessment of whether the reasoning or methodology underlying the testimony is scientifically valid and of whether that reasoning or methodology properly can be applied to the facts in issue."[10] Although the Court declined to set out a definitive list of factors to be considered by the trial judge, it noted several pertinent considerations. First, a "key question" is whether the scientific theory or technique has been, or can be, tested. A second factor is whether the theory or technique has been subjected to peer review. Third, the court ordinarily should consider the potential or known error rate of the technique or methodology. And fourth, a relevant scientific community's general acceptance of a theory or method can still have a bearing on the judge's inquiry.[11] The judge's inquiry, noted the Court, is a flexible one. Its primary focus should

---

6 *Frye v. United States*, 293 F. 1013 (D.C. Cir. 1923).

7 *See, e.g., In re Agent Orange Prod. Litig.*, 611 F.Supp. 1223, 1242 (E.D.N.Y. 1985).

8 509 U.S. 579 (1993).

9 509 U.S. at 592–93.

10 *Id.*

11 509 U.S. at 593–94.

be on scientific validity, and thus the reliability of the underlying principles supporting the proposed testimony.[12]

The Texas Court of Criminal Appeals has also adopted the reliability test. In *Kelly v. State*,[13] the court concluded that the *Frye* test was no longer a part of Texas law and in its place substituted a reliability test. To show that novel scientific evidence is reliable, the proponent must establish by clear and convincing evidence that the underlying theory is valid, that the technique applying the theory is valid, and that the technique was properly applied. Although the court's opinion addressed the issue of novel scientific evidence, the reliability model should also apply to other forms of underlying principles or theories relied upon, whether scientific or not.[14]

The Texas Supreme Court has also adopted the reliability test for civil cases. In *Du Pont De Nemours and Company, Inc. v. Robinson*,[15] the court indicated that in deciding whether to admit expert testimony concerning scientific evidence, the trial judge must assess the reliability and relevancy of the offered testimony. Citing *Daubert* and the Court of Criminal Appeals decision in *Kelly v. State, supra*, the court held that the trial judge is required under Rule 104(a) to determine whether the scientific evidence is based upon methods and procedures of science, as opposed to mere conjecture. To help make that decision, the court offered a nonexhaustive list of factors: (1) the degree to which the theory has been tested; (2) the extent to which the technique depends on the subjective interpretation of the expert; (3) whether the theory has been subjected to publication or peer review; (4) the potential error rate; (5) whether the relevant scientific community has generally accepted the theory; and (6) the nonjudicial uses that have been made of the theory or technique. Although the foregoing list varies slightly from the lists suggested in *Daubert* and *Kelly*, the approach is generally the same. The scientific evidence is not admissible if the trial court determines that it is not reliable.

Sometimes the foundation will require two witnesses. If the theory and instrument are well known, the judge may judicially notice those elements of the predicate upon a proper timely request by counsel. When judicial notice is inapplicable, however, the proponent will probably have to call an expert with heavy academic credentials to lay those elements of the foundation. This is particularly true when the scientific principles or theories are novel. The proponent will then call a technician as the second witness to establish the balance of the predicate.

---

12 509 U.S. at 594.

13 824 S.W.2d 568 (Tex. Crim. App. 1992).

14 *Hartman v. State*, 946 S.W.2d 60 (Tex. Crim. App. 1997) (*Kelly* applies to all scientific evidence, whether novel or not).

15 923 S.W.2d 549 (Tex. 1995).

The Texas Court of Criminal Appeals, in *Nenno v. State*, 970 S.W.2d 549 (Tex. Crim. App. 1998), extended the principles set out in *Kelly* to *nonscientific* expert testimony. The court indicated that if the "field of study" is "based upon experience and training as opposed to the scientific method," then *Kelly's* requirement of reliability applies with less rigor than to the hard sciences. *Id.* at 561. The appropriate questions, the court said, are: "(1) whether the field of expertise is a legitimate one, (2) whether the subject matter of the expert's testimony is within the scope of that field, and (3) whether the expert's testimony properly relies upon and/or utilizes the principles involved in the field." *Id.*

In *Kuhmo Tire Company, Ltd. v. Carmichael*, 526 U.S. 137 (1999), the Supreme Court held that the "gatekeeping" principles articulated in *Daubert* extended to *all* forms of expert testimony, whether or not they embrace scientific principles. The Court noted that Federal Rule of Evidence 702 focuses on the "knowledge" of the expert and does not distinguish between the types of knowledge listed in the rule, i.e., "technical" or "other specialized." The Court indicated that it would be very hard for trial judges to administer the opinion evidence rules if they had to make distinctions between the types of expert knowledge involved. Although the proffered expert in *Kumho* was a mechanical engineer who had testified about the design of a tire, the trial court could nonetheless flexibly apply some of the *Daubert* factors in deciding whether the expert's testimony was reliable. The Court added that not all of the *Daubert* factors would necessarily fit. However, the trial court should apply those that are reasonable measures of reliability. Applying several of the *Daubert* factors, the Court concluded that the trial court had not abused its discretion in excluding the expert's testimony as unreliable. The defect, the Court said, was not his general methodology (visual and tactile inspection of the tire) but rather his specific mode of analysis. The expert had relied on a more particularized "two-factor test," and the plaintiff could not point to any "articles or paper that validate" that approach. The Court stressed that the trial judge should "make certain that an expert, whether basing testimony upon professional studies or personal experience, employs in the courtroom the same level of intellectual rigor that characterizes the practice of an expert in the relevant field."

As noted *supra*, the Texas Court of Criminal Appeals in *Nenno v. State* held that if the expert testimony involves a field of study apart from the hard sciences, the trial court must apply a three-pronged test for determining reliability. The *Nenno* decision, which predates the Supreme Court's decision in *Kumho,* varies from the *Daubert-Kelly* analysis and, according to the court, is less rigorous than those tests." In *Gammill v. Jack Williams Chevrolet, Inc.*, 972 S.W.2d 713 (Tex. 1998), the Texas Supreme Court held that the relevance and reliability requirements of Texas Rule of Evidence 702 apply to all expert evidence offered under that rule.

§ 9-3(C)(2) Elements of the Foundation—Scientific Evidence

The foundation for using the new "reliability" standard for verification of scientific evidence is as follows:

1. Witness #1 is qualified to establish the theory's validity and the instrument's reliability.
2. The underlying theory is valid. Testimony about the empirical validation of the theory is essential under *Daubert*.
3. The underlying theory is generally accepted as valid. Although this element is not absolutely required, the courts have indicated that this is a factor which may be considered. The fact that most specialists within a discipline subscribe to a theory is circumstantial evidence that the theory rests on sound scientific methodology; presumably they cannot find any substantial flaws in the research validating the theory.
4. The instrument or technique is reliable.
5. The instrument or technique is generally accepted as being reliable. Again, although not absolutely required, the courts have indicated that this is a relevant factor that may be considered.
6. Witness #2 is qualified to conduct and interpret test results.
7. The instrument that witness #2 used was in good working condition.
8. The witness used the instrument or technique.
9. The witness used the proper procedures.
10. The witness states the test results.

§ 9-3(C)(3) Sample Foundations—Scientific Evidence

§ 9-3(C)(3)(i) Sample Foundation—Psychiatric Testimony

The fact situation is a rape prosecution. The State alleges that the defendant, Mr. Marx, raped the complainant, Ms. Jane Whitlow. During her direct testimony, Ms. Whitlow described the rape and identified the defendant as the rapist. On cross-examination, she admitted that although on the day in question she reported the alleged rape to the police, the next day in a conversation with her mother, Ms. Whitlow refused to confirm or deny that there had been a rape. As their next witness, the State calls Dr. Herbert Dubowski, a licensed psychiatrist. The State proposes to elicit Dr. Dubowski's testimony about rape trauma syndrome (RTS) to rehabilitate Ms. Whitlow's credibility. Although Texas courts generally reject expert testimony on credibility, the courts may permit the prosecutor to introduce expert opinion evidence of syndrome evidence to rehabilitate a witness who had been impeached with prior inconsistent statements.[16] After stating his credentials, Dr. Dubowski testifies:

P Doctor, WHAT is your specialty? (1)

W For the past few years, I've concentrated my practice and research in the area of rape trauma syndrome.

P WHAT is rape trauma syndrome? (2)

W The theory holds that in most cases, after a rape, women cope with that traumatic event in a predictable manner.

P WHAT manner is that? (2)

W Their reaction usually progresses through two phases. The initial stage is the acute phase. They try to come to terms with the physical trauma and the immediate psychological impact. They experience disorganization in their lives. They become confused.

P WHAT do you mean by "confused?" (2)

W They're indecisive. Even if someone asks them point blank about the rape, out of shame or a sense of morality, they are often reluctant to discuss it. Again, that's the acute phase. That's followed by the long-term phase.

P WHAT happens during that phase? (1), (2)

W They begin reorganizing their lives. They may move, change their telephone number, and visit friends and family much more frequently to gain moral support. They often develop phobias. They may have a fear of being alone.

P WHAT research, if any, have you done on rape trauma syndrome? (2)

W I was fortunate enough to participate in the original research done on the subject. Before I moved to Dallas, I lived in Boston. That's where Burgess and Homstrom did the first intensive study of this subject.

P WHEN and WHERE did they conduct that study? (2)

W Between July 1992 and July 1993, they interviewed all the rape victims admitted to the emergency ward of Boston City Hospital.

P HOW many persons did they study? (2), (4)

W About 150 women were included in the data base.

P WHAT types of women were included in the study? (2), (4)

W All sorts. They were all races. About 70 percent were adult, and the rest were minors. In fact, there were three male children included in the study.

---

[16] *Schutz v. State*, 957 S.W.2d 52 (Tex. Crim. App. 1997). *See generally* WENDORF, SCHLUETER & BARTON, TEXAS RULES OF EVIDENCE MANUAL VII-38 to VII-41 (6th ed. 2002); Schlueter, *Criminal Evidence: Expert Testimony—The Human Lie Detector*, 54 TEX. B.J. 370 (April 1991).

P HOW did the researchers conduct the study? (2), (4)

W They initially interviewed these people, and they then followed up by studying the changes in the life patterns after the traumatic incident.

P WHAT findings did the researchers make? (2), (4)

W In the overwhelming majority of cases, there was a clear pattern.

P WHAT do you mean by "overwhelming majority?" (2), (4)

W I mean about 85 to 90 percent of the cases.

P WHAT was the pattern? (2), (4)

W It was the two stages, the acute and long-term phases, that I described a few moments ago.

P WHAT other research, if any, has been done on rape trauma syndrome? (2), (4)

W There have been several other studies, including those by Sutherland and Scherl.

P WHAT were the findings in those studies? (2), (4)

W About the same. You can quibble with percentages, but the virtually uniform finding is that in most cases, there is a definite pattern of coping behavior after a rape.

P Doctor, HOW valid is rape trauma syndrome? (2)

W It's very valid and is well documented.

P Is the theory of rape trauma syndrome generally accepted in the scientific community as being valid? (3)

W Yes. All of the latest editions of the leading, authoritative treatises on psychiatry recognize the syndrome.

P WHAT professional organizations are there in your field? (2), (3)

W One is the APA, the American Psychiatric Association.

P To WHAT extent has the American Psychiatric Association recognized the existence of rape trauma syndrome? (2), (3)

W The APA has an official manual, the Diagnostic and Statistical Manual of Mental Disorders. It's now in the fourth edition, the 1994 edition—DSM IV-TR.[17]

P WHAT, if anything, does DSM IV-TR say about rape trauma syndrome? (2), (3), (5)

W One of the examples of post-traumatic stress disorder in DSM IV-TR is its application after a rape.

---

[17] DSM IV-TR was published in 2000.

P Is the application of the rape trauma syndrome theory generally considered to be reliable? (5)

W Absolutely. As I mentioned, the studies have shown that an overwhelming number of rape victims are affected with the syndrome.

P HOW did you apply the theory of rape trauma syndrome to the facts in this case? (8)

W I carefully reviewed the documents in this case, interviewed the victim and those familiar with her, and then applied the criteria of the syndrome evidence to the victim's actions, and inactions in this case. Using that information, I prepared a chart showing how her actions fit the pattern found in the rape trauma syndrome.

§ 9-3(C)(3)(ii) Sample Foundation—Drug Identification

The following fact situation is a prosecution for possession of cocaine. The prosecutor presents the testimony of Mr. Holiday, a chemist for the local forensic science center, to identify the substance that was seized from the defendant. Note that in this hypothetical, the same witness lays all elements of the foundation. Further, when explaining complex devices or processes, such as a gas chromatography, mass spectrometer, or the mass spectrum, counsel should consider using a chart to help the jury visualize how the process or device works. Assume the chemist has already identified himself.

P WHAT is your occupation? (1)

W I am a forensic chemist for the Texas Department of Public Safety.

P WHAT is a forensic chemist? (1)

W Well, our basic function is to identify chemical substances by using appropriate scientific techniques.

P WHAT is your formal education? (1)

W I have both bachelor's and master of science degrees from the University of Texas Health Science Center.

P WHAT was your major area of study? (1)

W Chemistry and biology.

P HOW long have you been a forensic chemist? (1)

W I have been a forensic chemist for about 15 years. I worked for the Houston Police Crime Laboratory for about 5 years, and have been with the Department of Public Safety for the past 10 years.

P WHAT, if anything, have you published? (1)

W I have written over a dozen articles on general chemistry. I have also presented over two dozen papers to the American Academy of Forensic Sciences and the Southwestern Association of Forensic Scientists.

P WHAT is gas chromatography/mass spectrometry? (2)

W It is a method of purifying and identifying various chemical compounds, and actually involves two tests: gas chromatography followed by mass spectrometry. Gas chromatography does the separating and purifying by vaporization. Mass spectrometry does the identifying by measuring the mass of the compound and its fragments.

P HOW reliable are these tests? (2)

W They are very reliable. Gas chromatography, or GC, is unsurpassed as a method of separation, and mass spectrometry is a specific test that can identify the components of a sample mixture. When used together, these tests are extremely effective.

P Are these tests generally accepted in the scientific community as being valid ways of identifying drugs? (3), (5)

W Yes, definitely.

P WHAT is a specific, as opposed to a nonspecific, test? (2)

W A specific test yields a result that only one drug can produce, and therefore leads to few false positive results. A nonspecific test yields a result that more than one substance can produce, and leads to a large number of false positive results.

P WHAT is a false positive result? (2)

W A false positive result is a finding of one drug's presence when in fact another drug is present.

P WHAT type of test is gas chromatography/mass spectrometry? (2)

W Gas chromatography itself is nonspecific. This is why we follow up with mass spectrometry, which is a specific test.

P WHAT is a gas chromatograph and a mass spectrometer? (2), (5)

W They are the machines actually used to separate, purify, and identify a particular chemical compound.

P WHAT are the components of the gas chromatograph? (2), (4)

W The gas chromatograph has six components: the carrier gas, the injection port, the column tube, the sample splitter, the detector, and the recorder.

P HOW does the gas chromatograph work? (3), (4)

W First, a small, known quantity of the sample is dissolved in a solution. Second, the sample is introduced into the injection port with a hypodermic needle. The injection port is temperature controlled to ensure the sample is vaporized. Third, a high pressure gas cylinder sweeps the sample, now gaseous, into the column tube. The interior of the column tube is coated with a liquid, and each component of the sample has a different attraction to the liquid. This is how the compound is separated. The greater the attraction, the longer it takes the compound to travel the column. The GC measures the time it takes each component to proceed through the column tube. Fourth, when the gaseous component emerges from the column tube, a detector can identify and measure the component. We do not use this identification, however, because it is nonspecific. Instead, the sample splitter sends a portion of all separated compounds to the mass spectrometer.

P WHAT are the components of the mass spectrometer? (3), (4)

W The mass spectrometer, or MS, has four components: an ionization chamber, an analyzer tube and magnet, a detector, and a recorder.

P HOW does the mass spectrometer work? (3), (4)

W The gas chromatograph stream splitter feeds the purified and separated sample into an ionization chamber, where each component is electrically charged, causing it to break apart. Each component breaks apart in a unique, individual manner. The charged fragments are then forced into the analyzer tube and magnet region, where the fragments are affected by the magnet. As the fragments emerge from the tube and enter the detector, they lose their charge and activate the recorder. The recorder then produces a mass spectrum for each component.

P WHAT is a mass spectrum? (3)

W A mass spectrum is a visual display or graph of a sample's fragmentation pattern which is unique to that compound. If properly analyzed, the compound can be specifically identified.

P HOW is a mass spectrum analyzed? (3), (4)

W There are basically two methods. First, the sample spectrum can be compared with commercially prepared, known tables, either visually or by computer. Second, the analyst can make an original analysis of the spectrum.

P HOW is an original analysis performed? (3), (5)

W There are several steps. First, each peak is assigned a mass number. Second, the tallest peak is identified. Third, the parent peak, or peak with the highest mass number, is identified. The parent peak indicates the molecular weight that all the fragments must fit into, and the mass number of each individual fragment is known. Finally, the analyst must apply molecular structure and bonding theory to identify the compound.

P Is the use of these instruments generally accepted in the scientific community as a reliable means of testing for drugs? (5)

W Yes, it is. Virtually every laboratory that I am familiar with uses this technique and instrumentation.

P WHAT training, if any, have you had using the gas chromatograph/mass spectrometer? (4), (6)

W I completed the Department of Public Safety's required drug identification course.

P WHEN did you complete this course? (4)

W I completed the course in 1987, about one year after I began working for the Houston Police Crime Laboratory. Many local agencies often send their employees to the Department's training courses.

P WHAT drug identification techniques are taught at this course? (4)

W Most of the widely used tests today, including gas chromatography/mass spectrometry.

P HOW did you study these techniques? (6)

W This was primarily a hands-on training course because all of the students were well-versed in science generally. The instructors first explained the techniques and then demonstrated how to use the machinery. We were then required to use the machinery ourselves. We also received instruction on the proper maintenance of all machines.

P HOW was your proficiency in using the gas chromatograph/mass spectrometer measured? (6)

W During the testing phase, each student is given 20 sample compounds to identify, which may or may not be different. The instructors know what that sample is, but the student does not. To successfully complete the course, each student must properly identify all sample compounds.

P HOW many times have you used the gas chromatograph/mass spectrometer? (6)

W Hundreds of times.

P HOW long have you been using the gas chromatograph/mass spectrometer? (6)

W About 20 years.

P HAVE you ever identified illegal drugs with the gas chromatograph/mass spectrometer? (6)

W Yes.

P WHICH drugs have you identified? (6)

W Heroin, cocaine, marijuana, you name it and I've probably identified it.

P Your Honor, may I approach the witness?

J Yes.

Assume that the proponent establishes how the suspected drugs were received, marked, and handled by the chemist. Also assume that the proponent has had the specimen in question marked as State's exhibit six for identification.

P Mr. Holiday, I now show you what has been marked as State's exhibit six for identification. Do you recognize it? (8)

W Yes. This is the specimen I tested in this case.

P HOW do you recognize it? (8)

W I recognize my initials and case number date on the tag here.

P WHAT did you do after you received this exhibit? (8)

W I began preparing the gas chromatograph/mass spectrometer for operation.

P WHAT type of gas chromatograph/mass spectrometer is in your laboratory? (7)

W We have a standard, industry model common to most forensic laboratories.

P WHAT condition was the gas chromatograph/mass spectrometer in? (7)

W It was in good working condition.

P HOW do you know that? (7)

W Well, there are a number of other chemists who also use the same gas chromatograph/mass spectrometer. Before every use, each chemist is required to perform a series of preventive maintenance checks and services on the machines.

P WHAT deficiencies, if any, did you identify in the machines? (7)

W None.

P WHAT did you do then? (9)

W I dissolved a small sample from the vial in solvent, and introduced it into the injection port of the gas chromatograph.

P HOW did you conduct the test on this occasion? (9)

W In the same way I explained earlier. I performed an original analysis of the mass spectrum to specifically identify the compound.

P WHAT are "overlapping" peaks? (8)

W Overlapping peaks indicate that several compounds emerged from the mass spectrometer simultaneously. This would indicate that the gas chromatograph did not sufficiently purify and separate the sample, and the results would be questionable.

P WERE there any overlapping peaks during the analysis of this particular specimen—State's exhibit six for identification? (10)

W No.

P WHAT is a "peak cluster?" (10)

W A peak cluster occurs when certain chemical elements have the same atomic number but different mass numbers. This would indicate that a parent peak could be difficult to identify, and the results would be questionable.

P WERE there any peak clusters during the analysis of exhibit six for identification? (10)

W No.

P WHAT substance did you determine State's exhibit number six to be? (10)

W The substance in State's exhibit six was definitely cocaine.

§ 9-3(C)(3)(iii) Sample Foundation—DNA Validation

In the following sample foundation, samples of blood from the accused and a crime scene stain have already been marked as State's exhibits numbers one and two for identification during the testimony of an earlier witness, Officer Gonzalez. In this hypothetical three witnesses are required to lay the proper foundation. This sample foundation does not develop the chain of custody, which could be critical in a DNA case. The primary focus here is on demonstration of the scientific principles and methodology in DNA testing. The proponent's first witness establishes the scientific theory's validity.

Please also note that in the following sample foundation regarding DNA is the latest and third generation of tests. The first generation was RFLP. The second generation was PCR, the tests that took center stage in the O.J. Simpson case. STR is now the dominant technology. Because the FBI database includes information for 13 STR ("short tandem repeats") loci, this will remain the dominant technology for years.

WITNESS #1

P Please state your full name and spell your last name for the record.

W My name is John Gilmore. The surname is spelled G-I-L-M-O-R-E.

P WHAT is your address?

W I reside at 1433 Macmillan Avenue in Houston, Texas.

P WHAT is your occupation?

W I'm a professor at the University of Texas Health Science Center in Houston.

P Please describe your educational background for the ladies and gentlemen of the jury.

O Your Honor, this won't be necessary. We're perfectly willing to save the court some time by stipulating that Professor Gilmore is an expert.

(The Witness's Qualification as an Expert)

[*Pause for discussion during which the proponent successfully argues that the jury is entitled to hear the qualifications of the expert witness in order to intelligently determine how much weight to give to the witness's testimony.*]

P Professor Gilmore, let me repeat the last question. Please describe your educational background.

W Well, I received my B.S. from the University of Texas Health Science Center in Houston. I then obtained my master's degree from the same institution.

P When you studied for that degree, WHAT area of study, if any, did you concentrate in?

W Molecular biology.

P WHAT did you do after you obtained your master's degree?

W I then worked for my Ph.D. I obtained that degree in 1989 from the University of New Mexico.

P During your study for the doctorate, did you concentrate on any particular area?

W Certainly.

P And WHAT was that area?

W This time I narrowed my focus. I knew that DNA typing was a coming field, so I concentrated not only on molecular biology but more specifically on DNA typing. I wrote my thesis on that topic.

P WHAT did you do after you received your Ph.D. in 1989?

W I joined the University of Texas Health Science Center faculty. I've taught in the College of Sciences since late 1989.

P WHAT is your current title?

W I'm an associate professor in the College of Sciences.

P HOW many times, if ever, have you testified in court as an expert witness?

W I have testified as an expert on 20 other occasions.

P WHAT subjects did you testify on?

W On each occasion I testified as an expert on DNA.

(The General Scientific Theory the Expert Relies on)

P Professor, earlier in your testimony, you used the expression, on "DNA typing" In general terms, could you tell us WHAT that is?

W Certainly. As we all learn in high school biology, DNA is the basic building block of life. Each person's DNA accounts for his or her individuality. Everyone has a certain number of chromosomes. Each chromosome is composed of a DNA molecule. If you think back to high school, you'll remember that the molecule is usually thought of as a double helix—a sort of twisted ladder or spiral staircase.

P WHAT is this helix or ladder made of?

W The sides of the ladder are comprised of alternating molecules of sugar and phosphate. However, in DNA typing, what you're really interested in are the rungs of the ladder.

P WHAT are they made of?

W What we call nucleotides. There are four: adenine (A), thymine (f), cytosine (C), and guanine (G). Each rung consists of two of these. A always attaches to T, and C always attaches to G. A combination of two nucleotides forms each rung. The combination is called a base pair.

P HOW many base pairs does each individual have?

W Each person has about three billion. Most base pair sequences are common to all human beings. It's what makes us all human beings rather than horses. However, there are others that vary from person to person-approximately three million of them. They're the so-called polymorphic sites or locations. A person's DNA at any given location on the nucleotide chain wouldn't be unique to that person. But when you consider all the possible locations, each person's overall sequence is peculiar to that individual. The odds of a random, complete match in nucleotides are astronomical. They run well beyond the trillions. That unique nucleotide sequence is the basis of DNA typing. In a nutshell, that's the underlying theory of DNA typing.

P How WELL accepted is this theory?

W Universally by anyone who knows anything about molecular biology.

(The Specific Technique Implementing the Theory)

P HOW can you use this theory in practice to identify people?

W There are a number of techniques which implement the theory, but by a wide margin the one that's most widely used today is STR analysis—short tandem repeat analysis. It's a multi-step procedure that enables you to identify some of the parts of the nucleotide sequence that vary from person to person.

P Your Honor, I request that this be marked State's exhibit three for identification. [*Counsel hands exhibit to court reporter, who marks it and hands it back.*]

P Please let the record reflect that I am showing State's exhibit three for identification to the defense counsel.

P Permission to approach the witness?

J Granted.

P Professor, I now hand you what has been marked State's exhibit three for identification. Do you recognize it?

W Yes.

P WHAT is it?

W It's a chart showing the various steps in STR analysis. An oral description of the technique can be confusing if you don't visualize what's going on.

P WHO prepared this chart?

W I did.

P HOW accurate is the chart?

W It's a good basic depiction of all of the essential steps in STR.

P Your Honor, I now offer State's exhibit three for identification into evidence as State's exhibit three.

J Any objection?

O No, your Honor.

J Very well. It will be received.

P Your Honor, I would like your permission to distribute exact copies of the exhibit to each juror. They may find it helpful in following Professor Gilmore's testimony.

J May I see the copies? And give one to opposing counsel. [*Judge and opposing counsel examine copies to ensure that they conform to the exhibit.*] OK. You may proceed.

P Now, professor, using exhibit number three, please lead us through this process.

W OK. Start on the left-hand margin. That shows the double helix or ladder in the cell. Any cell with a nucleus will contain DNA-for example, white blood cells, sperm, saliva, and those surrounding hair roots. The first thing we've got to do is extract the DNA from the nucleus. Take a look at the second column from the left. We use chemical techniques to extract or remove the DNA.

P WHAT comes next?

W You target certain regions of the DNA and amplify or multiply them.

P WHICH regions do you target?

W They're parts of the DNA which have some short nucleotide sequences that are repeated—the short tandem repeats. We know that there are a number of these regions which are: (1) flanked by certain nucleotide sequences; and (2) include a varying number of repetitions or STRs. The number of repetitions varies from person to person. This multiplication step involves several procedures.

P WHAT is the first procedure?

W You create the reaction mixture.

P HOW do you do that?

W You place the original DNA in a test tube. Then you add two primers of two known nucleotide sequences. We know that those two sequences flank the specific STR.

P WHAT do you do after you mix the original DNA and the primers?

W You heat the mixture. As you can see on exhibit three, when the original DNA is heated, the double strand comes apart and yields two single strands. You then allow the mixture to cool.

P WHY do you do that?

W When the mixture cools, the two primers attach to the two strands. As the exhibit shows, one primer attaches toward one end of one strand; according to the binding rules I discussed earlier, the primer will attack to a known complementary nucleotide sequence. Thus, if part of the primer sequence is CA, it must attach to GT. The other primer attaches toward the opposite end of the other strand; again, that primer must attach at a binding site with a known complementary nucleotide sequence. The part of the original DNA nucleotide sequence between the two primers—in other words, flanked by the primers—is the target region containing the varying number of repeats.

P WHAT happens after the two primers attach to the two strands?

W As you can see on the exhibit, after binding to the single strands, the primers extend or elongate. Again, the two primers attached toward opposite ends of the two single strands. The primers now extend toward each other. Essentially, the extension ends when it reaches the other primer. Together, the original DNA strand and the extension form an exact copy of the original region that we wanted to amplify. We repeat this cycle until we have a large number of exact copies of that DNA fragment, that target region.

P After you have created all these copies of the target STR regions, WHAT is the next step?

W Separation. You need to separate or sort the fragments by size, as you can see in the column in the middle of exhibit three. You insert the fragments into a long tube. You also insert dyed fragments of known length. The number of repeats in the fragment determines the size of the fragment, and in turn the size of the fragment determines how quickly the fragment moves through the tube. The longer fragments move more slowly than the shorter fragments going through the tube.

P WHAT happens as the fragments pass through the tube?

W As I said earlier, they separate. The longer fragments take longer. At a certain point in the tube, an instrument scans the material.

P WHAT is the purpose of the scanning?

W The scanning determines when each fragment passes that point in the tube—in other words, how long it has taken that fragment to go through the tube. Again, the length of the fragment largely determines how much time it takes. The instrument scans both the fragments from the sample being analyzed and the dyed fragments of known length. Basically, instrument "sizes" the fragments, determines their length. By scanning both types of fragments and comparing the fragments being analyzed with the fragments of known length, the instrument determines the size. Ultimately, you get a printout which indicates when each fragment passes the scanner and, therefore, the size of the fragment.

P After you have determined the size, WHAT do you do?

W The sizing instrument is hooked up to a computer.

P WHAT does the computer do?

W The computer has a database of known genetic markers. The database contains the information as to the size or length of those markers. The computer compares the size of the analyzed samples to the information in the database to identify the genetic markers in the sample. That comparison confirms the identification of each fragment.

P WHY is this procedure called "DNA typing?"

W The analogy is to fingerprinting. Suppose you have a blood sample found at a crime scene and a sample taken from the accused who is suspected of committing the crime. You'd apply the procedure to both samples to see if the samples matched. In an STR test, if they match, you know that at least at the sites tested, the two samples have the same nucleotide sequence.

P WHAT, if anything, have you written about the procedure for conducting an STR test?

W I published an article on the subject in the 2001 issue of *BioTechniques* magazine. I actually coauthored the article with a Dr. Morgan.

P WHO is Dr. Morgan?

W He is the director of the Cellmatch laboratory in Houston. One of their specialties is DNA testing.

P Your Honor, I request that this be marked State's exhibit for identification next in order. [*Counsel hands to court reporter who marks it as State's exhibit four for identification and hands it back to counsel.*]

P Please let the record reflect that I am showing what the court reporter has marked as State's exhibit four for identification to the defense counsel.

P Permission to approach the witness?

J Yes.

P Professor, I hand you what has been marked as State's exhibit number four for identification. Do you recognize it?

W Yes, I most certainly do.

P WHAT is it?

W It's the appendix A from my article.

P HOW do you recognize it?

W I ought to know the contents, since I coauthored it with Dr. Morgan! Your Honor, I now offer State's exhibit four for identification into evidence as State's exhibit number four.

J Any objection?

O Yes, your Honor. This is incompetent hearsay.

P Your Honor, this isn't hearsay. I admit that it would be hearsay if we offered the body of the article, including assertions about molecular biology and the proper procedures for conducting an STR analysis. However, we're relying on the witness's in-court testimony for that. Instead, we're offering only Appendix A. Appendix A is a checklist for technicians conducting STR tests. It's a series of imperative sentences: "Do this. Then do this."

J May I see the exhibit? [*Counsel hands to judge.*] Thank you.

J I agree that this appendix doesn't constitute hearsay. Objection overruled. State's exhibit four for identification is admitted into evidence as State's exhibit four.

P Professor Gilmore, would you please describe appendix A, which appears in your article?

W It's a comprehensive checklist for technicians who conduct STR DNA testing.

P And HOW well accepted is reliability of the short tandem repeat analysis technique?

W Almost universally. It's not only employed in universities and colleges. It's also used by hospitals for genetic testing and by crime laboratories throughout the world.

WITNESS #2

(The Application of the STR Technique to Analyze the Samples in the Instant Case)

The proponent's second witness establishes the test results in the specific case.

P Please state your full name and spell your last name for the record.

W My name is Ralph Harrison.

P Would you please spell your last name for the court reporter?

W Harrison is spelled H-A-R-R-I-S-O-N.

P Thank you. WHERE do you live, Mr. Harrison?

W I live in Houston, Texas.

P Mr. Harrison, WHAT is your line of work?

W I'm a DNA genetic marker technician at Cell match Company in Houston, Texas.

P WHAT is your educational background?

W I have a B.S. degree from the University of Texas Health Science Center.

P WHEN did you receive your degree?

W 1995.

P WHAT did you do after receiving your degree?

W I went right to work for Cellmatch. Initially, I did bloodstain tests and electrophoretic analysis of enzymes and proteins. However, in 1999 when we set up our DNA unit, I helped establish the unit.

P WHAT, if any, special training did you receive when you joined the unit?

W I attended an intensive, three-week training program conducted by Dr. Morgan in conjunction with his good friend, Professor John Gilmore. Dr.

Gilmore flew down and spent two weeks with us going over every step of STR testing in great detail.

P I hand you what has been marked as State's exhibit number four. Do you recognize it?

W You bet I do.

P WHAT is it?

W It's an appendix from the 2001 article about STR procedures which Professor Gilmore and Dr. Morgan wrote.

P HOW do you recognize it?

W Professor Gilmore distributed a draft of it on the first day of class, and we used it throughout his instruction. I know every period and footnote in that article backwards and forwards by now.

P HOW, if at all, do you use the article in your work?

W I use it almost every day. Appendix A is a model protocol or test procedure for conducting STR tests. I use that protocol every time I conduct an RFLP test at Cellmatch.

P Now let's shift topics. WHERE were you on the afternoon of June 28, 2004?

W I was at work at Cellmatch.

P WHAT, if anything, happened that afternoon?

W Patrolman Gonzalez from the Houston Police Department stopped by. He delivered two blood samples and asked me to conduct a DNA test on them.

P I now hand you what have previously been marked as State's exhibits number one and number two for identification. Do you know WHAT these are?

W Yes.

P Could you please tell the jury what they are?

W They are the two samples which Patrolman Gonzalez gave me.

P HOW do you recognize them?

W I know his initials, and my initials are on the plastic container where I placed them at the time I tested the samples.

P WHAT did you do with the samples after Patrolman Gonzalez gave them to you?

W I immediately tested them.

P Between the time you received the samples from Patrolman Gonzalez and the time you tested the samples, WHO else handled the samples?

W No one else. I was the only one.

P During that same time, WHEN, if at all, were the samples out of your sight?

W They never were. It had been a quiet day, and I was able to get right to the test. When Gonzalez arrived, I met him at the receptionist's desk. I went straight from here to my bench in the DNA unit. I conducted the test almost immediately.

P Your Honor, I now offer State's exhibits numbers one and two for identification into evidence.

J Any objection?

O None, your Honor.

J All right. State's exhibits one and two are admitted into evidence.

P Thank you, your Honor. Mr. Harrison, WHAT equipment did you use in the test of these samples?

W There's a variety of instruments. You need some chemicals and the equipment to scan and size the fragments.

P WHAT condition were they in when used to test exhibits one and two?

W They all were in good condition.

P HOW do you know that?

W The chemicals were fresh.

P WHAT do you mean by "fresh?"

W We get a fresh shipment from the manufacturer on Monday morning. I conducted this test on a Monday afternoon. The chemicals certainly had not lost any of their potency by then.

P WHAT about the other apparatus and equipment?

W We have them serviced every Friday evening after work. Again, I conducted this test on a Monday afternoon. The equipment would have been checked shortly before that, and I know that I didn't encounter any problems in running the test.

P HOW did you conduct the test?

W I did it "by the book"—or I should say "by the article." As I always do, I followed the appendix to the Gilmore *BioTechniques* article step by step to ensure that I used the proper protocol.

P Mr. Harrison, HOW well do you remember the specific occasion when you tested these two samples?

W I guess I generally do, but I have to admit that I've tested hundreds of these samples and the tests tend to run together in my mind.

P Your Honor, I request that these be marked State's exhibit next in order for identification. [*Counsel hands exhibit to court reporter who marks it as State's exhibit five and six for identification and returns it to counsel.*]

P May the record reflect that I am showing what the court reporter has marked as State's exhibits five and six for identification to opposing counsel. [*Counsel shows exhibits to opposing counsel who briefly examines them.*]

P Your Honor, I request permission to approach the witness?

J Granted.

P Mr. Harrison, I now hand you what have been marked as State's exhibits numbers five and six for identification. WHAT are they?

W The printouts of the two STR samples which Patrolman Gonzalez delivered to me. Five is the printout for one sample, exhibit one, while six is the printout for the other sample, exhibit two.

P HOW do you recognize them?

W You can see my initials and the date on the bottom of both printouts. These are the printouts that I got when I subjected both samples to STR analysis.

P WHAT, if anything, did you do with the printouts?

W I compared them.

P WHAT was the purpose of the comparison?

W I wanted to see if they matched.

P WHAT do you mean when you say "match?"

W I mean that both samples contain fragments of the same size or length. In this case, they matched.

P HOW do you know?

W The scanning instrument compared them to the dyed fragments of known length, and then the computer compared the measurements to its database.

P WHAT did you do after declaring a match?

W I called in Dr. Morgan. He's in charge of the next step in the DNA unit, that is, calculating the probability of a random match.

WITNESS #3

5

(The Random Match Probability)

The proponent completes the DNA analysis with a third witness, Dr. Morgan.

P Please state your full name and spell your last name for the record.

W I'm Andrew J. Morgan. You spell that, M-O-R-G-A-N.

P WHERE do you live?

W In Houston.

P Dr. Morgan, WHERE do you work?

W I work at the Houston laboratory of Cellmatch, Inc. I am the director of the DNA typing unit of the laboratory.

P Please tell us your educational background.

W I attended undergraduate school at the University of California, Davis. I received a basic B.S. degree from U.C.D. Then I obtained my master's degree at Washington University in St. Louis. Finally, I obtained a doctorate.

P WHERE did you obtain that degree?

W At Yale.

P WHAT area, if any, did you specialize in during your doctoral program?

W Population genetics.

P Could you please tell us WHAT that specialty involves?

W In part, it involves the application of the laws of statistics to genetics problems.

P Please give us an example of such a problem.

W For instance, as in a case like this one, you might be interested in trying to figure out what percentage of the population has a certain DNA marker or a particular set of DNA markers. Population genetics experts attempt to answer that type of problem.

P Doctor, I hand you what has been admitted as State's exhibit six. Do you recognize it?

W Yes.

P WHAT is it?

W It's a printout which Mr. Harrison gave me to evaluate a few months ago.

P HOW do you recognize it?

W I recognize his initials and my initials on the comer of the printout. Also I recall the date that we ran the test.

P WHAT did you do with this printout after Mr. Harrison gave it to you? (9)

W The printout indicated which genetic markers were present in the sample. I determined the percentage of the Caucasian population that would have the set of DNA markers indicated on the printout.

P WHY did you attempt to determine that percentage in the Caucasian population rather than say, for example, the Hispanic population?

W I was told by Mr. Harrison that both the perpetrator and the suspect were identified as Caucasian.

O Objection, your Honor, that is hearsay.

P Your Honor, we are not offering the statement for the truth of the matter. Instead, we are offering it for the nonhearsay purpose of showing why this witness conducted the study. This is an example of a statement or information acted upon.

J Objection overruled.

P WHAT technique did you use to determine the percentage?

W used the multiplication or product rule.

P WHAT is that?

W Let me give you a simple example. Let's suppose that you want to know what percentage of the Caucasian population has blonde hair *and* a limp. You check the population frequencies, and you learn the following: Ten percent of the Caucasian population has blonde hair, and one percent has a limp. You multiply the two numbers, 10 percent by 1 percent. The multiplication yields the figure, one tenth of one percent. That is, he percentage of the Caucasian population that has both characteristics. That's the formula I used in this case.

P WHY did you use it?

W You use it when you're analyzing several "independent" factors.

P WHAT is an "independent" factor?

W When factors are independent, they don't affect one another. In my example, a person with a limp might have blonde hair, black hair, brown hair, or no hair; the color of the hair doesn't have any effect on the probability whether they limp. In contrast, suppose you wanted to know how many Caucasian men not only have a mustache but also have a beard. Those obviously aren't independent factors, and you consequently couldn't use the multiplication or product rule to determine the percentage.

P WHY did you apply the multiplication rule in this case to the various DNA markers shown on the printout?

W I was confident that each band, representing a different DNA marker, was independent of the other bands.

P WHY were you confident of that?

W Because in STR testing we target sites on different chromosomes. In early DNA analysis, they often used multi-locus probes. When you do that, the probe hits several locations or sites on the same chromosome. If the sites are close together, they might not be independent; your DNA marker at one location might in fact affect the likelihood you have a particular DNA marker at the nearby site. However, it's generally accepted in biology that when you target sites on separate chromosomes, you have adequate assurance that the bands are independent. We did that in this case.

P When you use this multiplication rule, exactly WHAT is it that you multiply?

W You identify each DNA marker, and you insert into the formula the population frequency for that marker for that ethnic group.

P WHERE did you get the numbers you used in this case?

W We have an agreement with Lifecodes, one of the largest DNA laboratories in the world. By virtue of their agreement, we can use the population frequencies in their database. They've built up the database over the years, and it now includes the results of thousands of DNA tests of persons of virtually every conceivable ethnic group.

P HOW many DNA markers did you identify?

W I could definitely identify 13.

P WHAT did you do once you identified them?

W I looked up the pertinent frequencies in the Lifecodes database and then inserted those frequencies as 13 variables in the multiplication rule.

P When you multiplied those 13 numbers, WHAT was the result?

W The multiplication indicated that only one thousandth of one percent of the Caucasian population would possess this set of DNA markers.

§ 9-3(C)(3)(iv) Sample Foundation—Horizontal Gaze Nystagmus Test

In the following fact situation, the defendant, Mr. Long, has been charged with driving under the influence of alcohol. The prosecutor presents the testimony of Officer Lopez, who stopped Mr. Long's vehicle and used the HGN test to determine if the defendant was intoxicated. Assume that the police officer has already identified himself.

P Officer Lopez, WHAT is your occupation? (1)

W I am currently a police officer with the Waco Police Department.

P HOW long have you worked for the Waco Police Department? (1)

W Five years.

P Officer Lopez, WHAT, if any, training have you received in connection with your duties as a police officer in conducting the field sobriety tests? (1)

W I have attended a number of programs. First, I received training at the Waco Police Academy when I first joined the force and then I attended a special three-day training program sponsored by the Waco Police Department. At that session I was taught the battery of field sobriety tests proposed by the National Highway Traffic Safety Administration, the NHTSA, which is a division of the United States Department of Transportation.

P WHAT do you mean by field sobriety tests? (2)

W We use several tests in the field to determine whether a driver is intoxicated. One is to ask the subject to walk a straight line or recite the alphabet. We also use what are referred to as the "one-leg stand" and the "walk-and-turn" test. Those tests give us information on whether the subject's coordination is affected by drugs or alcohol. Another test is the HGN test.

P WHAT is the HGN test? (2)

W HGN stands for Horizontal Gaze Nystagmus. It is a test for examining the eye movement of the subject to determine if the eyes jerk or move suddenly when the subject is asked to focus on a moving object.

P HOW does the test work? (2)

W We ask the subject to stand erect and cover one eye. We then hold an object, such as a pen light, in front of the subject level with his or her eyes and slowly move it laterally, from the center of their head to the side of their head. We watch the eye carefully to see if it jerks as it follows the object. We repeat the process with the other eye. We are basically looking for three things: first, the eye cannot move smoothly as it focuses on the moving object; second, the movement of the eye, when it is as far left or right as it can go, is moderate or distinct; and third, the eye jerks at less than 45 degrees from the center. We look for these three things in each eye, for a total of six factors. If we find a total of four or more factors, we conclude that the subject is intoxicated. We also screen the subjects to see if they are wearing contact lenses or glasses, whether they have brain damage, medical disorders, or blindness (things that might affect the HGN).

P WHAT, if any, specific training have you received on conducting that particular test? (1), (6)

W Well, as I said, I attended a special three-day training session on field sobriety tests. I was given specific instruction on the HGN and ultimately was certified by the State of Texas to conduct that test. As part of the training, I received about 24 hours of classroom training and 16 hours of field evaluations. During the field evaluation component, I completed and documented the required 35 cases of test administration. Those test results were sent to the Texas Department of Engineering Extension Service, Law Enforcement Training Division for grading. I then received my proficiency certification from the State.

P WHEN did you receive that certification? (1), (6)

W Approximately four and one-half years ago.

P Officer Lopez, HOW many times have you conducted the HGN test? (1), (6)

W Probably close to 100 times, not counting the 35 test cases I had to run.

P Your Honor, we request permission to ask Officer Lopez to show the jury how he conducts the HGN test. (1), (9)

J You may proceed.

The proponent asks the witness to step down out of the witness stand and demonstrate the test on the proponent or some other person in the courtroom. After the witness returns to the stand, the proponent continues questioning.

P Officer Lopez, WHY do you use those particular techniques for conducting the HGN test? (3), (9)

W Those are the techniques designed and specified by the National Highway Transportation Safety Administration, and those are the techniques that we, in the Waco Police Department, are required to follow.

P Your Honor, we request that you take judicial notice[18] that, first, the scientific theory underlying the HGN test is considered reliable under Rule of Evidence 702 and, second, that the technique for conducting the HGN test is a reliable indicator of intoxication. (2), (3), (4), (5).

O We object, your Honor.

P May we approach the bench, your Honor.

J Yes.

P Your Honor, here is a copy of the Court of Criminal Appeals decision in *State v. Emerson*, at 880 S.W.2d 759. I specifically draw your attention to pages 768 and 769 where the court concluded that the theory underlying the HGN test is sufficiently reliable under Rule of Evidence 702 and that the scientific references addressing the issue cannot reasonably be questioned. As the court concluded, those materials uniformly conclude that

---

[18] As noted in *Emerson v. State*, 880 S.W.2d at 764, 765, the court may take judicial notice of "legislative facts," i.e., the reliability of the theory and technique of scientific evidence. *See also* GIANELLI & IMWINKELRIED, SCIENTIFIC EVIDENCE § 1-2 (2d ed. 1993). Judicial notice of legislative facts is not controlled by Rule of Evidence 201. *See* WENDORF, SCHLUETER & BARTON, TEXAS RULES OF EVIDENCE MANUAL II-4 (6th ed. 2002).

there is direct correlation between intoxication and eye movement. (2) The court also concluded that the technique for conducting the HGN, as specified by the NHTSA, is a reliable indicator of intoxication. (3)

J [*To defense counsel*] Counsel, do you have any objection?

P Not on those specific points, your Honor.

J All right. I will take judicial notice that the underlying scientific theory of the HGN test is considered reliable and that the HGN testing technique, as specified by the NHTSA, is also a reliable method of determining intoxication.

The proponent then establishes the circumstances leading up to the officer stopping the defendant's car, asking the defendant to get out of his car, and conducting several field sobriety tests, which the defendant failed.

P After you conducted the sobriety tests, WHAT did you do next? (8)

W Well I decided to run the HGN test that I just described for you.

P Would you please tell us HOW you administered the test to the defendant. (8), (9)

W I followed the procedures specified by the National Highway Traffic Safety Administration. First, I checked to see if he was wearing contacts or if he needed corrective lenses. I also looked him over to see if he had any visible head injuries. I asked him to face me and stand erect, with his feet together, and to cover his left eye. I held my pen light in front of his face, at eye level, and asked him to follow the movement of the pen, without moving his head, as I slowly moved it toward the right. I made note of the three factors with regard to his right eye. Next, I asked him to switch eyes and I repeated the same steps on his left eye, looking for the three specified factors.

P WHAT was the result of your testing? (10)

O Objection, your Honor, there has been an insufficient showing that this witness is qualified to give an opinion on HGN test and that he properly applied the technique.

P Your Honor, as pointed out in the witness's testimony, he has been certified by the State of Texas to administer the test and he has testified that he followed the procedures outlined in the pertinent official standards. We also draw your attention to the *Emerson* decision again, your Honor, at page 769 where the court addressed the issue of expertise in this area.

J Objection overruled.

P Officer, let me repeat the question. WHAT was the result of the HGN test? (10)

W The defendant failed the test. Of the six factors, he failed all six. Based upon that, I concluded that he was intoxicated.

P Based upon your testing, WHAT would you estimate the defendant's blood alcohol content to have been? (10)

O Objection, your Honor. That is clearly inadmissible evidence. May we approach the bench?

J Yes.

O The *Emerson* case clearly states, and we quote, at page 769, that the "witness may not use the HGN evidence to quantify the defendant's BAC."

J Objection sustained.

P Your Honor, we have no further questions of this witness.

§ 9-3(C)(3)(v) Sample Foundation—Radar Speedmeter

The fact situation is a speeding prosecution. The prosecutor charges that the defendant, Mr. Berton, was going 45 miles per hour on a street posted for 30 miles per hour. He presents the testimony of Officer Jones, who used a radar speedmeter to clock the defendant. Some judges might judicially notice the validity of the underlying theory and the reliability of speedmeters. But, for illustrative purposes, the prosecutor will call a witness to lay those elements of the foundation.

The prosecutor first calls Professor Jerold Harter. Assume that the professor has already identified himself.

P WHAT is your occupation? (1)

W I teach at the University of Texas at San Antonio.

P WHAT do you teach? (1)

W I teach physics and electronics.

P WHAT is your formal education? (1)

W I have a B.S. from Ohio State and both a master's and a doctorate from University of California, Davis.

P WHAT was your major area of study? (1)

W My specialty has been radar and electronics.

P HOW long have you been teaching? (1)

W For approximately 10 years.

P WHAT, if anything, have you published? (1)

W I've published roughly 20 articles, most of them dealing with radar and electronics.

P Professor, WHAT is the Doppler shift principle? (2)

W It's a theory about beams of microwaves. If a beam bounces off an approaching object, the frequency of the beam changes; the change is an increase, and it is proportional to the speed of the approaching object.

P WHAT would be a simple example of the operation of this principle? (2)

W Well, suppose that you're standing at a train station. A train is coming, and it's blowing its whistle. When the train is approaching you, the pitch of the whistle sounds higher. As soon as the train passes you and begins receding, the pitch sounds lower. The whistle, of course, hasn't changed. It's the Doppler shift principle which explains why it sounds as if the whistle is changing.

P WHAT experiments, if any, have been conducted to verify this theory? (2)

W You couldn't count the number. The theory is one of the most fundamental principles in the field.

P HOW widely is the principle accepted? (3)

W It's regarded as a truism, a basic principle. Everyone in the field knows about and accepts the principle.

P Now, professor, WHAT is a radar speedmeter? (4)

W It's a device for measuring the speed of cars.

P WHAT are the components of a radar speedmeter? (4)

W It has a component for transmitting a beam of microwaves and another component for receiving.

P HOW does the speedmeter work? (4)

W For example, the transmitter sends a beam toward an approaching vehicle. The beam strikes the vehicle, shifts, and then bounces back to the receiver. The receiver measures the change in frequency, and the speedmeter then reads out the speed of the approaching vehicle.

P WHAT experiments, if any, have been conducted to test the reliability of the speedmeter? (4)

W There have been numerous experiments, particularly some at Northwestern and the University of North Carolina.

P WHAT has been the outcome of these experiments? (4)

W If the instrument is in good condition and the operator is qualified, the instrument will give you a very reliable speed estimate.

P HOW widely is the radar speedmeter accepted? (5)

W It's used extensively, and its reliability is almost universally accepted.

The second witness will be the officer who used a radar speedmeter to clock the defendant. The officer has already testified that he arrived at the scene and set up his equipment.

P WHAT equipment were you using? (6)

W A General Electric radar speedmeter.

P WHAT training, if any, have you had in using a speedmeter? (6)

W I spent a week studying the speedmeter at the Police Academy.

P HOW did you study the speedmeter? (6)

W First, we had several lectures on the speedmeter and its operation. Then we saw demonstrations of its use. Finally, we participated in exercises where we used the speedmeter and more experienced officers double-checked us.

P HOW many times have you used the speedmeter? (6)

W Hundreds of times.

P HOW long have you used a speedmeter? (6)

W I've been assigned to Traffic for three years, and you use the speedmeter almost daily in traffic detail.

P WHAT did you do after you arrived at the scene? (7)

W I checked to ensure that the speedmeter was in working order.

P WHAT condition was the speedmeter in? (7)

W It was in good operational condition.

P HOW do you know that? (9)

W I used a tuning fork test.

P WHAT is the tuning fork test? (5), (7)

W The manufacturer supplies you with several tuning forks. I have 30, 45, and 60 mile per hour forks. You set them off, and the speedmeter is supposed to register those speeds.

P HOW did you conduct the test on this occasion? (7)

W I used all three forks, and the machine checked out all three times. It registered the right speed.

P WHAT did you do then? (8)

W I let the machine warm up and then aimed the transmitter down the road.

P WHAT happened after you aimed the transmitter? (10)

W I saw the defendant's car approaching.

P WHO is the defendant?

W He's the gentleman sitting at the table over there in the grey suit.

P Please let the record reflect that the witness has identified the defendant.

J It will so reflect.

P HOW long did you have to observe the defendant at the scene? (9)

W About three minutes. I saw him as he passed by, and then later, after we stopped him, I talked to him for several minutes.

P WHAT did you do when you saw the defendant's car approaching? (9)

W I checked to ensure that the speedmeter was on, and then I clocked his car.

P WHAT does "clocked" mean? (9)

W It means that I measured his speed.

P WHAT was the clocking? (10)

W The speedmeter flashed a signal that his car was going 45 miles per hour.

§ 9-3(D) Basis of Expert's Opinion—In General

The expert should now state the minor premise, the factual data to which the theory will be applied. Texas Evidence Rule 703 governs the possible bases for an expert's opinion:

> The facts or data in the particular case upon which an expert bases an opinion or inference may be those perceived by or [made known to him] [reviewed by the expert] at or before the hearing. If of a type reasonably relied upon by experts in the particular field in forming opinions or inferences upon the subject, the facts or data need not be admissible in evidence.

Thus, there are three possible bases for an expert's opinion. The following discussion addresses those three possible bases: facts known, hearsay information, and hypotheticals.

§ 9-3(E) Basis of Expert's Opinion—Facts Expert Personally Knows

§ 9-3(E)(1) The Doctrine

Texas Rule 703 allows an expert to base an opinion on facts of which the expert has personal or firsthand knowledge. For instance, doctors usually base their opinions in part on conditions and symptoms they personally observed during an examination of the patient.

§ 9-3(E)(2) Elements of the Foundation

The foundation for showing facts the expert personally knows ordinarily includes these elements:

1. Where the witness observed the fact(s).
2. When the witness observed the fact(s).
3. Who was present.
4. How the witness observed the fact(s).
5. A description of the fact(s) observed.

§ 9-3(E)(3) Sample Foundation

The preceding hypothetical *supra* at § 9-3(B)(3) with the neurologist, Dr. Worth, is continued. Dr. Worth is testifying on behalf of the plaintiff, Mr. Nowick, who sustained a severe brain injury as a result of an automobile collision.

P WHERE were you on the afternoon of July 11, of last year? (1), (2)

W In my office.

P WHAT, if anything, happened that afternoon? (3), (4)

W I conducted an examination of the plaintiff, Mr. Nowick.

P WHO is Mr. Nowick? (3)

W He's the gentleman sitting over there at the end of the table.

P HOW is he dressed? (3)

W He's wearing the white suit with the gray tie.

P Your Honor, please let the record reflect that the witness has identified the plaintiff, Mr. Nowick.

J The record will reflect that.

P WHO was present during this examination? (3)

W Just Mr. Nowick, myself, and my nurse, Ms. Cartwright.

P WHAT happened during the examination? (4)

W I personally examined the plaintiff for any symptoms of brain damage.

P HOW did you conduct the examination? (4)

W I conducted a manual inspection of his cranium and then administered a battery of standard eye and coordination tests.

P HOW long did this examination take? (4)

W A good three hours. I conducted a very thorough examination.

P WHAT, if anything, did you observe during the examination? (5)

W I saw some symptoms and signs of brain damage.

P WHAT were the symptoms? (5)

W For one thing, there was a deep scar on the front, right side of Mr. Nowick's head.

P HOW deep? (5)

W Almost an eighth of an inch into the surface—easily deep enough to cause some damage.

P WHAT else did you observe? (5)

W There was a sort of vacancy in the plaintiff's eyes, again possibly indicating brain problems. Finally, the plaintiff exhibited real difficulty in the eye-to-hand coordination tests.

§ 9-3(F) BASIS OF EXPERT'S OPINION—HEARSAY REPORTS

§ 9-3(F)(1) The Doctrine

Before promulgation of the Texas Rules of Evidence, experts were not permitted to rely on reports from third parties, such as other experts, if the reports did not fall within any hearsay exception.[19] The Texas Rules now indicate, however, that the expert may do so in certain circumstances. Rule 703 allows an expert to rely on otherwise inadmissible evidence "[i]f of a type reasonably relied upon by experts in the particular field in forming opinions or inferences upon the subject . . . ." This means, in effect, that otherwise inadmissible hearsay evidence may be relied upon by the expert in forming his or her opinion. It must be remembered that under Rule 703, the evidence of the report is not admitted as substantive proof of the report's truth, unless the report is otherwise admissible, for example, under a hearsay exception. Under Rule 703, the report is admitted for the limited purpose of showing the basis of the expert's opinion. The fact that the expert has heard and considered the report is some evidence that the opinion is well grounded. Consequently, upon request, the opponent is entitled to a Rule 105 limiting instruction by the trial judge. Note that Rule 705 makes specific provisions for balancing the probative value of otherwise inadmissible evidence which may have been used to form the basis for the expert's opinion.

The December 1, 2000 amendment to Federal Rule of Evidence 703 settled the question in federal practice by adding the second sentence to the rule. That sentence announces a general rule that the expert may not give the jury a detailed description of the otherwise inadmissible information.

---

[19] *See* WENDORF, SCHLUETER & BARTON, TEXAS RULES OF EVIDENCE MANUAL VII-59-60 (6th ed. 2002).

§ 9-3(F)(2) Elements of the Foundation

The foundation for showing that the expert relied on reports from third parties includes these elements:

1. The source of the third party report.
2. The facts or data in the report.
3. If the facts or data are otherwise inadmissible, they are nonetheless of the type reasonably relied upon by experts in the particular field.

§ 9-3(F)(3) Sample Foundation

The preceding hypothetical involving expert testimony about Mr. Nowick's medical condition continues:

P Dr. Worth, in addition to the symptoms you personally observed during your examination of Mr. Nowick, WHAT else have you considered? (1)

W For one thing, I talked to Mr. Nowick's family physician, Dr. Stiles.

P WHO is Dr. Stiles? (1)

W Maynard Stiles is a general practitioner here in town.

P HOW long has he been in practice here? (1)

W Maybe 15 years. He's a well-respected member of our local medical community.

P WHEN did you talk with him? (1)

W The day after I examined the plaintiff.

P WHY did you talk to him? (3)

W I had to get Mr. Nowick's medical history. Specifically, I wanted to know whether he had that scar or displayed the vacant stare or lack of coordination before his car accident.

P WHAT is the importance of the medical history? (3)

W You just can't make an intelligent diagnosis without that.

P WHAT is the customary medical practice concerning the use of medical history? (3)

W I followed the custom here. It would be malpractice not to gather the history and consider it in evaluating your diagnosis. Use of the history is good, accepted practice.

P WHAT did Dr. Stiles tell you about the plaintiff's medical history? (2)

W He said that prior to the accident, there was no scar on the plaintiff's cranium. Further, prior to the collision, the plaintiff had not exhibited the symptoms of either vacancy of stare or lack of coordination.

O Your Honor, I request a limiting instruction. Counsel has made no showing that this information is otherwise admissible. Consequently, it is not admissible as substantive evidence.

J Ladies and gentlemen of the jury, Dr. Worth has just referred to a statement made by a Dr. Stiles. You may not consider Dr. Stiles's statement as proof that before the accident, the plaintiff had no scar or vacant stare or lack of coordination. You may consider Dr. Stiles's statement only for the limited purpose of showing one factor or element Dr. Worth considered in arriving at his opinion.

§ 9-3(G) BASIS OF EXPERT'S OPINION—THE HYPOTHETICAL

Sometimes the testifying expert has neither examined the party nor even talked with an expert who has personally examined the party. The testifying expert may still express an opinion in response to a hypothetical question. In the hypothesis, the proponent specifies the facts he or she wants the expert to assume. The expert then relies on his or her expert knowledge and skill to draw a proper inference from the facts in the hypothesis. After promulgation of the Texas Rules of Evidence, there is really no need to rely on hypothetical questions. Under Rule 705, an expert need not disclose the basis for his or her opinion during direct examination. In criminal cases, however, the opponent may request a voir dire examination, out of the presence of the jury, to determine the basis for the expert's opinion.

There are two potential limitations on hypothetical questions. The first limitation is that the trial court may limit the elements in the hypothetical question to testimony and exhibits which have already been introduced to support a finding that the assumed facts exist. The trial judge may permit the proponent to vary the order of proof and introduce proof of the assumed facts later. The second potential limitation is that the trial court may require the proponent to include disputed, material facts. The reason for this limitation is obvious. If the hypothesis is incomplete and omits critical facts, the ultimate opinion will be misleading rather than helpful.

Hypothetical questions can take two forms. In the first form, the proponent specifies the historical facts he or she wants the expert to assume. For example, the proponent could say:

P Dr. Worth, please assume the following facts as true. One, in the accident, the plaintiff sustained a cut three inches in length and one-eighth of an inch in depth on the right, front part of his head. Two, the plaintiff bled profusely from that cut. Three, immediately after the accident, the plaintiff began experiencing sharp, painful headaches in the right, front part of his head.

In the second form, the proponent asks the witness to assume the truth of the testimony of another witness or witnesses. Assume, for instance, that the ambulance attendant, Mr. Phelan, has already testified. During his testimony, Mr. Phelan stated that he observed the cut on plaintiff's head, noted the bleeding, and heard plaintiff complain about a headache. The plaintiff now calls Dr. Worth.

P Dr. Worth, WHERE were you this morning?

W Here in the courtroom.[20]

P WHAT were you doing?

W Listening to the testimony.

P WHOSE testimony did you listen to?

W Mr. Phelan, the ambulance attendant, was on the stand most of the morning.

P HOW well could you hear his testimony?

W Very well. I had no problems hearing what he was saying.

P Specifically, WHERE were you sitting?

W In the first row reserved for spectators.

P HOW often did you leave the room during Mr. Phelan's testimony?

W I didn't leave. I stayed in the courtroom the whole time.

P Dr. Worth, please assume the truth of Mr. Phelan's testimony about Mr. Nowick's condition immediately after the accident.

This form of hypothetical question is problematic. First, this form is ambiguous and may make it difficult for the jurors to determine the specific facts the expert witness is assuming. Second, if the proponent invites the expert to assume the truth of several witnesses' testimony and there are any conflicts between those witnesses' testimony, the proponent is really asking the expert to resolve those conflicts. In effect, the proponent is asking the expert to usurp the jury's function. This form, if used at all, should be used only where the assumed testimony is simple and internally consistent.

§ 9-3(H) THE STATEMENT OF THE OPINION ITSELF

§ 9-3(H)(1) The Doctrine

In the next part of the expert's testimony, the proponent should elicit the ultimate opinion. There is authority in Texas that the medical expert vouch that his or her opinion is "reasonably certain." The witness must be willing to testify

---

[20] This assumes that if one of the parties has invoked "The Rule" and has excluded all the witnesses from the courtroom, counsel is able to show a necessity for letting this witness remain. *See* TEX. R. EVID. 614.

that he or she has formed the opinion to a reasonable medical or scientific certainty. Other jurisdictions have abandoned these formal limitations. As long as the opinion is likely to be helpful to the jurors, these jurisdictions allow an expert to state a possibility, probability, or certainty.

There is now also authority in Texas case law which permits the expert to express an opinion on mixed questions of law and fact. That is, an expert may testify on matters such as proximate cause, negligence, gross negligence, and reckless conduct. Citing Rule 704, the Texas Supreme Court has indicated that such opinions are admissible if they are confined to the relevant facts and are based upon proper legal concepts.[21]

§ 9-3(H)(2) Elements of the Foundation

The complete foundation for the opinion includes these elements:

1. The witness has formed an opinion.
2. The witness states the opinion.
3. [*In cases involving medical opinions, the witness believes that the opinion is a reasonable medical or scientific certainty.*]

§ 9-3(H)(3) Sample Foundation

The preceding hypothetical fact situation concerning Mr. Nowick's medical condition continues:

P Dr. Worth, do you have an opinion as to whether Mr. Nowick suffered brain damage? (1)

W Yes.

P HOW positive are you of your opinion? (3)

W I'm fairly confident in it. I think that any competent neurologist would reach the same conclusion.

P WHAT is the degree of your certainty? (3)

W You can't treat this sort of question as an absolute, but I'm reasonably certain of my conclusion.

P WHAT is that conclusion? (2)

W In my opinion, Mr. Nowick has suffered permanent brain damage, located in the right, front part of his cranium.

P Doctor Worth, do you have an opinion on what caused the brain injury to Mr. Nowick? (1)

---

21 This assumes that if one of the parties has invoked "The Rule" and has excluded all of the witnesses from the courtroom, counsel is able to show a necessity for letting this witness remain. *See* TEX. R. EVID. 614.

W Yes, I do.

P WHAT is your opinion? (2)

W In my opinion, Mr. Nowick's injury was the direct result of the accident.

§ 9-3(I) THE EXPLANATION OF THE OPINION

§ 9-3(I)(1) The Doctrine

Evidence law does not require that the expert explain the opinion. Common sense tells the proponent, however, that unless the expert explains the opinion, the jurors will not be persuaded. The proponent cannot expect the jurors to make a blind act of faith in the expert. As a practical matter, the jury is unlikely to attach much weight to the opinion unless the expert explains his or her reasoning process in plausible, common sense terms. Consequently, the customary practice is for the proponent to invite the expert to explain the opinion. The expert should explain the opinion in general terms and specifically relate the opinion to the bases the expert previously recited. The opinion will be most persuasive if the expert can show the jurors that the opinion is firmly grounded in the facts that are the bases of the opinion.

§ 9-3(I)(2) Elements of the Foundation

In short, the foundation for this last part of the expert's testimony consists of two elements:

1. In general terms, the expert explains the opinion.
2. The expert explains the significance of each basis of the opinion. The expert demonstrates how each basis contributes to and supports the opinion.

§ 9-3(I)(3) Sample Foundation

The preceding hypothetical regarding Mr. Nowick finally concludes:

P Dr. Worth, WHY did you reach that conclusion? (1)

W The symptoms evidence the existence of brain damage, and the medical history discloses only one possible cause.

P WHAT symptoms are you referring to? (2)

W Well, the scar, the vacancy of gaze, and the lack of eye-to-hand coordination.

P WHAT is the significance of those symptoms? (2)

W The scar is deep enough to indicate a wound that probably would have applied damaging pressure to the brain. The part of the brain located under the scar is the part that controls vision and eye-to-hand coordination. The other symptoms of vacant stare and lack of manual coordination confirm that pressure in fact was applied, with resulting damage.

P WHAT medical history, if any, are you relying on? (2)

W My consultation with Dr. Stiles and the plaintiff's hospital records.

P WHAT is the significance of the medical history? (2)

W It establishes the causation. The scar was apparently inflicted in the accident. The other symptoms didn't exist before the accident. They arose immediately after the accident. The timing is conclusive in my mind.

Chapter 10
The Hearsay Rule and Its Exemptions

PART 1
THE HEARSAY RULE

§ 10-1 INTRODUCTION

The hearsay doctrine is the last major exclusionary doctrine based on doubt about the reliability of a type of evidence. The best evidence rule's underlying rationale is a fear of secondary evidence. The opinion rule expresses the courts' doubts about the reliability of opinions. Underlying the hearsay rule is a fear about the reliability of in-court testimony about out-of-court statements when the proponent is attempting to use the statements as evidence in the case. The common law prefers that the third party (the declarant) appear in court and subject himself or herself to cross-examination. The common law assumes that evidence will be more trustworthy if the declarant testifies under oath, in the jury's view, and subject to cross-examination. The opponent may use cross-examination to expose any errors of perception, memory, narration, or sincerity.

Lay persons commonly think that the hearsay rule applies to any out-of-court statement. In truth, the rule has a relatively narrow scope. Evidence constitutes hearsay only if it is (1) a statement (2) by an out-of-court declarant (3) offered to prove the truth of the assertion. Texas Evidence Rule 801 follows this view. The rationale for the Rule explains the Rule's limited scope. We are interested in the declarant's credibility only when the out-of-court statement is being used to prove the truth of the assertion. That is, the Rule comes into play whenever the proponent is asking the jury to believe, as true, what was said or written. In that circumstance, the evidence's value depends on the credibility of the out-of-court declarant. For example, suppose that an in-court witness testifies that an out-of-court declarant said that the defendant's car ran a red light. The plaintiff wants to offer the testimony for the purpose of showing that, in fact, the defendant's car ran the red light. For that purpose, the testimony's value depends upon the perception and memory of the out-of-court declarant. The opponent thus needs to cross-examine the out-of-court declarant to test the evidence.

On the other hand, if the proponent does not offer the out-of-court declaration for its truth, the opponent does not need to cross-examine the declarant. If the declaration is logically relevant on some other theory, the evidence's value usually depends on the credibility of the in-court witness. Suppose that the plaintiff has sued a defendant for slander. The plaintiff alleges that the defendant repeated the slanderous statement to *X*. The plaintiff calls *X*, the in-court witness, to testify that the defendant made an out-of-court statement that the plaintiff bribed a public official. The plaintiff does not want to offer the statement for its truth. Quite to the contrary, if the defendant can show that the statement is true, the defendant has a complete defense to tort liability. The plaintiff wants to show only that at a particular time and place, the defendant made the slanderous statement. The value of *X*'s testimony depends on *X*'s credibility. Did *X* hear the statement correctly? Does *X* remember the statement correctly? If *X* testifies in court, the defendant can test the value of the evidence. Hence, the limitation on the hearsay rule's scope is a corollary of the rule's rationale: the rule is limited to statements offered to prove their truth because then and only then does the opponent need to cross-examine the out-of-court declarant.

Even if a statement falls within the definition of hearsay, the statement may be admissible. There are numerous exemptions from, and exceptions to, the hearsay rule. Texas Rule 801(e) sets out the admission and witness-declarant exemptions, and Texas Rules 803 and 804 contain a lengthy list of exceptions. Part 2 of this chapter discusses the admission and witness-declarant exemptions. As that discussion explains, to bring a statement within the admission exemption, the proponent need not show that the statement was reliable or that there is any necessity for resorting to the statement. All the proponent has to do is to show that the statement should be imputed to the party-opponent.

Chapter 11 describes a series of hearsay exceptions based primarily on an inference of the reliability of the statement and also addresses a number of exceptions resting in large part on a showing of necessity. All of these exceptions require proof that the out-of-court declarant is unavailable at the time of trial.

§ 10-2 THE DEFINITION OF HEARSAY—IN GENERAL

As previously stated, the definition of *hearsay* is narrow. Texas Evidence Rule 801(d) states that "[h]earsay is a statement, other than one made by the declarant while testifying at the trial or hearing, offered in evidence to prove the truth of the matter asserted." Rule 801(a) adds that "[a] 'statement' is (1) an oral or written expression or (2) nonverbal conduct of a person, if it is intended by him as a substitute for verbal expression."

Under the Texas Rules, evidence constitutes hearsay only if three conditions are present:

1. The evidence is either a written or oral statement or an act intended as a substitute for a statement;
2. The statement was made or the act was committed by a person out of court; and
3. The evidence is being used to prove the truth of the statement or act.

Evidence falls within the hearsay definition only if all three elements are present. If any element is missing, the evidence is not hearsay, and there is no need to search for a hearsay exemption or exception. Thus, the option for the proponent seeking to introduce an out-of-court statement is to show that the statement does not satisfy the *hearsay definition*. If this is not possible, the next option is to establish that an *exemption* exists. That failing, the proponent should be prepared to show that an *exception* applies. Note that the judge decides, under Rule 104(a), whether the offered evidence is hearsay.

The next sections examine each of the three elements of the hearsay definition.

§ 10-3 THE DEFINITION OF HEARSAY—A "STATEMENT"

§ 10-3(A) THE DOCTRINE

§ 10-3(A)(1) Verbal or Written Expressions

Under Rule 801(a), a "statement" consists of a written or verbal expression. Thus, any oral statements or written statements potentially fall within the definition of hearsay. The question is whether any verbal or written expression constitutes a statement.

All courts agree that explicit, assertive expressions fall within the hearsay definition. Thus, the oral or written statement, "The road was wet," would normally fall within the definition. It must be remembered, however, that not all statements are assertive. Grammar rules indicate that there are four types of sentences: declarative, imperative, exclamatory, and interrogatory. As a practical matter, only declarative sentences, or statements, ordinarily fall within the hearsay definition. They declare or assert facts, including states of mind. Imperative statements giving orders, exclamations, and questions usually fall outside the hearsay definition. There is little or no need to cross-examine the declarant of an imperative, exclamatory, or interrogatory sentence about perception or memory.

Texas Rule 801, however, is written in such a manner to raise the possibility that an order, exclamation, or question might constitute a statement for purposes of the hearsay rule. While Federal Rule 801 uses the term "assertion," the Texas Rule uses the broader term "expression," which could include something other than an assertive, declarative statement.

§ 10-3(A)(2) Nonverbal Conduct Amounting to a "Statement"

Sometimes a person intends an act to be a true substitute for speech. For instance, persons sometimes nod or shake their heads in response to questions. In principle, these acts should be treated in the same fashion as verbal hearsay statements. These acts present the same probative dangers of perception, memory, narration, and sincerity. For this reason, all courts agree that like assertive statements, assertive acts fall within the hearsay definition. Texas Evidence Rule 801(a)(2) is illustrative. That rule includes within the hearsay definition "nonverbal conduct of a person, if it is intended by the person as an assertion."

§ 10-3(B) Elements of the Foundation

To show that an expression is not a statement within Rule 801(a), the proponent should be prepared to establish that:

1. The offered evidence is not a written or verbal expression; or
2. If the offered evidence is nonverbal conduct, it did not amount to an intentional substitute for a verbal expression.

§ 10-3(C) Sample Foundation

The following hypothetical illustrates the scope of the hearsay definition. The fact situation is a robbery prosecution. The witness is a police officer. The officer, Patrolman Glancy, has already identified himself. He testifies that he investigated the crime, interviewed the victim, and brought the victim to the police station. Assume that under these facts a witness's prior identification of a person is not admissible to bolster the witness's credibility. The proponent is the prosecutor.

P WHAT happened after you took the victim, Mr. Clayton, to the police station?

W I talked to him, and then I took him to the lineup room.

P WHAT is the lineup room?

W It's the room in the station where we permit victims and eyewitnesses to view suspects. We hope that they can pick the criminal out of the lineup parade.

P WHAT happened after you took Mr. Clayton into the interview room?

O Your Honor, I object to that question on the ground that it calls for hearsay.

P Your Honor, may we approach the bench?

J Yes.

P Your Honor, the witness is prepared to testify that at the lineup, Mr. Clayton became visibly shaken and nervous and left the room without saying anything. The evidence can't be hearsay because Mr. Clayton didn't say anything.

O Mr. Clayton's actions are an assertive act, your Honor. Assertive acts fall within the hearsay definition under Rule 801(a). Further, the prosecutor is clearly attempting to use this evidence to show that the victim's actions amounted to a statement that the person who attacked him is in the lineup.

P Your Honor, Rule 801(a)(2) indicates that in order to constitute a statement for purposes of the hearsay rule, the declarant must have intended to use his or her action as a substitute for a verbal expression. Here, the victim's actions were not intended as a substitute. In effect, the nervous reaction was involuntary. I agree with counsel, we do want the jury to hear about the victim's reaction upon viewing the lineup. But if the victim did not say anything, the hearsay definition is incomplete and the hearsay objection is not available to the defense.

J Under Rule 104(a), I find that the act was not subjectively intended to be the functional equivalent of an assertive statement. The objection will be overruled.

§ 10-4 THE DEFINITION OF HEARSAY—"OUT-OF-COURT DECLARANT"

§ 10-4(A) THE DOCTRINE

The second key element to the definition of hearsay is the requirement that the statement was made by an out-of-court declarant. This element includes the definition of *declarant* and the definition of *out-of-court.*

§ 10-4(A)(1) "Declarant"

Texas Rule 801(b) defines declarant as "a person who makes a statement." Thus, bloodhounds, clocks, and machines are not considered declarants for purposes of the hearsay rule.[1] Only people can make hearsay statements. Thus, what a clock or meteorological instrument "says" is not hearsay. That is not to say, however, that devices such as computers may not be implicated in the hearsay definition. For example, if a person has entered data or information, i.e., statements, into a computer, a printout of that data would be a statement by a "declarant" within the definition of Rule 801(a).

§ 10-4(A)(2) "Out-of-Court"

The term *out-of-court* addresses the time and location of the statement. Any statements made outside *this courtroom* are potentially hearsay, regardless of the fact that the speaker is now in this courtroom as a witness.

Assume that the proponent is offering testimony about an out-of-court statement for the truth of the assertion. Offering the evidence for that purpose creates an acute need to cross-examine the declarant about his or her perception, memory, and other testimonial qualities. Suppose, however, that the declarant becomes a witness at trial. If so, the opposing attorney can cross-examine the person both about the person's in-court testimony and about his or her earlier out-of-court statements. The person's current availability seemingly satisfies the need for

[1] *See* Schlueter, *Criminal Evidence: Hearsay—When Machines Talk,* 53 TEX. B.J. 1135 (Oct. 1990).

cross-examination. Does the person's current availability for cross-examination remove the earlier statements from the definition of hearsay? Not necessarily.

The traditional view is "once an out-of-court declarant, always an out-of-court declarant." If the person was not on the stand when he or she made the statement, it is immaterial that the person later becomes a witness and subjects himself or herself to cross-examination. Consider this example. On Monday, Jones tells a friend that the he saw the defendant's car run the red light. On Tuesday, Jones becomes a witness in the suit between plaintiff and defendant. Jones testifies that he saw the defendant's car run the red light. To increase the impact of the testimony, the plaintiff's attorney attempts to elicit the Jones's testimony that on Monday, Jones told the friend the same story. If the proponent attempts to use Jones's statement on Monday as substantive proof of the defendant's fault, the statement is hearsay. Although Jones is now the witness, Jones was not on the witness stand when he made the statement being offered into evidence.

As discussed *infra* at § 10-7(A), Texas Rule 801(e) recognizes that under limited circumstances, a witness's prior out-of-court statement may be admissible as "nonhearsay" if certain criteria are satisfied.

§ 10-4(B) ELEMENTS OF THE FOUNDATION

To establish this part of the hearsay definition, counsel must show the following:

1. The offered statement was made by a person.
2. At the time the statement was made, the person was not in this courtroom.

§ 10-4(C) SAMPLE FOUNDATION

The following hypothetical centers on a chemical plant explosion. One of the issues at trial is the exact temperature reading in boiler #21 just before the explosion. The plaintiff has alleged that the company was negligent in not shutting down the boiler when it learned that the internal temperatures had reached a danger zone. Mr. Wilson, the plant safety manager, is on the stand as a witness for the defendant to show that just before the explosion, the temperature readings were in the normal range for that boiler. The proponent is the defendant.

P Mr. Wilson, when you arrived in the control room, WHAT did you do?

W I walked over to the temperature gauges and read the readings.

P And WHAT was the temperature reading for boiler #21?

O Your Honor, I object. The question clearly calls for hearsay information.

P Your Honor, this is not hearsay. Rule of Evidence 801(b) clearly states that only persons can be hearsay declarants. The temperature gauge was not a "declarant." (1)

J Objection overruled.

P Mr. Wilson, let me repeat the question. WHAT did the temperature gauge say?

W It read 260 degrees.

P And WHAT time was it when you read the gauge?

W I looked at the clock in the control room and it said that it was 2:06 P.M.

O We object again, your Honor. This is hearsay.

J Objection overruled.

P WHAT did you do next?

W I turned to my assistant manager and told him . . .

O Objection, hearsay, your Honor.

J Counsel?

P Your Honor, we are offering this statement to confirm the witness's reading of the temperature gauge. We offer to prove that the witness immediately told his assistant manager what the temperature was at a crucial time. He is only repeating what he himself said and he is now subject to cross-examination.

O Your Honor, that is clearly hearsay. The fact that the declarant, Mr. Wilson, is now on the stand does not satisfy the hearsay rule. The key is that at the time he made the statement in question he was not on the stand in this court. (2) Thus, his statement clearly constitutes an out-of-court statement. And, because counsel is offering it for the truth of the matter asserted, the hearsay definition is satisfied.

J Objection sustained.

§ 10-5 THE STATEMENT IS OFFERED FOR A HEARSAY PURPOSE—PROVING THE TRUTH OF THE MATTER ASSERTED

§ 10-5(A) THE DOCTRINE

§ 10-5(A)(1) In General

The third element of the hearsay definition focuses on why the statement is being offered by the proponent. Assuming the offered statement was made by an out-of-court declarant, the statement is not hearsay unless the proponent offers the statement to prove the truth of the assertion.

Offering the statement for that purpose creates the need to cross-examine the declarant about perception or memory. This step in hearsay analysis parallels the second step in best evidence analysis: just as the best evidence rule does not come into play unless the writing's terms are in issue, a statement is not hearsay unless the proponent offers the statement to prove the truth of an assertion contained in the statement. The statement is deemed hearsay only when the immediate inference the proponent wants to draw is the truth of the assertion in the statement.

If the proponent can demonstrate that the statement is logically relevant on any other theory, the statement is nonhearsay. When the proponent offers the statement for a nonhearsay purpose, we are primarily interested simply in the fact that the statement was made. The only need to cross-examine is the need to question on the stand the witness who heard the statement made.

§ 10-5(A)(2) Implied Assertions

Normally, a statement is measured at its face value in determining whether it amounts to hearsay. Thus, if the declarant said, "It's cold," the statement would be treated as an explicit assertion by the declarant. But what if, instead of that explicit assertion, the declarant said, "I am going to wear my heavy coat this morning?" Is that hearsay? The answer depends on what use the proponent intends to make of the statement. Under Texas Rule 801(c), it would be considered as being offered for a hearsay purpose if the proponent wanted the jury to believe that the declarant thought it was cold outside and therefore it must have been cold at the time the statement was made. Rule 801(c) states: "[m]atter asserted includes any matter explicitly asserted, and any matter implied by a statement, if the probative value of the statement as offered flows from the declarant's belief as to the matter."

A classic English case, *Wright v. Tatham,*[2] is considered the genesis of the implied assertion doctrine. The facts were these: The issue was a testator's mental capacity to execute his will. The proponent of the will was attempting to prove that the testator was mentally competent. To prove that point, the proponent offered to show that several persons had written serious business letters to the testator. Although the act of writing the letter incidentally involved assertions in the letters, the act itself was nonassertive. The persons did not subjectively intend their act to substitute for the verbal statement that the testator was competent. The authors of the letters assumed that the testator was competent, and the proponent of the will offered the evidence to show the truth of their

[2] 5 Clark & Finley 670 (House of Lords 1838).

assumption and belief. The proponent of the will reasoned that they would not have mailed the testator serious letters unless they believed he was competent. And if they, his close acquaintances, believed him to be competent, he probably was competent. The English court held that the evidence fell within the hearsay definition. The court indicated that even though the act was nonassertive, it presented probative dangers of perception and memory. This case was the landmark case for the traditional common-law view that evidence of a nonassertive act is hearsay if (1) the act is apparently actuated or prompted by a certain belief, and (2) the proponent offers the evidence to prove the truth of the belief.

Although the trend in the statutes and case law has been to the contrary, Texas Rule of Evidence 801(c) adopts the rule in *Wright* to the extent that the probative value of the statements in the letters flowed from the writers' beliefs that the reader of the letters was sane. The Texas drafters apparently did not intend to extend the implied assertions doctrine to nonassertive acts.[3] Reading Rules 801(c) and 801(a) together, an implied assertion arises only when there is a verbal expression or an act which was intended as a substitute for a verbal expression.[4]

§ 10-5(A)(3) Common Nonhearsay Uses of Statements

There are three common nonhearsay uses of out-of-court statements. First, the proponent may argue that the statement is circumstantial evidence of the declarant's state of mind. If the declarant's state of mind is logically relevant in the case, the proponent may use the declarant's statements as circumstantial proof of such states of mind as malice, hatred, premeditation, and love. Sometimes the mere fact that a person makes a certain statement gives us insight into that person's frame of mind.

Second, the statement may be an operative fact or verbal act in the case. In some situations, legal consequences flow directly from the use of certain words such as the offer in a contract suit or the slander in a tort action. Again, the mere fact that the declarant uttered the words is logically relevant. The words themselves have legal consequences. Examples of this type of use would be any document which had independent legal significance, such as a contract, a will, a trust instrument, and commercial paper instruments.

Third, the proponent can prove the statement to show its effect on the state of mind of the hearer or reader. For example, if it is disputed whether the

---

[3] TEXAS RULES OF EVIDENCE HANDBOOK, 20 HOUS. L. REV. 477, 492 (1983).

[4] Note that Federal Rule 801 excludes this evidence, sometimes called Morgan hearsay, from its hearsay definition. *See, e.g.*, Morgan, *Hearsay Dangers and the Application of the Hearsay Concept*, 62 HARV. L. REV. 177 (1948). The Advisory Committee for the Federal Rule took the position that the dangers of this type of evidence are minimal in the absence of an intent to assert and do not justify the loss of the evidence on hearsay grounds. *See also* Park, *"I Didn't Tell Them Anything About You": Implied Assertions as Hearsay Under the Federal Rules of Evidence*, 74 MINN. L. REV. 783 (1990).

defendant knew of a certain dangerous condition, it is logically relevant to prove that someone told him of the condition. Quite apart from the truth of the third party's statement, the statement puts the defendant on notice. A classic example of nonhearsay use is information relied upon by the police in developing probable cause.

§ 10-5(B) ELEMENTS OF THE FOUNDATION

When the proponent is going to argue a nonhearsay theory for admitting a statement, the foundation includes these elements:

1. Where the statement was made.
2. When the statement was made.
3. Who was present.
4. The tenor of the statement.
5. In an offer of proof, the proponent states that he or she intends to use the statement for a nonhearsay purpose.
6. In the same offer of proof, the proponent shows that under nonhearsay theory, the statement is logically relevant.

§ 10-5(C) SAMPLE FOUNDATIONS

The following hypothetical demonstrate several nonhearsay uses of out-of-court statements. The final hypothetical focuses on the topic of implied assertions.

§ 10-5(C)(1) The Statement Is Circumstantial Proof of the Declarant's State of Mind—Mental Output

The fact situation is a dispute over title to real property. The decedent, Joan Furlow, formerly owned the land. Before she died, she gave her nephew, Garrett Furlow, a deed to the property; she gave him the deed on April 14, 1998. The executor claims that although Ms. Furlow gave Garrett the deed, she did not intend the deed to be immediately effective. And because she did not have the intent required by real property law, the deed was ineffective. The nephew calls Ms. Barbara Peterson as a witness. Ms. Peterson identifies herself and states that she knew the decedent for several years. The nephew is the proponent.

P WHERE were you on April 13, 1998? (1), (2)

W I was visiting Joan at her house on Dwight Street.

P WHO else was there? (3)

W Only the two of us.

P WHAT happened while you were there? (4)

W We just had a nice chat.

P WHAT did you chat about? (4)

W A lot of things, including Joan's nephew, Garrett.

P WHAT did Ms. Furlow say about her nephew, Garrett? (4)

O Your Honor, I object to that question on the ground that it calls for hearsay.

P Your Honor, may we approach the bench?

J Yes.

P Your Honor, I offer to prove that Ms. Peterson will testify that Ms. Furlow said that her nephew was a man in a million. (4) I want to offer that testimony for a nonhearsay purpose, as circumstantial proof of Ms. Furlow's affection for Garrett. (5) The testimony is logically relevant to show that she had donative intent when she gave him the deed the next day. (6)

J The objection will be overruled. I will admit the evidence for that nonhearsay purpose.

P Ms. Peterson, let me repeat the question. WHAT did Ms. Furlow say about her nephew, Garrett? (4)

W She said that he was a man in a million.

O Your Honor, I request a limiting instruction.

J Yes. Ladies and gentlemen of the jury, you have just heard Ms. Peterson's testimony about Ms. Furlow's statement. I am admitting the evidence of Ms. Furlow's statement only for the purpose of showing Ms. Furlow's state of mind, her feeling of affection for her nephew.

Given the trial judge's limiting instruction, during closing argument the proponent's attorney could legitimately use the testimony about the decedent's statement to prove her donative intent:

> Ladies and gentlemen, in her instructions the judge informed you that we need to prove that on April 14, 1998, when Ms. Furlow handed Garrett the deed to the house on Dwight Street, she actually intended to make a gift to Garrett. Think back to Ms. Peterson's testimony. She told you that on April 13th—one day before—Ms. Furlow told her that Garrett was a man in a million. Obviously, you don't have to decide whether Garrett is one man in a million. However, the fact that Ms. Furlow said that the day before tells you how much affection she had for her nephew Garrett—such strong affection and love that she wanted him to have the property on Dwight Street.

§ 10-5(C)(2) The Statement is an Operative Fact or Verbal Act

In this hypothetical, the plaintiff, Mr. Hernandez, owns a farm that he leased to Mr. Shotz. There are a number of large bins on the ranch for storing sorghum, and Mr. Shotz intends to use the ranch to raise sorghum. Mr. Shotz falls behind in his rent and enters into an agreement with Mr. Hernandez. Under the agreement, Mr. Hernandez will accept the sorghum stored in two bins, numbers five and seven, in lieu of rent due for June and July. When they enter into the agreement at the ranch, Mr. Shotz says, "It's a deal. The sorghum in bins five and seven is yours." In this suit for conversion of the sorghum, Mr. Hernandez has taken the stand to testify about the deal he had with Mr. Shotz. He explained that he was Mr. Shotz's landlord, and testifies that Mr. Shotz was delinquent on his rent. The plaintiff is the proponent.

P Mr. Hernandez, WHERE were you on the afternoon of July 6th? (1), (2)

W I was at the ranch, the one I rented to Mr. Shotz.

P WHO else was there? (3)

W Shotz was the only one around. I didn't see his wife or kids.

P WHY were you there? (4)

W As I said, he'd fallen behind in his rent. He was supposed to pay at the beginning of the month, and he'd missed the June and July payments. I asked him what he intended to do about the delinquent rent.

P WHAT happened when you asked him that? (4)

W He offered me a deal.

O Your Honor, I move to strike that last answer on the ground that it is hearsay.

P Your Honor, may we approach the bench?

J Yes.

P Your Honor, I offer to prove that Mr. Hernandez will testify that Mr. Shotz offered to give my client the sorghum in two bins, numbers five and seven, in exchange for the delinquent rent. (4) I want to use the statement for a nonhearsay purpose, namely, to show the offer itself. (5) The words constituting the offer are an operative fact or verbal act. Legal consequences flow simply from the fact that Mr. Shotz uttered those words. (6)

J The motion will be denied.

P Mr. Hernandez, let me repeat the question. WHAT happened when you asked him about the delinquent rent? (4)

W He offered to give me the sorghum in two bins in exchange for the late rent.

P WHAT were his words? (4)

W As best I recall, he said, "It's a deal. The sorghum in bins five and seven is yours."

P WHAT did you say then? (4)

W I just said that I accepted the offer, and we shook on it.

§ 10-5(C)(3) The Effect of the Statement on the Mind of the Hearer or Reader—Mental Input

Suppose that the plaintiff, Mr. Arneson, alleges that the defendant has been negligent in two respects. First, the defendant was speeding. Second, the defendant carelessly drove the car although he knew that the car had bad brakes. Under the second theory, one issue would be whether the defendant knew that the brakes were defective. The plaintiff calls Mr. John Horne. Mr. Horne testifies that he manages the auto repair shop near the defendant's house. Mr. Horne adds that on January 14th, the defendant dropped off his car for regular maintenance and that he picked it up two days later, on the 16th. Several days later the defendant was involved in an automobile accident. The plaintiff is the proponent.

P Mr. Horne, WHERE were you on January 16th of this year? (1), (2)

W I was at my repair shop.

P WHO else was there? (3)

W We had several customers, including the defendant.

P WHAT happened when the defendant came into the shop? (4)

W He was there to pick up his car.

P WHAT happened while he was there? (4)

W He got the car, and we talked for a while.

P WHAT did you talk about? (4)

W Mostly his car.

P WHAT did you tell him about the car? (4)

O Your Honor, I object to that question on the ground that it calls for hearsay.

P Your Honor, may we approach the bench?

J Yes.

P Your Honor, I offer to prove that the witness will testify that he told the defendant his brakes were bad. (4) I want to use the witness's prior statement for a nonhearsay purpose, namely, to show its effect on the defendant's state of mind. It gave him knowledge that his brakes were bad. (5) Under our second cause of action, this evidence is logically relevant. Our second cause of action is that the defendant negligently drove the car when he knew it had defective brakes. (6)

J The objection will be overruled.

P Mr. Horne, let me repeat the question. WHAT did you tell defendant about his car? (4)

W I told him that the brakes were bad and could go out any time.

P HOW close were you standing to the defendant when you told him that?

W Only a foot or two away.

P HOW noisy was the repair shop at the time?

W It was very quiet.

P HOW were you facing when you told him about his brakes?

W I was talking right at him.

P WHO else was talking to him at the time?

W No one else. We were the only two talking.

P HOW did he react when you told him about the bad brakes?

W He nodded his head, shrugged his shoulders, and got into his car.

O Your Honor, I request a limiting instruction.

J Yes. Ladies and gentlemen of the jury, you have just heard the witness's testimony that he told the defendant that the defendant's brakes were bad. You may not consider the witness's testimony as evidence that in fact, the brakes were bad. You may consider the witness's testimony only in deciding whether the next day, the defendant knew the car was defective and acted negligently in driving the car. If other evidence in this case establishes that the brakes were bad, then and only then may you consider the witness's testimony, and then only in deciding whether the next day, the defendant knew the brakes were bad and acted negligently in driving the car.

Of course, to get to the jury, the proponent will have to introduce other, independent evidence that the brakes were defective. The plaintiff could call the repairman who actually worked on the brakes to describe the condition of the brakes. It is clear, however, that the plaintiff could use Mr. Horne's testimony for the limited, nonhearsay purpose of proving that the defendant knew of the brakes' hazardous condition.

Thus, in closing argument, the plaintiff's attorney might state:

In his instructions to you, the judge told you that we have the burden of proving that before the collision, the defendant knew that his brakes were bad. Ladies and gentlemen, we've proven that. Remember the testimony by Mr. Horne, the owner of the repair shop that the defendant took his car to. Mr. Horne told you that on January 16th—several days before the accident—he had a conversation with the defendant. Mr. Horne added that in that conversation, he told the defendant point blank that the defendant's brakes were bad and could go out at anytime. When the defendant drove away from Mr. Horne's shop, the defendant knew good and well that his brakes were defective.

§ 10-5(C)(4) Implied Assertions—Relevancy Flows from Declarant's Belief

The following hypothetical illustrates the doctrine of implied assertions. Whether the assertions are hearsay depends on how the proponent intends to use them. This fact situation is an adaptation of the basic fact situation in *Wright*, discussed *supra* at § 10-5(A)(2), which gave rise to the doctrine. The testator is the decedent, Mr. Marsden. The decedent owned a large car dealership. The proponent of the will is Mr. Wright. Mr. Wright calls Mr. Toscher as a witness. Mr. Toscher owns a janitorial services company. Mr. Wright wants to show that Mr. Toscher sent Mr. Marsden a serious business proposal for janitorial services on the decedent's car lot. During closing argument, Mr. Wright's attorney wants to use Mr. Toscher's conduct as evidence of Mr. Marsden's competency: Mr. Toscher would not have sent Mr. Marsden the letter unless he believed that Mr. Marsden was mentally competent. Mr. Toscher has already identified himself and stated his line of business.

P Mr. Toscher, WHERE were you on the morning of April 16th of last year?

W In my office in downtown Lubbock.

P WHAT were you doing there?

W I was getting some bids ready on some new contracts for janitorial services.

P WHAT did you do after you finished the bids?

W I mailed them.

P WHOM did you mail them to?

W Several people, including the decedent, Mr. Marsden.

O Your Honor, I move to strike the last question and answer on the ground that they are irrelevant.

P Your Honor, may we approach the bench?

J Yes.

P Your Honor, the evidence shows that Mr. Toscher mailed a serious business proposal to Mr. Marsden. That conduct shows Mr. Toscher's belief in Mr. Marsden's mental competency. He wouldn't have mailed him that sort of letter unless he thought Mr. Marsden was competent.

O Now I object on the ground that the act of mailing the bids is hearsay.

P The act of mailing the bids is nonassertive, nonverbal conduct The witness did not intend to make a "statement" by mailing the bids. Under the Texas Rules of Evidence, nonassertive, nonverbal conduct is not hearsay.

J Your objection is overruled.

P Mr. Toscher, WHAT did the bids say?

O Your Honor, I object on hearsay grounds.

J Counsel?

P Your Honor, we are not offering the statements in the bids themselves for the truth of the matter asserted. We are only offering the contents of the bids to show that Mr. Toscher believed that Mr. Marsden was competent to read and understand the contents of the bids.

O That is our point, your Honor. Counsel has just indicated that the probative value of the statements in the bids flows from Mr. Toscher's belief. Under Rule 801(c), counsel is therefore offering the assertive, verbal statements for the truth of the matter asserted and it is therefore being offered for a hearsay purpose.

J Let me see a copy of that rule. [*Judge reads*] The hearsay objection is sustained.

Note that even if counsel can introduce the fact that the witness mailed the bids, and thereafter hopes to argue to the jury that the witness's actions demonstrate a belief that the reader was competent, there is still another hurdle to overcome. The proper objection would be that the proponent has not laid a proper foundation for skilled lay observer opinion testimony. On the witness stand, a lay person may not express an opinion of another person's sanity unless he or she is intimately familiar with that person.

Assume that, as the preceding hypothetical indicates, the trial judge has permitted evidence that Mr. Toscher mailed the bids. The opponent now makes the opinion objection.

O My last objection is that the proponent hasn't shown that the witness knew Mr. Marsden well enough to express an opinion about Mr. Marsden's competency. Your Honor, if you admit this evidence, you are in effect permitting Mr. Toscher to give opinion testimony about Mr. Marsden's competency or sanity. I request permission to take the witness on voir dire.

J Permission granted.

O Mr. Toscher, ISN'T IT TRUE THAT you never personally met the decedent, Mr. Marsden?

W Yes.

O ISN'T IT A FACT THAT the only letters you ever received from his company were signed by other persons?

W Yes.

O ISN'T IT CORRECT THAT you never had a telephone conversation with Mr. Marsden?

W Yes.

O ISN'T IT TRUE THAT your only information about Mr. Marsden is what other people told you about him?

W Yes.

O Your Honor, I have no further voir dire questions of this witness. I renew my objection that the question calls for improper lay opinion testimony.

J The objection will be sustained.

This hypothetical demonstrates the point made in the first chapter, that the proponent must be prepared to lay multiple foundations, i.e., overcome multiple objections, for a single piece of evidence.

PART 2
EXEMPTIONS FROM THE HEARSAY RULE

§ 10-6 EXEMPTIONS FROM THE HEARSAY RULE—INTRODUCTION

This part of the chapter addresses *exemptions* from the hearsay rule. The preceding sections focused on the question of whether an offered statement even constituted hearsay. Assuming that an offered statement satisfies the three elements for hearsay, the statement may fall within one of the categories of exemptions: the witness-declarant exemption, the party admission exemption, and the deposition exemption (in civil cases only).

It is important to note that if the proponent can show that the offered statements are exempt from the hearsay rule, they are considered nonhearsay, by operation of Rule 801, and can be treated as substantive evidence. There would be no need in that case to look further to one of the exceptions to the hearsay rule.

§ 10-7 THE WITNESS-DECLARANT EXEMPTIONS

§ 10-7(A) The Doctrine

As noted in the preceding discussion concerning out-of-court declarants, *supra* at § 10-4(A)(2), the general rule is, "Once an out-of-court declarant, always an out-of-court declarant." For purposes of determining whether the statement is hearsay, the proponent must determine where and when the statement in question was made. This area becomes confusing when the witness now on the stand, subject to oath and cross-examination, testifies as to his or her own prior out-of-court statement. Under the general rule cited above, the statement is still considered to be an out-of-court statement for purposes of the hearsay rule.

Several commentators, including Professor Morgan, argue that the definition of hearsay should not include prior statements made by witnesses now on the stand and subject to cross-examination. These commentators begin with the premise that the primary purpose of the hearsay rule is to protect the opponent's right to cross-examine. They then argue that the opportunity to cross-examine is adequate even if the opportunity is delayed until trial. On Tuesday, the opponent can cross-examine the witness about Monday's statement. These commentators conclude that if the person is now a witness available for examination in court, the person should no longer be considered an out-of-court declarant, and the hearsay rule should not apply to the witness's prior statements.[5]

There is a compromise view. The compromise view is that if the witness's prior statement is otherwise admissible for a nonhearsay purpose (as a prior identification to bolster, as a prior inconsistent statement to impeach, or as a prior consistent statement to rehabilitate), the statement should be admitted as substantive evidence. Texas Rule of Evidence 801, like the Federal Evidence Rule 801, embraces the compromise view. Texas Rule 801(e)(1) exempts certain prior statements of the witness from the hearsay definition and permits their use as substantive evidence:

> *A statement is not hearsay if* . . . the declarant testifies at the trial or hearing and is subject to cross-examination concerning the statement, and the statement is (A) inconsistent with the declarant's testimony, and was given under oath subject to the penalty of perjury at a trial, hearing, or other proceeding, or in a deposition, or (B) consistent with the declarant's testimony and is offered to rebut an express or implied charge against the declarant of recent fabrication or improper influence or motive, or (C) one of identification of a person made after perceiving the person (emphasis added).

---

[5] To date, only one jurisdiction, Kansas, has adopted this view.

This compromise view reflects two beliefs. First, its supporters believe that there is substantial merit in Morgan's position. Second, they frankly believe that limiting instructions are largely ineffective. Although the judge tells the jurors to use the prior statement for the limited purpose of bolstering, impeaching, or rehabilitating, many jurors will use the statement as substantive evidence of the assertion. These two beliefs lead the supporters of the compromise view to admit prior statements as substantive evidence when the statements are otherwise admissible, usually on a credibility theory.

§ 10-7(B) ELEMENTS OF THE FOUNDATIONS

§ 10-7(B)(1) Elements—Prior Inconsistent Statement by Witness

In order to rely upon the hearsay exemption for prior inconsistent statements, under Rule 801(e)(1)(A), the proponent must establish:

1. The witness is on the stand subject to cross-examination.
2. The testifying witness made an inconsistent statement.[6]
3. The inconsistent statement was made under oath subject to the penalty of perjury.
4. The inconsistent statement was made at a trial, hearing, proceeding, or deposition. (Rule 801(e)(1)(A) specifically excludes statements made at grand jury proceedings in criminal cases.)

If the proponent can introduce the prior inconsistent statement under Rule 801, the opponent is not entitled to a limiting instruction. The prior out-of-court inconsistent statement can be used both to impeach and as substantive evidence.

§ 10-7(B)(2) Elements—Prior Consistent Statement by Witness

To establish the exemption for a testifying witness's prior consistent statements, under Rule 801(e)(1)(B), the proponent must establish the following:

1. The witness is on the stand and is subject to cross-examination.
2. The testifying witness has been impeached through evidence of an express or implied charge of recent fabrication or improper influence or motive.
3. The witness made a prior consistent statement.[7]
4. The prior consistent statement was made before the alleged fabrication, influence, or motive arose.

---

[6] In laying the foundation for this element, counsel will, of course, have to follow the requirements of Rule 613, discussed in Chapter 5.

[7] *See also* Rule 613(c).

Note that unlike the foundation for a prior inconsistent statement, *supra* at § 10-7(B)(1) there is no requirement here that the prior consistent statement was made under oath at another proceeding.

§ 10-7(B)(3) Elements—Prior Identification of Person by Witness

To rely upon the exemption for a testifying witness's prior identification of a person under Rule 801(e)(1)(C), counsel must show the following:

1. The witness is on the stand and is subject to cross-examination.
2. The testifying witness made a prior out-of-court identification of a person.
3. Where the identification occurred.
4. Who was present at the identification.
5. When the identification occurred.

Unlike the exemption for prior inconsistent statements, there is no requirement here that the out-of-court identification occurred while the witness was under oath at a prior proceeding. Nor must the proponent wait until the witness-identifier has been impeached before relying on this exemption, as is required before relying on the prior consistent statement exemption.[8]

§ 10-7(B)(4) Use of Prerecorded Videotaped and Closed-Circuit Testimony of Child Victims (Used in Criminal Cases)

Article 38.071 of the Texas Code of Criminal Procedure permits the proponent to offer videotaped testimony of a child victim. In 1987, the Texas Court of Criminal Appeals invalidated a major section of that provision. It was later revised by the state legislature.

§ 10-7(C) SAMPLE FOUNDATIONS—WITNESS-DECLARANT EXEMPTIONS

§ 10-7(C)(1) Sample Foundation—Prior Inconsistent Statement

The following fact situation demonstrates the prior inconsistent statement exemption, probably the most common of the witness-declarant exemptions under Rule 801. The witness-declarant, Ms. Kurth, testified on direct examination under questioning by the counsel for the defendant that at the time of the accident, the road conditions were terrible. Cross-examination has begun. The proponent is the plaintiff's counsel.

P I AM CORRECT, AM I NOT, Ms. Kurth, in saying that you testified on direct examination a little while ago that at the time of the accident, the road conditions were terrible?

---

[8] As noted in Chapter 5, the proponent may introduce evidence of a witness-identifier's prior identification without violating the "no bolstering" rule.

W Yes.

P And IT IS ALSO CORRECT TO SAY that on December 12, 2004, you gave your deposition testimony in another related case involving this accident?

W Yes.

P There were several people present at that time. Mr. Jones, a Ms. Smith, and myself. ISN'T THAT CORRECT?

W Yes, that is correct.

P And IT'S TRUE, IS IT NOT, that you testified at the deposition under oath?

W Yes.

P And IT IS TRUE, IS IT NOT, that you were asked by me what the road conditions were and you testified that the road was just fine at the time of the accident?

W Yes, I made that statement.[9]

O Your Honor, I request a limiting instruction under Rule 105 to the effect that counsel's attempt to discredit this witness with her prior hearsay statement is only admissible on the issue of the weight to be given to her testimony.

P Your Honor, this witness's prior inconsistent statement is admissible as substantive evidence under Rule 801(e)(1)(A). First, she is now on the stand subject to cross-examination. (1) Second, she has admitted making the inconsistent statement. (2) And third, that statement was made under oath at a deposition. (3), (4) We are therefore permitted to argue to the jury that they may believe the prior statement.

J The requested instruction will be denied.

§ 10-7(C)(2) Sample Foundation—Prior Consistent Statement

The prior consistent statement exemption in Rule 801 is commonly used to rehabilitate a witness who has been impeached with a prior inconsistent statement. See *supra* at § 5-14(A). Evidence of prior consistent statements, however, may arise in other contexts as well. For example, a codefendant's prior statement given before the codefendant entered into plea bargain negotiations is admissible to rebut the defendant's claim that the codefendant's testimony was recently fabricated or improperly influenced by a successful plea bargain.

---

[9] As noted in Chapter 5, by admitting the inconsistency, the witness precluded the proponent from introducing extrinsic evidence of the prior statement.

The following fact situation demonstrates another common use of this evidence, a child's prior consistent statement in a sexual assault case. Uncle Johnny sexually assaulted his niece, Amy, on April 28th. On May 1st, Amy told her friend Alice what Uncle Johnny had done. On May 5th, Alice relayed that information to Amy's mother, Martha. Martha asked Amy what Uncle Johnny had done. However, Amy became fearful of retribution from Uncle Johnny and refused to say anything to her mother. On May 15th, Martha promised her daughter, Amy, a new bicycle if she would tell the police what happened. On May 20th, Amy made accusatory statements to the authorities.

The prosecutor is the proponent, the defense is the opponent, and Amy is the witness. Assume that on direct examination, the prosecutor has already elicited the desired accusatory statements from Amy, and that the defense counsel, the opponent, is cross-examining Amy.

O ISN'T IT TRUE, Amy, that your mother promised you a new bicycle if you told the police what Uncle Johnny did to you?

W Yes.

O And your mother got that bicycle for you, DIDN'T SHE?

W Yes.

P And you got the new bicycle right after you talked to the police, DIDN'T YOU?

W Yes.

O I have no further questions.

J Prosecutor? Any redirect examination?

P Yes, your Honor. Amy, did you tell anyone about what Uncle Johnny did to you before your mother promised you a new bicycle?

O Your Honor, I object on hearsay grounds.

J Prosecutor?

P Your Honor, the witness's prior consistent statements to Alice and the police are admissible, both to rehabilitate her and as substantive evidence under Rules 613(c) and 801(e)(1)(B). First, she is now on the stand subject to cross-examination. (1) Second, the defendant during cross-examination alleged an improper motive, the bicycle, for her testimony. (2) And third, the witness made a statement, consistent with her testimony today, before this alleged improper motive arose. (3), (4)

O Your Honor, the witness's statement to the police was dearly made after Amy's mother promised to buy her a new bicycle, and is clearly not admissible under the rule. (4)

J Okay. I will allow the prior statement made by the witness to her friend, Alice, but not the prior statement made to the police.

P Amy, did you tell anyone about what Uncle Johnny did to you before your mother promised you a new bicycle?

W Yes.

P WHO did you tell?

W I told my friend Alice.

P WHAT did you tell her?

W I told her that Uncle Johnny had touched me in a bad way.

§ 10-7(C)(3) Sample Foundation—Prior Identification

The fact situation is a criminal prosecution for robbery. At 7:30 A.M., the robbery occurred. At 8:45 A.M., the defendant was apprehended. At 11:15 A.M., in a police lineup, the victim identified the defendant as the assailant. At trial, the witness is prepared to testify that the defendant was in fact his assailant. The witness has already described the robbery.

P WHO was the individual who took your wallet and car keys? (1)

W The defendant.

P WHERE is the defendant now? (1)

W He is sitting at the table over there.

P HOW is he dressed? (1)

W He is wearing a gray tweed jacket, a white shirt, and a red tie.

P Please let the record reflect that the witness has identified the defendant, William Bonnie. (1)

P Mr. Johnson, HOW many times have you seen the defendant? (2)

W I have seen him three times.

P WHICH times were those? (2)

W I saw him when he robbed me, today in court, and at a lineup at the police station.

P WHEN did this lineup occur? (2)

W It was about 11:00 A.M. on the morning of the robbery.

P WHERE did the police hold this lineup? (2)

W It was on a stage in one of the downstairs rooms at the police department.

P HOW was the lighting in the room? (3)

W It was fine.

P HOW close were you to the stage? (3)

W I was about 10 feet away.

P HOW were you facing? (3)

W I was facing straight ahead and looking at all the men in the lineup.

P HOW long were you permitted to observe the lineup? (3)

W As much time as I wanted. I didn't need long.

P HOW many men were in the lineup? (4)

W There were six.

P HOW were they dressed? (4)

W They were all wearing dark clothes.

P HOW tall were they? (4)

W They were roughly the same height, five feet-eight inches to five feet ten inches.

P WHAT, if anything, did the police say about the men in the lineup? (4)

W They didn't say anything. They just ushered me into the room and asked me if I recognized anyone.

P WHAT did the men in the lineup do while they were on the stage? (4)

W Nothing. They just stood there.

P WHAT happened after the lineup? (5)

W The police asked me if I recognized the robber in the lineup.

P WHAT did you say? (5)

W I told them that I did.

P WHO did you identify at the lineup? (5)

W The defendant, the same person I just pointed out in court.

O Your Honor, I object. This prior identification constitutes improper bolstering.

P Your Honor, may we be heard?

J Yes.

P Under Texas Rule of Evidence 801(e)(1)(C), we are permitted to introduce this witness's pretrial identification as nonhearsay, substantive evidence. Because the witness made the out-of-court identification and is now testifying, we are in compliance with the rule, and opposing counsel's bolstering objection is misplaced.

J The objection is overruled.

§ 10-8 THE ADMISSION EXEMPTIONS—IN GENERAL

As noted *supra* at § 10-4(A)(2), if an out-of-court statement falls within the definition of hearsay, the proponent of the statement must find an applicable hearsay exemption or exception. One of the most frequently used exemptions is that for the admissions of a party-opponent which is reflected in Texas Rule of Evidence 801(e)(2). For example, in a tort action the plaintiff can prove the defendant's out-of-court statements acknowledging fault. From the plaintiff's perspective, the defendant's statements are admissions of the party-opponent. The same hearsay exemption permits prosecutors to introduce defendants' confessions acknowledging guilt.

Although the common law treats the admission doctrine as a hearsay exception, the admission doctrine differs from most hearsay exceptions. Commentators have had some difficulty explaining the admission doctrine. Unlike most hearsay exceptions, admissions do not have to have a circumstantial guarantee of trustworthiness. Although the admission is obviously disserving at the time of trial, the admission is admissible even if it was self-serving when made. Nor is there any need to show a necessity for resorting to the hearsay. The opposing party may be available and perfectly willing to testify about the subject matter of the earlier statement. The truth of the matter is that the admission doctrine is a product of the adversary litigation system. The opponent can hardly complain that he or she does not have an opportunity to cross-examine himself or herself. The opponent can always take the stand to deny or explain the statement.

As with the witness-declarant exemption, discussed *supra* at § 10-7, if the proponent can establish the foundation for a party-opponent admission, it is admissible as nonhearsay.

There are three basic kinds of admissions: personal, adoptive, and vicarious. The basis of the classification is the reason for which we attribute the statement to the party-opponent. In the case of personal admissions, the statement is attributed to the party-opponent because it is his or her own words or acts. In the case of adoptive admissions, a third party makes the statement. But it is imputed to the party-opponent because the party-opponent manifests agreement with the statement. The opponent thereby "adopts" the statement. Finally, in the case of vicarious admissions, again a third party makes the statement, but the party-opponent does not manifest agreement. Rather, the statement is attributed to the party-opponent because of the legal relationship such as agency between the third party and the party-opponent. The following sections examine in more detail the foundations for these various types of admissions.

§ 10-9 THE PERSONAL ADMISSION EXEMPTION

§ 10-9(A) IN GENERAL

Texas Rule of Evidence 801(e)(2)(A) admits the party-opponent's own personal admissions in civil and criminal cases. It permits the proponent to introduce a statement when "[t]he statement is offered against a party and is . . . the party's own statement, in either an individual or a representative capacity." The courts tend to be liberal in admitting personal admissions. The phrasing of the admission can be highly opinionated, and the admission need not even be based on personal knowledge.

It is important to distinguish between admissions by a party-opponent and the hearsay exception for statements against interest located in Rule 803(24). In the case of admissions, the party's prior statement must be offered against that party. It does not matter that the statement was in the best interest of the party at the time it was made. In the case of statements against interest, the statement must have been against the declarant's interest at the time it was made. For example, in order for a criminal defendant to introduce his own, out-of-court exculpatory statement, he will not be able to rely upon the party admission exemption. Instead, he will have to find a hearsay exception to do so. Depending on the tenor of the offered statement, it might be admissible as a statement against interest.

§ 10-9(B) PERSONAL ADMISSIONS IN CIVIL CASES

§ 10-9(B)(1) The Doctrine

Express party admissions in Texas civil cases are governed by Rule 801(e)(2)(A). Note that express admissions may take the form of conduct. Thus, if the officer investigating the accident asks who was driving the green car, and the defendant raised his hand, that would constitute an admission.

§ 10-9(B)(2) Elements of the Foundation

In civil cases, the foundation for personal admissions is very simple. The foundation includes these elements:

1. The witness heard a declarant make a statement.
2. The witness identifies the declarant as the present party-opponent.
3. The statement is inconsistent with the position the party-opponent is taking at trial.[10]

---

[10] Although the appellate courts usually phrase this requirement negatively and purport to insist upon inconsistency, in practice trial judges apply the requirement affirmatively. Trial judges ask whether the statement is logically relevant to an issue the proponent has a right to prove in the case. The phrasing of the question eliciting the statement usually ensures the statement's logical relevance; the question inquires "about" a specific topic.

§ 10-9(B)(3) Sample Foundation

The following fact situation is a civil tort action. The case arose from a collision. The plaintiff, Ms. Langdale, alleges that the defendant, Mr. Maire, caused the collision by speeding. The speed limit in this section of town is 25 miles per hour. The plaintiff calls the investigating officer, Patrolman Lopez. The witness has already identified himself and testified that he went to the accident scene. The proponent is the plaintiff.

P Officer Lopez, WHAT did you do when you arrived at the scene of the collision?

W I investigated the accident.

P HOW did you investigate the accident? (1)

W I viewed the debris and interviewed the persons involved.

P WHO did you interview? (2)

W Ms. Langdale and Mr. Maire.

P WHERE is Mr. Maire now? (2)

W In the courtroom.

P Specifically, WHERE in the courtroom? (2)

W He's sitting at the table.

P HOW is he dressed? (2)

W In a green suit and blue tie.

P Your Honor, please let the record reflect that the witness has correctly identified the defendant.

J It will so reflect.

P Officer Lopez, WHAT did the defendant say about the accident? (3)

O Your Honor, I object on the ground that the question calls for hearsay.

P Your Honor, may I be heard?

J Yes.

P The statement is exempt from the hearsay rule under Rule 801(e)(2) because it is the admission of a party-opponent.

J The objection will be overruled.

P Let me repeat the question. WHAT did the defendant say about the accident? (3)

W He said he was really sorry about it because he thought he caused it by going too fast.

P HOW fast did he say he was going? (3)

W He said maybe 40 miles an hour.

§ 10-9(C) PERSONAL ADMISSIONS IN CRIMINAL CASES

§ 10-9(C)(1) The Doctrine

The foundation for a criminal defendant's confession is usually more complex than the foundation for admissions in civil cases. The foundation is more complex because in a criminal case, the prosecutor must also comply with constitutional and statutory requirements as well as evidentiary hearsay requirements. The prosecutor must first demonstrate that the confession was voluntary. The Fifth and Fourteenth Amendment Due Process Clauses and Texas Code of Criminal Procedure bar the admission of involuntary confessions. In addition, if the defendant's statement resulted from custodial questioning, the prosecutor must demonstrate that the police administered proper *Miranda*[11] warnings. *Miranda* imposes requirements in addition to traditional voluntariness. Finally, the prosecutor must prove that the defendant properly waived his *Miranda* rights. As noted *supra* at § 10-9(B)(1), conduct can amount to an admission. Thus, if the victim asks, "Who stole my car?" and the defendant raises his hand, that act could constitute an admission for purposes of Rule 801.

The emphasis here is on the hearsay aspects of the defendant's statements. For a more complete discussion of meeting the constitutional and statutory requirements for admitting a defendant's statements made to government agents, see § 13-15 et seq.

§ 10-9(C)(2) Elements of the Foundation

The foundation for a defendant's personal admission made to the police under Rule of Evidence 801(e)(2)(A) includes these elements:

1. The declarant made a statement.
2. The witness identifies the declarant as the present defendant.
3. The statement was voluntary.
4. The statement was in writing.
5. The police administered proper *Miranda* warnings to the defendant.
6. The defendant waived his or her rights.
7. The statement is inconsistent with the position the defendant takes at trial.[12]

---

[11] *Miranda v. Arizona*, 384 U.S. 436 (1966). *In Dickerson v. United States*, 530 U.S. 428 (2000), the Supreme Court affirmed that *Miranda* is still good law.

[12] The statement is logically relevant to some issue the prosecution has a right to prove at trial.

§ 10-9(C)(3) Sample Foundation

The fact situation is a prosecution for robbery. The defendant is Mr. Walters. The prosecution calls Officer Gannon as a witness. Officer Gannon identifies himself and then testifies that he is assigned to the robbery detail of the El Paso Police Department. The proponent is the prosecutor.

P Officer Gannon, WHERE were you on the afternoon of January 20th?

W I was at our station on duty.

P WHAT happened that afternoon?

W Some other officers brought in someone for questioning.

P WHO was that person? (2)

W James Walters.

P WHERE is James Walters now? (2)

W Here in the courtroom.

P Specifically, WHERE in the courtroom? (2)

W He's sitting right there.

P HOW is he dressed? (2)

W He's dressed in a brown shirt and green pants.

P Your Honor, please let the record reflect that the witness identified the defendant.

J It will so reflect.

P WHAT happened after the officers brought Mr. Walters in? (3)

W I took him to the interrogation room.

P WHAT happened then? (3)

W I began questioning him.

P WHAT promises did you make to him during the questioning? (3)

W None.

P WHAT force did you use during the interrogation? (3)

W None. I never touched him.

P WHAT threats did you make? (3)

W I didn't make any. I didn't threaten him or his family in any way.

If the defendant pleads not guilty, the defendant requires the prosecution to prove all the elements of the crime. By pleading not guilty, the defendant takes the general position that all the facts alleged are false.

P WHAT requests did he make during the questioning? (3)

W He asked for a cigarette, for coffee, and to go to the bathroom, that sort of thing.

P HOW did you respond to his requests? (3)

W I granted them. I gave him cigarettes and coffee. I let him go to the bathroom. I tried to make him as comfortable as possible.

P WHAT, if anything, did you say to Mr. Walters? (5)

W I read him his rights.

P HOW did you read him his rights? (5)

W I read them verbatim from a warning card.

P [*To court reporter*] Would you please mark this as an exhibit for the State? [*Court reporter marks exhibit and hands it back to counsel.*]

P Thank you. Please let the record reflect that I am showing State's exhibit number three for identification to opposing counsel. [*Opposing counsel briefly examines exhibit and hands it back to counsel.*]

P I request permission to approach the witness.

J Permission granted.

P Officer Gannon, I now hand you State's exhibit number three for identification. WHAT is it? (5)

W It's the warning card I just referred to.

P HOW can you recognize it? (5)

W I initialed it, and I had the defendant initial it as well. I see the initials and the date we wrote in pencil on the card.

P HOW did you use the card during the questioning? (5)

W I read from it verbatim to make certain I gave the suspect the correct warnings.

P Your Honor, I now offer State's exhibit number three for identification into evidence.

J It will be received.

P Officer Gannon, please read State's exhibit number three.

W [*Witness reads rights warnings.*]

P WHAT happened after you read Mr. Walters these rights? (5)

W I asked him whether he understood his rights.

P WHAT was his answer? (5)

W He said he did.

P WHAT happened then? (5)

W I asked him whether he wanted an attorney.

P WHAT was his response?

W He said no.

P WHAT happened then? (1), (3), (6)

W I asked him whether he was willing to talk about the robbery.

P WHAT was his response? (1), (6)

W He told me about the robbery.

P WHAT did you do next? (1), (3), (4)

W I typed up what he told me and showed it to him. He read it over and then signed it without making any changes.

P [*To court reporter*] Would you please mark this as a State's exhibit? [*Court reporter marks exhibit and hands it back to prosecutor.*]

P Thank you. Please let the record reflect that I am showing what has been marked as State's exhibit number four for identification to the defense counsel. [*Shows to counsel.*]

P Officer Gannon, I now show you State's exhibit number four for identification. WHAT IS IT?

W It is the defendant's written statement.

P HOW do you know that?

W Well, this is his signature, and my initials are located here in the top portion of the first page.

P Your Honor, we offer into evidence what has been marked as State's exhibit number four for identification.

O We have no objections, Your Honor.

J Then it will be received into evidence as State's exhibit number four.

P Your Honor, may we have permission to show State's exhibit number four to the jury?

J Yes.

There is an additional requirement for the admission of confessions. The confession or statement must be corroborated. See § 13-19(D), *infra*. That is, there must be independent evidence that a crime was committed, the corpus delicti. For example, in a robbery case, the store owner would have to testify that he found his locks broken and discovered money or merchandise missing. The corroboration need not show the identity of the perpetrator of the crime. It need show only that a crime was committed. The prosecutor may present the corroborating evidence first and then call the witness who will testify about the defendant's confession to the crime.

§ 10-10 THE ADOPTIVE ADMISSION EXEMPTIONS

§ 10-10(A) In General

In personal admissions, the party-opponent himself or herself says or writes the statement constituting the admission. In adoptive admissions, a third party says or writes the statement. The party-opponent then manifests assent to the statement in some fashion. In the words of Texas Evidence Rule 801(e)(2)(B), the party "manifest(s) an adoption or belief in its truth . . . ." When a criminal defendant signs a confession typed by a secretary at the police station, the defendant is manifesting assent to the contents of the writing. A party-opponent can manifest assent expressly or impliedly, even by silence.

§ 10-10(B) Express Adoption by a Party

§ 10-10(B)(1) The Doctrine

The doctrine supporting the express adoption is fairly straightforward. The party has said or done something which in effect says, "That is my statement."

§ 10-10(B)(2) Elements of the Foundation

The foundation for an admission which has been expressly adopted by a party includes these elements:

1. A declarant made a statement.
2. The declarant made the statement in the party's presence.[13]
3. The party heard and understood the statement.
4. The party made a statement which expressed agreement with the declarant's statement.
5. The declarant's statement is inconsistent with a position the party is taking at trial.

Most jurisdictions treat these foundational facts as Rule 104(b) issues. Hence, for example, the proponent need only present sufficient evidence to create a permissive inference that the party-opponent heard the declarant's statement. The jury ultimately decides whether the party opponent heard the statement.

---

[13] The declarant's statement itself is thus offered for a nonhearsay purpose, to show its effect on the state of mind of the party.

§ 10-10(B)(3) Sample Foundation

To illustrate this doctrine, we shall use a tort action involving a hit-and-run accident. On July 1, 2005, the plaintiff, Ms. Waylen, was crossing a street in downtown Dickinson when a car struck her and fled the scene. The plaintiff's complaint alleges that the driver of the car was the defendant, Brad Benton. Benton works as a salesperson at an electronics store and denies any involvement in the accident. In his pretrial deposition, he claimed that he was on vacation in Mexico on the date of the accident. The plaintiff is the proponent. The plaintiff calls Mr. George Nickmeyer as her next witness. Mr. Nickmeyer testifies that he is the manager of the store where Mr. Benton works.

P Mr. Nickmeyer, WHAT are your duties as manager?

W I'm generally in charge of everything: purchasing, finance, personnel. You name it, and I do it at the store. It's a pretty small operation.

P Please tell us more about your personnel responsibilities.

W It's a big area. I make sure that everyone is signed up for fringe benefits, medical plans, and the like. I also keep track of work days and vacations. We don't have an old-fashioned time clock.

P HOW do you keep track of vacation days? (1)

W I keep a personal log of when people work and when they're off. Then, at the end of each month I prepare a summary for each employee and have them verify its accuracy.

P HOW do you do that? (2), (3)

W I hand them the statement. At the end of each month, everyone checks by my office to inspect their work and vacation statement. They read it, and then they sign it.

P [*To court reporter*] Would you please mark this as an exhibit for the plaintiff? [*Court reporter marks exhibit and hands it back to proponent.*]

P Thank you. Please let the record reflect that I am showing what has been marked as plaintiff's exhibit number one for identification to the opposing counsel.

P May I have permission to approach the witness?

J Granted.

P Mr. Nickmeyer, I now hand you plaintiff's exhibit number one for identification. WHAT is it? (1), (4)

W It's Brad Benton's statement for the month of July 2005.

P HOW do you recognize it? (1)

W I was the one who prepared it; I recognize the contents and the form. In addition, I see Brad's signature at the bottom. He's worked for me for over three years.

P HOW many times have you seen the defendant sign his name? (4)

W I can't give you a precise number, but I've probably seen him do it dozens of times during that period. Like I said, the employees come by at the end of every month to sign these statements right in my presence.

P HOW was this form prepared? (2), (3), (4)

W I always do it the same way. I don't want any hassles with them over their vacation time. I call them into the office or they stop by on their own, read the statement while I'm present, and then put their John Hancock on it.

P Your Honor, I now offer plaintiff's exhibit number one for identification into evidence.

O Your Honor, I must object on the ground that this is inadmissible hearsay. This is obviously an inadequate foundation for a business entry.

P Your Honor, may I be heard?

J Yes.

P I'm not offering this exhibit as a business entry. I'm offering it as an adoptive admission. Mr. Nickmeyer prepared the form, but his testimony shows that the defendant had an opportunity to read and check it before signing it. By signing it, the defendant manifested his assent to the accuracy of the form. The form lists July 1, 2005, as a work day for the defendant, not a vacation day. (4)

J Objection overruled. The exhibit will be received.

P Mr. Nickmeyer, let me direct your attention to the extreme left-hand margin of plaintiff's exhibit number one. WHAT is listed on that margin?

W That margin lists each day of the month.

P Now let me direct your attention to the middle column of the form and the column on the extreme right-hand margin. WHAT do those columns represent?

W The middle column is for checkmarks indicating workdays. The column on the right is for vacation days. If someone works a particular day, I place a checkmark in the middle of the form. If they're on vacation, I place the check in the right-hand column.

P Please look at the columns for July 1, 2005.

W O.K.

P WHERE is the checkmark for July 1, in the middle or on the right hand margin?

W It's in the middle.

P Your Honor, I now request permission to circulate the exhibit to the jurors for their inspection.

J You may do so.

§ 10-10(C) IMPLIED ADOPTION BY SILENCE—THE "TACIT ADMISSION"

§ 10-10(C)(1) The Doctrine

Sometimes, if a person stands silent in the face of an accusation, we may infer the person's assent to the accusation from his or her silence. Thus, there can be an implied adoption by silence. The courts sometimes refer to this doctrine as "tacit admission."

§ 10-10(C)(2) Elements of the Foundation

The foundation for a tacit admission includes these elements:

1. The declarant made a statement.[14]
2. The statement was an accusation against the party-opponent.
3. The declarant made the statement in the party's presence.
4. The party heard and understood the statement.
5. The party had the opportunity to deny the statement.
6. The party either remained silent or made an evasive or equivocal reply.
7. Under similar circumstances, a reasonable innocent person would have immediately denied the accusation.
8. The declarant's statement is inconsistent with a position the party is taking at trial.

§ 10-10(C)(3) Sample Foundation

The fact situation is a tort case arising from a collision. The plaintiff, Mr. Girard, alleges that the defendant, Ms. Ratner, caused the accident by disregarding a stop sign. The investigating officer was Highway Patrolman Merle Kuhns. The plaintiff calls Patrolman Kuhns. He has already identified himself and testified that he responded to the accident scene. The plaintiff is the proponent.

---

[14] The declarant's statement, which triggered the party's response, could be admissible for the nonhearsay purpose of showing the effect it had on the hearer, the party.

P WHAT did you do when you responded to the scene?

W I immediately looked for the two drivers.

P WHO were the drivers?

W Your client, Mr. Girard, and Ms. Ratner.

P WHERE is Mr. Girard now?

W At the table over there.

P HOW is he dressed?

W He's wearing a gray business suit and blue tie.

P Your Honor, please let the record reflect that the witness has identified the plaintiff.

J It will so reflect.

P WHERE is Ms. Ratner now?

W At the other table there.

P HOW is she dressed?

W She has on a pink dress and red shoes.

P Your Honor, please let the record reflect that the witness has also identified the defendant.

J It will so reflect.

P WHERE did you find the plaintiff and defendant at the accident scene?

W They were standing on the northeast corner of the intersection.

P HOW close were they to each other?

W Right next to each other.

P WHAT were they doing?

W They were talking.

P WHAT were they talking about?

W The accident.

P WHAT, if anything, did Mr. Girard tell the defendant about the accident? (1), (2)

O Your Honor, I object to that question on the ground that it calls for hearsay.

P Your Honor, may we approach the bench?

J Yes.

P I offer to prove that Mr. Girard confronted the defendant and accused her of running a stop sign and that the defendant adopted the statement by remaining silent. I am using Mr. Girard's statement for a nonhearsay purpose; I am not offering his statement itself for its truth. I simply want to prove that the plaintiff made the statement and the defendant then adopted it.

O There's been no foundation for an adoptive admission yet.

J I will admit the statement subject to a motion to strike.[15]

P Officer Kuhns, let me repeat the question. WHAT, if anything, did Mr. Girard tell the defendant about the accident? (1), (2)

W He told her that she had caused the accident by running a stop sign. He said she was as blind as a bat.

P WHAT language was Mr. Girard speaking in? (4)

W English.

P HOW close was Mr. Girard to the defendant when he made that statement? (3)

W Two feet away at most. As I said, they were standing talking.

P HOW much noise was there when Mr. Girard made the statement? (4), (5)

W It was pretty quiet. The traffic congestion had died down.

P HOW many other people were talking to the defendant at the time? (4), (5)

W No one else.

P WHO was Mr. Girard facing when he made the statement? (4), (5)

W He was looking right at Ms. Ratner.

P HOW was she facing? (4), (5)

W She was facing him.

P WHAT was Mr. Girard's tone of voice when he made the statement? (5), (7)

W He was obviously excited.

P WHAT threats did Mr. Girard make against the defendant at the time? (5), (7)

W None. He was upset, but he wasn't threatening or anything like that.

P WHAT gestures did Mr. Girard make? (5), (7)

W He was animated, but he wasn't making a fist or pointing a finger in Ms. Ratner's face. He was just exasperated.

---

[15] Note that many judges may hesitate to admit evidence subject to being connected up later. Certainly, the safer course is to wait until the entire foundation has been laid before admitting the evidence.

P WHAT was the defendant's facial expression immediately after Mr. Girard made the statement? (7)

W She looked worried.

P WHERE did she look? (4), (5), (7)

W Right after he made the statement, she looked down and away from the plaintiff.

P WHAT, if anything, did the defendant say then? (6)

W Nothing.

P WHAT was her response to Mr. Girard's statement that she had run the stop sign? (6)

W None. She didn't say anything in response to his remark.

§ 10-11 THE VICARIOUS ADMISSION EXEMPTIONS

§ 10-11(A) In General

Vicarious admissions by a party-opponent are covered in Rule 801(e)(2)(C), (D), and (E). The basis for imputing a declarant's statement to the party-opponent is the party's relationship with the declarant. A principal debtor's statement, for example, may be admitted against a surety, the statements of a predecessor in title against the present titleholder, and the statements of an agent against the principal. The foundation consists of demonstrating the relation between the declarant and the party-opponent. Once the relation has been demonstrated, the declarant's statements are vicariously admissible against the party-opponent.

§ 10-11(B) Statements by Authorized Spokesperson

§ 10-11(B)(1) The Doctrine

Most vicarious admissions, especially in civil cases, are statements made by agents and admitted against the agent's principal. The traditional view is that the declarant must have been a spokesperson for the principal. It is not sufficient that the declarant was an agent or employee of the party-opponent. The declarant must have been a special type of agent, authorized to make statements on the principal's behalf. In the words of Texas Evidence Rule 801(e)(2)(C), the statement was made "by a person authorized by the party to make a statement concerning the subject."

§ 10-11(B)(2) Elements of the Foundation

The foundation for a vicarious admission by an authorized spokesperson for the party includes the following elements:

1. The declarant was an agent of the party-opponent.
2. The party-opponent authorized the declarant to make the particular statements.
3. The statement is inconsistent with a position the party-opponent is taking at trial; the statement is logically relevant to an issue the proponent has a right to prove at trial.

§ 10-11(B)(3) Sample Foundation

The fact situation is a suit against an insurance company. Delta Corporation sues Grant Insurance Company. The complaint alleges that the defendant insured the plaintiff against fire. A fire occurred on the plaintiff's premises but the defendant has wrongfully refused to compensate the plaintiff. The policy excluded any fire which the plaintiff's employee negligently started. In discovery, the defendant obtained a copy of a report the plaintiff's safety investigator, Mr. Grant Richards, prepared. The report includes the finding that one contributing cause of the fire was some careless welding by plaintiff's employees. The welder negligently cut into a furnace and permitted flames to escape. During its case-in-chief, the defendant calls Mr. Richards. Note that the defendant could treat him as an adverse witness and conduct the direct examination as cross-examination and use leading questions. For purposes of this sample foundation, the defense attorney will use nonleading questions. The defendant is the proponent. Mr. Richards has already identified himself.

P WHERE do you work? (1)

W I work for Delta Corporation in Amarillo.

P HOW long have you worked for them? (1)

W Seven years, give or take a few months.

P WHAT is your job with Delta Corporation? (2)

W I am a safety and accident investigator.

P HOW long have you held that position? (2)

W The last five years.

P WHERE were you on November 13, 2005? (2)

W At our plant in Arlington.

P WHAT were you doing there? (2)

W I was investigating the fire that had occurred the day before.

P HOW long did you spend investigating the fire? (2)

W The whole day.

P WHAT did you do when you finished the investigation? (2)

W As is my normal practice, I prepared a report of the investigation.

P [*To court reporter*] Would you please mark this as an exhibit for the defense? [*Court reporter marks exhibit and hands it back to proponent.*]

P Thank you. Please let the record reflect that I am showing what has been marked as defense exhibit F for identification to the opposing counsel.

J The record will so reflect.

P I request permission to approach the witness.

J Permission granted.

P Mr. Richards, I now hand you defense exhibit F for identification. WHAT is it? (2)

W It's my report on the fire.

P HOW can you recognize it? (2)

W I recognize my handwriting on the last page. I also generally recall the report's contents.

P Again, WHAT are your duties for Delta Corporation? (2)

W As I said before, I'm the safety and accident investigator.

P In general terms, WHAT is the subject of this particular report?

W It relates to the fire I investigated as part of my duties.

P WHY did you prepare this particular report? (2)

W It's part of my job. In fact, the vice president for operations ordered me to get that report finished and submitted as soon as possible.

P Your Honor, I now offer defense exhibit F for identification into evidence.

J It will be received.

P Mr. Richards, please turn to page 18 of exhibit F and read finding #4 to the jury. (3)

W The report reads, "Another contributing factor may have been our own employees' carelessness. Some of our welders were evidently working next to furnace #3 on the second floor. Some eyewitness reports indicated that the welders accidentally cut into the furnace, releasing the flames that started the fire."

§ 10-11(C) Statements Made by Agent Within Course of Employment

§ 10-11(C)(1) The Doctrine

Texas Rule 801(e)(2)(D) reflects the emerging view that the party-opponent need not have authorized the particular statement. The declarant need not be a spokesperson. Under the emerging view, it is sufficient that the declarant was an agent of the party-opponent and the statement relates to the agent's employment duties.

Rule 801(e)(2)(D) authorizes the admission of a statement by the party's agent or servant concerning a matter within the scope of the agency or employment, made during the existence of the relationship.

§ 10-11(C)(2) Elements of the Foundation

To prove a party-opponent admission under this view, the foundational elements are:

1. The declarant was an agent of the party-opponent.
2. The declarant made the statement while he or she was an agent.
3. The statement related to the agent's employment duties. The proponent first elicits testimony about the agent's employment duties. The proponent then asks the agent about a topic related to the duties.
4. The statement is inconsistent with a position the party-opponent is taking at trial. The statement is logically relevant to an issue the proponent has a right to prove at trial.

§ 10-11(C)(3) Sample Foundation

The fact situation is a tort action arising from a collision. Ms. Cantu, the plaintiff, alleges that Carrington Company's driver, Mr. Julius, negligently caused the accident. The only named defendant is the company, Carrington. During the plaintiff's case-in-chief, she calls Mr. Julius as a witness. As in the previous hypothetical, many courts would permit the proponent to treat the witness as hostile and conduct the direct examination as if it were cross-examination. For purposes of this example, however, the proponent will use nonleading questions. Mr. Julius has already identified himself.

P WHERE do you work? (1)

W I work for the Carrington warehouse here in Beaumont.

P HOW long have you worked there? (1)

W Eight years.

P WHAT are your duties? (1)

W I'm a driver. I haul our deliveries all over the United States. I do mostly intrastate moves, but I occasionally do cross-country moves.

P Mr. Julius, WHERE were you on the afternoon of October 13th? (2)

W I was driving along Highway 84 headed for Colorado.

P WHO were you working for that day? (2)

W My regular employer, Carrington.

P WHAT happened that afternoon? (2)

W I was involved in an accident with a Ms. Henning. [*Here the proponent would elicit facts about the collision itself.*]

P WHAT happened immediately after the accident? (3)

W I talked to the police officer who investigated the accident.

P WHAT was his name? (3)

W I think his name was Patrolman Blue.

P WHAT, if anything, did you tell him about your speed just before the collision? (3), (4)

O Your Honor, I object to that question on the ground that it calls for hearsay.

P Your Honor, may we approach the bench?

J Yes.

P Your Honor, I offer to prove that the witness will admit he said he was going 70 miles an hour. My theory of admissibility is that Mr. Julius's statement about his speed is a vicarious admission against his employer.

O Carrington hires drivers to drive rather than to act as spokespersons.

P As you know, your Honor, Rule 801(e)(2)(D) authorizes the admission of agent's statements so long as they relate to the agent's employment duties. This statement relates to the speed at which Mr. Julius was driving.

J The objection will be overruled.

P Mr. Julius, let me repeat the question. WHAT, if anything, did you tell Patrolman Blue about your speed just before the collision? (3), (4)

W I told him I thought I was going about 70 miles an hour. I was a little behind schedule, and I was trying to make up time.

P WHAT is the posted speed limit on the stretch of highway where the collision occurred?

W Fifty-five miles per hour.

§ 10-11(D) Co-conspirator's Statements

§ 10-11(D)(1) The Doctrine

The practitioner is most likely to confront this issue in a criminal case. Like the other vicarious admissions discussed *supra* at § 10-11(A), the co-conspirator doctrine rests on an agency principle. Texas Evidence Rule 801(e)(2)(E) states the doctrine. The Rule excepts "a statement by a co-conspirator of a party during the course and in furtherance of the conspiracy."

§ 10-11(D)(2) Elements of the Foundation

The foundation for a co-conspirator hearsay exemption includes these elements:

1. There was a conspiracy.
2. The conspiracy was in progress when the declarant made the statement. The conspiracy continues at least until the conspirators attempt to commit the crime. If the crime is a theft offense, the conspiracy also continues until the conspirators divide the proceeds of the theft.
3. The declarant was a co-conspirator.
4. The declarant made the statement in furtherance of the conspiracy. The declarant furthers the conspiracy by attempting to recruit new conspirators or updating current conspirators on the state of their plans. If the declarant has already been arrested, his or her confession is usually not deemed to promote the conspiracy.
5. The defendant was a member of the conspiracy. The defendant need not be a member of the conspiracy when the declarant makes the statement. If the defendant later joins the conspiracy, the defendant is deemed to ratify the earlier statements.
6. The statement is inconsistent with a position the defendant is taking at trial.

In *Bourjaily v. United States*,[16] the Supreme Court announced that in deciding whether the prosecution has established all the foundational elements, under Rule 104(a), the trial judge may consider the content of the proffered statement itself.[17] There is Texas case law for the proposition, however, that the proponent may not use the statements themselves to bootstrap a showing of the underlying conspiracy.[18] To lay the foundation, the prosecutor usually calls an informer or a conspirator who has turned state's evidence.

[16] 483 U.S. 171 (1987).

[17] The Court stopped short of saying that the statement, standing alone, would be a sufficient foundation. In 1997, Federal Rule of Evidence 801(d)(2) was amended to explicitly state that the contents of the statement "shall be considered but are not alone sufficient to establish the declarant's authority" to make the statement.

[18] *See, e.g., Sorce v. State*, 736 S.W.2d 851 (Tex. App.—Houston [14th Dist.] 1987, pet. ref.); *see also* WENDORF, SCHLUETER & BARTON, TEXAS RULES OF EVIDENCE MANUAL VIII-51 (6th ed. 2002).

§ 10-11(D)(3) Sample Foundations

The fact situation is a prosecution for conspiracy to sell cocaine. The defendant is Mr. George Sherr. The indictment alleges that the defendant conspired with Mr. James Blanton. The prosecution calls Mr. Donald Peterson as a witness. The prosecutor hopes to use Mr. Peterson's testimony to prove the intent to sell. The witness has already identified himself. The prosecutor is the proponent.

P WHAT is your occupation?

W I am a police officer, a member of the Austin Police Department.

P WHAT are your duties?

W I specialize in undercover work for the Narcotics Division.

P HOW long have you done that type of work?

W For the last three years.

P WHERE were you on the evening of September 3rd of last year? (1)

W I was at James Blanton's house in Austin.

P WHO else was there? (1), (3), (5)

W It was just me, Mr. Blanton, and the defendant.

P WHAT happened while you were there? (1)

W Mr. Blanton showed me some bags containing a drug. Both he and the defendant referred to it as cocaine.

P WHAT happened after Mr. Blanton showed you the bags? (1)

W I pretended to get high on some marijuana. And while I was doing that, Mr. Blanton and the defendant discussed their plans for getting more cocaine.

P WHAT plans did they discuss? (1)

W Mr. Blanton said he had a contact in Mexico for good cocaine; the defendant said he could fly down, pick up the cocaine, and smuggle it back across the border.

P WHEN did they say they would carry out these plans? (2)

W Over the next couple of months.

P WHAT happened after they discussed their plans?

W The defendant took me home.

P WHAT happened the next day? (2)

W I met Mr. Blanton for lunch.

P WHAT happened during the lunch? (4)

W Mr. Blanton invited me to help the defendant and him carry out their plans.

P HOW did he want you to help him? (4)

W He said he wanted me to hide some bags of cocaine in my apartment. He said he thought it would be a good idea to divide up his cache rather than storing it in only one place.

P HOW did you respond? (4)

W I said that I wanted to make certain there was something in it for me.

P WHAT, if anything, did Mr. Blanton say then? (4)

O Your Honor, I object to that question on the ground that it calls for hearsay.

P Your Honor, may we approach the bench?

J Yes.

P Your Honor, I offer to prove that the witness will testify that Mr. Blanton said he and the defendant were going to sell the cocaine and make enough money to pay the witness $10,000. The testimony is directly relevant to prove the intent to sell. Since Mr. Blanton was the defendant's co-conspirator, Mr. Blanton's statement is vicariously admissible against the defendant under Texas Rule of Evidence 801(e)(2)(E).

J The objection will be overruled.

P Mr. Peterson, let me repeat the question. WHAT did Mr. Blanton say when you said you wanted to make certain there was something in the proposal for you? (4)

W He said that he and the defendants weren't simply piling up the cocaine supply for their personal use. He told me that they intended to sell the cocaine. He was certain that they would make enough money to pay me $10,000 for the use of my apartment.

The next fact situation is also a criminal prosecution. The government charges that Mr. Cetina and Mr. Britton conspired to sell and actually sold heroin. The witness is Ms. Grace. Ms. Grace identifies herself. She then testifies that she is a government informant and infiltrated the meeting of a drug ring. The prosecutor is the proponent. Note in this sample how the issue of implied assertions, which under Texas Rule 801 may constitute hearsay, arises in conjunction with the co-conspirator's exemption.

P Ms. Grace, WHERE were you on the evening of January 17, 2005?

W I was at 70 Aberdeen Court in Longview.

P WHO else was there? (1), (2)

W The two defendants, Mr. Cetina and Mr. Britton.

P WHERE are they now? (1), (2)

W In the courtroom.

P Specifically, WHERE in the courtroom?

W At that table over there.

P HOW are they dressed?

W Mr. Cetina is wearing a blue suit with red tie. Mr. Britton has a brown suit and yellow tie.

P Your Honor, please let the record reflect that the witness has correctly identified the two defendants.

J It will so reflect.

P Ms. Grace, WHAT happened during this meeting? (1), (2), (3)

W The defendants were making plans to sell drugs.

P WHAT plans did they discuss? (4)

O Your Honor, I object to that question on the ground that it calls for hearsay.

P Your Honor, may we approach the bench and be heard?

J Yes.

P [*Out of the jury's hearing*] Your Honor, I offer to prove that the witness will testify that the defendant Mr. Cetina ordered the defendant Mr. Britton to get some bags of heroin out of Mr. Britton's car, and that Mr. Britton did so. (4) The statement is logically relevant to prove the existence of a conspiracy between them. That is, Mr. Cetina's words to Mr. Britton impliedly stated that Mr. Cetina knew there were drugs in the car and that a conspiracy existed. We realize that this is probably an implied assertion, but Mr. Cetina's statement is nonhearsay under Rule 801 because first, his statement can be admitted as a party-opponent, personal assertion under Rule 801(e)(2)(A). And second, his statement should be admissible under the co-conspirator exemption in Rule 801(e)(2)(E).

J The objection will be overruled.

P Ms. Grace, let me repeat the question. WHAT plans did they discuss? (4)

W The plans for a drug sale. Mr. Cetina ordered Mr. Britton to get some bags of heroin out of Mr. Britton's car to get them ready for sale.

P WHAT happened then?

W Mr. Britton left for a couple of minutes and then came back with some bags.

P WHAT was the appearance of the bags?

W The bags themselves were transparent.

P WHAT, if anything, could you see in the bags?

W There was a white, powdery substance in each bag.

§ 10-12 THE DEPOSITION EXEMPTION IN CIVIL CASES

§ 10-12(A) THE DOCTRINE

Rule 801(e)(3) includes a provision for civil cases only which is not found in the Federal Rule counterpart. The Rule provides that a statement is not hearsay if "[i]t is a deposition taken in the same proceeding, as same proceeding is defined in Rule 207, Texas Rules of Civil Procedure." Unavailability of the deponent is not a requirement of admissibility. The significance of this provision is that first, the proponent is not required to show, as in Rule 801(e)(1), that the prior deposition testimony is inconsistent. Second, the deponent need not even be on the stand to introduce his or her deposition. Nor does the proponent have to show, as under Rule 804, that the deponent is unavailable. Texas Rule of Civil Procedure 207 provides that such depositions may be introduced for any purpose against any party who was present at the deposition, who was represented at the deposition, or who had reasonable notice that it was being conducted. In short, the proponent does not have to show the necessity for introducing the deposition. Indeed, even if the deponent is available to testify, counsel may find that using his or her deposition is the most convenient and easiest method of presenting the evidence. It is not difficult to see how this one exemption can virtually swallow the hearsay rule as it might otherwise apply to out-of-court statements made in depositions.

The one limitation is that the deposition must have been taken in the same proceeding. Texas Rule of Civil Procedure 207 indicates that "same proceeding" includes suits in any Texas or other state's court or federal court involving the same parties, their representatives, or their successors in interest, and involving the same subject matter.

If the requirements of Civil Procedure Rule 207 are not met, the deposition is considered to be from a "different proceeding," and the proponent must rely on one of the other exemptions or exceptions to the hearsay rule.

When the deposition is read into evidence at trial, the Rules of Evidence will be applied to each question and answer as though the deponent was present and testifying. Thus, although Rule 801(e)(3) helps the proponent clear the hearsay hurdle, the other rules governing relevancy, privileges, etc., must still be satisfied.

§ 10-12(B) ELEMENTS OF THE FOUNDATION

To introduce a deposition using the hearsay exemption in Rule 801(e)(3), the proponent must show:

1. A deposition was taken.

2. The deposition was taken in the "same proceeding."
   a. The deposition was taken in a case in a federal or state court;
   b. The deposition involved the same subject matter as the present trial; and
   c. The deposition involved the same parties as this suit, or their representatives or successors in interest.
3. The party against whom the deposition is being offered was present or represented at the deposition, or was given reasonable notice of the deposition.
4. The deposition is authentic.

Assuming that opposing counsel is not willing to stipulate to the authenticity of the deposition, the proponent will probably have to call a witness to the stand to testify that the deposition is authentic. The witness could be the custodial attorney (the attorney who initiated the deposition and has the original) or someone who was present at the deposition or who is familiar with the document. That could include the court reporter who served as the deposition officer.

Because a written deposition, or excerpts from the deposition, are *not admissible as exhibits*,[19] counsel will have to make some provision for having the pertinent portions *read* to the jury. This may be done by counsel reading the selection or by asking a witness to do so. Both the questions and the answers should be read. Other counsel prefer to use a surrogate witness (who, at the discretion of the trial judge, may be permitted to sit in the witness chair) to serve in the role of the person answering the questions. If the excerpts are lengthy, the proponent should be prepared to provide copies of the deposition to opposing counsel and the trial judge so that they might follow along. Regardless of the method used, the questions and answers are subject to objection.

§ 10-12(C) SAMPLE FOUNDATION

The fact situation involves a lawsuit in which there is a dispute as to whether the parties adequately anticipated adverse soil conditions at a construction site. The plaintiff is Acme Construction and the defendant is Mother's Excavation Company. Depositions were taken in accordance with the Texas Rules of Civil Procedure. The proponent is the plaintiff, who is introducing the deposition testimony of Mr. Tom Worthy, who was the on-site engineer for the plaintiff construction company. The witness on the stand is Ms. Melba Jones, the deposition officer for Mr. Worthy's deposition. Assume that the defendant's counsel has been unwilling to stipulate to the deposition.

---

[19] *See* TEX. R. CIV. P. 281 and 287.

P Ms. Jones, WHAT is your occupation?

W I am a certified court reporter.

P In that capacity, WHAT, if any, depositions were you involved in for this case? (1), (2a)

W I served as the deposition officer for a deposition taken of Mr. Tom Worthy.

P WHEN was that deposition taken? (1)

W It was taken on March 9, 2005.

P WHERE was it taken? (1)

W It was taken in the Milam Building, here in town. It was in your law firm's conference room.

P WHO requested the deposition? (1)

W You did.

P WHO was present at Mr. Worthy's deposition? (3)

W You were, Mr. Worthy, of course, myself, and the attorney for the other side, the defendant company. His name was Mr. Drokes.

P WHAT was the subject, or purpose, for that deposition? (2b), (2c)

W It was taken for this case, this same lawsuit.

P Your Honor, I request that this be marked as an exhibit for the plaintiff. [*Proponent hands exhibit to court reporter, who marks exhibit and hands it back to proponent.*]

P Thank you. We also request that the record reflect that I am showing plaintiff's exhibit number 31 for identification to counsel for the defendant.

J It will so reflect.

P Now, Ms. Jones, I show you plaintiff's exhibit number 31 for identification. Do you recognize this exhibit?

W Yes, I do.

P Would you please tell the court WHAT you recognize it to be?

W This is a copy of Mr. Worthy's deposition.

P HOW do you recognize it?

W Well, the cover sheet clearly indicates that it is his deposition and a copy of my certificate is attached. [*Witness scans through contents.*] I can also tell by some of the questions and answers that this is the deposition we have been talking about.

P HOW accurate is this copy?

W Very accurate.

P HOW can you tell?

W I ran this off on my own photocopy machine. There are no extraneous marks and it appears to include every page of the deposition.

P Your Honor, I now request permission to read portions of the deposition, from pages 3 and 13.

O Your Honor, we object on hearsay grounds. Counsel has failed to show that Mr. Worthy is not available. In fact we have reason to believe that he is available right now to come in here and testify. Further, this deposition will be obviously self-serving to the plaintiff.

P Your Honor, may we approach the bench?

J Yes.

P Your Honor, we are offering this deposition under Texas Rule of Evidence 801(e)(3) and Civil Procedure Rule 207. Rule 801 treats a deposition taken in the same proceeding as nonhearsay if it otherwise complies with Civil Procedure Rule 207. We believe that we have established a sufficient foundation for showing that this deposition satisfies both of those rules. Regarding the self-serving nature of the deposition, Civil Procedure Rule 207 and Evidence Rule 801, read together, permit us to use this deposition against the opposing party for any purpose, whether it is self-serving or not.

J The statements are admissible. You may read the pertinent portions.

P Ladies and gentlemen, I will be reading two questions and answers from Mr. Worthy's deposition. First, on page 3, I asked the question: "What was the condition of the soil around the footings on the south side of building?"

O Your Honor, I object to that question on the ground that it calls for mere speculation on the part of the deponent.

P Your Honor, under Rule 701 the deponent should be permitted to offer lay opinion on the condition of the soil.

J Objection overruled.

P The answer given by Mr. Worthy was: "It was very saturated." The next question is on page 13 and reads as follows: "Did you say anything about the soil to anyone from the defendant's company?" And his answer was: "Yes, I warned them that the soil was saturated."

Note that the deposition transcript itself is not offered into evidence as an exhibit.[20]

---

[20] *See* TEX. R. CIV. P. 281 and 287.

CHAPTER 11
EXCEPTIONS TO THE HEARSAY RULE

PART 1
HEARSAY EXCEPTIONS BASED PRIMARILY ON A SHOWING OF RELIABILITY

§ 11-1 INTRODUCTION

§ 11-1(A) HEARSAY EXCEPTIONS—IN GENERAL

Chapter 10 addresses the question of what types of evidence constitute hearsay and whether there are any exemptions from that definition. The fact that an out-of-court statement is hearsay does not necessarily mean that it is inadmissible. The common law, and now the Texas Rules of Evidence, specifically recognize a long list of *exceptions* to the hearsay rule. If the proponent can fit the offered statement into at least one recognized exception, the statement becomes admissible hearsay.

There are two general categories of hearsay exceptions: (1) exceptions grounded on the theory that they are reliable; and (2) those that are based on a showing of necessity caused by the unavailability of the declarant. Part 1 of this chapter addresses the first category of exceptions, which appear in Texas Rule of Evidence 803, and Part 2 focuses on the second category, which are located in Texas Rule 804.

§ 11-1(B) Hearsay Exceptions Based on Reliability—Rule 803

As noted in Chapter 10, a proponent offering a statement as the admission of a party-opponent need not establish the reliability of the statement or any necessity to resort to the statement. In contrast, some hearsay exceptions require a showing of reliability. These exceptions in turn fall into two subcategories. In one category, the exception is usually a spinoff of the old *res gestae* doctrine. In this category, there is an inference of sincerity on the part of the declarant. Sections 11-6 through 11-10 of this chapter focus on the exceptions falling into this category. The second category includes primarily documentary statements. There is something about the process of generating the writing which creates an inference of the reliability of the statement. Sections 11-2 through 11-5 of this chapter discuss those hearsay exceptions.

§ 11-2 BUSINESS RECORDS EXCEPTION

§ 11-2(A) The Doctrine

At common law, business entries are admissible as an exception to the hearsay rule. Texas Evidence Rule 803(6) restates the modern doctrine:

> A memorandum, report, record, or data compilation, in any form, of acts, events, conditions, opinions, or diagnoses, made at or near the time by, or from information transmitted by, a person with knowledge, if kept in the course of a regularly conducted business activity, and if it was the regular practice of that business activity to make the memorandum, report, record, or data compilation, all as shown by the testimony of the custodian or other qualified witness, unless the source of the information or the method or circumstances of preparation indicate lack of trustworthiness. The term "business" as used in this paragraph includes business, institution, association, profession, occupation, and calling of every kind, whether or not conducted for profit.

In the case of business entries, the circumstantial guarantee of trustworthiness is that since the entry is routine, the business's employees have developed habits of precision in gathering and reporting the data. The employees' habits help to ensure the reliability of the report. There is also necessity for resorting to the hearsay report. If a business conducts hundreds or thousands of similar transactions during a year, it is doubtful whether any employee will remember the particular transaction recorded in the entry. Even if an employee remembers, the employee's memory is likely to be incomplete or hazy. Thus, the business entry is probably the most reliable evidence available.

§ 11-2(B) ELEMENTS OF THE FOUNDATION

To lay the foundation for a business record exception, the proponent must establish the following foundational elements:

1. The report was prepared by a person who has a business relationship with the company. It is ideal if the person is an employee of the company. However, the person might also work for a parent, subsidiary, or affiliated company.
2. The informant (the ultimate source of the report) had a business duty to report the information.[1]
3. The informant had personal knowledge of the facts or events reported.
4. The written report was prepared contemporaneously with the facts or events.
5. It was a routine practice of the business to prepare such reports.
6. The report was reduced to written form.
7. The report was made in the regular course of business.[2]

The foundation or predicate witness need not have personal knowledge of the entry's preparation. In fact, the witness rarely has such knowledge. The witness is ordinarily the business's records custodian. The witness testifies to his or her connection with the business and then describes the habitual method with which the business prepares and maintains its reports. The proponent lays the foundation for such habit by following the procedure outlined in Chapter 6. The habit evidence has sufficient probative value to support a finding that the business followed that procedure on the occasion in question. As noted in Chapter 4, Texas

[1] This requirement is not specifically noted in Rule 803(6), but has generally been required by case law. The business duty requirement is traceable to the leading case of *Johnson v. Lutz*, 253 N.Y. 124, 170 N.E. 517 (1930), cited with approval in the Advisory Committee's Note to Federal Rule of Evidence 803. There, the court held that a report is not prepared in the course of business unless all the persons contributing to the report have a business duty to do so. In that case, the business entity was the police department. The parts of the police report reflecting bystanders' statements did not qualify as business entries, because the civilian bystanders were not employees of the police department. The informant's business duty is one of the guarantees of the report's trustworthiness.

[2] The expression "regular course of business" requires at least that the entry be related to the nature of the business. For instance, a sales slip is obviously related to the nature of a retail merchandise business. *Palmer v. Hoffman*, 318 U.S. 109 (1943), adds another level of meaning to "regular course of business." The lower courts and commentators have construed *Palmer* as meaning that reports specially prepared for litigation are not made "in the regular course of business." If the trial judge finds that the business entry is, in reality, a special litigation report, the judge has discretion to exclude the entry as being suspect and unreliable. The Advisory Committee Note to Federal Rule 803 seems to adopt *Palmer*.

Rule of Evidence 902(10) also permits the proponent to authenticate a business record through the use of an affidavit.

It is important to remember that showing that a particular document is admissible under the business records exception does not automatically satisfy the requirement that the document be authenticated (see Chapter 4) and also satisfy the original writing rule (see Chapter 8). For all practical purposes, however, laying the foundation for the business records exception also authenticates the records.

§ 11-2(C) SAMPLE FOUNDATIONS

The following fact situation is a contract suit. The plaintiff is Armor Corporation. Its complaint alleges that it delivered 500 stereophonic speakers to Hyatt Corporation and that the defendant wrongfully failed to pay for the speakers. The defendant has generally denied those allegations. The plaintiff wants to introduce a delivery sheet stating that its employees delivered the 500 speakers to the defendant. The plaintiff calls Mr. James Merton as a witness. Mr. Merton has already identified himself. The plaintiff is the proponent.

P WHERE do you work?

W I am the records custodian for Armor Corporation.

P HOW long have you held that position?

W About six years.

P WHAT are your duties as records custodian?

W I establish company-wide procedures for preparing records, I ensure that the prepared records are properly filed, and, finally, I'm in charge of records retirement and destruction.

P [*To court reporter*] Would you please mark this as an exhibit for the plaintiff? [*Court reporter marks and hands exhibit back to proponent.*]

P Thank you. Please let the record reflect that I am showing what has been marked as plaintiff's exhibit number three for identification to the opposing counsel.

J The record will so reflect.

P I request permission to approach the witness.

J Permission granted.

P Mr. Merton, I now hand you plaintiff's exhibit number three for identification. WHAT is it?

The complete foundation would include proof of the document's authenticity. See Chapter 4. The complete foundation will also include proof of compliance with the original writing rule. See Chapter 8. The foundation for the hearsay component is as follows:

P WHO prepared this document? (1)

W Well, it seems to have been prepared by Bob Grant.

P HOW do you know that? (1)

W I recognize his handwriting style. I've seen his writing on hundreds of occasions.

P WHO is Bob Grant? (1)

W He's one of our delivery personnel.

P As a delivery man, WHAT are Mr. Grant's duties? (2)

W He picks up merchandise in our warehouse in Scranton, makes sure that it gets to the customer, and prepares the paperwork on the delivery.

P WHICH of your employees are authorized to prepare the paperwork? (3)

W Only the delivery person in charge of that particular delivery. That's the employee who fills out the delivery report or sheet.

P WHEN does the delivery person make out the report? (4)

W He's supposed to make it out as soon as they make the delivery. At the very latest, they make it out when they get back to our office.

P HOW often do your employees prepare these reports? (5)

W Every time they make a delivery. I'd say that they send us 50 to 80 of those delivery sheets each week.

P WHAT form does the report take? (6)

W It's a standard, written report we call a delivery sheet. Like the one we have here, exhibit number three.

P WHY do you require that the delivery personnel prepare these reports? (7)

W There are all sorts of business reasons for the reports: accounting, inventory, taxes. You just can't run an efficient, profitable business establishment unless you keep very, very close tabs on your deliveries.

P WHAT does the delivery person do with the report after he or she prepares it?

W They hand it to someone in our office.

P WHAT does your office do with it?

W We store it in a separate file, including all the delivery sheets for that week.

P WHERE did you find plaintiff's exhibit number three for identification?

W In the file for that week's delivery sheets.

P WHEN did you remove it from that file?

W Just this morning before trial.

P Your Honor, I now offer plaintiff's exhibit number three for identification into evidence.

O Your Honor, I object to the exhibit's introduction on the ground that the exhibit is hearsay.

P The objection will be overruled, and plaintiff's exhibit number three will be received.

P Mr. Merton, please read the circled part of the exhibit to the jury.

W That part reads, "January 18—delivered 500 stereo speakers to Hyatt Corp."

P Your Honor, I request permission to submit plaintiff's exhibit number three to the jurors for their personal inspection.

J Permission granted.

§ 11-3 PUBLIC RECORDS AND REPORTS

§ 11-3(A) THE DOCTRINE

The second major documentary exception to the hearsay rule is the public record doctrine, also sometimes referred to as the official records doctrine. Just as business employees presumably are careful in gathering and recording information for their employers, public employees presumably are diligent in gathering and recording information for their employer, the government. For this reason, the Texas Rules admit public records as well as business entries. Texas Rule of Evidence 803(8) states the basic doctrine:

> The following are not excluded by the hearsay rule, even though the declarant is available as a witness . . .: Records, reports, statements, or data compilations, in any form, of public offices or agencies, setting forth
>
> (A) the activities of the office or agency;
>
> (B) matters observed pursuant to duty imposed by law as to which matters there was a duty to report, excluding in criminal cases matters observed by police officers and other law enforcement personnel; or
>
> (C) in civil cases as to any party and in a criminal case as against the state, factual findings resulting from an investigation made pursuant to authority granted by law;

unless the sources of information or other circumstances indicate lack of trustworthiness.

Note that within Rule 803(8) there are really three types of information which may fall within the exception for public records and that the rule applies differently in civil and criminal cases.

Chapter 4 discusses the authentication of public and official records. As noted in that discussion, the proponent of such a record rarely presents live, sponsoring testimony to authenticate the record. In most instances, live testimony is similarly unnecessary to lay the foundation for the public record exception to the hearsay rule. Two doctrines usually make the live testimony unnecessary. The first doctrine is judicial notice. The judge may judicially notice the statute, regulation, or custom requiring that the public official prepare the record. Second, Rule 902 recognizes that certain public and official records may be authenticated by an attesting certificate. If the attested copy is fair on its face (complete with no erasures), the document's face creates a permissive inference that the officials followed the proper procedures in preparing the particular record.

§ 11-3(B) ELEMENTS OF THE FOUNDATION

§ 11-3(B)(1) In General

Although there are points of commonality in laying the foundation for the three types of public records, in Rule 803(8), they are listed here separately for purposes of clarity. Note that for each of them, the trial court, under Rule 803(8), may exclude the offered evidence if it determines that the sources of information or other circumstances indicate lack of trustworthiness.

§ 11-3(B)(2) Elements—Activities of the Office or Agency

The foundation for establishing the activities of the office or agency under Rule 803(8)(A) is as follows:

1. There is a particular public office or agency.
2. The public office or agency prepared a record, report, statement, or data compilation, in any form.
3. The record, report, etc., describes the office's or agency's activities.

§ 11-3(B)(3) Elements—Matters Observed Pursuant to Duty

The foundation for the public records exception relating to matters observed by an office or agency, under Rule 803(8)(B), is as follows:

1. There is a particular public office or agency.
2. The public office or agency prepared a record, report, statement, or data compilation, in any form.

3. The office or agency had a duty, by law, to report certain matters it observed.
4. The record, report, etc., contains matters so observed. In criminal cases, Rule 803(8)(B) specifically excludes matters observed by police officers or other law enforcement personnel.[3]

§ 11-3(B)(4) Elements—Factual Findings

The foundation for the public records exception relating to factual findings under Rule 803(8)(C) is as follows:

1. There is a particular public office or agency.
2. The public office or agency prepared a record, report, statement, or data compilation, in any form.
3. The office or agency has been authorized by law to conduct investigations.
4. The report, statement, etc., contains factual findings resulting from that investigation.[4] In criminal cases, Rule 803(8)(C) is limited to use by a party offering the factual findings *against* the state.

While the proponent of a business record must, under Rule 803(6), show that the document was prepared at or near the time of the event recorded, Rule 803(8) contains no such requirement. Thus, if, long after the original event, the official discovers an error in the record and follows prescribed procedures for making a corrected entry, the corrected entry should still qualify as a public or official record.

§ 11-3(C) SAMPLE FOUNDATION

The following hypothetical demonstrates use of a foundation witness to introduce a public record under Rule 803(8). Assume that an issue in the case is the exact angle of an exit ramp off a state highway. The proponent wants to introduce a report through the testimony of Mr. Justin, an engineer working for the State Department of Highways and Public Transportation, which lists the grade of slope on the curve as 19 degrees. The proponent calls Mr. Justin as a witness.

---

[3] The Texas courts have concluded that a record inadmissible under Rule 803(8)(B) in a criminal case, is likewise inadmissible as a business record under Rule 803(6). *Cole v. State*, 839 S.W.2d 798 (Tex. Crim. App. 1990) (on rehearing). *See generally* WENDORF, SCHLUETER & BARTON, TEXAS RULES OF EVIDENCE MANUAL VIII-115 (6th ed. 2002).

[4] In *Beech Aircraft Corp. v. Rainey*, 488 U.S. 153 (1988), the Supreme Court indicated that "opinions" included in an official investigation report would be admissible as well. In *Rainey*, the Court was construing factual findings and stopped short of sanctioning the admission of legal conclusions.

P WHAT is your name, please?

W Mr. Tom Justin.

P Would you please spell your last name for the record?

W It is J-U-S-T-I-N.

P WHAT is your educational background?

W I have bachelor's and master's degrees in civil engineering from Texas A & M University.

P WHERE do you work? (2)

W I am a civil engineer for the Department of Highways and Public Transportation.

P WHAT is the Department of Highways and Public Transportation? (1)

W It's an official department of our state government.

P Briefly, WHAT are its responsibilities? (3)

W Well, it actually has a broad range of responsibilities. One of them is to monitor the state's highway system. We do that by periodically testing and surveying the roads and highways for potential problem areas.

P HOW long have you worked there? (2)

W The past seven years.

P [*To court reporter*] Would you please mark this as an exhibit for the plaintiff? [*Court reporter marks exhibit and hands it back to counsel.*]

P Thank you. Please let the record reflect that I am showing what has been marked as plaintiff's exhibit number six for identification to the opposing counsel. [*Shows to counsel.*]

P I request permission to approach the witness.

J Permission granted.

P Mr. Justin, I now hand you plaintiff's exhibit number six for identification. WHAT is it? (4)

W It's a survey report our office prepared on the curve on Texas Highway 87 seven-tenths of a mile north of the I-10 cutoff at Comfort.

P WHEN was the survey conducted? (4)

W In early 2000.

P WHY was it made? (2), (3)

W The regional office decided to conduct a safety inspection of the area, and the local supervisor ordered our office to do the field work.

P WHO actually inspected the curve? (3)

W A Mr. Wilson, who no longer works for the Department.

P WHO actually prepared the report? (2)

W He did.

P WHAT procedures are you supposed to follow in conducting this type of survey and preparing the report? (4)

W The practice is that you both drive the road and walk it with appropriate surveying equipment. You take detailed notes and then have them immediately transcribed.

P WHERE is this report ordinarily kept? (2)

W In our office files at the Department's local office. That is where I found it before coming to court this morning.

P Your Honor, I now offer plaintiff's exhibit number six for identification into evidence.

O Your Honor, I object to the introduction of the exhibit on the ground that the exhibit is hearsay.

P Your Honor, may we approach the bench?

J Yes.

P Your Honor, I concede that the exhibit is hearsay, but I submit that I've laid a complete foundation for the public record exception to the hearsay rule.

O In general, that's true. However, an additional requirement is that the entry offered be factual. Page 10 of the report has a lot of conclusory opinions. I want to know whether the plaintiff's counsel intends to read that page to the jury.

J [*To the proponent*] What is your intention?

P Our view is that both factual and opinion evidence is admissible under Rule 803(8). Under *Beech Aircraft Corp. v. Rainey*, opinions included in the report are admissible.

J The exhibit will be received, and you have permission to have the witness read the pertinent portions to the jury.

P Mr. Justin, please read the first measurement on page 7 to the jurors.

W The report reads, "While at the scene, I measured the slope of the curve. I determined the angle to be 19 degrees."

§ 11-4 LEARNED TREATISES

§ 11-4(A) THE DOCTRINE

Under pre-Rules Texas law, statements in learned treatises could only be used to impeach expert witnesses.[5] They were treated like inconsistent statements in the sense that the jury was not permitted to consider the statements in the treatise as substantive evidence. Texas Rule of Evidence 803(18) now includes a specific hearsay exception for learned treatises. Under the exception, the proponent may use statements in a treatise either on direct examination or on cross-examination of an *expert* witness. For a discussion of expert witnesses, see Chapter 9. The underlying reliability rationale for this exception is that treatises and similar publications are normally written by impartial and professional individuals who are willing to place their reputations on the line by subjecting their published works for public scrutiny. Thus, like the other hearsay exceptions based on trustworthiness principles, published treatises and like publications considered as reliable authority are more likely to be accurate.

The exception is not broad enough to include every book or periodical. It applies only to published treatises, periodicals, or pamphlets on a subject of history, medicine, or other science or art. The Rule does not define what "published" means. But read in the context of the Rule, which requires that the material must be "established as reliable authority," it probably means something more than the expert witness's locally photocopied materials.[6]

Rule 803(18) permits some leeway to the proponent in showing that the treatise is an established and reliable authority. That element may be shown through the testimony (or admission) of the expert witness on the stand, another expert's testimony, or by judicial notice.

Because there are dangers associated with the jury being able to read the entire treatise during its deliberations, the rule only permits the proponent to *read* statements in the treatise. That means that the proponent should be selective in choosing what statements will be read. Reading an entire chapter, for example, out of a complicated medical text might be permissible under this hearsay exception. But it would normally not be a good trial tactic.

If the proponent lays the foundation for a learned treatise under this exception, the statements in the treatise or other publication are admitted as substantive evidence, i.e., the proponent may argue to the jury that they should believe the statements as being true.

---

[5] *See* WENDORF, SCHLUETER & BARTON, TEXAS RULES OF EVIDENCE MANUAL VIII-129-30 (6th ed. 2002).

[6] In *United States v. Jones*, 712 F.2d 115 (5th Cir. 1983), the court indicated that Rule 803(18) is confined to published works that have been subjected to widespread collegial scrutiny.

§ 11-4(B) ELEMENTS OF THE FOUNDATION

The elements for establishing the learned treatise exception under Rule 803(18) are as follows:

1. An expert witness, qualified under Rule 702, is testifying.
2. There is a treatise, periodical, or pamphlet on the subject of history, medicine, or other science or art.
3. The treatise, periodical, or pamphlet is brought to the attention of the testifying expert witness during direct or cross-examination.
4. The treatise, periodical, or pamphlet is published.
5. The treatise, periodical, or pamphlet is considered an established reliable authority. This may be shown through the testimony of the expert on the stand, through another expert, or through judicial notice.

It is generally preferred that counsel treat the treatise as an exhibit by having it marked and identified. This assists the participants and the appellate court in sorting out what evidence and statements came from which exhibits. It is usually not important that the entire treatise be formally admitted into evidence. What the proponent is offering here are *statements* in the treatise. As noted *supra* at § 11-4(A), if the statements are admitted, they may be read into evidence but may not be, in the words of Rule 803(18), "received as exhibits."

§ 11-4(C) SAMPLE FOUNDATION

The following fact situation involves a medical malpractice case in which the plaintiff was permanently disabled following brain surgery to remove a cancerous brain tumor. One of the issues before the court is whether the defendant surgeon, Dr. Morts, adequately apprised the plaintiff of the risks of the particular method of surgery. The plaintiff has called its expert witness, Dr. Wilson, to the stand to testify that under the circumstances, Dr. Morts should have apprised the plaintiff of the mathematical risks of this particular type of surgery. The proponent is the plaintiff. Dr. Wilson has already been established as an expert witness under Rule 702. The direct examination continues.

P Dr. Wilson, are you familiar with Welby on *Modern Brain Surgery*, the fifth edition, 1999? (1), (2), (3), (4)

W Yes, very much so.

P Do you know WHO published it? (4)

W I believe it has been published by Medical Books Publishing out of New York City.

P HOW familiar are you with it? (3)

W Very. It is one of the leading national texts on brain surgery. It is used in most medical schools; I first read and studied from it in medical school. I have a personal copy in my office.

P HOW reliable is it? (5)

W Very. Not only is it used by surgeons as a reliable reference tool, it is often cited as authority in medical journal articles.

P WHAT attention is given in that text to brain cancer surgery? (2)

W There are two chapters on the subject.

P Your Honor, we request that this be marked as an exhibit for the plaintiff. [*Counsel hands exhibit to court reporter, who marks it and hands it back to counsel.*]

P Thank you. Please let the record reflect that I am showing what has been marked as plaintiff's exhibit four for identification to opposing counsel. [*Shows to counsel.*]

P Dr. Wilson, I now show you plaintiff's exhibit four for identification. Would you please tell us WHAT it is?

W This is the treatise by Dr. Welby on brain surgery that you were just asking me about.

P Your Honor, I now move that this text be admitted into evidence as plaintiff's exhibit number four.

O Your Honor, we object. Under Rule 803(18), counsel is not permitted to actually introduce the text as an exhibit.

J I will sustain the objection.

P Your Honor, then we move the admission of statements made on page 321 in plaintiff's exhibit number four for identification—specifically, the second and third sentences in the first paragraph.

J Those statements will be admitted. But the exhibit itself will not be received into evidence.

P Dr. Wilson, would you please turn to page 321 and read the second and third sentences in the first paragraph at the top of the page? [*Counsel points to part to be read.*]

W It says, "In deciding whether to operate, it must be remembered that the success rate of [the type of surgery performed in this case] is extremely low, and very risky. Any good surgeon will carefully explain that fact to the patient."

§ 11-5 PAST RECOLLECTION RECORDED AND PRESENT RECOLLECTION REFRESHED

§ 11-5(A) Past Recollection Recorded

§ 11-5(A)(1) The Doctrine

The next documentary hearsay exception is the past recollection recorded doctrine. Suppose that the witness on the stand cannot recall a particular fact or event. The witness's inability to recall supplies the necessity for resorting to hearsay evidence. If, at the time of the event, the witness had made a record of the fact or event, the record would be a reliable substitute for the witness's present recollection. The recognition of this necessity and reliability led to the development of the past recollection recorded doctrine.

Texas Evidence Rule 803(5) states the doctrine succinctly:

> A memorandum or record concerning a matter about which a witness once had knowledge but now has insufficient recollection to enable the witness to testify fully and accurately, shown to have been made or adopted by the witness when the matter was fresh in the witness' memory and to reflect that knowledge correctly.

If the proponent can show that the exhibit satisfies the doctrine, the real evidence is the document. Under Texas Rule 803(5), however, the proponent can only read the statements. If the document is to be admitted, it must be offered by the opponent. The reason for this rule is that the document is the functional equivalent of oral testimony and that it would place undue emphasis on that evidence to permit the jury to examine the document.

§ 11-5(A)(2) Elements of the Foundation

The foundation for the past recollection recorded hearsay exception includes these elements:

1. The witness formerly gained personal knowledge of the fact or events recorded.
2. The witness subsequently prepared, or adopted, a record of the facts.[7]

---

[7] It is possible under Rule 803(5) to have one person prepare the document and then have the witness verify it, or adopt it, while the event was still fresh in the witness's mind. This process is sometimes referred to as a cooperative report. There is apparently still a requirement, however, that the witness had personal knowledge about the event, even though it was initially recorded by someone else. *See, e.g.*, *Phea v. State*, 767 S.W.2d 263 (Tex. App.—Amarillo 1989, pet. refused).

3. The witness prepared the record while the events were still fresh in his or her memory.[8]
4. The witness can vouch that when he or she prepared the record, the record was accurate.[9]
5. At trial, the witness cannot completely and accurately recall the facts even after reviewing the document.[10]

§ 11-5(A)(3) Sample Foundation

The fact situation is a bank robbery prosecution. The government charges that Mr. Gary Vincent robbed a teller in the First National Bank in downtown New Braunfels. The witness is Ms. Jane Millot. Ms. Millot has already identified herself. She has testified that she works as a teller at the First National Bank. The prosecution is the proponent.

P Ms. Millot, WHERE were you on the morning of February 14, 2005? (1)

W I was at work at the bank.

P WHAT happened that morning? (1)

W One of the bank's tellers was robbed.

P HOW were the robbers dressed? (1)

W They all had masks on. That's why I can't identify any faces.

P WHAT happened immediately after the robbers took the money? (1)

W They made their getaway.

P HOW did they make their getaway? (1)

W In a white car parked in front of the bank.

P WHAT was the car's license number? (1), (5)

---

[8] Some courts have interpreted Rule 803(5) as liberalizing this timing requirement. In *United States v. Patterson*, 678 F.2d 774 (9th Cir. 1982), the court found a declarant's memory sufficiently fresh despite a 10-month time lapse.

[9] Ideally, the witness will recall the very occasion on which he or she prepared the document. Alternatively, the witness may testify that he or she habitually records that type of information and that their habit is to record the information carefully. A police officer assigned to the traffic detail could give that type of testimony about measurements at accident scenes. Finally, it may be acceptable if the witness at least recognizes his or her handwriting on the document. In this last situation, in reality, the witness is vouching for his or her own honesty. The witness is really testifying that he or she is an honest person and would not knowingly record false data.

[10] The early view was that the witness had to completely forget the event. Most modern courts are of the view that it is sufficient if the witness's memory is partial or hazy. In the words of Texas Rule 803(5), the witness cannot remember fully and accurately. The requirement is that the witness has made a good faith effort to remember.

W I can't remember. I saw it, but I can't remember it now.

P WHAT, if anything, might help you remember? (2)

W I made a note on a slip of paper I had at the time.

P WHAT did you note on this slip of paper? (2)

W The license number of the getaway car.

P WHO prepared this slip? (3)

W I did it myself.

P WHEN did you prepare this slip? (3)

W Right after the car got away.

P HOW many minutes passed between the time the car left and the time you wrote on the slip? (3)

W One or two. Not any more than that. I had the slip of paper and a pen in the pocket of my dress.

P HOW clear was your memory of the license number when you wrote the number down? (3), (4)

W I don't remember making any mistakes. I looked at it carefully, and it seemed okay at the time.

P [*To court reporter*] Would you please mark this as an exhibit for the State? [*Court reporter marks exhibit and hands it back to proponent.*]

P Please let the record reflect that I am showing State's exhibit number five for identification to the opposing counsel. [*Counsel shows exhibit to opposing counsel.*]

P Ms. Millot, I now hand you State's exhibit number five for identification. WHAT is it?

W It's the slip of paper I mentioned.

P HOW can you recognize it?

W I recognize my handwriting.

P Please read the exhibit silently to yourself. [*Pause*] Have you done so?

W Yes.

P Now please hand it to me. [*The witness does so.*] Your Honor, please let the record reflect that I am holding the exhibit away from the witness and out of her view.

J The record will so reflect.

P Ms. Millot, you've had a chance to read the exhibit and refresh your memory. Now, without relying on the exhibit, WHAT was the car's license number? (5)

W I still can't remember apart from the exhibit.

P WHY can't you remember? (5)

W I have a bad memory for numbers. I can't honestly say that I now remember the license number.

P Please read the slip of paper to the jury.

W It reads, "JSC 247."

P WHAT does that stand for?

W That's the license number of the getaway car.

§ 11-5(B) PRESENT RECOLLECTION REFRESHED

§ 11-5(B)(1) The Doctrine

In past recollection recorded, even after viewing the document, the witness cannot recall the relevant fact or event. Suppose that viewing the document refreshes the witness's recollection. Then the witness may testify from his or her revived recollection. The courts use the expressions *present recollection refreshed* or *present recollection revived* to describe the use of exhibits to refresh present memory. Under this theory, the real evidence is the witness's oral testimony, and the exhibit serves only as a memory aid or jogger.[11] Although it is usually a document which is used to refresh a witness's memory, virtually any object will do. Texas Rule of Evidence 612 governs this practice in Texas courts.

§ 11-5(B)(2) Elements of the Foundation

The foundation for present recollection refreshed or revived is quite simple:

1. The witness states that he or she cannot recall a fact or event.
2. The witness states that a certain writing or object could help refresh his or her memory. Many trial attorneys think that it is good practice to have the witness first mention the writing or object.
3. The proponent tenders the writing or object to the witness.
4. The proponent asks the witness to read the writing silently or to study the object.
5. The witness states that viewing the document or object refreshes his or her memory.

[11] *See* WENDORF, SCHLUETER & BARTON, TEXAS RULES OF EVIDENCE MANUAL VI-75 to VI-84 (6th ed. 2002) (noting the distinction between past recollection recorded and present memory refreshed).

6. The witness then testifies from revived memory.

On this theory, the evidence is the witness's oral testimony, and the proponent does not formally offer the writing or object into evidence. For purposes of making a good record, many trial judges prefer that the proponent at least mark the writing or object as an exhibit for identification.

The rule contains provisions for the opposing counsel to examine any writing used to jog the witness's memory, to cross-examine the witness on the writing, and to introduce pertinent portions of the writing into evidence.

§ 11-5(B)(3) Sample Foundation

The preceding robbery hypothetical can be used to illustrate present recollection refreshed. In this variation of the hypothetical, Ms. Millot has a better memory for numbers.

P WHAT was the getaway car's license number? (1)

W I can't honestly remember right now.

P WHAT, if anything, might help you remember? (2)

W I wrote the number down on a slip of paper.

P Your Honor, I request that this be marked by the court reporter as an exhibit for the State. [*Court reporter marks exhibit.*]

P Please let the record reflect that I am showing what has been marked as State's exhibit number five for identification to the opposing counsel.

J The record will so reflect.

P I request permission to approach the witness.

J Granted.

P Ms. Millot, I now hand you State's exhibit number five for identification. (3) WHAT is it? (2)

W It's the slip of paper I mentioned.

P HOW can you recognize it? (2)

W I ought to know my own handwriting style.

P Please read the exhibit silently to yourself. (4) [*Pause*] Have you done so?

W Yes.

P Now hand it to me. [*The witness does so.*] Your Honor, please let the record reflect that I am holding the exhibit away from the witness and out of her view.

J It will so reflect.

P Ms. Millot, you've had a chance to read the exhibit to refresh your memory. Now, without relying on the exhibit, can you remember the license number? (5)

W Yes.

P WHAT was the license number? (6)

W JSC 247.

Many experienced trial attorneys use this combination of past recollection recorded and present recollection refreshed. As soon as a witness states that he or she cannot recall a fact or event, the proponent lays elements one through four of the past recollection recorded foundation. The proponent then tenders the writing to the witness in an attempt to revive present recollection. If the attempt is successful, the witness testifies from present, refreshed memory. If the attempt is unsuccessful, the witness's inability to recall lays the last element of the past recollection recorded foundation. Whichever response the witness gives, the proponent elicits the desired testimony.

§ 11-6 EXCITED OR STARTLED UTTERANCES

§ 11-6(A) THE DOCTRINE

In the preceding sections, the focus was on documentary hearsay exceptions resting primarily on a showing of reliability. In each case, the showing is based on testimony describing the trustworthy manner in which the document was generated. The next sections address other hearsay exceptions recognized principally because of an inference of reliability. In these exceptions, however, the inference of reliability has a different basis. Each exception in this category is a variation of the old res gestae doctrine,[12] and rests on an inference of the declarant's sincerity. This category includes excited utterances under Rule 803(2), present sense impressions under Rule 803(1), declarations of bodily condition under Rule 803(4), and statements of mental condition under Rule 803(3).

The exception for excited utterances illustrates the common rationale of the exceptions in this category. A startling event occurs, an observer becomes excited, and the observer then makes a spontaneous statement about the event. The statement's spontaneity is the circumstantial guarantee of the declarant's sincerity. Texas Evidence Rule 803(2) describes the doctrine in this fashion: "[t]he following [is] not excluded by the hearsay rule, even though the declarant is available as a witness: A statement relating to a startling event or condition made while the declarant was under the stress of excitement caused by the event or condition."

---

[12] For a discussion of the problems associated with using the term res gestae, *see* WENDORF, SCHLUETER & BARTON, TEXAS RULES OF EVIDENCE MANUAL VIII-86 (6th ed. 2002).

§ 11-6(B) ELEMENTS OF THE FOUNDATION

The foundation for an excited utterance under Rule 803(2) includes the following elements:

1. An event occurred.[13]
2. The event was startling, or at least stressful.[14]
3. The declarant had personal knowledge of the event.[15]
4. The declarant made a statement about the event.[16]
5. The declarant made the statement while he or she was in a state of nervous excitement. This element is the subjective guarantee of the statement's sincerity.

§ 11-6(C) SAMPLE FOUNDATION

The fact situation is a tort action arising from a collision at an intersection. The plaintiff was driving a blue car. The defendant was driving a red car. The issue was which way each car was facing and which car ran a red light. The plaintiff calls Mr. Reynolds as a witness. Mr. Reynolds has already identified himself. The plaintiff is the proponent.

P WHERE were you on the afternoon of March 13th of last year? (1)

W I was in downtown Bryan at the intersection of Cedar Street and Sixth Avenue.

---

13 In the past, Texas courts required independent evidence of the event. The federal courts generally do not require any independent, corroborating evidence that the event occurred; these courts accept the declarant's assertion of the event's occurrence at face value. Assuming that adoption of Rule 803(2) has not abrogated the pre-Rules requirement, the quantum of required corroboration is usually slight. For example, if the declaration refers to an assault on the declarant and, at the time, the declarant's clothing was dirty and disheveled, the declarant's appearance might be sufficient proof that an assault occurred.

14 This element is the objective guarantee of the statement's sincerity. The nature of the event was likely to inspire nervous excitement.

15 The declarant must have been a participant in or an observer of the event. Again, the courts apply this element laxly. In some cases, the declarants have been unidentified bystanders. The courts have admitted the bystanders' excited statements so long as the time and place of the statement suggest that the bystander actually observed the event. Thus, if a person made a statement a few minutes after an accident and at the same intersection where the accident occurred, the court might assume that the declarant observed the accident.

16 At the end of the foundational questioning, the proponent usually asks the witness whether the out-of-court declarant made a statement about the event. The federal courts seem to be relaxing this requirement. In *United States v. Napier*, 518 F.2d 316 (9th Cir. 1975), a kidnapping victim was injured and became unconscious. Weeks later she saw a newspaper article containing a photograph of the defendant. She immediately stated, "He killed me, he killed me." The court admitted the statement as evidence of the defendant's identity as the kidnapper.

P WHY were you there? (1)

W I just happened to be walking my dog.

P WHAT, if anything, happened at the intersection while you were there? (1), (2)

W There was a collision.

P HOW noisy was the collision? (1), (2)

W It was an awful, shattering sound.

P HOW many bystanders were there? (1)

W I'd say that there were about 20 people in the immediate vicinity.

P WHAT was their reaction to the collision? (2)

W We were all shocked. It happened so fast, and the noise was so loud. And as soon as we looked, we could see that some people were injured and bleeding. It was just an awful sight.

P WHO else besides yourself was in the crowd of bystanders? (3)

W There were a number of people mingling around, but there was one guy in particular who stuck in my mind.

P WHAT was his name? (3)

W I never got his name.

P WHAT did he look like?

W He was a Caucasian male, maybe 30 or 35.

P WHERE was he at the time of the collision? (3)

W Standing right next to me.

P HOW was he facing? (3)

W He was looking right into the intersection. He was evidently waiting for the light to change to walk across.

P WHAT was his condition right after the collision? (5)

W He was just like the rest of us—shocked and frightened.

P WHAT was his facial expression? (5)

W He had his mouth open. I guess he was dumbfounded at first.

P WHAT was his tone of voice? (5)

W He was shouting in a loud voice.

P WHAT were his gestures? (5)

W He was pointing at the wreck and gesturing wildly.

P WHAT, if anything, did he say about the accident?

O Your Honor, I object to that question on the ground that it calls for hearsay.

P Your Honor, may I be heard?

J Yes.

P Although the statement is hearsay, it clearly falls within the excited utterance exception under Rule 803(2).

J The objection will be overruled.

P Mr. Reynolds, let me repeat the question. WHAT, if anything, did this man say about the accident? (4)

W He said that the fellow in the red car had gone right through the red light and caused the collision.

§ 11-7 PRESENT SENSE IMPRESSIONS OR CONTEMPORANEOUS STATEMENTS

§ 11-7(A) THE DOCTRINE

The spontaneity of the statement is the basic rationale for the excited utterance exception. The statement's contemporaneity can also serve as proof of the declarant's sincerity. The fact that the declarant makes the statement at roughly the same time the event occurs is some evidence of the statement's reliability. Texas Rule 803(1) provides: "[t]he following [is] not excluded by the hearsay rule, even though the declarant is available as a witness: . . . A statement describing or explaining an event or condition made while the declarant was perceiving the event or condition, or immediately thereafter."

The present sense impression doctrine differs from the excited utterance doctrine in two important respects. First, the timing requirement is more rigorous under the present sense impression doctrine. To qualify as a contemporaneous statement, the declaration must usually be made within minutes after the event. If the declarant is still excited or in pain, an excited utterance can be made hours after the event. Second, the event need not be startling to prompt a present sense impression statement. The guarantee of trustworthiness is contemporaneity rather than nervous spontaneity.

Note that there is no requirement in Rule 803(1) that the declarant be a participant in the event described.

§ 11-7(B) ELEMENTS OF THE FOUNDATION

The foundation for present sense impression, Rule 803(1), includes these elements:

1. An event occurred.[17]
2. The declarant had personal knowledge of the event.
3. The declarant made the statement during or very shortly after the event.
4. The statement relates to the event.

§ 11-7(C) SAMPLE FOUNDATION

To illustrate this doctrine, we can use the same hypothetical of the red and blue cars colliding as in § 11-6(C). In this variation of the hypothetical, the proponent omits the questions designed to show the declarant's nervous excitement.

P WHERE were you on the afternoon of March 13th of last year? (1)

W I was in downtown Bryan at the intersection of Cedar Street and Sixth Avenue.

P WHY were you there? (1)

W I just happened to be walking my dog there.

P WHAT, if anything, happened at the intersection while you were there? (1)

W There was a collision.

P HOW far were you from the collision when it occurred? (1)

W I was about 30 feet from the point of impact. That's just a rough estimate.

P HOW were you facing? (1)

W I was waiting for the light to change, so I was looking right into the intersection.

P HOW clear was your line of sight to the collision? (1)

W It was clear. I don't think there were any cars obstructing my view.

P HOW much of the collision did you see? (1)

W Just about the whole thing. I saw the cars approaching the intersection and actually collide.

P HOW many other bystanders were there? (2)

W I'd say that there were about 20 people in the immediate vicinity.

P WHO were the bystanders? (2)

W I didn't know any by name, but one guy in particular stuck in my mind.

---

17 As in the case of excited utterances, it is not clear whether the proponent must present independent, corroborating evidence that the event occurred. In most cases, as a practical matter, there will be such evidence. The declarant's appearance and demeanor can constitute evidence.

P WHAT did he look like? (2)

W He was a Caucasian male, maybe 30 or 35.

P WHERE was he at the time of the collision? (2)

W He was standing right next to me.

P HOW was he facing? (2)

W He was looking right into the intersection. He was evidently waiting for the light to change to walk across.

P WHAT did he do after the collision? (3)

W He was pointing to the wreck, and we talked about the collision.

P WHEN did you and this bystander talk about the collision? (3)

W Right after it happened.

P HOW many minutes elapsed between the collision and your discussion of the collision with this bystander? (3)

W It may have been a minute or two, but it was no longer than that.

P WHAT, if anything, did this bystander say about the accident? (4)

O Your Honor, I object to that question on the ground that it calls for hearsay.

P Your Honor, may I be heard?

J Yes.

P I will concede that the question calls for hearsay, but the record shows that any statement by the bystander qualifies as a present sense impression or contemporaneous statement under Rule 803(1).

J The objection will be overruled.

P Mr. Reynolds, let me repeat the question. WHAT, if anything, did this bystander say about the accident? (4)

W He said that the fellow in the red car had gone right through the red light and caused the collision.

§ 11-8 DECLARATIONS OF STATE OF MIND OR EMOTION OFFERED TO PROVE STATE OF MIND OR EMOTION

§ 11-8(A) Statements Offered to Prove State of Mind or Emotion

§ 11-8(A)(1) The Doctrine

One of the most difficult things for a trial attorney to prove is a person's state of mind. The attorney must usually rely on circumstantial proof, such as conduct which evidences a certain state of mind. Sometimes, however, a person openly declares his or her state of mind. Because of the difficulty of proving state of mind, the courts have been especially inclined to admit any apparently sincere declarations of state of mind or emotion. These declarations often give us the best insight into the declarant's state of mind or emotion. Thus, the courts have developed a general rule that these declarations are admissible. If a person declares his or her then existing state of mind or emotion, the declaration is admissible to prove the existence of that state of mind or emotion.

Texas Evidence Rule 803(3) provides: "[t]he following [is] not excluded by the hearsay rule, even though the declarant is available as a witness: . . . A statement of the declarant's then existing state of mind [or] emotion."

Ideally, the declarant will make the statement at the pivotal time under the substantive law. For example, under real property law, the grantor must have the intent to pass title when he hands the deed to the grantee. If at the very instant he hands the deed to the grantee, the grantor states that he intends to pass title, the statement is certainly admissible. What if the grantor makes such a statement shortly before or shortly after the manual delivery of the deed? The courts still admit the statement on the theory of continuity of state of mind; the time lapse between the statement and the critical event is so short that we may assume that the declarant's state of mind was the same at both times.

§ 11-8(A)(2) Elements of the Foundation

The foundation for this doctrine is simple. The proponent need only establish the normal foundation for an event:

1. Where the statement was made.
2. When the statement was made. The declarant must make the statement at or near the pivotal time under the substantive law.
3. Who was present.
4. Who made the statement.
5. The tenor of the statement.

§ 11-8(A)(3) Sample Foundation

The fact situation is a quiet title action. The plaintiff, Ms. Sheila Morris, has brought suit against the defendant, Ms. Marilyn Winters. Ms. Morris claims title from the original titleholder, Mr. Forest Morris, her grandfather. She claims that on December 25, 2003, her grandfather gave her a deed to the property as a Christmas present. The plaintiff calls Mr. Thomas Morris, her brother, as a witness. The plaintiff is the proponent.

P WHERE were you on December 25, 2003? (1), (2)

W I was at our family Christmas party at Lufkin.

P WHO else was there? (3)

W All the close relatives, including Grandfather and my sister, Sheila.

P WHAT, if anything, unusual happened during the party?

W As an unexpected Christmas gift, Grandfather handed Sheila a deed to his land near Fredericksburg.

P WHAT, if anything, did he do when he handed her the deed? (4)

W Well, he did say something.

P WHAT did he say? (5)

W He said that he wanted her to have the land because, ever since she was a little girl, she had loved to vacation there.

In the next variation of the hypothetical, the grantor makes the statement shortly before delivery of the deed.

P WHERE were you on December 25, 2003? (1), (2)

W I was at our family Christmas party at Lufkin.

P WHO else was there? (3)

W All the close relatives, including Grandfather and my sister, Sheila.

P WHAT, if anything, unusual happened during the party?

W As an unexpected Christmas gift, Grandfather handed Sheila a deed to his land in Fredericksburg.

P WHAT, if anything, did he say about the deed during the party? (5)

O Objection, your Honor. That question calls for hearsay.

P Your Honor, may we approach the bench?

J Yes.

P Your Honor, I offer to prove that the witness will say the grandfather said he wanted Sheila to have the land. The witness will also testify the grandfather made this statement only an hour before handing the deed to Sheila. The time lapse is so short that we may assume that the grandfather's state of mind was the same at both times.

J The objection will be overruled.

P Mr. Morris, let me repeat the question. WHAT, if anything, did your grandfather say about the deed during the party? (5)

W He said he wanted Sheila to have the land because, ever since she was a little girl, she had loved to vacation there.

P WHEN did your grandfather say that? (4)

W A little while before he handed the deed to her.

P Specifically, HOW many minutes or hours before he handed her the deed? (4)

W About an hour, maybe a little less.

§ 11-8(B) STATEMENTS OFFERED TO PROVE CONDUCT

§ 11-8(B)(1) The Doctrine

In § 11-8(A)(1), *supra*, the declarations of state of mind are used when state of mind itself is in issue. There is another use for state of mind declarations. Suppose that the declaration is a statement of present plan, intention, or design: "I plan to," "I intend to," or "I am going to."

These declarations indicate that the declarant currently plans to engage in subsequent conduct. Moreover, the fact that the declarant expressed that intent increases the probability that the declarant subsequently performed the planned act. Texas Evidence Rule 803(3) also sanctions this use of state of mind declarations; it expressly authorizes the admission of statements of "intent, plan, . . . [or] design . . . ."

It should be added that the exception is not broad enough to include a declarant's out-of-court statements of memory, or a past state of mind. In other words, the exception only looks forward, not backwards. For example, an out-of-court statement by the declarant that she remembered being angry on a prior occasion would not fall within this exception.

§ 11-8(B)(2) Elements of the Foundation

The foundation for introducing a declarant's statements to prove subsequent conduct is as follows:

1. Where the statement was made.
2. When the statement was made.
3. Who was present.
4. Who made the statement.
5. The tenor of the statement.

§ 11-8(B)(3) Sample Foundation

The fact situation is a burglary prosecution. The government alleges that the defendant, Mr. Michael Waylen, burglarized a drug store in Hondo on August 17th. The defendant raises an alibi defense. The defendant testifies that he was with his girlfriend in Oklahoma City on the day of the burglary. His girlfriend testifies to the same effect. Now the defendant calls Mr. John Farmer as a witness. Mr. Farmer has already identified himself. The defendant is the proponent:

P Mr. Farmer, WHERE were you on the evening of August 15th? (1), (2)

W I was at a party at a friend's here in Hondo.

P WHO else was at the party? (3)

W A lot of people, including the defendant, Michael Waylen.

P WHERE is the defendant now? (3)

W He's in the courtroom.

P Specifically, WHERE in the courtroom? (3)

W He's sitting at that table.

P HOW is he dressed? (3)

W He's wearing a gray sweater and black pants.

P Your Honor, please let the record reflect that the witness has identified the defendant.

J It will so reflect.

P Mr. Farmer, WHAT happened during the party? (4)

W It was just a quiet party. I drank a little and talked with some friends.

P WHOM did you talk with? (4)

W I had a nice long talk with Michael, the defendant.

P WHAT did you talk about? (5)

W A lot of things, especially his plans for the future.

P WHAT, if anything, did the defendant say about his immediate plans? (5)

O Your Honor, I object to that last question on the ground that it calls for self-serving hearsay.

P Your Honor, may we approach the bench to be heard?

J Yes.

P Your Honor, I offer to prove that the witness will testify that the defendant said he intended to visit his girlfriend in Oklahoma City the weekend of the alleged crime. The defendant's statement falls within the hearsay exception for declarations of present state of mind under Rule 803(3).

J The objection will be overruled. You may proceed.

P WHAT, if anything, did the defendant say about his immediate plans? (5)

W He said that weekend he was going to visit his girlfriend, Norma, in Oklahoma City.

P WHICH weekend was he referring to? (5)

W He mentioned the weekend of August 17 and 18.

Assume that a murder victim made a statement that she presently intended to meet the defendant at a particular location. Later the victim's body is found at that location. Under this exception, the victim's statement is certainly admissible to prove that she carried out her plan and went to that location. Is the statement also admissible as evidence that the defendant met her at that location? The courts have divided over this question. If the court holds that the statement is inadmissible for that purpose, the judge must either remove the reference to the defendant or give the jury a limiting instruction about the proper use of the statement.

In the limiting instruction, the judge would tell the jury that although it could treat the statement as the basis for an inference as to the declarant's own later conduct, it could not use the statement as evidence of the accused's conduct. Thus, in closing argument the prosecutor could employ the statement as evidence that the declarant went to the location she mentioned, but the prosecutor could not utilize the statement as evidence that the accused went to that location.

§ 11-9 DECLARATIONS OF BODILY CONDITION

§ 11-9(A) Present Bodily Condition

§ 11-9(A)(1) The Doctrine

The courts are almost as willing to admit evidently sincere statements of bodily condition as they are to admit statements of mental condition. Texas Rule 803(3) specifically authorizes the admission of statements of "pain and bodily health . . . ." Ordinarily, if a declarant proclaims his or her present bodily sensation or condition, the declaration is admissible. There is no requirement that the statement be made to a physician or health care provider. Those types of statements are discussed *infra* at § 11-9(B). Rule 803(3) is silent concerning statements made after the controversy arose. If it appears to the trial judge that the circumstances in the making of the statement are suspect, the judge could, in theory, exclude the evidence as not being reliable.

§ 11-9(A)(2) Elements of the Foundation

The foundation for establishing the present bodily condition exception under Rule 803(3) includes these elements:

1. Where the statement was made.

2. When the statement was made.
3. Who was present.
4. Who made the statement.
5. To whom the statement was made.
6. The tenor of the statement. The statement must refer to the person's present bodily condition.

§ 11-9(A)(3) Sample Foundation

This fact situation will illustrate the doctrine. The plaintiff, Ms. Joan Gillette, brings a products liability action against Miller Pharmaceuticals. The plaintiff alleges that the defendant sold her defective medication and that the medication caused her serious internal injuries. Her complaint prayed for $5,000 for pain and suffering. At the trial, she calls Mr. Leonard Wright as a witness. Mr. Wright identifies himself and states that he is her employer and that shortly after she took the medication she showed up in his office. The plaintiff is the proponent.

P Mr. Wright, WHERE were you on the afternoon of January 28th? (1), (2)

W In my office.

P WHO else was there? (3)

W The plaintiff, Ms. Gillette.

P WHERE is the plaintiff now? (3)

W In this courtroom.

P Specifically, WHERE in the courtroom? (3)

W She's sitting at that table to your right.

P HOW is she dressed? (3)

W She's wearing a white blouse and a green skirt.

P Your Honor, please let the record reflect that the witness identified the plaintiff.

J It will so reflect.

P WHAT happened while the plaintiff was at your office? (3), (4), (5), (6)

W Well, she came in and complained that she had a terrible headache and felt sick to her stomach.

P Specifically, WHAT did she say to you? (4), (5), (6)

O Your Honor, I object to that question on the ground that it calls for hearsay.

P Your Honor, may we approach the bench?

J Yes.

P I agree that the question calls for hearsay. However, I offer to prove that the witness will testify that the plaintiff said she was then in terrible pain. That statement qualifies as a declaration of present bodily condition under Rule 803(3).

J Objection overruled.

P Let me repeat the question. WHAT did Ms. Gillette say to you? (6)

W She said that she was experiencing tremendous pressure and pain in the back of her head. She also said that she was feeling nauseous and that there was a tingling sensation in her left arm.

§ 11-9(B) PAST BODILY CONDITION

§ 11-9(B)(1) The Doctrine

A majority of jurisdictions now admit statements of past bodily condition as substantive proof in limited circumstances. The Texas Rules commit the Texas courts to this view. Texas Evidence Rule 803(4) states:

> The following are not excluded by the hearsay rule, even though the declarant is available as a witness: . . . Statements made for purposes of medical diagnosis or treatment and describing the medical history, or past or present symptoms, pain, or sensations, or the inception or general character of the cause or external source thereof insofar as reasonably pertinent to diagnosis or treatment.

This particular exception is grounded on the assumption that declarants will make reliable statements when they are seeking medical assistance. It is not necessary that the statements be made to a doctor, or even to medical personnel. For example, a man's statements to his wife who in turn transmits them over the phone to a nurse would probably be covered. But statements by medical personnel to the declarant would probably not be covered.[18]

The key requirement here is that the statements be "pathologically germane" to treatment. That is, the statement must be "reasonably pertinent to diagnosis or treatment." Thus, the courts will usually admit statements regarding the cause of an injury or condition. But they will almost always exclude statements regarding fault.[19]

---

18 *See Bulthuis v. Rexall Corp.*, 777 F.2d 1315 (9th Cir. 1985).

19 Texas courts, however, have admitted statements made by a child abuse victim which identified the attacker. The rationale for receiving such statements is that where child abuse or injury is involved, physical, psychological, and emotional treatment is aided by identification of the defendant. *See, e.g., Tissier v. State*, 792 S.W.2d 120 (Tex. App.—Houston [1st Dist.] 1990, pet. refused).

The Advisory Committee's Note to Federal Rule 803(4) explains that "a patient's statement that he was struck by an automobile would qualify but not his statement that the car was driven through a red light." Statements of past medical history and present bodily condition fall within this exception.

§ 11-9(B)(2) Elements of the Foundation

The foundation for the medical diagnosis exception under Rule 803(4) usually includes these elements:

1. The declarant made the statement to a proper addressee.
2. The declarant made the statement for purposes of diagnosis or treatment.[20]
3. The subject matter of the statement was proper.

§ 11-9(B)(3) Sample Foundation

The fact situation is a personal injury action. The plaintiff, Ms. Norton, alleges that she sustained severe internal injuries after ingesting some of the defendant's medicine. The defendant is Shaevers Drug Company. The plaintiff wants to introduce a hospital record. The record contains the following entry in section #15, Medical History: "[t]he patient stated she experienced intense pain after drinking from a bottle of cough medicine." The plaintiff calls Mr. Florence as a witness. Mr. Florence identifies himself, states that he is University Hospital's records librarian, and lays a proper business entry foundation for the hospital record itself. The exhibit has already been marked for identification as plaintiff's exhibit number four. The plaintiff is the proponent.

P Now, Doctor, permit me to direct your attention to this section on exhibit number four for identification, the section labeled #15. WHAT is that section?

W That's the case history part of the patient's record.

P WHAT is case history?

W The patient's past medical history.

P WHO took this medical history? (1)

---

[20] The Rule does not specifically exclude statements which might have been made for purposes of litigation. The Federal Rules opt for a more liberal view. The Federal Rules permit the statement's admission if the declarant sought diagnosis or treatment. A diagnosis for purpose of trial is sufficient. The Advisory Committee Note expressly repudiates the "[c]onventional doctrine . . . exclud[ing] from the hearsay exception, as not within its guarantee of truthfulness, statements to a physician consulted only for the purpose of enabling him to testify." If it appears that this was the only motive for the statement, the jury may take that into account in determining what weight, if any, to give to the statement.

W Dr. Morrell, one of our internists.

P HOW do you know he took it? (1)

W I recognize his signature and handwriting style.

P WHO normally takes the history? (1)

W The intern.

P WHEN does the intern ordinarily take the history from the patient? (2)

W As soon as the patient arrives at the first processing station.

P WHY does the intern take the history? (2)

W It's often critical to diagnosis and treatment. The case history helps you make a much more informed evaluation of the patient's condition.

P WHAT, if anything, does the intern usually tell the patient about the purpose of taking the case history? (2)

W Some patients are very resentful of prying, and we always tell them that we are taking the history to give them better treatment. We tell them we need to know everything about their medical past.

P Now, Doctor, without disclosing to the jury the precise entry on the exhibit, WHY would this particular entry have been included in the patient's case history? (2)

W Well, it describes how the patient suffered the injuries. The treating doctor has to have that sort of data to do a professional, competent job.

P Your Honor, I now offer plaintiff's exhibit number four for identification into evidence.

O Your Honor, I object to the introduction of the exhibit on the ground that it is hearsay. In fact, it is double hearsay.

P Your Honor, may we approach the bench?

J Yes.

P Your Honor, under Rule 805, even double hearsay is admissible if each statement falls within a hearsay exception. The first statement, the hospital record itself, qualifies as a business entry.

J Are we in agreement on that point?

O Yes, your Honor.

P The second statement, of course, is my client's statement reflected in section #15 of the report. I feel that it qualifies as a statement of past bodily condition under Rule 803(4). My client made the statement to a physician in order to obtain treatment. And statements of past condition and external cause are admissible.

J The objection will be overruled, and the exhibit will be received.

P Dr. Florence, would you please read section #15 to the jury? (3)

W It reads, "The patient stated she experienced intense pain after drinking from a bottle of cough medicine."

§ 11-10 DECLARATIONS AGAINST INTEREST

§ 11-10(A) THE DOCTRINE

Admissions of a party-opponent are disserving to the declarant's interest at the time of trial. The admission is inconsistent with some position the party-opponent is defending at the time of trial. So long as the statement is disserving at that time, it is admissible as nonhearsay under Rule 801, even if it was highly self-serving when made.

Declarations against interest, under Rule 803(24), contrast with admissions in several respects. Declarations against interest are admissible only if, at the time of the statement, the declarant believed the statement was contrary to his or her interest. The declarant's belief is the guarantee of the reliability of declarations against interest. Secondly, the declarant of an admission must be the party-opponent, while any person can make a declaration against interest.

Texas Rule 803(24) states the doctrine:

> The following are not excluded by the hearsay rule, even if the declarant is available as a witness: . . . A statement which was at the time of its making so far contrary to the declarant's pecuniary or proprietary interest, or so far tended to subject the declarant to civil or criminal liability, or to render invalid a claim by the declarant against another, or to make him an object of hatred, ridicule, or disgrace, that a reasonable person in his position would not have made the statement unless believing it to be true.

It is important to note that under the Federal Rules, this provision is located in Rule 804, which covers hearsay exceptions requiring that the declarant be unavailable at trial.

§ 11-10(B) ELEMENTS OF THE FOUNDATION

The foundation for the statement against interest hearsay exception includes the following elements:

1. The declarant subjectively believed that the statement was contrary to his or her interest.
2. The interest was a recognized type of interest (civil or criminal liability, proprietary interest, social interest, etc.).

3. In criminal cases, if either side offers a statement in which the declarant is exposed to criminal liability, there must be corroboration to show that the statement is trustworthy.

§ 11-10(C) SAMPLE FOUNDATION

The fact situation is a robbery prosecution. The state alleges that the defendant, Mr. Charles Bosley, robbed the manager of the Midland Stereo Store in Amarillo on February 17th. The defense theory is that Mr. Gregory Bennett actually committed the robbery. During the defense case-in-chief, the defense calls Mr. William Store. Mr. Store has already identified himself. The defendant is the proponent.

P WHAT is your occupation?

W I am a member of the Amarillo Police Department.

P HOW long have you held that position?

W For about eight years.

P WHERE were you on the morning of February 19th?

W I was on duty at the station.

P WHAT happened while you were on duty that morning?

W Some patrolmen brought in a suspect for questioning.

P WHO was the suspect?

W A Gregory Bennett.

P WHAT happened after the patrolmen brought in Mr. Bennett?

W As is my custom, I first informed him of his rights.

P WHAT rights did you tell him about? (1), (2)

W I told him he had a privilege against self-incrimination and a right to counsel—all of the *Miranda* warnings.

P WHAT was his condition when you informed him of his rights? (1)

W He seemed okay. He was alert, and there didn't seem to be anything physically wrong with him.

P HOW did he react when you informed him of his rights? (1)

W He seemed concerned.

P WHAT did you do after you informed Mr. Bennett of his rights? (1)

W I asked him if he understood his rights.

P HOW did he respond? (1)

W He said he understood them and did not want a lawyer, and then he gave me some factual information I wanted.

P WHAT did you do after you spoke with Mr. Bennett? (3)

W I attempted to verify some of the facts Mr. Bennett had told me.

P WHAT facts? (3)

W He told me about the location of some of the stolen property, some receivers and speakers.

P WHAT did Mr. Bennett say about the location of the stolen property? (3)

W He said that several of the stolen receivers and speakers were in his apartment.

P WHAT steps did you take to verify his statement? (3)

W With his consent, I visited and searched his apartment.

P WHAT did you find in his apartment? (3)

W I found his personal effects. In addition, I found several receivers and speakers. I checked the serial numbers against the list supplied by Midland Stereo. The numbers matched.

P Mr. Store, during your questioning of Mr. Bennett, WHO did he say robbed the manager of the Midland Stereo Store on February 17th?

O Your Honor, I object to that question on the ground that it calls for hearsay.

P Your Honor, may we approach the bench?

J Yes.

P Your Honor, I offer to prove that the witness will testify that Mr. Bennett confessed to the robbery my client is charged with. In light of the warnings Officer Store gave Mr. Bennett, Mr. Bennett must have realized his confession was contrary to his penal interest. There is corroboration that Mr. Bennett was involved in the robbery. Some of the stolen property was found in his apartment. Therefore, his statements are admissible under Rule 803(24) as a statement against interest.

J The objection will be overruled.

P Officer Store, let me repeat the question. WHO did Mr. Bennett say robbed the manager of the Midland Stereo Store?

W He said that he did.

PART 2
HEARSAY EXCEPTIONS BASED ON A SHOWING OF UNAVAILABILITY

§ 11-11 HEARSAY EXCEPTIONS BASED ON UNAVAILABILITY—RULE 804

§ 11-11(A) INTRODUCTION

The preceding sections analyze hearsay exceptions recognized primarily because of an inference of the reliability of the hearsay statement. Other exceptions, though, depend to a greater degree for their recognition on a showing of necessity for resorting to the hearsay. These exceptions require proof of the declarant's unavailability at the time of trial. The following section discusses the test for unavailability. §§ 11-12 and 11-13 then describe two hearsay exceptions requiring proof of unavailability as part of their foundation: dying declarations and former testimony.

§ 11-11(B) ESTABLISHING UNAVAILABILITY OF THE DECLARANT AT TRIAL

§ 11-11(B)(1) The Doctrine

At common law, the exceptions requiring proof of unavailability emerged at different times and developed varying tests for unavailability. Some exceptions demanded proof of the declarant's death, while others were satisfied by proof that the declarant was beyond the reach of compulsory process. Texas Rule of Evidence 804(a) establishes a single, uniform definition of unavailability. That Rule provides:

"Unavailability as a witness" includes situations in which the declarant:

(1) is exempted by ruling of the court on the ground of privilege from testifying concerning the subject matter of his statement;

(2) persists in refusing to testify concerning the subject matter of his statement despite an order of the court to do so; (3) testifies to a lack of memory of the subject matter of his statement;

(4) is unable to be present or to testify at the hearing because of death or then existing physical or mental illness or infirmity; or

(5) is absent from the hearing and the proponent of statement has been unable to procure the declarant's attendance or testimony by process or other reasonable means.

A declarant is not unavailable as a witness if exemption, refusal, claim of lack of memory, inability, or absence is due to the procurement or wrongdoing of the proponent of a statement for the purpose of preventing the witness from attending or testifying.

Whether any of these reasons for unavailability is present is a decision for the trial judge under Rule of Evidence 104(a).

§ 11-11(B)(2) Elements of the Foundation

Under Rule 804(a), there are numerous methods of demonstrating the prior witness's unavailability. In the first three subsections of Rule 804(a), the witness is technically unavailable, but actually present at hearing #2. Under Rule 804(a)(1), the witness is deemed unavailable if the witness "is exempted by ruling of the court on the ground of privilege from testifying concerning the subject matter of the declarant's statement." The prior witness from hearing #1 actually takes the stand in hearing #2, but the witness properly refuses to testify on the ground of privilege.

Under Rule 804(a)(2), the witness is considered unavailable if he or she "persists in refusing to testify concerning the subject matter of the declarant's statement despite an order of the court to do so." Here, the witness does not have a legitimate ground for refusing to answer. But if the witness refuses an order to answer, as a practical matter the witness is unavailable.

Under Rule 804(a)(3), the witness is unavailable if the witness "testifies to a lack of memory of the subject matter of the declarant's statement." Here also, the witness is physically present, but as a practical matter the witness's testimony is unavailable. When the proponent is relying on one of these three grounds to show unavailability, the proponent need ensure only that the witness's refusal or failure to recall is reflected on the record. The proponent should ask point blank about the topic of the prior statement or testimony, "WHAT was the color of the defendant's car?" If the witness responds "I refuse to answer" or "I cannot remember," there is a sufficient showing of unavailability.

Rule 804(a)(4) declares that the prior witness is unavailable if the witness "is unable to be present or to testify at the hearing because of death or then existing physical or mental illness or infirmity." If the witness is now dead, the proponent may introduce a properly attested death certificate. The death certificate qualifies as an official record. If the witness is ill, under Rule 104(a), the court may permit the proponent to prove the illness by a physician's affidavit, declaration, or letter. Otherwise, the proponent may have to call the physician at hearing #2 to prove the illness of the prior witness. The proponent would have to lay the expert opinion testimony foundation outlined in Chapter 9: the physician's qualifications, the physician's major premise, the basis of the expert's opinion, the ultimate opinion that the former witness is now too ill to appear and testify, and the expert's explanation of the opinion. (Remember that in determining the existence of preliminary facts under Rule 104(a), the trial judge need not follow the technical exclusionary rules such as hearsay.)

Finally, Rule 804(a)(5) announces that a declarant is considered unavailable if the witness "is absent from the hearing and the proponent of a statement has been unable to procure the declarant's attendance . . . by process or other reasonable means."

§ 11-11(B)(3) Sample Foundations

The following examples demonstrate how the proponent might show that a declarant is unavailable under Rule 804(a)(5). The first situation is the case in which the proponent simply cannot locate the former witness. The proponent could use a process server's testimony to establish the former witness's unavailability.

P WHAT is your name?

W Michael Senet.

P Would you please spell your last name for the record?

W Yes, it's spelled S-E-N-E-T.

P WHERE do you live?

W At 1440 Alsworth Street here in El Paso.

P HOW long have you lived there?

W For the past five years.

P WHAT is your occupation?

W I am a process server.

P WHERE do you work?

W I work for the Speedy Process Service Company downtown.

P HOW long have you worked there?

W Three years.

P HOW long have you been a process server?

W Three years.

P Mr. Senet, WHERE were you on the morning of January 17th of this year?

W I stopped by your office.

P WHY did you visit my office?

W You had phoned and asked me to pick up a subpoena.

P WHOM was the subpoena for?

W John Milton.

P WHAT was his address?

W Both the subpoena and the telephone directory listed his address as 40 Paradise Lost, Apartment 201.

P WHAT did you do after you picked up the subpoena?

W I went directly to the address given.

P WHAT happened when you arrived there?

W I inquired whether he still lived there.

P WHAT was the result of your inquiry?

O Your Honor, I object to that question on the ground that it calls for hearsay.

P Your Honor, may we approach the bench?

J Yes.

P Your Honor, I offer to prove that this witness will testify that the manager said Mr. Milton had moved. I want to use the testimony for a nonhearsay purpose, its effect on the process server's state of mind. The issue is whether the process server acted reasonably and diligently. We have to judge his diligence in light of the information about Mr. Milton he was given by other persons such as the apartment manager.

J The objection will be overruled.

P Mr. Senet, let me repeat the question. WHAT was the result of your inquiry at Mr. Milton's apartment?

W The manager said he had moved.

P WHAT was Mr. Milton's new address?

W Unfortunately, he did not leave a forwarding address.

P WHAT did you do then?

W Over the next few days, I contacted other companies and agencies that might have Milton's new address.

P WHICH companies and agencies did you contact?

W To list just some, I talked to people at the telephone company, the gas company, the electric company, and the welfare department.

P WHAT was the result of your contact with these companies and agencies?

W It was negative. None of them knew where I could locate Mr. Milton.

P HOW many hours did you spend talking to people at these companies and agencies?

W Over the period of days, I'd estimate I spent at least 10 full hours trying to hunt him down.

P Mr. Senet, WHERE is Mr. Milton now?

W I'm afraid that I have no idea.

The second situation is the case in which the former witness is in another jurisdiction. In order to rely on this basis for unavailability, the proponent must show that good faith efforts have been used to obtain the declarant. The judge can, of course, judicially notice the constitutional and statutory provisions setting out the territorial limits of the court's compulsory process. Note that Rule 804(a)(5) expressly requires the proponent to attempt to use "other reasonable means."

Suppose that Mr. Watson has sued Ms. Belson for personal injuries resulting from a traffic accident. A Mr. Green was a passing acquaintance of the plaintiff and happened to be in the plaintiff's car at the time of the accident. But Mr. Green now lives in Minnesota. At trial, assume that the plaintiff wants to use Mr. Green's former testimony. The plaintiff himself takes the stand to establish Mr. Green's unavailability.

P WHERE does Mr. Green live now?

W In St. Paul, Minnesota.

P HOW do you know that?

W For one thing, I've received letters from him postmarked St. Paul, Minnesota.

P HOW do you know the letters came from Mr. Green?

W I recognized his handwriting.

P HOW did you recognize his handwriting?

W I'm familiar with it. We worked together for several years, and I saw his handwriting on numerous occasions.

P WHY else do you think he now lives in Minnesota?

W I tried to contact him by telephone. I went through the operator in St. Paul and eventually reached him.

P HOW do you know you were speaking with Mr. Green?

W I recognized his voice just as I recognized his handwriting.

P WHERE is Mr. Green today?

W I don't know for sure.

P WHERE was he when you last spoke with him?

W In St. Paul.

P WHY isn't he here?

W He refused to come.

P HOW do you know that?

W I asked him to come during our last telephone conversation, and he said he was too tied up with his business to come.

P WHAT efforts have you made to persuade him to attend this trial?

W I phoned him several times. I even volunteered to pick up the tab for his airline ticket. He just won't cooperate.

Assuming that the proponent can establish that the declarant is unavailable under Rule 804(a), he or she must still fit the offered statement into one of the exceptions in Rule 804(b). Two of those exceptions are addressed in the following discussion.

§ 11-12 DYING DECLARATIONS

§ 11-12(A) THE DOCTRINE

Another type of evidently sincere statement that is exceptionally admissible is a dying declaration. At early common law, the courts admitted the decedent's dying declarations in homicide prosecutions. The courts reasoned that there was a peculiar need for dying declarations in homicide prosecutions. The courts feared that if they excluded the victim's dying declaration the murderer might go free. The circumstantial guarantee of the trustworthiness of dying declarations is the declarant's sense of impending death. At the point of death, the declarant should not have any reason to lie. There is a theistic belief that the decedent will not want to face the Creator with a last lie on his or her lips. At common law, the necessity for admitting the hearsay was that at the time of trial, the declarant was dead.

The most arbitrary limitation on the common-law doctrine was its restriction to homicide prosecutions. Under Federal Rule 804(b)(2), that limitation still exists in criminal, but not civil, cases. Under Texas Rule 804(b)(2), however, dying declarations are admissible in any type of criminal or civil case.

The dying declaration exception does not require a showing that the declarant is now dead. Thus, the proponent could use this exception to introduce the statement of a person who truly believed that he was really dying, but later fully recovered and then refused to testify.

§ 11-12(B) ELEMENTS OF THE FOUNDATION

The elements for the dying declaration exception under Rule 804(b)(2) include the following:

1. The declarant made a statement.

2. At the time of the statement, the declarant believed that his or her death was imminent.[21]
3. At the time of trial, the declarant is unavailable.
4. The statement relates to the cause or circumstances of what the declarant believed to be his impending death.

§ 11-12(C) SAMPLE FOUNDATION

The fact situation is an attempted murder prosecution. The indictment alleges that the defendant, Mr. James Ireland, attempted to murder Ms. Grace Shafer. The indictment thus supplies the first element of the foundation. The prosecution calls Mr. William Turner as a witness. Mr. Turner has already identified himself. The prosecutor is the proponent.

P Mr. Turner, WHAT is your occupation?

W I am an emergency medical technician. I work for the local fire department on their emergency rescue squad.

P WHERE were you on the morning of February 22nd?

W I was in my office.

P WHAT happened that morning?

W Our unit received an emergency call.

P WHAT was the nature of the call?

W Someone was hurt very badly and needed immediate medical attention.

P WHAT did you do after you received this call?

W We jumped in our emergency vehicle and drove to Garnet Street.

P WHAT did you find when you arrived there?

W I found several police surrounding a very badly injured person.

P WHO was that person? (1)

W A Ms. Grace Shafer.

P HOW do you know that? (1)

W She identified herself, and I also checked the identification that she had in her purse.

P WHAT condition was she in? (2)

---

[21] The declarant had abandoned all hope and had concluded that certain death was imminent. The declarant sometimes voices his or her belief. Alternatively, the proponent may rely on such circumstances as the nature of the wound, the administration of last rites, and the statements made by third parties to the declarant.

W Very bad. She had several stab wounds.

P HOW many stab wounds? (2)

W Five in her chest.

P HOW deep were the wounds? (2)

W Some were several inches deep.

P HOW much blood was she losing? (2)

W She was bleeding profusely.

P WHERE was she bleeding? (2)

W All over the chest area.

P WHAT did you do after you discovered these wounds? (2)

W I helped her as best I could.

P WHAT, if anything, did you tell her about her condition? (2)

O Your Honor, I object to that question on the ground that it calls for hearsay.

P Your Honor, may we approach the bench?

J Yes.

P Your Honor, I offer to prove that the witness will testify he told Ms. Shafer that she was dying. I want to use that statement for a nonhearsay purpose, namely, to show its effect on her state of mind. His statement helped produce a sense of imminent death in her mind. That is part of the foundation for the dying declaration I ultimately want to offer.

J The objection will be overruled.

P Mr. Turner, let me repeat the question. WHAT, if anything, did you tell Ms. Shafer about her condition? (2)

W Well, I was honest with her. She asked, and I told her that she appeared to have lost a lot of blood and that it did not look good.

P HOW did she respond? (2)

W She asked me if I thought she would die.

P And WHAT did you say? (2)

W I told her that it did not look good.

P HOW did she react to that? (2)

W She looked frightened. Then she started to cry and said that she knew that she was going to die from all of the blood she had lost.

P WHAT happened then? (2)

W She asked that I quickly contact a Catholic priest. She said that she wanted to receive the last rites of her church before she died. And she also said that I should tell her husband that she had loved him.

P WHAT, if anything, did she say about the cause of her injuries? (1), (4)

W She said someone had stabbed her with an ice pick.

P WHO did she say stabbed her? (4)

W She said it was Jim Ireland.

P WHAT happened next?

W She lapsed into unconsciousness as we were loading her into the ambulance.

P WHERE is Ms. Shafer now? (3)

W She's in Mercy Hospital, on life-support equipment.

P WHAT is her condition? (3)

W She has never awakened since she received her wounds. In a way, it is a miracle that she is still alive.

§ 11-13 FORMER OR PRIOR TESTIMONY

§ 11-13(A) THE DOCTRINE

§ 11-13(A)(1) In General

The next exception is former testimony which is reflected in Texas Rule of Evidence 804(b)(1). As noted in Chapter 10, the primary rationale for the hearsay rule is that the opponent has not had an opportunity to test the hearsay by cross-examination. What if the opponent had an opportunity to test the hearsay by cross-examination in a prior trial? Does that opportunity satisfy the hearsay rule and justify admitting the prior testimony in the present proceeding? Most courts have answered that question in the affirmative. Texas Rule of Evidence 804(b)(1) states the doctrine:

The following are not excluded by the hearsay rule if the declarant is unavailable as a witness:

> In civil cases, as a witness at another hearing of the same or a different proceeding, or in a deposition taken in compliance with law in the course of the same or another proceeding, if the party against whom the testimony is now offered, or a person with a similar interest, had an opportunity and similar motive to develop the testimony by direct, cross, or redirect examination. In criminal cases, testimony given as a witness at another hearing of the same or a different proceeding, if the party against whom the testimony is now offered had an opportunity to develop the testimony by direct, cross, or redirect examination. In criminal cases the use of depositions is controlled by Chapter 39 of the Code of Criminal Procedure.

§ 11-13(A)(2) Identity of Parties

The most controversial aspect of the former testimony exception to the hearsay rule has been the issue of whether the parties to the two hearings must be identical.[22] Early common law insisted upon complete identity of parties. The parties to hearing #2 were parties to hearing #1, and there were no additional parties at either hearing. The common law quickly realized that the complete identity requirement was unnecessarily strict. So long as the present parties were parties to hearing #1, the courts generally concluded it was immaterial that there were additional parties to either hearing.

Some courts and legislatures, including the drafters of Texas Rule 804(b)(1), recognize the "similar party" view for civil cases only. They still begin their analysis by focusing on the party to hearing #2 that the former testimony is offered against. Then, however, they pose a different question. Under the prevailing view, the pivotal question is whether that party had an opportunity in hearing #1 to probe the testimony. Under this new view, the question is whether there was a party to hearing #1 who had a similar motive to probe the testimony. The present opponent need not have had that opportunity. It is sufficient if there was a similarly situated party, with a motive and interest similar to that of the present opponent.

The following example illustrates this view. Suppose that several passengers are injured when a plane crashes during landing. In hearing #1, passenger *A* sues the airline. The airline introduces the testimony of a safety engineer against *A*. The engineer dies before passenger *B* sues. Under Rule 804(b)(1), at hearing #2 between passenger *B* and the same airline, the airline could use the engineer's testimony against passenger *B*. It is true that passenger *B* was not a party to hearing #1. Passenger *A* was a party, however, and the two plaintiffs' motive and interest are sufficiently similar. We can assume with fair assurance that passenger *A* attacked the engineer's testimony as vigorously as passenger *B* would have. This view applies only in Texas civil cases.

According to Rule 804(b)(1), in criminal cases, the party against whom the former testimony is offered must have had an opportunity and similar motive to develop or attack the testimony at hearing #1. For example, in criminal trial #1, defendant *A* is on trial for transfer of drugs. Officer Jones testifies against defendant *A*. The appellate court authorizes a new trial for defendant *A*. In the interim, Officer Jones becomes unavailable under Rule 804(a). May the state now use the police officer's prior testimony against *A* in criminal trial #2? Probably, assuming that the offered testimony generally focuses on the same issues. At trial #1, *A* had a fair opportunity for confrontation and cross-examination of the

---

22 *See generally* WENDORF, SCHLUETER & BARTON, TEXAS RULES OF EVIDENCE MANUAL VIII-158 (6th ed. 2002).

police officer. Under Rule 804(b)(1), the identity of parties requirement would thus be met.

§ 11-13(A)(3) Other Nonhearsay Uses of Prior Testimony or Depositions

The assumption here is that the proponent wishes to offer the prior testimony for the truth of the matter asserted. If counsel is using the prior testimony solely for purposes of impeachment, no hearsay issue is presented. Even if counsel is attempting to use the prior testimony for the truth of the matter asserted, the hearsay exemptions for prior inconsistent statement, Rule 801(e)(1)(A), may be used in both criminal and civil trials. And the hearsay exemption for depositions taken in the "same proceeding," Rule 801(e)(3), may be used in Texas civil cases.

§ 11-13(B) ELEMENTS OF THE FOUNDATION

The elements for introducing prior testimony under Rule 804(b)(1) are as follows:

§ 11-13(B)(1) Civil Cases

1. Hearing #1 was a fair, adversarial hearing.
2. The witness testified under oath at hearing #1.
3. Either the opponent was a party in hearing #1, or a person with an interest similar to the opponent's was a party to hearing #1.
4. The opponent, or similar party, had an opportunity[23] to develop the witness's testimony on direct, cross, or redirect examination in hearing #1.
5. The opponent, or similar party, had a motive to develop the witness's testimony at hearing #1.[24]
6. At hearing #2, the witness is unavailable.

§ 11-13(B)(2) Criminal Cases

1. Hearing #1 was a fair, adversarial hearing.
2. The witness testified under oath at hearing #1.

---

[23] All that is required is that the opportunity was available at hearing #1. If the opponent waived, for example, the right to cross-examine the witness at hearing #1, that waiver will not prevent the introduction of that prior testimony.

[24] This can be translated into a requirement that the issues in both hearings should match. If the issues are dramatically different, it is more difficult to show that the examination of the witness in hearing #1 was motivated by the same reasons for doing so in hearing #2.

3. The opponent was a party to hearing #1.
4. The opponent had an opportunity to develop the witness's testimony on direct, cross, or redirect examination in hearing #1.
5. The opponent had a motive to develop the witness's testimony at hearing #1.
6. At hearing #2, the witness is unavailable.

In some cases, the proponent may need two witnesses. One witness will establish the unavailability of the prior witness. The second witness will then lay the foundation for the prior witness's testimony. The second witness may have been a spectator at hearing #1 who simply remembers the substance of the prior testimony; the witness need not be able to recite the testimony verbatim. Or, the second witness may be the court reporter, who describes the testimony with or without relying on notes. Finally, the proponent may dispense entirely with live testimony if the proponent can authenticate the documentary record of hearing #1. The transcript may be self-authenticating under Rule 902.

§ 11-13(C) SAMPLE FOUNDATION

Assume that the proponent has already established the declarant's unavailability. In the following hypothetical, the proponent is laying the other elements of the foundation.

The first hypothetical illustrates the testimony of a participant in hearing #1 who happens to remember the substance of the witness's testimony at hearing #1. The fact situation is a homicide prosecution. The government charges that Mr. John Gentile murdered his wife. An eyewitness to the killing, Mr. John Walton, testified at the preliminary hearing. Mr. Walton died after the hearing and before the trial. The prosecution has already proved Mr. Walton's unavailability by introducing a properly attested death certificate. Now the prosecutor calls Ms. Pamela Martin to lay the other elements of the foundation. The prosecutor is the proponent. Ms. Martin has already identified herself.

P Ms. Martin, WHERE were you on the afternoon of March 12, 2005?

W I was in another courtroom in this building.

P WHAT were you doing there?

W I was a spectator at a court proceeding.

P WHY were you there?

W I had read a lot about the case in the papers, and I was interested in watching it.

P WHAT proceeding did you see the afternoon of March 12, 2005? (1)

W It was the preliminary hearing in this case.

P WHO was there attending the hearing? (3)

W For one, the defendant himself, Mr. Gentile.

P WHERE is Mr. Gentile now? (3)

W He's in the courtroom right now.

P Specifically, WHERE in the courtroom? (3)

W Over there at the end of that table.

P HOW is he dressed? (3)

W He's wearing a blue suit, white shirt, and red tie.

P Please let the record reflect that the witness has identified the defendant.

J It will so reflect.

P WHAT happened at this hearing you attended on March 12th? (1)

W They called a witness to testify.

P WHAT did they do when they first called the witness to the stand? (1), (2)

W They swore him in.

P WHO questioned the witness? (4)

W Usually the prosecutor would start, and then the defense counsel would ask questions.

P WHO asked questions on behalf of the defendant? (4), (5)

W An attorney. I honestly can't remember her name.

P WHO was the witness that day? (2), (5)

W An eyewitness named John Walton.

P HOW long was he on the stand? (2)

W About one hour.

P HOW much of his testimony did you hear? (2)

W All of it.

P HOW well could you hear Mr. Walton while he testified? (2)

W Very well. I didn't have any problem hearing him.

P HOW loudly was he speaking?

W In a normal voice, but his voice carried well.

P HOW close were you sitting to him while he was on the stand?

W About 15 feet away. I was in the very first row for the spectators.

P HOW well do you remember his testimony?

W Very well. I was really enthralled. As I said, it was real exciting.

P WHAT did he say during his testimony? (2)

O Your Honor, I object to that question on the ground that it calls for hearsay.

P Your Honor, may we approach the bench?

J Yes.

P Your Honor, I concede that the testimony will be hearsay. However, it falls within the former testimony exception under Rule 804(b)(1). The witness's testimony shows that there was an oath, cross-examination, and counsel at the preliminary hearing. Since it was the preliminary hearing in this case, there's obviously identity of issues and parties. Finally, the death certificate shows that the former witness is now unavailable. (6)

J The objection will be overruled.

P Ms. Martin, let me repeat the question. WHAT did Mr. Walton say during his testimony? [*The proponent should now elicit all the important facts Mr. Walton previously testified to.*]

The next example illustrates the use of a properly attested or certified transcript of the former testimony. The previous hypothetical is continued. In this variation of the hypothetical, there is a documentary transcript of the preliminary hearing. Again, assume that the prosecutor has already introduced Mr. Walton's death certificate.

P Your Honor, I request that this be marked as a prosecution exhibit by the court reporter. [*Court reporter marks exhibit.*]

P Please let the record reflect that I am showing State's exhibit number three for identification to the opposing counsel.

J The record will so reflect.

P I now offer State's exhibit number three for identification into evidence.

O Your Honor, I object to the introduction of the exhibit on the ground that the exhibit is hearsay.

P Your Honor, may we approach the bench?

J Yes.

P Your Honor, I concede that the exhibit is hearsay. But it is a copy of that portion of the transcription of testimony which contains Mr. Walton's testimony. The attesting certificate was completed by Ms. Warth, this court's court reporter. Thus, it is a properly certified copy of the transcription of testimony under Rule 902(4). Finally, it falls within the former testimony exception under Rule 804.

J Where is the foundation for the former testimony exception?

P The transcription is a record of the preliminary hearing in this case. There is obviously identity of issues and parties. I've already introduced Mr. Walton's death certificate, showing his unavailability. Page 2 of the transcription shows that the defendant had counsel at the hearing, page 16 shows that Mr. Walton was sworn before he testified, and page 142 shows that the defense had an opportunity to cross-examine Mr. Walton.

J The objection will be overruled, and the exhibit will be received.

P Your Honor, I request permission to read pages 22–53 to the jurors. I shall read the questions, and my clerk will take the witness stand and read the answers.

J Permission granted.

Part 3
IMPEACHMENT AND REHABILITATION OF THE HEARSAY DECLARANT

§ 11-14 INTRODUCTION

Assuming that counsel is able to introduce a hearsay statement under one of the exceptions identified in the preceding questions, Rule 806 permits the opposing counsel to impeach the credibility of the hearsay declarant. For example, plaintiff's counsel introduces the hearsay statement of a bystander who saw the automobile accident as a present sense impression under Rule 803(1). The defense counsel has learned through pretrial discovery that the declarant has a prior perjury conviction from the State of Illinois. Even though the hearsay declarant never takes the stand, the defense counsel may rely on Rule 806 and use extrinsic evidence to show the jury that the declarant's statement should receive little or no weight because she is not a truthful person. Alternatively, the defense counsel could call the declarant to the stand and ask her directly about her prior conviction for perjury. For example, the proponent may have decided not to call the hearsay declarant to the stand because the declarant does not appear to be a credible witness. Indeed, counsel may have decided as a tactical matter not to call the declarant to the stand precisely because the declarant is highly impeachable.[25] This tactic presents some risks, however, and should be rarely used.[26]

Of course, Rule 806 also provides that if a hearsay declarant has been impeached, the other side may attempt to rehabilitate the declarant's credibility

---

[25] *See* IMWINKELRIED & SCHLUETER, FEDERAL EVIDENCE TACTICS, § 8.06[4] (1998).

[26] *Id.* For example, if counsel uses the declarant's deposition to impeach the absent declarant, the opponent may be able to use Rules 106 and 107 to introduce other portions of the deposition, under the rule of optional completeness. Or if counsel impeaches the absent declarant, the opponent may decide to actually call the declarant to the stand—especially if the declarant has a strong demeanor and makes an otherwise excellent witness.

§ 11-15 IMPEACHING THE ABSENT HEARSAY DECLARANT

When using Rule 806, counsel should remember that hearsay declarants are in effect witnesses, whether or not they are in the courtroom. That is, if the judge has admitted a hearsay statement for substantive purposes, the declarant's credibility is always relevant. For instance, the proponent might establish through cross-examination of the opponent's witness that the hearsay declarant is biased or has made inconsistent statements about the case.

Although it may be awkward to impeach a person who has never actually appeared in the courtroom, Rule 806 contemplates that possibility. In laying the foundation for impeachment evidence, the other rules of evidence generally apply. Thus, counsel must show that the foundation witness has personal knowledge and that the proffered evidence is relevant to the hearsay declarant's credibility. One impeachment rule does not apply, however. When counsel attempts to introduce extrinsic evidence of a prior inconsistent statement to impeach a witness on the stand, Texas Rule 613(a) requires counsel first to provide the witness with an opportunity to deny or explain the prior statement. If the witness admits making the prior inconsistent statement, counsel is barred from actually introducing extrinsic evidence of the statement. Under Rule 806, however, the declarant need not be given that opportunity.

§ 11-15(A) Impeaching the Absent Hearsay Declarant—Bias

§ 11-15(A)(1) The Doctrine

Just as any witness may be impeached with evidence that he or she is biased in favor of, or against, a party to the case, the credibility of a hearsay declarant be may be attacked on that ground. As discussed at § 5-12, bias may be proved through evidence of either statements or acts. Normally, counsel may both cross-examine the witness to be impeached and use extrinsic evidence. Texas follows the traditional view, which requires that the opponent lay a foundation on cross-examination as a predicate for extrinsic evidence. If the witness fully admits all the facts, the judge may exercise discretion to limit or exclude extrinsic evidence. When the witness denies any of the relevant impeaching facts or equivocates, however, the opponent may introduce extrinsic evidence. However, Rule 806 explicitly provides that in the case of impeaching a hearsay declarant, the declarant need not be given an opportunity to deny or explain.

§ 11-15(A)(2) Elements of the Foundation

The foundational requirements for impeaching a hearsay declarant through bias evidence in the form of a statement are as follows:

1. The hearsay declarant made an earlier statement at a certain place.

2. The hearsay declarant made a statement at a certain time.
3. The statement was made to a certain person.
4. The statement was of a certain tenor that demonstrates bias.

The foundation for showing bias through circumstance, event, or condition include the following elements:

1. Where the event or condition occurred.
2. When the event or condition occurred.
3. Who was present.
4. What occurred.

§ 11-15(A)(3) Sample Foundation

In the following sample foundation, the opponent has called Mr. Juarez to the stand to testify that he heard Ms. Smith make a hearsay statement in which she stated that she had seen the defendant take a gun out of his pocket just before confronting the victim. The trial judge admitted the statement under Rule 803(2) as an excited utterance. The proponent wishes to show that Ms. Smith was biased against the defendant.

P ISN'T IT TRUE, Mr. Juarez, that several months ago you had a conversation concerning this case with a Ms. Smith at her apartment? (1), (2), (3)

W Yes, we talked.

P IT IS TRUE, ISN'T IT, Mr. Juarez, that Ms. Smith told you that she had a score to settle with the defendant in this case? (4)

W Well, maybe not in those exact words.

P WHAT words did she use? (4)

W She said that she was mad at the defendant and that she was going to make life very hard for him. She didn't say anything about settling any scores.

In the following sample foundation, the defendant is charged with aggravated assault. During its case-in-chief, the prosecution presented the testimony of Officer Jones to the effect that Bobby Wilson, the victim, stated that while he lay bleeding on the ground that he thought that he was dying and that the defendant had shot him. The judge admitted the hearsay statement under Rule 804 as a dying declaration; although the victim recovered from his wounds, he was not available to testify at trial. The defense counsel has evidence that the victim and the defendant had a long-standing feud. Now, during its case-in-chief the defense counsel has called a mutual friend of the two to the stand: Charlie Juarez.

P Mr. Juarez, are you familiar with the victim in this case and the defendant?

W Yes, I am.

P How long have you known them?

W For over 20 years. We were in school together.

P Do you have any knowledge about whether they may have had any disagreements over a women named Rosa Lopez? (1), (2), (3), (4)

O Objection, Your Honor. This evidence is not in any way relevant to this case.

P Your Honor, we intend to question this witness about the relationship between the victim and the defendant. It is our position that the victim was biased against the defendant and because of that has falsely implicated the defendant in this case. (1), (2), (3), (4)

O Your Honor, in that case we also object that counsel is not permitted to prove the bias of someone who has not actually testified in this courtroom.

P Your Honor, the victim in this case is a hearsay declarant. And under Rule of Evidence 806 we are entitled to impeach him under any of the traditional methods, including proof of bias.

J Objection overruled.

P Again, did these two people have any disagreements over a woman named Rosa Lopez. (4)

W Definitely. The victim was angry with the defendant because he thought that the defendant had taken Rosa away from him about five years ago. Even though that was not true, the victim kept thinking that and constantly harassed the defendant over it.

§ 11-15(B) Impeaching the Absent Hearsay Declarant—Prior Inconsistent Statement

§ 11-15(B)(1) The Doctrine

A hearsay declarant may also be impeached with his or her prior inconsistent statements. Although Texas Rule of Evidence 613 normally bars extrinsic evidence of a witness's prior inconsistent statement unless the witness is first reminded of the particulars of the statement and provided an opportunity to deny or explain the statement, Rule 806 explicitly states that such impeachment of a hearsay declarant may occur without providing the declarant with that opportunity. In any event, the proponent of the impeaching evidence must still be prepared to lay the foundation for the statement, such as when and to whom it was made.

§ 11-15(B)(2) Elements of the Foundation

1. The hearsay declarant made an earlier oral or written statement at a certain place.
2. The hearsay declarant made the statement at a certain time.
3. The statement was made to a certain person.
4. The statement was of a certain tenor that is inconsistent with a statement offered at trial.

§ 11-15(B)(3) Sample Foundation

The fact situation involves impeachment of an absent hearsay declarant with an oral inconsistent statement. The hearsay declarant, Ernst Wilson (who is not present), observed an automobile accident and made a statement to a Mr. Williams that "the red car just ran the red light." That statement was repeated in court by Mr. Williams and the judge, over objection, admitted it under Rule 803(1) as a present sense impression. The proponent of the impeachment evidence is the defense counsel who is cross-examining Mr. Williams.

P Mr. Williams, if I correctly understood your testimony on direct examination, you said that Mr. Wilson told you that the red car—my client's car—was the car that ran a red light. IS THAT CORRECT? (1)

W Yes.

P ISN'T IT A FACT THAT several days after the accident, you had a another conversation with Mr. Wilson at your house? (2), (3), (4)

W Yes.

P ISN'T IT CORRECT THAT during that conversation, you discussed the collision between my client's car and the plaintiff's car? (5)

W Right.

P ISN'T IT ALSO TRUE THAT during the conversation, Mr. Jensen told you . . .

O Objection, Your Honor, counsel is calling for hearsay. Further, this is completely irrelevant to the case.

P Your Honor, under Rule 806 we are permitted to impeach a hearsay declarant with his or her prior inconsistent statement. In this instance, Mr. Wilson made two statements, which are inconsistent with each other. Further, we are not offering the statement for its truth, and therefore, it is not hearsay under Rule 801.

J Objection overruled.

P Let me repeat the question. ISN'T IT ALSO TRUE THAT during the conversation, Mr. Wilson told you that it was the defendant's car—the blue car—that had run a red light? (5)

W Yes.

P Your Honor, may I please have a limiting instruction under Rule 105 that the jurors may use this evidence only in evaluating Mr. Wilson's credibility?

J The court will grant the request for a limiting instruction.

§ 11-15(C) IMPEACHING THE HEARSAY DECLARANT—CHARACTER EVIDENCE

§ 11-15(C)(1) The Doctrine

As discussed at § 5-8, a witness may be impeached through testimony of someone who knows the witness or someone who is familiar with the reputation of the witness for telling the truth. So too may a hearsay declarant be impeached. Because of the nature of this type of credibility evidence, at least one other witness will be involved. This method generally follows the steps used for impeaching any witness who has testified in the case: either through a reputation character witness or an opinion character witness.

§ 11-15(C)(2) Elements of the Foundation

The foundation for impeaching a hearsay declarant through reputation testimony is as follows:

1. The witness is a member of the same community (residential or social) as the hearsay declarant.
2. The hearsay declarant has a reputation for untruthfulness in the community.
3. The witness knows hearsay declarant's reputation for untruthfulness.

The foundation elements for impeaching a hearsay declarant through opinion testimony are as follows:

1. The witness is personally acquainted with the hearsay declarant.
2. The witness knows the hearsay declarant well enough to have formed an opinion of the declarant's truthfulness.
3. The witness has an opinion of the hearsay declarant's untruthfulness.
4. The witness has the opinion that the hearsay declarant is an untruthful person.

§ 11-15(C)(3) Sample Foundation

In the following situation, the statement of an absent hearsay declarant, Oliver Harding, was admitted against the plaintiff during the defense's case-in-chief. The court has granted the plaintiff the opportunity to rebut that evidence through the testimony of a character witness. The plaintiff's counsel is the proponent of the character evidence concerning the hearsay declarant.

P WHO is Mr. Harding? (1)

W He's an acquaintance of mine.

P WHEN is the last time you saw him?

W Several days ago.

P HOW did you come to know him? (2)

W We've worked in the same company for a long time. I've had a lot of contact with him.

P HOW many years have you known him? (2)

W I'd say easily nine years.

P In WHAT contexts have you known him? (2)

W As I said, we've worked for the same company, Jon's Pools, for a long time. I see him at least several times a day around the plant.

P HOW often do you talk with him? (2)

W Usually several times a week. We're always bumping into each other on various projects.

P Do you have an opinion of his truthfulness? (3)

W Yes, I do.

P WHAT is that opinion? (4)

W In my opinion, he's an untruthful person.

P Given that opinion, would you believe Mr. Harding? (5)

W No.

§ 11-16 IMPEACHINGTHE HEARSAY DECLARANT CALLED AS A WITNESS BY THE OPPONENT

Rule 806 indicates that if the party against whom the hearsay statement was admitted calls the hearsay declarant as a witness, then the party may question that declarant as though it were cross-examination. That means that counsel may use leading questions when questioning the declarant-witness.

§ 11-16(A) IMPEACHING THE HEARSAY DECLARANT CALLED AS A WITNESS BY THE OPPONENT—BIAS

§ 11-16(A)(1) The Doctrine

As with any witness, a hearsay declarant may be called to the stand and impeached with evidence that the declarant is biased. Under the second sentence of Rule 806, apparently no foundation is required to allow the declarant the opportunity to explain or deny the bias alleged.

§ 11-16(A)(2) Elements of the Foundation

Impeaching a hearsay declarant with evidence that the declarant is biased is the same as for any other witness. The foundation for impeaching a declarant-witness through bias exhibited in statements by the declarant is:

1. The hearsay declarant-witness made an earlier statement at a certain place.
2. The hearsay declarant-witness made a statement at a certain time.
3. The statement was made to a certain person.
4. The statement was of a certain tenor that demonstrates bias.

The foundation for showing bias through circumstance, event, or condition include the following elements:

1. Where the event or condition occurred.
2. When the event or condition occurred.
3. Who was present.
4. What occurred.

§ 11-16(A)(3) Sample Foundation

In the following sample foundation, the defendant is charged with shooting the victim in the back during an altercation at a bar. The defendant testified that he never had a gun in his possession at the time of the offense. To rebut that testimony, the prosecution presented the testimony of Mr. Juarez that he heard a hearsay statement of Mr. Smith at the time of the shooting to the effect that he had seen the defendant take a gun out of his pocket just before confronting the victim. The trial judge admitted the statement under Rule 803(2) as an excited utterance. The prosecution did not call the declarant, Mr. Smith, to the stand to testify. The defense now wishes to impeach the hearsay declarant by showing that he is biased against the defendant. To do so, counsel has called the declarant to the stand as a defense witness. The proponent is the defense counsel.

P ISN'T IT TRUE, Mr. Smith, that several months ago you had a conversation concerning this case with a Mr. Juarez at his apartment? (1), (2), (3)

W I did.

P IT IS TRUE, ISN'T IT, Mr. Smith, that you told Mr. Juarez that you had a score to settle with the defendant in this case? (4)

W Well, maybe not in those exact words.

P WHAT words did you use? (4)

W I said that I was mad at the defendant and that I was going to make life very hard for him. I didn't say anything about settling any scores.

CHAPTER 12
SUBSTITUTES FOR EVIDENCE

§ 12-1 INTRODUCTION

The preceding chapters analyze the legal restrictions on the process of admitting evidence during a trial. There are substitutes, however, for conventional evidence. The parties may stipulate to certain propositions, the judge may judicially notice a proposition, or the jurors themselves may be taken outside the courtroom to view a scene or object that is relevant to the case. This chapter discusses the limitations on those substitutes.

§ 12-2 STIPULATIONS

§ 12-2(A) THE DOCTRINE

It is very common for the parties to stipulate before or during a trial. A stipulation can save both parties time, and, by stipulating in the jury's presence, a party can attempt to create the impression in the jurors' minds that he or she is a reasonable, fair person.

There are several types of stipulations. For example, the parties may stipulate to procedural matters, such as continuances. The focus here, however, is on evidentiary stipulations: stipulations to evidentiary foundations, stipulations of fact, and stipulations of expected testimony.

§ 12-2(A)(1) Stipulations to Evidentiary Foundations

The first type of evidentiary stipulation is a stipulation that a particular evidentiary foundation or predicate exists. For example, after having a letter marked as an exhibit for identification, the proponent may ask if opposing counsel is willing to stipulate to the authenticity of the letter. Or, the opposing counsel may volunteer to stipulate to certain evidentiary foundations. Such stipulations may be partial. That is, the opposing counsel may stipulate that the letter is authentic, but may not be willing to waive any possible hearsay or relevancy objections.

§ 12-2(A)(2) Stipulations of Fact

The second type of evidentiary stipulation is a stipulation of fact: the parties agree that a certain fact existed or that a certain event occurred. If the parties enter a stipulation of fact, neither party can ordinarily introduce evidence to contradict the stipulated fact. In fact, the courts may consider such stipulations as an admission.[1]

The fact that a party has agreed to stipulate to certain facts does not prohibit that party from introducing other noncontradictory evidence on the same issues. For example, in a murder prosecution, the prosecutor may agree to stipulate to the fact that a particular witness is an expert in the field of pathology, that he performed an autopsy on the deceased, and that he determined that the cause of death was strangulation. Despite that stipulation, the prosecutor may still call the witness to the stand and develop more fully his testimony about the cause of death.

§ 12-2(A)(3) Stipulations of Expected Testimony

The third type of evidentiary stipulation is a stipulation of expected testimony: the parties agree that if a particular person were present in court as a witness, the person would give certain testimony. The parties are not stipulating that the testimony is truthful or correct. The parties may introduce evidence to contradict the expected testimony. The parties are agreeing upon only what the person's testimony would be if the person appeared and testified in court.

---

[1] *See, e.g.*, *Mendoza v. Fidelity & Guar. Ins. Underwriters, Inc.*, 606 S.W.2d 692, 694 (Tex. 1980).

§ 12-2(B) ELEMENTS OF THE FOUNDATION

The procedure for introducing stipulations varies. Texas Rule of Civil Procedure 11 requires that stipulations be written or made in open court. Although it is common for counsel to enter into oral stipulations in court, some judges may prefer that the parties reduce their stipulations to writing. Written pretrial stipulations obviously reduce the possibility for disagreement at trial over the content of the stipulations.

The final procedural question is whether the judge accepting the stipulation must personally question the parties. May the judge accept the attorneys' assurances that the parties assent? Most judges routinely do so when the stipulation is made in open court.

The issue is more complex in criminal cases. In *Boykin v. Alabama*,[2] the Supreme Court held that because a defendant waives certain constitutional rights by pleading guilty, the trial record must reflect that the defendant knowingly waived the rights. Texas follows this principle. A defendant pleading guilty or nolo contendere must be advised of what rights are being waived by pleading guilty.[3] Additionally, Article 1.15 of the Texas Code of Criminal Procedure specifies that a defendant's guilty plea in a felony case must be substantiated by evidence. That provision also indicates that a plea may be substantiated by a stipulation if the defendant consents in writing to waive the appearance, cross-examination, and confrontation of the witnesses and further consents to an oral stipulation of the evidence and testimony. The question is what procedures should be followed where the defendant pleads not guilty but offers to stipulate to evidence which amounts to a confession. If the stipulation amounts to proof of the prosecution's entire case, then an argument could be made that the stipulation is really more in the nature of a guilty plea and the trial court should determine if the defendant is voluntarily waiving his or her constitutional rights. Although some federal and state cases follow this reasoning, Texas courts have not yet embraced this requirement.[4]

The procedure for entering a stipulation includes these steps:

1. One attorney announces to the judge that there has been a stipulation.
2. The judge then inquires of the other attorney whether there has been a stipulation.

---

[2] 395 U.S. 238 (1969).

[3] *See* TEX. CODE CRIM. PROC. art. 26.13.

[4] *See* Annotation, *Guilty Plea Safeguards as Applicable to Stipulation Allegedly Amounting to Guilty Plea in State Trial*, 17 ALR 4th 61 (1982) (collecting state cases); Annotation, *Standards of Rule 11 of Federal Rules of Criminal Procedure, Requiring Personal Advice to Accused from Court Before Acceptance of Guilty Plea, as Applicable Where Accused's Stipulations or Testimony Allegedly Amounts to Guilty Plea*, 53 A.L.R. FED. 919 (1981).

3. The second attorney answers in the affirmative.
4. The proponent of the stipulation establishes the tenor or content of the agreement. If the stipulation is oral, the proponent simply states the nature of the agreement on the record. If the stipulation is in writing, the proponent introduces the writing.
5. When required, the judge personally questions the party or parties before accepting the stipulation. The judge ensures that the party understands the nature and consequences of the stipulation.

After the judge accepts the stipulation, the judge informs the jury of the stipulation and instructs the jury on the legal effect of the stipulation.

§ 12-2(C) Sample Foundations

The first fact situation is a suit for breach of contract. The plaintiff, Bennett Industries, alleges that on January 10, 2005, it entered into a contract with the defendant, Jura Company. The complaint alleges that under the terms of the contract, Jura Company promised to excavate a site, lay a foundation, and build a two-story shopping center for the plaintiff. In its answer, the defendant raises the affirmative defenses of impossibility and financial impracticability. The answer alleges that a week after beginning excavation, the defendant discovered a subsoil condition that made it prohibitively expensive for it to do the promised construction work. The proponent is the plaintiff.

P Your Honor, I would like to announce that the parties in this case have reached a stipulation as to their actual knowledge of the existence of the subsoil condition that the defendant discovered in March 2005. (1)

J [*To the defense attorney*] Is that true? (2)

O Yes, your Honor. (3)

J What is the nature of this stipulation? (4)

P We have stipulated that before the defendant's discovery of the layer of granite in March 2005, none of the employees of either the plaintiff or the defendant had actual, subjective knowledge that the layer of granite existed.

J [*To the defense attorney*] Is that the tenor of the stipulation?

O Yes.

J And both of your clients consent to this stipulation?

O Yes, your Honor.

J Has this agreement been reduced to writing?

P No, your Honor.

O No—it's an oral stipulation.

J I shall accept the stipulation of fact. Ladies and gentlemen of the jury, the plaintiff and the defendant have just entered into an agreement or stipulation. All parties agree that before the defendant discovered the layer of granite at the construction site in March 2005, none of the employees of the plaintiff or defendant had actual, subjective knowledge that the granite was there. Will both parties state for the record that I have correctly described the stipulation for the jury?

O Certainly, your Honor.

P I concur.

J Ladies and gentlemen of the jury, because of the stipulation, you will not hear any evidence on that issue. However, I am instructing you that you are simply to assume the truth of the stipulated fact. All right, let's proceed with the evidence.

The second fact situation is a criminal prosecution for theft. The State alleges that the defendant, Mr. David Miles, stole $1,700 from an Albertsons grocery store. An acquaintance of the defendant saw him leave the store in a furtive, hurried fashion immediately after the alleged theft. Unfortunately for the prosecution, that person is now vacationing in Florida. Rather than forcing the witness to return or seeking a continuance, the parties entered into a stipulation of expected testimony. On this occasion, the parties decided to reduce the stipulation to writing before trial.

Continued on the next page.

[Caption of Case]

STIPULATION OF EXPECTED TESTIMONY

It is hereby stipulated between the State and the defense in the above numbered cause, with the defendant's express consent, and the defendant's waiver of the appearance, confrontation, and cross-examination of the witness, that if Robert Prothero, 77 Sunset Street, San Antonio, Texas, were present in court and sworn as a witness, he would testify substantially as follows:

> I know the defendant, David Miles. We have been members of the same labor union for the past three years. I can recognize him by sight. On the afternoon of July 28, 2005, as I was walking by the entrance to the Albertsons Store on Wurzbach in San Antonio, I saw the defendant exit the store. As soon as he stepped outside, he looked both ways—up and down the street. He seemed to be nervous. Then he stuck his hand in his right pants pocket; there was a big bulge in the pocket. As soon as he removed his hand from his pocket, he began running away from the store.

____

/s/ Assistant District Attorney

____

/s/ Defense Counsel

____

/s/ Defendant

____

Dated: November 1, 2005

The parties now offer the stipulation at trial. The prosecutor is the proponent. Although it is apparently not required by Texas case law, the judge in this case decides to conduct an inquiry of the defendant concerning his right to confront and cross-examine the witness.

P Your Honor, the parties in this case have reached a stipulation as to the expected testimony of an unavailable witness. (1)

J [*To the defense counsel*] Is that true? (2)

O Yes, your Honor. (3)

J What is the stipulation? (4)

P [*To court reporter*] Would you please mark this as a State's exhibit for identification? [*Court reporter marks exhibit and hands it back to proponent.*]

P Thank you. Please let the record reflect that I am showing State's exhibit number 13 for identification to the opposing counsel. [*Defense counsel briefly examines exhibit.*]

P I now offer State's exhibit number 13 for identification into evidence as prosecution exhibit 13.

J [*To the defense counsel*] Is this the stipulation?

O Yes, your Honor.

J [*To the defendant*] Mr. Miles, please hold State's exhibit number 13 in your hands while I ask you a few questions. (5)

D Yes, sir.

J Have you ever seen this document before? (5)

D Yes.

J When? (5)

D My attorney showed it to me when he asked me to sign it.

J Are you familiar with the contents? (5)

D Yes.

J Is that your signature on the bottom of the page? (5)

D Yes, your Honor.

J Has your lawyer advised you that you do not have to enter into this stipulation? (5)

D Yes. He told me that.

J Has your lawyer informed you that you have a right to insist that the prosecution produce Mr. Prothero at this trial? (5)

D Yes.

J Do you realize that if Mr. Prothero appeared at this trial, he would have to testify under oath? (5)

D Yes.

J Do you understand that if he testified at trial, he would have to testify in view of the jury? (5)

D Yes, your Honor.

J Do you realize that if he testified at trial, you would have an opportunity to cross-examine him? (5)

D Yes.

J Do you understand that you are waiving the right of appearance, confrontation, and cross-examination of Mr. Prothero by agreeing to this stipulation? (5)

D Yes, sir.

J Has your counsel advised you that even if you stipulate to Mr. Prothero's testimony, you can introduce evidence to rebut or contradict what Mr. Prothero says? (5)

D Yes.

J Has your counsel told you that even if you stipulate to Mr. Prothero's testimony, your counsel can make objections on evidentiary grounds to the testimony? (5) [*As a practical matter, there will rarely be evidentiary objections after the entry of the stipulation; the parties usually eliminate any objectionable material during the bargaining over the content of the stipulation.*]

D Yes.

J Do you voluntarily consent to this stipulation? (5)

D Yes.

J Well, then the stipulation will be accepted. State's exhibit number 13 will be received into evidence.

P Your Honor, I request permission to read State's exhibit number 13 to the jurors.

J Permission granted.

P Both parties, the State and defense, have agreed and stipulated that if Mr. Robert Prothero, of 77 Sunset Street, San Antonio, Texas, were present in court, he would give the following testimony: "I know the defendant, David Miles. We have been members of the same labor union for the past three years. I can recognize him on sight. On the afternoon of July 28, 2005, I was walking by the entrance to the Albertsons store on Wurzbach. I saw the defendant exit the store. As soon as he stepped outside, he looked both ways—up and down the street. He seemed to be nervous. Then he stuck his hand in his right pants pocket; there was a big bulge in the pocket. As soon as he removed his hand from his pocket, he began running away from the store."

O Your Honor, will you please instruct the jury about the stipulation?

J Yes. Ladies and gentlemen of the jury, the prosecutor has just read a stipulation of expected testimony. The parties have agreed as to what the testimony of Mr. Prothero would be if he appeared here and testified under oath. The stipulation does not admit the truth of the testimony, and does not add anything to the weight of Mr. Prothero's testimony. The defense may attack, contradict, or explain Mr. Prothero's testimony. In deciding how much weight to attach to Mr. Prothero's testimony, you may consider the fact that you have not had an opportunity to personally observe his demeanor.

§ 12-3 JUDICIAL NOTICE

§ 12-3(A) THE DOCTRINE

Like the stipulation technique, judicial notice of facts is an alternative to the presentation of formal evidence. The judge relieves the parties of the duty to present evidence by noting a fact and informing the jury of the fact's existence. What types of facts may be judicially noticed? Texas Evidence Rule 201(b) indicates that to be judicially noticeable, a fact must be "either (1) generally known within the territorial jurisdiction of the trial court or (2) capable of accurate and ready determination by resort to sources whose accuracy cannot reasonably be questioned." The Rule typifies the modern common law of judicial notice and recognizes two separate, independent bases for judicial notice: (1) the fact is a matter of common knowledge within the court's territorial jurisdiction; and (2) the fact is a readily verifiable certainty.[5] The Texas Rules of Evidence do include several Rules governing judicial notice of legal matters.[6] The focus here, however, is on judicial notice of "facts."

The procedure for judicial notice varies from court to court. Some courts permit attorneys to request judicial notice orally during trial. Other courts prefer that the attorneys submit judicial notice requests in writing before trial. Perhaps the best rule of thumb is that the procedure depends on the basis for judicial notice the party is invoking. If the party claims that the fact is a matter of common knowledge, the request can be informal. If the knowledge of the fact is widespread in the territorial area, the judge and attorneys should know the fact, and a formal hearing would be a waste of time. On the other hand, if the party claims that the fact is a readily verifiable certainty, the request should be written and supported by documentary material. For example, if the party requests judicial notice of a scientific principle, the party should submit at least documentary proof of the principle's validity. Courts usually relax the hearsay rule when the parties are litigating the propriety of judicial notice. Some judges may permit the parties to use affidavits, declarations, and letters that would usually be considered inadmissible hearsay.[7]

Rule 201 provides that a court may take judicial notice, whether requested or not. But the court must take judicial notice if a party requests that the court take judicial notice and supplies the court with the necessary information.

---

[5] *See* WENDORF, SCHLUETER & BARTON, TEXAS RULES OF EVIDENCE MANUAL II-1 (6th ed. 2002).

[6] *See* TEX. R. EVID. 202, 203, 204.

[7] *See* TEX. R. EVID. 104(a).

§ 12-3(B) ELEMENTS OF THE FOUNDATION

In requesting the court to take judicial notice of a fact, the proponent must do the following:

1. Request the court to take judicial notice of a fact which is either (a) generally known within the territory of the court, or (b) can be verified by sources whose accuracy cannot reasonably be questioned.
2. If necessary, supply the court with any supporting information, e.g., an almanac.

§ 12-3(C) SAMPLE FOUNDATIONS

The first fact situation illustrates the first basis for judicial notice: matter of common knowledge. The fact situation is a tort action arising from a traffic accident. The plaintiff, Ms. Garnet, alleges that the defendant, Mr. Simmons, was speeding and carelessly struck her as she was crossing the street. The plaintiff has already called Mr. James Farnsworth as a witness. Mr. Farnsworth testifies that he observed the accident. He testifies that the defendant's car struck the plaintiff at the intersection of F and Girard Streets in downtown Houston. Mr. Farnsworth also expresses his opinion that the defendant was driving 35 miles an hour just before the accident. Mr. Farnsworth leaves the witness stand, and the following occurs. The plaintiff is the proponent.

P Your Honor, I now request that you judicially notice two facts. (1)

J What are the facts?

P The first is that there is major road construction at the intersection of F and Girard Streets and that it has been in progress for at least the last several years. Second, we ask that you judicially notice that at that particular intersection, the speed limit has been reduced to 15 miles per hour. Both facts are matters of common knowledge in this area.

J Any objections?[8]

O Yes, your Honor. While we agree that it is common knowledge that that particular intersection has been under repair for some time, we cannot agree that it is commonly known that the speed limit in that intersection is 15 miles per hour. Indeed, we intend to offer evidence that no speed limit signs were posted there.

J [*To proponent*] Do you have any supporting evidence which would permit me, in the words of Rule 201(b), to ensure that the speed limit in that intersection is not subject to reasonable dispute?

---

[8] Texas Rule of Evidence 201(e) provides that the opponent is entitled, upon request, to be heard on the question of whether judicial notice should be taken.

P Not at this time, your Honor.

J Then I will only take judicial notice of the fact that the intersection of F and Girard Streets here in Houston has been under construction for the last several years.

P Would you please instruct the jury about the judicially noticed fact?

J Yes. Ladies and gentlemen of the jury, I am now judicially noticing a fact. The intersection where this accident occurred—F and Girard Streets, here in Houston, has been under construction for the last several years. Because this fact is a matter of common knowledge, I am authorized to note this fact without requiring formal evidence from the parties. You are to accept this fact and assume it to be true even though you may not hear any other evidence on this fact.

The second fact situation illustrates the second basis for judicial notice: verifiable certainty. The second situation is a continuation of the first. The plaintiff ultimately wants to offer the testimony of Officer Celeste Ripley. Officer Ripley had her police car parked near the intersection when the accident occurred. Her police car was equipped with a radar speedmeter. The speedmeter clocked the defendant's car at 36 miles per hour just before the accident. As § 4-11, *supra*, points out, part of the foundation for an offer of scientific evidence is proof of the theory's validity and the instrument. The plaintiff must lay those two elements of the foundation in our hypothetical. Because those facts are readily verifiable certainties, however, the plaintiff need not present live testimony; the plaintiff can use judicial notice to supply the first two elements of the scientific evidence foundation. Before trial, the plaintiff could obtain this affidavit.

Continued on the next page.

STATE OF TEXAS
COUNTY OF BEXAR

AFFIDAVIT

I, the undersigned, being duly sworn, depose and say that:

1. My name is Glenda Schneider. I reside at 7144 Frontier Boulevard, Houston, Texas.

2. I teach Electronics at the University of Houston. I have taught that subject there for the past seven years. I have a B.S., a master's, and a doctorate in that field from Texas A & M University.

3. The underlying theory of the radar speedmeter is the Doppler shift principle. The principle states that if a beam of microwaves of known frequency strikes an approaching or receding object, the beam changes frequency. The change in frequency is proportional to the speed of the object. This theory has been verified through hundreds of experiments throughout the world. It is accepted as a valid theory by all experts in the field.

4. The radar speedmeter applies the Doppler shift principle. The speedmeter consists of a transmitter and a receiver. The transmitter generates and sends out the beam of microwaves. The receiver measures the frequency change after the beam strikes an object and bounces back to the car containing the radar speedmeter. Like the underlying theory, the radar speedmeter instrument has been subjected to numerous experiments. The conclusion of the experiments is that if the speedmeter is in proper, working order and operated properly, the instrument will accurately measure speed to within a few hundredths of a mile per hour. At one time or another, speedmeters have been used by law enforcement agencies in every state in the United States. Experts in my field almost universally accept the reliability of radar speedmeters.

____

/s/ Glenda Schneider

On September 17, 2005, before the undersigned, a Notary Public for the State of Texas, personally appeared Glenda Schneider, known to me to be the person whose name is subscribed to the within instrument, and acknowledged that she executed the same.

____

/s/ Mildred Adams
Notary Public

My license expires October 17, 2007

In addition to using affidavits from experts, the party can sometimes use an affidavit from a professional school librarian. The librarian's affidavit is attached to photocopies of the title page and the pertinent pages from a learned treatise in the scientific field. The librarian's affidavit states the librarian's position, lists the credentials of the author of the treatise, and, finally, asserts that the treatise is a standard, authoritative text in its field. The party then uses the excerpts from the treatise to establish that the principle's validity or the instrument's reliability is a verifiable certainty.

The plaintiff would use the affidavit at trial in the following fashion. As soon as the judge granted the first request for judicial notice, the plaintiff could make this request before calling Officer Ripley as a witness. The plaintiff is still the proponent.

P Your Honor, I have one last request for judicial notice. (1)

J What is that?

P May we approach the bench?

J Yes.

P Your Honor, I request that you judicially notice the validity of the theory underlying radar speedmeters and the general reliability of speedmeters. Both facts are verifiable certainties. (1)

J [*To the opposing attorney*] Did you have advance notice that the plaintiff was going to make this request?

O Yes, your Honor. He gave me notice a week ago.

P Your Honor, I request that the court reporter mark this as a plaintiff's exhibit for identification.

J Go ahead. [*Court reporter marks exhibit and hands it back to counsel.*]

P Please let the record reflect that I am showing what has been marked as plaintiff's exhibit number nine for identification to the opposing counsel.

J The record will so reflect.

P I now offer plaintiff's exhibit number nine for identification into evidence.

J [*To the opposing attorney*] Have you seen this exhibit before today?

O Yes. The plaintiff's attorney gave me a copy about a week ago.

J Do you have any objections?

O Yes, your Honor. We do object. This affidavit is gross hearsay.

P Your Honor, at this point, we're litigating the propriety of judicial notice. Under Texas Rule of Evidence 104(a), the hearsay rule doesn't apply to your determination whether these facts are verifiable certainties.

J The objection will be overruled, and plaintiff's exhibit number nine will be received.

P The exhibit establishes that the validity of the underlying principle and the reliability of the instrument are verifiable, scientific certainties. For that reason, judicial notice is appropriate. (2)

J I will grant your request.

P I request that you inform the jury of these facts.

J Yes. Ladies and gentlemen of the jury, I am now going to judicially notice two more facts. One fact is the validity of the theory underlying radar speedmeters. As you may know, the police in this jurisdiction use radar speedmeters to measure the speed of cars. The technical theory underlying speedmeters has been accepted by scientists. Secondly, the speedmeter itself is a reliable instrument if it's in working order and operated correctly. You are to assume the validity of the theory and the general reliability of the instrument. I understand that we are about to hear some testimony about a radar speedmeter clocking of the defendant's car. I want to make it clear that I am not deciding whether this speedmeter was in good, working condition or whether the officer used the correct procedures. You will have to listen to the testimony and make those decisions. I am instructing you only that you must assume the validity of the scientific principle and the general reliability of speedmeters even though you won't hear any evidence on these topics.

The above hypothetical assumes a civil action. In a civil action, Rule of Evidence 201(g) permits the judge to direct the jury to assume the existence of the noticed fact. Evidence Rule 201(g) prescribes a different rule for criminal cases, however: the court shall instruct the jury that it may, but is not required to, accept as conclusive any fact judicially noticed.

§ 12-4 JURY VIEWS

§ 12-4(A) THE DOCTRINE

Sometimes the attorneys want the jurors and judge to view an object or location that cannot feasibly be brought into the courtroom. In most cases, the attorney will be content to offer either a witness's oral description of the object, a diagram of the object, or a photograph of the object. In some cases, however, the object is so complex and plays such a pivotal role in the case that the attorney wants the trier of fact to observe the object or location personally. This procedure is known as a *jury view*.

Although Texas commentators have recognized that there is no rule barring jury views,[9] many judges are reluctant to take the jury out of the courtroom.[10] There are obvious problems with conducting jury views. In addition to logistical questions, there is always the problem that the jury will see or hear something that is otherwise inadmissible. If jury views are to be used, there is a greater burden on the court and the counsel to ensure that does not occur.

If a jury view is to be conducted, it is important that the jurors not view the scene on their own. They should visit the scene as a group, accompanied by court personnel who can monitor and record what is said and observed.

§ 12-4(B) ELEMENTS OF THE FOUNDATION

The proponent of a jury view should preferably make a pretrial motion for a view and submit affidavits or declarations in support of the motion. The declarations should show that:

1. Certain property exists.
2. The property is logically relevant to the pending case.
3. It is impossible or inconvenient to bring the property into the court-room.
4. The features of the property are so complex or detailed that an oral description, diagram, or photograph would be inadequate.
5. The property is in substantially the same condition as at the time of the relevant event. If the property has changed materially, the judge usually exercises discretion by denying the motion. If the property has changed markedly, a view might mislead the jury. When there is potential for misleading the jury, Rule 403 cuts against granting the motion.

§ 12-4(C) SAMPLE FOUNDATION

The fact situation is a personal injury action arising from a collision in February 2005 on a winding, rural road in Bexar County. The plaintiff moves for a jury view of the section of road where the collision occurred. In support of the motion, the plaintiff submits two declarations. Both declarations refer to the same section of road mentioned in the pleadings. For that reason, both declarations lay the first three elements of the foundation. The date of the hearing on the motion is August 1, 2005.

---

[9] *See, e.g.*, Wendorf, *Some Views on Jury Views*, 15 BAYLOR L. REV. 379, 381 n.11 (1963).

[10] Jury views are rarely held in Texas criminal cases.

AFFIDAVIT

1. My name is George Wasterson. I live at 1444 Court Street, San Antonio, Texas.

2. I am a professional photographer. I am the proprietor of the Wasterson Photography Studio, 1456 Court Street, in San Antonio. I have owned that company for 15 years. While I was on active duty in the United States Army between 1997 and 2000, I received formal training in photography. I have since taken seven photography classes at Trinity University in San Antonio.

3. On July 1, 2005, an attorney, Ms. Eileen Richards, contacted me by phone. She asked me to meet her at the intersection of FM 1604 and Range Road outside the city limits of San Antonio. (1), (2), (3) I met her there later that afternoon.

4. While we were at the intersection, Ms. Richards explained to me that she represented the plaintiff in a civil action arising from a collision at the intersection. She also explained that she was interested in showing the jurors the 200 yards of Range Road immediately to the west of the intersection with FM 1604. She asked whether I could photograph or videotape that section of road.

5. I carefully inspected the two hundred yards of road in question. I walked the stretch of road twice and drove it twice. I then advised Ms. Richards that in my professional opinion, neither still photographs nor a videotape would be adequate. The section of road in question is not only winding; the road is also uneven—any car traveling that section of road is constantly riding up and then down and then up again. Even if I took a hundred still photographs and submitted them to a jury, the stills would not adequately convey to the jury the sense of traveling down that stretch of road. In addition, since the road is both curvy and uneven, even a videotape would convey only a limited sense of perspective of a driver on that stretch of road. I declare under penalty of perjury that the above statements are true and correct.

Executed this 14th day of July 2005, in San Antonio, Texas.

____

/s/ George Wasterson

AFFIDAVIT

1. My name is Doris Kingman. I reside at 723 Range Road in Bexar County, Texas. I have lived at that residence for the past 37 years.

2. I am intimately familiar with the intersection of Range Road and FM 1604 outside San Antonio in Bexar County. It is the intersection closest to my house. I have driven through that intersection thousands of times.

3. I can recall the condition of the two hundred yards of Range Road immediately to the west of the intersection with FM 1604 since February 2005. I generally remember the condition of the road and the foliage on both sides of the road. I inspected that area again today. To the best of my recollection, the condition of the foliage and road today is substantially the same as the condition in February 2005.

I declare under penalty of perjury that the above statements are true and correct.

Executed this 29th day of July 2005 in San Antonio, Bexar County, Texas.

/s/ Doris Kingman

CHAPTER 13
CONSTITUTIONAL PRIVILEGES—THE EXCLUSIONARY RULES

PART 1
THE PRODUCTS OF SEARCHES AND SEIZURES

§ 13-1 INTRODUCTION

Chapter 7 covers the topic of the privilege rules, and other rules of evidence, which require the exclusion of otherwise relevant evidence in order to promote some extrinsic policy. This chapter focuses on the topic of what might be referred to as constitutional privileges, i.e., the exclusionary rules. The exclusionary rules are designed to enforce a person's right to be free from unreasonable searches and seizures, involuntary confessions and admissions, and certain identification procedures. Whether based upon constitutional (federal or state) or statutory provisions, the overarching purpose is generally the same: deterrence of improper governmental actions and incentive to government agents to be more careful in the future. If the defense objects, and the trial judge concludes that the evidence being offered by the government was illegally obtained, it is excluded.

Although the topics of searches and seizures and confessions are not explicitly mentioned in the Texas Rules of Evidence, they share many common attributes with other evidentiary issues insofar as the prosecutor bears the burden of "proving up" the contraband seized or statements obtained from the defendant. To that extent there are evidentiary foundations, or predicates, to be proved. There are still other similarities. First, the burden rests on the defendant to object to the prosecutor's evidence; failure to do so will normally result in a waiver. Secondly, the prosecutor must be proficient in walking and talking the object or statement into evidence. And thirdly, the prosecutor must be proficient in questioning his or her witnesses in a nonleading fashion to show that the seizure or interrogation was legal.

Because the exclusionary rules operate almost exclusively in criminal trials, this chapter is unlike preceding chapters to the extent that the proponent is usually the prosecutor and the defense is usually the opponent. The material should be helpful to both sides, however. Although the prosecutor has the burden as the proponent, this material should serve as an important checklist for the defense to make sure that the prosecutor has met that burden.

Volumes have been written on the substantive aspects of the constitutional and statutory principles involved. Those texts and materials should provide ample discussion of the applicable law.[1] As with other chapters, the discussion here focuses on a brief statement of the applicable legal doctrine, with some citation of authority, a list of the elements to be proved, and a sample foundation which demonstrates suggested lines of questions for the prosecutor.

The chapter is divided into three parts; the first part addresses searches and seizures, the second part focuses on self-incrimination and confessions, and the third part addresses eyewitness identification.

§ 13-2 THE EXCLUSIONARY RULES REGARDING SEARCHES AND SEIZURES

§ 13-2(A) CONSTITUTIONAL GROUNDS FOR EXCLUDING PRODUCTS OF SEARCHES AND SEIZURES

The judicial decisions interpreting the Fourth Amendment generally address two fundamental topics. The first topic is the rules governing the legality of searches and seizures. In some instances, the prosecutor need not justify a search or seizure. For example, the Fourth Amendment is inapplicable if the person conducting the search is a private citizen rather than a government agent. Even when there is sufficient government involvement to trigger the Fourth Amendment, there may be other reasons why that amendment is not involved, i.e., where the government action did not impinge on any reasonable expectation of privacy.

---

[1] *See* BARTON, TEXAS SEARCH AND SEIZURE (2d ed. 1999); Dix & Dawson, CRIMINAL PRACTICE AND PROCEDURE, chs. 4–12 (2d ed. 2001).

For example, the prosecutor may be able to justify the seizure on the ground that the defendant abandoned the personal property or that the search occurred in an open field.

In other cases, however, the prosecutor must prove inculpatory facts particularized to the defendant. By way of illustration, the prosecutor must demonstrate founded or reasonable suspicion to justify a stop or frisk. If the intrusion amounts to a full-fledged arrest or search, the prosecutor must go further and establish probable cause.

The second topic in the judicial decisions is the scope of the exclusionary rule barring the admission of the products of illegal searches and seizures. Even if an illegal search or seizure has occurred, the prosecutor may be able to introduce a product of the search or seizure by using the good faith exception.

Both the Fourth Amendment and article I, section 9 of the Texas Constitution generally forbid unreasonable searches and seizures. To a lesser extent they provide guidance on the procedure for issuing warrants and the contents of such warrants.

With respect to both searches and seizures, the requirement of reasonableness has three parts: (1) it must be supported by probable cause; (2) it must be conducted pursuant to a warrant or a recognized exception to the warrant requirement; and (3) the manner of conducting the search or seizure must be reasonable.

Article I, section 9 of the Texas Constitution may be construed as affording greater rights than the Fourth Amendment of the United States Constitution.[2] The cases generally hold that a defendant arguing for a broader construction of the state provision bears the burden of persuading the state court of the inaccuracy or inappropriateness of the federal court's approach or result.

§ 13-2(B) STATUTORY GROUNDS FOR EXCLUDING PRODUCTS OF SEARCHES AND SEIZURES

The Texas statutory exclusionary rule, article 38.23(a) of the Code of Criminal Procedure, states:

> No evidence obtained by an officer or other person in violation of any provisions of the Constitution or laws of the State of Texas, or of the Constitution or laws of the United States of America, shall be admitted in evidence against the accused on the trial of any criminal case.

Its primary purpose is to deter unlawful police conduct by rendering inadmissible evidence obtained by exploitation of an unlawful search or seizure. For the

---

[2] *Autran v. State*, 887 S.W.2d 31 (Tex. Crim. App. 1994); *Richardson v. State*, 865 S.W.2d 944 (Tex. Crim. App. 1993); *Heitman v. State*, 815 S.W.2d 681 (Tex. Crim. App. 1991).

exclusionary statute to be invoked, there must exist a causal connection between the unlawful police conduct and the way in which the challenged evidence was obtained.

§ 13-3 EXCEPTIONS TO THE EXCLUSIONARY RULES GOVERNING SEARCHES AND SEIZURES

§ 13-3(A) THE GOOD FAITH EXCEPTION

§ 13-3(A)(1) The Doctrine

The primary purpose of the exclusionary rule is to deter illegal searches by the police. If the police illegally seize evidence in good faith, and the intrusion is otherwise lawful, the exclusionary rule may not serve the purpose for which it was intended. That was the reasoning relied upon by the United States Supreme Court in recognizing a good faith exception to the exclusionary rule in warranted searches. In short, the exception applies when the police rely on a facially valid search warrant which is later found to be invalid. The seized evidence is admissible if the police have acted in objective good faith in conducting the search.[3]

The good faith exception has been partially extended to warrantless searches, in situations where the police have conducted a warrantless search authorized by a state statute which is later found to be unconstitutional. In such a case the Court has sustained the admission of evidence seized under the statute.[4]

The Texas good faith exception, contained in article 38.23(b) of the Code of Criminal Procedure, recognizes the exception to the exclusionary statute if "the evidence was obtained by a law enforcement officer acting in objective good faith reliance upon a warrant issued by a neutral magistrate based on probable cause." There is authority for the view, however, that the Texas good faith exception is not coextensive with the federal good faith exception to the extent that the Texas version is only available if in fact the search was supported by probable cause.[5] The federal version permits the government to invoke the exception even if it is later determined that the federal magistrate erred in concluding that there was probable cause. Thus, the exception under Texas law

---

[3] The Court adopted that exception in *United States v. Leon*, 468 U.S. 897 (1984) and *Massachusetts v. Sheppard*, 468 U.S. 981 (1984).

[4] *See Illinois v. Krull*, 480 U.S. 340 (1987), in which the police conducted a warrantless search pursuant to an Illinois statute permitting inspection of the records of licensed sellers of motor vehicles and motor vehicle parts. The Court held that the statute clearly authorized the officers' action and that the officers' reliance on the statute was in objective good faith.

[5] *See Gordon v. State*, 801 S.W.2d 899 (Tex. Crim. App. 1990) (plurality opinion); *Flores v. State*, 827 S.W.2d 416 (Tex. App.—Corpus Christi 1992, pet. ref.).

will probably only be available where there was probable cause supporting the search but there was a technical violation of the rules governing searches and seizures.[6]

§ 13-3(A)(2) Elements of the Foundation

To invoke the good faith exception, the prosecutor must demonstrate that:

1. The officer who originally received the report about the crime neither knew the information was false nor acted in reckless disregard for the truth.
2. The evidence must have been obtained through the execution of a warrant.
3. The warrant was issued by a neutral magistrate based on an affidavit presented by an officer which was supported by probable cause.
4. The officer executing the warrant relied on the validity of the warrant.
5. In executing the warrant, the police did not exceed the scope of the warrant.

At each stage of the process, the officers must act in objective good faith. All elements must be proven in order to invoke the good faith exception.

§ 13-3(A)(3) Sample Foundation

In the following sample foundation, the State has charged the defendant, Mr. David Kline, with possession of heroin. On July 31, 2005, an informant told the police that the previous day she had seen a large quantity of heroin at the defendant's apartment. When the police drafted the warrant for the judge's signature, they listed the wrong apartment number for the defendant's residence. The affidavit listed the residence as Apartment 121 and the warrant listed the residence as 212. The officers nonetheless searched the apartment actually occupied by the defendant and found heroin. The defendant moves to suppress the evidence. For purposes of the motion, the prosecutor argues that the search was based on probable cause but concedes that the warrant contained a typographical error. The prosecutor argues, however, that the search was in objective good faith.

The witness is Officer Garcia, who received the informant's report, drafted the affidavit, and executed the warrant. The proponent is the prosecutor.

P Officer Garcia, WHERE were you on the morning of July 31, 2005? (1)

W I was on duty at the Narcotics Detail Office.

---

[6] *See, e.g., Rios v. State*, 901 S.W.2d 704 (Tex. App.—San Antonio 1995, no pet.) (search warrant inadvertently identified place to be searched as vehicle and not house).

P WHAT, if anything, unusual happened that morning? (1)

W I got a phone call from Sally.

P WHO is Sally? (1)

W She is one of my informants. She gives me leads for drug arrests and seizures. I've used her many times in the past.

P HOW often have you used her? (1)

W At least 15 times over the past two years. I've relied on her tips in investigations.

P WHAT have been the results of those investigations? (1)

W She always gives me good, solid leads. She double checks any hearsay. Most of the information she relays to me is based on her personal observation.

P WHAT did Sally say when she called that morning? (1)

W She said that the day before she'd been at the defendant's apartment and had seen a large quantity of heroin in the bedroom.

P HOW did you know she was referring to this defendant? (1)

W She gave me the address, 1440 Blanco, Apartment 121. I'd driven by that area and seen the defendant walking around. I knew we were talking about the same guy.

P WHAT did you do after you spoke with Sally? (1)

W I wrote up an affidavit for a search warrant.

P WHY did you do that? (1)

W I was convinced at that point that I had probable cause for a good search.

P [*To court reporter.*] Would you please mark this as an exhibit for the State? [*Reporter marks exhibit and hands it back to counsel.*]

P Thank you. Please let the record reflect that I am showing State's exhibit number one for identification to the opposing counsel. [*Opposing counsel examines exhibit and hands it back to the proponent.*]

P Officer, I now hand you what has been marked State's exhibit number one for identification. WHAT is it? (3)

W It's the affidavit I just mentioned.

P HOW can you recognize it? (3)

W I know my own handwriting. That's definitely my signature at the bottom of the page.

P I now offer State's exhibit number one for identification into evidence.

J Any objections?

O None, your Honor.

J It will be received.

P Officer, please read the third paragraph of that affidavit to yourself.

W Yes.

P WHAT, if anything, does the affidavit say about the location of where Sally saw the heroin? (3)

W It says Apartment 121.

P WHAT did you do after you typed the affidavit? (3)

W I walked it over to Judge Lorenzo's chambers.

P WHAT happened then? (3)

W She was in her office. She took a couple of minutes to read it, and I remember her asking me when I had this conversation with Sally. I told her that I had just gotten off the phone with Sally and immediately typed up the affidavit.

P WHAT did Judge Lorenzo do then? (3)

W She issued a warrant to me.

P [*To court reporter.*] Would you please mark this State's exhibit number two for identification? [*Reporter marks exhibit and hands it back to counsel.*]

P Thank you. Please let the record reflect that I am showing State's exhibit number two for identification to the defense attorney. [*Opposing counsel examines exhibit and hands it back to the proponent.*]

P Officer, WHAT is the exhibit? (4)

W It's the search warrant the judge gave me.

P HOW do you recognize it? (4)

W I know the contents—the date and the rest of it. I also recognize the judge's handwriting. I typed this warrant out for the judge's signature.

P I now offer State's exhibit number two for identification into evidence.

J Objections?

O None.

J State's exhibit number two will be received.

P Officer please read the portion of the warrant which describes the place to be searched. WHAT does it say?

W It says Apartment 212.

P Officer, why is there is a discrepancy between the location in the affidavit and the location listed in the search warrant?

W That was my mistake. I thought I had typed in the right address. I drafted the thing in pencil and then typed it. I'm not the world's best typist. I'm afraid that I didn't proofread it carefully. It had been a hectic day, there was a lot going on, and I just slipped up when I was typing it up for the judge.

P WHAT did you do after the judge gave you this warrant?

W Officer Marshall and I executed it.

P WHY did you do that? (4)

W I assumed that we had authority to go get the heroin. I had a warrant in my hands.

P WHERE did you go after you got the warrant in your hands? (4)

W We went straight to 1440 Blanco, Apartment 121, the place where the defendant lives.

P WHY did you go there? (4)

W Because I was familiar with that location and the number "121" had stuck in my mind.

P WHAT did you do when you arrived at 1440 Blanco, Apartment 121? (5)

W We knocked and showed the defendant the warrant. He let us in and then we searched.

P WHAT did you search for? (4)

W The only stuff we looked for was heroin.

P WHY? (4)

W Again, right here in the warrant—it says that's what we were authorized to search for. That's the only contraband we were looking for.

P WHAT happened while you were searching? (2), (5)

W We found a large quantity of heroin.

P WHAT did you do when you found it? (2), (5)

W We seized it.

P WHY? (2), (5)

W I just assumed that it was perfectly proper and lawful for us to grab it. I thought I had probable cause and a good warrant for a seizure.

§ 13-3(B) RESERVED

§ 13-4 MOTIONS TO SUPPRESS

§ 13-4(A) IN GENERAL

A motion to suppress is one method by which a defendant may obtain the exclusion of evidence recovered as the result of an unlawful arrest. Although the defense is not required to file a pretrial motion to suppress, it may, and usually does so. The motion to suppress may be heard, at the trial court's discretion, either before or during trial.

§ 13-4(B) THE DEFENDANT'S BURDEN

The defendant is not required to file a pretrial motion to suppress; he or she may wait until trial and object to the admission of the evidence at the time it is offered by the State. The defendant's objection must be both timely and specific in order to preserve error on appeal.

If the defendant files a pretrial motion to suppress and presents evidence, and the motion is denied, the defendant is not required to object at trial to the admission of the disputed evidence in order to preserve error. On the other hand, if no pretrial hearing is conducted on the motion, or the defendant does not present evidence at the pretrial hearing, and the motion is denied, the defendant must object at trial to the admission of the evidence in order to preserve error.

A motion to suppress may be accompanied by an offer of proof in the form of affidavits of persons the defense intends to call to testify on the motion.

§ 13-4(C) THE PROSECUTION'S BURDEN

If the defendant has filed a motion to suppress or raises an objection that the offered evidence was illegally obtained, the State has the burden of showing by clear and convincing evidence that the evidence is admissible.[7] Regardless of the trial judge's ruling out of the presence of the jury, either pretrial or during the trial, if the defendant raises a factual issue before the jury about the legality of the search or seizure, the State is required to prove beyond a reasonable doubt that the evidence was lawfully obtained.[8]

§ 13-4(D) ROLE OF THE JUDGE AND JURY

Once the defendant has either filed a motion to suppress or raised an objection at trial, the trial judge rules on the admissibility of the evidence. Whether to hold a hearing on the matter is discretionary with the judge. In this text the sample foundations assume that the trial judge has decided to hold a "hearing" and the

---

[7] *LaLande v. State*, 676 S.W.2d 115, 117–18 (Tex. Crim. App. 1984).

[8] *See* TEX. CRIM. PROC CODE ANN. § 38.22.

prosecution has called witnesses to establish the legality of the government agent's actions. Assuming that the trial judge has ruled that the evidence is admissible, if trial evidence raises an issue about the legality of the search or seizure the jury must be instructed (upon the defendant's request) that it cannot consider the evidence unless it first finds beyond a reasonable doubt that it was legally obtained.[9] In effect, that procedure permits the defendant a second bite at the apple and in that case the prosecution would almost certainly have to call live witnesses to show how and why the search or seizure occurred.

§ 13-5 THE DEFENDANT'S STANDING TO CHALLENGE THE GOVERNMENT'S INTRUSION

§ 13-5(A) THE REASONABLE EXPECTATION OF PRIVACY REQUIREMENT

Assume the defense establishes that there was a government search or seizure. Does the defendant automatically have a right to challenge the legality of the search or seizure? In both federal and Texas practice, the answer is "No." In *Jones v. United States*, 362 U.S. 257, 261 (1960), the Supreme Court announced that only "a victim of a search or seizure, one against whom the search was directed," has standing to challenge the intrusion. To be the "victim," the person must be (1) the defendant against whom the evidence obtained by the search or seizure is offered, and (2) the person whose reasonable expectation of privacy was invaded.[10] The defendant has the burden of proving that the search was unreasonable and that it violated his reasonable expectation of privacy. Texas law has these same requirements.[11]

A defendant has standing if he or she had a subjective and reasonable expectation of privacy in the place searched. Factors relevant to determining the defendant's standing include the following: (1) whether the defendant had a proprietary or possessory interest in the place searched; (2) whether the defendant's presence in or on the place searched was legitimate; (3) whether the defendant had such control of the place as to be entitled to exclude others; (4) whether the defendant took normal precautions, prior to the search, which are customarily taken by a person seeking privacy; (5) whether the place searched was put to a private use; and (6) whether the defendant's claim of privacy is consistent with historical notions of privacy.[12]

---

[9] TEX. CRIM. PROC CODE ANN. § 38.23.

[10] *Rakas v. Illinois*, 439 U.S. 128, 133 (1978).

[11] In *Fuller v. State*, 829 S.W.2d 191, 202 (Tex. Crim. App. 1992), *cert. denied*, 498 U.S. 951, the Court of Criminal Appeals stated that the Texas exclusionary statute does not preclude the requirement of standing.

[12] *Calloway v. State*, 743 S.W.2d 645, 651 (Tex. Crim. App. 1988).

§ 13-5(B) The Nature of the Governmental Intrusion

The Fourth Amendment and article I, section 9 of the Texas Constitution apply only to searches and seizures made by the *government*. For a defendant to have standing to challenge the legality of a search or seizure, the search or seizure must have been conducted by government officials or by someone acting as an agent of the government.

The Texas exclusionary statute, article 38.23(a) of the Code of Criminal Procedure, operates to exclude evidence unlawfully obtained by an officer or "other person." The term "other person," however, should be interpreted to mean a private person acting at the request of a government agent. To determine whether the person acted as an agent of the State, the following factors must be considered: (1) whether a government agent initiated, knew of, or acquiesced in the search or seizure, and (2) whether the private person intended to assist law enforcement efforts, or to further his own ends in conducting the search or seizure.[13]

§ 13-5(C) Search and Seizure of Property by a Private Citizen

§ 13-5(C)(1) The Doctrine

The Fourth Amendment and article I, section 9 of the Texas Constitution do not apply to the activities of private persons who act independently.[14] It follows that the prosecution may use evidence procured by the wrongful conduct of private persons in cases where the government had no role.[15]

§ 13-5(C)(2) Elements of the Foundation

A prosecutor attempting to introduce the product of a search and seizure under this doctrine must prove the following foundational elements:

1. Someone searched the defendant's property.
2. That person acted as a private citizen.
3. During the search, the person seized certain personal property or made certain incriminating observations.
4. The scope of any later government intrusion was essentially the same as the scope of the private citizen's intrusion. To prove this, the prosecutor will probably have to call the police officer to whom the private citizen surrendered the personal property.

---

[13] *Dawson v. State*, 868 S.W.2d 363, 369 (Tex. App.—Dallas 1993, pet. refused).

[14] *State v. Comeaux*, 818 S.W.2d 46 (Tex. Crim. App. 1991) (plurality opinion).

[15] *Stoker v. State*, 788 S.W.2d 1, 11 (Tex. Crim. App. 1989), *cert. denied*, 496 U.S. 951 (1990).

§ 13-5(C)(3) Sample Foundation

The State has charged the defendant Lynch with illegal possession of crack cocaine. The witness is Mr. Winthrop Johnson. Mr. Johnson has already testified that he is a porter at the Yachtsman Hotel in Houston. The proponent is the prosecutor.

P Mr. Johnson, WHERE were you on the morning of July 13, 2005?

W I was on duty in the hotel lobby.

P WHAT happened that morning?

W People were checking in and out. I remember one customer in particular who checked in.

P WHO is that?

W The defendant, Lynch, over there.

P WHERE is he sitting?

W At the table over there.

P HOW is he dressed?

W He's wearing a blue suit with a yellow tie.

P Your Honor, please let the record reflect that the witness has correctly identified the defendant, Charles Lynch.

J The record will so reflect.

P WHAT happened after the defendant checked in? (1)

W He gave me his suitcases and told me to take them up to his room while he went to park his car.

P WHAT did you do after he gave you the suitcases? (1)

W I got into the elevator and started taking his suitcases to the 14th floor where his room was. I guess he didn't have the suitcases locked properly. When the elevator got to the 14th floor and I started to pick them up to take to his room, one came partially open and I saw two plastic bags.

P WHAT was the appearance of the bags? (1)

W The bags were clear, and you could see the contents.

P WHAT was the appearance of the contents? (1)

W They were a white, chunky substance. It looked to me as if it might be crack cocaine.

P WHY do you say that? (1)

W Two weeks before, the head of hotel security had given a class on identifying and handling illegal drugs. She told us to be on the lookout for that sort of junk. She showed us photographs of various illegal drugs and a local policeman showed us some actual samples. This stuff looked just like the crack cocaine in the photograph she showed us.

P WHAT did you do after you saw the bags in defendant's luggage? (3)

W I immediately called hotel security and the police.

P WHY did you do that? (2)

W That was what we had been told to do by hotel security. And I don't want that sort of stuff going on in the hotel.

P WHEN did you first contact the police—before or after you met the defendant? (2)

W Afterwards.

P WHO else was present when you discovered the bags containing the drugs? (2)

W No one—just me.

P After you called the police, WHAT happened? (3)

W They came to the hotel room.

P WHAT were their names? (3)

W Officers Lopez and Crump.

P WHAT did you do after the two police officers arrived? (3)

W I gave them the luggage and the bags containing the white chunks.

§ 13-5(D) SEARCH AND SEIZURE OF ABANDONED PROPERTY

§ 13-5(D)(1) The Doctrine

If a defendant voluntarily abandons property, he or she relinquishes any protected expectation of privacy in the property,[16] and has no standing to argue the lawfulness of its recovery.[17] The central problem for the prosecutor is establishing that the defendant's physical act was not prompted by an illegal action by government officials.

§ 13-5(D)(2) Elements of the Foundation

The elements for showing that the defendant abandoned the property in question are as follows:

---

16 *California v. Greenwood*, 486 U.S. 35, 41 (1988); *Crawford v. State*, 769 S.W.2d 331, 333 (Tex. App.—San Antonio 1989, pet. ref.).

17 *Sullivan v. State*, 564 S.W.2d 698, 702 (Tex. Crim. App. 1978); *See also Salcido v. State*, 758 S.W.2d 261 (Tex. Crim. App. 1988).

1. The defendant physically abandoned the property.[18]
2. The defendant performed the act voluntarily.[19]
3. The police lawfully proceeded to the location where the property was abandoned.[20]
4. The police seized the abandoned item.

§ 13-5(D)(3) Sample Foundation

In the following scenario, the State has charged the defendant Ruiz with carrying an unlicensed, concealed weapon. The witness is Officer Trail. Officer Trail has already testified that on the morning of January 3rd, he was on duty on foot patrol near the corner of Commerce and St. Mary's streets in downtown San Antonio. The proponent is the prosecutor.

P Officer Trail, WHAT, if anything, unusual happened that morning?

W I saw someone approach the northwest corner, and I noticed that he had a suspicious looking bulge in the front of his jacket.

P WHO was that person?

W The defendant.

P WHERE is he sitting now?

W He's the guy in the green shirt at the table to my right.

P Your Honor, please let the record reflect that the witness has identified the defendant, Mario Ruiz.

J The record will so reflect.

P WHAT happened next?

W He was walking along, and then he caught sight of me.

P HOW were you dressed?

W I was in full uniform, as I am now.

P WHAT did he do then?

W He looked at me for a second or two. Then he abruptly turned and walked in the other direction.

P WHAT did you do? (2)

---

18 Abandonment is a question of intent, which may be inferred from statements, conduct, or other objective facts. *See Sullivan v. State*, 564 S.W.2d 698 (Tex. Crim. App. 1977).

19 In many cases, when a police officer approaches, the defendant throws contraband to the ground. The act is involuntary if it was the result of illegal action by the police.

20 If the location is a public street, the police officer does not need a warrant to walk over and pick up the property.

W I just stood and watched him carefully.

P WHAT happened next? (1)

W Next, I saw his left hand reach down and throw something on the ground.

P WHERE was he standing at the time? (3)

W On the public sidewalk.

P WHAT happened to the thing he threw down?

W It just fell to the ground.

P WHERE did it land? (3)

W It landed on the public sidewalk.

P HOW could you tell that the defendant threw the object down? (4)

W I saw his hand move, and I saw an object fall from his hand.

P WHAT did you do then? (4)

W I walked over quickly and picked it up.

P WHAT was the object? (4)

W It was a pistol.

P HOW would you describe the pistol? (4)

W It was a police special with serial number A14744.

P HOW can you remember the serial number? (4)

W I have an almost photographic memory for numbers. It's easy for me to remember serial numbers.

P [*To court reporter.*] Would you please mark this as an exhibit for the State? [*Reporter marks exhibit and hands it back to counsel.*]

P Thank you. Please let the record reflect that I am showing State's exhibit number one for identification to the defense attorney. [*Opposing counsel examines exhibit and hands it back to the proponent.*]

J The record will so reflect.

P Permission to approach the witness?

J Granted.

P Officer, I now hand you State's exhibit number one for identification. WHAT is it? (4)

W It's the pistol I picked up after the defendant threw it down.

P HOW can you recognize it? (4)

W I recognize the general type of weapon and the serial number—just like I said, A14744.

P Officer, WHAT did you say to the defendant before he threw his pistol to the ground? (2)

W Nothing.

P HOW far away from the defendant were you when he threw the pistol down? (2)

W About 20 feet or so.

P WHAT gestures did you make toward him before he threw the pistol down? (2)

W None. I just stood there and watched him carefully.

P WHAT were you doing when he threw the pistol down? (2)

W Nothing—I didn't chase him or even make a move toward him. I was just watching the guy.

§ 13-5(E) SEARCH OF OPEN FIELDS

§ 13-5(E)(1) The Doctrine

The Fourth Amendment protects both a person's residence and the curtilage, the area immediately adjacent to the house and used in connection with the house. In *Hester v. United States*, 265 U.S. 57 (1924), however, the Supreme Court held that the Fourth Amendment does not protect property located in an open field. Article I, section 9 of the Texas Constitution contains the same exception to the warrant requirement. The reasoning behind the exception is that a person has no reasonable or legitimate expectation of privacy in open fields.

Because of the phrasing of Texas Code of Criminal Procedure article 38.23(a), which states in part, "No evidence obtained by an officer or other person in violation of *any* provisions of the Constitution or laws of the State of Texas, or of the Constitution or laws of the United States . . . ." (emphasis added), a conflict in the Texas courts of appeals has resulted. One court of appeals has held that if an officer commits the offense of criminal trespass when entering an open field, the evidence recovered as a result of the offense should be suppressed.[21] Another court of appeals has disagreed, saying that if an officer reasonably believes that the entry onto the property is required to discharge his statutory duties, the officer's action is justified by the "public duty" justification.[22] Therefore, the officer has not trespassed and the exclusionary statute is not invoked.[23]

---

21 *State v. Hobbs*, 824 S.W.2d 317, 319 (Tex. App.—San Antonio 1992, pet. ref.).

22 TEX. PENAL CODE § 9.21(a) ("Conduct is justified if the actor reasonably believes the conduct is required or authorized by law, by the judgment or order of a competent court or other governmental tribunal, or in the execution of legal process.")

23 *Rosalez v. State*, 875 S.W.2d 705, 715–17 (Tex. App.—Dallas 1993, pet. ref). *See also Carroll*

§ 13-5(E)(2) Elements of the Foundation

The elements for showing that the evidence was located in an "open field" are as follows:

1. The defendant's property where the evidence was located was an open field.[24]
2. The police searched the open field.
3. The police discovered and seized certain property in the open field.

§ 13-5(E)(3) Sample Foundation

The State has charged the defendant Wyatt with bank robbery. The State alleges that on October 13th, the defendant robbed the NationsBank branch in Waco, Texas. The witness is Deputy Sheriff Elizabeth Cameron. She has already testified that she drove to the defendant's farm in a rural area outside of Waco on a tip that the defendant was involved in the robbery. The prosecutor is the proponent.

P Deputy Cameron, HOW did you get to the defendant's farm?

W I drove there on Highway 6.

P WHERE is the defendant's farm?

W It's right by the FM 121 turnoff.

P HOW well do you know the area? (1)

W Quite well. I've been a deputy sheriff in that area for 13 years.

P HOW well do you know the defendant's farm? (1)

W I know the lay of the land pretty well.

P HOW did you become acquainted with the layout of the farm? (1)

W I hunt in that area, and I often hunt on the farm right next to the defendant's. You get a good view of the place from Gavin's farm. Gavin is a good friend of mine, and I've hunted on his property many times.

P [*To court reporter.*] Would you please mark this diagram as an exhibit for the State? [*Reporter marks exhibit and hands it back to counsel.*]

P Please let the record reflect that I am showing what the reporter has marked as State's exhibit number two for identification to opposing counsel. [*Opposing counsel examines exhibit and hands it back to the proponent.*]

---

v. State, 911 S.W.2d 210 (Tex. App.—Austin 1995, no pet.) (violation of just any law does not invoke article 38.23(a)).

24 The prosecutor usually establishes the fact by process of elimination, that is, the prosecutor shows that the location was neither a residence house nor the area immediately connected to the residence. The prosecutor may introduce a chart or diagram of the defendant's property for this purpose.

J The record will so reflect.

P I request permission to approach the witness.

J Granted.

P Deputy Cameron, I now hand you what has been marked as State's exhibit number two for identification. WHAT is it? (1)

W It's a diagram of the defendant's farm.

P HOW well does the diagram depict the area? (1)

W All the features it shows are correct—Highway 6 running along the northern border, FM 121 cutting down the eastern border, and the square shape of the piece of property. It's not to scale, but other than that, it's accurate.

P WHAT buildings are located on the property? (1)

W There are only three. The main residence, a barn, and a little storage shed. They're all located on the western edge of the property.

P Please take this black marker and indicate their location with a capital R for the residence, a capital B for barn, and a capital S for shed. [*The witness complies.*] Thank you. Please let the record reflect that the witness has so marked the diagram.

P HOW are those buildings connected? (1)

W There are paths from the residence house to both the barn and the shed. There's a wooden fence around all three buildings. All three buildings are located in a small area on the western edge of the property, and they're all surrounded by this fence.

P Please use the black marker to indicate the paths with Ps, and then please use this red marker to draw the fence around all three buildings. [*Witness marks diagram as requested.*] Please let the record reflect that the witness has complied with my request.

P Deputy Cameron, please describe the eastern half of this farm. (1)

W It's nothing but a big, uncultivated field. There aren't even many weeds.

P HOW is the field separated from the buildings on the western edge of the property? (1)

W The fence—the one I drew in red—cuts off those buildings from the field.

P WHAT paths, if any, connect the field to the buildings? (1)

W As far as I know, there aren't any. The paths from the residence house dead end at the shed and the barn. The paths don't continue into the field.

P HOW is the field separated from the highway? (1)

W There's a short, maybe three-foot wire fence around the edge of the entire property, including the field.

P To WHAT extent does the fence block the view of the field from the highway? (1)

W Really not at all. It's a three-strand fence that you can see through.

P On the morning of October 28th, when you drove to the defendant's farm, WHERE did you park your car? (2)

W Right here near the northeast corner of the property.

P WHY did you do that? (2)

W As I was approaching the property from Highway 6, I thought I noticed something peculiar in the middle of the field.

P WHAT? (2)

W As I recalled, it was just an empty field. But when I approached it that morning, there was something piled in the middle of the field that I hadn't noticed before.

P Please use the green marker and indicate the location where you parked with C1. [*The witness complies.*] Please let the record reflect that the witness has so marked the diagram. Deputy Cameron, WHAT did you do after you parked? (2)

W I walked to the pile in the field.

P HOW did you get onto the defendant's property? (2)

W I stepped over the fence here.

P Please mark that location with C2. [*Witness marks chart as requested.*] Please let the record reflect that the witness has complied.

W There. This is where I stepped over the fence.

P Thank you. WHAT did you do after you stepped over the fence? (2)

W I walked straight toward the pile.

P Please indicate your path with an arrow and mark that arrow C3.

W Okay. [*Witness complies.*]

P Thank you. Please let the record reflect that the witness has so marked the diagram. WHAT happened then?

W I reached the pile.

P Please mark that location with C4. (3)

W [*Witness marks the diagram.*] Right here at the end of the arrow.

P Thank you. Please let the record reflect that the witness has complied.

P WHAT is the distance between the spot where you saw the suspicious pile and the closest building or structure on the farm? (1)

W Oh, I would say at least 200 or 300 yards.

P Your Honor, I now offer State's exhibit number two for identification into evidence.

J Any objections?

O None, your Honor.

J It will be received.

P WHAT, if anything, did you find at the pile? (3)

W There was a cardboard box with the top open. Inside, I could see some discarded cloth bags.

P WHAT type of bags were they? (3)

W They were bank bags. There were three bags, and they all bore the inscription, "NationsBank."

P Your Honor, I request that these be marked State's exhibits number three, number four, and number five for identification. (The prosecutor would continue the foundation to identify the three bank bags.)

§ 13-5(F) SEARCH OF GOVERNMENT PROPERTY

§ 13-5(F)(1) The Doctrine

If the government decides to search its own property, a defendant who has had possession or control of that property may not have any standing to object to the intrusion because of a lack of expectation of privacy. The question is whether the government has in any way indicated to the defendant, usually a government employee, that there is some expectation of privacy. In *O'Connor v. Ortega*, 480 U.S. 709 (1987), the Supreme Court recognized that searches and seizures conducted by government employers of the property of their employees are subject to Fourth Amendment restraints. The question of whether an employee has a reasonable expectation of privacy in his or her office is to be decided on a case-by-case basis. Determining what is a reasonable search depends on the context in which the search takes place. The Court developed a test for balancing the employee's legitimate expectation of privacy against the government's need for supervision, control, and the efficient operation of the workplace. Examples of areas where the employee would most likely have a privacy right would include his or her desk and file cabinets.[25]

---

25 The Fourth Amendment also applies to the search of the office of a member of the military. *See United States v. Muniz*, 23 M.J. 201 (CMA 1987) (search of a locked credenza, located in Muniz's office and designated for his personal use, was held to be reasonable under the circumstances).

§ 13-5(F)(2) Elements of the Foundation

If the governmental intrusion involved a search of government property then the following elements would have to be met:

1. The public employer's intrusion on the constitutionally protected privacy interest of the government employee was for noninvestigative, work-related purposes or for investigations of work-related misconduct.
2. The search of the employee's office was reasonable under the circumstances.

§ 13-5(F)(3) Sample Foundation

The State has charged the defendant, Juan Solis, with theft of prescription drugs from a hospital pharmacy. The defendant is an employee of the main pharmacy of the state hospital in Lubbock, Texas. He had been under investigation for several weeks, and on May 29th, hospital officials entered his office and searched it for evidence of the stolen drugs. A large box of the stolen drugs was found. The witness is Katherine Gray, the executive director of the hospital. The proponent is the prosecutor.

P Ms. Gray, WHAT happened on May 29th? (1)

W Some other hospital officials and I entered the defendant's office, located on the second floor of the hospital.

P WHAT was the purpose of your entry into his office? (1)

W We had been investigating Mr. Solis's activities for the past five weeks, and we had good information from eyewitnesses that he had been taking drugs from the pharmacy. We wanted to see if this was true.

P WHAT happened when you went into his office? (1)

W We looked around the office, in his file cabinets, and in his desk drawers.

P WHY did you look in his file cabinets and desk drawers? (2)

W The drugs we were looking for are small and easily concealed. Also, we felt he would be more likely to place them in a private location.

P WHAT, if anything, did you find? (2)

W We found a box of the stolen drugs.

P [*To court reporter.*] Would you please mark this as an exhibit for the State? [*Reporter marks exhibit and hands it back to counsel.*] Please let the record reflect that I am showing what the reporter has marked as State's exhibit number two for identification to opposing counsel. [*Opposing counsel examines exhibit and hands it back to the proponent.*] Ms. Gray, WHAT is State's exhibit number two for identification? (2)

W It's the box of drugs we found in Solis's office.

P HOW do you recognize it? (2)

W I recognize the markings on the box itself, as well as the types of drugs inside the box.

P Your Honor, I now offer State's exhibit number two for identification into evidence.

J Any objections?

O No, your Honor.

J State's exhibit number two for identification will be received as State's exhibit number two.

P Ms. Gray, WHY did you look into what you considered to be private areas of the defendant's office? (1), (2)

W Under the circumstances, we felt we should look through everything in the office in order to find any drugs he may have hidden. The drugs he took are highly addictive and we did not want them to fall into the wrong hands.

P WHAT did you do once you located the drugs? (2)

W I immediately called the police department. They came and took over from there.

§ 13-6 SEARCHES BASED UPON PROBABLE CAUSE—SEARCH WARRANT REQUIRED

§ 13-6(A) THE DOCTRINE

Assume that an officer believes there is probable cause for an arrest or search.[26] If time permits, the officer can contact a judge or magistrate and seek a search warrant. The law prefers that the officer obtain judicial authorization for an arrest or search. Although a person with law enforcement responsibilities may be overzealous in assessing the information, a judge or magistrate is presumably neutral and detached. The judge's intervention helps ensure that privacy will be invaded only if there is in fact probable cause justifying the intrusion. The officer reduces the information to a written affidavit and submits the affidavit to a judicial officer. The judge or magistrate then applies the credibility and probability tests to the information set out in the affidavit.

---

[26] Probable cause exists when the facts and circumstances within the searching or seizing officer's knowledge and of which the officer has reasonably trustworthy information would lead a person of reasonable caution and prudence to believe that he or she will find the instrumentality of a crime or evidence pertaining to a crime. *Brown v. State*, 481 S.W.2d 106, 110 (Tex. Crim. App. 1972).

Warranted searches must be reasonable. The scope of the search must be "strictly tied to and justified by" the circumstances which caused its initiation to be permissible,[27] and restricted to the object of the search and the places in which there is probable cause to believe it may be found.[28]

§ 13-6(B) ELEMENTS OF THE FOUNDATION

The prosecutor can use a simple, chronological organization for this foundation:

1. The officer received certain information.
2. The officer reduced the information to affidavit form.
3. The officer submitted the affidavit to a judge or magistrate and requested a warrant.
4. The magistrate approved the request and issued a written warrant.
5. The officer executed the warrant.

After executing the warrant, the officer signs a return on the warrant and files an inventory with the court. If the prosecutor anticipates a defense argument that the officer violated these procedures, the prosecutor can lengthen the foundation to include the officer's testimony about the return and inventory.

§ 13-6(C) SAMPLE FOUNDATION

The following sample foundation addresses a fact situation where the State has charged the defendant, Mr. Hatcher, with the burglary of a gun store in Mission, Texas. The witness is Officer Ramos. She has already testified that she is an employee of the Mission Police Department. The proponent is the prosecutor.

P Officer Ramos, WHERE were you on the afternoon of July 30th of last year? (1)

W I was on duty at our main station.

P WHAT, if anything, unusual happened that afternoon? (1)

W I received a telephone call from one of our informants, whom we call Mel.

P HOW did you know that it was Mel? (1)

W I've met with him and spoken with him over the telephone on many prior occasions.

---

27 *Terry v. Ohio*, 392 U.S. 1, 18 (1968).

28 *Joseph v. State*, 807 S.W.2d 303, 307 (Tex. Crim. App. 1991).

P WHAT did Mel tell you during this telephone call? (1)

W He gave me some information indicating that some of the weapons stolen from Tony's Gun Shop two days before were located at the defendant's apartment.

P WHAT did you do after you received the call from Mel? (2)

W I immediately wrote down everything he told me. I put it in affidavit form so that we could apply for a search warrant.

P [*To court reporter.*] Would you please mark this as an exhibit for the State? [*Reporter marks exhibit and hands it back to counsel.*] Please let the record reflect that I am showing the exhibit to the defense attorney. [*Opposing counsel examines exhibit and hands it back to the proponent.*]

P Permission to approach the witness?

J Granted.

P Now, Officer Ramos, I hand you what has been marked State's exhibit number one for identification. WHAT is it? (2)

W It's the affidavit I just mentioned.

P HOW can you recognize it? (2)

W I recognize the contents and my signature at the bottom.

P Your Honor, I now offer State's exhibit number one for identification into evidence.

J Any objections?

O None, your Honor.

J It will be received.

P WHAT did you do with the affidavit after you drafted it? (3)

W I walked over to Judge Jackson's chambers in the courthouse across the street and applied for a search warrant for the defendant's apartment.

P HOW did you make the application? (3)

W I handed the affidavit to the judge and asked her to read it.

P WHAT, if anything, did Judge Jackson do? (4)

W Initially, she seemed to read the affidavit. Then she told me she would grant the application.

P WHAT happened then? (4)

W After telling me that orally, she signed a warrant for the search.

P [*To court reporter.*] Would you please mark this as an exhibit for the State? [*Reporter marks exhibit and hands it back to counsel.*] Please let the record reflect that I am showing the exhibit to opposing counsel. [*Opposing counsel examines exhibit and hands it back to the proponent.*]

P Officer, I now hand you what has been marked as State's exhibit number two for identification. WHAT is it? (4)

W It is Judge Jackson's warrant.

P HOW can you recognize it? (4)

W I recognize the contents and her signature. I saw her sign it.

P HOW well do you know the judge's signature style?

W Very well. She was an Assistant District Attorney for several years before going on the bench, and we worked on a couple of cases together.

P Your Honor, I now offer State's exhibit number two for identification into evidence.

J Any objection?

O None, your Honor.

J Very well. It will be admitted.

P Officer Ramos, WHAT did you do after Judge Jackson gave you this warrant? (5)

W I carried it out.

P WHEN did you do that? (5)

W The same afternoon. As soon as she gave me the warrant, I jumped in a police car and drove over there with two other officers.

P WHERE is "there?" (5)

W I'm sorry. I mean the defendant's apartment. The warrant was for Apartment 3A, 1000 Hazel Street in Mission. That's the address named in the warrant.

P WHAT did you do when you arrived there? (5)

W We knocked, and the defendant came to the door. We showed him the warrant, gave him a copy, and explained that we were searching for certain types of pistols and revolvers.

P WHAT did you do after you told the defendant that? (5)

W The two other officers and I searched the apartment.

P WHAT was the result of the search? (5)

W We found four weapons of the type, make, and caliber that the warrant mentioned. We seized them.

P [*To court reporter.*] Would you please mark these as exhibits for the State? [*Reporter marks exhibit and hands it back to counsel.*] Please let the record reflect that I am showing what the reporter has marked as State's exhibit number three for identification, State's exhibit number four for identification, State's exhibit number five for identification, and State's exhibit number six for identification to opposing counsel. [*Opposing counsel examines the exhibits and hands them back to the proponent.*]

P Officer, I now hand you State's exhibits number three, number four, number five, and number six for identification. WHAT are they? (5)

W They're the pistols and revolvers we found at the defendant's apartment.

P HOW can you recognize them? (5)

W When we found them, I put my initials and the date on an evidence tag and stuck it on the handle of each weapon. I recognize the caliber, shape, and markings of all the weapons.

P I now offer State's exhibits number three, number four, number five, and number six for identification into evidence.

J Objections?

O None, your Honor.

J Received.

P WHAT did you do after you found these weapons? (5)

W I immediately made out an inventory of the four weapons. I gave one copy to the defendant.

P WHAT did you do after you gave him a copy of the inventory? (5)

W I filled out the last part of the warrant, the return, on the spot. I returned the warrant and the original inventory to Judge Jackson's court clerk. Then I took the weapons over to the physical evidence custodian at the main station.

P [*To court reporter.*] Would you please mark this as an exhibit for the State? [*Reporter marks exhibit and hands it back to counsel.*] Please let the record reflect that I am showing what the reporter has marked as State's exhibit number seven for identification to opposing counsel. [*Opposing counsel examines exhibit and hands it back to the proponent.*]

P Officer Ramos, I now hand you State's exhibit number seven for identification. WHAT is it? (5)

W It's the inventory of the items seized, listing the make, type, and serial number of each weapon.

P HOW do you recognize the inventory? (5)

W It's in my handwriting.

P Thank you, Officer. I now offer State's exhibit number seven for identification into evidence.

J Any objection?

O No.

J It will be received as State's exhibit number seven.

§ 13-7 SEARCHES BASED UPON PROBABLE CAUSE—SEARCH WARRANT NOT REQUIRED

§ 13-7(A) EMERGENCY SEARCHES

§ 13-7(A)(1) The Doctrine

The existence of exigent circumstances, often referred to as the emergency doctrine, serves as an exception to the warrant requirement. The need for immediate action makes obtaining a warrant unfeasible. Examples of situations where an emergency situation will justify a warrantless entry and search are: (1) rendering emergency aid to persons whom police officers reasonably believe are in need of assistance;[29] (2) preventing the destruction of evidence or contraband;[30] (3) protecting officers from persons whom they reasonably believe to be dangerous;[31] (4) investigating the cause of a fire;[32] and (5) hot pursuit of a fleeing felony suspect.[33] The State bears the burden of demonstrating the existence of the exigent circumstance. If the search is lawful, the plain view doctrine comes into play.

§ 13-7(A)(2) Elements of the Foundation

The foundation for showing that officers acted in an emergency situation requires the prosecutor to prove the following elements.

1. The police had objectively reasonable grounds to believe that an emergency existed at the time of the warrantless entry.
2. The police were not motivated primarily by a desire to arrest a suspect or seize evidence.
3. There was a reasonable basis to connect the emergency to the place or area entered.[34]

[29] *Pine v. State*, 889 S.W.2d 625, 631 (Tex. App.—Houston [14th Dist.] 1994, pet. refused).

[30] *Moss v. State*, 878 S.W.2d 632, 641–642 (Tex. App.—San Antonio 1994, pet. refused).

[31] *Lockhart v. State*, 847 S.W.2d 568, 575 n.14 (Tex. Crim. App. 1992), *cert. denied*, 114 S.Ct. 146.

[32] *Michigan v. Clifford*, 464 U.S. 287, 293 (1984).

[33] *United States v. Richard*, 994 F.2d 244, 247 (5th Cir. [La] 1993).

[34] If the entry is for the purpose of searching for evidence of criminal activity or contraband, the State must prove, in addition to the exigency, that there was probable cause for the entry. *Cammack v. State*, 808 S.W.2d 253, 256 (Tex. App.—Houston [1st Dist.] 1991, pet. ref.).

§ 13-7(A)(3) Sample Foundation

This sample foundation demonstrates an example of an exigent or emergency search by government agents. The State has charged the defendant, Mr. Tattaglia, with the attempted murder of his wife. The witness is Deputy Sheriff Womack. The proponent is the prosecutor.

P Deputy Womack, WHERE were you at approximately 5:00 P.M. on March 12th of this year?

W I was on duty at the Sheriff's Office on Panghorn Road.

P WHAT, if anything, unusual happened then? (1)

W We got a call on the emergency 911 line.

P WHO was the caller?

W The caller identified herself as a Mrs. Urick. She said she was the landlady of the Malcolm Motor Lodge on Highway 113.

P WHAT did she say? (1), (3)

W She said that it sounded as if there was a real violent argument going on in one of the motel rooms, Room 22.

P WHAT did she say about the argument? (1), (2), (3)

W She said she heard a man scream something like, "Shut up, bitch." Then she heard a loud noise, and it sounded as if a woman cried out just then. She said that there were still loud noises coming from that room just as she was on the telephone with us.

P WHAT did you do then?

W Deputy Gibson and I jumped into the Sheriff's car and drove over there as fast as we could.

P HOW long did it take you to get there?

W We were over there in under five minutes.

P WHAT did you do when you arrived at the motel?

W We went straight to Room 22.

P WHAT, if anything, did you hear when you reached Room 22? (1), (3)

W We heard loud voices. Then there was a silent pause for a second. Then all of a sudden a shot rang out.

P HOW could you tell that?

W I've been on the Sheriff's force for almost 15 years, and during that time, I have become very familiar with the sound of a weapon being discharged.

P WHAT did you do after you heard that sound? (2)

W Gibson and I drew our revolvers and ran to the door of the motel room. I cried out that we were officers and that we wanted to come in to investigate the noise.

P WHAT happened then? (1), (2)

W There was no response, but I thought I could hear moaning as if someone were in pain.

P WHAT did you do after you heard the moaning? (1), (2)

W I kicked in the door, and Gibson and I both went in.

P WHAT did you find when you entered the room? (2)

W This woman was stretched out on the floor. She had been shot in the throat and was bleeding profusely. Right by her side was a handgun.

P WHAT did you do after you found her and the handgun? (2)

W We immediately called an ambulance for her. I picked up the gun to take it to the lab for fingerprinting.

P [*To court reporter.*] Would you please mark this as an exhibit for the State? [*Reporter marks exhibit and hands it back to counsel.*] Please let the record reflect that I am showing what the reporter has marked as State's exhibit number four for identification to opposing counsel. [*Opposing counsel examines exhibit and hands it back to the proponent.*] Permission to approach the witness?

J Yes.

P Deputy, I now hand you State's exhibit number four for identification. WHAT is it?

W It's the handgun we found lying by the woman's body.

P HOW can you recognize it?

W I recognize the deep scratches on the handle.

P I now offer State's exhibit number four for identification into evidence.

J Any objections?

O None, your Honor.

J It will be received as State's exhibit number four.

§ 13-7(B) AUTOMOBILE SEARCHES

§ 13-7(B)(1) The Doctrine

Warrantless searches of vehicles are allowed when there is probable cause to believe that a vehicle contains evidence of criminal activity, and the possibility exists that the automobile will be moved out of the jurisdiction before a warrant may be procured. Of course, the vehicle must be either moving or movable to justify such a search. Factors to consider are: (1) whether the car is parked in a public place, and (2) whether the vehicle is occupied, or if unoccupied, someone with access to the vehicle is at large. The exigency created by the actual or potential mobility of the automobile must exist at the time the car is seized, stopped, or detained.[35] Another justification to the automobile exception to the warrant requirement is the lesser expectation of privacy people have in their vehicles than in their homes or offices.

§ 13-7(B)(2) Elements of the Foundation

In order to rely on the automobile exception to the warrant requirement, the prosecutor must show the following:

1. Probable cause existed to believe that a vehicle contained evidence of criminal activity.
2. The vehicle is actually or readily mobile at the time of its warrantless seizure.
3. There was no delay in conducting the search. The vehicle may be searched immediately or taken to the police station and searched, but may not be left unsecured in a place accessible to the public.[36]

§ 13-7(B)(3) Sample Foundation

The State has charged the defendant, Mr. Harrison, with burglary of an appliance store. The State alleges that the defendant burglarized the store on the evening of August 10, 2005. The owner of the store has already testified. During his testimony, the prosecutor introduced a list of the missing appliances. The description describes the serial numbers of each missing item. An eyewitness has also testified as to the description of a man he saw carrying appliances from the back door of the store and placing them in a 2000 grey Oldsmobile, Texas license plate number JFF538. The next witness is Officer Scott. Scott is the officer who spotted the defendant's car and searched it, finding several of the stolen appliances in the trunk. The prosecutor is the proponent.

P Officer Scott, WHAT, if anything, unusual happened on August 10, 2005? (1)

W I was on night duty and received notice to keep an eye out for a grey 2000 Oldsmobile, license plate number JFF538.

---

[35] *California v. Acevedo*, 500 U.S. 565 (1991).

[36] If this is done, the automobile exception will not justify a warrantless search because the delay demonstrates a lack of exigent circumstances. *Stine v. State*, 787 S.W.2d 82, 84–87 (Tex. App.—Waco 1990, pet. ref.).

P WHY were you told to look for this car? (1)

W It matched the description of a car reported to have been used in a burglary earlier that night.

P WHAT happened next? (1)

W As I was on patrol in my unmarked car, I saw a vehicle matching the description I had been given. It was parked in a grocery store parking lot. (1)

P WHAT did you do next? (1)

W I drove up next to the car and read the license plate, and it was the same number we had been told to look for.

P WHAT was the number of the license plate on the car? (1)

W JFF538.

P HOW do you remember the number?

W I have a good memory for numbers, and I reviewed my report before coming in to testify.

P WHERE was the driver of the car at the time you pulled up next to it? (2)

W I don't know. He was not in or near the car.

P In WHAT condition did the car appear to be? (2)

W It appeared to be mobile. The tires were all in good condition and it was parked in a public parking lot.

P WHAT did you do next? (3)

W Well, because the car exactly matched the description I had been given, I called that information in on my radio. Just then I saw someone approaching the car.

P WHAT happened next? (2)

W The defendant came back to the car, opened the trunk and put some groceries in it, then closed the trunk. I then approached him, identified myself, and told him I was going to search his vehicle.

P WHERE is the defendant now?

W He's in the courtroom, seated at counsel table to my right, wearing a gray suit.

P Your Honor, please let the record reflect that the witness has identified the defendant.

J The record will so reflect.

P WHAT happened next? (3)

W I opened the trunk and saw that it was full of appliances. I then arrested the defendant on suspicion of possessing stolen goods. The car was taken immediately to the police station and searched.

§ 13-8 SEARCHES NOT REQUIRING PROBABLE CAUSE

§ 13-8(A) INVENTORY SEARCHES

§ 13-8(A)(1) The Doctrine

Suppose that the defendant unlawfully parks his car so as to obstruct traffic. The traffic obstruction justifies the police in moving and impounding the car. Once the police take the car, a number of interests come into play. As bailee of the car, the police department has some liability to the defendant; the police should also protect the government from claims liability. Also, the police have a duty to safeguard the defendant's property, as he or she is a citizen entitled to police protection. In *South Dakota v. Opperman*, 428 U.S. 364 (1976), the Supreme Court held that these interests permit a police inventory of a lawfully impounded car.

§ 13-8(A)(2) Elements of the Foundation

To rely on an inventory search the prosecution must prove the following elements:

1. There was a legitimate basis for impounding the vehicle.
2. The police conducting the inventory follow standard police policy and procedures.
3. The scope of the search was reasonable.
4. During the search, the police seized the item in question.

§ 13-8(A)(3) Sample Foundation

In the following sample, the State has charged Mr. Barnes, the defendant, with the burglary of a gun store. The State alleges that the defendant burglarized the store on the evening of May 12, 2005. The owner of the store has already testified. During his testimony, the prosecutor introduced a list describing the missing weapons. The description includes the serial number of each missing weapon. The second witness was Officer Malone. Malone testified that while he was driving on a public street in Post, Texas, he noticed a car stopped, partially blocking a lane of traffic. He testified that he found the defendant slumped behind the wheel. The officer adds that the defendant was obviously intoxicated. He arrested the defendant and called the Post Police Department Impound Lot to seize the car. The next witness is Officer Saucedo. She testifies that she was the officer on duty at the lot on the evening of May 12, 2005. The prosecutor is the proponent.

P Officer Saucedo, WHAT, if anything, unusual happened that evening? (1)

W I got the phone call from Officer Malone to pick up a car stopped in a traffic lane on Main Street.

P HOW do you know that the caller was Officer Malone? (1)

W We've worked together for years. I know his voice very well.

P WHAT did you do after you received the call? (1)

W I drove the tow truck over to Main Street to pick up the car.

P WHAT did you find when you arrived at Main Street? (1)

W Just as Malone had told me, the car was stopped part of the way into a traffic lane. Malone was just driving off with the defendant in his patrol car.

P WHERE is the defendant now? (1)

W He's over there. He's the guy in the orange jumpsuit at the table to my right.

P Your Honor, please let the record reflect that the witness has identified the defendant, John Barnes.

J The record will so reflect.

P WHAT did you do after you found the car in the traffic lane? (1)

W I followed the standard operating procedure.

P WHAT is that procedure? (2)

W I hooked it up to the tow truck and took it back to the impound lot.

P WHAT did you do when you reached the lot? (2)

W I continued to follow standard procedure and inventoried the contents of the car.

P WHY did you do that? (2)

W Our department has a regulation requiring me to do that.

P [*To court reporter.*] Would you please mark this as an exhibit for the State? [*Reporter marks exhibit and hands it back to counsel.*] Please let the record reflect that I am showing what the reporter has marked as State's exhibit number three for identification to opposing counsel. [*Opposing counsel examines exhibit and hands it back to the proponent.*] Permission to approach the witness?

J Permission granted.

P Officer, I now hand you what has been marked as State's exhibit number three for identification. WHAT is this? (2)

W It's our departmental regulation that I referred to. It governs the operation of our impound lot.

P HOW do you recognize it? (2)

W I work with it every night. The chief handed it to me when he put me in charge of the night shift at the lot, and I have it right on my desk all the time.

P Your Honor, I now offer State's exhibit number three for identification into evidence.

J Any objections?

O None, your Honor.

J It will be received.

P Officer, please read paragraph four of the regulation. (3)

W Sure. It says: "Within 24 hours of the impoundment of any vehicle, the officer in charge of the lot shall inventory any and all objects in the car that are either in plain view or in unlocked compartments."

P WHAT did you do after you brought the defendant's car to the impound lot? (3)

W I did exactly what the regulation says. I inventoried the car for those contents.

P WHAT, if anything, did you find inside the defendant's car? (4)

W I found a pistol.

P WHERE did you find the pistol? (4)

W Under the front seat.[37]

The prosecutor should continue by having the witness identify the pistol. See § 4-8(B).

§ 13-8(B) CONSENT SEARCHES

§ 13-8(B)(1) The Doctrine

The inventory doctrine allows the police to search a defendant's vehicle even if there are no objective indications that the automobile contains incriminating

[37] There is authority for the view that under art. I, § 9, an inventory search in Texas may not be used to open any closed containers. *Autran v. State*, 887 S.W.2d 31 (Tex. Crim. App. 1994) (plurality opinion).

evidence against the defendant. The consent doctrine also permits the police to search when they lack incriminating information about the particular defendant.

If the defendant consents to a search, in effect the defendant waives the protection of the Fourth Amendment. The prosecutor has the burden of demonstrating consent. If a person who has authority to consent to a search or seizure gives his or her consent, a third person is not entitled to complain about the admission of the fruits of the search or seizure.[38]

§ 13-8(B)(2) Elements of the Foundation

To prove that the government conducted a search based upon consent, the prosecution must prove the following:

1. The police contacted the defendant.
2. The police requested the defendant's consent to search his residence, his car, or another constitutionally protected area.
3. The defendant consented.
4. Under the totality of the circumstances, the consent was voluntary.
5. The scope of the search was limited to the scope of the consent given by the defendant.
6. During the search, the police seized a particular object.

§ 13-8(B)(3) Sample Foundation

The State has charged Brian Vega with possession of a picklock, a criminal instrument. The witness is Officer DeLeon. He has already testified that he is assigned to the burglary detail of the Marshall Police Department. He testifies further that there has been a series of burglaries in a large apartment complex on Martin Luther King Boulevard. He adds that during the afternoon of July 6th, he visited the apartment complex to investigate the burglaries. The proponent is the prosecutor.

P Officer DeLeon, WHAT did you do after you arrived at the apartment complex? (1)

W I went door-to-door on one floor where there had been a number of break-ins.

P WHAT did you do as you went door-to-door? (1)

W I talked to the residents of the various apartments and asked if I could look around a bit.

P WHICH residents did you talk to? (1)

38 *Potter v. State*, 481 S.W.2d 101, 105 (Tex. Crim. App. 1972).

W As I recall, I spoke with six of them, including the defendant.

P WHERE is the defendant now? (1)

W He's in the courtroom.

P WHERE is he seated? (1)

W He's at the counsel table to my right. He's wearing a brown suit and a brown tie.

P Your Honor, please let the record reflect that the witness has identified the defendant, Brian Vega.

J The record will reflect that.

P WHAT happened when you met the defendant? (1), (2)

W I introduced myself and asked whether I could look around a bit in his apartment.

P HOW did the defendant respond? (3)

W He said it was okay. Then he asked me not to look in the bedroom because his girlfriend had just been there and it was a mess.

P Before he said that it was okay to search, WHAT, if anything, did you tell him about his rights? (4)

W I told him that he didn't have to let me in. I made it clear that I didn't have a warrant. I said I'd just appreciate his cooperation.

P WHAT, if any, weapons did you display during your conversation with the defendant? (4)

W I had my pistol, but it was in my holster. I never drew it or even put my hand on it while I was talking to him.

P WHAT, if any, threats did you make if he did not allow you to search? (4)

W None.

P WHAT, if anything, did you say about a warrant? (4)

W I said I didn't have one. And I didn't say that I was going to try and get one. I just asked for his voluntary cooperation.

P WHAT did you do after he said okay? (5)

W I searched the apartment.

P WHAT parts of the apartment did you search? (5)

W I searched all the rooms except the bedroom that he told me to stay out of.

P WHAT, if anything, did you find during the search? (6)

W I found a picklock.

P WHAT is a picklock? (6)

W It's a tool that professional burglars use.

P HOW do you know that? (6)

W I've been assigned to the burglary detail for several years. I know that from my professional training and experience. For example, they show you picklocks and other specialized burglary tools during your basic training at the police academy. (This testimony is an expert opinion, and the prosecutor must establish the officer's qualification as an expert.)

P WHERE did you find the picklock? (5)

W It was sitting on the top of a pile of magazines in one corner of the living room in the apartment.

P WHERE were you standing when you saw it? (5)

W Right in the middle of the living room by his couch.

P From your position there, HOW clear a view did you have of the picklock? (5)

W It was in plain view.

P WHAT did you do after you saw it? (6)

W I seized it. It's contraband. It's illegal to have one.

P WHAT furniture, if any, did you have to move to seize the picklock? (6)

W None. It was right on top of the stack of magazines. You couldn't see it from the front door, but once you were in the living room, it was right there for anyone to see.

The prosecutor would complete the foundation by eliciting testimony to identify the exhibit as the picklock the witness seized.

§ 13-8(C) Search Incident to an Arrest

§ 13-8(C)(1) The Doctrine

The incidental search doctrine permits a warrantless seizure when there is probable cause in conjunction with other factors. The key factor is that the police have lawfully arrested the defendant. The arrest reduces the defendant's privacy expectation. Especially when the police transport the defendant to jail they have a legitimate interest in ensuring that he is not armed.

§ 13-8(C)(2) Elements of the Foundation

The elements for the foundation are as follows:

1. There was a lawful arrest or at least probable cause for an arrest.
2. The arrest was custodial.
3. The officer searched the arrestee.
4. The scope of the search was spatially reasonable.[39]
5. The search was reasonably contemporaneous with the arrest.
6. During the search, the police discovered an object subject to seizure.

§ 13-8(C)(3) Sample Foundation

The State has charged the defendant, Mr. Wilson, with burglarizing a residence in Corpus Christi. The witness is Officer Rivas. He has already testified that he was instructed by his superior to execute an arrest warrant that had just been issued for the defendant. The prosecutor is the proponent.

P Officer Rivas, WHAT did you do after receiving the arrest warrant? (1)

W I asked Officer Torres to go with me and we got in my patrol car and headed for Logan's Bar on Fourth Street. That was where the defendant allegedly worked so I thought that I would look there first.

P WHAT did you do when you arrived there? (1)

W We walked into the bar and searched for the defendant. He was sitting at the counter.

P WHAT did you do then? (1)

W Torres and I walked straight up to him and informed him that we had a warrant for his arrest and that he was under arrest for burglary. We told him we were taking him to the local police station for booking.

P WHAT did you do then? (2), (3)

W We took the defendant outside, and before we put him in the patrol car, we searched him.

P WHEN did you search him? (5)

W On the spot.

P HOW many minutes passed between the arrest and the search? (5)

W Two or three at the most.

P HOW did you conduct the search? (4)

---

[39] In *Chimel v. California*, 395 U.S. 752 (1969), the Court declared that the arresting officer may search the arrestee's person and the area within the arrestee's immediate control—the area from which the arrestee might grab a weapon or destructible evidence. *See Linnett v. State*, 1982 Tex. Crim. App. LEXIS 1172 (applying *Chimel* to a custodial arrest).

W We had him spread his legs and lean up against the patrol car. We patted him down and searched all his pockets.

P WHAT, if anything, did you find? (6)

W I reached into his right front pant pocket. I could feel his wallet. As I removed the wallet, a picklock fell out of the wallet.

P WHAT is a picklock? (6)

W It's a tool that professional burglars use.

P HOW do you know that? (6)

W I've investigated dozens of burglaries over the years, and I've had training at the Police Academy in the modus operandi of burglars.

P [*To court reporter.*] Would you please mark this as an exhibit for the State? [*Reporter marks exhibit and hands it back to counsel.*] Please let the record reflect what has been marked as State's exhibit number five for identification to the defense counsel. [*Opposing counsel examines exhibit and hands it back to the proponent.*] May I have permission to approach the witness?

J Granted.

P Officer, I now hand you what has been marked as State's exhibit number five for identification. WHAT is it? (6)

W It's the picklock I found in the defendant's pocket.

P HOW can you recognize it? (6)

W My evidence tag is on it, and it has some peculiar scratches. There are seven deep parallel scratches. I've never seen any other picklock with those unique markings.

P Your Honor, I now offer State's exhibit number five for identification into evidence.

J Any objection?

O None, your Honor.

J It will be received.

§ 13-8(D) FRISK INCIDENT TO LAWFUL STOP

§ 13-8(D)(1) The Doctrine

An arrest requires probable cause, but in cases such as *Terry v. Ohio*, 392 U.S. 1 (1968), the Supreme Court has declared the police may stop and frisk an individual on a lesser justification than probable cause, namely, founded or reasonable suspicion. No "stop" occurs until the suspect is somehow physically restrained or submits to police authority.

The typical procedure is that the officer stops the suspect, temporarily detains him for questioning, and conducts a pat-down frisk of the exterior of the suspect's clothing if the officer believes that the suspect may be armed. If the frisk reveals the presence of an item subject to seizure, the officer may then reach in to grab the object.

§ 13-8(D)(2) Elements of the Foundation

In the elements for proving a valid frisk incident to a stop, the prosecutor must show the following:

1. The officer encountered the defendant.
2. There were articulable, objective facts indicating that the defendant had committed, was committing, or was about to commit a crime.
3. The facts led the officer to conclude that it was necessary to stop the defendant.
4. The officer temporarily detained and questioned the defendant. If the officer lawfully stops a vehicle, the officer may remove the occupants from the vehicle.
5. There were articulable, objective facts indicating that the defendant was armed. There must be a specific justification to look for weapons.
6. The facts listed in element number five led the officer to conduct an exploratory pat-down frisk. In an appropriate case, after detaining the driver of an automobile, the officer may "frisk" the vehicle's passenger compartment for a weapon.
7. The frisk revealed the presence of a weapon or another object subject to seizure on the defendant's person.
8. The officer reached in and seized the item.

§ 13-8(D)(3) Sample Foundation

In the following sample foundation, defendant, Mr. Clayton, has been charged with a series of assaults. The witness is Officer Connelly. Officer Connelly testifies that there had been a series of assaults on elderly people late at night near the intersection of Mission Street and San Fernando Avenue in Brownsville. The officer testifies that he was on foot patrol in the vicinity at 11:00 P.M. The proponent is the prosecutor.

P Officer Connelly, WHAT, if anything, unusual happened while you were on patrol? (1)

W I ran into the defendant.

P HOW do you know that the person was the defendant? (1)

W I saw him up close. I spoke with him.

P WHERE is the defendant now? (1)

W He's in the courtroom at the table over there. He is wearing a plaid shirt with a green tie.

P Your Honor, please let the record reflect that the witness has identified the defendant, Kenneth Clayton.

J The record will so reflect.

P WHAT initially attracted your attention to the defendant? (1), (2)

W As you can see, he's a young guy in his 20s. In that area there are mostly homes for the aged. It was a bit unusual to see him just loitering in that area late at night.

P HOW was he dressed at the time? (2)

W He was wearing what appeared to be a heavy coat. That was suspicious.

P WHY was that suspicious? (2)

W We were having a hot spell in town, and it was still pretty warm at that time of night. Most people were walking around in short sleeves, and he was dressed as if it were the dead of winter.

P WHAT did you do when you first saw the defendant? (2)

W I just looked at him, and then he seemed to notice that I was watching him. As soon as he saw me, he turned around and walked in the opposite direction.

P WHAT did you do then? (3)

W I decided that this needed investigating. I suspected that criminal activity was in progress or had already taken place. I called out to him to stop.

P WHAT did you say? (4)

W I called out something like, "Mister, I'd like to talk to you for a second."

P WHAT happened then? (4)

W After another step or two, he stopped and waited for me to catch up with him.

P WHAT did you do when you caught up with him? (4)

W I informed him who I was and asked him for some identification. I told him that there had been some attacks on elderly people in the area, and I thought it was a bit peculiar that he was just hanging around at that hour of the night.

P WHAT, if anything, did the defendant say? (5)

W He told me that he was sorry, but he had left his wallet at home and didn't have any identification on him.

P HOW did the defendant act while you questioned him? (5)

W He seemed to tense up.

P WHY do you say that? (5)

W At the same time that he was giving me the excuse that he had no identification, I noticed that he clenched one of his fists and the other fist was moving around to his back where I could not see it. He wouldn't look me straight in the eye either.

P HOW close were you standing to the defendant at this time? (5)

W I was only about two feet or so away.

P From that position, WHAT, if anything, did you observe about the defendant? (5)

W One of the pockets of his coat was bulging out. There was a raised line that suggested a long knife.

P WHY do you say it suggested that? (5)

W I've been a police office for almost 20 years. I've investigated lots of crimes involving knives, and I know the shape of one when I see it.

P WHAT did you think when you saw that shape? (6)

W I concluded that he was armed and that I'd better check it out before I continued questioning him.

P WHAT did you do then? (6)

W I told him that I suspected he had a knife. I then frisked him. I patted down his clothing, especially the pocket where the bulge was.

P WHAT was the result of the pat-down? (7)

W The object seemed hard and metallic. The frisk confirmed my belief that he was carrying a knife.

P WHAT did you do then? (8)

W I immediately reached into the pocket to grab the weapon. I wanted to make sure that he didn't have a chance to use it against me.

At this point, the prosecutor would elicit testimony to identify the exhibit as the knife found on the defendant's person as an item of physical evidence. See § 4-8(B).

§ 13-8(E) PROTECTIVE SWEEPS

§ 13-8(E)(1) The Doctrine

Under some circumstances when a full search of a premises is not otherwise permissible without a warrant, officers may make a cursory search of the premises in order to be sure that the location does not contain persons who may endanger the officers' safety during the course of an otherwise lawful entry.

§ 13-8(E)(2) Elements of the Foundation

To justify the protective sweep, the prosecutor must be prepared to demonstrate the following elements:

1. Officers were making an arrest at a residence.
2. The officers can articulate facts which would warrant a reasonably prudent officer in believing that the premises contained a potentially dangerous person.[40]
3. The scope, intensity, and duration of the protective sweep was limited to its protective rationale.

§ 13-8(E)(3) Sample Foundation

In the following sample foundation, the State has charged the defendant, Jack Hanna, with manufacturing a controlled substance. The defendant was arrested in his home. While one officer arrested Hanna, another officer conducted a protective sweep of the premises. While doing so, they found evidence that implicated the defendant. The witness is Officer Contreras, who arrested the defendant in his home. The proponent is the prosecutor.

P Officer Contreras, WHAT happened on that night? (1)

W My partner, Officer Morales, and I received a call to go to the home of the defendant, Mr. Hanna, and arrest him with a warrant that had been issued for him. We were told that he was one of 10 people who were being arrested as part of a drug manufacturing ring.

P WHAT did you do? (1)

W We went to the address and knocked on the door. When the defendant answered, we identified ourselves as police officers. Officer Morales asked if we could enter the house and the defendant said sure. Just after we stepped inside, Morales told him that he was under arrest.

P WHERE is the defendant now? (1)

---

[40] *Janicek v. State*, 634 S.W.2d 687, 690 (Tex. Crim. App. 1982).

W He's in the courtroom. He's sitting at the table to my right, wearing a plaid shirt.

P Your Honor, please let the record reflect that the witness has identified the defendant, Jack Hanna.

J The record will so reflect.

P After you arrested the defendant, WHAT happened? (2)

W While Morales was cuffing the defendant, I quickly conducted a protective sweep of the premises.

P WHAT is a protective sweep? (2)

W It's a quick and limited search of the premises, which we conduct when we arrest someone, to make sure that no one else is there who may pose a threat to our safety.

P WHY did you conduct a protective sweep in this instance? (2)

W Because the defendant was suspected of manufacturing a controlled substance, we had good reason to think that he had accomplices working with him. We wanted to be cautious in case there was an armed person in the home.

P WHAT specific information did you have that indicated another person might be in the house? (2)

W Before we left our supervisor told us that he had received information that some of the people being arrested, including the defendant, were known to carry guns. Also, we heard music coming from one of the other rooms in the house.

P WHAT was the nature of your protective sweep? (3)

W It was brief. We separated and quickly went through each of the rooms of the house.

P WHAT did you see during your protective sweep? (3)

W We did not find any other people. A radio was on in the back bedroom but no one was there. We did find evidence of a methamphetamine lab in one of the rooms of the house, as we were conducting our sweep.

P Did you go into the other rooms of the house with the intention of looking for evidence? (3)

W No. We were simply conducting a protective sweep to ensure that no one else was present who may have presented a threat.

§ 13-9 SEIZURES OF PERSONS AND PROPERTY—IN GENERAL

Both the Fourth Amendment and article I, section 9 of the Texas Constitution require that each search and seizure performed by law enforcement officers be reasonable within the meaning of those provisions. It is possible to have a search without a seizure and vice versa. Typically the two terms are almost always used in tandem. But as the following discussion points out, the two concepts are distinct and may require separate analysis and application.

§ 13-10 SEIZURE OF THE DEFENDANT—ARRESTS AND TEMPORARY DETENTIONS

§ 13-10(A) PROBABLE CAUSE ARRESTS

§ 13-10(A)(1) The Doctrine

The Fourth Amendment and article I, section 9 of the Texas Constitution require that every "traditional" or "custodial" arrest whether made with or without a warrant be based on probable cause. Probable cause for an arrest requires that, at the time of the arrest, the facts and circumstances within the knowledge of the arresting officer and of which the officer has reasonably trustworthy information would justify a reasonable and prudent person to believe that a particular person has committed or is committing a crime.[41]

§ 13-10(A)(2) Elements of the Foundation

The following elements must be shown if the prosecutor is arguing that the defendant's arrest was based upon probable cause:

1. The person was arrested by an officer.
2. The arrest was reasonable.
3. The arrest was based on probable cause.

§ 13-10(A)(3) Sample Foundation

The State has charged the defendant, Tony Barlow, with aggravated assault. The defendant is accused of stabbing a convenience store clerk on January 8th, causing him serious bodily injury. The witness is Officer Joe Newman, who was driving by on patrol when he saw the defendant running from the Stop-N-Pay with a knife in his hand. Officer Newman arrested the defendant immediately. The proponent is the prosecutor.

---

[41] *McCray v. Illinois*, 386 U.S. 300, 304 (1967).

P Officer Newman, WHAT happened on the night of January 8th of this year? (1)

W I was on patrol in my squad car. I was driving through my assigned area, and I decided to drive by the Stop-N-Pay, as I often do. It's not located in a very safe neighborhood.

P WHAT happened next? (1)

W As I drove by, I saw the defendant running out of the store. He had a knife in his hand. I could see a man stumbling out of the store clutching his chest and reaching after the defendant.

P WHAT did you think was going on? (2), (3)

W I believed that something might have happened inside the store. I felt that at that point I had probable cause to stop the defendant, because his actions led me to believe he may have just committed a crime. When I saw the blood on the knife, I arrested him.

P WHERE is the defendant now?

W He's in the courtroom. He's seated at counsel table to my right, wearing a navy blue suit and a red tie.

P Your Honor, please let the record reflect that the witness has identified the defendant, Tony Barlow.

J The record will so reflect.

§ 13-10(B) STOPS BASED UPON REASONABLE SUSPICION

§ 13-10(B)(1) The Doctrine

Stops based on reasonable suspicion are often referred to as "*Terry* stops," named after the famous Supreme Court case *Terry v. Ohio*, 392 U.S. 1 (1968). As a result of this case, the Court allows police to briefly detain a suspicious person whom they encounter during routine patrolling functions, without having to have probable cause for arrest. The Court said that the detainment of a person on the street for questioning is a sufficient intrusion on his or her freedom to constitute a "seizure" within the meaning of the Fourth Amendment. Probable cause, however, is not required because of the exigency of the circumstances. The only constitutional test to consider is whether the stop was unreasonable.

§ 13-10(B)(2) Elements of the Foundation

The elements of the foundation for showing a valid *Terry* stop are as follows:

1. The officer was on routine patrol.
2. While on patrol, the officer encountered the defendant.

3. The defendant appeared suspicious.
4. The officer briefly detained the defendant for questioning.
5. The officer's conduct was reasonable under the circumstances.

§ 13-10(B)(3) Sample Foundation

The State has charged the defendant, Wade Lyons, with the unlawful carrying of a weapon. The defendant was arrested by Officer Huston and a gun was found on his person. The issue is whether he was lawfully stopped and questioned by the officer. The proponent is the prosecutor.

P Officer Huston, WHERE were you on the night of September 2nd? (1)

W I was on foot patrol in the area of downtown Austin.

P WHAT, if anything, unusual happened while you were on patrol? (2)

W I was walking down Sixth Street when I encountered the defendant, who was walking in my direction.

P WHERE is the defendant now? (2)

W He's in the courtroom. He is sitting at the table to my right, wearing a white shirt and dark pants.

P Your Honor, please let the record reflect that the witness has identified the defendant, Wade Lyons.

J The record will so reflect.

P WHAT happened next? (3)

W When the defendant saw me, he quickly stopped, turned around, and walked in the opposite direction at a brisk pace. I noticed that he was wearing a jacket, which is unusual attire for a hot June night.

P WHAT did you do next? (4)

W I felt he looked suspicious, so I called out to him to stop. He did.

P WHAT did you do then? (4)

W I identified myself as a police officer and asked him for some identification. He said he didn't have any with him, and he appeared extremely nervous. At that point I noticed a bulky object in the pocket of his jacket.

P WHAT happened next? (5)

W I felt that it might be a weapon, so for my own safety I reached into the pocket. I felt a metallic object, and pulled it out. It was a gun.

At this point the prosecutor would lay the foundation for a "frisk." See § 13-8(D)(3).

§ 13-11 PLAIN-VIEW SEIZURES OF PROPERTY

§ 13-11(A) THE DOCTRINE

A warrant is not required to observe or seize that which is open or in plain view because neither its observation nor its seizure involves any invasion of privacy.[42] The plain-view exception applies in both public and private places. Its justification lies in the need to relieve police officers of the delay and risk of having to obtain a warrant in order to seize the object.[43]

§ 13-11(B) ELEMENTS OF THE FOUNDATION

To prove that the object was seized as an item in plain view, the prosecution must prove the following elements:

1. The officer was standing in a position and place where he or she had a lawful right to be.
2. From that position, the officer saw the object in question.
3. As soon as the officer saw the object, it was immediately apparent that the object was subject to seizure.[44]
4. The officer then seized the object.

§ 13-11(C) SAMPLE FOUNDATION

The following sample foundation involves a case where the State has charged the defendant, Mr. Nettles, with bank robbery. The witness is Officer Aiken. The proponent is the prosecutor. The witness has already testified that he was investigating a bank robbery committed by two men armed with Luger pistols. Based on an informant's report, he obtained a warrant to search the defendant's apartment for cash in bank bags. Then he drove to the defendant's apartment to execute the warrant. The proponent is the prosecutor.

P Officer Aiken, WHAT did you do when you arrived at the apartment? (1)

W We knocked. The defendant came to the door. After we explained that we had a warrant and showed it to him, he let us in.

P WHAT did you do after you entered the apartment? (1)

---

[42] *Horton v. California*, 496 U.S. 128, 133 (1990).

[43] *Arizona v. Hicks*, 480 U.S. 321, 326, 327 (1987).

[44] This means that the officer must have probable cause to believe that the item constitutes contraband, or the fruits, instrumentalities, or evidence of a crime. *Arizona v. Hicks*, 480 U.S. 321, 326–327 (1987).

W From the door, we stepped right into a small living room.

P WHAT happened then? (2)

W We just looked around. As I was turning to walk into the bedroom, I caught sight of a pistol.

P WHERE did you see the pistol? (2)

W It was sitting on top of a suitcase on the living room floor.

P HOW well could you see the pistol from where you stood? (2)

W Very well. There was nothing obstructing my view, and it was daylight. I could see the pistol clearly.

P WHAT type of pistol was it? (3)

W It was a Luger.

P HOW do you know that? (3)

W As police officers, we get a lot of training in weapons. We have to be able to differentiate by sight between the common types of weapons.

P WHAT did you do after you saw the Luger? (3), (4)

W I seized it.

P WHY did you do that? (3)

W The eyewitnesses to the crimes had mentioned that the robbers used Lugers. I believed that the Luger was evidence that the defendant was one of the robbers, but I hadn't included weapons in my warrant application.

P [*To court reporter.*] Would you please mark this as an exhibit for the State? [*Reporter marks exhibit and hands it back to counsel.*] Please let the record reflect that I am showing State's exhibit number two for identification to the defense counsel. [*Opposing counsel examines exhibit and-hands it back to the proponent.*] Permission to approach the witness?

J Granted.

P Officer Aiken, I now hand you what has been marked as State's exhibit number two for identification. WHAT is it? (4)

W It's the Luger I seized in the defendant's apartment.

P HOW can you recognize it? (4)

W I put my initials and the date on an evidence tag on the handle. I can see them right here.

P Your Honor, I now offer State's exhibit number two for identification into evidence.

J Is there any objection?

O No, your Honor.

J It will be received.

§§ 13-12–13-14 RESERVED

PART 2
THE DEFENDANT'S STATEMENTS TO GOVERNMENT AGENTS

§ 13-15 IN GENERAL

This part of the chapter deals with constitutional and statutory constraints on the admissibility of a defendant's statements. While federal constitutional law creates the minimal standard for criminal jurisprudence, Texas law has surpassed these standards in certain areas and has created additional protection for the accused.

The following sections first briefly address the procedural aspects of deciding the admissibility of confessions. They are followed by discussions on reasons for excluding a defendant's statements—the Texas "confession statute," the Due Process Clauses, the *Miranda* doctrine, and the Sixth Amendment right to counsel. The final section addresses the use of otherwise inadmissible statements to impeach defendants.

§ 13-16 PROCEDURAL ASPECTS OF DECIDING ADMISSIBILITY OF CONFESSIONS

§ 13-16(A) AN OVERVIEW

As with any challenges to any piece of evidence, the burden of raising objections to the admissibility of a defendant's statements to law enforcement personnel rests on the defense. Once the issue is raised, either through a motion to suppress or an objection at trial, the prosecution must then offer proof to rebut the defendant's objection. Procedural requirements vary depending on the argument advanced by the defendant.

§ 13-16(B) RAISING THE ISSUE; MOTIONS TO SUPPRESS AND TRIAL OBJECTIONS

The defense may raise the issue regarding the admissibility of a confession or statement by either making a pretrial motion to suppress and/or objecting when the evidence is offered at trial. Under article 28.01 of the Texas Code of Criminal Procedure, a judge may schedule a pretrial hearing requiring a defendant to file any and all motions to suppress. Such motions must be filed at least seven days before the hearing; failure to do so will preclude a defendant from raising such arguments except by permission of the court for good cause shown.

§ 13-16(C) Hearings Outside the Jury's Presence

Article 38.22, sections 6 and 7 of the Texas Code of Criminal Procedure provide the procedures for challenging the admissibility of confessions and statements. A defendant is entitled to a hearing, outside the presence of the jury, when a challenge is made regarding the voluntariness of a confession or statement. Such a hearing is mandatory based on the defendant making a timely objection to the introduction of such confession or statement as evidence at trial. Failure to timely object constitutes waiver of the right to a hearing.

Furthermore, a court is required to conduct subsequent hearings for each separate ground raised by a defendant in challenging the voluntariness of a confession or statement, if the separate ground was not argued in the previous hearings. Subsequent hearings must also follow the procedure outlined in article 38.22.

§ 13-16(D) Burdens of Proof

Challenging the admissibility of a confession or statement entails various burdens of proof, depending on the issue in question. A defendant who contends that a confession or statement was not made voluntarily puts the burden on the prosecution to prove by a preponderance of the evidence that the confession or statement was voluntary. But if the issue of voluntariness is submitted to the trial jury pursuant to article 38.22, section 6, the prosecution is required to prove voluntariness beyond a reasonable doubt.

Upon an objection by the defendant, the prosecution also bears the burden of proving that a defendant was given the required warnings and the defendant effectively waived those rights when attempting to introduce a confession or statement obtained by custodial interrogation. Presently, the Supreme Court of the United States and the Texas Court of Criminal Appeals require the prosecution to meet this burden by a mere preponderance of the evidence. The prosecution is relieved of its duty to give a defendant the required warnings and waivers if the confession or statement is not obtained during custodial interrogation.

With regards to the admissibility of a defendant's oral statements resulting from custodial interrogation, which are generally inadmissible, the defendant carries the burden of raising the objection or risking waiver. Article 38.22, section 3(a). Once the issue has been raised, article 38.22, section 3(e) places the burden on the prosecution to establish an exception to the rule of exclusion by a preponderance of the evidence.

§ 13-16(E) RULINGS BY THE TRIAL COURT

Under section 6, article 38.22 of the Texas Code of Criminal Procedure, the trial judge is required to make independent findings, in absence of the jury, regarding the voluntariness of a confession or statement. See Texas Rule of Evidence 104(c). If the trial judge concludes that a statement was made voluntarily, article 38.22 requires the judge to enter an order stating its conclusion along with specific findings of fact upon which the conclusion was made. A trial judge will not be required to make findings and conclusions if the evidence offered at the hearing does not raise a factual issue.

§ 13-16(F) SUBMISSION OF ISSUE TO JURY

At trial, the defense may raise the issue of voluntariness of the defendant's statement by presenting evidence on the issue. See article 38.22, sections 6 and 7. If the issue is raised, the trial judge must instruct the jury on the law pertaining to such statement and must instruct the jury that unless it finds, beyond a reasonable doubt, that the statement was made voluntarily, the jury must not consider such statement for any purpose.[45]

§ 13-17 THE TEXAS "CONFESSION STATUTE"—IN GENERAL

Most of the statements offered by the prosecution will fall into one of the categories of statements discussed in article 38.22 of the Texas Code of Criminal Procedure, which is often referred to as the "confession statute." In many respects, it is more protective than the constitutional, case law requirements. Article 38.22 establishes the statutory requirements for the admissibility of a statement, made by a defendant, during custodial interrogation. It provides detailed requirements for the admissibility of a defendant's written statements and addresses the admissibility of a defendant's oral statements.

---

[45] In order to raise an issue regarding voluntariness, the defendant must undermine or discredit the prosecution's evidence before the jury. An issue will not be raised by the prosecution merely admitting evidence illustrating the voluntariness of a confession or statement. A defendant must present evidence that would allow a jury to cast a reasonable doubt regarding the voluntariness of a confession or statement.

A jury issue in the form of a general instruction regarding voluntariness is usually sufficient, because specific instructions may be an improper comment on the weight of the evidence. A general instruction should include a definition of voluntariness, and, depending upon the circumstances, whether defendant was given proper warnings and whether defendant knowingly, intelligently, and voluntarily waived his rights. The jury issue must also instruct the jury to disregard the statement and any evidence obtained as a result thereof if it finds that the statement was made involuntarily. The jury issue should not require the jury to make special or specific findings regarding the voluntariness of the statement.

The statutory provision applies only to statements resulting from "custodial interrogation" by a magistrate or other government agent. Thus, if a voluntary statement was not the result of custodial interrogation, it is probably admissible. In interpreting what amounts to custody interrogation, the Texas Court of Criminal Appeals has generally followed the Supreme Court definitions of "custody" and "interrogation" as enunciated under *Miranda* case law. Article 38.22 does not prevent the admissibility of a statement given by the accused in open court at his trial, before a grand jury, or at an examining trial.

§ 13-18 THE TEXAS "CONFESSION STATUTE"—WRITTEN STATEMENTS

§ 13-18(A) THE DOCTRINE

Article 38.22, section 1 states that a written statement "means a statement signed by the accused or a statement made by the accused in his own handwriting." Section 1 also covers the situation where the defendant is unable to write. In that instance, the defendant's written statement will be admissible if it bears "his mark" and it is witnessed by someone other than a peace officer.

Section 2 of article 38.22 requires that specific information to be "shown on the face of the written statement" before it may be deemed admissible. The statement must recite that the accused, "prior to making the statement . . . received from the person to whom the statement is made a warning that:

1. [H]e has the right to remain silent and not make any statement at all and that any statement he makes may be used against him at his trial;
2. [A]ny statement he makes may be used as evidence against him in court;
3. [H]e has the right to have a lawyer present to advise him prior to and during any questioning;
4. [I]f he is unable to employ a lawyer, he has the right to have a lawyer appointed to advise him prior to and during any questioning; and
5. [H]e has the right to terminate the interview at any time . . . ."

The face of the statement must also show that the accused made the statement knowingly, intelligently, and voluntarily waived his rights set out above.[46] There is authority for the view that an accused may also argue that someone else, other than the person to whom he made the statement, gave him the required warnings. This requires officers to state the name of the individual taking the statement and states that the person also gave the appropriate warnings to the accused.

---

[46] Art. 38.22, § 2(b).

§ 13-18(B) ELEMENTS OF THE FOUNDATION

To establish the admissibility of a written statement made during custodial interrogation by a government agent, the prosecutor should lay these foundational elements.

1. The defendant made a statement;
2. The statement:
   a. Is in the defendant's own handwriting; or
   b. Was reduced to writing;
3. The written statement was signed by the defendant or bears the mark of the defendant;
4. The statement, on its face, states that the statutory warnings were given to the defendant, either by a magistrate[47] or by the person to whom the statement was made;[48]
5. The statutory warnings were actually conveyed to the defendant; and
6. The defendant made the statement knowingly, intelligently, and voluntarily.

§ 13-18(C) SAMPLE FOUNDATION

In the following sample foundation, the State has charged the defendant, Jackson, with robbery. The defendant made a written statement to Officer Smith during a custodial interrogation. Officer Smith is the witness, and the prosecutor is the proponent.

P Officer Smith, after you gave the defendant the cigarettes and coffee, WHAT, if anything, did the defendant say to you? (1)

W He informed me that he wanted to make a statement regarding the robbery in question.

P WHAT did you do then?

W I obtained a police form used for taking statements.

P Your Honor, I request that this be marked State's exhibit number 10 for identification.

J It will be so marked. [*Prosecutor presents exhibit to court reporter who marks exhibit and hands back to counsel who in turn shows it to the defense counsel.*]

---

[47] *See* art. 15.17.

[48] The warnings must be those specified in art. 38.22, § 2(a).

P Please let the record reflect that I am showing the State's exhibit number 10 for identification to the defense counsel.

J It will so reflect.

P I request permission to approach the witness.

J Permission granted.

P Officer Smith, I now hand you State's exhibit number 10 for identification. WHAT is it? (1), (2)

W It's the police form I took the defendant's statement on.

P HOW can you recognize it? (2), (3)

W It has my name on it, and it has the defendant's signature on it as well.

P WHAT warnings, if any, did you give to the defendant? (4), (5)

W I gave him the warnings that are written out here on the front of the form. These are required by law.

P HOW did you use the police form during the questioning? (4), (5)

W I read from it verbatim to make certain I gave the defendant the correct warnings.

P WHAT happened after you read Mr. Jackson these rights? (4), (5), (6)

W I asked him if he understood these rights and he said that he did. I then asked him if he had any questions and he said no. I asked him if he wanted me to repeat any of the warnings. And again, he said no.

P WHAT, if anything, did he specifically say about waiving his rights? (4), (6)

W The defendant stated he was waiving his rights. He said he did not want to see a lawyer and that he wanted to give me his statement. He then proceeded to give me a statement regarding his participation in the robbery.

P WHAT, if any, threats did you make to him? (6)

W Absolutely none.

P WHAT, if any, promises did you make to him? (6)

W None.

P WHAT happened then? (2)

W As he gave me his statement, I typed it. After I typed it, I read it back to him to make sure I had typed his statement correctly. He said it was correct. Then he signed the statement.

P Is that his signature at the bottom of page two? (3)

W Yes, that is it.

P Your Honor, I now offer State's exhibit number 10 for identification into evidence as exhibit number 10.

J Any objections, defense counsel?

D Not at this point, your Honor.

J Then, State's exhibit number 10 will be received.

§ 13-19 THE TEXAS "CONFESSION STATUTE"—ORAL STATEMENTS

§ 13-19(A) THE GENERAL RULE OF EXCLUSION

Section 3 of article 38.22 prohibits the admission of any oral statements made by the defendant during a custodial interrogation. However, the bulk of section 3 deals with exceptions

§ 13-19(B) ORAL STATEMENTS—ELECTRONICALLY RECORDED

§ 13-19(B)(1) The Doctrine

Although article 38.22 generally prohibits the introduction of a defendant's oral statements, whether verbal or by sign language, section 3 of that article makes an exception for oral statements that have been preserved in the form of an electronic recording, whether audio or video. As noted in the next section, however, there are detailed requirements to be met before the recording may be admitted.

§ 13-19(B)(2) Elements of the Foundation

The foundation for the electronic recording exception to the general rule of exclusion is set out in article 38.22, section 3. That provision requires that the prosecutor show that:

1. The defendant made an oral statement during custodial interrogation;
2. Prior to making the statement, but during the recording, the accused was:
   a. Given his statutory warnings,[49] their "fully effective equivalent;"[50] and
   b. He knowingly, intelligently, and voluntarily waived his rights given by the statutory warnings;

---

[49] Art. 38.22, § 3(a)(2).

[50] *See* art. 38.22, § 3(e)(2).

3. The recording device was capable of making an accurate recording;
4. The operator was competent to operate the recording device;
5. The recording is accurate;
6. The recording has not been altered;
7. All material voices[51] on the recording are identified; and
8. The statement was provided to the defense attorney via a true, complete, and accurate copy of all recordings of the accused not later than twenty days before the date of the proceeding.

Under section 3(e), article 38.22, the courts are instructed to strictly construe the requirements stated above. Failure to comply with such requirements will make a statement inadmissible. Furthermore, the prosecution must preserve every electronic recording until the defendant's conviction is final.

§ 13-19(B)(3) Sample Foundation

The following sample foundation is a variation of the foundation used, *supra*, for a written statement. Officer Smith has testified about the general conditions of the custodial interrogation. The proponent is the prosecutor.

P Officer Smith, after you gave the defendant the cigarettes and coffee, WHAT, if anything, did the defendant say to you? (1)

W He informed me that he was willing to talk to me about the robbery in question.

P WHAT did you do then? (2)

W I told him that I was going to advise him of his rights and make a videotape of his statement and started to set up the equipment.

P WHAT equipment did you use? (3)

W I used a Sony 3000, a standard VHS video recorder which was mounted on a tripod about 10 feet away from where the defendant and I were sitting. I set it up, turned it on, inserted a new tape, hit the record button, and let it run.

P WHAT experience do you have in operating the video camera? (4)

W Well, I have used it about 30 times in the last six months and I have never had a problem with it. It is very easy to use.

P HOW do you know if it recorded accurately? (5)

W I ran a short test and checked it out. After the defendant had completed giving me his statement, I rewound it and watched the tape to make sure that it was accurate.

---

[51] Art. 38.22, § 3(e)(1).

P WHAT, if any, changes have been made to the recording? (6)

W None. I reviewed it again this morning and it is just as I recorded it.

P WHO else is included in this recording? (7)

W No one. Just the defendant and myself.

P WHAT, if any, warnings did you give the defendant? (2)

W I gave him the statutory warnings advising him of his right to remain silent and his right to counsel. The warnings are actually shown on the tape.

P I request that this be marked as a State's exhibit for identification [*Prosecutor hands exhibit to court reporter who marks it and hands it back.*] Thank you. Please let the record reflect that I am showing what has been marked as State's exhibit number nine for identification to the defense counsel. [*Counsel examines exhibit and hands back to Prosecutor.*]

P Officer, I now hand you State's exhibit number nine for identification. Do you recognize it?

W Yes I do. This is the rights warnings card that I used in this case.

P HOW did you use it?

W I read the warnings printed here verbatim to the defendant. These are the warnings that are on the tape I made.

P Your Honor, I now offer into evidence State's exhibit number nine for identification.[52]

J Objections?

D Not at this point, your Honor.

J State's exhibit number nine for identification will be admitted into evidence.

P Your Honor, I now request that this next item be marked State's exhibit number 10 for identification.

J It will be so marked. [*Prosecutor presents exhibit to court reporter who marks exhibit and hands back to counsel who in turn shows it to the defense counsel.*]

P Please let the record reflect that I am showing the exhibit to the defense counsel.

J It will so reflect.

P I request permission to approach the witness.

---

[52] As shown here, it may be better for the prosecutor to ask the officer to state specifically what warnings were given. Of course, the judge should be able to review the electronic recording of the tape itself to determine what warnings were given, before ruling on the tape's admissibility.

J Permission granted.

P Officer Smith, I now hand you State's exhibit number 10 for identification. WHAT is it? (1)

W It's the videotape I made of the defendant's statement.

P HOW can you recognize it?

W It has my name on it, and it has the defendant's name on it along with the date I recorded it.

P WHAT happened after you read Mr. Jackson these rights? (2)

W I asked him if he understood those rights and he said that he did. I then asked him if he had any questions and he said no. I asked him if he wanted me to repeat any of the warnings. And again, he said no.

P WHAT, if anything, did he say specifically about waiving his rights? (2b)

W The defendant stated he was waiving his rights. He said he did not want to see a lawyer and that he wanted to give me his statement. He then proceeded to give me a statement regarding his participation in the robbery.

P WHAT happened then? (1)

W He made his statement.

P Your Honor, I would make an offer of proof that 30 days ago, in compliance with article 38.22, section 3(a)(5), I gave the defense counsel an exact copy of the defendant's recorded statement, which is on State's exhibit number 10 for identification. (8)

J Defense counsel?

D That is correct, your Honor, we have received a copy of the tape.

P Your Honor, I now offer State's exhibit number 10 for identification into evidence as exhibit number 10.

J Any objections, defense counsel?

D Not at this point, your Honor.

J Then, State's exhibit number 10 for identification will be received as State's exhibit number 10.

§ 13-19(C) ORAL STATEMENTS—THE "RES GESTAE" EXCEPTION

§ 13-19(C)(1) The Doctrine

A res gestae,[53] or more accurately, "spontaneous" statement is another exception to the general prohibition of oral statements. The exception, which is

[53] For a discussion on use of the term *res gestae*, see WENDORF, SCHLUETER & BARTON, TEXAS RULES OF EVIDENCE MANUAL IV-81 et seq. (6th ed. 2002).

specifically mentioned in section 5 of article 38.22, typically arises where the defendant has made a spontaneous, unwarned statement to a police officer at the time of the offense or the time of arrest. As with the hearsay exception for excited utterances,[54] the key here is spontaneity. The longer the interval of time between the startling event and the statement, the less likely it will be viewed as being spontaneous. Likewise, if it appears that the statement was in direct response to an attempt to obtain an incriminating statement—without the benefit of warnings—the statement will probably be viewed as an otherwise inadmissible oral statement. Note that the statement might fall within this exception even if the defendant was in custody at the time of making the statement.[55]

§ 13-19(C)(2) Elements of the Foundation

In order to make the spontaneous oral statement admissible, the prosecution must show the following elements:

1. The defendant's arrest or the alleged offense amounted to an exciting event (either physically or emotionally);
2. The defendant's statement was a spontaneous response to the stimulating event; and
3. The statement related to the arrest or offense.[56]

§ 13-19(C)(3) Sample Foundation

In the following sample foundation, the defendant, Chuck Watson, has been charged with aggravated assault. The witness is Officer Gannon, who after receiving a call on his police radio responded by driving to the location of a reported fight. The proponent is the prosecutor. Officer Gannon has already identified himself and established that he was on duty and received the call. He has also established that he knows and recognizes the defendant. In this foundation, the defendant has made two statements to the policeman. While the prosecutor might argue that both statements are related to, and the result of, the startling event of the assault itself, the second statement follows the defendant's arrest. Thus, even if the court determines for some reason that the first statement was the result of custodial interrogation and not spontaneous, the second statement should be treated separately.

P Officer Gannon, after you received the call on your radio, WHAT did you do? (1)

W I immediately proceeded to the scene.

---

[54] *See* § 11-6 (discussion of excited or startled utterances).

[55] *See, e.g., Etheridge v. State*, 903 S.W.2d 1 (Tex. Crim. App. 1994).

[56] *See, e.g., Hood v. State*, 490 S.W.2d 549, 550–51 (Tex. Crim. App. 1973).

P WHAT was the location? (1)

W 1222 West Main Street in Texarkana.

P HOW long after you received the report did you actually arrive at the scene? (2)

W It took me less than five minutes to get there.

P WHAT did you observe when you arrived at the scene? (2)

W I noticed a group of people looking at someone lying on the ground. One person saw me drive up and motioned for me to come quickly to help. I ran over and saw a woman lying in a pool of blood and moaning.

P WHAT happened next? (2)

W Well, I immediately checked her condition and called for an ambulance. I then asked the people standing there what had happened. At that point, the defendant stepped up and said that he had cut her because he caught her with another man.

P WHAT was the defendant's condition when he made that statement? (2), (3)

W Well, he was really excited. His eyes were wide open, he appeared to be short of breath, and his hands were shaking slightly. Also, his voice seemed strained to me and he talked really fast.

P Was the defendant in custody at the time he made his statement?

W No.

P WHAT happened next? (2), (3)

W When the ambulance arrived, I took the defendant back to my patrol car and placed him under arrest. I had him empty his pockets and get in the back seat.

P WHAT, if any, statements did the defendant make at that time? (3)

W He repeated that he felt good that he had cut his girlfriend and that he would do it again if given the chance.

P WHAT was his emotional condition at the time he made that statement? (2)

W He still seemed excited and nervous about what was happening.

P WHAT, if any, questions did you ask of him to prompt that statement? (2)

W None. I had only told him he was under arrest and that I was going to take him downtown for booking.

§ 13-19(D) ORAL STATEMENTS—PARTIAL CORROBORATION EXCEPTION

§ 13-19(D)(1) The Doctrine

A partially corroborated oral statement is another exception to the general rule of exclusion.[57] Under section 3(c) of article 38.22, the rule of exclusion does not apply to "any statement which contains assertions of facts or circumstances that are found to be true and which conduce to establish the guilt of the accused, such as the finding of secreted or stolen property or the instrument with which he states the offense was committed." This exception allows the admission of an entire unrecorded oral statement, if the information given in the statement is corroborated by information found elsewhere. Two things must be kept in mind: First, it only takes the discovery of one piece of corroborated information to make the entire oral statement admissible, and, second, the Texas Court of Criminal Appeals requires the corroborated evidence to be discovered *after* the statement is made.[58]

It is important to see how this doctrine relates to the *Miranda* doctrine, discussed *infra*. Although the police will almost always give them, the statutory rights warnings specified for written and electronically recorded statements in article 38.22 are not required. But the *Miranda* warnings are applicable if the oral statement was the result of a custodial interrogation. If the element of custody or the element of interrogation is missing, then neither the Texas confession statute nor *Miranda* apply.

§ 13-19(D)(2) Elements of the Foundation

In order to rely on the corroborated oral statement exception, the prosecution must be prepared to show the following elements;

1. The defendant was subjected to custodial interrogation;
2. The defendant received rights warnings;
3. The defendant made an oral statement to government agents;
4. The oral statement includes assertions of facts or circumstances;
5. The prosecutor uses independent evidence, discovered after the statement was made, to prove that the defendant's assertions of facts or circumstances are true; and

---

[57] *See* Barton, *The Code Means What it Says: Revisiting the Admissibility of Corroborated Unwritten Custodial Statements*, 26 TEX. TECH. L. REV. 780 (1995) (discussing exception to general rule of exclusion of custodial oral statements).

[58] *See McGilvery v. State*, 533 S.W.2d 24, 26 (Tex. Crim. App. 1976). *Cf.* DIX AND DAWSON, CRIMINAL PRACTICE AND PROCEDURE 558–60 (2d ed, 2001) (questioning whether this requirement is still viable). *See also Gunter v. State*, 858 S.W.2d 430 (Tex. Crim. App. 1993) (citing *Port v. State*, 791 S.W.2d 103, 106 (Tex. Crim. App. 1990) which discusses the plain meaning of 38.22).

6. The assertions of facts or circumstances "conduce"[59] to establish the guilt of the defendant.

§ 13-19(D)(3) Sample Foundation

The State has charged the defendant, Hernandez, with murder. Before trial, the defendant gave the police an oral statement during a custodial interrogation, after which he was advised of his rights warnings. (1), (2), (3), In his statement, the defendant admitted that he had killed the victim and had struck the victim five times in the back with a large hunting knife. (4) The defense argues that the statement is inadmissible under article 38.22 because it is oral and uncorroborated. An earlier witness, Officer Johnston, testified that he found a body at the defendant's apartment and helped transport the body to the medical examiner's office. (5) The witness is Dr. Garner, the assistant medical examiner. The proponent is the prosecutor. Dr. Garner has already described his qualifications; he has testified that he is a physician licensed to practice in Texas and is board certified in the specialty of forensic pathology.

P Doctor, WHERE were you on the afternoon of October 15th last year?

W I was at my office downtown.

P WHAT happened that afternoon? (5)

W I received word from the front desk that the police would soon be delivering a cadaver that they had discovered.

P WHAT happened then? (5)

W I went to the receiving dock to meet the police vehicle. It arrived about 10 minutes later.

P WHO did you meet when the police arrived? (5)

W There were several officers, including Officer Johnston, who just left the witness stand.

P WHAT happened then? (5)

W The police delivered the cadaver to us.

P I request that this be marked as State's exhibit number two for identification. [*Proponent hands exhibit to court reporter, who marks it and hands back to counsel.*]

P Please let the record reflect that I am showing State's exhibit number two to both the defense counsel and the judge. [*Counsel hands exhibit to defense counsel and judge.*]

P Doctor, I now show you what has been marked as State's exhibit number two for identification. WHAT is it? (5)

---

59 Article 38.22 uses the term "conduce," which means leads to or contributes to a result.

W It's a photograph of the cadaver. This is the body they delivered to me that afternoon.

P WHAT did you do after they delivered the body? (1)

W I had some of our attendants load the body onto a cart and wheel it to Examination Room #3 on the first floor.

P WHAT did you do after the body reached the examination room? (1)

W The first thing I did was to examine the body carefully for any signs of life.

P WHAT was the result of the examination? (1)

W The person was unquestionably dead. There were no signs of circulatory, respiratory, or brain activity.

P WHAT else, if anything, did you observe about the body? (2)

W There were two observations in particular that were significant.

P WHAT were they? (2)

W One was a number of stab wounds—five, to be exact—in the back. They were also made by what appeared to be a large knife.

P WHY were those wounds significant? (2)

W It would have been physically impossible for the victim to have stabbed himself in those locations. The location of the wounds immediately ruled out any possibility of suicide as the manner or mode of death. I knew at that point that we had either a homicide or a remote possibility of an accident on our hands.

P WHAT was the other observation you made? (2)

W I carefully examined all the extremities, especially the hands. There were a number of cuts on the back of both hands in the form of short lacerations.

P WHY were those lacerations significant? (2)

W They're what we call "defense wounds," the sort of cuts that a victim often gets when he's trying to fight off an attacker with a knife. These wounds result when the victim tries to grab the knife away from the attacker. You often find them on the hands, fingers, and forearms. The location and depth of the lacerations both were indicative of defense wounds. Together, the location of the stab wounds on the back and the presence of characteristic defense wounds on the backs of both hands lead me to conclude that this was a homicide rather than either a suicide or an accident.

To complete the picture, the prosecutor would probably use other evidence to establish that the body examined by the doctor was in fact the victim in the case.

§ 13-20 INVOLUNTARY CONFESSIONS BARRED BY CONSTITUTIONAL DUE PROCESS CLAUSES AND STATUTE

§ 13-20(A) THE DOCTRINE

Even if a defendant's statement has been preceded by the necessary rights warnings, it may be inadmissible on due process grounds. Relying on the due process clauses of the Fifth and Fourteenth Amendments, courts have historically forbidden the use of confessions which were involuntarily given by the defendant. See also article 38.21, Texas Code of Criminal Procedure. If threats or improper inducements overcome the defendant's will to resist, the confession is involuntary, and the prosecutor may not introduce the confession against the defendant.

One substantive question is whether the doctrine applies only when the persons applying pressure to the defendant are government agents. In *Colorado v. Connelly*, 479 U.S. 157 (1986), the Court held that only coercive police conduct violates the federal due process clause. Whether the Texas Due Process Clause requires official coercion is uncertain. Texas courts, however, have declared that the Texas statutory requirement of voluntariness applies even when the pressure on the defendant was exerted by private citizens.

The pivotal question is whether, under the totality of the circumstances, the suspect's ability to make a free choice was overborne by the coercion or inducement. The trial judge should consider the defendant's age, intelligence, and mental or physical condition. Other factors the judge may take into account include the length of interrogation, whether interrogation was continuous and rigorous, and whether defendant was denied access to communicate with others.

What types of coercion and inducement are forbidden by the Due Process Clauses and statute? The clauses unquestionably forbid physical torture. The troublesome problems arise when the police obtain statements induced by promises or deception.

Under the federal Due Process Clause, any promise made by the police will be examined as a factor in applying the totality of the circumstances analysis when a defendant contends that such confession or statement, based on a promise, was given involuntarily. Texas voluntariness law consists of a four-prong test which a defendant must satisfy for a confession or statement to be found involuntary based on a promise by the police. The promise must convey some positive benefit to the defendant, made or approved by a person in authority, and likely to influence the defendant to speak untruthfully.

With regards to statements induced by deception, the federal Due Process Clause also considers the deception as a mere factor to be applied in the totality of the circumstances analysis. Texas law has held confessions or statements, induced by deception, to be involuntary when the police misrepresent information about the offense to the defendant. Several Texas courts of appeals have also declared that deception in interrogation will render a confession or statement involuntary when the police employ methods to produce an untruthful statement or offensive to due process. The courts, however, have not enunciated what types of deception produce untruthful statements or offend due process.

§ 13-20(B) ELEMENTS OF THE FOUNDATION

To establish that the defendant's statement was voluntary, i.e., there was no coercion or improper inducement, the prosecutor should lay these foundational elements.

1. Negatively, the police did not
    a. Use violence or threats against the defendant;
    b. Make improper promises to the defendant; or
    c. Misrepresent information to the defendant.
2. Affirmatively, the police treated the suspect decently and afforded the suspect at least minimum conveniences.

§ 13-20(C) SAMPLE FOUNDATION

The following fact pattern involves a prosecution for robbery. The defendant is Mr. Johnson. The prosecution calls Officer Gannon as a witness. Officer Gannon identifies himself and then testifies that he is assigned to the robbery detail of the Austin Police Department. The proponent is the prosecutor.

P Officer Gannon, WHERE were you on the afternoon of January 20th last year?

W I was at our downtown station on duty in the robbery detail office.

P WHAT happened that afternoon?

W Some other officers brought in someone for questioning.

P WHO was that person?

W Jim Johnson.

P WHERE is Jim Johnson now?

W Here in the courtroom.

P Specifically, WHERE in the courtroom?

W He's sitting right there.

P HOW is he dressed?

W He's wearing a brown shirt and green pants.

P Your Honor, please let the record reflect that the witness identified the defendant.

J It will so reflect.

P WHAT happened after the officers brought in Mr. Johnson?

W I took him to the interrogation room.

P WHAT happened then?

W I gave him his rights warnings, obtained a waiver, and then began questioning him.

P WHAT promises did you make to him during the questioning? (1b)

W None.

P WHAT representations regarding the robbery did you make to him during the interrogation? (1c)

W I simply told him that we suspected him of committing the robbery and that I wanted to question him about it. I did not say anything to him about why we suspected him.

P WHAT force did you use during this interrogation? (1a)

W None, I never touched him. I never did anything to indicate that I would even consider using force against him.

P WHAT threats did you make? (1a)

W I didn't make any. I didn't threaten him or his family or his friends in any way.

P WHEN did your questioning begin? (2)

W He was brought in at about 4:00 in the afternoon and I started talking to him about 4:15.

P HOW long did you question him? (2)

W Altogether, from start to finish, about two hours. I finished at about 6:30 or so.

P WHAT were the physical surroundings of the room where you questioned him? (2)

W It was in one of our conference rooms. It measures about 8 feet by 12 feet with a table in the center. There is one large window with blinds in the center of the wall. Because it was in the afternoon, I probably had the blinds closed slightly. There is a large window in the door so people can see in and anyone in the room can see clearly into the hallway. The room is air-conditioned as well.

P WHAT requests did he make during the questioning? (2)

W Well, after we had talked for about an hour, he asked for a cigarette, for coffee, and to go to the bathroom—that sort of thing.

P HOW did you respond to his requests? (2)

W I granted them. I gave him cigarettes and coffee. I let him go to the bathroom. I tried to make him as comfortable as possible.

P WHAT, if any, comments did he make about his condition during the questioning? (2)

W None. He did not say anything to lead me to think that he was hungry, cold, hot, or otherwise uncomfortable.

§ 13-21 CONFESSIONS BARRED BY THE *MIRANDA* DOCTRINE

§ 13-21(A) THE DOCTRINE

In *Miranda v. Arizona*, 384 U.S. 436 (1966), the Supreme Court noted that custodial interrogation is inherently coercive and, therefore, held that when the police interrogate a defendant, they must advise him of certain rights and obtain a knowing, intelligent waiver of the rights. There are two types of commonly litigated *Miranda* situations. In one type, the prosecutor argues that *Miranda* does not apply and, in the other type, the prosecution contends that the police complied with *Miranda* and obtained an effective waiver.

Because *Miranda* is a limited doctrine, prosecutors can argue various reasons why *Miranda* warnings were not required.

First, *Miranda* applies only when interrogators are government agents. This includes private citizens acting as government agents. Second, *Miranda* applies only when the defendant's statement results from police questioning. The Supreme Court has defined this as any words or actions by the police which the police should know are likely to invoke an incriminating answer from the defendant. Third, *Miranda* applies only if the defendant is "in custody." The test is whether the police make a formal arrest or restrain one's freedom of movement comparable to a formal arrest. In deciding whether a person is in custody, the courts consider several factors: the place, time of day, and length of the interrogation; the use of weapons or other physical restraint; whether the suspect was present voluntarily; and whether the suspect was or felt free to leave.

Prosecutors may also find assistance in exceptions to *Miranda* which have been recognized by the Supreme Court. The Supreme Court has recognized a public safety exception to *Miranda*: the Court permitted an officer to question an individual about a weapon without a *Miranda* warning when the weapon posed a threat to the public safety.[60] The Supreme Court has also declared that *Miranda*

[60] *New York v. Quarles*, 467 U.S. 649 (1984).

does not apply to routine questions asked during booking; thus, prosecutors may introduce incriminating evidence obtained during booking without *Miranda* warnings being given.[61]

In the second situation, the prosecutor argues that the police satisfied the requirements of *Miranda*. Typically, the argument requires proof of proper warnings, the defendant's understanding of the warnings, and a waiver of his rights.

Police usually warn suspects in the following fashion:

1. You have the right to remain silent.
2. Anything you say can and will be used against you in court.
3. You have the right to speak with an attorney and to have the attorney with you during questioning.
4. If you cannot afford an attorney, one will be appointed for you.

The Supreme Court made it clear that the police need not quote the exact language used in the *Miranda* opinion; communicating the substance of the warning is sufficient. In testifying about the warnings, police often vouch that they read warnings verbatim from a card. The prosecutor can then introduce the card to corroborate the officer's testimony.

The second element of the foundation is proof that the suspect understood the warnings. Officers usually meet this requirement by asking the defendant, point blank, whether he understands the rights explained to him. An affirmative answer is admissible to prove the defendant's understanding of his rights.

Lastly, the defendant must waive his rights. Officers can accomplish this by asking the defendant whether he wants a lawyer or wants to make a statement. A negative response to the former question and an affirmative answer to the latter question is ordinarily adequate to establish a defendant's knowing and intelligent waiver of his rights. Should a defendant, however, clearly assert his right to counsel, the police must terminate questioning about any criminal conduct. Questioning can begin again only if the defendant initiates further communications with the police. On the other hand, if defendant asserts his right to remain silent, the Supreme Court has held that this does not cut off all questioning. The police may renew interrogation on a different subject after a fresh warning.

As noted in § 13-19(D), *supra*, in most cases officers will give the warnings specified in article 38.22 as a matter of course; as a practical matter they will not always know whether the resulting statement will be admissible as a written statement, an electronically recorded statement, or a partially corroborated oral statement. To be admissible as either a written statement or an electronically recorded statement, the statutory rights warnings are required. They are not

---

[61] *Pennsylvania v. Muniz*, 496 U.S. 582 (1990).

needed if the prosecution is relying on the partially corroborated oral statement exception. But *Miranda* will be applicable if that type of statement resulted from a custodial interrogation.

§ 13-21(B) ELEMENTS OF THE FOUNDATION

To prove a valid *Miranda* foundation, i.e., a waiver of the right to remain silent, the prosecutor must show the following elements:

1. The police conducted a custodial interrogation of the defendant;
2. Before the interrogation, the police administered proper warnings;
3. The suspect understood the warnings; and
4. The suspect knowingly and intelligently waived his rights.

§ 13-21(C) SAMPLE FOUNDATION

The following sample foundation is a continuation of the preceding foundation. The defendant is Mr. Johnson, who was in custody at the time of the initial interrogation (1), and the witness is Officer Gannon.

P [*Continued questioning.*] Officer Gannon, after you gave the defendant the cigarettes and coffee, WHAT, if anything, did you say to him? (2)

W I read him his rights.

P HOW did you read him his rights? (2)

W I read them verbatim from a warning card.

P [*To court reporter.*] We request that this be marked as State's exhibit number three for identification. [*Reporter marks exhibit and hands it back to the prosecutor who shows it to the defense counsel.*]

P Thank you. Please let the record reflect that I have shown what has been marked as State's exhibit number three to the defense counsel.

P I request permission to approach the witness.

J Permission granted.

P Officer Gannon, I now hand you State's exhibit number three for identification. WHAT is it? (2)

W It's the warning card I just referred to.

P HOW can you recognize it? (2)

W I initialed it, and I had the defendant initial it as well. I see the initials and the date we wrote in pencil on the card.

P HOW did you use the card during questioning? (2)

W I read from it verbatim to make certain I gave the suspect the correct warnings.

P Your Honor, I now offer State's exhibit number three for identification into evidence as exhibit number three. (2)

J Any objections to this exhibit, counsel?

D No, your Honor.

J State's exhibit number three for identification will be received into evidence.

P Officer Gannon, please read prosecution exhibit number three. (2)

W It says: "You have the right to remain silent. Anything you say can and will be used against you in a court of law. You also have a right to an attorney. You have a right to consult an attorney before any questioning. You have a right to have an attorney present during any questioning. If you cannot afford an attorney, one will be appointed to represent you."

P WHAT happened after you read Mr. Johnson these rights? (3)

W I asked him whether he understood his rights.

P WHAT was his answer? (3)

W He said he did.

P HOW would you describe the defendant's demeanor when he said that he understood his rights? (4)

W He seemed calm and clear headed.

P WHAT happened then? (4)

W I asked him whether he was willing to talk about the robbery.

P WHAT was his response? (4)

W He told me about the robbery.

P WHAT did he say about the robbery? (4)

W He said he had held up the McDonald's on 4th Street, and he was very sorry he had done it. He said he desperately needed money for rent, and he couldn't figure out any other way to get it.

§ 13-22 CONFESSIONS BARRED BY THE SIXTH AMENDMENT RIGHT TO COUNSEL

§ 13-22(A) THE DOCTRINE

The Sixth Amendment right to counsel does not attach until the initiation of adversary judicial proceedings against the accused. At that point the police may not interrogate the defendant in the absence of counsel. *Massiah v. United States*, 377 U.S. 201 (1964). The limitation applies to both overt police interrogation and questioning of the defendant by an undercover informant. In regards to undercover informants, the Sixth Amendment right to counsel bars the admissibility of self-incriminating statements elicited by informants in the absence of counsel. However, the Sixth Amendment right to counsel does not bar statements which an informant received by merely listening to what the defendant had to say and not asking the defendant any questions. *Kuhlmann v. Wilson*, 477 U.S. 436 (1986). The Sixth Amendment right to counsel is "offense-specific," which means officers may continue to question the defendant regarding other crimes for which no judicial proceedings have been initiated. Furthermore, the Sixth Amendment right to counsel may be waived by the defendant.

§ 13-22(B) ELEMENTS OF THE FOUNDATION

Suppose that the prosecutor decides to respond to a *Massiah* objection by arguing that the police informant did not actively question the defendant. The prosecutor should show that:

1. Before placing the informant in the defendant's cell, the police instructed the informant not to question the defendant. They instructed him to merely talk about his own background and listen carefully to the defendant's statements.
2. The informant carried out those instructions.
3. While listening to the defendant, the informant overheard an incriminating statement.

§ 13-22(C) SAMPLE FOUNDATION

In the following sample foundation, the State has charged the defendant, Williams, with robbery. The defendant was indicted on July 31st. As of that date, he had an assigned counsel. On August 2nd, the police placed an informant in the defendant's cell. The informant was Mr. Anderson, who is the witness. The prosecutor is the proponent.

P Mr. Anderson, WHERE were you on the morning of August 2nd?

W I was in my cell on the second floor of the detention center downtown.

P WHAT happened that morning? (1)

W I was called into one of the interrogation rooms on the first floor.

P WHAT happened there? (1)

W I met an Assistant District Attorney by the name of Joe. He told me that they had a proposition for me.

P WHAT was the proposition? (1)

W They told me that they might be willing to help me with my pending charges if I helped them nail the defendant.

P Specifically, WHAT did they ask you to do? (1)

W They said that all I was supposed to do was go into the defendant's cell and keep my ears open.

P WHAT instructions, if any, did they give you? (1)

W They said under no circumstances was I to question the guy about the robbery or any other crime. I was just to stay in the cell, tell him about myself, and listen for anything incriminating that he might say.

P WHAT did you say after the Assistant District Attorney told you this? (1)

W I said that I'd do it.

P WHAT happened after you said you'd do it? (2)

W The guards came in and led me to the defendant's cell on the third floor.

P WHERE is the defendant now? (2)

W He's sitting over there at the table to my right. He's the guy in the green jacket.

P Your Honor, please let the record reflect that the witness has identified the defendant, Mark Williams.

J The record will so reflect.

P Mr. Anderson, WHAT happened after you entered the defendant's cell?

W I did just what the D.A. told me to do.

P Please be more specific. WHAT did you do? (2)

W All I did was talk about my background—primarily my own criminal record—and keep my ears open.

P WHAT questions, if any, did you pose to the defendant? (2)

W None. I may have asked the guy for a cigarette, but I didn't ask the guy anything about the robbery or any other crimes. I did what I was told.

P While you were in the defendant's cell . . . [*The prosecutor would continue the questioning to elicit the defendant's incriminating statement.*] (3)

§ 13-23 USE OF OTHERWISE INADMISSIBLE CONFESSION TO IMPEACH THE DEFENDANT

§ 13-23(A) THE DOCTRINE

Suppose that the police obtain a defendant's statement in violation of *Miranda* or *Massiah* but that the statement is voluntary in the traditional, due process sense. At trial, the defendant testifies to facts inconsistent with the pretrial statement. The prosecutor may introduce the statement, in rebuttal, for the limited purpose of impeaching the defendant's credibility. In *Harris v. New York*, 401 U.S. 222 (1971) the Court reasoned that if the statement is voluntary, it is probably reliable. The Court concluded that the government interest in exposing the defendant's perjury at trial outweighs the policies inspiring *Miranda*. The Supreme Court has not answered whether a statement taken in violation of *Massiah* can be used for impeachment purposes. Article 38.22, section 5 of the Texas Code of Criminal Procedure is consistent with the constitutional rule enunciated in *Harris*.

§ 13-23(B) ELEMENTS OF THE FOUNDATION

The only required foundation would be the proof of the voluntariness of the statement. The prosecutor should lay these foundational elements.

1. Negatively, the police did not:
    a. Use violence or threats against the defendant;
    b. Make improper promises to the defendant; or
    c. Misrepresent information to the defendant.
2. Affirmatively, the police treated the suspect decently and afforded the suspect at least minimum conveniences.

§ 13-23(C) SAMPLE FOUNDATION

The sample foundation involves a prosecution for robbery. The defendant is Mr. Johnson. At a pretrial hearing, the court ruled that the defendant's statements to the police were inadmissible for lack of proper rights warnings. During the defense case-in-chief the defendant testified that he could not have committed the robbery because he was in Detroit visiting his grandmother at the time. In rebuttal, the prosecution calls Officer Gannon to impeach that testimony. Officer Gannon identifies himself and then testifies that he is assigned to the robbery detail of the Austin Police Department. The proponent is the prosecutor.

P Officer Gannon, WHERE were you on the afternoon of January 20th of last year?

W I was at our downtown station on duty in the robbery detail office.

P WHAT happened that afternoon?

W Some other officers brought in someone for questioning.

P WHO was that person?

W Jim Johnson.

P WHERE is Jim Johnson now?

W Here in the courtroom.

P Specifically, WHERE in the courtroom?

W He's sitting right there.

P HOW is he dressed?

W He's wearing a brown shirt and green pants.

P Your Honor, please let the record reflect that the witness identified the defendant.

J It will so reflect.

P WHAT happened after the officers brought Mr. Johnson in?

W I took him to the interrogation room.

P WHAT happened then?

W I began questioning him.

P WHAT promises did you make to him during the questioning? (1b)

W None.

P WHAT misrepresentations regarding the robbery did you make to him during the interrogation? (1c)

W None.

P WHAT force did you use during this interrogation? (1a)

W None, I never touched him.

P WHAT threats did you make? (1a)

W I didn't make any. I didn't threaten him or his family in any way.

P WHAT requests did he make during the questioning? (2)

W He asked for a cigarette, for coffee, and to go to the bathroom—that sort of thing.

P HOW did you respond to his requests? (2)

W I granted them. I gave him cigarettes and coffee. I let him go to the bathroom. I tried to make him as comfortable as possible.

P WHAT, if anything, did he say about his whereabouts during the time of the robbery?

W He said that he could not have committed the robbery because at the time he was visiting his brother in Dallas. He was very positive about that and told me to check out his alibi.

§§ 13-24–13-29 RESERVED

PART 3
EYEWITNESS IDENTIFICATION

§ 13-30 IN GENERAL

Because every criminal charge requires that the prosecution prove beyond a reasonable doubt that the defendant was the actor who committed the crime,[62] the defendant's identity is an issue in every criminal prosecution. Absent a stipulation or a concession by the defendant that he committed the act, the prosecutor must introduce evidence bearing on identification.

During an investigation, police use a variety of devices to link the defendant to the crime. Sometimes defendants admit their involvement during interrogation, but more often law enforcement authorities must resort to physical descriptions by witnesses, photo-spread identifications, one-on-one encounters, and lineups to prove that the defendant committed the offense. At trial, the prosecutor offers the results of these pretrial identification procedures, as well as the eyewitness's "in-court" identification of the defendant.

Part 3 addresses pretrial identification techniques used by law enforcement officers. Usually these techniques involve citizen eyewitnesses, but the rules also extend to police officers asked to identify the defendant.

Identification procedures raise two broad issues. First, did the pretrial procedures comport with Due Process protections designed to safeguard against erroneous identifications? Second, did the government violate the defendant's Sixth Amendment right to counsel?

§ 13-31 PROCEDURAL ASPECTS OF DECIDING ADMISSIBILITY OF EYEWITNESS IDENTIFICATION EVIDENCE

§ 13-31(A) AN OVERVIEW

The state uses the testimony of a witness who observed the crime or the perpetrator to connect the defendant to the charged crime. The possible lack of certainty on the part of that witness's identification of the defendant usually goes

---

[62] *In re Winship*, 397 U.S. 358 (1970).

to the weight and credibility of the testimony, not the testimony's admissibility.[63] Trial courts generally have the discretionary authority to refuse to hold pretrial lineups in order to verify the witness's ability to identify the defendant, using only the witness's memory.[64] The Texas Court of Criminal Appeals has also decided that Due Process and the right to counsel do not require that the identification by the state's witness be made while the defendant is part of an in-court group or any other in-court "test."[65]

Because of courts' tendency to allow eyewitness identification both out-of-court and in-court, despite its likelihood of unreliability, the constitutionally protected Due Process procedures and the right to counsel at critical stages of the adjudicatory phase form the best basis for an objection by the defendant.

§ 13-31(B) RAISING THE ISSUE; MOTIONS TO SUPPRESS AND TRIAL OBJECTIONS

Counsel for the defendant should raise any objection to the pretrial procedure used to identify the defendant in a Motion to Suppress Eyewitness Identification and request a hearing on this motion under Texas Code of Criminal Procedure 28.10. Generally, the objection should be made under the Sixth and Fourteenth Amendments of the United States Constitution, article I, section 19 of the Texas Constitution, and article 38.23 of the Texas Code of Criminal Procedure. The trial judge will determine the admissibility of the proposed eyewitness testimony under Texas Rule of Evidence 104(a).

A Motion to Suppress Eyewitness Identification should be clear and specific as to which testimony will not be allowed. Testimony can be brought by witnesses other than the identifying witness as to what was said out-of-court if the identifying witness also testifies at trial.[66] Such testimony is not considered bolstering.[67]

§ 13-31(C) HEARINGS OUTSIDE THE JURORS' PRESENCE

Counsel should request that a hearing be conducted outside the presence of the jury pursuant to Texas Rule of Evidence 104(c). If testimony is given within the presence of the jury, the defense should offer its objection into the record and request a limiting instruction if appropriate.

---

63 *See Livingston v. State*, 739 S.W.2d 311, 329 (Tex. Crim. App. 1987).

64 *See Sapp v. State*, 476 S.W.2d 321, 323 (Tex. Crim. App. 1972).

65 *Johnson v. State*, 462 S.W.2d 955 (Tex. Crim. App. 1971).

66 *See* TEX. R. EVID. 801(e)(1)(C) (certain out-of-court identifications are not hearsay).

67 *See Thomas v. State*, 811 S.W.2d 201, 208 (Tex. App.—Houston [1st Dist.] 1991, pet. ref.).

§ 13-31(D) BURDENS OF PROOF

Challenging the identification process under either Due Process or right to counsel grounds begins with the defense shouldering the burden of proof. If the defense is successful in its challenge, the state may try to rehabilitate the witness's testimony if the objection was based upon Due Process. If the successful objection was based upon right to counsel, the eyewitness identification testimony is automatically excluded. The respective burdens of proof are included in the discussion of the doctrines supporting the two possible challenges to the identification evidence, *infra*.

§ 13-31(E) RULINGS BY THE TRIAL COURT

Generally, a witness who observed the perpetrator or the crime in progress will be permitted to testify at trial. Trial judges are free to allow a state's witness to make in-court identifications based upon the witness's claim of excellent memory even if the courtroom context, i.e. the defendant is the only person sitting at the defense table, is very suggestive.[68]

Trial courts are also not barred from attempting to ascertain the capacity of the witness's memory to identify the defendant. The trial judge's general discretionary authority allows for certain in-court procedures to prove or disprove the witness's ability to identify the defendant, but such methods are not used often. Even so, it is generally left to the defense to impeach the witness's testimony or demonstrate the unconstitutionality of an out-of-court identification procedure.

§ 13-31(F) SUBMISSION OF ISSUE TO JURY

Article 38.23 of the Texas Code of Criminal Procedure implicitly gives counsel opportunity to re-litigate some eyewitness identification issues is if there still remains a controversy as to a material fact, e.g., whether the witness had an adequate opportunity to observe the defendant. This method of last resort can be especially helpful to the defendant if the witness's testimony—whose credibility is questionable—has been allowed as legally admissible. The jury can be informed that it may believe or disregard the testimony it has heard.

---

[68] *See Ward v. State*, 474 S.W.2d 471, 474 (Tex. Crim. App. 1971); *Mullen v. State*, 722 S.W.2d 808, 812 (Tex. App.—Houston [14th Dist.] 1987, no writ); *Baskin v. State*, 672 S.W.2d 312, 314 (Tex. App.—San Antonio 1984, no writ).

§ 13-32 EYEWITNESS IDENTIFICATION PROCEDURES—THE DUE PROCESS ANALYSIS

§ 13-32(A) THE DOCTRINE

The Due Process Clauses of the Fifth and Fourteenth Amendments provide some measure of protection against unfair identification procedures by law enforcement officers. The Due Process rights are analytically distinct from the Sixth Amendment right to counsel, which may also apply to identification procedures.

In *Stovall v. Denno*,[69] the Supreme Court held that a Due Process violation occurs if the pretrial identification procedures are "unnecessarily suggestive and conducive to irreparable mistaken identification." The following year, the Supreme Court clarified the contours of the Due Process right related to identification procedures. In *Simmons v. United States*,[70] the Court explained that evidence of an identification procedure offends the Due Process clause only if the pretrial identification was so "impermissibly suggestive as to give rise to a very substantial likelihood of irreparable misidentification."

Thus, the linchpin of the Due Process analysis became the existence of a substantial likelihood of an *irreparable* misidentification of the suspect. In both *Neil v. Biggers*,[71] and *Manson v. Brathwaite*,[72] the Court ruled that an identification procedure that was both suggestive and unnecessary did not require per se exclusion. If an identification arising from the unnecessarily suggestive procedure was reliable under the totality of the circumstances, testimony about the out-of-court identification is nevertheless admissible at trial. The same analysis applies to the admissibility of a later in-court identification by the same witness.

The Texas Court of Criminal Appeals has used a five-element analysis in determining whether an impermissibly suggestive identification procedure has caused an in-court identification to be so unreliable as to be inadmissible:

1. The witness's opportunity to view the criminal at the time of the crime,
2. the witness's degree of attention,
3. the accuracy of his out-of-court description of the criminal prior to the procedure,
4. the level of certainty demonstrated at the trial confrontation, and
5. the time between the crime and the confrontation.[73]

---

[69] 388 U.S. 293 (1967).

[70] 390 U.S. 377 (1968).

[71] 409 U.S. 188 (1972).

[72] 432 U.S. 98 (1977).

[73] *Webb v. State*, 760 S.W.2d 263 (Tex. Crim. App. 1988); *see also Ibarra v. State*, 11 S.W.3d 189 (Tex. Crim. App. 1999) and *Delk v. State*, 855 S.W.2d 700, 706 (Tex. Crim. App. 1993).

This list is not considered to be exclusive and other elements can be relevant but not necessarily controlling.

The *Stovall* analysis contemplates two inquiries: (1) were the procedures "suggestive," and, if so, (2) were they "necessary" despite their suggestive nature? The defendant bears the burden of proving that the procedures used by law enforcement officers were suggestive and unnecessary.

Courts often merge considerations of suggestiveness and necessity even though they are analytically distinct. Perhaps it is more accurate to say that the permissible suggestiveness of a procedure is a function of its necessity under the circumstances; the more suggestive the procedure, the more compelling the justification for having used it. Further, the Due Process right is limited to deliberately staged governmental identification procedures. Purely private conduct, such as a chance encounter between the witness and the defendant in a courtroom hallway, are not subject to Due Process scrutiny.

The burden of establishing unnecessary suggestiveness is a heavy one.[74] The courts are inclined to treat suggestive procedures and even the risk of mistaken identification as weight issues best left for adversary sparring at trial. Evidence of out-of-court procedures or in-court identifications is suppressed only in "extraordinary cases." Suggestiveness alone is insufficient to show a Due Process violation.[75]

The courts have refused to find per se suggestiveness even where police have carelessly lost the photographs on which the witness based her identification. In the absence of testimony revealing suggestive procedures, the court will not presume suggestiveness. When assembling a lineup or a photo array, police are not required to exhaust all possibilities to find people physically comparable to the defendant. The suggestiveness of any given technique turns entirely on the facts of the particular case.[76]

Once the court determines that the procedures used were suggestive, the next issue is whether the suggestive procedures were necessary under the circumstances. This opens an inquiry into the police investigation itself. Why did the law enforcement officers use the procedures in question? What was the status of the investigation at the time of the identification? What alternatives were available?

---

74 *Jackson v. State*, 628 S.W.2d 446, 448 (Tex. Crim. App. 1982).

75 *See Holloway v. State*, 691 S.W.2d 608, 615 (Tex. Crim. App. 1984); *Herrera v. State*, 682 S.W.2d 313, 318 (Tex. Crim. App. 1984) (citing *Jackson*).

76 For examples of case-by-case analysis see *Hudson v. State*, 675 S.W.2d 507, 510 (Tex. Crim. App. 1984); *Cantu v. State*, 738 S.W.2d 249, 252 (Tex. Crim. App. 1987); *Tapley v. State*, 673 S.W.2d 284, 286–287 (Tex. App.—San Antonio 1984, pet. ref.); *Rawlings v. State*, 720 S.W.2d 561 (Tex. App.—Austin 1986, pet. ref.).

Case law stops far short of demanding a showing of emergency or exigent circumstances in justifying suggestive procedures. For example, the one-on-one showup approved in *Stovall* did not involve a death-bed identification despite the Court's intimation that police were uncertain whether the victim would survive. In *Simmons* the Supreme Court found the use of a suggestive photographic array justified. In describing the justification, the Court said only that a serious felony had occurred, the perpetrators were still at large, circumstantial evidence pointed toward the defendant, and police had to act "swiftly to determine whether they were on the right track."

Although unnecessarily suggestive procedures are suspect, they do not per se exclude evidence about either the pretrial identification or an in-court identification by the witness. As long as the witness's identification was reliable under the totality of the circumstances, the pretrial identification is admissible regardless of the procedure's unnecessary suggestiveness.

The prosecution bears the burden of proving that an unnecessarily suggestive pretrial identification procedure nevertheless resulted in a reliable identification. Defense attacks on a witness's in-court identification are subject to a similar but more demanding standard. The in-court identification is admissible so long as the pretrial procedure did not create a "*very* substantial likelihood of *irreparable* misidentification."[77] The Court observed:

It is, first of all, apparent that the primary evil to be avoided is "a very substantial likelihood of irreparable misidentification." While the phrase was coined as a standard for determining whether an in-court identification would be admissible in the wake of a suggestive out-of-court identification, with the deletion of "irreparable" it serves equally well as a standard for the admissibility of testimony concerning the out-of-court identification itself.[78]

In *Manson v. Brathwaite*,[79] the Court explained that the *Stovall* Due Process right shields a limited "evidentiary interest" in reliable identifications that is protected through the adversary system.

What does the Court mean by the "totality of the circumstances"? In *Manson v. Brathwaite*, the Court adopted the factors first set forth in *Biggers* for evaluating pretrial identifications.[80] The same factors are relevant to the admissibility of both the out-of-court procedures and any later in-court identification. Although the factors outlined in *Biggers* and *Brathwaite* are not exhaustive, they provide a useful touchstone for considering most issues relating to the reliability of identifications.[81]

---

77 *Neil v. Biggers*, 409 U.S. 188, 197 (quoting *Simmons*) (emphasis added).

78 409 U.S. at 198 (citation omitted).

79 432 U.S. 98 (1977).

80 432 US at 114. See discussion, *supra*, at § 13-31(A).

81 *See, e.g.*, *United States v. Concepcion*, 983 F.2d 369, 377 (2d Cir. 1992) ("A good or poor rating with respect to any one of these factors will generally not be dispositive").

These factors relate not only to a motion to suppress the identifications, but also to the weight of the identification at trial. Pretrial suppression motions serve the ancillary purpose of providing useful discovery for defense counsel. When conducting a suppression hearing, counsel for both sides should be alert to the implications for trial of the evidence elicited at the hearing.

§ 13-32(B) ELEMENTS OF THE FOUNDATION

Identification procedures raise the following elements relating to the defendant's due process rights:

1. The defense must establish to the satisfaction of the court that law enforcement officers used "suggestive" procedures. This must include the assertion that the procedures gave rise to a substantial likelihood of misidentification.
2. The defense must prove that the suggestive procedure used was also unnecessary under the "totality of circumstances."
3. If the first two elements are met to the satisfaction of the court, then the prosecutor must demonstrate that even though the procedures were both suggestive and unnecessary, the identification is nevertheless reliable under the "totality of the circumstances" because of:
    a. The witness's opportunity to view the criminal at the time of the crime;
    b. The witness's degree of attention;
    c. The accuracy of any description of the criminal prior to the procedure;
    d. The level of certainty shown at the trial; and
    e. The time lapse between the crime and the confrontation.

An in-court identification will be suppressed only where the pretrial identification procedure created a *very* substantial likelihood of *irreparable* misidentification.

§ 13-32(C) SAMPLE FOUNDATION

The defendant, Winters, has been charged with armed robbery in Montgomery County, Texas. The police conducted a photo array procedure at which an eyewitness singled out the defendant as the robber. The defense has filed a pretrial motion to suppress any testimony about the photo array procedure and the identification of the defendant. The prosecutor decides to argue that the identification was nevertheless reliable based upon other circumstances. The witness is Officer Norris of the Woodlands Police Department who was in charge of the photo array procedure. The defense is the opponent.

O Officer Norris, before conducting this photographic lineup, WHAT connection did you have with this case?

W None. I wasn't at all involved in the investigation. The first I heard about it was that morning.

O WHAT happened that morning?

W The deputy chief's office phoned to say that they wanted me to arrange a photographic lineup which included the defendant.

O WHY does the Department use photographic arrays for identification?

W A lineup gives witnesses a chance to observe the suspect among a group of other people who are similar in appearance. It doesn't take much time to put together, and we have a large pool of photographic resources to pool together.

O WHY doesn't the Department use a live lineup? (2)

W Lineups involving actual people usually take too long to put together.

O Do lineups involving real persons provide a witness with a better chance for an accurate identification? (1)

W Probably, but I'm not aware of any hard proof of that.

O WHAT did you do after you were assigned to create a photographic array?

W The first thing I did was to read the reports about the crime. I wanted to make sure I knew the eyewitness's descriptions of the robber. After reading them, I knew that the witness had described the robber as a white male, approximately 5 feet 10 inches tall, maybe 160–170 pounds, brown hair with two scars on his left cheek.

O After you learned that, WHAT did you do?

W I looked through the binders containing booking photographs to pick out which photos would be best for the identification procedure.

O HOW did you choose the photographs which were used? (1)

W I tried to look for inmate photographs which were similar to the given description, but they were hard to find because of the two scars on the suspect's face.

O HOW well did they match the description? (1)

W The photographs I used were mostly within the general description of the suspect as best as I could manage. Of course, I couldn't find anyone else who had two scars on his left cheek.

O WHAT was the race of each person in the photographic array? (1)

W They all were black or Hispanic except for the suspect who was described as being fair-skinned. (1)

O WHY wasn't an effort made to make sure that all of the persons in these photographs were of the same skin color? (2)

W I didn't have that much time to put the photo array together, and my resources were somewhat limited at the time.

O HOW was the actual identification procedure conducted?

W The procedure is real simple. We lay out the photos on a table in one of the briefing rooms. The witness is brought in and sits alone at the table for a few minutes or however long he or she wants to take in order to examine each photograph. Then, the witness is asked to identify which photograph he believes is the suspect. The process is usually repeated a few times, involving different photographs.

O Was the process repeated in this instance? (1)

W No, because the witness had to leave quickly for some other matter.

O HOW long did the witness take in examining the photographs and identifying the defendant? (1)

W Probably only about 4 or 5 minutes.

O WHAT is the normal amount of time taken by an eyewitness during this procedure? (1)

W Anywhere from 8 to 15 minutes, I suppose.

O I show you what has been marked as exhibit number one for identification. WHAT is it?

W This was the card that was filled out by the witness. I watched her write the number of the photograph she identified as the robber and sign her name at the bottom. She also wrote that she was positive of her identification.

O Your Honor, I offer exhibit number one into evidence for purposes of this hearing.

J It will be received.

O Your Honor, the defense objects to any use of the out-of-court identification procedure used in this case. And the defense would also reassert its motion that the out-of-court identification procedure used to identify the defendant as the robber be suppressed in its entirety based upon the foregoing testimony. The procedure used was very suggestive your Honor, probably leading to a misidentification of my client, and the police could have used other means to ensure a proper identification. They simply did not take the time to do so. (1), (2)

J Your objection is so noted, as well as your motion to suppress. Does the State have any answer to this objection?

P Yes, your Honor. The State would argue that the procedure used was not suggestive, nor unnecessarily suggestive simply because it may not have been a perfect procedure. In the alternative, the State would argue that even if the procedure in question was suggestive, the eyewitness's identification of the defendant is still reliable based upon several factors. In support of this argument, the State would like to call Ms. Sinclair, the eyewitness, to the stand.

J Very well. Officer Norris may be excused if there are no further questions for Officer Norris at this time. Officer Norris, you are excused. Ms. Sinclair, you may take the stand. [*Ms. Sinclair is sworn in and states her identity for the record.*]

P Ms. Sinclair, HOW long after the robbery occurred did you participate in identifying the suspect in a photographic lineup? (3e)

W About one week.

P WHY were you able to pick out the defendant so quickly from all of the photographs presented to you by the police? (3c), (3d)

W I have a very good memory of what the robber looked like, so it was easy to pick out his picture. He has a very distinct face.

P WHY do you retain such an excellent memory of the robber's face? (3d)

W Because during the entire robbery, which lasted for about 10 to 15 minutes, the robber stood immediately in front of my counter about a foot-and-a-half away from me.

P Did you have time to view his face? (3a), (3b)

W Yes, I made a point out of staring at his face so that I could identify him later on if he was caught.

P HOW certain are you that you have properly identified the defendant as the robber, either out-of-court or in-court? (3d)

W I am very confident that the defendant was the robber. As I told the police, he has a very distinct face, and I have a very clear memory as to what he looked like.

P Thank you, Ms. Sinclair, I have no further questions. Your Honor, Ms. Sinclair's testimony makes it abundantly clear that her identification of the defendant as the robber was in no way tainted by any suggestive identification procedure. She is very sure of herself, and her ability to testify as to the identity of the robber should not be suppressed whether it was out-of-court or in-court.

J Based upon the testimony just given and the totality of the circumstances surrounding Ms. Sinclair's out-of-court identification of the defendant, the photographic array procedure used, will not be suppressed from the record.

§ 13-33 EYEWITNESS IDENTIFICATION—THE SIXTH AMENDMENT RIGHT TO COUNSEL

§ 13-33(A) THE DOCTRINE

The Sixth Amendment provides the criminal defendant with a right to representation by counsel. The right extends beyond the confines of the criminal trial itself. In *United States v. Wade*,[82] the Supreme Court provided that the right to counsel applies to the "critical stages" of the prosecution, including pretrial identifications procedures, the results of which "might well settle the accused's fate and reduce the trial itself to a mere formality."[83]

Counsel can play two roles at an identification procedure. First, defense counsel can prevent prejudicial identification procedures by pointing them out to police or objecting to their use. This normally motivates the police to alter procedures in order to avoid impeachment or suppression at the trial stage. Second, counsel can serve as the defendant's eyes and ears at the lineup, observing how the lineup is conducted for purposes of reconstructing and challenging the procedures later at trial.

It should be remembered that, even if the lineup procedures meet constitutional requirements and thereby escape suppression, they are nevertheless subject to impeachment later at trial. Insights gained by observing lineups (and the like) might provide a fertile basis for cross-examination or other impeaching attacks.

Counsel should, however, be sensitive to the risk that his or her presence at the identification procedure could result in counsel becoming a witness in the case, and thus having to withdraw as attorney of record.

The Sixth Amendment right to counsel does not extend to all pretrial identification procedures. Rather, the right is hedged by three significant limitations.

First, the right to counsel is limited to those identification procedures that occur after the formal commencement of adversary criminal proceedings. Usually the issuance of an indictment, information, or complaint marks formal commencement, but the procedural rules vary from jurisdiction to jurisdiction. In Texas, exactly when a defendant's Sixth Amendment right begins depends largely upon a case-by-case analysis of when the "adjudicatory process" has been initiated.[84]

---

[82] 388 U.S. 218 (1967).

[83] 388 U.S. at 224.

[84] While the cases have been seemingly inconsistent, formal adjudicatory procedures can begin at an art. 15.17 hearing, after a formal indictment, or other formal hearings before a magistrate. *See Holloway v. State*, 780 S.W.2d 787 (Tex. Crim. App. 1989) (en banc); *Nehman v. State*, 721 S.W.2d 319 (Tex. Crim. App. 1986); *Higginbotham v. State*, 769 S.W.2d 265, 269 (Tex. App.—Houston [14th Dist.] 1989), *reversed on other grounds*, 807 S.W.2d 732 (Tex. Crim. App. 1991) (plurality opinion).

Article 1, section 10 of the Texas Constitution also applies to lineups and identification procedures which are consistent with the Sixth Amendment without providing a broader protection.[85]

Second, the Sixth Amendment right to counsel applies only to those procedures that involve the physical (corporeal) presence of the defendant. Physical confrontations may occur at a "live" lineup or where the defendant is personally brought before the witness for identification (a so-called "showup" procedure). The physical presence requirement demands a literal face-to-face encounter between the defendant and the witness.

Of course, witnesses are often asked to identify suspects from an array of various photographs. But neither the presentation of the photos to the witness nor any later questioning concerning the witness's identification is subject to the right to counsel. Similarly, the videotape of a lineup may be shown to other witnesses outside the presence of defense counsel because the viewing does not involve the actual (corporeal) presence of the defendant.[86]

The right to counsel is not applicable to inadvertent or accidental encounters between the defendant and a witness. For example, a witness waiting in a courtroom hallway who observes the shackled defendant entering the courtroom is not involved in an identification "procedure." In short, the deterrent effect of the exclusionary rule is reserved for deliberately staged identification procedures.

It also appears that the right to counsel endures only for the duration of the face-to-face contact. After a witness has viewed a lineup in the presence of defendant's counsel, the witness may be interviewed by law enforcement authorities outside the gaze or hearing of counsel.[87]

Third, the right to counsel is "charge-specific." That is, the right applies only to those crimes that have been formally charged. For example, assume that a defendant charged with armed robbery is identified at a lineup in violation of his right to counsel. Assume also that two of the witnesses were involved in the pending robbery but one other witness saw the defendant steal a car. After

---

[85] *See Foster v. State*, 787 S.W.2d 385, 386 (Tex. Crim. App. 1990).

[86] *See United States v. Tolliver*, 569 F.2d 724, 728 (2d Cir. 1978) ("We now join our sister circuits in holding that the actual identification from a line-up (as well as a photographic spread), if made outside the presence of the defendant, is constitutionally valid, since the actual confrontation is the only 'critical stage' requiring the presence of counsel").

[87] For example, in *Sams v. Walker*, 18 F.3d 167, 170 (2d Cir. 1994), the petitioner in a federal habeas action unsuccessfully argued that his attorney had a right to be present when the witness "declared" whether she could identify anyone in the lineup. Nor was it constitutional error that the prosecution failed to record the witness's statements on an audiotape. The Second Circuit had "suggested" in an earlier decision that where counsel is precluded from listening to the witness's "declaration" of identification, a recording should be made. The court clarified that its "supervisory recommendation" had been directed only at federal prosecutors and was not a "constitutional mandate."

the lineup the defendant is also charged with the car theft. Although the prosecution cannot introduce any evidence of the lineup as to the armed robbery charge, it can offer evidence about the third witness's lineup identification on the car theft charge.

The penalty for violating the right to counsel is suppression of the evidence. The law distinguishes, however, between the suppression of the pretrial (out-of-court) identification itself and suppression of a later in-court identification by the same witness involved in the tainted procedure. The out-of-court procedure is completely suppressed; moreover, the state is not even entitled to demonstrate that the out-of-court identification "had an independent source."[88] The exclusionary rule also extends to an in-court identification of the defendant by the witnesses involved in the illegal identification procedure, unless the in-court identification is based on sources independent of the tainted identification. The prosecution bears the burden of convincing the trial judge by clear and convincing evidence that the in-court identification is based on sources independent of the tainted lineup.

Among the factors for the trial court to consider in deciding whether there is an independent basis for admitting the in-court identification are the following:

> [F]or example, the prior opportunity to observe the alleged criminal act, the existence of any discrepancy between any pre-lineup description and the defendant's actual description, any identification prior to lineup of another person, the identification by picture of the defendant prior to the lineup, failure to identify the defendant on a prior occasion, and the lapse of time between the alleged act and the lineup identification.[89]

These are the same factors the courts grapple with in deciding whether an unnecessarily suggestive identification procedure nevertheless resulted in a reliable identification. See § 13-31, *supra*.

The initial burden of proof lies with the defendant. The defendant merely needs to demonstrate to the court that there was no counsel present during the procedure in question. The state can either make a contrary factual argument or can argue that the defendant waived his rights to counsel.

If the determination is made that there was no counsel present during the procedure and that there was not a knowing and voluntary waiver by the defendant, then the entire out-of-court procedure is suppressed for the purposes of identification. The state then has the burden to show that there was some "independent" source to provide a basis for the witness's identifying the defendant. If the independent source argument does not persuade the court, the

---

[88] *Gilbert v. California*, 388 U.S. 263, 273 (1967).

[89] *Wade*, 388 U.S. at 241.

witness also cannot make an in-court identification of the defendant, as discussed *supra*.

Unlike a due process violation, the Sixth Amendment right to counsel can be waived by the defendant.[90] A valid waiver must be one that is made knowingly, intelligently, and voluntarily. It must be shown that the defendant understood that he had the right to an attorney at the lineup (or other identification procedure), and that one would have been appointed to represent him at no cost if he was indigent. A *Miranda* warning is not independently necessary at the time of the procedure because the lineup procedures, absent custodial interrogation, do not implicate the *Miranda* doctrine or the Fifth Amendment right against self-incrimination.[91] The burden is on the prosecution to show a valid waiver by a preponderance of the evidence.

§ 13-33(B) Elements of the Foundation

The following elements shape the contours of the Sixth Amendment right to counsel:

1. The prosecution must have formally commenced adversary criminal proceedings against the defendant at the time of identification procedure.
    a. The right to counsel attaches only to the pending charges.
2. The right extends only to "corporeal" (face-to-face) identifications such as lineups.
    a. It is not applicable to photographic identifications.
    b. The confrontation must have been "staged" for purposes of identification; that is, "accidental" or inadvertent physical confrontations between the witness and the defendant are not subject to suppression.
3. The defendant can knowingly and voluntarily waive the right to counsel.
4. Sixth Amendment violations result in the suppression of the tainted pretrial identification.
    a. The witness involved in the tainted procedure can make an in-court identification, provided the prosecution establishes an

[90] *Martinez v. State*, 437 S.W.2d 842, 846 (Tex. Crim. App. 1969); *see also Barnhill v. State*, 657 S.W.2d 131, 132 (Tex. Crim. App. 1983).

[91] Even so, the Supreme Court has found that waiver of rights as they are outlined in a *Miranda* warning can also constitute a valid waiver of Sixth Amendment right to counsel. *Patterson v. Illinois*, 487 U.S. 285 (1988).

independent basis for the identification by clear and convincing evidence.

§ 13-33(C) SAMPLE FOUNDATION

The defendant, Mr. Byron, was arrested on a warrant for rape. The day after the arrest, the police placed Byron in a lineup viewed by the rape victim. It is undisputed that Byron did not have counsel at the lineup, which occurred after the formal commencement of adversary proceedings. The witness is Officer Sheehan, who was in charge of the lineup. The prosecutor is the proponent. She is attempting to establish that Byron waived his right to counsel at the lineup.

P WHERE were you early in the afternoon of October 16th of this year?

W I was at headquarters on Drum Street.

P WHAT were you doing then? (2)

W I was arranging a lineup in connection with a rape that occurred the day before.

P WHO was going to be in this lineup? (2)

W The defendant and four other guys who matched the description of the rapist.

P WHEN did you see the defendant that afternoon? (2)

W Actually, I first met with him late that morning.

P WHY did you meet with him then? (3)

W I knew we had scheduled the lineup, and I wanted to know whether he wanted an attorney present.

P WHAT, if anything, did you tell him about his right to have an attorney at the lineup? (3)

W I said that he had a right to have one there. I told him that if he couldn't afford an attorney, we'd get one for him. I told him that the attorney could make sure that the lineup was fair and everything was on the up and up.

P WHAT else did you say to him? (3)

W I asked him directly whether he understood that he had the right to have an attorney there.

P HOW did the defendant respond? (3)

W He said he realized that.

P At the time, WHAT was the defendant's demeanor? (3)

W He seemed calm enough. He acted as if he knew what was going on.

P WHAT else did you say? (3)

W Finally, I asked him to tell me whether he wanted an attorney.

P WHAT did he say? (3)

W He said, "No." He insisted he was innocent. To use his words, he didn't need "any damn lawyer" to protect his rights.

P Was the lineup later conducted?

W Yes, it was. The victim positively identified Mr. Byron as the man who sexually assaulted her.

P At any point during the course of the lineup did Mr. Byron request an attorney? (3)

W No, he never said anything about a lawyer in my presence.

APPENDIX A
TEXAS RULES OF EVIDENCE

ARTICLE I. GENERAL PROVISIONS

RULE 101. TITLE AND SCOPE

(a) Title. These rules shall be known and cited as the Texas Rules of Evidence.

(b) Scope. Except as otherwise provided by statute, these rules govern civil and criminal proceedings (including examining trials before magistrates) in all courts of Texas, except small claims courts.

(c) Hierarchical Governance in Criminal Proceedings. Hierarchical governance shall be in the following order: the Constitution of the United States, those federal statutes that control states under the supremacy clause, the Constitution of Texas, the Code of Criminal Procedure and the Penal Code, civil statutes, these rules, and the common law. Where possible, inconsistency is to be removed by reasonable construction.

(d) Special Rules of Applicability in Criminal Proceedings.

(1) *Rules not applicable in certain proceedings.* These rules, except with respect to privileges, do not apply in the following situations:

(A) the determination of questions of fact preliminary to admissibility of evidence when the issue is to be determined by the court under Rule 104;

(B) proceedings before grand juries;

(C) proceedings in an application for habeas corpus in extradition, rendition, or interstate detainer;

(D) a hearing under Code of Criminal Procedure article 46.02, by the court out of the presence of a jury, to determine whether there is sufficient evidence of incompetency to require a jury determination of the question of incompetency;

(E) proceedings regarding bail except hearings to deny, revoke or increase bail;

(F) a hearing on justification for pretrial detention not involving bail;

(G) proceedings for the issuance of a search or arrest warrant; or

(H) proceedings in a direct contempt determination.

(2) *Applicability of privileges.* These rules with respect to privileges apply at all stages of all actions, cases, and proceedings.

(3) *Military justice hearings.* Evidence in hearings under the Texas Code of Military Justice, TEX. GOV'T CODE § 432.001–432.195, shall be governed by that Code.

Notes and Comments

Comment to 1998 change: "Criminal proceedings" rather than "criminal cases" is used since that was the terminology used in the prior Rules of Criminal Evidence. In subpart (b), the reference to "trials before magistrates" comes from prior Criminal Rule 1101(a). In the prior Criminal Rules, both Rule 101 and Rule 1101 dealt with the same thing—the applicability of the rules. Thus, Rules 101(c) and (d) have been written to incorporate the provisions of former Criminal Rule 1101 and that rule is omitted.

RULE 102. PURPOSE AND CONSTRUCTION

These rules shall be construed to secure fairness in administration, elimination of unjustifiable expense and delay, and promotion of growth and development of the law of evidence to the end that the truth may be ascertained and proceedings justly determined.

RULE 103. RULINGS ON EVIDENCE

(a) **Effect of Erroneous Ruling.** Error may not be predicated upon a ruling which admits or excludes evidence unless a substantial right of the party is affected, and

(1) *Objection.* In case the ruling is one admitting evidence, a timely objection or motion to strike appears of record, stating the specific ground of objection, if the specific ground was not apparent from the context. When the court hears objections to offered evidence out of the presence of the jury and rules that such evidence be admitted, such objections shall be deemed to apply to such evidence when it is admitted before the jury without the necessity of repeating those objections.

(2) *Offer of proof.* In case the ruling is one excluding evidence, the substance of the evidence was made known to the court by offer, or was apparent from the context within which questions were asked.

(b) **Record of Offer and Ruling.** The offering party shall, as soon as practicable, but before the court's charge is read to the jury, be allowed to make, in the absence of the jury, its offer of proof. The court may add any other or further statement which shows the character of the evidence, the form in which it was offered, the objection made, and the ruling thereon. The court may, or at the request of a party shall, direct the making of an offer in question and answer form.

(c) **Hearing of Jury.** In jury cases, proceedings shall be conducted, to the extent practicable, so as to prevent inadmissible evidence from being suggested to the jury by any means, such as making statements or offers of proof or asking questions in the hearing of the jury.

(d) **Fundamental Error in Criminal Cases.** In a criminal case, nothing in these rules precludes taking notice of fundamental errors affecting substantial rights although they were not brought to the attention of the court.

Notes and Comments

Comment to 1998 change: The exception to the requirement of an offer of proof for matters that were apparent from the context within which questions were asked, found in paragraph (a)(2), is now applicable to civil as well as criminal cases.

RULE 104. PRELIMINARY QUESTIONS

(a) **Questions of Admissibility Generally.** Preliminary questions concerning the qualification of a person to be a witness, the existence of a privilege, or the admissibility of evidence shall be determined by the court, subject to the provisions of subdivision (b). In making its determination the court is not bound by the rules of evidence except those with respect to privileges.

(b) **Relevancy Conditioned on Fact.** When the relevancy of evidence depends upon the fulfillment of a condition of fact, the court shall admit it upon, or subject to, the introduction of evidence sufficient to support a finding of the fulfillment of the condition.

(c) **Hearing of Jury.** In a criminal case, a hearing on the admissibility of a confession shall be conducted out of the hearing of the jury. All other civil or criminal hearings on preliminary matters shall be conducted out of the hearing of the jury when the interests of justice so require or in a criminal case when an accused is a witness and so requests.

(d) **Testimony by Accused Out of the Hearing of the Jury.** The accused in a criminal case does not, by testifying upon a preliminary matter out of the hearing of the jury, become subject to cross-examination as to other issues in the case.

(e) **Weight and Credibility.** This rule does not limit the right of a party to introduce before the jury evidence relevant to weight or credibility.

RULE 105. LIMITED ADMISSIBILITY

(a) **Limiting Instruction.** When evidence which is admissible as to one party or for one purpose but not admissible as to another party or for another purpose is admitted, the court, upon request, shall restrict the evidence to its proper scope and instruct the jury accordingly; but, in the absence of such request the court's action in admitting such evidence without limitation shall not be a ground for complaint on appeal.

(b) **Offering Evidence for Limited Purpose.** When evidence referred to in paragraph (a) is excluded, such exclusion shall not be a ground for complaint on appeal unless the proponent expressly offers the evidence for its limited, admissible purpose or limits its offer to the party against whom it is admissible.

RULE 106. REMAINDER OF OR RELATED WRITINGS OR RECORDED STATEMENTS

When a writing or recorded statement or part thereof is introduced by a party, an adverse party may at that time introduce any other part or any other writing or recorded statement which ought in fairness to be considered contemporaneously with it. "Writing or recorded statement" includes depositions.

RULE 107. RULE OF OPTIONAL COMPLETENESS

When part of an act, declaration, conversation, writing or recorded statement is given in evidence by one party, the whole on the same subject may be inquired into by the other, and any other act, declaration, writing or recorded statement which is necessary to make it fully understood or to explain the same may also be given in evidence, as when a letter is read, all letters on the same subject between the same parties may be given. "Writing or recorded statement" includes depositions.

Notes and Comments

Comment to 1998 change: This rule is the former Criminal Rule 107 except that the example regarding "when a letter is read" has been relocated in the rule so as to more accurately indicate the provision it explains. While this rule appeared only in the prior criminal rules, it is made applicable to civil cases because it accurately reflects the common law rule of optional completeness in civil cases.

ARTICLE II. JUDICIAL NOTICE

RULE 201. JUDICIAL NOTICE OF ADJUDICATIVE FACTS

(a) **Scope of Rule.** This rule governs only judicial notice of adjudicative facts.

(b) **Kinds of Facts.** A judicially noticed fact must be one not subject to reasonable dispute in that it is either (1) generally known within the territorial jurisdiction of the trial court or (2) capable of accurate and ready determination by resort to sources whose accuracy cannot reasonably be questioned.

(c) **When Discretionary.** A court may take judicial notice, whether requested or not.

(d) **When Mandatory.** A court shall take judicial notice if requested by a party and supplied with the necessary information.

(e) **Opportunity to Be Heard.** A party is entitled upon timely request to an opportunity to be heard as to the propriety of taking judicial notice and the tenor of the matter noticed. In the absence of prior notification, the request may be made after judicial notice has been taken.

(f) **Time of Taking Notice.** Judicial notice may be taken at any stage of the proceeding.

(g) **Instructing Jury.** In civil cases, the court shall instruct the jury to accept as conclusive any fact judicially noticed. In criminal cases, the court shall instruct the jury that it may, but is not required to, accept as conclusive any fact judicially noticed.

RULE 202. DETERMINATION OF LAW OF OTHER STATES

A court upon its own motion may, or upon the motion of a party shall, take judicial notice of the constitutions, public statutes, rules, regulations, ordinances, court decisions, and common law of every other state, territory, or jurisdiction of the United States. A party requesting that judicial notice be taken of such matter shall furnish the court sufficient information to enable it properly to comply with the request, and shall give all parties such notice, if any, as the court may deem necessary, to enable all parties fairly to prepare to meet the request. A party is entitled upon timely request to an opportunity to be heard as to the propriety of taking judicial notice and the tenor of the matter noticed. In the absence of prior notification, the request may be made after judicial notice has been taken. Judicial notice of such matters may be taken at any stage of the proceeding. The court's determination shall be subject to review as a ruling on a question of law.

RULE 203. DETERMINATION OF THE LAWS OF FOREIGN COUNTRIES

A party who intends to raise an issue concerning the law of a foreign country shall give notice in the pleadings or other reasonable written notice, and at least 30 days prior to the date of trial such party shall furnish all parties copies of any written materials or sources that the party intends to use as proof of the foreign law. If the materials or sources were originally written in a language other than English, the party intending to rely upon them shall furnish all parties both a copy of the foreign language text and an English translation. The court, in determining the law of a foreign nation, may consider any material or source, whether or not submitted by a party or admissible under the rules of evidence, including but not limited to affidavits, testimony, briefs, and treatises. If the court considers sources other than those submitted by a party, it shall give all parties notice and a reasonable opportunity to comment on the sources and to submit further materials for review by the court. The court, and not a jury, shall determine the laws of foreign countries. The court's determination shall be subject to review as a ruling on a question of law.

RULE 204. DETERMINATION OF TEXAS CITY AND COUNTY ORDINANCES, THE CONTENTS OF THE TEXAS REGISTER, AND THE RULES OF AGENCIES PUBLISHED IN THE ADMINISTRATIVE CODE

A court upon its own motion may, or upon the motion of a party shall, take judicial notice of the ordinances of municipalities and counties of Texas, of the contents of the Texas Register, and of the codified rules of the agencies published in the Administrative Code. Any party requesting that judicial notice be taken of such matter shall furnish the court sufficient information to enable it properly to comply with the request, and shall give all parties such notice, if any, as the court may deem necessary, to enable all parties fairly to prepare to meet the request. A party is entitled upon timely request to an opportunity to be heard as to the propriety of taking judicial notice and the tenor of the matter noticed. In the absence of prior notification, the request may be made after judicial notice has been taken. The court's determination shall be subject to review as a ruling on a question of law.

ARTICLE III. PRESUMPTIONS

[No rules adopted at this time.]

ARTICLE IV. RELEVANCY AND ITS LIMITS

RULE 401. DEFINITION OF "RELEVANT EVIDENCE"

"Relevant evidence" means evidence having any tendency to make the existence of any fact that is of consequence to the determination of the action more probable or less probable than it would be without the evidence.

RULE 402. RELEVANT EVIDENCE GENERALLY ADMISSIBLE; IRRELEVANT EVIDENCE INADMISSIBLE

All relevant evidence is admissible, except as otherwise provided by Constitution, by statute, by these rules, or by other rules prescribed pursuant to statutory authority. Evidence which is not relevant is inadmissible.

RULE 403. EXCLUSION OF RELEVANT EVIDENCE ON SPECIAL GROUNDS

Although relevant, evidence may be excluded if its probative value is substantially outweighed by the danger of unfair prejudice, confusion of the issues, or misleading the jury, or by considerations of undue delay, or needless presentation of cumulative evidence.

RULE 404. CHARACTER EVIDENCE NOT ADMISSIBLE TO PROVE CONDUCT; EXCEPTIONS; OTHER CRIMES

(a) Character Evidence Generally. Evidence of a person's character or character trait is not admissible for the purpose of proving action in conformity therewith on a particular occasion, except:

(1) *Character of accused.* Evidence of a pertinent character trait offered:

(A) by an accused in a criminal case, or by the prosecution to rebut the same, or

(B) by a party accused in a civil case of conduct involving moral turpitude, or by the accusing party to rebut the same;

(2) *Character of victim.* In a criminal case and subject to Rule 412, evidence of a pertinent character trait of the victim of the crime offered by an accused, or by the prosecution to rebut the same, or evidence of peaceable character of the victim offered by the prosecution in a homicide case to rebut evidence that the victim was the first aggressor; or in a civil case, evidence of character for violence of the alleged victim of assaultive conduct offered on the issue of self-defense by a party accused of the assaultive conduct, or evidence of peaceable character to rebut the same;

(3) *Character of witness.* Evidence of the character of a witness, as provided in rules 607, 608 and 609.

(b) **Other Crimes, Wrongs or Acts.** Evidence of other crimes, wrongs or acts is not admissible to prove the character of a person in order to show action in conformity therewith. It may, however, be admissible for other purposes, such as proof of motive, opportunity, intent, preparation, plan, knowledge, identity, or absence of mistake or accident, provided that upon timely request by the accused in a criminal case, reasonable notice is given in advance of trial of intent to introduce in the State's case-in-chief such evidence other than that arising in the same transaction.

RULE 405. METHODS OF PROVIDING CHARACTER

(a) **Reputation or Opinion.** In all cases in which evidence of a person's character or character trait is admissible, proof may be made by testimony as to reputation or by testimony in the form of an opinion. In a criminal case, to be qualified to testify at the guilt stage of trial concerning the character or character trait of an accused, a witness must have been familiar with the reputation, or with the underlying facts or information upon which the opinion is based, prior to the day of the offense. In all cases where testimony is admitted under this rule, on cross-examination inquiry is allowable into relevant specific instances of conduct.

(b) **Specific Instances of Conduct.** In cases in which a person's character or character trait is an essential element of a charge, claim or defense, proof may also be made of specific instances of that person's conduct.

RULE 406. HABIT; ROUTINE PRACTICE

Evidence of the habit of a person or of the routine practice of an organization, whether corroborated or not and regardless of the presence of eyewitnesses, is relevant to prove that the conduct of the person or organization on a particular occasion was in conformity with the habit or routine practice.

RULE 407. SUBSEQUENT REMEDIAL MEASURES; NOTIFICATION OF DEFECT

(a) **Subsequent Remedial Measures.** When, after an injury or harm allegedly caused by an event, measures are taken that, if taken previously, would have made the injury or harm less likely to occur, evidence of the subsequent remedial measures is not admissible to prove negligence, culpable conduct, a defect in a product, a defect in a product's design, or a need for a warning or instruction. This rule does not require the exclusion of evidence of subsequent remedial measures when offered for another purpose, such as proving ownership, control, or feasibility of precautionary measures, if controverted, or impeachment.

(b) **Notification of Defect.** A written notification by a manufacturer of any defect in a product produced by such manufacturer to purchasers thereof is admissible against the manufacturer on the issue of existence of the defect to the extent that it is relevant.

RULE 408. COMPROMISE AND OFFERS TO COMPROMISE

Evidence of (1) furnishing or offering or promising to furnish or (2) accepting or offering or promising to accept, a valuable consideration in compromising or attempting to compromise a claim which was disputed as to either validity or amount is not admissible to prove liability for or invalidity of the claim or its amount. Evidence of conduct or statements made in compromise negotiations is likewise not admissible. This rule does not require the exclusion of any evidence otherwise discoverable merely because it is presented in the course of compromise negotiations. This rule also does not require exclusion when the evidence is offered for another purpose, such as proving bias or prejudice or interest of a witness or a party, negativing a contention of undue delay, or proving an effort to obstruct a criminal investigation or prosecution.

RULE 409. PAYMENT OF MEDICAL AND SIMILAR EXPENSES

Evidence of furnishing or offering or promising to pay medical, hospital, or similar expenses occasioned by an injury is not admissible to prove liability for the injury.

RULE 410. INADMISSIBILITY OF PLEAS, PLEA DISCUSSIONS AND RELATED STATEMENTS

Except as otherwise provided in this rule, evidence of the following is not admissible against the defendant who made the plea or was a participant in the plea discussions:

(1) a plea of guilty that was later withdrawn;

(2) in civil cases, a plea of *nolo contendere*, and in criminal cases, a plea of *nolo contendere* that was later withdrawn;

(3) any statement made in the course of any proceedings under Rule 11 of the Federal Rules of Criminal Procedure or comparable state procedure regarding, in a civil case, either a plea of guilty that was later withdrawn or a plea of *nolo contendere*, or in a criminal case, either a plea of guilty that was later withdrawn or a plea of *nolo contendere* that was later withdrawn; or

(4) any statement made in the course of plea discussions with an attorney for the prosecuting authority, in a civil case, that do not result in a plea of guilty or that result in a plea of guilty later withdrawn, or in a criminal case, that do not result in a plea of guilty or a plea of *nolo contendere* or that results in a plea, later withdrawn, of guilty or *nolo contendere*.

However, such a statement is admissible in any proceeding wherein another statement made in the course of the same plea or plea discussions has been introduced and the statement ought in fairness be considered contemporaneously with it.

RULE 411. LIABILITY INSURANCE

Evidence that a person was or was not insured against liability is not admissible upon the issue whether the person acted negligently or otherwise wrongfully. This rule does not require the exclusion of evidence of insurance against liability when offered for another issue, such as proof of agency, ownership, or control, if disputed, or bias or prejudice of a witness.

RULE 412. EVIDENCE OF PREVIOUS SEXUAL CONDUCT IN CRIMINAL CASES

(a) **Reputation or Opinion Evidence.** In a prosecution for sexual assault or aggravated sexual assault, or attempt to commit sexual assault or aggravated sexual assault, reputation or opinion evidence of the past sexual behavior of an alleged victim of such crime is not admissible.

(b) **Evidence of Specific Instances.** In a prosecution for sexual assault or aggravated sexual assault, or attempt to commit sexual assault or aggravated sexual assault, evidence of specific instances of an alleged victim's past sexual behavior is also not admissible, unless:

(1) such evidence is admitted in accordance with paragraphs (c) and (d) of this rule;

(2) it is evidence:

(A) that is necessary to rebut or explain scientific or medical evidence offered by the State;

(B) of past sexual behavior with the accused and is offered by the accused upon the issue of whether the alleged victim consented to the sexual behavior which is the basis of the offense charged;

(C) that relates to the motive or bias of the alleged victim;

(D) is admissible under Rule 609; or

(E) that is constitutionally required to be admitted; and

(3) its probative value outweighs the danger of unfair prejudice.

(c) **Procedure for Offering Evidence.** If the defendant proposes to introduce any documentary evidence or to ask any question, either by direct examination or cross-examination of any witness, concerning specific instances of the alleged victim's past sexual behavior, the defendant must inform the court out of the hearing of the jury prior to introducing any such evidence or asking any such question. After this notice, the court shall conduct an in camera hearing, recorded by the court reporter, to determine whether the proposed evidence is admissible under paragraph (b) of this rule. The court shall determine what evidence is admissible and shall accordingly limit the questioning. The defendant shall not go outside these limits or refer to any evidence ruled inadmissible in camera without prior approval of the court without the presence of the jury.

(d) **Record Sealed.** The court shall seal the record of the in camera hearing required in paragraph (c) of this rule for delivery to the appellate court in the event of an appeal.

(e) **Sexual Conduct of Child as Defense.** This rule does not limit the right of the accused to produce evidence of promiscuous sexual conduct of a child 14 years old or older as a defense to sexual assault, aggravated sexual assault, indecency with a child or an attempt to commit any of the foregoing crimes. If such evidence is admitted, the court shall instruct the jury as to the purpose of the evidence and as to its limited use.

ARTICLE V. PRIVILEGES

RULE 501. PRIVILEGES RECOGNIZED ONLY AS PROVIDED

Except as otherwise provided by Constitution, by statute, by these rules, or by other rules prescribed pursuant to statutory authority, no person has a privilege to:

(1) refuse to be a witness;

(2) refuse to disclose any matter;

(3) refuse to produce any object or writing; or

(4) prevent another from being a witness or disclosing any matter or producing any object or writing.

RULE 502. REQUIRED REPORTS PRIVILEGED BY STATUTE

A person, corporation, association, or other organization or entity, either public or private, making a return or report required by law to be made has a privilege to refuse to disclose and to prevent any other person from disclosing the return or report, if the law requiring it to be made so provides. A public officer or agency to whom a return or report is required by law to be made has a privilege to refuse to disclose the return or report if the law requiring it to be made so provides. No privilege exists under this rule in actions involving perjury, false statements, fraud in the return or report, or other failure to comply with the law in question.

RULE 503. LAWYER-CLIENT PRIVILEGE

(a) Definitions. As used in this rule:

(1) A "client" is a person, public officer, or corporation, association, or other organization or entity, either public or private, who is rendered professional legal services by a lawyer, or who consults a lawyer with a view to obtaining professional legal services from that lawyer.

(2) A "representative of the client" is:

(A) a person having authority to obtain professional legal services, or to act on advice thereby rendered, on behalf of the client, or

(B) any other person who, for the purpose of effectuating legal representation for the client, makes or receives a confidential communication while acting in the scope of employment for the client.

(3) A "lawyer" is a person authorized, or reasonably believed by the client to be authorized, to engage in the practice of law in any state or nation.

(4) A "representative of the lawyer" is:

(A) one employed by the lawyer to assist the lawyer in the rendition of professional legal services; or

(B) an accountant who is reasonably necessary for the lawyer's rendition of professional legal services.

(5) A communication is "confidential" if not intended to be disclosed to third persons other than those to whom disclosure is made in furtherance of the rendition of professional legal services to the client or those reasonably necessary for the transmission of the communication.

(b) Rules of Privilege.

(1) *General rule of privilege.* A client has a privilege to refuse to disclose and to prevent any other person from disclosing confidential communications made for the purpose of facilitating the rendition of professional legal services to the client:

(A) between the client or a representative of the client and the client's lawyer or a representative of the lawyer;

(B) between the lawyer and the lawyer's representative;

(C) by the client or a representative of the client, or the client's lawyer or a representative of the lawyer, to a lawyer or a representative of a lawyer representing another party in a pending action and concerning a matter of common interest therein;

(D) between representatives of the client or between the client and a representative of the client; or

(E) among lawyers and their representatives representing the same client.

(2) *Special rule of privilege in criminal cases.* In criminal cases, a client has a privilege to prevent the lawyer or lawyer's representative from disclosing any other fact which came to the knowledge of the lawyer or the lawyer's representative by reason of the attorney-client relationship.

(c) Who May Claim the Privilege. The privilege may be claimed by the client, the client's guardian or conservator, the personal representative of a deceased client, or the successor, trustee, or similar representative of a corporation, association, or other organization, whether or not in existence. The person who was the lawyer or the lawyer's representative at the time of the communication is presumed to have authority to claim the privilege but only on behalf of the client.

(d) Exceptions. There is no privilege under this rule:

(1) *Furtherance of crime or fraud.* If the services of the lawyer were sought or obtained to enable or aid anyone to commit or plan to commit what the client knew or reasonably should have known to be a crime or fraud;

(2) *Claimants through same deceased client.* As to a communication relevant to an issue between parties who claim through the same deceased client, regardless of whether the claims are by testate or intestate succession or by *inter vivos* transactions;

(3) *Breach of duty by a lawyer or client.* As to a communication relevant to an issue of breach of duty by a lawyer to the client or by a client to the lawyer;

(4) *Document attested by a lawyer.* As to a communication relevant to an issue concerning an attested document to which the lawyer is an attesting witness; or

(5) *Joint clients.* As to a communication relevant to a matter of common interest between or among two or more clients if the communication was made by any of them to a lawyer retained or consulted in common, when offered in an action between or among any of the clients.

Notes and Comments

Comment to 1998 change: The addition of subsection (a)(2)(B) adopts a subject matter test for the privilege of an entity, in place of the control group test previously used. See *National Tank Co. v. Brotherton*, 851 S.W.2d 193, 197–198 (Tex. 1993).

RULE 504. HUSBAND-WIFE PRIVILEGES

(a) Confidential Communication Privilege.

(1) *Definition.* A communication is confidential if it is made privately by any person to the person's spouse and it is not intended for disclosure to any other person.

(2) *Rule of privilege.* A person, whether or not a party, or the guardian or representative of an incompetent or deceased person, has a privilege during marriage and afterwards to refuse to disclose and to prevent another from disclosing a confidential communication made to the person's spouse while they were married.

(3) *Who may claim the privilege.* The confidential communication privilege may be claimed by the person or the person's guardian or representative, or by the spouse on the person's behalf. The authority of the spouse to do so is presumed.

(4) *Exceptions.* There is no confidential communication privilege:

(A) *Furtherance of crime or fraud.* If the communication was made, in whole or in part, to enable or aid anyone to commit or plan to commit a crime or fraud.

(B) *Proceeding between spouses in civil cases.* In (A) a proceeding brought by or on behalf of one spouse against the other spouse, or (B) a proceeding between a surviving spouse and a person who claims through the deceased spouse, regardless of whether the claim is by testate or intestate succession or by *inter vivos* transaction.

(C) *Crime against spouse or minor child.* In a proceeding in which the party is accused of conduct which, if proved, is a crime against the person of the spouse, any minor child, or any member of the household of either spouse.

(D) *Commitment or similar proceeding.* In a proceeding to commit either spouse or otherwise to place that person or that person's property, or both, under the control of another because of an alleged mental or physical condition.

(E) *Proceeding to establish competence.* In a proceeding brought by or on behalf of either spouse to establish competence.

(b) Privilege Not to Testify in Criminal Case.

(1) *Rule of privilege.* In a criminal case, the spouse of the accused has a privilege not to be called as a witness for the state. This rule does not prohibit the spouse from testifying voluntarily for the state, even over objection by the accused. A spouse who testifies on behalf of an accused is subject to cross-examination as provided in rule 611(b).

(2) *Failure to call as witness.* Failure by an accused to call the accused's spouse as a witness, where other evidence indicates that the spouse could testify to relevant matters, is a proper subject of comment by counsel.

(3) *Who may claim the privilege.* The privilege not to testify may be claimed by the person or the person's guardian or representative but not by that person's spouse.

(4) *Exceptions.* The privilege of a person's spouse not to be called as a witness for the state does not apply:

(A) *Certain criminal proceedings.* In any proceeding in which the person is charged with a crime against the person's spouse, a member of the household of either spouse, or any minor.

(B) *Matters occurring prior to marriage.* As to matters occurring prior to the marriage.

Notes and Comments

Comment to 1998 change: The rule eliminates the spousal testimonial privilege for prosecutions in which the testifying spouse is the alleged victim of a crime by the accused. This is intended to be consistent with Code of Criminal Procedure article 38.10, effective September 1, 1995.

RULE 505. COMMUNICATIONS TO MEMBERS OF THE CLERGY

(a) Definitions. As used in this rule:

(1) A "member of the clergy" is a minister, priest, rabbi, accredited Christian Science Practitioner, or other similar functionary of a religious organization or an individual reasonably believed so to be by the person consulting with such individual.

(2) A communication is "confidential" if made privately and not intended for further disclosure except to other persons present in furtherance of the purpose of the communication.

(b) General Rule of Privilege. A person has a privilege to refuse to disclose and to prevent another from disclosing a confidential communication by the person to a member of the clergy in the member's professional character as spiritual adviser.

(c) Who May Claim the Privilege. The privilege may be claimed by the person, by the person's guardian or conservator, or by the personal representative of the person if the person is deceased. The member of the clergy to whom the communication was made is presumed to have authority to claim the privilege but only on behalf of the communicant.

RULE 506. POLITICAL VOTE

Every person has a privilege to refuse to disclose the tenor of the person's vote at a political election conducted by secret ballot unless the vote was cast illegally.

RULE 507. TRADE SECRETS

A person has a privilege, which may be claimed by the person or the person's agent or employee, to refuse to disclose and to prevent other persons from disclosing a trade secret owned by the person, if the allowance of the privilege will not tend to conceal fraud or otherwise work injustice. When disclosure is directed, the judge shall take such protective measure as the interests of the holder of the privilege and of the parties and the furtherance of justice may require.

RULE 508. IDENTITY OF INFORMER

(a) **Rule of Privilege.** The United States or a state or subdivision thereof has a privilege to refuse to disclose the identity of a person who has furnished information relating to or assisting in an investigation of a possible violation of a law to a law enforcement officer or member of a legislative committee or its staff conducting an investigation.

(b) **Who May Claim.** The privilege may be claimed by an appropriate representative of the public entity to which the information was furnished, except the privilege shall not be allowed in criminal cases if the state objects.

(c) **Exceptions.**

(1) *Voluntary disclosure; informer a witness.* No privilege exists under this rule if the identity of the informer or the informer's interest in the subject matter of the communication has been disclosed to those who would have cause to resent the communication by a holder of the privilege or by the informer's own action, or if the informer appears as a witness for the public entity.

(2) *Testimony on merits.* If it appears from the evidence in the case or from other showing by a party that an informer may be able to give testimony necessary to a fair determination of a material issue on the merits in a civil case to which the public entity is a party, or on guilt or innocence in a criminal case, and the public entity invokes the privilege, the court shall give the public entity an opportunity to show in camera facts relevant to determining whether the informer can, in fact, supply that testimony. The showing will ordinarily be in the form of affidavits, but the court may direct that testimony be taken if it finds that the matter cannot be resolved satisfactorily upon affidavit. If the court finds that there is a reasonable probability that the informer can give the testimony, and the public entity elects not to disclose the informer's identity, the court in a civil case may make any order that justice requires, and in a criminal case shall, on motion of the defendant, and may, on the court's own motion, dismiss the charges as to which the testimony would relate. Evidence submitted to the court shall be sealed and preserved to be made available to the appellate court in the event of an appeal, and the contents shall not otherwise be revealed without consent of the public entity. All counsel and parties shall be permitted to be present at every stage of proceedings under this subdivision except a showing in camera, at which no counsel or party shall be permitted to be present.

(3) *Legality of obtaining evidence.* If information from an informer is relied upon to establish the legality of the means by which evidence was obtained and the court is not satisfied that the information was received from an

informer reasonably believed to be reliable or credible, it may require the identity of the informer to be disclosed. The court shall, on request of the public entity, direct that the disclosure be made in camera. All counsel and parties concerned with the issue of legality shall be permitted to be present at every stage of proceedings under this subdivision except a disclosure in camera, at which no counsel or party shall be permitted to be present. If disclosure of the identity of the informer is made in camera, the record thereof shall be sealed and preserved to be made available to the appellate court in the event of an appeal, and the contents shall not otherwise be revealed without consent of the public entity.

RULE 509. PHYSICIAN-PATIENT PRIVILEGE

(a) Definitions. As used in this rule:

(1) A "patient" means any person who consults or is seen by a physician to receive medical care.

(2) A "physician" means a person licensed to practice medicine in any state or nation, or reasonably believed by the patient so to be.

(3) A communication is "confidential" if not intended to be disclosed to third persons other than those present to further the interest of the patient in the consultation, examination, or interview, or those reasonably necessary for the transmission of the communication, or those who are participating in the diagnosis and treatment under the direction of the physician, including members of the patient's family.

(b) Limited Privilege in Criminal Proceedings. There is no physician-patient privilege in criminal proceedings. However, a communication to any person involved in the treatment or examination of alcohol or drug abuse by a person being treated voluntarily or being examined for admission to treatment for alcohol or drug abuse is not admissible in a criminal proceeding.

(c) General Rule of Privilege in Civil Proceedings. In a civil proceeding:

(1) Confidential communications between a physician and a patient, relative to or in connection with any professional services rendered by a physician to the patient are privileged and may not be disclosed.

(2) Records of the identity, diagnosis, evaluation, or treatment of a patient by a physician that are created or maintained by a physician are confidential and privileged and may not be disclosed.

(3) The provisions of this rule apply even if the patient received the services of a physician prior to the enactment of the Medical Liability and Insurance Improvement Act, Tex. Rev. Civ. Stat. art. 4590i.

(d) Who May Claim the Privilege in a Civil Proceeding. In a civil proceeding:

(1) The privilege of confidentiality may be claimed by the patient or by a representative of the patient acting on the patient's behalf.

(2) The physician may claim the privilege of confidentiality, but only on behalf of the patient. The authority to do so is presumed in the absence of evidence to the contrary.

(e) Exceptions in a Civil Proceeding. Exceptions to confidentiality or privilege in administrative proceedings or in civil proceedings in court exist:

(1) when the proceedings are brought by the patient against a physician, including but not limited to malpractice proceedings, and in any license revocation proceeding in which the patient is a complaining witness and in which disclosure is relevant to the claims or defense of a physician;

(2) when the patient or someone authorized to act on the patient's behalf submits a written consent to the release of any privileged information, as provided in paragraph (f);

(3) when the purpose of the proceedings is to substantiate and collect on a claim for medical services rendered to the patient;

(4) as to a communication or record relevant to an issue of the physical, mental or emotional condition of a patient in any proceeding in which any party relies upon the condition as a part of the party's claim or defense;

(5) in any disciplinary investigation or proceeding of a physician conducted under or pursuant to the Medical Practice Act, TEX. REV. CIV. STAT. art. 4495b, or of a registered nurse under or pursuant to TEX. REV. CIV. STAT. arts. 4525, 4527a, 4527b, and 4527c, provided that the board shall protect the identity of any patient whose medical records are examined, except for those patients covered under subparagraph (e)(1) or those patients who have submitted written consent to the release of their medical records as provided by paragraph (f);

(6) in an involuntary civil commitment proceeding, proceeding for court-ordered treatment, or probable cause hearing under TEX. HEALTH & SAFETY CODE ch. 462; tit. 7, subtit. C; and tit. 7, subtit. D;

(7) in any proceeding regarding the abuse or neglect, or the cause of any abuse or neglect, of the resident of an "institution" as defined in TEX. HEALTH & SAFETY CODE § 242.002.

(f) Consent.

(1) Consent for the release of privileged information must be in writing and signed by the patient, or a parent or legal guardian if the patient is a minor, or a legal guardian if the patient has been adjudicated incompetent to manage personal affairs, or an attorney ad litem appointed for the patient, as authorized by TEX. HEALTH & SAFETY CODE tit. 7, subtits. C and D; TEX. PROB. CODE ch. V; and TEX. FAM. CODE § 107.011; or a personal representative if the patient is deceased, provided that the written consent specifies the following:

(A) the information or medical records to be covered by the release;

(B) the reasons or purposes for the release; and

(C) the person to whom the information is to be released.

(2) The patient, or other person authorized to consent, has the right to withdraw consent to the release of any information. Withdrawal of consent does not affect any information disclosed prior to the written notice of the withdrawal.

(3) Any person who received information made privileged by this rule may disclose the information to others only to the extent consistent with the authorized purposes for which consent to release the information was obtained.

Notes and Comments

Comment to 1998 change: This comment is intended to inform the construction and application of this rule. Prior Criminal Rules of Evidence 509 and 510 are now in subparagraph (b) of this Rule. This rule governs disclosures of patient-physician communications only in judicial or administrative proceedings. Whether a physician may or must disclose such communications in other circumstances is governed by TEX. REV. CIV. STAT. ANN. art. 4495b, § 5.08. Former subparagraph (d)(6) of the Civil Evidence Rules, regarding disclosures in a suit affecting the parent-child relationship, is omitted, not because there should be no exception to the privilege in suits affecting the parent-child relationship, but because the exception in such suits is properly considered under subparagraph (d)(4), as construed in *R.K. v. Ramirez*, 887 S.W.2d 836 (Tex. 1994). In determining the proper application of an exception in such suits, the trial court must ensure that the precise need for the information is not outweighed by legitimate privacy interests protected by the privilege. Subparagraph (d) does not except from the privilege information relating to a nonparty patient who is or may be a consulting or testifying expert in the suit.

RULE 510. CONFIDENTIALITY OF MENTAL HEALTH INFORMATION IN CIVIL CASES

(a) Definitions. As used in this rule:

(1) "Professional" means any person:

(A) authorized to practice medicine in any state or nation;

(B) licensed or certified by the State of Texas in the diagnosis, evaluation or treatment of any mental or emotional disorder;

(C) involved in the treatment or examination of drug abusers; or

(D) reasonably believed by the patient to be included in any of the preceding categories.

(2) "Patient" means any person who:

(A) consults, or is interviewed by, a professional for purposes of diagnosis, evaluation, or treatment of any mental or emotional condition or disorder, including alcoholism and drug addiction; or

(B) is being treated voluntarily or being examined for admission to voluntary treatment for drug abuse.

(3) A representative of the patient is:

(A) any person bearing the written consent of the patient;

(B) a parent if the patient is a minor;

(C) a guardian if the patient has been adjudicated incompetent to manage the patient's personal affairs; or

(D) the patient's personal representative if the patient is deceased.

(4) A communication is "confidential" if not intended to be disclosed to third persons other than those present to further the interest of the patient in the diagnosis, examination, evaluation, or treatment, or those reasonably necessary for the transmission of the communication, or those who are participating in the diagnosis, examination, evaluation, or treatment under the direction of the professional, including members of the patient's family.

(b) General Rule of Privilege.

(1) Communication between a patient and a professional is confidential and shall not be disclosed in civil cases.

(2) Records of the identity, diagnosis, evaluation, or treatment of a patient which are created or maintained by a professional are confidential and shall not be disclosed in civil cases.

(3) Any person who received information from confidential communications or records as defined herein, other than a representative of the patient acting on the patient's behalf, shall not disclose in civil cases the information except to the extent that disclosure is consistent with the authorized purposes for which the information was first obtained.

(4) The provisions of this rule apply even if the patient received the services of a professional prior to the enactment of TEX. REV. CIV. STAT. art. 5561h (Vernon Supp. 1984) (now codified as TEX. HEALTH & SAFETY CODE §§ 611.001–611.008).

(c) Who May Claim the Privilege.

(1) The privilege of confidentiality may be claimed by the patient or by a representative of the patient acting on the patient's behalf.

(2) The professional may claim the privilege of confidentiality but only on behalf of the patient. The authority to do so is presumed in the absence of evidence to the contrary.

(d) Exceptions. Exceptions to the privilege in court or administrative proceedings exist:

(1) when the proceedings are brought by the patient against a professional, including but not limited to malpractice proceedings, and in any license revocation proceedings in which the patient is a complaining witness and in which disclosure is relevant to the claim or defense of a professional;

(2) when the patient waives the right in writing to the privilege of confidentiality of any information, or when a representative of the patient acting on the patient's behalf submits a written waiver to the confidentiality privilege;

(3) when the purpose of the proceeding is to substantiate and collect on a claim for mental or emotional health services rendered to the patient;

(4) when the judge finds that the patient after having been previously informed that communications would not be privileged, has made communications to a professional in the course of a court-ordered examination relating to the patient's mental or emotional condition or disorder, providing that such communications shall not be privileged only with respect to issues involving the patient's mental or emotional health. On granting of the order, the court, in determining the extent to which any disclosure of all or any part of any communication is necessary, shall impose appropriate safeguards against unauthorized disclosure;

(5) as to a communication or record relevant to an issue of the physical, mental or emotional condition of a patient in any proceeding in which any party relies upon the condition as a part of the party's claim or defense;

(6) in any proceeding regarding the abuse or neglect, or the cause of any abuse or neglect, of the resident of an institution as defined in TEX. HEALTH AND SAFETY CODE § 242.002.

Notes and Comments

Comment to 1998 change: This comment is intended to inform the construction and application of this rule. This rule governs disclosures of patient-professional communications only in judicial or administrative proceedings. Whether a professional may or must disclose such communications in other circumstances is governed by TEX. HEALTH & SAFETY CODE §§ 611.001–611.008. Former subparagraph (d)(6) of the Civil Evidence Rules, regarding disclosures in a suit affecting the parent-child relationship, is omitted, not because there should be no exception to the privilege in suits affecting the parent-child relationship, but because the exception in such suits is properly considered under subparagraph (d)(5), as construed in *R.K. v. Ramirez*, 887 S.W.2d 836 (Tex. 1994). In determining the proper application of an exception in such suits, the trial court must ensure that the precise need for the information is not outweighed by legitimate privacy interests protected by the privilege. Subparagraph (d) does not except from the privilege information relating to a nonparty patient who is or may be a consulting or testifying expert in the suit.

RULE 511. WAIVER OF PRIVILEGE BY VOLUNTARY DISCLOSURE

A person upon whom these rules confer a privilege against disclosure waives the privilege if:

(1) the person or a predecessor of the person while holder of the privilege voluntarily discloses or consents to disclosure of any significant part of the privileged matter unless such disclosure itself is privileged; or

(2) the person or a representative of the person calls a person to whom privileged communications have been made to testify as to the person's character or character trait insofar as such communications are relevant to such character or character trait.

RULE 512. PRIVILEGED MATTER DISCLOSED UNDER COMPULSION OR WITHOUT OPPORTUNITY TO CLAIM PRIVILEGE

A claim of privilege is not defeated by a disclosure which was (1) compelled erroneously or (2) made without opportunity to claim the privilege.

RULE 513. COMMENT UPON OR INFERENCE FROM CLAIM OF PRIVILEGE; INSTRUCTION

(a) Comment or Inference Not Permitted. Except as permitted in Rule 504(b)(2), the claim of a privilege, whether in the present proceeding or upon a prior occasion, is not a proper subject of comment by judge or counsel, and no inference may be drawn therefrom.

(b) Claiming Privilege Without Knowledge of Jury. In jury cases, proceedings shall be conducted, to the extent practicable, so as to facilitate the making of claims of privilege without the knowledge of the jury.

(c) Claim of Privilege Against Self-Incrimination in Civil Cases. Paragraphs (a) and (b) shall not apply with respect to a party's claim, in the present civil proceeding, of the privilege against self-incrimination.

(d) Jury Instruction. Except as provided in Rule 504(b)(2) and in paragraph (c) of this Rule, upon request any party against whom the jury might draw an adverse inference from a claim of privilege is entitled to an instruction that no inference may be drawn therefrom.

Notes and Comments

Comment to 1998 change: Subdivision (d) regarding a party's entitlement to a jury instruction about a claim of privilege is made applicable to civil cases.

ARTICLE VI. WITNESSES

RULE 601. COMPETENCY AND INCOMPETENCY OF WITNESSES

(a) General Rule. Every person is competent to be a witness except as otherwise provided in these rules. The following witnesses shall be incompetent to testify in any proceeding subject to these rules:

(1) *Insane persons.* Insane persons who, in the opinion of the court, are in an insane condition of mind at the time when they are offered as a witness, or who, in the opinion of the court, were in that condition when the events happened of which they are called to testify.

(2) *Children.* Children or other persons who, after being examined by the court, appear not to possess sufficient intellect to relate transactions with respect to which they are interrogated.

(b) "Dead Man's Rule" in Civil Actions. In civil actions by or against executors, administrators, or guardians, in which judgment may be rendered for or against them as such, neither party shall be allowed to testify against the others as to any oral statement by the testator, intestate or ward, unless that testimony to the oral statement is corroborated or unless the witness is called at the trial to testify thereto by the opposite party; and, the provisions of this article shall extend to and include all actions by or against the heirs or legal representatives of a decedent based in whole or in part on such oral statement. Except for the foregoing, a witness is not precluded from giving evidence of or concerning any transaction with, any conversations with, any admissions of, or statement by, a deceased or insane party or person merely because the witness is a party to the action or a person interested in the event thereof. The trial court shall, in a proper case, where this rule prohibits an interested party or witness from testifying, instruct the jury that such person is not permitted by the law to give evidence relating to any oral statement by the deceased or ward unless the oral statement is corroborated or unless the party or witness is called at the trial by the opposite party.

RULE 602. LACK OF PERSONAL KNOWLEDGE

A witness may not testify to a matter unless evidence is introduced sufficient to support a finding that the witness has personal knowledge of the matter. Evidence to prove personal knowledge may, but need not, consist of the testimony of the witness. This rule is subject to the provisions of Rule 703, relating to opinion testimony by expert witnesses.

RULE 603. OATH OR AFFIRMATION

Before testifying, every witness shall be required to declare that the witness will testify truthfully, by oath or affirmation administered in a form calculated to awaken the witness's conscience and impress the witness's mind with the duty to do so.

RULE 604. INTERPRETERS

An interpreter is subject to the provisions of these rules relating to qualification as an expert and the administration of an oath or affirmation to make a true translation.

RULE 605. COMPETENCY OF JUDGE AS A WITNESS

The judge presiding at the trial may not testify in that trial as a witness. No objection need be made in order to preserve the point.

RULE 606. COMPETENCY OF JUROR AS A WITNESS

(a) **At the Trial.** A member of the jury may not testify as a witness before that jury in the trial of the case in which the juror is sitting as a juror. If the juror is called so to testify, the opposing party shall be afforded an opportunity to object out of the presence of the jury.

(b) **Inquiry into Validity of Verdict or Indictment.** Upon an inquiry into the validity of a verdict or indictment, a juror may not testify as to any matter or statement occurring during the jury's deliberations, or to the effect of anything on any juror's mind or emotions or mental processes, as influencing any juror's assent to or dissent from the verdict or indictment. Nor may a juror's affidavit or any statement by a juror concerning any matter about which the juror would be precluded from testifying be admitted in evidence for any of these purposes. However, a juror may testify: (1) whether any outside influence was improperly brought to bear upon any juror; or (2) to rebut a claim that the juror was not qualified to serve.

RULE 607. WHO MAY IMPEACH

The credibility of a witness may be attacked by any party, including the party calling the witness.

RULE 608. EVIDENCE OF CHARACTER AND CONDUCT OF A WITNESS

(a) Opinion and Reputation Evidence of Character. The credibility of a witness may be attacked or supported by evidence in the form of opinion or reputation, but subject to these limitations:

(1) the evidence may refer only to character for truthfulness or untruthfulness; and

(2) evidence of truthful character is admissible only after the character of the witness for truthfulness has been attacked by opinion or reputation evidence or otherwise.

(b) Specific Instances of Conduct. Specific instances of the conduct of a witness, for the purpose of attacking or supporting the witness's credibility, other than conviction of crime as provided in Rule 609, may not be inquired into on cross-examination of the witness nor proved by extrinsic evidence.

RULE 609. IMPEACHMENT BY EVIDENCE OF CONVICTION OF CRIME

(a) General Rule. For the purpose of attacking the credibility of a witness, evidence that the witness has been convicted of a crime shall be admitted if elicited from the witness or established by public record but only if the crime was a felony or involved moral turpitude, regardless of punishment, and the court determines that the probative value of admitting this evidence outweighs its prejudicial effect to a party.

(b) Time Limit. Evidence of a conviction under this rule is not admissible if a period of more than ten years has elapsed since the date of the conviction or of the release of the witness from the confinement imposed for that conviction, whichever is the later date, unless the court determines, in the interests of justice, that the probative value of the conviction supported by specific facts and circumstances substantially outweighs its prejudicial effect.

(c) Effect of Pardon, Annulment, or Certificate of Rehabilitation. Evidence of a conviction is not admissible under this rule if:

(1) based on the finding of the rehabilitation of the person convicted, the conviction has been the subject of a pardon, annulment, certificate of rehabilitation, or other equivalent procedure, and that person has not been convicted of a subsequent crime which was classified as a felony or involved moral turpitude, regardless of punishment;

(2) probation has been satisfactorily completed for the crime for which the person was convicted, and that person has not been convicted of a subsequent crime which was classified as a felony or involved moral turpitude, regardless of punishment; or

(3) based on a finding of innocence, the conviction has been the subject of a pardon, annulment, or other equivalent procedure.

(d) **Juvenile Adjudications.** Evidence of juvenile adjudications is not admissible, except for proceedings conducted pursuant to Title III, Family Code, in which the witness is a party, under this rule unless required to be admitted by the Constitution of the United States or Texas.

(e) **Pendency of Appeal.** Pendency of an appeal renders evidence of a conviction inadmissible.

(f) **Notice.** Evidence of a conviction is not admissible if after timely written request by the adverse party specifying the witness or witnesses, the proponent fails to give to the adverse party sufficient advance written notice of intent to use such evidence to provide the adverse party with a fair opportunity to contest the use of such evidence.

RULE 610. RELIGIOUS BELIEFS OR OPINIONS

Evidence of the beliefs or opinions of a witness on matters of religion is not admissible for the purpose of showing that by reason of their nature the witness's credibility is impaired or enhanced.

Notes and Comments

Comment to 1998 change: This is prior Rule of Criminal Evidence 615.

RULE 611. MODE AND ORDER OF INTERROGATION AND PRESENTATION

(a) **Control by Court.** The court shall exercise reasonable control over the mode and order of interrogating witnesses and presenting evidence so as to (1) make the interrogation and presentation effective for the ascertainment of the truth, (2) avoid needless consumption of time, and (3) protect witnesses from harassment or undue embarrassment.

(b) **Scope of Cross-Examination.** A witness may be cross-examined on any matter relevant to any issue in the case, including credibility.

(c) **Leading Questions.** Leading questions should not be used on the direct examination of a witness except as may be necessary to develop the testimony of the witness. Ordinarily leading questions should be permitted on cross-examination. When a party calls a hostile witness, an adverse party, or a witness identified with an adverse party, interrogation may be by leading questions.

RULE 612. WRITING USED TO REFRESH MEMORY

If a witness uses a writing to refresh memory for the purpose of testifying either

(1) while testifying;

(2) before testifying, in civil cases, if the court in its discretion determines it is necessary in the interests of justice; or

(3) before testifying, in criminal cases;

an adverse party is entitled to have the writing produced at the hearing, to inspect it, to cross-examine the witness thereon, and to introduce in evidence those portions which relate to the testimony of the witness. If it is claimed that the writing contains matters not related to the subject matter of the testimony the court shall examine the writing in camera, excise any portion not so related, and order delivery of the remainder to the party entitled thereto. Any portion withheld over objections shall be preserved and made available to the appellate court in the event of an appeal. If a writing is not produced or delivered pursuant to order under this rule, the court shall make any order justice requires, except that in criminal cases when the prosecution elects not to comply, the order shall be one striking the testimony or, if the court in its discretion determines that the interests of justice so require, declaring a mistrial.

RULE 613. PRIOR STATEMENTS OF WITNESSES: IMPEACHMENT AND SUPPORT

(a) **Examining Witness Concerning Prior Inconsistent Statement.** In examining a witness concerning a prior inconsistent statement made by the witness, whether oral or written, and before further cross-examination concerning, or extrinsic evidence of, such statement may be allowed, the witness must be told the contents of such statement and the time and place and the person to whom it was made, and must be afforded an opportunity to explain or deny such statement. If written, the writing need not be shown to the witness at that time, but on request the same shall be shown to opposing counsel. If the witness unequivocally admits having made such statement, extrinsic evidence of same shall not be admitted. This provision does not apply to admissions of a party-opponent as defined in Rule 801(e)(2).

(b) **Examining Witness Concerning Bias or Interest.** In impeaching a witness by proof of circumstances or statements showing bias or interest on the part of such witness, and before further cross-examination concerning, or extrinsic evidence of, such bias or interest may be allowed, the circumstances supporting such claim or the details of such statement, including the contents and where, when and to whom made, must be made known to the witness, and the witness must be given an opportunity to explain or to deny such circumstances or statement. If written, the writing need not be shown to the witness at that time, but on request the same shall be shown to opposing counsel. If the witness unequivocally admits such bias or interest, extrinsic evidence of same shall not be admitted. A party shall be permitted to present evidence rebutting any evidence impeaching one of said party's witnesses on grounds of bias or interest.

(c) **Prior Consistent Statements of Witnesses.** A prior statement of a witness which is consistent with the testimony of the witness is inadmissible except as provided in Rule 801(e)(1)(B).

RULE 614. EXCLUSION OF WITNESSES

At the request of a party the court shall order witnesses excluded so that they cannot hear the testimony of other witnesses, and it may make the order of its own motion. This rule does not authorize exclusion of:

(1) a party who is a natural person or in civil cases the spouse of such natural person;

(2) an officer or employee of a party in a civil case or a defendant in a criminal case that is not a natural person designated as its representative by its attorney;

(3) a person whose presence is shown by a party to be essential to the presentation of the party's cause; or

(4) the victim in a criminal case, unless the victim is to testify and the court determines that the victim's testimony would be materially affected if the victim hears other testimony at the trial.

RULE 615. PRODUCTION OF STATEMENTS OF WITNESSES IN CRIMINAL CASES

(a) Motion for Production. After a witness other than the defendant has testified on direct examination, the court, on motion of a party who did not call the witness, shall order the attorney for the state or the defendant and defendant's attorney, as the case may be, to produce, for the examination and use of the moving party, any statement of the witness that is in their possession and that relates to the subject matter concerning which the witness has testified.

(b) Production of Entire Statement. If the entire contents of the statement relate to the subject matter concerning which the witness has testified, the court shall order that the statement be delivered to the moving party.

(c) Production of Excised Statement. If the other party claims that the statement contains matter that does not relate to the subject matter concerning which the witness has testified, the court shall order that it be delivered to the court in camera. Upon inspection, the court shall excise the portions of the statement that do not relate to the subject matter concerning which the witness has testified, and shall order that the statement, with such material excised, be delivered to the moving party. Any portion withheld over objection shall be preserved and made available to the appellate court in the event of appeal.

(d) Recess for Examination of Statement. Upon delivery of the statement to the moving party, the court, upon application of that party, shall recess proceedings in the trial for a reasonable examination of such statement and for preparation for its use in the trial.

(e) Sanction for Failure to Produce Statement. If the other party elects not to comply with an order to deliver a statement to the moving party, the court shall order that the testimony of the witness be stricken from the record and that the trial proceed, or, if it is the attorney for the state who elects not to comply, shall declare a mistrial if required by the interest of justice.

(f) Definition. As used in this rule, a "statement" of a witness means:

(1) a written statement made by the witness that is signed or otherwise adopted or approved by the witness;

(2) a substantially verbatim recital of an oral statement made by the witness that is recorded contemporaneously with the making of the oral statement and that is contained in a stenographic, mechanical, electrical, or other recording or a transcription thereof; or

(3) a statement, however taken or recorded, or a transcription thereof, made by the witness to a grand jury.

Notes and Comments

Comment to 1998 change: This is prior Rule of Criminal Evidence 614.

ARTICLE VII. OPINIONS AND EXPERT TESTIMONY

RULE 701. OPINION TESTIMONY BY LAY WITNESSES

If the witness is not testifying as an expert, the witness's testimony in the form of opinions or inferences is limited to those opinions or inferences which are (a) rationally based on the perception of the witness and (b) helpful to a clear understanding of the witness's testimony or the determination of a fact in issue.

RULE 702. TESTIMONY BY EXPERTS

If scientific, technical, or other specialized knowledge will assist the trier of fact to understand the evidence or to determine a fact in issue, a witness qualified as an expert by knowledge, skill, experience, training, or education may testify thereto in the form of an opinion or otherwise.

RULE 703. BASES OF OPINION TESTIMONY BY EXPERTS

The facts or data in the particular case upon which an expert bases an opinion or inference may be those perceived by, reviewed by, or made known to the expert at or before the hearing. If of a type reasonably relied upon by experts in the particular field in forming opinions or inferences upon the subject, the facts or data need not be admissible in evidence.

Notes and Comments

Comment to 1998 change: The former Civil Rule referred to facts or data "perceived by or reviewed by" the expert. The former Criminal Rule referred to facts or data "perceived by or made known to" the expert. The terminology is now conformed, but no change in meaning is intended.

RULE 704. OPINION ON ULTIMATE ISSUE

Testimony in the form of an opinion or inference otherwise admissible is not objectionable because it embraces an ultimate issue to be decided by the trier of fact.

RULE 705. DISCLOSURE OF FACTS OR DATE UNDERLYING EXPERT OPINION

(a) Disclosure of facts or data. The expert may testify in terms of opinion or inference and give the expert's reasons therefor without prior disclosure of the underlying facts or data, unless the court requires otherwise. The expert may in any event disclose on direct examination, or be required to disclose on cross-examination, the underlying facts or data.

(b) Voir dire. Prior to the expert giving the expert's opinion or disclosing the underlying facts or data, a party against whom the opinion is offered upon request in a criminal case shall, or in a civil case may, be permitted to conduct a *voir dire* examination directed to the underlying facts or data upon which the opinion is based. This examination shall be conducted out of the hearing of the jury.

(c) Admissibility of opinion. If the court determines that the underlying facts or data do not provide a sufficient basis for the expert's opinion under Rule 702 or 703, the opinion is inadmissible.

(d) Balancing test; limiting instructions. When the underlying facts or data would be inadmissible in evidence, the court shall exclude the underlying facts or data if the danger that they will be used for a purpose other than as explanation or support for the expert's opinion outweighs their value as explanation or support or are unfairly prejudicial. If otherwise inadmissible facts or data are disclosed before the jury, a limiting instruction by the court shall be given upon request.

Notes and Comments

Comment to 1998 change: Paragraphs (b), (c), and (d) are based on the former Criminal Rule and are made applicable to civil cases. This rule does not preclude a party in any case from conducting a *voir dire* examination into the qualifications of an expert.

RULE 706. AUDIT IN CIVIL CASES

Despite any other evidence rule to the contrary, verified reports of auditors prepared pursuant to Rule of Civil Procedure 172, whether in the form of summaries, opinions, or otherwise, shall be admitted in evidence when offered by any party whether or not the facts or data in the reports are otherwise admissible and whether or not the reports embrace the ultimate issues to be decided by the trier of fact. Where exceptions to the reports have been filed, a party may contradict the reports by evidence supporting the exceptions.

ARTICLE VIII. HEARSAY

RULE 801. DEFINITIONS

The following definitions apply under this article:

(a) Statement. A "statement" is (1) an oral or written verbal expression or (2) nonverbal conduct of a person, if it is intended by the person as a substitute for verbal expression.

(b) Declarant. A "declarant" is a person who makes a statement.

(c) Matter Asserted. "Matter asserted" includes any matter explicitly asserted, and any matter implied by a statement, if the probative value of the statement as offered flows from declarant's belief as to the matter.

(d) Hearsay. "Hearsay" is a statement, other than one made by the declarant while testifying at the trial or hearing, offered in evidence to prove the truth of the matter asserted.

(e) Statements Which Are Not Hearsay. A statement is not hearsay if:

(1) *Prior statement by witness.* The declarant testifies at the trial or hearing and is subject to cross-examination concerning the statement, and the statement is:

(A) inconsistent with the declarant's testimony, and was given under oath subject to the penalty of perjury at a trial, hearing, or other proceeding except a grand jury proceeding in a criminal case, or in a deposition;

(B) consistent with the declarant's testimony and is offered to rebut an express or implied charge against the declarant of recent fabrication or improper influence or motive;

(C) one of identification of a person made after perceiving the person; or

(D) taken and offered in a criminal case in accordance with Code of Criminal Procedure article 38.071.

(2) *Admission by party-opponent.* The statement is offered against a party and is:

(A) the party's own statement in either an individual or representative capacity;

(B) a statement of which the party has manifested an adoption or belief in its truth;

(C) a statement by a person authorized by the party to make a statement concerning the subject;

(D) a statement by the party's agent or servant concerning a matter within the scope of the agency or employment, made during the existence of the relationship; or

(E) a statement by a co-conspirator of a party during the course and in furtherance of the conspiracy.

(3) *Depositions.* In a civil case, it is a deposition taken in the same proceeding, as same proceeding is defined in Rule of Civil Procedure 207. Unavailability of deponent is not a requirement for admissibility.

RULE 802. HEARSAY RULE

Hearsay is not admissible except as provided by statute or these rules or by other rules prescribed pursuant to statutory authority. Inadmissible hearsay admitted without objection shall not be denied probative value merely because it is hearsay.

RULE 803. HEARSAY EXCEPTIONS; AVAILABILITY OF DECLARANT IMMATERIAL

The following are not excluded by the hearsay rule, even though the declarant is available as a witness:

(1) **Present Sense Impression.** A statement describing or explaining an event or condition made while the declarant was perceiving the event or condition, or immediately thereafter.

(2) **Excited Utterance.** A statement relating to a startling event or condition made while the declarant was under the stress of excitement caused by the event or condition.

(3) **Then Existing Mental, Emotional, or Physical Condition.** A statement of the declarant's then existing state of mind, emotion, sensation, or physical condition (such as intent, plan, motive, design, mental feeling, pain, or bodily health), but not including a statement of memory or belief to prove the fact remembered or believed unless it relates to the execution, revocation, identification, or terms of declarant's will.

(4) **Statements for Purposes of Medical Diagnosis or Treatment.** Statements made for purposes of medical diagnosis or treatment and describing medical history, or past or present symptoms, pain, or sensations, or the inception or general character of the cause or external source thereof insofar as reasonably pertinent to diagnosis or treatment.

(5) **Recorded Recollection.** A memorandum or record concerning a matter about which a witness once had personal knowledge but now has insufficient recollection to enable the witness to testify fully and accurately, shown to have been made or adopted by the witness when the matter was fresh in the witness' memory and to reflect that knowledge correctly, unless the circumstances of preparation cast doubt on the document's trustworthiness. If admitted, the memorandum or record may be read into evidence but may not itself be received as an exhibit unless offered by an adverse party.

(6) **Records of Regularly Conducted Activity.** A memorandum, report, record, or data compilation, in any form, of acts, events, conditions, opinions, or diagnoses, made at or near the time by, or from information transmitted by, a person with knowledge, if kept in the course of a regularly conducted business activity, and if it was the regular practice of that business activity to make the memorandum, report, record, or data compilation, all as shown by the testimony of the custodian or other qualified witness, or by affidavit that complies with Rule 902(10), unless the source of information or the method or circumstances of preparation indicate lack of trustworthiness. "Business" as used in this paragraph includes any and every kind of regular organized activity whether conducted for profit or not.

(7) **Absence of Entry in Records Kept in Accordance with the Provisions of Paragraph (6).** Evidence that a matter is not included in the memoranda, reports, records, or data compilations, in any form, kept in accordance with the provisions of paragraph (6), to prove the nonoccurrence or nonexistence of the matter, if the matter was of a kind of which a memorandum, report, record, or data compilation was regularly made and preserved, unless the

sources of information or other circumstances indicate lack of trustworthiness.

(8) Public Records and Reports. Records, reports, statements, or data compilations, in any form, of public offices or agencies setting forth:

(A) the activities of the office or agency;

(B) matters observed pursuant to duty imposed by law as to which matters there was a duty to report, excluding in criminal cases matters observed by police officers and other law enforcement personnel; or

(C) in civil cases as to any party and in criminal cases as against the state, factual findings resulting from an investigation made pursuant to authority granted by law; unless the sources of information or other circumstances indicate lack of trustworthiness.

(9) Records of Vital Statistics. Records or data compilations, in any form, of births, fetal deaths, deaths, or marriages, if the report thereof was made to a public office pursuant to requirements of law.

(10) Absence of Public Record or Entry. To prove the absence of a record, report, statement, or data compilation, in any form, or the nonoccurrence or nonexistence of a matter of which a record, report, statement, or data compilation, in any form, was regularly made and preserved by a public office or agency, evidence in the form of a certification in accordance with Rule 902, or testimony, that diligent search failed to disclose the record, report statement, or data compilation, or entry.

(11) Records of Religious Organizations. Statements of births, marriages, divorces, deaths, legitimacy, ancestry, relationship by blood or marriage, or other similar facts of personal or family history, contained in a regularly kept record of a religious organization.

(12) Marriage, Baptismal, and Similar Certificates. Statements of fact contained in a certificate that the maker performed a marriage or other ceremony or administered a sacrament, made by a member of the clergy, public official, or other person authorized by the rules or practices of a religious organization or by law to perform the act certified, and purporting to have been issued at the time of the act or within a reasonable time thereafter.

(13) Family Records. Statements of fact concerning personal or family history contained in family Bibles, genealogies, charts, engravings on rings, inscriptions on family portraits, engravings on urns, crypts, or tombstones, or the like.

(14) Records of Documents Affecting an Interest in Property. The record of a document purporting to establish or affect an interest in property, as proof of the content of the original recorded document and its execution and delivery by each person by whom it purports to have been executed, if the record is a record of a public office and an applicable statute authorizes the recording of documents of that kind in that office.

(15) Statements in Documents Affecting an Interest in Property. A statement contained in a document purporting to establish or affect an interest in property if the matter stated was relevant to the purpose of the document, unless dealings with the property since the document was made have been inconsistent with the truth of the statement or the purport of the document.

(16) Statements in Ancient Documents. Statements in a document in existence twenty years or more the authenticity of which is established.

(17) Market Reports, Commercial Publications. Market quotations, tabulations, lists, directories, or other published compilations, generally used and relied upon by the public or by persons in particular occupations.

(18) Learned Treatises. To the extent called to the attention of an expert witness upon cross-examination or relied upon by the expert in direct examination, statements contained in published treatises, periodicals, or pamphlets on a subject of history, medicine, or other science or art established as a reliable authority by the testimony or admission of the witness or by other expert testimony or by judicial notice. If admitted, the statements may be read into evidence but may not be received as exhibits.

(19) Reputation Concerning Personal or Family History. Reputation among members of a person's family by blood, adoption, or marriage, or among a person's associates, or in the community, concerning a person's birth, adoption, marriage, divorce, death, legitimacy, relationship by blood, adoption, or marriage, ancestry, or other similar fact of personal or family history.

(20) Reputation Concerning Boundaries or General History. Reputation in a community, arising before the controversy, as to boundaries of or customs affecting lands in the community, and reputation as to events of general history important to the community or state or nation in which located.

(21) Reputation as to Character. Reputation of a person's character among associates or in the community.

(22) Judgment of Previous Conviction. In civil cases, evidence of a judgment, entered after a trial or upon a plea of guilty (but not upon a plea of *nolo contendere*), judging a person guilty of a felony, to prove any fact essential to sustain the judgment of conviction. In criminal cases, evidence of a judgment, entered after a trial or upon a plea of guilty or *nolo contendere*, adjudging a person guilty of a criminal offense, to prove any fact essential to sustain the judgment of conviction, but not including, when offered by the state for purposes other than impeachment, judgments against persons other than the accused. In all cases, the pendency of an appeal renders such evidence inadmissible.

(23) Judgment as to Personal, Family, or General History, or Boundaries. Judgments as proof of matters of personal, family or general history, or boundaries, essential to the judgment, if the same would be provable by evidence of reputation.

(24) Statement Against Interest. A statement which was at the time of its making so far contrary to the declarant's pecuniary or proprietary interest, or so far tended to subject the declarant to civil or criminal liability, or to render invalid a claim by the declarant against another, or to make the declarant an object of hatred, ridicule, or disgrace, that a reasonable person in declarant's position would not have made the statement unless believing it to be true. In criminal cases, a statement tending to expose the declarant to criminal liability is not admissible unless corroborating circumstances clearly indicate the trustworthiness of the statement.

RULE 804. HEARSAY EXCEPTIONS; DECLARANT UNAVAILABLE

(a) Definition of Unavailability. "Unavailability as a witness" includes situations in which the declarant:

(1) is exempted by ruling of the court on the ground of privilege from testifying concerning the subject matter of the declarant's statement;

(2) persists in refusing to testify concerning the subject matter of the declarant's statement despite an order of the court to do so;

(3) testifies to a lack of memory of the subject matter of the declarant's statement;

(4) is unable to be present or to testify at the hearing because of death or then existing physical or mental illness or infirmity; or

(5) is absent from the hearing and the proponent of the declarant's statement has been unable to procure the declarant's attendance or testimony by process or other reasonable means.

A declarant is not unavailable as a witness if the declarant's exemption, refusal, claim of lack of memory, inability, or absence is due to the procurement or wrong-doing of the proponent of the declarant's statement for the purpose of preventing the witness from attending or testifying.

(b) Hearsay Exceptions. The following are not excluded if the declarant is unavailable as a witness:

(1) *Former testimony.* In civil cases, testimony given as a witness at another hearing of the same or a different proceeding, or in a deposition taken in the course of another proceeding, if the party against whom the testimony is now offered, or a person with a similar interest, had an opportunity and similar motive to develop the testimony by direct, cross, or redirect examination. In criminal cases, testimony given as a witness at another hearing of the same or a different proceeding, if the party against whom the testimony is now offered had an opportunity and similar motive to develop the testimony by direct, cross, or redirect examination. In criminal cases the use of depositions is controlled by Chapter 39 of the Code of Criminal Procedure.

(2) *Dying declarations.* A statement made by a declarant while believing that the declarant's death was imminent, concerning the cause or circumstances of what the declarant believed to be impending death.

(3) *Statement of personal or family history.*

(A) A statement concerning the declarant's own birth, adoption, marriage, divorce, legitimacy, relationship by blood, adoption, or marriage, ancestry, or other similar fact of personal or family history even though declarant had no means of acquiring personal knowledge of the matter stated; or

(B) A statement concerning the foregoing matters, and death also, of another person, if the declarant was related to the other by blood, adoption, or marriage or was so intimately associated with the other's family as to be likely to have accurate information concerning the matter declared.

RULE 805. HEARSAY WITHIN HEARSAY

Hearsay included within hearsay is not excluded under the hearsay rule if each part of the combined statements conforms with an exception to the hearsay rule provided in these rules.

RULE 806. ATTACKING AND SUPPORTING CREDIBILITY OF DECLARANT

When a hearsay statement, or a statement defined in Rule 801(e)(2)(C), (D), or (E), or in civil cases a statement defined in Rule 801(e)(3), has been admitted in evidence, the credibility of the declarant may be attacked, and if attacked may be supported by any evidence which would be admissible for those purposes if declarant had testified as a witness. Evidence of a statement or conduct by the declarant at any time, offered to impeach the declarant, is not subject to any requirement that the declarant may have been afforded an opportunity to deny or explain. If the party against whom a hearsay statement has been admitted calls the declarant as a witness, the party is entitled to examine the declarant on the statement as if under cross-examination.

ARTICLE IX. AUTHENTICATION AND IDENTIFICATION

RULE 901. REQUIREMENT OF AUTHENTICATION OF IDENTIFICATION

(a) General Provision. The requirement of authentication or identification as a condition precedent to admissibility is satisfied by evidence sufficient to support a finding that the matter in question is what its proponent claims.

(b) Illustrations. By way of illustration only, and not by way of limitation, the following are examples of authentication or identification conforming with the requirements of this rule:

(1) *Testimony of witness with knowledge.* Testimony that a matter is what it is claimed to be.

(2) *Nonexpert opinion on handwriting.* Nonexpert opinion as to the genuineness of handwriting, based upon familiarity not acquired for purposes of the litigation.

(3) *Comparison by trier or expert witness.* Comparison by the trier of fact or by expert witness with specimens which have been found by the court to be genuine.

(4) *Distinctive characteristics and the like.* Appearance, contents, substance, internal patterns, or other distinctive characteristics, taken in conjunction with circumstances.

(5) *Voice identification.* Identification of a voice, whether heard firsthand or through mechanical or electronic transmission or recording, by opinion based upon hearing the voice at anytime under circumstances connecting it with the alleged speaker.

(6) *Telephone conversations.* Telephone conversations, by evidence that a call was made to the number assigned at the time by the telephone company to a particular person or business, if:

(A) in the case of a person, circumstances, including self-identification, show the person answering to be the one called; or

(B) in the case of a business, the call was made to a place of business and the conversation related to business reasonably transacted over the telephone.

(7) *Public records or reports.* Evidence that a writing authorized by law to be recorded or filed and in fact recorded or filed in a public office, or a purported public record, report, statement, or data compilation, in any form, is from the public office where items of this nature are kept.

(8) *Ancient documents or data compilation.* Evidence that a document or data compilation, in any form, (A) is in such condition as to create no suspicion concerning its authenticity, (B) was in a place where it, if authentic, would likely be, and (C) has been in existence twenty years or more at the time it is offered.

(9) *Process or system.* Evidence describing a process or system used to produce a result and showing that the process or system produces an accurate result.

(10) *Methods provided by statute or rule.* Any method of authentication or identification provided by statute or by other rule prescribed pursuant to statutory authority.

RULE 902. SELF-AUTHENTICATION

Extrinsic evidence of authenticity as a condition precedent to admissibility is not required with respect to the following:

(1) Domestic Public Documents Under Seal. A document bearing a seal purporting to be that of the United States, or of any State, district, Commonwealth, territory, or insular possession thereof, or the Panama Canal Zone, or the Trust Territory of the Pacific Islands, or of a political subdivision, department, officer, or agency thereof, and a signature purporting to be an attestation or execution.

(2) Domestic Public Documents Not Under Seal. A document purporting to bear the signature in the official capacity of an officer or employee of any entity included in paragraph (1) hereof, having no seal, if a public officer having a seal and having official duties in the district or political subdivision of the officer or employee certifies under seal that the signer has the official capacity and that the signature is genuine.

(3) Foreign Public Documents. A document purporting to be executed or attested in an official capacity by a person, authorized by the laws of a foreign country to make the execution or attestation, and accompanied by a final certification as to the genuineness of the signature and official position (A) of the executing or attesting person, or (B) of any foreign official whose certificate of genuineness of signature and official position relates to the execution or attestation or is in a chain of certificates of genuineness of signature and official position relating to the execution or attestation. A final certification may be made by a secretary of embassy or legation, consul general, consul, vice consul, or consular agent of the United States, or a diplomatic or consular official of the foreign country assigned or accredited to the United States. If reasonable opportunity has been given to all parties to investigate the authenticity and accuracy of official documents, the court may, for good cause shown, order that they be treated as presumptively authentic without final certification or permit them to be evidenced by an attested summary with or without final certification. The final certification shall be dispensed with whenever both the United States and the foreign country in which the official record is located are parties to a treaty or convention that abolishes or displaces such requirement, in which case the record and the attestation shall be certified by the means provided in the treaty or convention.

(4) Certified Copies of Public Records. A copy of an official record or report or entry therein, or of a document authorized by law to be recorded or filed and actually recorded or filed in a public office, including data compilations in any form certified as correct by the custodian or other person authorized to make the certification, by certificate complying with paragraph (1), (2) or (3) of this rule or complying with any statute or other rule prescribed pursuant to statutory authority.

(5) Official Publications. Books, pamphlets, or other publications purporting to be issued by public authority.

(6) Newspapers and Periodicals. Printed materials purporting to be newspapers or periodicals.

(7) Trade Inscriptions and the Like. Inscriptions, signs, tags, or labels purporting to have been affixed in the course of business and indicating ownership, control, or origin.

(8) Acknowledged Documents. Documents accompanied by a certificate of acknowledgment executed in the manner provided by law by a notary public or other officer authorized by law to take acknowledgments.

(9) Commercial Paper and Related Documents. Commercial paper, signatures thereon, and documents relating thereto to the extent provided by general commercial law.

(10) Business Records Accompanied by Affidavit.

(a) *Records or photocopies; admissibility; affidavit; filing.* Any record or set of records or photographically reproduced copies of such records, which would be admissible under Rule 803(6) or (7) shall be admissible in evidence in any court in this state upon the affidavit of the person who would otherwise provide the prerequisites of Rule 803(6) or (7), that such records attached to such affidavit were in fact so kept as required by Rule 803(6) or (7), provided further, that such record or records along with such affidavit are filed with the clerk of the court for inclusion with the papers in the cause in which the record or records are sought to be used as evidence at least fourteen days prior to the day upon which trial of said cause commences, and provided the other parties to said cause are given prompt notice by the party filing same of the filing of such record or records and affidavit, which notice shall identify the name and employer, if any, of the person making the affidavit and such records shall be made available to the counsel for other parties to the action or litigation for inspection and copying. The expense for copying shall be borne by the party, parties or persons who desire copies and not by the party or parties who file the records and serve notice of said filing, in compliance with this rule. Notice shall be deemed to have been promptly given if it is served in the manner contemplated by Rule of Civil Procedure 21a fourteen days prior to commencement of trial in said cause.

(b) *Form of affidavit.* A form for the affidavit of such person as shall make such affidavit as is permitted in paragraph (a) above shall be sufficient if it follows this form though this form shall not be exclusive, and an affidavit which substantially complies with the provisions of this rule shall suffice, to-wit:

No. ______

John Doe (Name of Plaintiff) v. John Roe (Name of Defendant)	IN THE ________ COURT IN AND FOR ________ COUNTY, TEXAS

AFFIDAVIT

Before me, the undersigned authority, personally appeared ________, who, being by me duly sworn, deposed as follows:

My name is ________, I am of sound mind, capable of making this affidavit, and personally acquainted with the facts herein stated:

I am the custodian of the records of ________. Attached hereto are ______ pages of records from ________. These said ______ pages of records are kept by ________ in the regular course of business, and it was the regular course of business of ________ for an employee or representative of ________, with knowledge of the act, event, condition, opinion, or diagnosis, recorded to make the record or to transmit information thereof to be included in such record; and the record was made at or near the time or reasonably soon thereafter. The records attached hereto are the original or exact duplicates of the original.

____
Affiant

SWORN TO AND SUBSCRIBED before me on the ______ day of ________, 19____.

____
Notary Public, State of Texas
Notary's printed name:

____

My commission expires:

____

(11) **Presumptions Under Statutes or Other Rules.** Any signature, document, or other matter declared by statute or by other rules prescribed pursuant to statutory authority to be presumptively or prima facie genuine or authentic.

RULE 903. SUBSCRIBING WITNESS' TESTIMONY UNNECESSARY

The testimony of a subscribing witness is not necessary to authenticate a writing unless required by the laws of the jurisdiction whose laws govern the validity of the writing.

ARTICLE X. CONTENTS OF WRITINGS, RECORDINGS, AND PHOTOGRAPHS

RULE 1001. DEFINITIONS

For purposes of this article the following definitions are applicable:

(a) **Writings and Recordings.** "Writings" and "recordings" consist of letters, words, or numbers or their equivalent, set down by handwriting, typewriting, printing, photostating, photographing, magnetic impulse, mechanical or electronic recording, or other form of data compilation.

(b) **Photographs.** "Photographs" include still photographs, X-ray films, video tapes, and motion pictures.

(c) **Original.** An "original" of a writing or recording is the writing or recording itself or any counterpart intended to have the same effect by a person executing or issuing it. An "original" of a photograph includes the negative or any print therefrom. If data are stored in a computer or similar device, any printout or other output readable by sight, shown to reflect the data accurately, is an "original."

(d) **Duplicate.** A "duplicate" is a counterpart produced by the same impression as the original, or from the same matrix, or by means of photography, including enlargements and miniatures, or by mechanical or electronic re-recording, or by chemical reproduction, or by other equivalent techniques which accurately reproduce the original.

RULE 1002. REQUIREMENT OF ORIGINALS

To prove the content of a writing, recording, or photograph, the original writing, recording, or photograph is required except as otherwise provided in these rules or by law.

RULE 1003. ADMISSIBILITY OF DUPLICATES

A duplicate is admissible to the same extent as an original unless (1) a question is raised as to the authenticity of the original or (2) in the circumstances it would be unfair to admit the duplicate in lieu of the original.

RULE 1004. ADMISSIBILITY OF OTHER EVIDENCE OF CONTENTS

The original is not required, and other evidence of the contents of a writing, recording, or photograph is admissible if:

(a) **Originals Lost or Destroyed.** All originals are lost or have been destroyed, unless the proponent lost or destroyed them in bad faith;

(b) **Original Not Obtainable.** No original can be obtained by any available judicial process or procedure;

(c) **Original Outside the State.** No original is located in Texas;

(d) **Original in Possession of Opponent.** At a time when an original was under the control of the party against whom offered, that party was put on notice, by the pleadings or otherwise, that the content would be a subject of proof at the hearing, and that party does not produce the original at the hearing; or

(e) **Collateral Matters.** The writing, recording or photograph is not closely related to a controlling issue.

RULE 1005. PUBLIC RECORDS

The contents of an official record or of a document authorized to be recorded or filed and actually recorded or filed, including data compilations in any form, if otherwise admissible, may be proved by copy, certified as correct in accordance with Rule 902 or testified to be correct by a witness who has compared it with the original. If a copy which complies with the foregoing cannot be obtained by the exercise of reasonable diligence, then other evidence of the contents may be given.

RULE 1006. SUMMARIES

The contents of voluminous writings, recordings, or photographs, otherwise admissible, which cannot conveniently be examined in court may be presented in the form of a chart, summary, or calculation. The originals, or duplicates, shall be made available for examination or copying, or both, by other parties at a reasonable time and place. The court may order that they be produced in court.

RULE 1007. TESTIMONY OR WRITTEN ADMISSION OF PARTY

Contents of writings, recordings, or photographs may be proved by the testimony or deposition of the party against whom offered or by that party's written admission, without accounting for the nonproduction of the original.

RULE 1008. FUNCTIONS OF COURT AND JURY

When the admissibility of other evidence of contents of writings, recordings, or photographs under these rules depends upon the fulfillment of a condition of fact, the question whether the condition has been fulfilled is ordinarily for the court to determine in accordance with the provisions of Rule 104. However, when an issue is raised (a) whether the asserted writing ever existed, or (b) whether another writing, recording, or photograph produced at the trial is the original, or (c) whether other evidence of contents correctly reflects the contents, the issue is for the trier of fact to determine as in the case of other issues of fact.

RULE 1009. TRANSLATION OF FOREIGN LANGUAGE DOCUMENTS

(a) **Translations.** A translation of foreign language documents shall be admissible upon the affidavit of a qualified translator setting forth the qualifications of the translator and certifying that the translation is fair and accurate. Such affidavit, along with the translation and the underlying foreign language documents, shall be served upon all parties at least 45 days prior to the date of trial.

(b) **Objections.** Any party may object to the accuracy of another party's translation by pointing out the specific inaccuracies of the translation and by stating with specificity what the objecting party contends is a fair and accurate translation. Such objection shall be served upon all parties at least 15 days prior to the date of trial.

(c) **Effect of Failure to Object or Offer Conflicting Translation.** If no conflicting translation or objection is timely served, the court shall admit a translation submitted under paragraph (a) without need of proof, provided however that the underlying foreign language documents are otherwise admissible under the Texas Rules of Evidence. Failure to serve a conflicting translation under paragraph (a) or failure to timely and properly object to the accuracy of a translation under paragraph (b) shall preclude a party from attacking or offering evidence contradicting the accuracy of such translation at trial.

(d) **Effect of Objections or Conflicting Translations.** In the event of conflicting translations under paragraph (a) or if objections to another party's translation are served under paragraph (b), the court shall determine whether there is a genuine issue as to the accuracy of a material part of the translation to be resolved by the trier of fact.

(e) **Expert Testimony of Translator.** Except as provided in paragraph (c), this Rule does not preclude the admission of a translation of foreign language documents at trial either by live testimony or by deposition testimony of a qualified expert translator.

(f) **Varying of Time Limits.** The court, upon motion of any party and for good cause shown, may enlarge or shorten the time limits set forth in this Rule.

(g) **Court Appointment.** The court, if necessary, may appoint a qualified translator, the reasonable value of whose services shall be taxed as court costs.

Notes and Comments

Comment to 1998 change: This is a new rule.

INDEX

[References are to sections.]

[References are to sections.]

B

[References are to sections.]

[References are to sections.]

[References are to sections.]

[References are to sections.]

[References are to sections.]

[References are to sections.]

[References are to sections.]

I

[References are to sections.]

[References are to sections.]

[References are to sections.]

P

[References are to sections.]

[References are to sections.]

Q

R

[References are to sections.]

S

[References are to sections.]

[References are to sections.]

[References are to sections.]

[References are to sections.]

X